PRELIMINARY CLASS-TEST EDITION: PARTIAL
Chapters 1–14 of 22

microeconomics

Paul Krugman

Princeton University

Robin Wells

Princeton University

WORTH PUBLISHERS

To beginning students everywhere, which we all were at one time.

Publisher: Catherine Woods

Executive Editor: Craig Bleyer

Acquisitions Editor: Charlie Van Wagner

Executive Development Editor: Sharon Balbos

Development Editors: Marilyn Freedman, Becky Kohn

Consultant: Andreas Bentz

Director of Market Development: Steven Rigolosi

Senior Marketing Manager: Jeffrey Rucker

Associate Managing Editor: Tracey Kuehn

Art Director, Cover Designer: Babs Reingold

Interior Designer: Babs Reingold

Layout Designer: Lee Ann Mahler

Illustrations: TSI Graphics, Paul Lacy

Photo Research Manager: Patricia Marx

Photo Editor: Ted Szczepanski

Photo Researcher: Julie Tesser

Production Manager: Barbara Anne Seixas

Composition: TSI Graphics

Printing and Binding: R. R. Donnelley and Sons

ISBN: 0-7167-5997-7 (Preliminary Edition only)

This preliminary edition contains the first 14 chapters of the text and is not available after December 2004. **To order the complete** *Microeconomics* **text (Chapters 1–22),** please use the following ISBN: **0-7167-5229-8.**

Worth Publishers
41 Madison Avenue
New York, NY 10010
www.worthpublishers.com

About the Authors

Paul Krugman is Professor of Economics at Princeton University, where he regularly teaches the principles course. He received his BA from Yale and his PhD from MIT. Prior to his current position, he taught at Yale, Stanford, and MIT. He also spent a year on the staff of the Council of Economic Advisers in 1982–1983. His research is mainly in the area of international trade, where he is one of the founders of the "new trade theory," which focuses on increasing returns and imperfect competition. He also works in international finance, with a concentration in currency crises. In 1991, Krugman received the American Economic Association's John Bates Clark medal. In addition to his teaching and academic research, Krugman writes extensively for nontechnical audiences. Krugman is a regular op-ed columnist for the *New York Times*. His latest trade book is a best-selling collection of his *Times* articles entitled *The Great Unraveling: Losing Our Way in the New Century*. His earlier books, *Peddling Prosperity* and *The Age of Diminished Expectations,* have become modern classics.

Robin Wells is Researcher in Economics at Princeton University, where she regularly teaches undergraduate courses. She received her BA from the University of Chicago and her PhD from the University of California at Berkeley; she then did postdoctoral work at MIT. She has taught at the University of Michigan, the University of Southampton (United Kingdom), Stanford, and MIT. Her teaching and research focus on the theory of organizations and incentives. She writes regularly for academic journals.

Preface

"What is above all needed is to let the meaning choose the word, and not the other way about."

George Orwell,
"Politics and the English Language," 1946

FROM PAUL

Robin and I like to think that we wrote this book with a similar principle in mind. We wanted to write a different sort of book, one in which making sure the student understands how the models apply to the real world is given as much attention as the models themselves. We wanted to adapt Orwell's principle to the writing of an economics textbook: to let the purpose of economics—to achieve a deeper understanding of the world—rather than the mechanics of economics dictate the writing.

We believe that writing in this style reflects a commitment to the reader—a commitment to approach the material from a beginner's point of view, to make the material entertaining and accessible, to make discovery a joy. That's the fun part. But we also believe that there is another, equally compelling obligation on the part of an author of a principles of economics text. Economics is an extremely powerful tool. Many of us who are economists originally started in other disciplines (I started in history, Robin in chemistry). And we fell in love with economics because we believed it offers what most other disciplines don't—a coherent worldview that offers real guidelines to making the world a better place. (Yes, most economists are idealists at heart.) But like any powerful tool, economics should be treated with great care. For us, this obligation became a commitment that students would learn the appropriate use of the models—understand their assumptions and know their limitations as well as their positive uses. Why do we care about this? Because we don't live in a "one model of the economy fits all" world. To achieve deeper levels of understanding of the real world through economics, students must learn to appreciate the kinds of trade-offs and ambiguities that economists and policy makers face when applying their models to real-world problems. We hope this approach will make students more insightful and more effective participants in our common economic, social, and political lives.

To those familiar with my academic work, this perspective will probably look familiar. There I tried to make the problem to be solved the focus, and to avoid unnecessary technique. I tried to simplify. And I tried to choose topics that had important real-world implications. Writing for a large, nontechnical audience has only reinforced and expanded these tendencies. I had to begin with the working assumption that readers initially have no reason to care about what I am writing about—that it is my responsibility to show them why they should care. So the beginning of each chapter of this book is written according to the dictum: "If you haven't hooked them by the third sentence, then you've lost them." I've also learned that about all you can take for granted in writing for a lay audience is basic numeracy—addition and subtraction, but no more than that. Concepts must be fully explained; likely confusions must be anticipated and headed off. And most of all, you must be judicious in choosing the content and pacing of the writing—don't overwhelm your reader.

FROM ROBIN

Like Paul, I wanted to write a book that appeals to students without unduly sacrificing an instructor's obligation to teach economics well. I arrived at a similar perspective on how this book should be written, but by a different path. It came from my experiences teaching economics in a business school for a few years. Facing students who were typically impatient with abstraction and often altogether unhappy to be taking economics (and who would often exact bloody revenge in teaching evaluations), I learned how important it is to "hook" the students into the subject matter. Teaching with case studies, I found that concepts had been truly learned only when students could successfully apply them. And one of the most important lessons I learned was not to patronize. We—economists, that is—often assume that people who aren't familiar with conceptual thinking aren't smart and capable. Teaching in a business school showed me otherwise. The majority of my students were smart and capable, and many had shouldered a lot of responsibility in their working lives. Although adept at solving practical problems, they weren't trained to think conceptually. I had to learn to acknowledge the practical skills that they did have, but also show them the importance of the conceptual skills they didn't have. Although I eventually returned to an economics department, the lessons I learned about teaching economics in a business school stayed with me and, I believe, have been crucial ingredients in writing this textbook.

Advantages of This Book

Despite our fine words, why should any instructor use our text? We believe our book distinguishes itself in several ways that will make your introductory economics course an easier and more successful undertaking for the following reasons:

➤ **Chapters build intuition through realistic examples.** In every chapter, we use real-world examples, stories, applications, and case studies to teach the core concepts and motivate student learning. We believe that the best way to introduce concepts and reinforce them is through real-world examples; students simply relate more easily to them.

➤ **Pedagogical features reinforce learning.** We've worked hard to craft a set of features that will be genuinely helpful to students. We describe these features in the next section, "Tools for Learning."

➤ **Chapters have been written to be accessible and entertaining.** We have used a fluid and friendly writing style that makes the concepts accessible. And we have tried whenever possible to use examples that are familiar to students: for example, choosing which course to take, buying a used textbook, or deciding where to eat at the food court at the local shopping mall.

➤ **Although easy to understand, the book also prepares students for further coursework.** Too often, instructors find that selecting a textbook means choosing between two unappealing alternatives: a textbook that is "easy to teach" but leaves major gaps in students' understanding, or a textbook that is "hard to teach" but adequately prepares students for future coursework. We have worked very hard to create an easy-to-understand textbook that offers the best of both worlds.

➤ **The book permits flexible yet conceptually structured use of chapters.** We recognize that many instructors will prefer to teach the chapters in a sequence different from the one found in the book. Chapters were written with this in mind. Instructors can use the chapters in any order they wish. Our overarching goal was flexibility of organization for everyone. For a detailed look at the organization of chapters and ways to use them, see pages vii through xii of this preface.

Tools for Learning

We have structured each of the chapters around a common set of features. The following features are intended to help students learn better while also keeping them engaged.

"What You Will Learn in This Chapter"

To help readers get oriented, the first page of each chapter contains a preview of the chapter's contents, in an easy-to-review bulleted list format, that alerts students to the critical concepts and details the objectives of the chapter.

Opening Story

In contrast to other books in which each chapter begins with a recitation of some aspect of economics, we open each chapter with a compelling story that often extends through the entire chapter. Stories were chosen to accomplish two things: to illustrate important concepts in the chapter and then to encourage students to want to read on to learn more.

As we've mentioned, one of our main goals is to build intuition with realistic examples. Because each chapter is introduced with a real-world story, students will relate more easily to the material. For example, Chapter 3 teaches supply and demand in the context of a market for scalped tickets to a sports event (our opening story on page 56 is "Gretzky's Last Game").

"Economics in Action" Case Studies

In addition to introducing chapters with vivid stories, we conclude virtually every major text section with still more examples: a real-world case study called "Economics in Action." This feature provides a short but compelling application of the major concept just covered in that section. Students will experience an immediate payoff from being able to apply the concepts they've just read about to real phenomena. For example, in Chapter 6 we use the case of eBay, the online auctioneer, to communicate the concept of efficiency (see the "Economics in Action" entitled "eBay and Efficiency" on page 151). For a complete list of all the "Economics in Action" cases in the text, see the table of contents; the cases appear in the outline for each chapter.

Unique End-of-Section Review: "Quick Review" and "Check Your Understanding" Questions

In contrast to most other textbooks, which offer a review of concepts only at the end of each chapter, we include review material at the end of each major section within a chapter.

Economics contains a lot of jargon and abstract concepts that can quickly overwhelm the principles student. So we provide **Quick Reviews**, a short bulleted summary of concepts at the end of each major section. This review helps ensure that students understand what they have just read.

The **Check Your Understanding** feature, which appears along with every Quick Review, consists of a short set of review questions; solutions to these questions appear at the back of the book. These questions allow students to immediately test their understanding of the section just read. If they're not getting the questions right, it's a clear signal for them to go back and reread before moving on.

The "Economics in Action" cases, followed by the "Quick Reviews" and "Check Your Understanding" questions comprise our unique end-of-section pedagogical set that encourages students to apply what they've learned (via the "Economics in Action") and then review it (with the "Quick Reviews" and "Check Your Understanding" questions). Our hope is that students will be more successful in the course if they make use of this carefully constructed set of study aids.

"For Inquiring Minds" Boxes

To further our goal of helping students build intuition with real-world examples, each chapter contains one or more "For Inquiring Minds" boxes, in which concepts are applied to real-world events in unexpected and sometimes surprising ways, generating a sense of the power and breadth of economics. These boxes help impress on students that economics can be fun despite being labeled "the dismal science."

In a Chapter 10 box, for example, students learn how prices in a budget line serve the same function as the number of points assigned to a particular food in a Weight Watchers' diet plan (see the "For Inquiring Minds" entitled "Food for Thought on Budget Constraints," on page 240.) For a list of all "For Inquiring Minds" boxes, see the table of contents.

"Pitfalls" Boxes

Certain concepts are prone to be misunderstood when students are beginning their study of economics. We have tried to alert students to these mistakes in the "Pitfalls" boxes. Here common misunderstandings are spelled out and corrected—for example, the difference between increasing total cost and increasing marginal cost (see the "Pitfalls" box on this topic on page 167). For a list of all the "Pitfalls" boxes in chapters, see the table of contents.

Student-Friendly Graphs

Comprehending graphs is often one of the biggest hurdles for principles students. To help alleviate that problem, this book has been designed so that figures are large,

clear, and easy for students to follow. Many contain helpful annotations—in an easy-to-see balloon label format—that link to concepts within the text. Figure captions have been written both to complement the text discussion of figures and also to help students more readily grasp what they're seeing.

We've worked hard to make these graphs student-friendly. For example, to help students navigate one of the stickier thickets—the distinction between a shifting curve and movement along a curve—we encourage students to see this difference by using two types of arrows: a shift arrow (⟶) and what we call a "movement-along" arrow (⟶). You can see these arrows at work in Figures 3-12 and 3-13 on pages 73 and 74.

In addition, several graphs in each chapter are accompanied by the following icon: **>web**... This icon indicates that these graphs are available online as simulations (the graphs are animated in a Flash format and can be manipulated by students). Every interactive graph is accompanied by a quiz on key concepts to further help students in their work with graphs.

Helpful Graphing Appendix For students who would benefit from an explanation of how graphs are constructed, interpreted, and used in economics, we've included a detailed graphing appendix after Chapter 2 on page 41. This appendix is more comprehensive than most because we know that some students need this kind of helpful background, and we didn't want to breeze through the material. Our hope is that this comprehensive graphing appendix will better prepare students to use and interpret the graphs in this textbook and then out in the real world (in newspapers, magazines, and elsewhere).

Definitions of Key Terms

Every key term, in addition to being defined in the text, is also placed and defined in the accompanying margin to make it easier for students to study and review.

A Look Ahead

The text of each chapter ends with an "A Look Ahead" section, a short overview of what lies ahead in upcoming chapters. This concluding section provides students with a sense of continuity among chapters.

End-of-Chapter Review

In addition to the "Quick Review" at the end of each major section, each chapter ends with a complete but brief **Summary** of the key terms and concepts. In addition, a list of the **Key Terms** is placed at the end of each chapter along with page references.

Finally, we have created for each chapter a comprehensive set of **End-of-Chapter Problems**—problems that test intuition as well as the ability to calculate important variables. Much care and attention have been devoted to the creation of these problems so that instructors can be assured that they provide a true test of students' learning.

Upcoming Variations of This Book

The text you are now holding is our introduction to microeconomics, intended for the one-semester principles course in microeconomics.

Here is an overview of other textbooks in this series:

> *Economics:* The complete version of this textbook, containing all microeconomics chapters plus the full complement of macroeconomics chapters, is intended for the two-semester principles course.

> *Macroeconomics:* The complete introduction to macroeconomics is intended for a one-semester principles course in macroeconomics.

The Organization of This Book and How to Use It

This book is organized as a series of building blocks in which conceptual material learned at one stage is clearly built upon and then integrated into the conceptual material covered in the next stage. These building blocks correspond to the ten parts into which the chapters are divided. It's equally important to remember that an instructor need not teach these parts in the same sequence as they are found in the book. We recognize that a number of chapters will be considered optional and that many instructors will prefer to teach the chapters using a different order. Chapters and sections have been written to incorporate a degree of flexibility in the sequence in which they are taught, without sacrificing conceptual continuity. So an instructor can achieve some course customization through the choice of which chapters to cover and in which order to cover them. We will give a brief overview of each part and chapter, followed by a discussion of the various ways in which an instructor can tailor this book to meet his or her needs.

Part 1: What Is Economics?

In the **Introduction, "The Ordinary Business of Life,"** students are initiated into the study of economics in the context of a shopping trip on any given Sunday in everyday America. It provides students with basic definitions of

terms such as *economics*, the *invisible hand*, and *market structure*. In addition it serves as a "tour d'horizon" of economics, explaining the difference between microeconomics and macroeconomics.

In **Chapter 1, "First Principles,"** nine principles are presented and explained: four principles of individual choice, covering concepts such as opportunity cost, marginal analysis, and incentives; and five principles of interaction between individuals, covering concepts such as gains from trade, market efficiency, and market failure. In later chapters, we build intuition by frequently referring to these principles in the explanation of specific models. Students learn that these nine principles form a cohesive conceptual foundation for all of economics.

Chapter 2, "Economic Models: Trade-offs and Trade," shows students how to think like an economist by using three models—the production possibility frontier, comparative advantage and trade, and the circular-flow diagram—to analyze the world around them. It gives students an early introduction to gains from trade and to international comparisons. The **Chapter 2 appendix** contains a comprehensive math and graphing review for those students and instructors who wish to cover this material.

Part 2: Supply and Demand

Chapter 3, "Supply and Demand," covers the standard material in a fresh and compelling way: supply and demand, market equilibrium, and surplus and shortage are all illustrated using an example of the market for scalped tickets to a sports event. Students learn how the demand and supply curves of scalped tickets shift in response to the announcements of a star player's impending retirement.

Chapter 4, "The Market Strikes Back," covers various types of market interventions and their consequences: price and quantity controls, inefficiency and deadweight loss, and excise taxes. Through tangible examples such as New York City rent control regulations and New York City taxi licenses, the costs generated by attempts to control markets are made real to students.

In **Chapter 5, "Elasticity,"** the actions of OPEC and their consequences for the world market for oil taken together are the real-world motivating example in our discussion of the price elasticity of demand. There we introduce the various elasticity measures and show how elasticities are used to evaluate the incidence of an excise tax.

Part 3: Individuals and Markets

Through examples such as a market for used textbooks and eBay, students learn how markets increase welfare in **Chapter 6, "Consumer and Producer Surplus."** Although the concepts of market efficiency and deadweight loss are strongly emphasized, we also preview the ways in which a market can fail.

Chapter 7, "Making Decisions," is a unique chapter. Microeconomics is fundamentally a science of how to make decisions. But that aspect is rarely highlighted in introductory microeconomics. Rather, other textbooks place much of the emphasis on comprehending the consequences of decision making instead of on developing an understanding of how decisions should be made in any context. For example, due to the almost exclusive emphasis that economics textbooks place on marginal analysis, we believe that students are often unable to distinguish between what is and what isn't a marginal decision. To remedy this, we have included an entire section on "either-or" versus "how much" decisions—a distinction that is particularly useful in later chapters where we compare a firm's output decision to its entry/exit decision. In addition, in Chapter 7 we reprise the concept of opportunity cost; present a thorough treatment of marginal analysis; explain the concept of sunk cost; and, for instructors who wish to teach it, cover present discounted value. Full coverage of sunk cost at this point will help students later in understanding the irrelevance of fixed cost in the firm's short-run output decision. We think this chapter will be an important teaching aid because it helps students develop a deeper intuition about the common conceptual foundations of microeconomic models.

What Comes Next: The Firm or the Consumer? You may have noticed that we have placed the chapters covering the producer before the chapters covering the consumer. Why have we done this? Because we believe that it is a more natural conceptual progression to cover the producer after Chapter 7, "Making Decisions," than it is to cover the consumer. Since students have just studied opportunity cost, economic profit versus accounting profit, marginal benefit and marginal cost, and sunk cost, we think examining the firm's cost curves, its output decision, and its entry/exit decision is an easier next step for them to undertake.

We are aware that some instructors are likely to be skeptical of this approach. We have often heard instructors say that the consumer should be studied before the producer because students can relate to being a consumer but not to being the owner of a firm. We hope, however, to change that viewpoint because what we really want students to do is not just relate to being a consumer but *think like a rational consumer—a consumer who maximizes utility subject to scarce resources.* And we believe that it is easier for students to understand utility maximization (utility being an inherently slippery concept) after they have come to understand profit maximization.

Nonetheless, we want to strongly emphasize that it is very easy for instructors who wish to follow a traditional chapter sequence—with the consumer before the firm—to do just that. We wrote the chapters so that there is no loss whatsoever if an instructor follows Chapter 7 with Chapter 10, "The Rational Consumer," and Chapter 11, "Consumer Preferences and Consumer Choice" (an optional chapter).

Part 4: The Producer

In Chapter 8, "Behind the Supply Curve: Inputs and Costs," we develop the production function and the various cost measures of the firm. There is an extensive discussion of the difference between average cost and marginal cost, illustrated by examples such as a student's grade point average. Chapter 9, "Perfect Competition and the Supply Curve," explains the output decision of the perfectly competitive firm, its entry/exit decision, the industry supply curve, and the equilibrium of a perfectly competitive market. We draw on examples such as generic pharmaceuticals and the California energy crisis of 2000–2001 to contrast the behavior of oligopolists and monopolists.

Part 5: The Producer

Chapter 10, "The Rational Consumer," provides a complete treatment of consumer behavior for instructors who don't cover indifference curves. There is a simple, intuitive exposition of the budget line, the optimal consumption choice, diminishing marginal utility, and income and substitution effects and their relationship to market demand. Students learn, for example, that a budget line constructed using prices is much like a Weight Watchers diet plan constructed using a "point" system. Chapter 11, "Consumer Preferences and Consumer Choice," offers a more detailed treatment for those who wish to cover indifference curves. It contains an analysis of the optimal consumption choice using the marginal rate of substitution as well as income and substitution effects.

What Comes Next: Markets and Efficiency or Market Structure? Many instructors are likely to consider the next two chapters—Chapter 12, "Factor Markets and the Distribution of Income," and Chapter 13 "Efficiency and Equity"—optional. For those who wish to skip them, their next topic area will be market structure beyond perfect competition: monopoly, oligopoly, and monopolistic competition. Chapters 12 and 13 are likely to be used by instructors who want a more in-depth coverage of microeconomics, as well as those who wish to emphasize labor markets, welfare, and public policy issues.

Instructors who prefer a traditional sequence of topics may wish to go from Part 5 ("The Consumer") to Part 4 ("The Producer") to Part 7 ("Market Structure: Beyond Perfect Competition"), bypassing Part 6 ("Markets and Efficiency") altogether or covering it later. This is a good choice for those who wish to contrast the difference between the perfectly competitive firm's output decision and the monopolist's output decision. But, those who follow the existing chapter sequence—"The Producer" followed by "The Consumer" followed by "Market Structure: Beyond Perfect Competition"—will be able to draw a tighter connection among consumer behavior, monopoly pricing, price discrimination, product differentiation, and monopolistic competition. We have written the chapters so that either sequence works equally well.

Part 6: Markets and Efficiency

Chapter 12, "Factor Markets and the Distribution of Income," covers the competitive factor market model and the factor distribution of income. It also contains modifications and alternative interpretations of the labor market: the efficiency-wage model of the labor market is discussed, and the influences of education, discrimination, and market power are also addressed. It presents, we hope, a balanced and well-rounded view of the strengths and limitations of the competitive market model of labor markets and leads to a greater appreciation of the issues of efficiency and equity discussed in the next chapter. For instructors who covered indifference curves in Chapter 11, the **Chapter 12 appendix** offers a detailed examination of the labor-leisure trade-off and the backward-bending labor supply curve.

In **Chapter 13, "Efficiency and Equity,"** after recapping efficiency in a single market, we compare and contrast this to what it means to have efficiency in a market economy as a whole. Some may wonder why it is useful to draw the distinction between partial equilibrium and general equilibrium in a principles course. We believe that doing so gives students a deeper understanding of the often-conflicting objectives of efficiency and equity—something that really can't be fully explored in a partial equilibrium setting. As a real-world example, we discuss the reunification of West and East Germany in terms of the trade-offs faced by German policy makers, who sacrificed some efficiency-enhancing measures in order to reduce the income differences between East and West Germans. Students should come away from this chapter with a fuller appreciation of the complexity of real-world economic policy making—that is, how democracies may sometimes choose to sacrifice some efficiency for equity purposes.

Part 7: Market Structure: Beyond Perfect Competition

Chapter 14, "Monopoly," is a full treatment of monopoly, including topics such as price discrimination and the welfare effects of monopoly. We provide an array of compelling examples, such as De Beers Diamonds, price manipulation by California power companies, and airline ticket–pricing. In **Chapter 15, "Oligopoly,"** we present basic game theory in both a one-shot and repeated-game context, as well as an integrated treatment of the kinked demand curve model. The models are applied to a wide set of actual examples, such as Archer-Daniels-Midland, a European vitamin cartel, OPEC, and airline ticket–pricing wars. In **Chapter 16, "Monopolistic Competition and Product Differentiation,"** students are brought face to face early on with an example of monopolistic competition that is a familiar feature of their lives: the food court at the local mall. We go on to cover entry and exit, efficiency considerations, and advertising in monopolistic competition.

What Comes Next: Extending Market Boundaries or Microeconomics and Public Policy? The next section of the book, "Extending Market Boundaries," is devoted to applications and extensions of the competitive market model: Chapter 17, "International Trade," and Chapter 18, "Uncertainty, Risk, and Private Information." Both of these chapters are entirely optional. Instructors who prefer to skip one or both of these chapters can proceed to the following section, "Microeconomics and Public Policy."

Part 8: Extending Market Boundaries

In Chapter 2, we presented a full exposition of gains from trade and the difference between comparative and absolute advantage, illustrated with an international example (trade between high-wage and low-wage countries). **Chapter 17, "International Trade,"** builds on that material. It contains a recap of comparative advantage, traces the sources of comparative advantage, considers tariffs and quotas, and explores the politics of trade protection. In response to current events, we give in-depth coverage to the controversy over imports from low-wage countries.

The inclusion in a principles text of **Chapter 18, "Uncertainty, Risk, and Private Information,"** may come as a surprise to some—a common reaction being "Isn't this material too hard for principles students?" We believe that, with our treatment, the answer is "no" for many more students than is typically expected. In this chapter we explain attitudes toward risk in a careful and methodical way, grounded in the basic concept of diminishing marginal utility. This allows us to analyze a simple competitive insurance market, and to examine the benefits and limits of diversification. Next comes an easily comprehensible and intuitive presentation of private information in the context of adverse selection and moral hazard, with illustrations drawn from the market for lemons (used cars) and franchising. We believe that instructors will be surprised by how easy it is to teach this material and how much it will enlighten students about the relevance of economics to their everyday lives.

Part 9: Microeconomics and Public Policy

Chapter 19, "Externalities," covers negative externalities and solutions such as Coasian private trades, emissions taxes, and a system of tradable permits. We also examine positive externalities, technological spillovers, and the resulting arguments for industrial policy. **Chapter 20, "Public Goods and Common Resources,"** makes an immediate impression by opening with the story of how "The Great Stink of 1858" compelled Londoners to build a public sewer system. Students learn how to classify goods into four categories (private goods, common resources, public goods, and artificially scarce goods) based on two dimensions: excludability and rivalry in consumption. With this system, they can develop an intuitive understanding of why some goods but not others can be efficiently managed by markets.

Chapter 21, "Taxes, Social Insurance, and Income Distribution," begins with a review of the burden of taxation and considerations of equity versus efficiency. Next, it examines the structure of taxes, current tax policy, and public spending in the United States. This is followed by an investigation into the sources of poverty and their implications for government tax and transfer policies. From this chapter students can gain an appreciation of the difficult questions policy makers face in addressing issues of economic efficiency and welfare.

Part 10: New Directions for Markets

The final section of the book contains one chapter, **Chapter 22, "Technology, Innovation, and Network Externalities."**

We believe that Chapter 22, even though providing real economic models and relevant cases, will be enjoyable for both instructors and students. Starting with the example of sharing music files over the Internet, it introduces the concept of information goods and network externalities and analyzes the problems they cause for efficient pricing. We discuss the implications for standard-setting and the ambiguities that network externalities present for regulatory policy. Students will see how these issues affect their daily lives through references to Kazaa, Apple Computers, and Microsoft.

What's Core, What's Optional?

As noted earlier, we realize that some of our chapters will be considered optional. On the facing page is a listing of what we view as core chapters and those that could be considered optional chapters. We've annotated the list of optional chapters to indicate what they cover should you wish to consider incorporating them into your course.

A Selection of Possible Outlines

To illustrate how instructors can use this book to meet their specific goals, we've constructed a selection of three possible outlines (see page xii). By no means exclusive, these outlines reflect a likely range of different ways in which this book could be used:

> **Traditional Outline** (consumer first, producer second)
> **Public Policy and Welfare Outline** (includes factor markets and efficiency)
> **Applied Microeconomics Outline** (includes international trade and uncertainty, risk, and private information)

Although we don't outline it here, we also offer a Decision-Based Outline. The choice between a Traditional Outline and the Decision-Based Outline is primarily a choice about the sequencing of Parts 4 and 5. An instructor who prefers to cover "The Consumer" before "The Producer" will choose the Traditional Outline. An instructor who wants to emphasize decision making should instead cover "The Producer" before "The Consumer," just covering Parts 4 and 5 as ordered.

At this point, instructors can skip immediately to Part 7, to cover monopoly, oligopoly, and monopolistic competition. However, instructors who wish to focus more intensely on international economics, tools of microeconomics, or public policy (the Applied Microeconomics Outline or the Public Policy and Welfare Outline) may choose to teach Part 6, which addresses factor markets and economy-wide efficiency, before moving on to Part 7. After Part 7, instructors who have adopted an applied microeconomics or public policy focus may wish to cover some or all of Part 8, which contains a chapter on international trade and a chapter on risk and private information. Others, however, will prefer to skip to Part 9, which covers externalities, public goods, common resources, and tax policy. Finally, Part 10, consisting solely of Chapter 22, which covers the network economy, is a suitable choice for any of these outlines. But it will be a particularly good chapter for those who wish to focus on public policy.

WHAT'S CORE, WHAT'S OPTIONAL: AN OVERVIEW

Core	Optional

Core

1. First Principles
2. Economic Models: Trade-offs and Trade

3. Supply and Demand
4. The Market Strikes Back
5. Elasticity
6. Consumer and Producer Surplus

8. Behind the Supply Curve: Inputs and Costs
9. Perfect Competition and the Supply Curve
10. The Rational Consumer

14. Monopoly
15. Oligopoly
16. Monopolistic Competition and Product Differentiation

19. Externalities
20. Public Goods and Common Resources
21. Taxes, Social Insurance, and Income Distribution

Optional

Introduction: The Ordinary Business of Life

Appendix: Graphs in Economics
A comprehensive review of graphing and math for students who would find such a refresher helpful.

7. Making Decisions
A unique chapter aimed at helping students understand how decisions should be made in any context. Includes coverage of marginal analysis and cost-benefit analysis. Pairs well with Chapter 6. Prepares students for coverage of models in upcoming chapters.

11. Consumer Preferences and Consumer Choice
This chapter offers a more detailed treatment of consumer behavior for instructors who wish to cover indifference curves.

12. Factor Markets and the Distribution of Income Plus Appendix: Indifference Curve Analysis of Labor Supply
For instructors who want to go more in-depth, this chapter covers the efficiency-wage model of the labor market as well as the influences of education, discrimination, and market power. The appendix examines the labor-leisure trade-off and the backward-bending labor supply curve.

13. Efficiency and Equity
A unique chapter that explores what it means to have efficiency in a market economy as a whole. Gives students a deeper understanding of the often-conflicting objectives of efficiency and equity. Intended for instructors who emphasize welfare and public policy issues.

17. International Trade
This chapter recaps comparative advantage, considers tariffs and quotas, and explores the politics of trade protection. Coverage here links back to international coverage in Chapter 2.

18. Uncertainty, Risk, and Private Information
A unique, applied chapter that explains attitudes toward risk, examines the benefits and limits of diversification, and considers private information in the context of adverse selection and moral hazard.

22. Technology, Innovation, and Network Externalities
A unique chapter that shows students how to use economic models to analyze information goods. A nice treat for students and instructors!

THREE POSSIBLE OUTLINES

Traditional	Public Policy and Welfare	Applied Microeconomics

Part 1
1. First Principles
2. Economic Models: Tradeoffs and Trade
   Appendix: Graphs in Economics
	Part 1
	1. First Principles
	2. Economic Models: Tradeoffs and Trade
	   Appendix: Graphs in Economics
		Part 1
		1. First Principles
		2. Economic Models: Tradeoffs and Trade
		   Appendix: Graphs in Economics

Part 2 3. Supply and Demand 4. The Market Strikes Back 5. Elasticity	**Part 2** 3. Supply and Demand 4. The Market Strikes Back 5. Elasticity	**Part 2** 3. Supply and Demand 4. The Market Strikes Back 5. Elasticity
Part 3 6. Consumer and Producer Surplus 7. Making Decisions	**Part 3** 6. Consumer and Producer Surplus 7. Making Decisions	**Part 3** 6. Consumer and Producer Surplus 7. Making Decisions
Part 5* 10. The Rational Consumer 11. Consumer Preferences and Consumer Choice	Either **Part 4, then 5** Or, **Part 5, then Part 4**	Either **Part 4, then 5** Or, **Part 5, then Part 4**

Part 4*
8. Behind the Supply Curve: Inputs and Costs
9. Perfect Competition and the Supply Curve
	Part 6
	12. Factor Markets and Distribution of Income
	   Appendix: Indifference Curve Analysis of Labor Supply
	13. Efficiency and Equity
		Part 6
		12. Factor Markets and the Distribution of Income
		   Appendix: Indifference Curve Analysis of Labor Supply
		13. Efficiency and Equity

Part 7 14. Monopoly 15. Oligopoly 16. Monopolistic Competition and Product Differentiation	**Part 7** 14. Monopoly 15. Oligopoly 16. Monopolistic Competition and Product Differentiation	**Part 7** 14. Monopoly 15. Oligopoly 16. Monopolistic Competition and Product Differentiation
Part 9 19. Externalities 20. Public Goods and Common Resources 21. Taxes, Social Insurance, and Income Distribution	**Part 8** 17. International Trade 18. Uncertainty, Risk, and Private Information	**Part 8** 17. International Trade 18. Uncertainty, Risk, and Private Information
	Part 9 19. Externalities 20. Public Goods and Common Resources 21. Taxes, Social Insurance, and Income	**Part 9** 19. Externalities 20. Public Goods and Common Resources 21. Taxes, Social Insurance, and Income
	Part 10 22. Technology, Innovation, and Network Externalities	

*Instructors who wish to follow a decision-based sequence should use the parts of this text as we've ordered them: Part 4, "The Producer," followed by Part 5, "The Consumer."

Supplements and Media

Worth Publishers is pleased to offer an exciting and useful supplements and media package to accompany this textbook. The package has been crafted to help instructors teach their principles course and to help students grasp concepts more readily.

The entire package has been coordinated by Martha Olney, University of California-Berkeley, to provide consistency in level and quality. Rosemary Cunningham, Agnes Scott College, has coordinated all of the quizzing materials in the Study Guide, Test Bank, and all the online materials to guarantee uniformity.

Since accuracy is so critically important, all the supplements have been scrutinized and double-checked by members of the supplements team, reviewers, and a team of additional accuracy checkers. The time and care that have been put into the supplements and media ensure a seamless package.

Companion Website for Students and Instructors

econ✕change

(www.worthpublishers.com/krugmanwells)
The companion website for the Krugman/Wells text offers valuable tools for both the instructor and students.

For instructors, this completely customized website offers many opportunities for quizzing and, most important, powerful grading tools. The site gives you the ability to track students' interaction with the Homework Advantage Center, the Practice Quizzing Center, and the Graphing Center by accessing separate online gradebooks for each category.

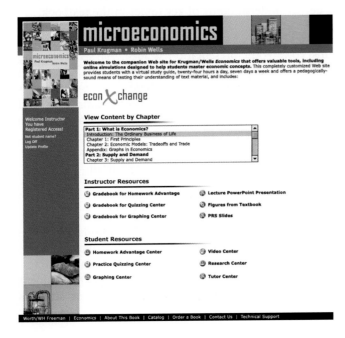

For students, the site offers many opportunities to practice, practice, practice. On the site, students can find online simulations, practice quizzes, video resources, graphing tutorials, and links to many other resources designed to help them master economic concepts. In essence, this site provides students with a virtual study guide, twenty-four hours a day, seven days a week by offering a pedagogically sound means of testing their understanding of text material.

This helpful, powerful site contains the following:

Homework Advantage Center This section of the site offers a secure, interactive, online environment. It allows you to create customized homework assignments, quizzes, or tests.

Selected end-of-chapter questions from the textbook have been incorporated into an online quizzing engine that allows the variables of each question to be algorithmically generated. Questions from the textbook's Test Bank are also incorporated into this engine with the same algorithmic generation capabilities. You can add your own questions or edit the questions provided by Worth.

The Homework Advantage Center enables you to create a customized test for each and every student. Although each student will be asked the same question, the values of those questions will be completely different. Using the Homework Advantage Center, you can easily create and assign tests for automatic grading. You can also use the Homework Advantage Center to allow students to test their own skills and diagnose their understanding of the material.

All the student responses are stored in an electronic gradebook so that you can easily grade exams and generate reports. The gradebook has the following features that allow for flexibility in assessing students' abilities.

➤ Grades can be organized into as many as 25 related categories (tests, papers, homework, etc.).

➤ Assignments can be independently weighted.

➤ Letter grade cutoffs can be adjusted, and custom grading created ("Fair," "Good," "Excellent," and so on).

➤ Assignment scores and category averages can be entered or displayed as percentages, points, letter grades, or according to your own customized grading scheme.

➤ Gradebooks can be set up to report final averages as points earned across all categories.

➤ Student properties can include ID number, password (for online testing), e-mail address, and status (active, withdraw, incomplete).

➤ Grades can be dropped manually or automatically.

➤ Assignment, category, and final scores can be curved.

➤ Numerous reports can be customized and printed with an interactive print preview.

➤ Results can be merged from TheTestingCenter.Com.

➤ Student rosters can be imported and exported.

Practice Quizzing Center Developed by Debbie Mullin, University of Colorado-Colorado Springs, this quizzing engine provides 20 multiple-choice questions per chapter with appropriate feedback and page references to the textbook. The questions as well as the answer choices are randomized to give students a different quiz with every refresh of the screen. All student answers are saved in an online database that can be accessed by instructors.

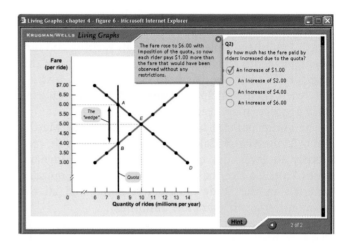

Research Center Created and continually updated by Jules Kaplan, University of Colorado-Boulder, the Research Center allows students to easily and effectively locate outside resources and readings that relate to topics covered in the textbook. It lists web addresses that hotlink to relevant websites; each URL is accompanied by a detailed description of the site and its relevance to each chapter, allowing students to conduct research and explore related readings on specific topics with ease. Also hotlinked are relevant articles by Paul Krugman and other leading economists.

Video Center In video interviews, the text's authors, Paul Krugman and Robin Wells, comment on specific aspects of each chapter and their relevance to students' lives. Each video is embedded in a Flash format with other pedagogical features and a running transcript of the authors' remarks. Videos can be presented in class to generate discussion or assigned as homework to give students a deeper understanding of key topics in the textbook.

Tutor Center Created by Can Erbil, Brandeis University, this PowerPoint presentation is ideal for students who need extra help in understanding the concepts in each chapter. The PowerPoint presentations for each chapter come complete with animations, notes, summaries, and graphics. This tool enables students to review and practice and helps them to more readily grasp economic concepts. The Tutor Center nicely complements the already extensive learning apparatus within the text itself.

Additional Student Supplements

Graphing Center Developed by Cadre LLC in conjunction with Debbie Mullin, University of Colorado-Colorado Springs, the Graphing Center includes selected graphs from the textbook that have been animated in a Flash format, allowing students to manipulate curves and plot data points when appropriate. About five to seven graphs from each chapter have been animated and are identified in the textbook by a web icon **>web...** within the appropriate figure. Having the ability to manipulate graphs and observe the results of the manipulation provides students with a keen understanding of the effects of the shifts and movements of the curves. Every interactive graph is accompanied by questions that quiz students on key concepts from the textbook and provide instructors with feedback on student progress. Student responses and interactions are tracked and stored in an online database that can be accessed by the instructor.

Student CD-ROM This CD-ROM contains all of the multimedia content found on the Krugman/Wells Companion website, including the practice quizzes, interactive graphs, Krugman/Wells videos, and the student PowerPoint slides. This CD-ROM is ideal for students with limited web access or for use in a lab setting. Available upon request, this CD can be packaged with the textbook at no additional cost to the student.

Study Guide Prepared by Rosemary Cunningham, Agnes Scott College, and Elizabeth Sawyer-Kelley, University of Wisconsin-Madison, and coordinated by Martha Olney, University of California-Berkeley, the Study Guide reinforces the topics and key concepts covered in the text. For each chapter, the Study Guide provides an introduction, fill-in-the-blank chapter review, learning tips with graphical analysis, four or five comprehensive problems and exercises, 20 multiple-choice questions, and solutions to all fill-in-the-blank reviews, problems, exercises, and quizzes found within the Study Guide.

Additional Instructor Supplements

Instructor's Resource Manual The Instructor's Resource Manual written by Diane Keenan, Cerritos Community College, and coordinated by Martha Olney, University of California-Berkeley, is an ideal resource for instructors teaching principles of economics. The manual includes:

➤ Chapter-by-chapter learning objectives

➤ Chapter outlines

➤ Teaching tips and ideas

➤ Hints on how to create student interest

➤ Common misunderstandings that are typical among students

➤ Activities that can be conducted in or out of the classroom

➤ Detailed solutions to every end-of-chapter problem from the textbook

Printed Test Bank The Test Bank, coordinated by Rosemary Cunningham, Agnes Scott College, with contributing authors Jack Chambless, Valencia Community College; Ardeshir Dalal, Northern Illinois University; Mark Funk, University of Arkansas-Little Rock; Lynn Gillette, University of Kentucky; Gus W. Herring, Brookhaven College; and Regina Wyatt, Dallas Community College District, provides a wide range of creative and versatile questions ranging in levels of difficulty. Selected questions are paired with original graphs and graphs from the textbook to reinforce comprehension. Totaling over 2,500 questions, the Test Bank offers 60 multiple-choice questions and 20 true/false questions per chapter assessing comprehension, interpretation, analysis, and synthesis. Each question is conveniently cross referenced to the page number in the text where the appropriate topic is discussed. Questions have been

checked by the entire supplements team, reviewed extensively, and checked again for accuracy.

Diploma 6.3 Computerized Test Bank The Krugman/Wells printed Test Bank is also available in CD-ROM format, powered by Brownstone, for both Windows and Macintosh users. With Diploma, you can easily create tests, write and edit questions, and create study sessions for students. You can add an unlimited number of questions, scramble questions, and include pictures, equations, and multimedia links. Tests can be printed in a wide range of formats or administered to students with Brownstone's network or Internet testing software. The software's unique synthesis of flexible word-processing and database features creates a program that is extremely intuitive and capable. With the new Diploma 6.3, you can:

➤ Work with complete word processing functions (including creating tables).

➤ Work with myriad question formats, including multiple choice, true/false, short answer, matching, fill in the blank, and essay.

➤ Attach feedback (rationales) to questions (or answers).

➤ Create, install, and use an unlimited number of question banks.

➤ Incorporate references (including tables, figures, and case studies).

➤ Attach customized instructions.

➤ Use multiple graphic formats (BMP, DIB, RLE, DXF, EPS, FPX, GIF, IMG, JPG, PCD, PCX, DCX, PNG, TGA, TIF, WMF, and WPG).

➤ Take advantage of a powerful algorithm engine for complex, dynamic question types and dynamic equations.

➤ Export self-grading tests (in HTML formats) for use with web browsers.

➤ Export test files in Rich Text File format for use with any word-processing program.

➤ Export test files to EDU, WebCT, and Blackboard course management systems.

➤ Preview and re-format tests before printing them.

➤ Include custom splash screens that feature graphics or images.

➤ Post tests to Diploma's online testing site, TheTestingCenter.com.

This computerized Test Bank is accompanied by a gradebook that enables you to record students' grades throughout a course; it also includes the capacity to track student records and view detailed analyses of test items, curve tests, generate reports, add weights to grades, and allows you to:

➤ Organize grades into as many as 25 related categories.
➤ Adjust letter grade cutoffs and create customized grading.
➤ Enter/display assignment scores and category averages as percentages, points, letter grades, or according to your own customized grading scheme.
➤ Report final averages as points earned across all categories.
➤ Customize student properties (including ID number, password, e-mail address, and status).
➤ Drop grades either manually or automatically.
➤ Import and export student rosters.

Diploma Online Testing at www.brownstone.net is another useful tool within the Brownstone software that allows instructors to provide online exams for students using Test Bank questions. With Diploma, you can easily create and administer secure exams over a network and over the Internet, with questions that incorporate multimedia and interactive exercises. The program allows you to restrict tests to specific computers or time blocks, and it includes an impressive suite of gradebook and result-analysis features.

PowerPoint Slides Created by Can Erbil, Brandeis University, the enhanced PowerPoint presentation slides are designed to assist you with lecture preparation and presentation by providing original animations, graphs from the textbook, data tables, and bulleted lists of key concepts suitable for large lecture presentation. Although the slides are organized by topic from the text's table of contents, you can customize these slides to suit your individual needs by adding your own data, questions, and lecture notes. You can access these files on the instructor's side of the website or on the Instructor's Resource CD-ROM.

Instructor's Resource CD-ROM Using the Instructor's Resource CD-ROM, you can easily build classroom presentations around a variety of still and moving images—from the Krugman/Wells text, from your own sources, and even from the web. This customized presentation CD-ROM contains all text figures (in JPEG and GIF formats), video clips of interviews with Paul Krugman and Robin Wells, animated graphs, and enhanced PowerPoint slides. All of these resources are compatible with Microsoft PowerPoint software but can also be used independently to create a classroom presentation providing an unbeatable combination of convenience and power. This CD allows you to combine all of the publisher-provided instructor materials with your own materials into a customized presentation suitable for all lecture needs.

Overhead Transparencies Worth is also happy to provide you with more than 200 vivid color acetates of text figures designed for superior projection quality.

Web-CT E-pack The Krugman/Wells WebCT E-Packs enable you to create a thorough, interactive, and pedagogically-sound online course or course website. The Krugman/Wells E-Pack provides you with cutting-edge online materials that facilitate critical thinking and learning including course outlines, preprogrammed quizzes, links, activities, threaded discussion topics, animated graphs, and a whole array of other materials. Best of all, this material is pre-programmed and fully functional in the WebCT environment. Prebuilt materials eliminate hours of course-preparation work and offer significant support as you develop your online course. You can also obtain a WebCT-formatted version of the text's test bank.

Blackboard The Krugman/Wells Blackboard Course Cartridge allows you to combine Blackboard's popular tools and easy-to-use interface with the Krugman/Wells' text-specific, rich web content, including course outlines, preprogrammed quizzes, links, activities, interactive graphs, and a whole array of other materials. The result: an interactive, comprehensive online course that allow for effortless implementation, management, and use. The Worth electronic files are organized and prebuilt to work within the Blackboard software and can be easily downloaded from the Blackboard content showcases directly onto your department server. You can also obtain a Blackboard-formatted version of the book's test bank.

Aplia Aplia, founded by Paul Romer, Stanford University, is the first web-based company to integrate pedagogical features from a textbook with interactive media. Specifically designed for use with the Krugman/Wells text, the figures, end-of-chapter problems, boxes, text, and other pedagogical resources have been combined with Aplia's interactive media to save time for professors and encourage students to exert more effort in their learning.

The integrated online version of the Aplia media and the Krugman/Wells text includes:

➤ Extra problem sets suitable for homework and keyed to specific topics from each chapter
➤ Regularly updated news analyses
➤ Real-time online simulations of market interactions
➤ Interactive tutorials to assist with math
➤ Graphs and statistics
➤ Instant online reports that allow instructors to target student trouble areas more efficiently

With Aplia, you retain complete control and flexibility for your course. You choose the topics you want students to cover, and you decide how to organize it. You decide whether online activities are practice (ungraded or graded). You can even edit the Aplia content—making cuts or addtions as you see fit for your course.

For a preview of Aplia materials and to learn more, visit http://www.aplia.com.

Dallas TeleLearning videos The Krugman/Wells text was chosen to accompany the economics telecourse developed by the Dallas Community College District (DCCCD). For use in class, instructors have access to videos produced by the DCCCD, the nation's leading developer of distance-learning materials. These videos dramatize key economic concepts and can be used in a classroom setting.

EduCue Personal Response System (PRS)—"Clickers"
Instructors can create a dynamic, interactive classroom environment with a personal response system, powered by EduCue. This wireless remote system allows you to ask your students questions, record their responses, and calculate grades instantly during lectures. Students use a hand-held wireless device (about the size of a television remote control) to transmit immediate feedback to a lecture hall receiver.

Wall Street Journal **Edition** For adopters of the Krugman/Wells text, Worth Publishers and the *Wall Street Journal* are offering a ten-week subscription to students at a tremendous savings. Professors also receive their own free *Wall Street Journal* subscription plus additional instructor supplements created exclusively by the *Wall Street Journal*. Please contact your local sales rep for more information or go to the *Wall Street Journal* online at www.wsj.com.

Financial Times **Edition** For adopters of the Krugman/ Wells text, Worth Publishers and the *Financial Times* are offering a fifteen-week subscription to students at a tremendous savings. Professors also receive their own free *Financial Times* subscription for one year. Students and professors may access research and archived information at www.ft.com.

Acknowledgments

Writing a textbook is a team effort and we could never have reached this point without all of the talented and thoughtful consultants, reviewers, focus-group participants, class testers, and others who have been so generous with their insights on our work.

We are indebted to the following reviewers and other consultants for their suggestions and advice on portions of our manuscript:

Lee Adkins, *Oklahoma State University*
Elena Alvarez, *State University of New York, Albany*
David A. Anderson, *Centre College*
Sheryl Ball, *Virginia Polytechnic Institute and State University*
Charles L. Ballard, *Michigan State University*
Daniel Barszcz, *College of DuPage*
Charles A. Bennett, *Gannon University*
Andreas Bentz, *Dartmouth College*
Harmanna Bloemen, *Houston Community College*
Michael Bordo, *Rutgers University, NBER*
William Branch, *University of Oregon*
Michael Brandl, *University of Texas, Austin*
Charles Callahan, III, *State University of New York, College at Brockport*
Leonard A. Carlson, *Emory University*
Shirley Cassing, *University of Pittsburgh*
Jim Cobbe, *Florida State University*
Eleanor D. Craig, *University of Delaware*
Rosemary Thomas Cunningham, *Agnes Scott College*
Ardeshir Dalal, *Northern Illinois University*
A. Edward Day, *University of Texas, Dallas*
Stephen J. DeCanio, *University of California, Santa Barbara*
J. Bradford DeLong, *University of California, Berkeley*
Jim Eden, *Portland Community College*
Can Erbil, *Brandeis University*
Joe Essuman, *University of Wisconsin, Waukesha*
Oliver Franke, *Athabasca University*
Rhona Free, *Eastern Connecticut State University*
Susan Gale, *New York University*
J. Robert Gillette, *University of Kentucky*
Lynn G. Gillette, *University of Kentucky*
Robert Godby, *University of Wyoming*
David Goodwin, *University of New Brunswick*
Lisa Grobar, *California State University, Long Beach*
Philip Grossman, *St. Cloud State University*
Wayne Grove, *Syracuse University*
Jang-Ting Guo, *University of California, Riverside*
Jonathan Hamilton, *University of Florida*
Julie Heath, *University of Memphis*
Jill M. Hendrickson, *University of the South*
David Horlacher, *Middlebury College*
Robert Horn, *James Madison University*
Scott Houser, *California State University, Fresno*
Patrik T. Hultberg, *University of Wyoming*
Nancy Jianakoplos, *Colorado State University*
Donn Johnson, *Quinnipiac University*
Bruce Johnson, *Centre College*
James Jozefowicz, *Indiana University of Pennsylvania*
Matthew Kahn, *Columbia University*
Barry Keating, *University of Notre Dame*
Diane Keenan, *Cerritos College*

Bill Kerby, *California State University, Sacramento*

Kyoo Kim, *Bowling Green University*

Philip King, *San Francisco State University*

Kala Krishna, *Penn State University, NBER*

Tom Larson, *California State University, Los Angeles*

Jim Lee, *Texas A&M University—Corpus Christi*

Tony Lima, *California State University, Hayward*

Rachel McCulloch, *Brandeis University*

Diego Mendez-Carbajo, *Illinois Wesleyan University*

Juan Mendoza, *State University of New York at Buffalo*

Jeffrey Michael, *Towson University*

Jenny Minier, *University of Miami*

Ida A. Mirzaie, *John Carroll University*

Kristen Monaco, *California State University, Long Beach*

W. Douglas Morgan, *University of California, Santa Barbara*

Peter B. Morgan, *University of Michigan*

John A. Neri, *University of Maryland*

Seamus O'Cleireacain, *Columbia University / State University of New York, Purchase*

Martha Olney, *University of California, Berkeley*

Chris Papageorgiou, *Louisiana State University*

John Pharr, *Dallas County Community College*

Raymond E. Polchow, *Zane State College*

Jeffrey Racine, *University of South Florida*

Matthew Rafferty, *Quinnipiac University*

Dixie Watts Reaves, *Virginia Polytechnic Institute and State University*

Siobhán Reilly, *Mills College*

Thomas Rhoads, *Towson University*

Libby Rittenberg, *Colorado College*

Christina Romer, *University of California Berkeley*

Patricia Rottschaefer, *California State University, Fullerton*

Jeff Rubin, *Rutgers University*

Henry D. Ryder, *Glouchester Community College*

Allen Sanderson, *University of Chicago*

Rolando Santos, *Lakeland Community College*

Christine Sauer, *University of New Mexico*

Elizabeth Sawyer-Kelly, *University of Wisconsin, Madison*

Edward Sayre, *Agnes Scott College*

Robert Schwab, *University of Maryland*

Stanley Sedo, *University of Maryland*

Eugene Silberberg, *University of Washington*

Marcia S. Snyder, *College of Charleston*

John Solow, *University of Iowa*

David E. Spencer, *Brigham Young University*

Denise Stanley, *California State University, Fullerton*

Richard Startz, *University of Washington*

Jill Stowe, *Texas A&M University, Austin*

Rodney Swanson, *University of California, Los Angeles*

Jason Taylor, *University of Virginia*

Mark Thoma, *University of California, San Diego*

Karen Travis, *Pacific Lutheran University*

Arienne Turner, *Fullerton College*

Abu Wahid, *Tennessee State University*

Stephan Weiler, *Colorado State University*

Jonathan B. Wight, *University of Richmond*

Mark Wohar, *University of Nebraska, Omaha*

Cemile Yavas, *Pennsylvania State University*

We must also thank the following graduate student reviewers for their assistance: Casey Rothschild, Massachusetts Institute of Technology; Naomi E. Feldman, University of Michigan, Ann Arbor; and, Malte Loos, Massachusetts Institute of Techology.

And there are undergraduate student reviewers to thank—students at Princeton taking our principles course who used and reviewed early drafts of chapters. We'd like to thank these following former students for their suggestions and honest criticisms (both on paper and in person): Todd Beattie, Maura Bolger, James Brandt, Allison Bryan, Jenness I. Crawford, Adam Dressner, Catherine Farmer, Liz Federowicz, Katherine Griswold, Elizabeth S. Irwin, Crystal Jiang, Caitlin Loomis, Akshay Mahajan, Veronika Musilova, Brendon O'Donnell Carrington, Kaitlyn Parlin, Darlyn Pirakitikulr, Lisa A. Pugh, Sasha S. Rao, Robert Richardson, Dena Rachel Schlamowitz, Emily Scott, Samuel Spector, Suzanne Sprague, Michael Tibbetts, Joseph Tursi, Fei Wang, and Julie Zankel.

Thanks, too, to the following students who reviewed the design for our book: Devin Cohen at New York University; Vishal Dave at the University of California, Berkeley; Melissa Duelks at Rutgers; Chloe Gale at Cambridge University; Mike Geier at New York University; Jaret Gronczewski at Rutgers; and Becky Zissel at University of California, Berkeley.

During the course of drafting our manuscript, we met with instructors of principles courses for face-to-face focus-group sessions that afforded us invaluable input. We appreciate the forthright advice and suggestions from these colleagues:

Michael Bordo, *Rutgers University*

Jim Cobbe, *Florida State University*

Tom Creahan, *Morehead State University*

Stephen DeCanio, *University of California, Santa Barbara*

Jim Eden, *Portland Community College, Sylvania*

David Flath, *North Carolina State University*

Rhona Free, *Eastern Connecticut State University*

Rick Godby, *University of Wyoming*

Wayne Grove, *Syracuse University*

Jonathan Hamilton, *University of Florida*

Robert Horn, *James Madison University*

Patrik Hultberg, *University of Wyoming*

Bruce Johnson, *Centre College*

Jim Jozefowicz, *Indiana University of Pennsylvania*

Jim Lee, *Texas A&M University, Corpus Christi*

Rachel McCulloch, *Brandeis University*

Ida Mirzaie, *John Carroll University*

Henry Ryder, *Gloucester Community College*

Marcia Snyder, *College of Charleston*

Brian Trinque, *University of Texas, Austin*

William C. Wood, *James Madison University*

Many thanks to the class testers who took the time to use early drafts of our chapters in their classrooms. The following instructors should know that we made use of their helpful suggestions. We also extend special thanks to so many of your students who filled out user surveys about our chapters. This student input inspired us.

Ashley Abramson, *Barstow College*

Terry Alexander, *Iowa State University*

Leon Battista, *Bronx Community College*

Richard Beil, *Auburn University*

Charles Bennett, *Gannon University*

Andreas Bentz, *Dartmouth College*

John Bockino, *Suffolk County Community College*

Ellen Bowen, *Fisher College, New Bedford*

Anne Bresnock, *University of California, Los Angeles*

Bruce Brown, *California State Polytechnic University, Pomona*

John Buck, *Jacksonville University*

Raymonda Burgman, *University of Southern Florida*

William Carlisle, *University of Utah*

Kevin Carlson, *University of Massachusetts, Boston*

Fred Carstensen, *University of Connecticut*

Shirley Cassing, *University of Pittsburgh*

Ramon Castillo-Ponce, *California State University, Los Angeles*

Emily Chamlee-Wright, *Beloit College*

Anthony Chan, *Santa Monica College*

Yuna Chen, *South Georgia College*

Maryanne Clifford, *Eastern Connecticut State University*

Gregory Colman, *Pace University*

Sarah Culver, *University of Alabama*

Rosa Lea Danielson, *College of DuPage*

Stephen Davis, *University of Minnesota, Crookston*

Tom DelGiudice, *Hofstra University*

Arna Desser, *United States Naval Academy*

Dorsey Dyer, *Davidson County Community College*

Mary Edwards, *St. Cloud State Univesity*

Fritz Efaw, *University of Tennessee at Chattanooga*

Herb Elliot, *Alan Hancock College*

Can Erbil, *Brandeis University*

Yee Tien Fu, *Stanford University*

Yoram Gelman, *Lehman College, The City University of New York*

E.B. Gendel, *Woodbury College*

Doug Gentry, *St. Mary's College*

Satyajit Ghosh, *University of Scranton*

Richard Gosselin, *Houston Community College, Central*

Patricia Graham, *University of Northern Colorado*

Kathleen Greer Rossman, *Birmingham Southern College*

Wayne Grove, *Syracuse University*

Eleanor Gubins, *Rosemont College*

Alan Haight, *State University of New York, Cortland*

Gautam Hazarika, *University of Texas, Brownsville*

Tom Head, *George Fox University*

Susan Helper, *Case Western Reserve University*

Paul Hettler, *Duquesne University*

Roger Hewett, *Drake University*

Jill Holman, *University of Wisconsin, Milwaukee*

Scott Houser, *California State University, Fresno*

Ray Hubbard, *Central Georgia Technical College*

Murat Iyigun, *University of Colorado*

Habib Jam, *Rowan University*

Louis Johnston, *College of St. Benedict/St. John's University*

Jack Julian, *Indiana University of Pennsylvania*

Soheila Kahkashan, *Towson University*

Charles Kaplan, *St. Joseph's College*

Bentzil Kasper, *Broome Community College*

Sinan Koont, *Dickinson College*

Kenneth Kriz, *University of Nebraska, Omaha*

Tom Larson, *California State University, Los Angeles*

Delores Linton, *Tarrant County College, Northwest*

Rolf Lokke, *Albuquerque Academy*

Ellen Magenheim, *Swarthmore College*

Diana McCoy, *Truckee Meadows Community College*

Garrett Milam, *Ryerson College*

Robert Miller, *Fisher College, New Bedford Campus*

Michael Milligan, *Front Range Community College*

Larry Miners, *Fairfield University*

Cathy Miners, *Fairfield University*

Kristen Monaco, *California State University, Long Beach*

Marie Mora, *University of Texas, Pan American*

James Mueller, *Alma College*

Ranganath Murthy, *Bucknell University*

Gerardo Nebbia, *Glendale College*

Anthony Negbenebor, *Gardner-Webb University*

Joseph Nowakowski, *Muskingum College*

Kimberley Ott, *Kent State University, Salem Campus*

Philip Packard, *St. Mary's College*

Jamie Pelley, *Mary Baldwin College*

Mary K. Perkins, *Howard University*

John Pharr, *Dallas Community College, Cedar Valley*

Ray Polchow, *Muskingum Area Technical College*

Ernest Poole, *Fashion Institute of Technology*

Reza Ramazani, *St. Michael's College*

Charles Reichheld, *Cuyahoga Community College*

Siobhan Reilly, *Mills College*

Malcolm Robinson, *Thomas More College*

Charles Rock, *Rollins College*

Richard Romano, *Broome Community College*

Jeff Romine, *University of Colorado, Denver*

Bernie Rose, *Rocky Mountain College*

Dan Rubenson, *Southern Oregon University*

Jeff Rubin, *Rutgers University*

Lynda Rush, *California State Polytechnic University, Pomona*

Martin Sabo, *Community College of Denver*

Sara Saderion, *Houston Community College, Southwest*

George Sawdy, *Providence College*

Ted Scheinman, *Mt. Hood Community College*

Russell Settle, *University of Delaware*

Anna Shostya, *Pace University*

John Somers, *Portland Community College*

Jim Spellicy, *Lowell High School*

Kurt Stephenson, *Virginia Tech*

Charles Stull, *Kalamazoo College*

Laddie Sula, *Loras College*

David Switzer, *University of Northern Michigan*

Deborah Thorsen, *Palm Beach Community College*

Andrew Toole, *Cook College/Rutgers University*

Arienne Turner, *Fullerton College*

Anthony Uremovic, *Joliet Junior College*

Jane Wallace, *University of Pittsburgh*

Tom Watkins, *Eastern Kentucky University*

Larry Wolfenbarger, *Macon State College*

James Woods, *Portland State University*

Mickey Wu, *Coe College*

Lou Zaera, *Fashion Institute of Technology*

Andrea Zanter, *Hillsborough Community College, Dale Mabry Campus*

We also appreciate the contributions of our Two-Year/Community College Advisory Panel:

Kathleen Bromley, *Monroe Community College*

Barbara Connolly, *Westchester Community College*

Will Cummings, *Grossmont College*

Richard Gosselin, *Houston Communty College, Central Campus*

Gus Herring, *Brookhaven College*

Charles Okeke, *Community College of Southern Nevada*

Charles Reichheld, *Cuyahoga Community College*

Sara Saderion, *Houston Community College, Southwest*

Ted Scheinman, *Mt. Hood Community College*

J. Ross Thomas, *Albuquerque Technical Vocational Institute*

Deborah Thorsen, *Palm Beach Community College*

Ranita Wyatt, *Dallas Community College*

We must thank the following instructors whose creativity and contributions helped to make the card deck—a lovely, thoughtful marketing piece—what it is:

Charles Antholt, *Western Washington University*

Richard Ball, *Haverford University*

Edward Blomdahl, *Bridgewater State College*

Michael Brace, *Jamestown Community College*

Tom Cooper, *Georgetown College*

James Craven, *Clark College*

Asif Dowla, *St. Mary's College of Maryland*

James Dulgeroff, *San Bernardino Valley Community College*

Tom Duston, *Keene State College*

Debra Dwyer, *State University of New York, Stony Brook*

Michael Ellis, *New Mexico State University*

Can Erbil, *Brandeis University*

Chuck Fischer, *Pittsburg State University*

Eric Fisher, *The Ohio State University*

Pat Graham, *University of Northern Colorado*

Hart Hodges, *Western Washington University*

Yu Hsing, *Southeastern Louisiana University*

Elia Kacapyr, *Ithaca College*

Farida Khan, *University of Wisconsin, Parkside*

Kent Klitgaard, *Wells College*

Margaret Landman, *Bridgewater State College*

Bill Lee, *St. Mary's College*

Nelson Nagai, *San Joaquin Delta College*

William O'Dea, *State University of New York, Oneonta*

Douglas Orr, *Eastern Washington University*

Brian Peterson, *Central College*

Kevin Quinn, *Bowling Green State University*

Richard Schatz, *Whitworth College*

Kathleen Segerson, *University of Connecticut*

Millicent Sites, *Carson-Newman College*

Herrick Smith, *Nease High School*

Maurice Weinrobe, *Clark University*

Gary Wolfram, *Hillsdale College*

Paul Zak, *Claremont Graduate University*

We would also like to thank the hundreds of instructors who took the time to offer their useful feedback to online marketing surveys about our project. There are nearly 800 of you out there. We only wish we had enough room in this small space to thank each and every one of you individually for your input and ideas. Please accept our deep gratitude for your role in our project.

The following key people critically read every page in virtually every chapter from many of our drafts and offered us so much: Andreas Bentz, Dartmouth College, oversaw accuracy checking, but his role turned into much more than that—a constant, tireless adviser who clarified our work at every step. It is extremely rare to find someone as faithful as Andreas has been to this project, and we are immensely grateful to him. Martha Olney, University of California, Berkeley, provided insightful input throughout—we had a number of moments when we realized that her advice saved us from a serious pedagogical misstep. Our deepest thanks also go to Martha. Development editor Marilyn Freedman helped us in shaping a book that instructors can really use and injected much-needed doses of common sense at crucial moments. We've even relied upon her to sort out pedagogical differences between the two of us. Elizabeth Sawyer-Kelly,

University of Wisconsin, Madison, has played, and continues to play, an invaluable role as a close reader of our chapters. Her detailed and wise input is enormously helpful to us. Thanks also to Becky Kohn, development editor in the early stages, who turned a rough idea into the beginnings of an actual book.

We've already thanked Rhona Free for her contributions as a reviewer and a focus-group participant. But, we must also thank her for the essential role she played in the development of our graphing appendix. We must also extend special thanks to Rosemary Cunningham for her many contributions to this text and its supplements.

We'd like to thank the current and former Worth people who made this project possible. Paul Shensa and Bob Worth suggested that we write this book. Alan McClare led us through the difficult transition from a vague intent into an actual writing process. Craig Bleyer, executive editor, kept that process moving, with just the right mix of patience and whip-cracking. Craig's able leadership and patience has helped us get this book finished.

Elizabeth Widdicombe, president of Freeman and Worth, and Catherine Woods, publisher at Worth, urged us on and kept faith with what must have been a very exasperating project at times.

We have had an incredible production and design team on this book. Tracey Kuehn, our associate managing editor, has worked tirelessly and with great skill to turn our rough manuscript into this beautiful textbook—and on a very tight schedule. Thank you, Tracey. Karen Osborne, our copyeditor, did a fine job helping us streamline and refine our writing. Babs Reingold created the spectacular cover for this book and came up with a design for the book that awed us each time we saw a new chapter in page proof. All we can say is "wow" and thanks. And, we would not have been so awed with the look of each and every spread, without the page-layout magic that Lee Mahler worked for us. Thanks, too, to Barbara Seixas, for her work on the manufacturing end. We've heard about some of the miracles you've worked for us, Barbara, and we appreciate all you've done. The lovely photos you see in this book come to us courtesy of Julie Tesser, our photo researcher. Thanks too, to Patricia Marx and Ted Szczepanski for their assistance with photos. And for all of her help, thanks to Sarah Fleischman, editorial assistant.

Many thanks to Charlie Van Wagner, acquisitions editor, for devising and coordinating the impressive collection of media and supplements that accompany our book. And, many thanks to the incredible team of supplements writers and coordinators who worked with Charlie to make the supplements and media package so strong.

Thanks to Steve Rigolosi, director of market development, and Jeffrey Rucker, senior marketing manager, for their energetic and creative work in marketing this book. Thanks to Tom Kling, national economics consultant, for his critical role in helping to seed business for this text. We would also like to thank the Sales Representative Advisory Board at Worth for their efforts. We met with this wonderful group of salespeople at critical points during our project's development and our heartfelt thanks go to Janet Alexander, Kevin Carlson, Greg David, Joe Diggins, Karita dos Santos, Kate Geraghty, Michael Krotine, Charles Linsmeier, Nikkole Meimbresse, Michelle Merlo, Tara Reifenheiser, Kimberly Smith, Chris Spavins, Bill Soeltz, Ed Tiefenthaler, Maureen Tomlin, and Mark Weber. And, thank you Barbara Monteiro of Monteiro and Company; as well as John Murphy and Dori Weintraub of St. Martin's Press for your help with publicity for the book.

And most of all, special thanks to Sharon Balbos, executive development editor on this project, who must have been as stressed out as we were—but kept her cool throughout many years of tough slogging. We hope that this book lives up to the level of dedication and professionalism that she put into this project.

Paul Krugman   Robin Wells

Credits

Photo Credits

Grateful acknowledgment is given for permission to reprint the following cover photos:

Front Cover
Row 1 (left to right): Fresh vegetables, Photodisc; Seagulls and cooling tower, EyeWire; Buying shoes, Photodisc; **Row 2 (left to right):** Electronic components assembly, Photodisc; Meeting with laptop, Photodisc; Happy graduates, ©image 100 Ltd.; Tractor hauling haybales, Stockbyte; **Row 3 (left to right):** Bar-B-Q Sign, Photodisc; Empty shopping cart, Photodisc; Man checking classified ads, Photodisc; Male college student pumping gas, Alden Pellet/ The Image Works; **Row 4:** Hip kids sharing headphones, ©image100 Ltd./Veer; **Row 5:** New York Stock Exchange interior, Image Source/Veer; **Row 6 (left to right):** Father carrying his baby boy on his shoulders, Photodisc; Business man on cell phone in front of Petronas Towers, Kuala Lumpur, Malaysia, ©image100 Ltd./Veer; Food stand, Photodisc; Oil-pumping rig, EyeWire; **Row 7 (left to right):** Big Ben and Commonwealth of Flags, Photodisc; Postal worker dropping letter in mail slot, Photodisc; Indian woman on cell phone and computer, Thinkstock/Getty Images; **Row 8 (left to right):** Satellite dish, Stockbyte; Couple crossing street with sales signs in background, Image Source/Picture Quest; Father kissing baby, Photodisc; Busy Hong Kong intersection, Photodisc; **Row 9 (left to right):** Portrait of a young woman, Photodisc; Office building under construction, EyeWire; Businesspeople paying taxi fare, Photodisc; Used car lot, Photodisc

Back Cover
Row 1 (left to right): Wood frame building under construction, EyeWire; Market fruit stand, Photodisc; Vancouver skyline, Photodisc; Nuclear plant cooling tower with steam, EyeWire; **Row 2 (left to right):** East River tugboat, EyeWire; Man making pizza at a pizza stand, Photodisc; Shoe repair window, Photodisc; **Row 3 (left to right):** Refinery, EyeWire; Plumber working, Photodisc; St. Louis Arch at sunset, Photodisc; Making cappuccino, Photodisc; **Row 4:** Bunches of asparagus, Photodisc; **Row 5:** Manhattan, Photodisc; **Row 6:** Fresh fish, Photodisc; **Row 7 (left to right):** European hotel, Photodisc; Sign for drive-up bank, Photodisc; Trishaw, Phnom Penh, Cambodia, Photodisc; **Row 8 (left to right):** Window display in men's shop, Photodisc; Logging truck, EyeWire; Chemical plant, EyeWire; **Row 9 (left to right):** Antique store, Photodisc; Dark meeting with laptop and videoconference, Photodisc; Woman holding bicycle on assembly line, EyeWire

Author photo
page iii: Ted Szczepanski

Text Credits

Chapter 5

Source information for Table 5-1, page 113:

Eggs, beef: Kuo S. Huang and Biing-Hwan Lin, Estimation of Food Demand and Nutrient Elasticities from Household Survey Data, United States Department of Agriculture Economic Research Service Technical Bulletin, No. 1887 (Washington, DC: U.S. Department of Agriculture, 2000);

Stationery, gasoline, airline travel, foreign travel: H. S. Houthakker and Lester D. Taylor, *Consumer Demand in the United States, 1929-1970: Analyses and Projections* (Cambridge, MA: Harvard University Press, 1966);

Housing, restaurant meals: H. S. Houthakker and Lester D. Taylor, *Consumer Demand in the United States: Analyses and Projections,* 2nd ed. (Cambridge, MA: Harvard University Press, 1970).

Chapter 12

Source article of "For Inquiring Minds" box on page 300:

C. Camerer et al., Labor Supply of New York City Cab Drivers: One Day at a Time. *Quarterly Journal of Economics, 112,* 407–471.

BRIEF CONTENTS

CONTENTS

Part 3 Individuals and Markets

>>Introduction: The Ordinary Business of Life

ANY GIVEN SUNDAY

I T'S SUNDAY AFTERNOON IN THE SUMMER of 2003, and Route 1 in central New Jersey is a busy place. Thousands of people crowd the shopping malls that line the road for 20 miles, all the way from Trenton to New Brunswick. Most of the shoppers are cheerful—and why not? The stores in those malls offer an extraordinary range of choice; you can buy everything from sophisticated electronic equipment to fashionable clothes to organic carrots. There are probably 100,000 distinct items available

The scene along Route 1 that summer day was, of course, perfectly ordinary—very much like the scene along hundreds of other stretches of road, all across America, that same afternoon. But the discipline of economics is mainly concerned with ordinary things. As the great nineteenth-century economist Alfred Marshall put it, economics is "a study of mankind in the ordinary business of life."

What can economics say about this "ordinary business"? Quite a lot, it turns

Delivering the goods: the market economy in action

along that stretch of road. And most of these items are not luxury goods that only the rich can afford; they are products that millions of Americans can and do purchase every day.

out. What we'll see in this book is that even familiar scenes of economic life pose some very important questions—questions that economics can help answer. Among these questions are:

- How does our economic system work? That is, how does it manage to deliver the goods?

- When and why does our economic system go astray, leading people into counterproductive behavior?

- Why are there ups and downs in the economy? That is, why does the economy sometimes have a "bad year"?

- Finally, why is the long run mainly a story of ups rather than downs? That is, why has America, along with other advanced nations, become so much richer over time?

Let's take a look at these questions and offer a brief preview of what you will learn in this book.

The Invisible Hand

That ordinary scene in central New Jersey would not have looked at all ordinary to an American from colonial times—say, one of the patriots who helped George Washington win the battle of Trenton in 1776. (At the time, Trenton was a small village with not a shopping mall in sight, and farms lined the unpaved road that would eventually become Route 1.)

Imagine that you could transport an American from the colonial period forward in time to our own era. (Isn't that the plot of a movie? Several, actually.) What would this time-traveler find amazing?

Surely the most amazing thing would be the sheer prosperity of modern America—the range of goods that ordinary families can afford. Looking at all that wealth, our transplanted colonial would wonder, "How can I get some of that?" Or perhaps he would ask himself, "How can my society get some of that?"

The answer is that to get this kind of prosperity, you need a well-functioning system for coordinating productive activities—the activities that create the goods and services people want and get them to the people who want them. That kind of system is what we mean when we talk about the **economy**. And **economics** is the study of economies, at the level both of individuals and of society as a whole.

An economy succeeds to the extent that it, literally, delivers the goods. A time-traveler from the eighteenth century—or even from 1950—would be amazed at how many goods the modern American economy delivers and at how many people can afford them. Compared with any past economy and with all but a few other countries today, America has an incredibly high standard of living.

So our economy must be doing something right, and the time-traveler might want to compliment the person in charge. But guess what? There isn't anyone in charge. The United States has a **market economy**, in which production and consumption are the result of decentralized decisions by many firms and individuals. There is no central authority telling people what to produce or where to ship it. Each individual producer makes what he or she thinks will be most profitable; each consumer buys what he or she chooses.

The alternative to a market economy is a *command economy,* in which there *is* a central authority making decisions about production and consumption. Command economies have been tried, most notably in the Soviet Union between 1917 and 1991. But they didn't work very well. Producers in the Soviet Union routinely found themselves unable to produce because they did not have crucial raw materials, or they succeeded in producing but then found that nobody wanted their products. Consumers were often unable to find necessary items—command economies are famous for long lines at shops.

Market economies, however, are able to coordinate even highly complex activities and to reliably provide consumers with the goods and services they want. Indeed, people quite casually trust their lives to the market system: residents of any major city

---

An **economy** is a system for coordinating society's productive activities. **Economics** is the study of economies, at the level both of individuals and of society as a whole.

A **market economy** is an economy in which decisions about production and consumption are made by individual producers and consumers.

would starve in days if the unplanned yet somehow orderly actions of thousands of businesses did not deliver a steady supply of food. Surprisingly, the unplanned "chaos" of a market economy turns out to be far more orderly than the "planning" of a command economy.

In 1776, in a famous passage in his book *The Wealth of Nations*, the pioneering Scottish economist Adam Smith wrote about how individuals, in pursuing their own interests, often end up serving the interests of society as a whole. Of a businessman whose pursuit of profit makes the nation wealthier, Smith wrote: "[H]e intends only his own gain, and he is in this, as in many other cases, led by an invisible hand to promote an end which was no part of his intention." Ever since, economists have used the term **invisible hand** to refer to the way a market economy manages to harness the power of self-interest for the good of society.

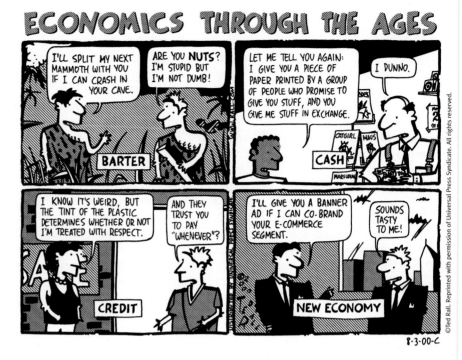

The study of how individuals make decisions and how these decisions interact is called **microeconomics**. One of the key themes in microeconomics is the validity of Adam Smith's insight: Individuals pursuing their own interests often do promote the interests of society as a whole.

So part of the answer to our time-traveler's question—"How can my society achieve the kind of prosperity you take for granted?"—is that his society should learn to appreciate the virtues of a market economy and the power of the invisible hand.

But the invisible hand isn't always our friend. It's also important to understand when and why the individual pursuit of self-interest can lead to counterproductive behavior.

The **invisible hand** refers to the way in which the individual pursuit of self-interest can lead to good results for society as a whole.

Microeconomics is the branch of economics that studies how people make decisions and how these decisions interact.

My Benefit, Your Cost

One thing that our time-traveler would not admire about modern Route 1 is the traffic. In fact, although most things have gotten better in America over time, traffic congestion has gotten a lot worse.

When traffic is congested, each driver is imposing a cost on all the other drivers on the road—he is literally getting in their way (and they are getting in his way). This cost can be substantial: in major metropolitan areas, each time someone drives to work, as opposed to taking public transportation or working at home, he can easily impose $15 or more in hidden costs on other drivers. Yet when deciding whether or not to drive, commuters have no incentive to take the costs they impose on others into account.

Traffic congestion is a familiar example of a much broader problem: sometimes the individual pursuit of one's own interest, instead of promoting the interests of society as a whole, can actually make society worse off. When this happens, it is known as **market failure**. Other important examples of market failure involve air and water pollution as well as the overexploitation of natural resources such as fish and forests.

The good news, as you will learn as you use this book to study microeconomics, is that economic analysis can be used to diagnose cases of market failure. And often, economic analysis can also be used to devise solutions for the problem.

When the individual pursuit of self-interest leads to bad results for society as a whole, there is **market failure**.

Good Times, Bad Times

Route 1 was bustling on that summer day in 2003—but it wasn't bustling quite as much as merchants would have liked, because in mid-2003 the U.S. economy wasn't doing all that well. The main problem was jobs: in early 2001, businesses began laying off workers in large numbers, and as of June 2003, employment had not yet started to recover.

Such troubled periods are a regular feature of modern economies. The fact is that the economy does not always run smoothly: it experiences *fluctuations,* a series of ups and downs. By middle age, a typical American will have experienced three or four downs, known as **recessions**. (The U.S. economy experienced serious recessions beginning in 1973, 1981, 1990, and 2001.) During a severe recession, millions of workers may be laid off.

Like market failure, recessions are a fact of life; but also like market failure, they are a problem to which economic analysis offers some solutions. Recessions are one of the main concerns of the branch of economics known as **macroeconomics**, which is concerned with the overall ups and downs of the economy. If you study macroeconomics, you will learn how economists explain recessions and how government policies can be used to minimize the damage from economic fluctuations.

Despite the occasional recession, however, over the long run the story of the U.S. economy contains many more ups than downs. And that long-run ascent is the subject of our final question.

A **recession** is a downturn in the economy.

Macroeconomics is the branch of economics that is concerned with overall ups and downs in the economy.

Onward and Upward

At the beginning of the twentieth century, most Americans lived under conditions that we would now think of as extreme poverty. Only 10 percent of homes had flush toilets, only 8 percent had central heating, only 2 percent had electricity, and nobody had a car, a washing machine, or air conditioning.

Such comparisons are a stark reminder of how much our lives have been changed by **economic growth**, the growing ability of the economy to produce goods and services.

Why does the economy grow over time? And why does economic growth occur faster in some times and places than in others? These are key questions for economics because economic growth is a good thing, as those shoppers on Route 1 can attest, and most of us want more of it.

Economic growth is the long-run trend toward production of more goods and services.

An Engine for Discovery

We hope we have convinced you that the "ordinary business of life" is really quite extraordinary, if you stop to think about it, and that it can lead us to ask some very interesting and important questions.

In this book, we will describe the answers economists have given to these questions. But this book, like economics as a whole, isn't a list of answers: it's an introduction to a discipline, a way to address questions like those we have just asked. Or as Alfred Marshall, who described economics as a study of the "ordinary business of life," put it: "Economics . . . is not a body of concrete truth, but an engine for the discovery of concrete truth."

So let's turn the key in the ignition.

KEY TERMS

>>First Principles

COMMON GROUND

THE ANNUAL MEETING OF THE AMERICAN Economic Association draws thousands of economists, young and old, famous and obscure. There are booksellers, business meetings, and quite a few job interviews. But mainly the economists gather to talk and listen. During the busiest times, 60 or more presentations may be taking place simultaneously, on questions that range from the future of the stock market to who does the cooking in two-earner families.

What do these people have in common? An expert on the stock market probably knows very little about the economics of housework, and vice versa. Yet an economist who wanders into the wrong seminar and ends up listening to presentations on some unfamiliar topic is nonetheless likely to hear much that is familiar. The reason is that all economic analysis is based on a set of common principles that apply to many different issues.

Some of these principles involve *individual choice*—for economics is, first of all, about the choices that individuals make. Do you choose to work over the summer or take a backpacking trip? Do you buy a new CD or go to a movie? These decisions involve *making a choice* among a limited number of alternatives—limited because no one can have everything that he or she wants. Every question in economics at its most basic level involves individuals making choices.

But to understand how an economy works, you need to understand more than how individuals make choices. None of us are Robinson Crusoe, alone on an island—we must make decisions in an environment that is shaped by the decisions of others. Indeed, in a modern economy even the simplest decisions you

One must choose.

Richard Hamilton Smith/Corbis

make—say, what to have for breakfast—are shaped by the decisions of thousands of other people, from the banana grower in Costa Rica who decided to grow the fruit you eat to the farmer in Iowa who provided the corn in your cornflakes. And because each of us in a market economy depends on

What you will learn in this chapter:

➤ A set of principles for understanding the economics of how individuals make choices.

➤ A set of principles for understanding how individual choices interact.

so many others—and they, in turn, depend on us—our choices interact. So although all economics at a basic level is about individual choice, in order to understand how market economies behave we must also understand economy-wide *interaction*—how my choices affect your choices, and vice versa.

In this chapter, we will look at nine basic principles of economics—four principles involving individual choice and five involving the way individual choices interact.

Individual Choice: The Core of Economics

Individual choice is the decision by an individual of what to do, which necessarily involves a decision of what not to do.

Every economic issue involves, on its most basic level, **individual choice**—decisions by an individual about what to do and what *not* to do. In fact, you might say that it isn't economics if it isn't about choice.

Step into a big store like a Wal-Mart or Home Depot. There are thousands of different products available, and it is extremely unlikely that you—or anyone else—could afford to buy everything you might want to have. And anyway, there's only so much space in your dorm room or apartment. So will you buy another bookcase or a mini-refrigerator? Given limitations on your budget and your living space, you must choose which products to buy and which to leave on the shelf.

The fact that those products are on the shelf in the first place involves choice—the store manager chose to put them there, and the manufacturers of the products chose to produce them. All economic activities involve individual choice.

Four economic principles underlie the economics of individual choice, as shown in Table 1-1. We'll now examine each of these principles in more detail.

TABLE 1-1

Principles that underlie the economics of individual choice

1. Resources are scarce.

2. The real cost of something is what you must give up to get it.

3. "How much?" is a decision at the margin.

4. People usually exploit opportunities to make themselves better off.

Resources Are Scarce

You can't always get what you want. Everyone would like to have a beautiful house in a great location (and help with the housecleaning), two or three luxury cars, and frequent vacations in fancy hotels. But even in a rich country like the United States, not many families can afford all that. So they must make choices—whether to go to Disney World this year or buy a better car, whether to make do with a small backyard or accept a longer commute in order to live where land is cheaper.

Limited income isn't the only thing that keeps people from having everything they want. Time is also in limited supply: there are only 24 hours in a day. And because the time we have is limited, choosing to spend time on one activity also means choosing not to spend time on a different activity—spending time studying for an exam means forgoing a night at the movies. Indeed, many people are so limited by the number of hours in the day that they are willing to trade money for time. For example, convenience stores normally charge higher prices than a regular supermarket. But they fulfill a valuable role by catering to time-pressured customers who would rather pay more than travel farther to the supermarket.

A **resource** is anything that can be used to produce something else.

Resources are **scarce**—the quantity available isn't large enough to satisfy all productive uses.

Why do individuals have to make choices? The ultimate reason is that *resources are scarce*. A **resource** is anything that can be used to produce something else. Lists of the economy's resources usually begin with land, labor (the available time of workers), and capital (machinery, buildings, and other man-made productive assets). A resource is **scarce** when the quantity of the resource available isn't large enough to satisfy all productive uses. There are many scarce resources. These include natural resources—resources that come from the physical environment, such as minerals, lumber, and petroleum. There is also a limited quantity of human resources—labor, skill, and intelligence. And in a growing world economy with a rapidly increasing human population, even clean air and water have become scarce resources.

Just as individuals must make choices, the scarcity of resources means that society as a whole must make choices. One way for a society to make choices is simply to allow them to emerge as the result of many individual choices, which is what usually happens in a market economy. For example, Americans as a group have only so many hours in a week: how many of those hours will they spend going to supermarkets to get lower prices, rather than saving time by shopping at convenience stores? The answer is the sum of individual decisions: each of the millions of individuals in the economy makes his or her own choice about where to shop, and the overall choice is simply the sum of those individual decisions.

But for various reasons, there are some decisions that a society decides are best not left to individual choice. For example, the authors live in an area that until recently was mainly farmland but is now being rapidly built up. Most local residents feel that the community would be a more pleasant place to live if some of the land were left undeveloped. But no individual has an incentive to keep his or her land as open space, rather than selling it to a developer. So a trend has emerged in many communities across the United States of local governments purchasing undeveloped land and preserving it as open space. We'll see in later chapters why decisions about how to use scarce resources are often best left to individuals but sometimes should be made at a higher, community-wide, level.

Opportunity Cost: The Real Cost of Something Is What You Must Give Up to Get It

It is the last term before you graduate, and your class schedule allows you to take only one elective. There are two, however, that you would really like to take: History of Jazz and Beginning Tennis.

Suppose you decide to take the History of Jazz course. What's the cost of that decision? It is the fact that you can't take Beginning Tennis. Economists call that kind of cost—what you must forgo in order to get something you want—the **opportunity cost** of that item. So the opportunity cost of the History of Jazz class is the enjoyment you would have derived from the Beginning Tennis class.

> The real cost of an item is its **opportunity cost**: what you must give up in order to get it.

The concept of opportunity cost is crucial to understanding individual choice because, in the end, all costs are opportunity costs. Sometimes critics claim that economists are concerned only with costs and benefits that can be measured in dollars and cents. But that is not true. Much economic analysis involves cases like our elective course example, where it costs no extra tuition to take one elective course—that is, there is no direct monetary cost. Nonetheless, the elective you choose has an opportunity cost—the other desirable elective course that you must forgo because your limited time permits taking only one.

You might think that opportunity cost is an add-on—that is, something *additional* to the monetary cost of an item. Suppose that an elective class costs additional tuition of $750; now there is a monetary cost to taking History of Jazz. Is the opportunity cost of taking that course something separate from that monetary cost?

Well, consider two cases. First, suppose that taking Beginning Tennis also costs $750. In this case, you would have to spend that $750 no matter which class you take. So what you give up to take the History of Jazz class is still the Beginning Tennis class, period—you would have to spend that $750 either way. But suppose there isn't any fee for the tennis class. In that case, what you give up to take the jazz class is the tennis class *plus* whatever you would have bought with the $750.

Either way, the cost of taking your preferred class is what you must give up to get it. *All* costs are ultimately opportunity costs.

Sometimes the money you have to pay for something is a good indication of its opportunity cost. But many times it is not. One very important example of how poorly monetary cost can indicate opportunity cost is the cost of attending college.

At many cash registers—for example, the one in our college cafeteria—there is a little basket full of pennies. People are encouraged to use the basket to round their purchases up or down: if it costs $5.02, you give the cashier $5 and take two pennies from the basket; if it costs $4.99, you pay $5 and the cashier throws in a penny. It makes everyone's life a bit easier. Of course, it would be easier still if we just abolished the penny, a step that some economists have urged.

But then why do we have pennies in the first place? If it's too small a sum to worry about, why calculate prices that exactly?

The answer is that a penny wasn't always such a negligible sum: the purchasing power of a penny has been greatly reduced by inflation. Forty years ago, a penny had more purchasing power than a nickel does today.

Why does this matter? Well, remember the saying: "A penny saved is a penny earned." But there are other ways to earn money, so you must decide whether saving a penny is a productive use of your time. Could you earn more by devoting that time to other uses?

Forty years ago, the average wage was about $2 an hour. A penny was equivalent to 18 seconds' worth of work—it was worth saving a penny if doing so took less than 18 seconds. But wages have risen along with overall prices, so that the average worker is now paid more than $17 per hour. A penny is therefore equivalent to just over 2 seconds of work—and so it's not worth the opportunity cost of the time it takes to worry about a penny more or less.

In short, the rising opportunity cost of time in terms of money has turned a penny from a useful coin into a nuisance.

Tiger Woods understood the concept of opportunity cost. The rest is history.

Tuition and housing are major monetary expenses for most students; but even if these things were free, attending college would still be an expensive proposition because most college students, if they were not in college, would have a job. That is, by going to college, students *forgo* the income they could have made if they had worked instead. This means that the opportunity cost of attending college is what you pay for tuition and housing *plus* the forgone income you would have earned in a job.

It's easy to see that the opportunity cost of going to college is especially high for people who could be earning a lot during what would otherwise have been their college years. That is why star athletes often skip college or, like Tiger Woods, leave before graduating.

"How Much?" Is a Decision at the Margin

Some important decisions involve an "either-or" choice—for example, you decide either to go to college or to begin working; you decide either to take economics or to take something else. But other important decisions involve "how much" choices—for example, if you are taking both economics and chemistry this semester, you must decide how much time to spend studying for each. When it comes to understanding "how much" decisions, economics has an important insight to offer: "how much" is a decision made at the *margin*.

Suppose you are taking both economics and chemistry. And suppose you are a pre-med student, so that your grade in chemistry matters more to you than your grade in economics. Does that therefore imply that you should spend *all* your study time on chemistry and wing it on the economics exam? Probably not; even if you think your chemistry grade is more important, you should put some effort into studying for economics.

Spending more time studying for economics involves a benefit (a higher expected grade in that course) and a cost (you could have spent that time doing something else, such as studying to get a higher grade in chemistry). That is, your decision involves a **trade-off**—a comparison of costs and benefits.

How do you decide this kind of "how much" question? The typical answer is that you make the decision a bit at a time, by asking how you should spend the next hour.

You make a **trade-off** when you compare the costs with the benefits of doing something.

Say both exams are on the same day, and the night before you spend time reviewing your notes for both courses. At 6:00 P.M., you decide that it's a good idea to spend at least an hour on each course. At 8:00 P.M., you decide you'd better spend another hour on each course. At 10:00 P.M., you are getting tired and figure you have one more hour to study before bed—chemistry or economics? If you are pre-med, it's likely to be chemistry; if you are pre-MBA, it's likely to be economics.

Note how you've made the decision to allocate your time: at each point the question is whether or not to spend *one more hour* on either course. And in deciding whether to spend another hour studying for chemistry, you weigh the costs (an hour forgone of studying for economics or an hour forgone of sleeping) versus the benefits (a likely increase in your chemistry grade). As long as the benefit of studying one more hour for chemistry outweighs the cost, you should choose to study for that additional hour.

Decisions of this type—what to do with your next hour, what to do with your next dollar, and so on—are **marginal decisions**. They involve making trade-offs *at the margin*: comparing the costs and benefits of doing a little bit more of an activity versus doing a little bit less. The study of such decisions is **marginal analysis**.

Many of the questions that we face in economics—as well as in real life—involve marginal analysis: How many workers should I hire in my shop? At what mileage should I change the oil in my car? What is an acceptable rate of negative side effects from a new medicine? Marginal analysis plays a central role in economics because it is the key to deciding "how much" of an activity to do.

> Decisions about whether to do a bit more or a bit less of an activity are **marginal decisions**. The study of such decisions is known as **marginal analysis**.

People Usually Exploit Opportunities to Make Themselves Better Off

One day, while listening to the morning financial news, the authors heard a great tip about how to park cheaply in Manhattan. Garages in the Wall Street area charge as much as $30 per day. But according to the newscaster, some people had found a better way: instead of parking in a garage, they had their oil changed at the Manhattan Jiffy Lube, where it costs $19.95 to change your oil—and they keep your car all day!

It's a great story, but unfortunately it turned out not to be true—in fact, there is no Jiffy Lube in Manhattan. But if there were, you can be sure there would be a lot of oil changes there. Why? Because when people are offered opportunities to make themselves better off, they normally take them—and if they could find a way to park their car all day for $19.95 rather than $30, they would.

When you try to predict how individuals will behave in an economic situation, it is a very good bet that they will exploit opportunities to make themselves better off. Furthermore, individuals will *continue* to exploit these opportunities until they have been fully exhausted—that is, people will exploit opportunities until those opportunities have been fully taken.

If there really was a Manhattan Jiffy Lube and an oil change really was a cheap way to park your car, we can safely predict that before long the waiting list for oil changes would be weeks, if not months.

In fact, the principle that people will exploit opportunities to make themselves better off is the basis of *all* predictions by economists about individual behavior. If the earnings of those who get MBAs soar while the earnings of those who get law degrees decline, we can expect more students to go to business school and fewer to go to law school. If the price of gasoline rises and stays high for an extended period of time, we can expect people to buy smaller cars with higher gas mileage—making themselves better off in the presence of higher gas prices by driving more fuel-efficient cars.

When changes in the available opportunities offer rewards to those who change their behavior, we say that people face new **incentives**. If the price of parking in Manhattan rises, those who can find alternative ways to get to their Wall Street jobs

> An **incentive** is anything that offers rewards to people who change their behavior.

TABLE 1-2

Principles that underlie the interaction of individual choices

1. There are gains from trade.

2. Markets move toward equilibrium.

3. Resources should be used as efficiently as possible to achieve society's goals.

4. Markets usually lead to efficiency.

5. When markets don't achieve efficiency, government intervention can improve society's welfare.

In a market economy, individuals engage in **trade**: They provide goods and services to others and receive goods and services in return.

There are **gains from trade**: people can get more of what they want through trade than they could if they tried to be self-sufficient. This increase in output is due to **specialization**: each person specializes in the task that he or she is good at performing.

---

prices have steadily fallen. These falling prices have reduced the incomes of many farmers, and as a result fewer and fewer people find farming worth doing. That is, an individual farmer who plants a better variety of corn is better off; but when many farmers plant a better variety of corn, the result may be to make farmers as a group worse off.

A farmer who plants a new, more productive corn variety doesn't just grow more corn. Such a farmer also affects the market for corn through the increased yields attained, with consequences that will be felt by other farmers, consumers, and beyond.

Just as there are four economic principles that fall under the theme of choice, there are five principles that fall under the theme of interaction. These five principles are summarized in Table 1-2. We will now examine each of these principles more closely.

There Are Gains from Trade

Why do the choices I make interact with the choices you make? A family could try to take care of all its own needs—growing its own food, sewing its own clothing, providing itself with entertainment, writing its own economics textbooks. But trying to live that way would be very hard. The key to a much better standard of living for everyone is **trade**, in which people divide tasks among themselves and each person provides a good or service that other people want in return for different goods and services that he or she wants.

The reason we have an economy, not many self-sufficient individuals, is that there are **gains from trade**: by dividing tasks and trading, two people (or 6 billion people) can each get more of what they each want than they could get by being self-sufficient. Gains from trade arise, in particular, from this division of tasks, which economists call **specialization**—a situation in which different people each engage in a different task.

The advantages of specialization, and the resulting gains from trade, were the starting point for Adam Smith's 1776 book *The Wealth of Nations*, which many regard as the beginning of economics as a discipline. Smith's book begins with a description of an eighteenth-century pin factory where, rather than each of the 10 workers making a pin from start to finish, each worker specialized in one of the many steps in pin-making:

> One man draws out the wire, another straights it, a third cuts it, a fourth points it, a fifth grinds it at the top for receiving the head; to make the head requires two or three distinct operations; to put it on, is a particular business, to whiten the pins is another; it is even a trade by itself to put them into the paper; and the important business of making a pin is, in this manner, divided into about eighteen distinct operations . . . Those ten persons, therefore, could make among them upwards of forty-eight thousand pins in a day. But if they had all wrought separately and independently, and without any of them having been educated to this particular business, they certainly could not each of them have made twenty, perhaps not one pin a day. . . .

The same principle applies when we look at how people divide tasks among themselves and trade in an economy. *The economy, as a whole, can produce more when each person specializes in a task and trades with others.*

The benefits of specialization are the reason a person typically chooses only one career. It takes many years of study and experience to become a doctor; it also takes many years of study and experience to become a commercial airline pilot. Many doctors might well have had the potential to become excellent pilots, and vice versa;

"I hunt and she gathers—otherwise we couldn't make ends meet."

but it is very unlikely that anyone who decided to pursue both careers would be as good a pilot or as good a doctor as someone who decided at the beginning to specialize in that field. So it is to everyone's advantage that individuals specialize in their career choices.

Markets are what allow a doctor and a pilot to specialize in their own fields. Because markets for commercial flights and for doctors' services exist, a doctor is assured that she can find a flight and a pilot is assured that he can find a doctor. As long as individuals know that they can find the goods and services that they want in the market, they are willing to forgo self-sufficiency and are willing to specialize. But what assures people that markets will deliver what they want? The answer to that question leads us to our second principle of economy-wide interaction.

Markets Move Toward Equilibrium

It's a busy afternoon at the supermarket; there are long lines at the checkout counters. Then one of the previously closed cash registers opens. What happens?

The first thing that happens, of course, is a rush to that register. After a couple of minutes, however, things will have settled down; shoppers will have rearranged themselves so that the line at the newly opened register is about the same length as the lines at all the other registers.

How do we know that? We know from our fourth principle of individual choice that people will exploit opportunities to make themselves better off. This means that people will rush to the newly opened register in order to save time standing in line. And things will settle down when shoppers can no longer improve their position by switching lines— that is, when the opportunities to make themselves better off have all been exploited.

A story about supermarket checkout lines may seem to have little to do with economy-wide interactions, but in fact it illustrates an important principle. A situation in which individuals cannot make themselves better off by doing something different—the situation in which all the checkout lines are the same length—is what economists call an **equilibrium**. An economic situation is in equilibrium when no individual would be better off doing something different.

Recall the story about the mythical Jiffy Lube, where it was supposedly cheaper to leave your car for an oil change than to pay for parking. If that opportunity had

Witness equilibrium in action at the checkout lines in your neighborhood supermarket.

An economic situation is in **equilibrium** when no individual would be better off doing something different.

FOR INQUIRING MINDS
CHOOSING SIDES

Why do people in America drive on the right side of the road? Of course, it's the law. But long before it was the law, it was an equilibrium.

Before there were formal traffic laws, there were informal "rules of the road," practices that everyone expected everyone else to follow. These rules included an understanding that people would normally keep to one side of the road. In some places, such as England, the rule was to keep to the left; in others, such as France, it was to keep to the right.

Why would some places choose the right and others, the left? That's not completely clear, although it may have depended on the dominant form of traffic. Men riding horses and carrying swords on their left hip preferred to ride on the left (think about getting on or off the horse, and you'll see why.) On the other hand, right-handed people walking but leading horses apparently preferred to walk on the right.

In any case, once a rule of the road was established, there were strong incentives for each individual to stay on the "usual" side of the road: those who didn't would keep colliding with oncoming traffic. So once established, the rule of the road would be self-enforcing—that is, it would

be an equilibrium. Nowadays, of course, which side you drive on is determined by law; some countries have even changed sides (Sweden went from left to right in 1967). But what about pedestrians? There are no laws—but there are informal rules. In the United States, urban pedestrians normally keep to the right. But if you should happen to visit Japan, watch out: the Japanese, who drive on the left, also typically walk on the left. So when in Japan, do as the Japanese do. You won't be arrested if you walk on the right, but you will be worse off than if you accept the equilibrium and walk on the left.

really existed and people were still paying $30 to park in garages, the situation would *not* have been an equilibrium.

And that should have been a giveaway that the story couldn't be true. In reality, people would have seized an opportunity to park cheaply, just as they seize opportunities to save time at the checkout line. And in so doing they would have eliminated the opportunity! Either it would have become very hard to get an appointment for an oil change or the price of a lube job would have increased to the point that it was no longer an attractive option (unless you really needed a lube job).

As we will see, markets usually reach equilibrium via changes in prices, which rise or fall until no opportunities for individuals to make themselves better off remain.

The concept of equilibrium is extremely helpful in understanding economic interactions because it provides a way of cutting through the sometimes complex details of those interactions. To understand what happens when a new line is opened at a supermarket, you don't need to worry about exactly how shoppers rearrange themselves, who moves ahead of whom, which register just opened, and so on. What you need to know is that any time there is a change, the situation will move to an equilibrium.

The fact that markets move toward equilibrium is why we can depend on them to work in a predictable way. In fact, we can trust markets to supply us with the essentials of life. For example, people who live in big cities can be sure that the supermarket shelves will always be fully stocked. Why? Because if some merchants who distribute food *didn't* make deliveries, a big profit opportunity would be created for any merchant who did—and there would be a rush to supply food, just like the rush to a newly opened cash register. So the market ensures that food will always be available for city dwellers. And, returning to our previous principle, this allows city dwellers to be city dwellers—to specialize in doing city jobs rather than living on farms and growing their own food.

A market economy also allows people to achieve gains from trade. But how do we know how well such an economy is doing? The next principle gives us a standard to use in evaluating an economy's performance.

Resources Should Be Used as Efficiently as Possible to Achieve Society's Goals

Suppose you are taking a course in which the classroom is too small for the number of students—many people are forced to stand or sit on the floor—despite the fact that large, empty classrooms are available nearby. You would say, correctly, that this is no way to run a college. Economists would call this an *inefficient* use of resources.

But if an inefficient use of resources is undesirable, just what does it mean to use resources *efficiently*? You might imagine that the efficient use of resources has something to do with money, maybe that it is measured in dollars-and-cents terms. But in economics, as in life, money is only a means to other ends. The measure that economists really care about is not money but people's happiness or welfare. Economists say that *an economy's resources are used efficiently when they are used in a way that has fully exploited all opportunities to make everyone better off.* To put it another way, an economy is **efficient** if it takes all opportunities to make some people better off without making other people worse off.

An economy is **efficient** if it takes all opportunities to make some people better off without making other people worse off.

In our classroom example, there clearly was a way to make everyone better off—moving the class to a larger room would make people in the class better off without hurting anyone else in the college. Assigning the course to the smaller classroom was an inefficient use of the college's resources, while assigning the course to the larger classroom would have been an efficient use of the college's resources.

When an economy is efficient, it is producing the maximum gains from trade possible given the resources available. Why? Because there is no way to rearrange how resources are used in a way that can make everyone better off. When an economy is efficient, one person can be made better off by rearranging how resources are used *only* by making someone else worse off. In our classroom example, if all larger classrooms were already occupied, the college would have been run in an efficient way: your class could be made better off by moving to a larger classroom only by making people in the larger classroom worse off by making them move to a smaller classroom.

Should economic policy makers always strive to achieve economic efficiency? Well, not quite, because efficiency is not the only criterion by which to evaluate an economy. People also care about issues of fairness or **equity**. And there is typically a trade-off between equity and efficiency: policies that promote equity often come at a cost of decreased efficiency in the economy, and vice versa.

To see this, consider the case of handicapped-designated parking spaces in public parking lots. Many people have great difficulty walking due to age or disability, so it seems only fair to assign closer parking spaces specifically for their use. You may have noticed, however, that a certain amount of inefficiency is involved. To make sure that there is always an appropriate space available should a handicapped person want one, there are typically quite a number of handicapped-designated spaces. So at any one time there are typically more such spaces available than there are handicapped people who want one. As a result, desirable parking spaces are unused. (And the temptation for nonhandicapped people to use them is so great that we must be dissuaded by fear of getting a ticket.) So, short of hiring parking valets to allocate spaces, there is a conflict between *equity*, making life "fairer" for handicapped people, and *efficiency*, making sure that all opportunities to make people better off have been fully exploited by never letting close-in parking spaces go unused.

Exactly how far policy makers should go in promoting equity over efficiency is a very difficult question that goes to the heart of the political process. As such, it is not a question that economists can answer. What is important for economists, however, is to always seek to use the economy's resources as efficiently as possible in the pursuit of society's goals, whatever those goals may be.

Equity means that everyone gets his or her fair share. Since people can disagree about what's "fair," equity isn't as well-defined a concept as efficiency.

Markets Usually Lead to Efficiency

No branch of the U.S. government is entrusted with ensuring the general economic efficiency of our market economy—we don't have agents who go around making sure that brain surgeons aren't plowing fields, that Minnesota farmers aren't trying to grow oranges, that prime beachfront property isn't taken up by used-car dealerships, that colleges aren't wasting valuable classroom space. The government doesn't need to enforce efficiency because in most cases the invisible hand does the job.

In other words, the incentives built into a market economy already ensure that resources are usually put to good use, that opportunities to make people better off are not wasted. If a college were known for its habit of crowding students into small classrooms while large classrooms go unused, it would soon find its enrollment dropping, putting the jobs of its administrators at risk. The "market" for college students would respond in a way that induces administrators to run the college efficiently.

A detailed explanation of why markets are usually very good at making sure that resources are used well will have to wait until we have studied how markets actually work. But the most basic reason is that in a market economy, in which individuals are free to choose what to consume and what to produce, opportunities for mutual gain are normally taken. If there is a way in which some people can be made better off, people will usually be able to take advantage of that opportunity. And that is exactly what defines efficiency: all the opportunities to make everyone better off have been exploited.

As we learned in the Introduction, however, there are exceptions to this principle that markets are generally efficient. In cases of *market failure*, the individual pursuit of self-interest found in markets makes society worse off—that is, the market outcome is inefficient. And, as we will see in examining the next principle, when markets fail, government intervention can help. But short of instances of market failure, the general rule is that markets are a remarkably good way of organizing an economy.

When Markets Don't Achieve Efficiency, Government Intervention Can Improve Society's Welfare

Let's recall from the Introduction the nature of the market failure caused by traffic congestion—a commuter driving to work has no incentive to take into account the cost that his or her act inflicts on other drivers in the form of increased traffic congestion. There are several possible remedies to this situation; examples include charging road tolls, subsidizing the cost of public transportation, or taxing sales of gasoline to individual drivers. All these remedies work by changing the incentives of would-be drivers—motivating them to drive less and use alternative transportation. But they also share another feature: each relies on government intervention in the market.

This brings us to our fifth and last principle of interaction: *When markets don't achieve efficiency, government intervention can improve society's welfare.* That is, when markets go wrong, an appropriately designed government policy can sometimes move society closer to an efficient outcome by changing how society's resources are used.

A very important branch of economics is devoted to studying why markets fail and what policies should be adopted to improve social welfare. We will study these problems and their remedies in depth in later chapters, but here we give a brief overview of why markets fail. They fail for three principal reasons:

- Individual actions have *side effects* that are not properly taken into account by the market.
- One party prevents mutually beneficial trades from occurring in the attempt to capture a greater share of resources for itself.
- Some goods, by their very nature, are unsuited for efficient management by markets.

An important part of your education in economics is learning to identify not just when markets work but also when they don't work—and to judge what government policies are appropriate in each situation.

economics in action

Restoring Equilibrium on the Freeways

In 1994 a powerful earthquake struck the Los Angeles area, causing several freeway bridges to collapse and thereby disrupting the normal commuting routes of hundreds of thousands of drivers. The events that followed offer a particularly clear example of interdependent decision making—in this case, the decisions of commuters about how to get to work.

In the immediate aftermath of the earthquake, there was great concern about the impact on traffic, since motorists would now have to crowd onto alternative routes or detour around the blockages by using city streets. Public officials and news programs warned commuters to expect massive delays and urged them to avoid unnecessary travel, reschedule their work to commute before or after the rush, or use mass transit. These warnings were unexpectedly effective. In fact, so many people heeded them that in the first few days following the quake, those who maintained their regular commuting routine actually found the drive to and from work faster than before.

Of course, this situation could not last. As word spread that traffic was actually not bad at all, people abandoned their less convenient new commuting methods and reverted to their cars—and traffic got steadily worse. Within a few weeks after the quake, serious traffic jams had appeared. After a few more weeks, however, the situation stabilized: the reality of worse-than-usual congestion discouraged enough drivers to prevent the nightmare of citywide gridlock from materializing. Los Angeles traffic, in short, had settled into a new equilibrium, in which each commuter was making the best choice he or she could, given what everyone else was doing.

This was not, by the way, the end of the story: fears that the city would strangle on traffic led local authorities to repair the roads with record speed. Within only 18 months after the quake, all the freeways were back to normal, ready for the next one. ∎

> > > > > > > > > > > > > > > > > >

>>CHECK YOUR UNDERSTANDING 1-2

1. Explain how each of the following situations illustrates one of the five principles of interaction.
   a. Using the college website, any student who wants to sell a used textbook for at least $X is able to sell it to another who is willing to pay $X.
   b. At a college tutoring co-op, students can arrange to provide tutoring in subjects they are good in (like economics) in return for receiving tutoring in subjects they are poor in (like philosophy).
   c. The local municipality imposes a law that requires bars and nightclubs near residential areas to keep their noise levels below a certain threshold.
   d. To provide better care for low-income patients, the city of Tampa has decided to close some underutilized neighborhood clinics and shift funds to the main hospital.
   e. On the college website, books of a given title with approximately the same level of wear and tear sell for about the same price.

2. Which of the following describes an equilibrium situation? Which does not? Explain your answer.
   a. The restaurants across the street from the university dining hall serve better-tasting and cheaper meals than those served at the university dining hall. The vast majority of students continue to eat at the dining hall.
   b. You currently take the subway to work. Although taking the bus is cheaper, the ride takes longer. So you are willing to pay the higher subway fare in order to save time.

Solutions appear at back of book.

• A LOOK AHEAD •

The nine basic principles we have described lie behind almost all economic analysis. Although they can be immediately helpful in understanding many situations, they are usually not enough. Applying the principles to real economic issues takes one more step.

That step is the creation of *models*—simplified representations of economic situations. Models must be realistic enough to provide real-world guidance but simple enough that they allow us to see clearly the implications of the principles described in this chapter. So our next step is to show how models are used to actually do economic analysis.

SUMMARY

1. All economic analysis is based on a short list of basic principles. These principles apply to two levels of economic understanding. First, we must understand how individuals make choices; second, we must understand how these choices interact.

2. Everyone has to make choices about what to do and what *not* to do. **Individual choice** is the basis of economics—if it doesn't involve choice, it isn't economics.

3. The reason choices must be made is that **resources**—anything that can be used to produce something else—are **scarce.** Individuals are limited in their choices by money and time; economies are limited by their supplies of human and natural resources.

4. Because you must choose among limited alternatives, the true cost of anything is what you must give up to get it—all costs are **opportunity costs.**

5. Many economic decisions involve questions not of "whether" but of "how much"—how much to spend on some good, how much to produce, and so on. Such decisions must be taken by performing a **trade-off** *at the margin*—by comparing the costs and benefits of doing a bit more or a bit less. Decisions of this type are called marginal decisions, and the study of them, **marginal analysis,** plays a central role in economics.

6. The study of how people *should* make decisions is also a good way to understand actual behavior. Individuals usually exploit opportunities to make themselves better off. If opportunities change, so does behavior: people respond to **incentives.**

7. **Interaction**—my choices depend on your choices, and vice versa—adds another level to economic understanding.

When individuals interact, the end result may be different from what anyone intends.

8. The reason for interaction is that there are **gains from trade:** by engaging in the **trade** of goods and services with one another, the members of an economy can all be made better off. Underlying gains from trade are the advantages of **specialization,** of having individuals specialize in the tasks they are good at.

9. Economies normally move toward **equilibrium**—a situation in which no individual can make himself or herself better off by taking a different action.

10. An economy is **efficient** if all opportunities to make someone better off without making others worse off are taken. Resources should be used as efficiently as possible to achieve society's goals. But efficiency is not the sole way to evaluate an economy: **equity,** or fairness, is also desirable, and there is often a trade-off between equity and efficiency.

11. Markets usually lead to efficiency, with some well-defined exceptions.

12. When markets fail and do not achieve efficiency, government intervention can improve society's welfare.

KEY TERMS

Individual choice, p. 6
Resource, p. 6
Scarce, p. 6
Opportunity cost, p. 7
Trade-off, p. 8

Marginal decisions, p. 9
Marginal analysis, p. 9
Incentive, p. 9
Interaction, p. 11
Trade, p. 12

Gains from trade, p. 12
Specialization, p. 12
Equilibrium, p. 13
Efficient, p. 14
Equity, p. 15

PROBLEMS

1. In each of the following situations, identify which of the nine principles is at work.

   a. You choose to shop at the local discount store rather than paying a higher price for the same merchandise at the local department store.

   b. On your spring vacation trip, your budget is limited to $35 a day.

   c. The student union provides a website on which departing students can sell items such as used books, appliances, and furniture rather than giving them away to their roommates as they formerly did.

   d. You decide how many cups of coffee to have when studying the night before an exam by considering how much more work you can do by having another cup versus how jittery it will make you feel.

   e. There is limited lab space available to do the project required in Chemistry 101. The lab supervisor assigns lab time to each student based on when that student is able to come.

   f. You realize that you can graduate a semester early by forgoing a semester of study abroad.

   g. At the student union, there is a bulletin board on which people advertise used items for sale, such as bicycles. Once you have adjusted for differences in quality, all the bikes sell for about the same price.

   h. You are better at performing lab experiments, and your lab-mate is better at writing lab reports. So the two of you agree that you will do all the experiments, and she will write up all the reports.

   i. State governments mandate that it is illegal to drive without passing a driving exam.

2. Describe some of the opportunity costs when you decide to do the following.

   a. Attend college instead of taking a job

   b. Watch a movie instead of studying for an exam

   c. Ride the bus instead of driving your car

3. Liza needs to buy a textbook for the next economics class. The price at the college bookstore is $65. One online site offers it for $55 and another site for $57. All prices include sales tax. The accompanying table indicates the typical shipping and handling charges for the textbook ordered online.

   a. What is the opportunity cost of buying online?

   b. Show the relevant choices for this student. What determines which of these options the student will choose?

Shipping method	Delivery time	Charge
Standard shipping	3–7 days	$3.99
Second-day air	2 business days	$8.98
Next-day air	1 business day	$13.98

4. Use the concept of opportunity cost to explain the following.

   a. More people choose to get graduate degrees when the job market is poor.

   b. More people choose to do their own home repairs when the economy is slow.

   c. There are more parks in suburban areas than in urban areas.

d. Convenience stores, which have higher prices than super-markets, cater to busy people.

e. Fewer students enroll in classes that meet before 10:00 A.M.

5. In the following examples, state how you would use the principle of marginal analysis to make a decision.

a. Deciding how many days to wait before doing your laundry

b. Deciding how much library research to do before writing your term paper

c. Deciding how many bags of chips to eat

d. Deciding how many lectures of a class to skip

6. This morning you made the following individual choices: you bought a bagel and coffee at the local café, you drove to school in your car during rush hour, and you typed your roommate's term paper because you are a fast typist—in return for which she will do your laundry for a month. In each of these actions, describe how your individual choices interacted with the individual choices made by others. Were other people left better off or worse off by your choices in each case?

7. On the east side of the Hatatoochie River lives the Hatfield family, while the McCoy family lives on the west side. Each family's diet consists of fried chicken and corn-on-the-cob, and each is self-sufficient, raising their own chickens and growing their own corn. Explain the conditions under which each of the following would be true.

a. The two families are made better off when the Hatfields specialize in raising chickens, the McCoys specialize in raising corn, and the two families trade.

b. The two families are made better off when the McCoys specialize in raising chickens, the Hatfields specialize in raising corn, and the two families trade.

8. Which of the following situations describes an equilibrium? Which does not? If the situation does not describe an equilibrium, what would an equilibrium look like?

a. Many people regularly commute from the suburbs to downtown Pleasantville. Due to traffic congestion, the trip is 30 minutes when you travel by highway, but only 15 minutes when you go by side streets.

b. At the intersection of Main and Broadway are two gas stations. One station charges $1.15 per gallon for regular gas and the other charges $1.00 per gallon. Customers can get service immediately at the first station, but must wait in a long line at the second.

c. Every student enrolled in Economics 101 must also attend a weekly tutorial. This year there are two sections offered: section A and section B, which meet at the same time in adjoining classrooms and are taught by equally competent instructors. Section A is overcrowded, with people sitting on the floor and often unable to see the chalkboard. Section B has many empty seats.

9. In each of the following cases, explain whether you think the situation is efficient or not. If it is not efficient, why not? What actions would make the situation efficient?

a. Some residents in your dorm leave lights, computers, and appliances on when they are not in their rooms.

b. Although they cost the same amount to prepare, the cafeteria in your dorm consistently provides too many dishes that diners don't like, such as tofu casserole, and too few dishes that diners do like, such as roast turkey with dressing.

c. The enrollment for a particular course exceeds the spaces available. Some students who need to take this course to complete their major are unable to get a space while others who are taking it as an elective do get a space.

10. Discuss the efficiency and equity implications of each of the following policies. How would you go about balancing the concerns of equity and efficiency in these areas?

a. The government pays the full tuition for every college student to study whatever subject he or she wishes.

b. When people lose their jobs, the government provides unemployment benefits until they find new ones.

11. Governments often adopt certain policies in order to promote desired behavior among their citizens. For each of the following policies, determine what the incentive is and what behavior the government wishes to promote. In each case, why do you think that the government might wish to change people's behavior, rather than allow their actions to be solely determined by individual choice?

a. A tax of $5 per pack is imposed on cigarettes.

b. The government pays parents $100 when their child is vaccinated for measles.

c. The government pays college students to tutor children from low-income families.

d. The government imposes a tax on the amount of air pollution that a company discharges.

12. In each of the following situations, explain how government intervention could improve society's welfare by changing people's incentives. In what sense is the market going wrong?

a. Pollution from auto emissions has reached unhealthy levels.

b. Everyone in Woodville would be better off if streetlights were installed in the town. But no individual resident is willing to pay for installation of a streetlight in front of his or her house because it is impossible to recoup the cost by charging other residents for the benefit they receive from it.

>**web**... To continue your study and review of concepts in this chapter, please visit the Krugman/Wells website for quizzes, animated graph tutorials, web links to helpful resources, and more.

www.worthpublishers.com/krugmanwells

>>Economic Models: Trade-offs and Trade

TUNNEL VISION

I N 1901 WILBUR AND ORVILLE WRIGHT built something that would change the world. No, not the airplane—their successful flight at Kitty Hawk would come two years later. What made the Wright brothers true visionaries was their wind tunnel, an apparatus that let them experiment with many different designs for wings and control surfaces. These experiments gave them the knowledge that would make heavier-than-air flight possible.

A miniature airplane sitting motionless in a wind tunnel isn't the same thing as an actual aircraft in flight. But it is a very useful model of a flying plane—a simplified representation of the real thing that can be used to answer crucial questions, such as how much lift a given wing shape will generate at a given airspeed.

Needless to say, testing an airplane design in a wind tunnel is cheaper and safer than building a full-scale version and hoping it will fly. More generally, models play a crucial role in almost all scientific research—economics very much included.

In fact, you could say that economic theory consists mainly of a collection of models, a series of simplified representations of economic reality that allow us to understand a variety of economic issues.

Clearly, the Wright brothers believed in their model.

Landov Photos

In this chapter, we will look at three economic models that are crucially important in their own right and also illustrate why such models are so useful. We'll conclude with a look at how economists actually use models in their work.

What you will learn in this chapter:

➤ Why **models**—simplified representations of reality—play a crucial role in economics

➤ Three simple but important models: the **production possibility frontier, comparative advantage,** and the **circular-flow diagram**

➤ The difference between **positive economics,** which tries to describe the economy and predict its behavior, and **normative economics,** which tries to prescribe economic policy

➤ When economists agree and why they sometimes disagree

Models in Economics: Some Important Examples

A **model** is any simplified representation of reality that is used to better understand real-life situations. But how do we create a simplified representation of an economic situation?

One possibility—an economist's equivalent of a wind tunnel—is to find or create a real but simplified economy. For example, economists interested in the economic role of money have studied the system of exchange that developed in World War II prison camps, in which cigarettes became a universally accepted form of payment even among prisoners who didn't smoke.

Another possibility is to simulate the workings of the economy on a computer. For example, when changes in tax law are proposed, government officials use *tax models*—large computer programs—to assess how the proposed changes would affect different types of people.

The importance of models is that they allow economists to focus on the effects of only one change at a time. That is, they allow us to hold everything else constant and study how one change affects the overall economic outcome. So the **other things equal assumption**, which means that all other relevant factors remain unchanged, is an important assumption when building economic models.

A **model** is a simplified representation of a real situation that is used to better understand real-life situations.

The **other things equal assumption** means that all other relevant factors remain unchanged.

FOR INQUIRING MINDS
MODELS FOR MONEY

What's an economic model worth, anyway? In some cases, quite a lot of money.

Although many economic models are developed for purely scientific purposes, others are developed to help governments make economic policies. And there is a growing business in developing economic models to help corporations make decisions.

Who models for money? There are dozens of consulting firms that use models to predict future trends, offer advice based on their models, or develop custom models for business and government clients. A notable example is Global Insight, the world's biggest economic consulting firm. It was created by a merger between Data Resources, Inc., founded by professors from Harvard and MIT, and Wharton Economic Forecasting Associates, founded by professors at the University of Pennsylvania.

One particularly lucrative branch of economics is finance theory, which helps investors figure out what assets, such as shares in a company, are worth. Finance theorists often become highly paid "rocket scientists" at big Wall Street firms because financial models demand a high level of technical expertise.

Unfortunately, the most famous business application of finance theory came spectacularly to grief. In 1994 a group of Wall Street traders teamed up with famous finance theorists—including two Nobel Prize winners—to form Long-Term Capital Management, a fund that used sophisticated financial models to invest the money of wealthy clients. At first, the fund did very well. But in 1998 bad news from all over the world—with countries as disparate as Russia, Japan, and Brazil in trouble at the same time—inflicted huge losses on LTCM's investments. For a few anxious days, many people feared not only that the fund would collapse but also that it would bring many other companies down with it. Thanks in part to a rescue operation organized by government officials, this did not happen; but LTCM was closed a few months later, with some of its investors losing most of the money they had put in.

What went wrong? Partly it was bad luck. But experienced hands also faulted the economists at LTCM for taking too many risks. Their models said that a run of bad news like the one that actually happened was extremely unlikely—but a sensible economist knows that sometimes even the best model misses important possibilities.

But you can't always find or create a small-scale version of the whole economy, and a computer program is only as good as the data it uses. (Programmers have a saying: garbage in, garbage out.) For many purposes, the most effective form of economic modeling is the construction of "thought experiments": simplified, hypothetical versions of real-life situations.

In Chapter 1 we illustrated the concept of equilibrium with the example of how customers at a supermarket would rearrange themselves when a new cash register opens. Though we didn't say it, this was an example of a simple model—an imaginary supermarket, in which many details were ignored (what are the customers buying? never mind), that could be used to answer a "what if" question: what if another cash register were opened?

As the cash register story showed, it is often possible to describe and analyze a useful economic model in plain English. However, because much of economics involves changes in quantities—in the price of a product, the number of units produced, or the number of workers employed in its production—economists often find that using some mathematics helps clarify an issue. In particular, a numerical example, a simple equation, or—especially—a graph can be key to understanding an economic concept.

Whatever form it takes, a good economic model can be a tremendous aid to understanding. The best way to make this point is to consider some simple but important economic models and what they tell us. First, we will look at the *production possibility frontier*, a model that helps economists think about the tradeoffs every economy faces. Then we will turn to *comparative advantage*, a model that clarifies the principle of gains from trade—trade both between individuals and between countries. Finally, we'll examine the *circular-flow model*, which helps economists analyze the monetary transactions taking place in the economy as a whole.

Note: in discussing these models, we make considerable use of graphs to represent mathematical relationships. Such graphs will play an important role throughout this book. If you are already familiar with the use of graphs, the material that follows should not present any problem. If you are not, this would be a good time to turn to the appendix of this chapter, which provides a brief introduction to the use of graphs in economics.

Trade-offs: The Production Possibility Frontier

The hit movie *Cast Away*, starring Tom Hanks, was an update of the classic story of Robinson Crusoe, the hero of Daniel Defoe's eighteenth-century novel. Hanks played the sole survivor of a plane crash, stranded on a remote island. As in the original story of Robinson Crusoe, the character played by Hanks had limited resources: the natural resources of the island, a few items he managed to salvage from the plane, and, of course, his own time and effort. With only these resources, he had to make a life. In effect, he became a one-man economy.

The first principle of economics we introduced in Chapter 1 was that resources are scarce and that, as a result, any economy—whether it contains one person or millions of people—faces trade-offs. For example, if a castaway devotes resources to catching fish, he cannot use those same resources to gather coconuts.

To think about the trade-offs that face any economy, economists often use the model known as the **production possibility frontier**. The idea behind this model is to improve our understanding of trade-offs by considering a simplified economy that produces only two goods. This simplification enables us to show the trade-off graphically.

What to do? Even a castaway faces tradeoffs.

Photo by 20th Century FOX Photo/ZUMA Press. © Copyright 2002 by 20th Century FOX

Figure 2-1 shows a hypothetical production possibility frontier for Tom, a castaway alone on an island, who must make a trade-off between production of fish and production of coconuts. The frontier—the curve in the diagram—shows the maximum number of fish Tom can catch during a week *given* the quantity of coconuts he gathers, and vice versa. That is, it answers questions of the form, "What is the maximum number of fish Tom can catch if he also gathers 20 (or 25, or 30) coconuts?" (We'll explain the bowed-out shape of the curve in Figure 2-1 shortly, after we've seen how to interpret the production possibility frontier.)

There is a crucial distinction between points *inside or on* the curve (the shaded area) and outside the curve. If a production point lies inside the frontier—like the point labeled C, at which Tom catches 20 fish and gathers 20 coconuts—it is feasible. After all, the frontier tells us that if Tom catches 20 fish, he could also gather a maximum of 25 coconuts, so he could certainly gather 20 coconuts. On the other hand, a production point that lies outside the frontier—such as the hypothetical production point shown in the figure as point D, where Tom catches 40 fish and gathers 30 coconuts—isn't feasible. (In this case, Tom could catch 40 fish and gather no coconuts *or* he could gather 30 coconuts and catch no fish, but he can't do both.)

In Figure 2-1 the production possibility frontier intersects the horizontal axis at 40 fish. This means that if Tom devoted all his resources to catching fish, he would catch 40 fish per week but would have no resources left over to gather coconuts. The production possibility frontier intersects the vertical axis at 30 coconuts; this means that if Tom devoted all his resources to gathering coconuts, he could gather 30 coconuts per week but would have no resources left over to catch fish.

The figure also shows less extreme trade-offs. For example, if Tom decides to catch 20 fish, he is able to gather 25 coconuts; this production choice is illustrated by point A. If Tom decides to catch 30 fish, he can gather at most only 20 coconuts, as shown by point B.

Thinking in terms of a production possibility frontier simplifies the complexities of reality. The real-world economy produces millions of different goods. Even a castaway on an island would produce more than two different items (for example, he would need clothing and housing as well as food). But in this model we imagine an economy that produces only two goods.

If we simplify reality, however, the production possibility frontier helps us understand some aspects of the real economy better than we could without the model.

> The **production possibility frontier** illustrates the trade-offs facing an economy that produces only two goods. It shows the maximum quantity of one good that can be produced for any given production of the other.

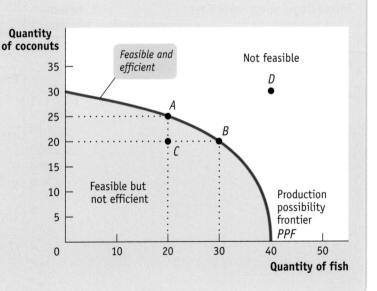

Figure 2-1

The Production Possibility Frontier

The production possibility frontier illustrates the trade-offs facing an economy that produces two goods. It shows the maximum quantity of one good that can be produced given the quantity of the other good produced. Here, the maximum number of coconuts that Tom can gather depends on the number of fish he catches, and vice versa. His feasible production is shown by the area *inside or on* the curve. Production at point C is feasible but not efficient. Points A and B are efficient and feasible, but point D is not feasible. **>web...**

>web... Throughout our book, this icon will be used to indicate which graphs are available in an interactive format on our text's website. You can work with these interactive graph tutorials and find additional learning resources if you go to www.worthpublishers.com/krugmanwells.

First of all, the production possibility frontier is a good way to illustrate the general economic concept of *efficiency*. Recall from Chapter 1 that an economy is efficient if there are no missed opportunities—there is no way to make someone better off without making others worse off. A key element of efficiency is that there are no missed opportunities in production—there is no way to produce more of one good without producing less of other goods.

As long as Tom is on the production possibility frontier, his production is efficient. At point *A*, the 25 coconuts he gathers are the maximum number he can get *given* that he has chosen to catch 20 fish; at point *B*, the 20 coconuts he gathers are the maximum he can get *given* his choice to catch 30 fish; and so on.

But suppose that for some reason Tom was at point *C*, producing 20 fish and 20 coconuts. Then this one-person economy would definitely be *inefficient*: it could be producing more of both goods.

The production possibility frontier is also useful as a reminder of the fundamental point that the true cost of any good is not just the amount of money it costs to buy, but everything else in addition to money that must be given up in order to get that good—the *opportunity cost*. If Tom were to catch 30 fish instead of 20, he would be able to gather only 20 coconuts instead of 25. So the opportunity cost of those 10 extra fish is the 5 coconuts not gathered. And if 10 extra fish have an opportunity cost of 5 coconuts, each 1 fish has an opportunity cost of $5/10 = 0.5$ coconuts.

We can now explain the bowed-out shape of the production possibility frontier in Figure 2-1: it reflects an assumption about how opportunity costs change as the mix of output changes. Figure 2-2 shows the same production possibility frontier as Figure 2-1. The arrows in Figure 2-2 illustrate the fact that with this bowed-out production possibility frontier, Tom faces *increasing opportunity cost*: the more fish he catches, the more coconuts he has to give up to catch an additional fish, and vice versa. For example, to go from producing zero fish to producing 20 fish, he has to give up 5 coconuts. That is, the opportunity cost of those 20 fish is 5 coconuts. But to increase his fish production to 40—that is, to produce an additional 20 fish—he must give up 25 more coconuts, a much higher opportunity cost.

Economists believe that opportunity costs are usually increasing. The reason is that when only a small amount of a good is produced, the economy can use

Figure 2-2

Increasing Opportunity Cost

The bowed-out shape of the production possibility frontier reflects increasing opportunity cost. In this example, to produce the first 20 fish, Tom must give up 5 coconuts. But to produce an additional 20 fish, he must give up 25 more coconuts. **>web...**

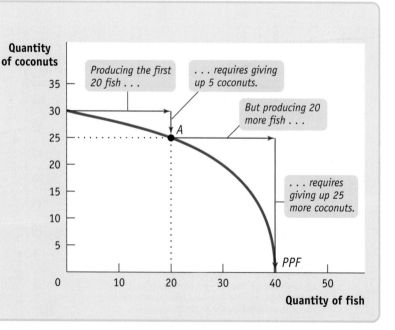

resources that are especially well suited for that production. For example, if an economy grows only a small amount of corn, that corn can be grown in places where the soil and climate are perfect for corn-growing but less suitable for growing anything else, like wheat. So growing that corn involves giving up only a small amount of potential wheat production. If the economy grows a lot of corn, however, land that isn't so great for corn and would have been well suited for wheat must be pressed into service, so the additional corn production will involve sacrificing considerably more wheat production.

Finally, the production possibility frontier helps us understand what it means to talk about *economic growth*. We introduced the concept of economic growth in the Introduction, defining it as *the growing ability of the economy to produce goods and services*. As we saw, economic growth is one of the fundamental features of the real economy. But are we really justified in saying that the economy has grown? After all, although the U.S. economy produces more of many things than it did a century ago, it produces less of other things—for example, horse-drawn carriages. Production of many goods, in other words, is actually down. So how can we say for sure that the economy as a whole has grown?

The answer, illustrated in Figure 2-3, is that economic growth means an *expansion of the economy's production possibilities*: the economy *can* produce more of everything. For example, if Tom's production is initially at point *A* (20 fish and 25 coconuts), economic growth means that he could move to point *E* (25 fish and 30 coconuts). *E* lies outside the original frontier; so in the production possibility frontier model, growth is shown as an outward shift of the frontier.

What the economy actually produces depends on the choices people make. After his production possibilities expand, Tom might not actually choose to produce both more fish and more coconuts—he might choose to increase production of only one good, or he might even choose to produce less of one good. But even if, for some reason, he chooses to produce either fewer coconuts or fewer fish than before, we would still say that his economy has grown—because he *could* have produced more of everything.

The production possibility frontier is a very simplified model of an economy. Yet it teaches us important lessons about real-life economies. It gives us our first clear sense of a key element of economic efficiency, it illustrates the concept of opportunity cost, and it makes clear what economic growth is all about.

Figure 2-3

Economic Growth

Economic growth results in an *outward shift* of the production possibility frontier because production possibilities are expanded. The economy can now produce more of everything. For example, if production is initially at point *A* (20 fish and 25 coconuts), it can move to point *E* (25 fish and 30 coconuts).

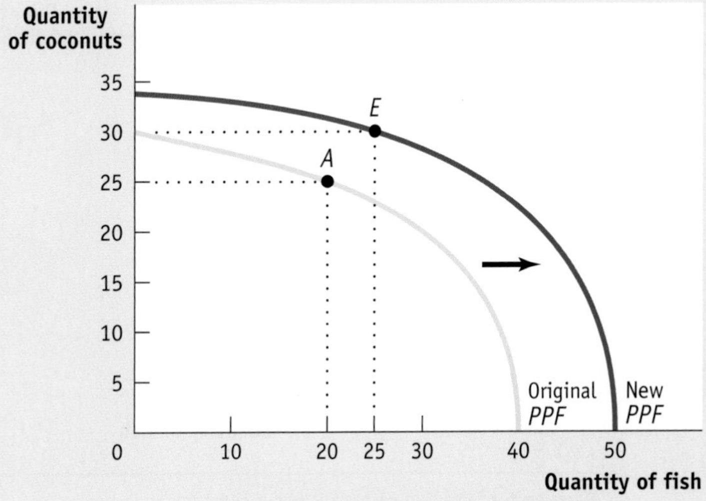

Comparative Advantage and Gains from Trade

Among the nine principles of economics described in Chapter 1 was that of *gains from trade*—the mutual gains that individuals can achieve by specializing in doing different things and trading with one another. Our second illustration of an economic model is a particularly useful model of gains from trade—trade based on *comparative advantage*.

Let's stick with Tom stranded on his island, but now let's suppose that a second castaway, who just happens to be named Hank, is washed ashore. Can they benefit from trading with each other?

It's obvious that there will be potential gains from trade if the two castaways do different things particularly well. For example, if Tom is a skilled fisherman and Hank is very good at climbing trees, clearly it makes sense for Tom to catch fish and Hank to gather coconuts—and for the two men to trade the products of their efforts.

But one of the most important insights in all of economics is that there are gains from trade even if one of the trading parties isn't especially good at anything. Suppose, for example, that Hank is less well suited to primitive life than Tom; he's not nearly as good at catching fish and compared to Tom even his coconut-gathering leaves something to be desired. Nonetheless, what we'll see is that both Tom and Hank can live better by trading with each other than either could alone.

For the purposes of this example, let's slightly redraw Tom's production possibilities represented by the production possibility frontier in panel (a) of Figure 2-4. According to this diagram, Tom could catch at most 40 fish, but only if he gathered no coconuts, and could gather 30 coconuts, but only if he caught no fish, as before.

In Figure 2-4, we have replaced the curved production possibility frontier of Figure 2-1 with a straight line. Why do this, when we've already seen that economists regard a bowed-out production possibility frontier as normal? The answer is that it simplifies our discussion—and as we have explained, modeling is all about simplification. The principle of comparative advantage doesn't depend on the assumption of straight-line production possibility frontiers, but it is easier to explain with that assumption.

The straight-line production possibility frontier in panel (a) of Figure 2-4 has a constant *slope* of −¾. (The appendix to this chapter explains how to calculate the slope of a line.) That is, for every 4 additional fish that Tom chooses to catch, he gathers 3 fewer coconuts. So Tom's opportunity cost of a fish is ¾ of a coconut regardless of how

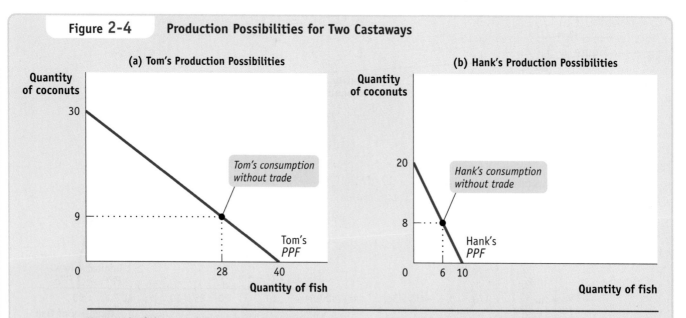

Figure 2-4   Production Possibilities for Two Castaways

(a) Tom's Production Possibilities

(b) Hank's Production Possibilities

Here, each of the two castaways has a constant opportunity cost of fish and a linear production possibility frontier: In Tom's case, each fish always has an opportunity cost of ¾ of a coconut. In Hank's case, each fish always has an opportunity cost of 2 coconuts. **>web...**

many or how few fish he catches. In contrast, a production possibility frontier is curved when the opportunity cost of a good changes according to how much of the good has already been produced. For example, you can see from Figure 2-2 that if Tom starts at the point of having caught zero fish and gathers 30 coconuts, his opportunity cost of catching 20 fish is 5 coconuts. But once he has already caught 20 fish, the opportunity cost of an additional 20 fish increases to 25 coconuts.

Panel (b) of Figure 2-4 shows Hank's production possibilities. Like Tom's, Hank's production possibility frontier is a straight line, implying a constant opportunity cost of fish in terms of coconuts. His production possibility frontier has a constant slope of −2. Hank is less productive all around: at most he can produce 10 fish or 20 coconuts. But he is particularly bad at fishing; whereas Tom sacrifices ¾ of a coconut per fish caught, for Hank the opportunity cost of a fish is 2 whole coconuts. Table 2-1 summarizes the two castaways' opportunity costs for fish and coconuts.

TABLE 2-1

Tom and Hank's Opportunity Costs of Fish and Coconuts

	Tom's Opportunity Cost	Hank's Opportunity Cost
One fish	3/4 coconut	2 coconuts
One coconut	4/3 fish	1/2 fish

Now Tom and Hank could go their separate ways, each living on his own side of the island, catching his own fish and gathering his own coconuts. Let's suppose that they start out that way and make the consumption choices shown in Figure 2-4: in the absence of trade, Tom consumes 28 fish and 9 coconuts per week, while Hank consumes 6 fish and 8 coconuts.

But is this the best they can do? No, it isn't. Given that the two castaways have different opportunity costs, they can strike a deal that makes both of them better off.

Table 2-2 shows how such a deal works: Tom specializes in the production of fish, catching 40 per week, and gives 10 to Hank. Meanwhile, Hank specializes in the production of coconuts, gathering 20 per week, and gives 10 to Tom. The result is shown in Figure 2-5 on page 30. Tom now consumes more of both goods than before: instead of 28 fish and 9 coconuts, he consumes 30 fish and 10 coconuts. And Hank also consumes more, going from 6 fish and 8 coconuts to 10 fish and 10 coconuts. As Table 2-2 also shows, both Tom and Hank experience gains from trade: Tom's consumption of fish increases by two, and his consumption of coconuts increases by one. Hank's consumption of fish increases by four, and his consumption of coconuts by two.

So both castaways are better off when they each specialize in what they are good at and trade. It's a good idea for Tom to catch the fish for both of them, because his opportunity cost of a fish in terms of coconuts not gathered is only ¾ of a coconut, versus 2 coconuts for Hank. Correspondingly, it's a good idea for Hank to gather coconuts for the both of them.

Or we could put it the other way around: Because Tom is so good at catching fish, his opportunity cost of gathering coconuts is high: 4/3 fish not caught for every coconut gathered. Because Hank is a pretty poor fisherman, his opportunity cost of gathering coconuts is much less, only ½ a fish per coconut.

TABLE 2-2

How the Castaways Gain from Trade

		Without Trade		With Trade		Gains from Trade
		Production	Consumption	Production	Consumption	
Tom	Fish	28	28	40	30	+2
	Coconuts	9	9	0	10	+1
Hank	Fish	6	6	0	10	+4
	Coconuts	8	8	20	10	+2

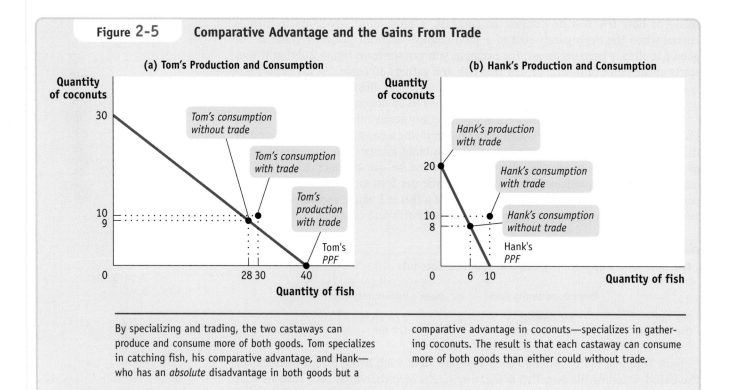

Figure 2-5   **Comparative Advantage and the Gains From Trade**

(a) Tom's Production and Consumption

Quantity
of coconuts

Tom's consumption
without trade

Tom's consumption
with trade

Tom's
production
with trade

Tom's
PPF

30

10
9

0   28 30   40

Quantity of fish

(b) Hank's Production and Consumption

Quantity
of coconuts

Hank's production
with trade

Hank's consumption
with trade

Hank's consumption
without trade

Hank's
PPF

20

10
8

0   6   10

Quantity of fish

By specializing and trading, the two castaways can produce and consume more of both goods. Tom specializes in catching fish, his comparative advantage, and Hank—who has an *absolute* disadvantage in both goods but a comparative advantage in coconuts—specializes in gathering coconuts. The result is that each castaway can consume more of both goods than either could without trade.

An individual has a **comparative advantage** in producing a good or service if the opportunity cost of producing the good is lower for that individual than for other people.

What we would say in this case is that Tom has a **comparative advantage** in catching fish and Hank has a comparative advantage in gathering coconuts. An individual has a comparative advantage in producing something if the opportunity cost of that production is less for that individual than for other people. In other words, Hank has a comparative advantage over Tom in producing a particular good or service if Hank's opportunity cost of producing that good or service is less than Tom's.

The story of Tom and Hank clearly simplifies reality. Yet it teaches us some very important lessons that apply to the real economy, too.

First, the model provides a clear illustration of the gains from trade: by agreeing to specialize and provide goods to each other, Tom and Hank can produce more and therefore both be better off than if they tried to be self-sufficient.

Second, the model demonstrates a very important point that is often overlooked in real-world arguments: as long as people have different opportunity costs, *everyone has a comparative advantage in something, and everyone has a comparative disadvantage in something.*

Notice that in our example Tom is actually better than Hank at producing both goods: Tom can catch more fish in a week, and he can also gather more coconuts. That is, Tom has an **absolute advantage** in both activities: he can produce more output with a given amount of input (in this case, his time) than Hank. You might therefore be tempted to think that Tom has nothing to gain from trading with the less competent Hank.

An individual has an **absolute advantage** in an activity if he or she can do it better than other people. Having an absolute advantage is not the same thing as having a comparative advantage.

But we've just seen that Tom can indeed benefit from a deal with Hank because *comparative,* not *absolute,* advantage is the basis for mutual gain. It doesn't matter that it takes Hank more time to gather a coconut; what matters is that for him the opportunity cost of that coconut is lower in terms of fish. So Hank, despite his absolute disadvantage, even in coconuts, has a comparative advantage in coconut-gathering. Meanwhile Tom, who can use his time better by catching fish, has a comparative *disadvantage* in coconut-gathering.

If comparative advantage were relevant only to castaways, it might not be that interesting. In fact, however, the idea of comparative advantage applies to many activities in the economy. Perhaps its most important application is to trade—not between individuals, but between countries. So let's look briefly at how the model of comparative advantage helps in understanding both the causes and the effects of international trade.

Comparative Advantage and International Trade

Look at the label on a manufactured good sold in the United States, and there's a good chance you will find that it was produced in some other country—in China, or Japan, or even in Canada, eh? On the other side, many U.S. industries sell a large fraction of their output overseas (this is particularly true of agriculture, high technology, and entertainment).

Should all this international exchange of goods and services be celebrated, or is it cause for concern? Politicians and the public often question the desirability of international trade, arguing that the nation should produce goods for itself rather than buying them from foreigners. Industries around the world demand protection from foreign competition: Japanese farmers want to keep out American rice, American steelworkers want to keep out European steel. And these demands are often supported by public opinion.

Economists, however, have a very positive view of international trade. Why? Because they view it in terms of comparative advantage.

Figure 2-6 shows, with a simple example, how international trade can be interpreted in terms of comparative advantage. Although the example as constructed is hypothetical, it is based on an actual pattern of international trade: American exports of pork to Canada and Canadian exports of aircraft to the United States. Panels (a) and (b) of Figure 2-6 illustrate hypothetical production possibility frontiers for the United States and

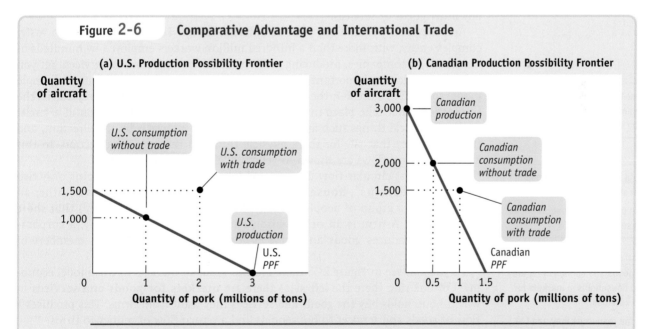

Figure 2-6   Comparative Advantage and International Trade

In this hypothetical example, Canada and the United States produce only two goods: pork and aircraft. Aircraft are measured on the vertical axis and tons of pork on the horizontal axis. Panel (a) shows the U.S. production possibility frontier. It is relatively flat, implying that the United States has a comparative advantage in pork production. Panel (b) shows the Canadian production possibility frontier. It is relatively steep, implying that Canada has a comparative advantage in aircraft production. Just like two individuals, both countries gain from specialization and trade. **>web...**

Canada, with tons of pork measured on the horizontal axis and aircraft measured on the vertical axis. The U.S. production possibility frontier is flatter than the Canadian frontier, implying that the United States has a comparative advantage in pork and Canada has a comparative advantage in aircraft.

Although the consumption points in Figure 2-6 are hypothetical, they illustrate a general principle: just like the example of Tom and Hank, the United States and Canada can both achieve mutual gains from trade. If the United States concentrates on producing pork and ships some of its output to Canada, while Canada concentrates on aircraft and ships some of its output to the United States, both countries can consume more than if they insisted on being self-sufficient.

Moreover, these mutual gains don't depend on each country being better at producing one kind of good. Even if one country has, say, higher output per person-hour in both industries—that is, even if one country has an absolute advantage in both industries—there are still mutual gains from trade.

But how does trade actually take place in market interactions? This brings us to our final model, the circular-flow diagram, which helps economists analyze the transactions that take place in a market economy.

Transactions: The Circular-Flow Diagram

The little economy created by Tom and Hank on their island lacks many features of the economy modern Americans live in. For one thing, though millions of Americans are self-employed, most workers are employed by someone else, usually a company with hundreds or thousands of employees. Also, Tom and Hank engage only in the simplest of economic transactions, **barter**, in which an individual directly trades a good or service he or she has for a good or service he or she wants. In the modern economy, simple barter is rare: usually people trade goods or services for money—pieces of colored paper with no inherent value—and then trade those pieces of colored paper for the goods or services they want. That is, they sell goods or services and buy other goods or services.

And they both sell and buy a lot of different things. The U.S. economy is a vastly complex entity, with more than a hundred million workers employed by hundreds of thousands of companies, producing millions of different goods and services. Yet you can learn some very important things about the economy by considering the simple model shown in Figure 2-7, the **circular-flow diagram.** This diagram represents the transactions that take place in an economy by two kinds of flows around a circle: flows of physical things such as goods, labor, or raw materials in one direction, and flows of money that pay for these physical things in the opposite direction. In this case the physical flows are shown in yellow, the money flows in green.

The simplest circular-flow diagram models an economy that contains only two kinds of "inhabitants": **households** and **firms.** A household consists of either an individual or a group of people (usually, but not necessarily, a family) that share their income. A firm is an organization (usually, but not necessarily, a corporation) that produces goods and services for sale—and that employs members of households.

As you can see in Figure 2-7, there are two kinds of markets in this model economy. On one side (here the left side) there are **markets for goods and services** in which households buy the goods and services they want from firms. This produces a flow of goods and services to households and a return flow of money to firms.

On the other side, there are **factor markets**. A **factor of production** is a resource used to produce goods and services. Economists usually use the term *factor of production* to refer to a resource that is not used up in production. For example, workers use sewing machines to convert cloth into shirts; the workers and the sewing machines are factors of production, but the cloth is not. Broadly speaking, the main factors of

Trade takes the form of **barter** when people directly exchange goods or services that they have for goods or services that they want.

The **circular-flow diagram** is a model that represents the transactions in an economy by flows around a circle.

A **household** is a person or a group of people that share their income.

A **firm** is an organization that produces goods and services for sale.

Firms sell goods and services that they produce to households in **markets for goods and services**.

Firms buy the resources they need to produce—**factors of production**—in **factor markets**.

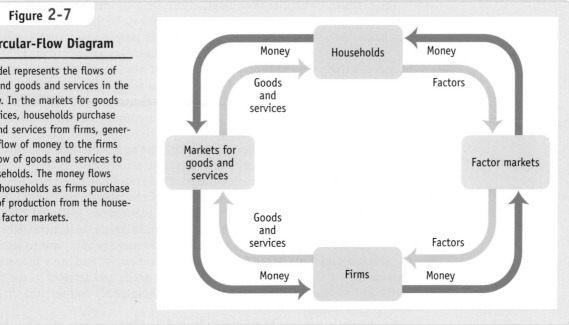

Figure 2-7

The Circular-Flow Diagram

This model represents the flows of money and goods and services in the economy. In the markets for goods and services, households purchase goods and services from firms, generating a flow of money to the firms and a flow of goods and services to the households. The money flows back to households as firms purchase factors of production from the households in factor markets.

production are labor, land, capital, and human capital. Labor is the work of human beings; land is a resource supplied by nature; capital refers to "created" resources such as machines and buildings; and human capital refers to the educational achievements and skills of the labor force, which enhance its productivity. Of course, each of these is really a category rather than a single factor: land in North Dakota is quite different from land in Florida.

The factor market most of us know best is the *labor market*, in which workers are paid for their time. Besides labor, we can think of households as owning and selling the other factors of production to firms. For example, when a corporation pays dividends to its stockholders, who are members of households, it is in effect paying them for the use of the machines and buildings that ultimately belong to those investors.

In what sense is Figure 2-7 a model? That is, in what sense is it a *simplified* representation of reality? The answer is that this picture ignores a number of real-world complications. A few examples:

■ In the real world, the distinction between firms and households isn't always that clear-cut. Consider a small, family-run business—a farm, a shop, a small hotel. Is this a firm or a household? A more complete picture would include a separate box for family businesses.

■ Many of the sales firms make are not to households but to other firms; for example, steel companies sell mainly to other companies such as auto manufacturers, not to households. A more complete picture would include these flows of goods and money within the business sector.

■ The figure doesn't show the government, which in the real world diverts quite a lot of money out of the circular flow in the form of taxes but also injects a lot of money back into the flow in the form of spending.

Figure 2-7, in other words, is by no means a complete picture either of all the types of "inhabitants" of the real economy or of all the flows of money and physical items that take place among these inhabitants.

Despite its simplicity, the circular-flow diagram, like any good economic model, is a very useful aid to thinking about the economy.

For example, a circular-flow diagram can help us understand how the economy manages to provide jobs for a growing population. To illustrate, consider the huge expansion in the U.S. labor force—the number of people who want to work—between the early 1960s and the late 1980s. This increase was partly caused by the 15-year baby boom that followed World War II; the first baby boomers began looking for jobs in the early 1960s and the last of them went to work in the late 1980s. In addition, social changes led a much higher fraction of women to seek paid work outside the home. As a result, between 1962 and 1988 the number of Americans employed or seeking jobs increased by 71 percent.

That's a lot of new job seekers. But luckily, the number of jobs also expanded during the same period, by almost exactly the same percentage.

Or was it luck? The circular-flow diagram helps us understand why the number of jobs available grew along with the expansion of the labor force. Figure 2-8 compares the money flows around the circle for the U.S. economy in 1962 and 1988. Both the money paid to households and the money spent by households increased enormously over the period—and that was no accident. As more people went to work—that is, as more labor was sold in the factor markets—households had more income to spend. They used that increased income to buy more goods and services in the market for goods and services. And in order to produce these goods and services, firms had to hire more workers!

So, despite being an extremely simple model of the economy, the circular-flow diagram helps us to understand some important facts about the real U.S. economy. The number of jobs isn't fixed, the model tells us, because it depends on how much households spend; and the amount households spend depends on how many people are working. It is, in other words, no accident that the economy somehow creates enough jobs even when the working population grows rapidly.

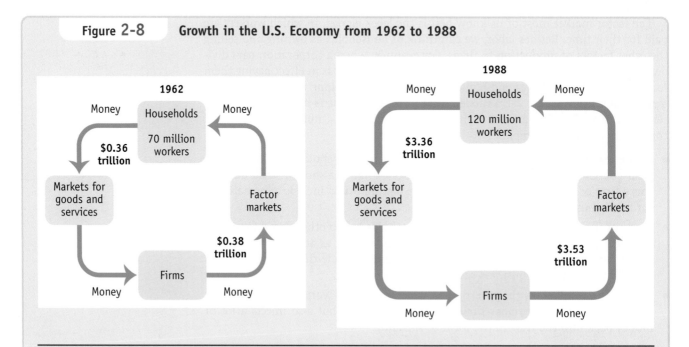

Figure 2-8   **Growth in the U.S. Economy from 1962 to 1988**

These two circular-flow diagrams—one corresponding to 1962, the other corresponding to 1988—help us understand how the U.S. economy was able to produce enough jobs for its rapidly growing labor force. A roughly twofold increase in the number of workers from 1962 to 1988 was accompanied by a ninefold increase in money flows between households and firms. As the labor force grew, money going to households increased and their spending on goods and services increased. This led firms to hire more workers to meet the increased desire for goods and services and generated more jobs for households.

economics in action

Rich Nation, Poor Nation

Try taking off your clothes—at a suitable time and in a suitable place, of course—and take a look at the labels inside that say where they were made. It's a very good bet that much, if not most, of your clothing was manufactured overseas, in a country that is much poorer than the United States—say, in El Salvador or in Bangladesh.

Why are these countries so much poorer than we are? The immediate reason is that their economies are much less *productive*—firms in these countries are just not able to produce as much from a given quantity of resources as comparable firms in the United States or other wealthy countries. Why countries differ so much in productivity is a deep question—indeed, one of the main questions that preoccupy economists. But in any case, the difference in productivity is a fact.

But if the economies of these countries are so much less productive than ours, how is it that they make so much of our clothing? Why don't we do it for ourselves?

The answer is "comparative advantage." Just about every industry in Bangladesh is much less productive than the corresponding industry in the United States. But the productivity difference between rich and poor countries varies across goods; it is very large in the production of sophisticated goods like aircraft but not that large in the production of simpler goods like clothing. So Bangladesh's position with regard to clothing production is like Hank's position with respect to coconut gathering: he's not as good at it as his fellow castaway, but it's the thing he does comparatively well.

The point is that Bangladesh, though it is at an absolute disadvantage compared with the United States in almost everything, has a comparative advantage in clothing production. This means that both the United States and Bangladesh are able to consume more because they specialize in producing different things, with Bangladesh supplying our clothing and the United States supplying Bangladesh with more sophisticated goods.

> > > > > > > > > > > > > > > > > > > >

Although less productive than American workers, Bengali workers have a comparative advantage in clothing production.

>> **QUICK REVIEW**

> Most economic *models* are "thought experiments" or simplified representations of reality, which rely on the *other things equal assumption.*

> An important economic model is the *production possibility frontier*, which illustrates the concepts of efficiency, opportunity cost, and economic growth.

> *Comparative advantage* is a model that explains the source of gains from trade but is often confused with *absolute advantage*. Every person and every country has a comparative advantage in something, giving rise to gains from trade.

> In the simplest economies people *barter* rather than trade with money as in a modern economy. The *circular-flow diagram* is a model representing transactions within the economy as flows of goods, services and money between *households* and *firms*. These transactions occur in *markets for goods and services* and *factor markets*, markets for *factors of production*, such as labor.

>> **CHECK YOUR UNDERSTANDING 2-1**

1. True or false? Explain your answer.
   a. An increase in the amount of resources available to Tom for use in producing coconuts and fish does not change his production possibility frontier.
   b. A technological change that allows Tom to catch more fish for any amount of coconuts gathered results in a change in his production possibility frontier.
   c. The production possibility frontier is useful because it illustrates how much of one good an economy must give up to get more of another good regardless of whether resources are being used efficiently.

2. In Italy, an automobile can be produced by 8 workers in one day and a washing machine by 3 workers in one day. In the United States, an automobile can be produced by 6 workers in one day, and a washing machine by 2 workers in one day.
   a. Which country has an absolute advantage in the production of automobiles? In washing machines?
   b. Which country has a comparative advantage in the production of washing machines? In automobiles?
   c. What pattern of specialization results in the greatest gains from trade between the two countries?

3. Use the circular-flow diagram to explain how an increase in the amount of money spent by households results in an increase in the number of jobs in the economy. Describe in words what the circular-flow model predicts.

Solutions appear at back of book.

Using Models

Economics, we have now learned, is mainly a matter of creating models that draw on a set of basic principles but add some more specific assumptions that allow the modeler to apply those principles to a particular situation. But what do economists actually *do* with their models?

Positive versus Normative Economics

Imagine that you are an economic adviser to the governor of your state. What kinds of questions might the governor ask you to answer?

Well, here are three possible questions:

1. How much revenue will the tolls on the state turnpike yield next year?

2. How much would that revenue increase if the toll were raised from $1 to $1.50?

3. Should the toll be raised, bearing in mind that a toll increase will reduce traffic and air pollution near the road but will impose some financial hardship on frequent commuters?

There is a big difference between the first two questions and the third one. The first two are questions about facts. Your forecast of next year's toll collection will be proved right or wrong when the numbers actually come in. Your estimate of the impact of a change in the toll is a little harder to check—revenue depends on other factors besides the toll, and it may be hard to disentangle the causes of any change in revenue. Still, in principle there is only one right answer.

But the question of whether tolls should be raised may not have a "right" answer—two people who agree on the effects of a higher toll could still disagree about whether raising the toll is a good idea. For example, someone who lives near the turnpike but doesn't commute on it will care a lot about noise and air pollution but not so much about commuting costs. A regular commuter who doesn't live near the turnpike will have the opposite priorities.

This example highlights a key distinction between two roles of economic analysis. Analysis that tries to answer questions about the way the world works, which have definite right and wrong answers, is known as **positive economics**. In contrast, analysis that involves saying how the world *should* work is known as **normative economics**. To put it another way, positive economics is about description, normative economics is about prescription.

Positive economics occupies most of the time and effort of the economics profession. And models play a crucial role in almost all positive economics. As we mentioned earlier, the U.S. government uses a computer model to assess proposed changes in national tax policy, and many state governments have similar models to assess the effects of their own tax policy.

It's worth noting that there is a subtle but important difference between the first and second questions we imagined the governor asking. Question 1 asked for a simple prediction about next year's revenue—a **forecast**. Question 2 was a "what if" question, asking how revenue would change if the tax law were to change. Economists are often called upon to answer both types of questions, but models are especially useful for answering "what if" questions.

The answers to such questions often serve as a guide to policy, but they are still predictions, not prescriptions. That is, they tell you what will happen if a policy is changed; they don't tell you whether that result is good or not. Suppose that your economic model tells you that the governor's proposed increase in highway tolls will raise property values in communities near the road but will hurt those people who must use the turnpike to get to work. Does that make this proposed toll increase a good idea or a bad one? It depends on whom you ask. As we've just seen, someone who is very concerned with the communities near the road will support the increase, but someone who is very concerned with the welfare of drivers will feel differently. That's a value judgment—it's not a question of economic analysis.

Positive economics is the branch of economic analysis that describes the way the economy actually works. **Normative economics** makes prescriptions about the way the economy *should* work.

A **forecast** is a simple prediction of the future.

Still, economists often do end up giving policy advice. That is, they do engage in normative economics. How can they do this when there may be no "right" answer?

One answer is that economists are also citizens, and we all have our opinions. But economic analysis can often be used to show that some policies are clearly better than others, regardless of anyone's opinions.

Suppose that policy A makes everyone better off than policy B—or at least makes some people better off without making others worse off. Then A is clearly more efficient than B. That's not a value judgment: we're talking about how best to achieve a goal, not about the goal itself.

For example, two different policies have been used to help low-income families obtain housing: rent control, which limits the rents landlords are allowed to charge, and rent subsidies, which provide families with additional money to pay rent. Almost all economists agree that subsidies are the more efficient policy. (In Chapter 4 we'll see why this is so.) And so the great majority of economists, whatever their personal politics, favor subsidies over rent control.

When policies can be clearly ranked in this way, then economists generally agree. But it is no secret that economists sometimes disagree. Why does this happen?

When and Why Economists Disagree

Economists have a reputation for arguing with each other. Where does this reputation come from?

One important answer is that media coverage tends to exaggerate the real differences in views among economists. If nearly all economists agree on an issue—for example, the proposition that rent controls lead to housing shortages—reporters and editors are likely to conclude that there is no story worth covering, and so the professional consensus tends to go unreported. But when there is some issue on which prominent economists take opposing sides—for example, whether cutting taxes right now would help the economy—that does make a good news story. So you hear much more about the areas of disagreement within economics than you do about the large areas of agreement.

It is also worth remembering that economics is, unavoidably, often tied up in politics. On a number of issues powerful interest groups know what opinions they want to hear; they therefore have an incentive to find and promote economists who profess those opinions, giving these economists a prominence and visibility out of proportion to their support among their colleagues.

But although the appearance of disagreement among economists exceeds the reality, it remains true that economists often *do* disagree about important things. For example, some very respected economists argue vehemently that the U.S. government should replace the income tax with a *value-added tax* (a national sales tax, which is the main source of government revenue in many European countries). Other equally respected economists disagree. Why this difference of opinion?

One important source of differences is in values: as in any diverse group of individuals, reasonable people can differ. In comparison to an income tax, a value-added tax typically falls more heavily on people of modest means. So an economist who values a society with less social and income equality for its own sake will tend to oppose a value-added tax. An economist with different values will be less likely to oppose it.

A second important source of differences arises from economic modeling. Because economists base their conclusions on models, which are simplified representations of reality, two economists can legitimately disagree about which simplifications are appropriate—and therefore arrive at different conclusions.

THE GLASS IS HALF FULL.

HALF EMPTY.

ECONOMISTS

THE CONSUMER IS HALF ALIVE.

"If all the economists in the world were laid end to end, they still couldn't reach a conclusion." So goes one popular economist joke. But do economists really disagree that much?

Not according to a classic survey of members of the American Economic Association, reported in the May 1992 issue of the *American Economic Review*. The authors asked respondents to agree or disagree with a number of statements about the economy; what they found was a high level of agreement among professional economists on many of the statements. At the top, with more than 90 percent of the economists agreeing, were "Tariffs and import quotas usually reduce general economic welfare" and "A ceiling on rents reduces the quantity and quality of housing available." What's striking about these two statements is that many non-economists disagree: tariffs and import quotas to keep out foreign-produced goods are favored by many voters, and proposals to do away with rent control in cities like New York and San Francisco have met fierce political opposition.

So is the stereotype of quarreling economists a myth? Not entirely: economists do disagree quite a lot on some issues, especially in macroeconomics. But there is a large area of common ground.

Suppose that the U.S. government were considering introducing a value-added tax. Economist A may rely on a model that focuses on the administrative costs of tax systems—that is, the costs of monitoring, processing papers, collecting the tax, and so on. This economist might then point to the well-known high costs of administering a value-added tax and argue against the change. But Economist B may think that the right way to approach the question is to ignore the administrative costs and focus on how the proposed law would change savings behavior. This economist might point to studies suggesting that value-added taxes promote higher consumer saving, a desirable result.

Because the economists have used different models—that is, made different simplifying assumptions—they arrive at different conclusions. And so the two economists may find themselves on different sides of the issue.

Most such disputes are eventually resolved by the accumulation of evidence showing which of the various models proposed by economists does a better job of fitting the facts. However, in economics as in any science, it can take a long time before research settles important disputes—decades, in some cases. And since the economy is always changing, in ways that make old models invalid or raise new policy questions, there are always new issues on which economists disagree. The policy maker must then decide which economist to believe.

The important point is that economic analysis is a method, not a set of conclusions.

economics in action

Economists in Government

Many economists are mainly engaged in teaching and research. But quite a few economists have a more direct hand in events.

As described in For Inquiring Minds on page 23, economists play a significant role in the business world, especially in the financial industry. But the most striking involvement of economists in the "real" world is their extensive participation in government.

This shouldn't be surprising: One of the most important functions of government is to make economic policy, and almost every government policy decision must take economic effects into consideration. So governments around the world employ economists in a variety of roles.

In the U.S. government, a key role is played by the Council of Economic Advisers, a branch of the Executive Office (that is, the staff of the president) whose sole purpose is to advise the White House on economic matters and to prepare the annual Economic Report of the President. Unusually for a government agency, most of the economists at the Council are not long-term civil servants; instead, they are mainly professors on leave for one or two years from their universities. Many of the nation's best-known economists have served on the Council of Economic Advisers at some point during their careers.

Economists also play an important role in many other parts of the U.S. government. Indeed, as the Bureau of Labor Statistics *Occupational Outlook Handbook* says, "Some economists work in almost every area of government." Needless to say, the Bureau of Labor Statistics is itself a major employer of economists.

It's also worth noting that economists play an especially important role in two international organizations headquartered in Washington, D.C.: the International Monetary Fund, which provides advice and loans to countries experiencing economic difficulties, and the World Bank, which provides advice and loans to promote long-term economic development.

Do all these economists in government disagree with each other all the time? Are their positions largely dictated by political affiliation? The answer to both questions is no. Although there are important disputes over economic issues in government, and politics inevitably plays some role, there is broad agreement among economists on many issues, and most economists in government try very hard to assess issues as objectively as possible.

> > > > > > > > > > > > > > > > > > > >

>>CHECK YOUR UNDERSTANDING 2-2

1. Which of the following statements is a positive statement? Which is a normative statement?
   a. Society should take measures to prevent people from engaging in dangerous personal behavior.
   b. People who engage in dangerous personal behavior impose higher costs on society through higher medical costs.

2. True or false? Explain your answer.
   a. Policy choice A and policy choice B attempt to achieve the same social goal. Policy choice A, however, results in a much less efficient use of resources than policy choice B. Therefore economists are more likely to agree on choosing policy choice B.
   b. When two economists disagree on the desirability of a policy, it's typically because one of them has made a mistake.
   c. Policy makers can always use economics to figure out which goals a society should try to achieve.

Solutions appear at back of book.

>>QUICK REVIEW

➤ Economists do mostly *positive economics*, analysis of the way the world works, in which there are definite right and wrong answers and which involve making *forecasts*. But in *normative economics*, which makes prescriptions about how things ought to be, there are often no right answers and only value judgments.

➤ Economists do disagree—though not as much as legend has it—for two main reasons. One, they may disagree about which simplifications to make in a model. Two, economists may disagree—like everyone else—about values.

• A LOOK AHEAD •

This chapter has given you a first view of what it means to do economics, starting with the general idea of models as a way to make sense of a complicated world and then moving on to three simple introductory models.

To get a real sense of how economic analysis works, however, and to show just how useful such analysis can be, we need to move on to a more powerful model. In the next two chapters we will study the quintessential economic model, one that has an amazing ability to make sense of many policy issues, predict the effects of many forces, and change the way you look at the world. That model is known as "supply and demand."

SUMMARY

1. Almost all economics is based on **models,** "thought experiments" or simplified versions of reality, many of which use mathematical tools such as graphs. An important assumption in economic models is the **other things equal assumption,** which allows analysis of the effect of a change in one factor by holding all other relevant factors unchanged.

2. One important economic model is the **production possibility frontier.** It illustrates: opportunity cost (showing how much of one good can be produced if less of the other good is produced); efficiency (an economy is efficient if it produces on the production possibility frontier); and economic growth (an expansion of the production possibility frontier).

3. Another important model is **comparative advantage,** which explains the source of gains from trade between individuals and countries. Everyone has a comparative advantage in something—some good or service in which that person has a lower opportunity cost than everyone else. But it is often confused with **absolute advantage,** an ability to produce a particular good or service better than anyone else. This confusion leads some to erroneously conclude that there are no gains from trade between people or countries.

4. In the simplest economies people **barter**—trade goods and services for one another—rather than trade them for money, as in a modern economy. The **circular-flow diagram** is a model representing transactions within the economy as flows of goods, services, and income between **households** and **firms.** These transactions occur in **markets for goods and services** and **factor markets,** markets for **factors of production** such as labor. It is useful in understanding how spending, production, employment, income, and growth are related in the economy.

5. Economists use economic models for both **positive economics,** which describes how the economy works, and for **normative economics,** which prescribes how the economy should work. Positive economics often involves making **forecasts.** Economists can determine correct answers for positive questions, but typically not for normative questions, which involve value judgments. The exceptions are when policies designed to achieve a certain prescription can be clearly ranked in terms of efficiency.

6. There are two main reasons economists disagree. One, they may disagree about which simplifications to make in a model. Two, economists may disagree—like everyone else—about values.

KEY TERMS

Model, p. 21
Other things equal assumption, p. 21
Production possibility frontier, p. 22
Comparative advantage, p. 28
Absolute advantage, p. 28

Barter, p. 30
Circular-flow diagram, p. 30
Household, p. 30
Firm, p. 30
Markets for goods and services, p. 30

Factor markets, p. 30
Factors of production, p. 30
Positive economics, p. 34
Normative economics, p. 34
Forecast, p. 34

PROBLEMS

1. Atlantis is a small, isolated island in the South Atlantic. The inhabitants grow potatoes and catch fresh fish. The accompanying table shows the maximum annual output combinations of potatoes and fish that can be produced. Obviously, given their limited resources and available technology, as they use more of their resources for potato production, there are fewer resources available for catching fish.

Maximum annual output options	Quantity of potatoes (pounds)	Quantity of fish (pounds)
A	1,000	0
B	800	300
C	600	500
D	400	600
E	200	650
F	0	675

a. Draw a production possibility frontier illustrating these options, showing points *A–F.*

b. Can Atlantis produce 500 pounds of fish and 800 pounds of potatoes? Explain. Where would this point lie relative to the production possibility frontier?

c. What is the opportunity cost of expanding the annual output of potatoes from 600 to 800 pounds?

d. What is the opportunity cost of increasing the annual output of potatoes from 200 to 400 pounds?

e. Can you explain why the answers to parts c and d are not the same? What does this imply about the slope of the production possibility frontier?

2. In the ancient country of Roma, only two goods, spaghetti and meatballs, were produced. There were two tribes in Roma, the Tivoli and the Frivoli. By themselves, the Tivoli each month could produce either 30 pounds of spaghetti and no meatballs,

or 50 pounds of meatballs and no spaghetti, or any combination in between, such as 15 pounds of spaghetti and 25 pounds of meatballs. The Frivoli, by themselves, each month could produce 40 pounds of spaghetti and no meatballs, or 30 pounds of meatballs and no spaghetti, or any combination in between, such as 20 pounds of spaghetti and 15 pounds of meatballs.

a. Assume that all production possibility frontiers are straight lines. Draw one diagram showing the monthly production possibility frontier for the Tivoli and another showing the monthly production possibility frontier for the Frivoli. Show how you calculated them.

b. Which tribe had the comparative advantage in spaghetti production? In meatball production?

In A.D. 100 the Frivoli discovered a new technique for making meatballs that doubled the quantity they could produce each month.

c. Draw the new monthly production possibility frontier for the Frivoli.

d. After the innovation, which tribe now had the absolute advantage in producing meatballs? In producing spaghetti? Which had the comparative advantage in meatball production? In spaghetti production?

3. Peter Pundit, an economics reporter, states that the European Union (EU) is increasing its productivity very rapidly in all major industries. He claims that this productivity advance is so rapid that output from the EU in these industries will soon exceed that of the United States and, as a result, the United States will no longer benefit from trade with the EU.

a. Do you think Peter Pundit is correct or not? If not, what do you think is the source of his mistake?

b. If the EU and the United States continue to trade, what do you think will characterize the goods that the EU exports to the United States and the goods that the United States exports to the EU?

4. You are in charge of allocating residents to your dormitory's baseball and basketball teams. You are down to the last four people, two of whom must be allocated to baseball and two to basketball. The accompanying table gives each person's batting average and free-throw average. Explain how you would use the concept of comparative advantage to allocate the players. Begin by establishing each player's opportunity cost of free throws in terms of batting average.

Name	Batting average	Free-throw average
Kelley	70%	60%
Jackie	50%	50%
Curt	10%	30%
Gerry	80%	70%

Why is it likely that the other basketball players will be unhappy about this arrangement but the other baseball players will be satisfied? Nonetheless, why would an economist say that this is an efficient way to allocate players for your dormitory's sports teams?

5. The economy of Atlantis has developed, and the inhabitants now use money in the form of cowry shells. Draw a circular-flow diagram showing households and firms. Firms produce potatoes and fish, and households buy potatoes and fish. Households also provide the land and labor to firms. Identify where in the flows of cowry shells or physical things (goods and services, or resources) each of the following impacts would occur. Describe how this impact spreads around the circle.

a. A devastating hurricane floods many of the potato fields.

b. A very productive fishing season yields a very large number of fish caught.

c. The inhabitants of Atlantis discover the Macarena and spend several days a month at dancing festivals.

6. An economist might say that colleges and universities "produce" education, using faculty members and students as inputs. According to this line of reasoning, education is then "consumed" by households. Construct a circular-flow diagram like the one found in this chapter to represent the sector of the economy devoted to college education: colleges and universities represent firms, and households both consume education and provide faculty and students to universities. What are the relevant markets in this model? What is being bought and sold in each direction? What would happen in the model if the government decided to subsidize 50 percent of all college students' tuition?

7. Your dormitory roommate plays loud music most of the time; you, however, would prefer more peace and quiet. You suggest that she buy some earphones. She responds that although she would be happy to use earphones, she has many other things that she would prefer to spend her money on right now. You discuss this situation with a friend who is an economics major. The following exchange takes place:
He: How much would it cost to buy earphones?
You: $15.
He: How much do you value having some peace and quiet for the rest of the semester?
You: $30.
He: It is efficient for you to buy the earphones and give them to your roommate. You gain more than you lose; the benefit exceeds the cost. You should do that.
You: It just isn't fair that I have to pay for the earphones when I'm not the one making the noise.

a. Which parts of this conversation contain positive statements and which parts contain normative statements?

b. Compose an argument supporting your viewpoint that your roommate should be the one to change her behavior. Similarly, compose an argument from the viewpoint of your roommate that you should be the one to buy the earphones. If your dormitory has a policy that gives residents the unlimited right to play music, whose argument is likely to win? If your dormitory has a rule that a person must stop playing music whenever a roommate complains, whose argument is likely to win?

8. A representative of the American clothing industry recently made the following statement: "Workers in Asia often work in sweatshop conditions earning only pennies an hour. American workers are more productive and as a result earn higher wages. In order to preserve the dignity of the American workplace, the government ought to enact legislation banning imports of low-wage Asian clothing."

   a. Which parts of this quote are positive statements? Which parts are normative statements?

   b. Is the policy that is being advocated consistent with the preceding statements about the wages and productivities of American and Asian workers?

   c. Would such a policy make some Americans better off without making any other Americans worse off? That is, would this policy be efficient from the viewpoint of all Americans?

   d. Would low-wage Asian workers benefit from or be hurt by such a policy?

9. Are the following statements true or false? Explain your answer.

   a. "When people must pay higher taxes on their wage earnings, it discourages their incentive to work" is a positive statement.

   b. "We should lower taxes to encourage more work" is a positive statement.

   c. Economics can never be used to completely decide what society ought to do.

   d. "The system of public education in this country generates greater benefits to society than the cost of running the system" is a normative statement.

   e. All disagreements among economists are generated by the media.

10. Evaluate the following statement: "It is easier to build an economic model that accurately reflects events that have already occurred than to build an economic model to forecast future events." Do you think that this is true or not? Why? What does this imply about the difficulties of building good economic models?

11. Economists who work for the government are often called on to make policy recommendations. Why do you think it is important for the public to be able to differentiate normative statements from positive statements in these recommendations?

12. The mayor of Gotham City, worried about a potential epidemic of deadly influenza this winter, asks an economic adviser the following series of questions. Does each question require the economic adviser to make a positive assessment or a normative assessment?

   a. How much vaccine will be in stock in the city by the end of November?

   b. If we offer to pay 10 percent more per dose to the pharmaceutical companies providing the vaccines, will they provide additional doses?

   c. If there is a shortage of vaccine in the city, whom should we vaccinate first—the elderly or the very young? (Assume that a person from one group has an equal likelihood of dying from influenza as a person from the other group.)

   d. If the city charges $25 per shot, how many people will pay?

   e. If the city charges $25 per shot, it will make a profit of $10 per shot, money that can go to pay for inoculating poor people. Should the city engage in such a scheme?

13. Assess the following statement: "If economists just had enough data, they could solve all policy questions in a way that maximizes the social good. There would be no need for divisive political debates, such as whether the government should provide free medical care for all."

>web... To continue your study and review of concepts in this chapter, please visit the Krugman/Wells website for quizzes, animated graph tutorials, web links to helpful resources, and more.

www.worthpublishers.com/krugmanwells

Chapter 2 Appendix:
>> Graphs in Economics

Getting the Picture

Whether you're reading about economics in the *Wall Street Journal* or in your economics textbook, you will see many graphs. Visual images can make it much easier to understand verbal descriptions, numerical information, or ideas. In economics, graphs are the type of visual image used to facilitate understanding. To fully understand the ideas and information being discussed, you need to be familiar with how to interpret these visual aids. This appendix explains how graphs are constructed and interpreted and how they are used in economics.

Graphs, Variables, and Economic Models

One reason to attend college is that a bachelor's degree provides access to higher-paying jobs. Additional degrees, such as MBAs or law degrees, increase earnings even more. If you were to read an article about the relationship between educational attainment and income, you would probably see a graph showing the income levels for workers with different amounts of education. And this graph would depict the idea that, in general, more education increases income. This graph, like most of those in economics, would depict the relationship between two economic variables. A **variable** is a quantity that can take on more than one value, such as the number of years of education a person has, the price of a can of soda, or a household's income.

> A quantity that can take on more than one value is called a **variable**.

As you learned in this chapter, economic analysis relies heavily on *models*, simplified descriptions of real situations. Most economic models describe the relationship between two variables, simplified by holding constant other variables that may affect the relationship. For example, an economic model might describe the relationship between the price of a can of soda and the number of cans of soda that consumers will buy, assuming that everything else that affects consumers' purchases of soda stays constant. This type of model can be described mathematically or verbally, but illustrating the relationship in a graph makes it easier to understand. Next we show how graphs that depict economic models are constructed and interpreted.

How Graphs Work

Most graphs in economics are based on a grid built around two perpendicular lines that show the values of two variables, helping you visualize the relationship between them. So a first step in understanding the use of such graphs is to see how this system works.

Two-Variable Graphs

Figure 2A-1 shows a typical two-variable graph. It illustrates the data in the accompanying table on outside temperature and the number of sodas a typical vendor can expect to sell at a baseball stadium during one game. The first column shows the values of outside temperature (the first variable) and the second column shows the values of the number of sodas sold (the second variable). Five combinations or pairs of the two variables are shown, each denoted by *A* through *E* in the third column.

Now let's turn to graphing the data in this table. In any two-variable graph, one variable is called the *x*-variable and the other is called the *y*-variable. Here we have made outside temperature the *x*-variable and number of sodas sold the *y*-variable. The solid

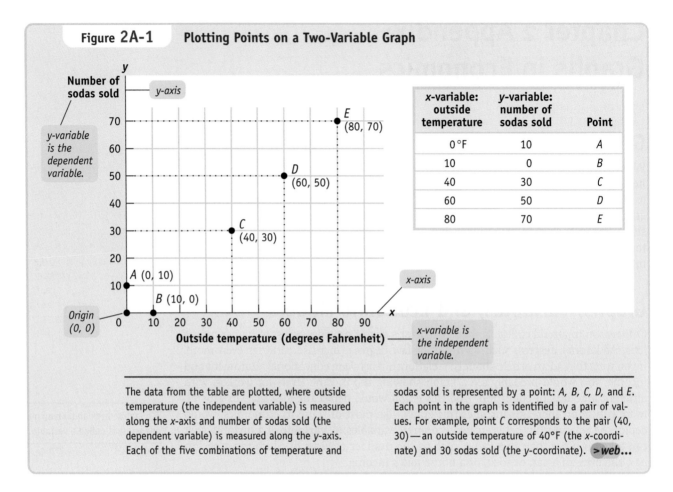

Figure 2A-1	Plotting Points on a Two-Variable Graph

x-variable: outside temperature	y-variable: number of sodas sold	Point
0°F	10	A
10	0	B
40	30	C
60	50	D
80	70	E

The data from the table are plotted, where outside temperature (the independent variable) is measured along the x-axis and number of sodas sold (the dependent variable) is measured along the y-axis. Each of the five combinations of temperature and sodas sold is represented by a point: A, B, C, D, and E. Each point in the graph is identified by a pair of values. For example, point C corresponds to the pair (40, 30)—an outside temperature of 40°F (the x-coordinate) and 30 sodas sold (the y-coordinate). **>web...**

The point where the axes of a two-variable graph meet is the **origin.**

The line along which values of the x-variable are measured is called the **horizontal axis** or **x-axis.** The line along which values of the y-variable are measured is called the **vertical axis** or **y-axis.**

A **causal relationship** exists between two variables when the value taken by one variable directly influences or determines the value taken by the other variable. In a causal relationship, the determining variable is called the **independent variable;** the variable it determines is called the **dependent variable.**

horizontal line in the graph is called the **horizontal axis** or **x-axis,** and values of the x-variable—outside temperature—are measured along it. Similarly, the solid vertical line in the graph is called the **vertical axis** or **y-axis,** and values of the y-variable—number of sodas sold—are measured along it. At the **origin,** the point where the two axes cross, each variable is equal to zero. As you move rightward from the origin along the x-axis, values of the x-variable are positive and increasing. As you move up from the origin along the y-axis, values of the y-variable are positive and increasing.

You can plot each of the five points A through E on this graph by using a pair of numbers—the values that the x-variable and the y-variable take on for a given point. In Figure 2A-1, at point C, the x-variable takes on the value 40 and the y-variable takes on the value 30. You plot point C by drawing a line straight up 40 on the x-axis and a horizontal line across from the 30 on the y-axis. We write point C as (40, 30). We write origin as (0, 0).

Looking at point A and point B in Figure 2A-1, you can see that when one of the variables for a point has a value of zero, it will lie on one of the axes. If the value of x is zero, the point will lie on the vertical axis, like point A. If the value of y is zero, the point will lie on the horizontal axis, like point B.

Most graphs that depict relationships between two economic variables represent a **causal relationship,** a relationship in which the value taken by one variable directly influences or determines the value taken by the other variable. In a causal relationship, the determining variable is called the **independent variable;** the variable it determines is called the **dependent variable.** In our example of soda sales, the outside temperature is the independent variable. It directly influences the number of sodas that are sold, the dependent variable in this case.

By convention, we put the independent variable on the horizontal axis and the dependent variable on the vertical axis. Figure 2A-1 is constructed consistent with this convention; the independent variable (outside temperature) is on the horizontal axis and the dependent variable (number of sodas sold) is on the vertical axis. An important exception to this convention is in graphs showing the economic relationship between the price of a product and quantity of the product: although price is generally the independent variable that determines quantity, it is always measured on the vertical axis.

Curves on a Graph

Panel (a) of Figure 2A-2 contains some of the same information as Figure 2A-1, with a line drawn through the points *B, C, D,* and *E.* Such a line on a graph is called a **curve,** regardless of whether it is a straight line or a curved line. If the curve that shows the relationship between two variables is a straight line, or linear, the variables have a **linear relationship.** When the curve is not a straight line, or nonlinear, the variables have a **nonlinear relationship.**

A point on a curve indicates the value of the *y*-variable for a specific value of the *x*-variable. For example, point *D* indicates that at a temperature of 60°F, a vendor can expect to sell 50 sodas. The shape and orientation of a curve reveal the general nature of the relationship between the two variables. The upward tilt of the curve in panel (a) of Figure 2A-2 suggests that vendors can expect to sell more sodas at higher outside temperatures.

> A **curve** is a line on a graph that depicts a relationship between two variables. It may be either a straight line or a curved line. If the curve is straight, the variables have a **linear relationship.** If the curve is not a straight line, the variables have a **nonlinear relationship.**

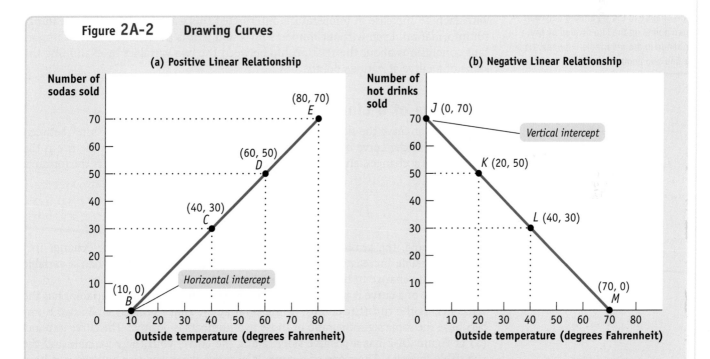

Figure 2A-2   Drawing Curves

(a) Positive Linear Relationship

(b) Negative Linear Relationship

The curve in panel (a) illustrates the relationship between the two variables, outside temperature and number of sodas sold. The two variables have a positive linear relationship: positive because the curve has an upward tilt, and linear because it is a straight line. It implies that an increase in *x* (outside temperature) leads to an increase in *y* (number of sodas sold). The curve in panel (b) is also a straight line, but it tilts downward. The two variables here, outside temperature and number of hot drinks sold, have a negative linear relationship: an increase in *x* (outside temperature) leads to a decrease in *y* (number of hot drinks sold). The curve in panel (a) has a horizontal intercept at point *B,* where it hits the horizontal axis. The curve in panel (b) has a vertical intercept at point *J,* where it hits the vertical axis and a horizontal intercept at point *M,* where it hits the horizontal axis. **>*web*...**

Two variables have a **positive relationship** when an increase in the value of one variable is associated with an increase in the value of the other variable. It is illustrated by a curve that slopes upward from left to right.

Two variables have a **negative relationship** when an increase in the value of one variable is associated with a decrease in the value of the other variable. It is illustrated by a curve that slopes downward from left to right.

The **horizontal intercept** of a curve is the point at which it hits the horizontal axis; it indicates the value of the *x*-variable when the value of the *y*-variable is zero.

The **vertical intercept** of a curve is the point at which it hits the vertical axis; it shows the value of the *y*-variable when the value of the *x*-variable is zero.

The **slope** of a line or curve is a measure of how steep it is. The slope of a line is measured by "rise over run"— the change in the *y*-variable between two points on the line divided by the change in the *x*-variable between those same two points.

When variables are related this way—that is, when an increase in one variable is associated with an increase in the other variable—the variables are said to have a **positive relationship.** It is illustrated by a curve that slopes upward from left to right. So the relationship between outside temperature and number of sodas sold illustrated by the curve in panel (a) of Figure 2A-2 is a positive linear relationship.

When an increase in one variable is associated with a decrease in the other variable, the two variables are said to have a **negative relationship.** It is illustrated by a curve that slopes downward from left to right, like the curve in panel (b) of Figure 2A-2. Because this curve is also linear, the relationship it depicts is a negative linear relationship. Two variables that might have such a relationship are the outside temperature and the number of hot drinks a vendor can expect to sell at a baseball stadium.

Return for a moment to the curve in panel (a) of Figure 2A-2 and you can see that it hits the horizontal axis at point *B*. This point, known as the **horizontal intercept,** shows the value of the *x*-variable when the value of the *y*-variable is zero. In panel (b) of Figure 2A-2 the curve hits the vertical axis at point *J*. This point, called the **vertical intercept,** indicates the value of the *y*-variable when the value of the *x*-variable is zero.

A Key Concept: The Slope of a Curve

The **slope** of a line or curve is a measure of how steep it is and indicates how sensitive the *y*-variable is to a change in the *x*-variable. In our example of outside temperature and the number of cans of soda a vendor can expect to sell, the slope of the curve would indicate how many more cans of soda the vendor could expect to sell with each 1° increase in temperature. Interpreted this way, the slope gives meaningful information. Even without numbers for *x* and *y*, it is possible to arrive at important conclusions about the relationship between the two variables by examining the slope of a curve at various points.

The Slope of a Linear Curve

Along a linear curve the slope, or steepness, is measured by dividing the "rise" between two points on the curve by the "run" between those same two points. The rise is the amount that *y* changes, and the run is the amount that *x* changes. Here is the formula:

$$\frac{\text{Change in } y}{\text{Change in } x} = \frac{\Delta y}{\Delta x} = \text{Slope}$$

In the formula, the symbol Δ (the Greek uppercase delta) stands for "change in." When a variable increases, the change in that variable is positive; when a variable decreases, the change in that variable is negative.

The slope of a curve is positive when the rise (the change in the *y*-variable) has the same sign as the run (the change in the *x*-variable). That's because when two numbers have the same sign, the ratio of those two numbers is positive. The curve in panel (a) of Figure 2A-2 has a positive slope: along the curve, both the *y*-variable and the *x*-variable increase. The slope of a curve is negative when the rise and the run have different signs. That's because when two numbers have different signs, the ratio of those two numbers is negative. The curve in panel (b) of Figure 2A-2 has a negative slope: along the curve, an increase in the *x*-variable is associated with a decrease in the *y*-variable.

Figure 2A-3 illustrates how to calculate the slope of a linear curve. Let's focus first on panel (a). From point *A* to point *B* the value of *y* changes from 25 to 20 and the value of *x* changes from 10 to 20. So the slope of the line between these two points is:

$$\frac{\text{Change in } y}{\text{Change in } x} = \frac{\Delta y}{\Delta x} = \frac{-5}{10} = -\frac{1}{2} = -0.5$$

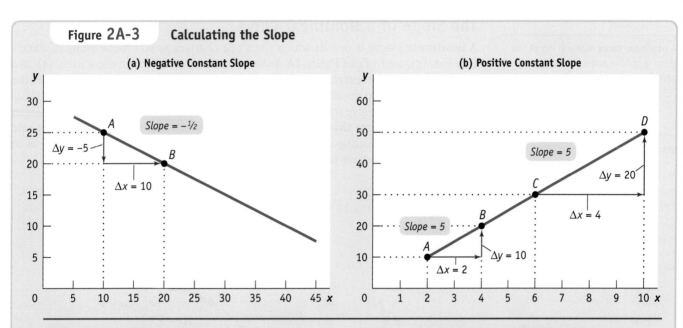

Figure 2A-3   **Calculating the Slope**

(a) Negative Constant Slope

(b) Positive Constant Slope

Panels (a) and (b) show two linear curves. Between points A and B on the curve in panel (a), the change in y (the rise) is −5 and the change in x (the run) is 10. So the slope from A to B is $\Delta y / \Delta x$ = −5/10 = −1/2 = −0.5, where the negative sign indicates that the curve is downward sloping. In panel (b), the curve has a slope from A to B of $\Delta y / \Delta x$ = 10/2 = 5. The slope from C to D is $\Delta y / \Delta x$ =

20/4 = 5. The slope is positive, indicating that the curve is upward sloping. Furthermore, the slope between A and B is the same as the slope between C and D, making this a linear curve. The slope of a linear curve is constant: it is the same regardless of where it is calculated along the curve. **>web...**

Because a straight line is equally steep at all points, the slope of a straight line is the same at all points. In other words, a straight line has a constant slope. You can check this by calculating the slope of the curve between points A and B and between points C and D in panel (b) of Figure 2A-3.

Between A and B: $\dfrac{\Delta y}{\Delta x} = \dfrac{10}{2} = 5$

Between C and D: $\dfrac{\Delta y}{\Delta x} = \dfrac{20}{4} = 5$

Horizontal and Vertical Curves and Their Slopes

When a curve is horizontal, the value of y along that curve never changes—it is constant. Everywhere along the curve, the change in y is zero. Now, zero divided by any number is zero. So, regardless of the value of the change in x, the slope of a horizontal curve is always zero.

If a curve is vertical, the value of x along the curve never changes—it is constant. Everywhere along the curve, the change in x is zero. This means that the slope of a vertical line is a ratio with zero in the denominator. A ratio with zero in the denominator is equal to infinity—that is, an infinitely large number. So the slope of a vertical line is equal to infinity.

A vertical or a horizontal curve has a special implication: it means that the x-variable and the y-variable are unrelated. Two variables are unrelated when a change in one of the variables (the independent variable) has no effect on the other variable (the dependent variable). Or to put it a slightly different way, two variables are unrelated when the dependent variable is constant regardless of the value of the independent variable. If, as is usual, the y-variable is the dependent variable, the curve is horizontal. If the dependent variable is the x-variable, the curve is vertical.

The Slope of a Nonlinear Curve

A **nonlinear curve** is one in which the slope is not the same between every pair of points.

A **nonlinear curve** is one in which the slope changes as you move along it. Panels (a), (b), (c), and (d) of Figure 2A-4 show various nonlinear curves. Panels (a) and (b) show nonlinear curves whose slopes change as you move along them, but the slopes always remain positive. Although both curves tilt upward, the curve in panel (a) gets steeper as you move from left to right in contrast to the curve in panel (b), which gets less steep. A curve that is upward sloping and gets steeper, as in panel (a), is said to have *positive increasing* slope. A curve that is upward sloping but gets flatter, as in panel (b), is said to have *positive decreasing* slope.

Figure 2A-4   **Nonlinear Curves**

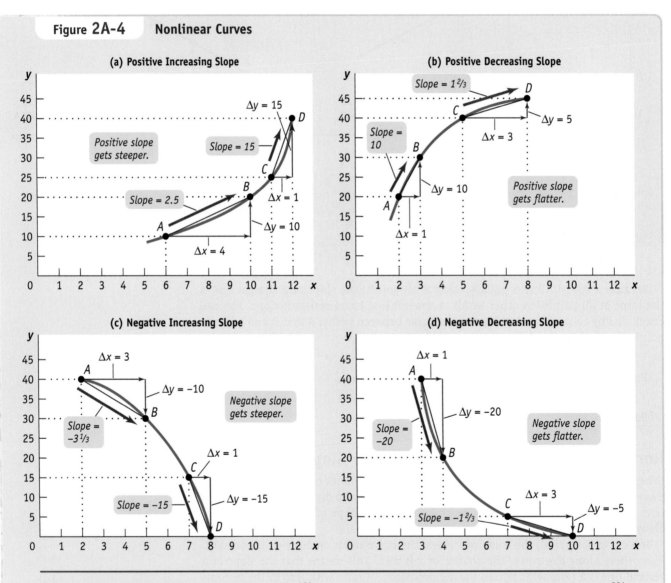

In panel (a) the slope of the curve from A to B is $\Delta y/\Delta x = {}^{10}\!/_4 = 2.5$, and from C to D it is $\Delta y/\Delta x = {}^{15}\!/_1 = 15$. The slope is positive and increasing; it gets steeper as you move to the right. In panel (b) the slope of the curve slope from A to B is $\Delta y/\Delta x = {}^{10}\!/_1 = 10$, and from C to D it is $\Delta y/\Delta x = {}^{5}\!/_3 = 1{}^{2}\!/_3$. The slope is positive and decreasing; it gets flatter as you move to the right. In panel (c) the slope from A to B is $\Delta y/\Delta x = {}^{-10}\!/_3 = -3{}^{1}\!/_3$, and from C to D it is $\Delta y/\Delta x = {}^{-15}\!/_1 = -15$. The slope is negative and increasing; it gets steeper as you move to the

right. And in panel (d) the slope from A to B is $\Delta y/\Delta x = {}^{-20}\!/_1 = -20$, and from C to D it is $\Delta y/\Delta x = {}^{-5}\!/_3 = -1{}^{2}\!/_3$. The slope is negative and decreasing; it gets flatter as you move to the right. The slope in each case has been calculated by using the arc method—that is, by drawing a straight line connecting two points along a curve. The average slope between those two points is equal to the slope of the straight line between those two points. **>web...**

When we calculate the slope along these nonlinear curves, we obtain different values for the slope at different points. How the slope changes along the curve determines the curve's shape. For example, in panel (a) of Figure 2A-4, the slope of the curve is a positive number that steadily increases as you move from left to right, whereas in panel (b), the slope is a positive number that steadily decreases.

The slopes of the curves in panels (c) and (d) are negative numbers. Economists often prefer to express a negative number as its **absolute value,** which is the value of the negative number without the minus sign. In general, we denote the absolute value of a number by two parallel bars around the number; for example, the absolute value of −4 is written as $|-4| = 4$. In panel (c), the absolute value of the slope steadily increases as you move from left to right. The curve therefore has *negative increasing* slope. And in panel (d), the absolute value of the slope of the curve steadily decreases along the curve. This curve therefore has *negative decreasing* slope.

> The **absolute value** of a negative number is the value of the negative number without the minus sign.

Calculating the Slope Along a Nonlinear Curve

We've just seen that along a nonlinear curve, the value of the slope depends on where you are on that curve. So how do you calculate the slope of a nonlinear curve? We will focus on two methods: the *arc method* and the *point method*.

The Arc Method of Calculating the Slope   An arc of a curve is some piece or segment of that curve. For example, panel (a) of Figure 2A-4 shows an arc consisting of the segment of the curve between points *A* and *B*. To calculate the slope along a nonlinear curve using the arc method, you draw a straight line between the two end-points of the arc. The slope of that straight line is a measure of the average slope of the curve between those two end-points. You can see from panel (a) of Figure 2A-4 that the straight line drawn between points *A* and *B* increases along the *x*-axis from 6 to 10 (so that $\Delta x = 4$) as it increases along the *y*-axis from 10 to 20 (so that $\Delta y = 10$). Therefore the slope of the straight line connecting points *A* and *B* is:

$$\frac{\Delta y}{\Delta x} = \frac{10}{4} = 2.5$$

This means that the average slope of the curve between points *A* and *B* is 2.5.

Now consider the arc on the same curve between points *C* and *D*. A straight line drawn through these two points increases along the *x*-axis from 11 to 12 ($\Delta x = 1$) as it increases along the *y*-axis from 25 to 40 ($\Delta y = 15$). So the average slope between points *C* and *D* is:

$$\frac{\Delta y}{\Delta x} = \frac{15}{1} = 15$$

Therefore the average slope between points *C* and *D* is larger than the average slope between points *A* and *B*. These calculations verify what we have already observed— that this upward-tilted curve gets steeper as you move from left to right and therefore has positive increasing slope.

The Point Method of Calculating the Slope   The point method calculates the slope of a nonlinear curve at a specific point on that curve. Figure 2A-5 on page 48 illustrates how to calculate the slope at point *B* on the curve. First, we draw a straight line that just touches the curve at point *B*. Such a line is called a **tangent line:** the fact that it just touches the curve at point *B* and does not touch the curve at any other point on the curve means that the straight line is *tangent* to the curve at point *B*. The slope of this tangent line is equal to the slope of the curve at point *B*.

> A **tangent line** is a straight line that just touches, or is tangent to, a nonlinear curve at a particular point. The slope of the tangent line is equal to the slope of the nonlinear curve at that point.

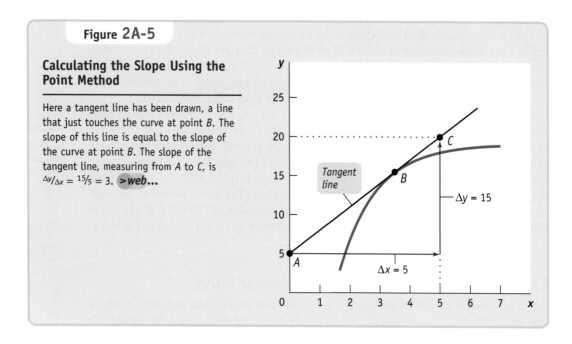

Figure 2A-5

Calculating the Slope Using the Point Method

Here a tangent line has been drawn, a line that just touches the curve at point B. The slope of this line is equal to the slope of the curve at point B. The slope of the tangent line, measuring from A to C, is $\Delta y/\Delta x = {}^{15}\!/_5 = 3$. **>web...**

You can see from Figure 2A-5 how the slope of the tangent line is calculated: from point A to point C, the change in y is 15 units and the change in x is 5 units, generating a slope of:

$$\frac{\Delta y}{\Delta x} = \frac{15}{5} = 3$$

By the point method, the slope of the curve at point B is equal to 3.

A natural question to ask at this point is how to determine which method to use—the arc method or the point method—in calculating the slope of a nonlinear curve. The answer depends on the curve itself and the data used to construct it. You use the arc method when you don't have enough information to be able to draw a smooth curve. For example, suppose that in panel (a) of Figure 2A-4 you have only the data represented by points A, C, and D and don't have the data represented by point B or any of the rest of the curve. Clearly, then, you can't use the point method to calculate the slope at point B; you would have to use the arc method to approximate the slope of the curve in this area by drawing a straight line between points A and C. But if you have sufficient data to draw the smooth curve shown in panel (a) of Figure 2A-4, then you could use the point method to calculate the slope at point B—and at every other point along the curve as well.

Maximum and Minimum Points

The slope of a nonlinear curve can change from positive to negative or vice versa. When the slope of a curve changes from positive to negative, it creates what is called a *maximum point* of the curve. When the slope of a curve changes from negative to positive, it creates a *minimum* point.

Panel (a) of Figure 2A-6 illustrates a curve in which the slope changes from positive to negative as you move from left to right. When x is between 0 and 50, the slope of the curve is positive. At x equal to 50, the curve attains its highest point—the largest value of y along the curve. This point is called the **maximum** of the curve. When x exceeds 50, the slope becomes negative as the curve turns downward. Many important curves in economics, such as the curve that represents how the profit of a firm changes as it produces more output, are hill-shaped like this.

In contrast, the curve shown in panel (b) of Figure 2A-6 is U-shaped: it has a slope that changes from negative to positive. At x equal to 50, the curve reaches its lowest

A nonlinear curve may have a **maximum** point, the highest point along the curve. At the maximum, the slope of the curve changes from positive to negative.

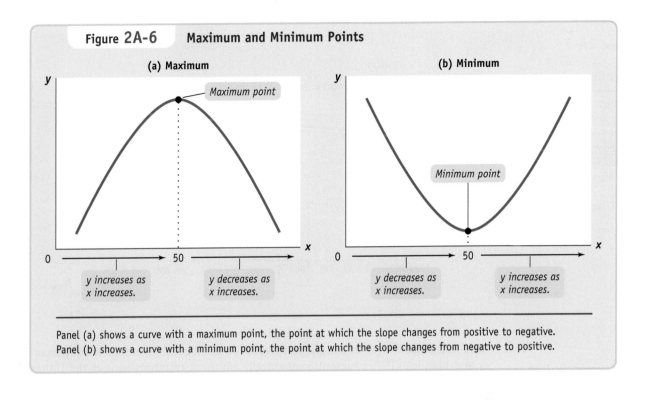

Figure 2A-6   Maximum and Minimum Points

(a) Maximum

Maximum point

y increases as x increases.   *y decreases as x increases.*

(b) Minimum

Minimum point

y decreases as x increases.   *y increases as x increases.*

Panel (a) shows a curve with a maximum point, the point at which the slope changes from positive to negative. Panel (b) shows a curve with a minimum point, the point at which the slope changes from negative to positive.

point—the smallest value of *y* along the curve. This point is called the **minimum** of the curve. Various important curves in economics, such as the curve that represents how the costs of some firms change as output increases, are U-shaped like this.

A nonlinear curve may have a **minimum** point, the lowest point along the curve. At the minimum, the slope of the curve changes from negative to positive.

Graphs That Depict Numerical Information

Graphs can also be used as a convenient way to summarize and display data without assuming some underlying causal relationship. Graphs that simply display numerical information are called *numerical graphs*. Here we will consider four types of numerical graphs: *time-series graphs*, *scatter diagrams*, *pie charts*, and *bar graphs*. These are widely used to display real, empirical data about different economic variables because they often help economists and policy makers identify patterns or trends in the economy. But as we will also see, you must be careful not to misinterpret or draw unwarranted conclusions from numerical graphs. That is, you must be aware of both the usefulness and the limitations of numerical graphs.

Types of Numerical Graphs

You have probably seen graphs in newspapers that show what has happened over time to economic variables such as the unemployment rate or stock prices. A **time-series graph** has successive dates on the horizontal axis and the values of a variable that occurred on those dates on the vertical axis. For example, Figure 2A-7 on page 50 shows the unemployment rate in the United States from 1989 to mid-2004. A line connecting the points that correspond to the unemployment rate for each year gives a clear idea of the overall trend in unemployment over these years.

Figure 2A-8 on page 50 is an example of a different kind of numerical graph. It represents information from a sample of 158 countries on average life expectancy and gross national product (GNP) per capita—a rough measure of a country's standard of living. Each point here indicates an average resident's life expectancy and the log of GNP per capita for a given country. (Economists have found that the log of GNP rather than the simple level of GNP is more closely tied to average life expectancy.) The points

A **time-series graph** has dates on the horizontal axis and values of a variable that occurred on those dates on the vertical axis.

Figure 2A-7

Time-Series Graph

Time-series graphs show successive dates on the *x*-axis and values for a variable on the *y*-axis. This time-series graph shows the seasonally adjusted unemployment rate in the United States from 1989 to mid-2004.

Source: Bureau of Labor Statistics.

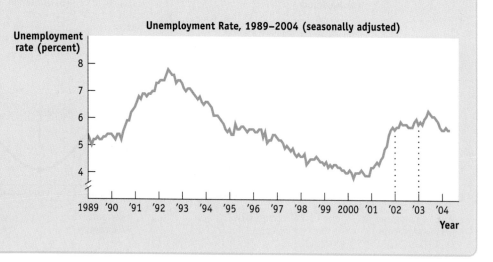

Unemployment Rate, 1989–2004 (seasonally adjusted)

Unemployment rate (percent)

Year

lying in the upper right of the graph, which show combinations of high life expectancy and high log GNP, represent economically advanced countries such as the United States. Points lying in the bottom left of the graph, which show combinations of low life expectancy and low log GNP, represent economically less advanced countries such as Afghanistan and Sierra Leone. The pattern of points indicates that there is a positive relationship between life expectancy and log GNP: on the whole, people live longer in countries with a higher standard of living. This type of graph is called a **scatter diagram,** a diagram in which each point corresponds to an actual observation of the *x*-variable and the *y*-variable. In scatter diagrams, a curve is typically fitted to the scatter of points; that is, a curve is drawn that approximates as closely as possible the general relationship between the variables. As you can see, the fitted curve in Figure 2A-8 is upward sloping, indicating the underlying positive relationship between the two variables. Scatter diagrams are often used to show how a general relationship can be inferred from a set of data.

A **scatter diagram** shows points that correspond to actual observations of the *x*- and *y*-variables. A curve is usually fitted to the scatter of points.

Figure 2A-8

Scatter Diagram

In a scatter diagram, each point represents the corresponding values of the *x*- and *y*-variables for a given observation. Here, each point indicates the observed average life expectancy and the log of GNP of a given country for a sample of 158 countries. The upward-sloping fitted line here is the best approximation of the general relationship between the two variables.

Source: Eduard Bos et al., *Health, Nutrition, and Population Indicators: A Statistical Handbook* (Washington, DC: World Bank, 1999).

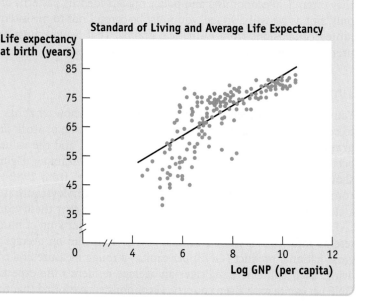

Standard of Living and Average Life Expectancy

Life expectancy at birth (years)

Log GNP (per capita)

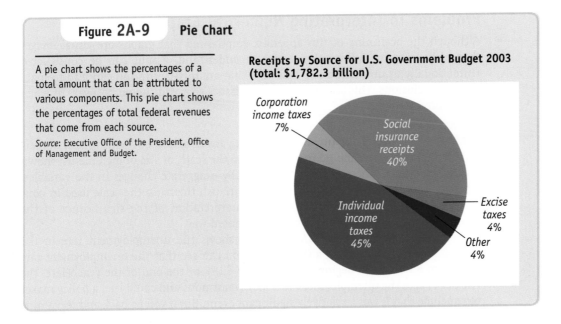

Figure 2A-9   Pie Chart

A pie chart shows the percentages of a total amount that can be attributed to various components. This pie chart shows the percentages of total federal revenues that come from each source.

Source: Executive Office of the President, Office of Management and Budget.

Receipts by Source for U.S. Government Budget 2003 (total: $1,782.3 billion)

Corporation income taxes 7%
Social insurance receipts 40%
Individual income taxes 45%
Excise taxes 4%
Other 4%

A **pie chart** shows the share of a total amount that is accounted for by various components, usually expressed in percentages. For example, Figure 2A-9 is a pie chart that depicts the various sources of revenue for the U.S. government budget in 2003, expressed in percentages of the total revenue amount, $1,782.3 billion. As you can see, social insurance receipts (the revenues collected to fund Social Security, Medicare, and unemployment insurance) accounted for 40% of total government revenue and individual income tax receipts accounted for 45%.

A **pie chart** shows how some total is divided among its components, usually expressed in percentages.

Bar graphs use bars of various heights or lengths to indicate values of a variable. In the bar graph in Figure 2A-10, the bars show the percent change in the number of unemployed workers in the United States from 2001 to 2002, separately for White, Black or African-American, and Asian workers. Exact values of the variable that is being measured may be written at the end of the bar as in this figure. For instance, the number of unemployed Asian workers in the United States increased by 35% between 2001 and 2002. But even without the precise values, comparing the heights or lengths of the bars can give useful insight into the relative magnitudes of the different values of the variable.

A **bar graph** uses bars of varying height or length to show the comparative sizes of different observations of a variable.

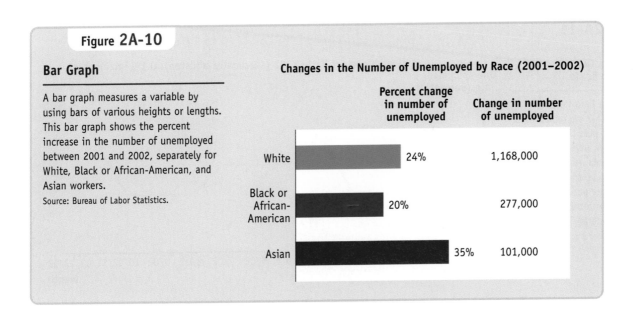

Figure 2A-10

Bar Graph

A bar graph measures a variable by using bars of various heights or lengths. This bar graph shows the percent increase in the number of unemployed between 2001 and 2002, separately for White, Black or African-American, and Asian workers.

Source: Bureau of Labor Statistics.

Changes in the Number of Unemployed by Race (2001–2002)

	Percent change in number of unemployed	Change in number of unemployed
White	24%	1,168,000
Black or African-American	20%	277,000
Asian	35%	101,000

Problems in Interpreting Numerical Graphs

Although the beginning of this appendix emphasized that graphs are visual images that make ideas or information easier to understand, graphs can be constructed (intentionally or unintentionally) in ways that are misleading and can lead to inaccurate conclusions. This section raises some issues that you should be aware of when you interpret graphs.

Features of Construction Before drawing any conclusions about what a numerical graph implies, you should pay attention to the scale, or size of increments, shown on the axes. Small increments tend to visually exaggerate changes in the variables, whereas large increments tend to visually diminish them. So the scale used in construction of a graph can influence your interpretation of the significance of the changes it illustrates—perhaps in an unwarranted way.

Take, for example, Figure 2A-11, which shows the unemployment rate in the United States in 2002 using a 0.1% scale. You can see that the unemployment rate rose from 5.6% at the beginning of 2002 to 6.0% by the end of the year. Here, the rise of 0.4% in the unemployment rate looks enormous and could lead a policy maker to conclude that it was a relatively significant event. But if you go back and reexamine Figure 2A-7 on page 50, which shows the unemployment rate in the United States from 1989 to 2004, you can see that this would be a misguided conclusion. Figure 2A-7 includes the same data shown in Figure 2A-11, but it is constructed with a 1% scale rather than a 0.1% scale. From it you can see that the rise of 0.4% in the unemployment rate during 2002 was, in fact, a relatively insignificant event, at least compared to the rise in unemployment during 1990 or during 2001. This comparison shows that if you are not careful to factor in the choice of scale in interpreting a graph, you can arrive at very different, and possibly misguided, conclusions.

An axis is **truncated** when some of the values on the axis are omitted, usually to save space.

Related to the choice of scale is the use of *truncation* in constructing a graph. An axis is **truncated** when part of the range is omitted. This is indicated by two slashes (//) in the axis near the origin. You can see that the vertical axis of Figure 2A-11 has been truncated—the range of values from 0 to 5.6 has been omitted and a // appears in the axis. Truncation saves space in the presentation of a graph and allows larger increments to be used in constructing it. As a result, changes in the variable depicted on a graph that has been truncated appear larger compared to a graph that has not been truncated and that uses smaller increments.

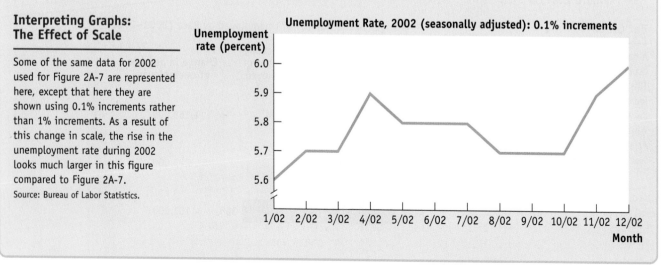

Figure 2A-11

Interpreting Graphs: The Effect of Scale

Some of the same data for 2002 used for Figure 2A-7 are represented here, except that here they are shown using 0.1% increments rather than 1% increments. As a result of this change in scale, the rise in the unemployment rate during 2002 looks much larger in this figure compared to Figure 2A-7.

Source: Bureau of Labor Statistics.

Unemployment Rate, 2002 (seasonally adjusted): 0.1% increments

You must also pay close attention to exactly what a graph is illustrating. For example, in Figure 2A-10, you should recognize that what is being shown here are percentage changes in the number of unemployed, not numerical changes. The unemployment rate for Asian workers increased by the highest percentage, 35% in this example. If you confused numerical changes with percentage changes, you would erroneously conclude that the greatest number of newly unemployed workers were Asian. But, in fact, a correct interpretation of Figure 2A-10 shows that the greatest number of unemployed workers were white: the total number of unemployed white workers grew by 1,168,000 workers, which is greater than the increase in the number of unemployed Asian workers, which is 101,000 in this example. Although there was a higher percentage increase in the number of unemployed Asian workers, the number of unemployed Asian workers in the United States in 2001 was much smaller than the number of white workers, leading to a smaller number of newly unemployed Asian workers than white workers.

Omitted Variables From a scatter diagram that shows two variables moving either positively or negatively in relation to each other, it is easy to conclude that there is a causal relationship. But relationships between two variables are not always due to direct cause and effect. Quite possibly an observed relationship between two variables is due to the *unobserved* effect of a third variable on each of the other two variables. An unobserved variable that, through its influence on other variables, creates the erroneous appearance of a direct causal relationship among those variables is called an **omitted variable.** For example, in New England, a greater amount of snowfall during a given week will typically cause people to buy more snow shovels. It will also cause people to buy more de-icer fluid. But if you omitted the influence of the snowfall and simply plotted the number of snow shovels sold versus the number of bottles of de-icer fluid, you would produce a scatter diagram that showed an upward tilt in the pattern of points, indicating a positive relationship between snow shovels sold and de-icer fluid sold. To attribute a causal relationship between these two variables, however, is misguided; more snow shovels sold do not cause more de-icer fluid to be sold, or vice versa. They move together because they are both influenced by a third, determining variable, the weekly snowfall—the omitted variable in this case. So before assuming that a pattern in a scatter diagram implies a cause-and-effect relationship, it is important to consider whether the pattern is instead the result of an omitted variable. Or to put it succinctly: Correlation is not causation.

> An **omitted variable** is an unobserved variable that, through its influence on other variables, creates the erroneous appearance of a direct causal relationship among those variables.

Reverse Causality Even when you are confident that there is no omitted variable and that there is a causal relationship between two variables shown in a numerical graph, you must also be careful that you don't make the mistake of **reverse causality**—coming to an erroneous conclusion about which is the dependent and which is the independent variable by reversing the true direction of causality between the two variables. For example, imagine a scatter diagram that depicts the grade point averages (GPAs) of 20 of your classmates on one axis and the number of hours that each of them spends studying on the other. A line fitted between the points will probably have a positive slope, showing a positive relationship between GPA and hours of studying. We could reasonably infer that hours spent studying is the independent variable and that GPA is the dependent variable. But you could make the error of reverse causality: you could infer that a high GPA causes a student to study more whereas a low GPA causes a student to study less.

> The error of **reverse causality** is committed when the true direction of causality between two variables is reversed.

The significance of understanding how graphs can mislead or be incorrectly interpreted is not purely academic. Policy decisions, business decisions, and political arguments are often based on interpretation of the types of numerical graphs that we've just discussed. Problems of misleading features of construction, omitted variables, and reverse causality can lead to very important and undesirable consequences.

PROBLEMS

1. Study the four accompanying diagrams. Consider the following statements and indicate which diagram matches each statement. Which variable would appear on the horizontal and which on the vertical axis? In each of these statements, is the slope positive, negative, zero, or infinity?

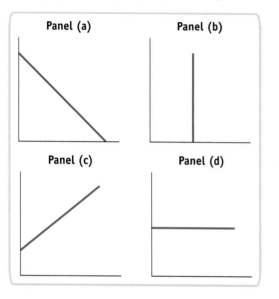

a. If the price of movies increases, fewer consumers go to see movies.

b. More experienced workers typically have higher incomes than less experienced workers.

c. Whatever the temperature outside, Americans consume the same number of hot dogs per day.

d. Consumers buy more frozen yogurt when the price of ice cream goes up.

e. Research finds no relationship between the number of diet books purchased and the number of pounds lost by the average dieter.

f. Regardless of its price, Americans buy the same quantity of salt.

2. During the Reagan administration, economist Arthur Laffer argued in favor of lowering income tax rates in order to increase tax revenues. Like most economists, he believed that at tax rates above a certain level, tax revenue would fall because high taxes would discourage some people from working and that people would refuse to work at all if they received no income after paying taxes. This relationship between tax rates and tax revenue is graphically summarized in what is widely known as the Laffer curve. Plot the Laffer curve relationship assuming that it has the shape of a nonlinear curve. The following questions will help you construct the graph.

a. Which is the independent variable? Which is the dependent variable? On which axis do you therefore measure the income tax rate? On which axis do you measure income tax revenue?

b. The minimum possible income tax rate is 0%. What would tax revenue be at a 0% income tax rate?

c. The maximum possible income tax rate is 100%. What would tax revenue be at a 100% income tax rate?

d. Estimates now show that the maximum point on the Laffer curve is (approximately) at a tax rate of 80%. For tax rates less than 80%, how would you describe the relationship between the tax rate and tax revenue, and how is this relationship reflected in the slope? For tax rates higher than 80%, how would you describe the relationship between the tax rate and tax revenue, and how is this relationship reflected in the slope?

3. In the accompanying figures, the numbers on the axes have been lost. All you know is that the units shown on the vertical axis are the same as the units on the horizontal axis.

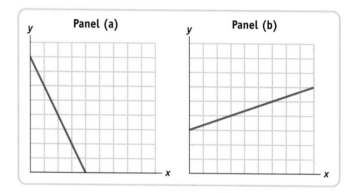

a. In panel (a), what is the slope of the line? Show that the slope is constant along the line.

b. In panel (b), what is the slope of the line? Show that the slope is constant along the line.

4. Answer each of the following questions by drawing a schematic diagram.

a. Taking measurements of the slope of a curve at three points farther and farther to the right along the horizontal axis, the slope of the curve changes from −0.3, to −0.8, to −2.5, measured by the point method. Draw a schematic diagram of this curve. How would you describe the relationship illustrated in your diagram?

b. Taking measurements of the slope of a curve at five points farther and farther to the right along the horizontal axis, the slope of the curve changes from 1.5, to 0.5, to 0, to −0.5, to −1.5, measured by the point method. Draw a schematic diagram of this curve. Does it have a maximum or a minimum?

5. The accompanying table shows the relationship between workers' hours of work per week and their hourly wage rate. Apart from the fact that they receive a different hourly wage rate and work different hours, these five workers are otherwise identical.

Name	Quantity of labor (hours per week)	Wage rate (per hour)
Athena	30	$15
Boris	35	30
Curt	37	45
Diego	36	60
Emily	32	75

a. Which variable is the independent variable? Which is the dependent variable?

b. Draw a scatter diagram illustrating this relationship. Draw a (nonlinear) curve that connects the points. Put the hourly wage rate on the vertical axis.

c. As the wage rate increases from $15 to $30, how does the number of hours worked respond according to the relationship depicted here? What is the average slope of the curve between Athena's and Boris's data points?

d. As the wage rate increases from $60 to $75, how does the number of hours worked respond according to the relationship depicted here? What is the average slope of the curve between Diego's and Emily's data points?

6. Studies have found a relationship between a country's yearly rate of economic growth and the yearly rate of increase in airborne pollutants. It is believed that a higher rate of economic growth allows a country's residents to have more cars and travel more, thereby releasing more airborne pollutants.

a. Which variable is the independent variable? Which is the dependent variable?

b. Suppose that in the country of Sudland, when the yearly rate of economic growth fell from 3.0% to 1.5%, the yearly rate of increase in airborne pollutants fell from 6% to 5%. What is the average slope of a nonlinear curve between these points using the arc method?

c. Now suppose that when the yearly rate of economic growth rose from 3.5% to 4.5%, the yearly rate of increase in airborne pollutants rose from 5.5% to 7.5%. What is the average slope of a nonlinear curve between these two points using the arc method?

d. How would you describe the relationship between the two variables here?

7. An insurance company has found that the severity of property damage in a fire is positively related to the number of firefighters arriving at the scene.

a. Draw a diagram that depicts this finding with number of firefighters on the horizontal axis and amount of property damage on the vertical axis. What is the argument made by this diagram? Suppose you reverse what is measured on the two axes. What is the argument made then?

b. In order to reduce its payouts to policyholders, should the insurance company therefore ask the city to send fewer firefighters to any fire?

8. The accompanying table illustrates annual salaries and income tax owed by five individuals. Apart from the fact that they receive different salaries and owe different amounts of income tax, these five individuals are otherwise identical.

Name	Annual salary	Annual income tax owed
Susan	$22,000	$3,304
Bill	63,000	14,317
John	3,000	454
Mary	94,000	23,927
Peter	37,000	7,020

a. If you were to plot these points on a graph, what would be the average slope of the curve between the points for Bill's and Mary's salaries and taxes using the arc method? How would you interpret this value for slope?

b. What is the average slope of the curve between the points for John's and Susan's salaries and taxes using the arc method? How would you interpret that value for slope?

c. What happens to the slope as salary increases? What does this relationship imply about how the level of income taxes affects a person's incentive to earn a higher salary?

>*web*... To continue your study and review of concepts in this chapter, please visit the Krugman/Wells website for quizzes, animated graph tutorials, web links to helpful resources, and more.

www.worthpublishers.com/krugmanwells

chapter

>> Supply and Demand

GRETZKY'S LAST GAME

THERE ARE SEVERAL WAYS YOU CAN GET tickets for a sporting event. You might have a season pass that gives you a seat at every home game, you could buy a ticket for a single game from the box office, or you could buy a ticket from a *scalper*. Scalpers buy tickets in advance—either from the box office or from season ticket-holders who decide to forgo the game—and then resell them shortly before the event.

Scalping is not always legal, but it is often profitable. A scalper might buy tickets at the box office and then, after the box office has sold out, resell them at a higher price to fans who have decided at the last minute to attend the event. Of course, the profits are not guaranteed. Sometimes an event is unexpectedly "hot" and scalped tickets can be sold for high prices, but sometimes an event is unexpectedly "cold" and scalpers end up selling at a loss.

Over time, however, even with some unlucky nights, scalpers can make money from eager fans.

Ticket scalpers in the Canadian city of Ottawa had a good few days in April 1999. Why? Because Wayne Gretzky, the Canadian hockey star, unexpectedly announced that he would retire from the sport and that the April 15 match between the Ottawa Senators and his team, the New York Rangers, would be his last game on Canadian soil. Many Canadian fans wanted to see the great Gretzky play one last time—and would not give up just because the box office had long since sold out.

Clearly, scalpers who had already stocked up on tickets—or who could acquire more tickets—were in for a bonanza. After the announcement, scalped tickets began selling for four or five times their face value. It was just a matter of supply and demand.

What you will learn in this chapter:

➤ What a **competitive market** is and how it is described by the **supply and demand model**

➤ What the **demand curve** is and what the **supply curve** is

➤ The difference between **movements along a curve** and **shifts of a curve**

➤ How the supply and demand curves determine a market's **equilibrium price** and **equilibrium quantity**

➤ In the case of a **shortage** or **surplus**, how price moves the market back to equilibrium

Shelly/Castellanos/Zuma

AFB/Corbis

Ronal Siemoneit/Corbis

Fans paid hundreds, even thousands, of dollars to see Wayne Gretzky and Michael Jordan play their last games. How much would you pay to see a music star, such as Jennifer Lopez, one last time? What about your favorite athlete?

But what do we mean by that? Many people use *supply and demand* as a sort of catchphrase to mean "the laws of the marketplace at work." To economists, however, the concept of supply and demand has a precise meaning: it is a *model of how a market behaves* that is extremely useful for understanding many—but not all—markets.

In this chapter, we lay out the pieces that make up the supply and demand model, put them together, and show how this model can be used to understand how many—but not all—markets behave.

Supply and Demand: A Model of a Competitive Market

Ticket scalpers and their customers constitute a market—a group of sellers and buyers. More than that, they constitute a particular type of market, known as a competitive market. Roughly, a **competitive market** is a market in which there are many buyers and sellers of the same good or service. More precisely, the key feature of a competitive market is that no individual's actions have a noticeable effect on the price at which the good or service is sold.

It's a little hard to explain why competitive markets are different from other markets until we've seen how a competitive market works. So let's take a rain check—we'll return to that issue at the end of this chapter. For now, let's just say that it's easier to model competitive markets than other markets. When taking an exam, it's always a good strategy to begin by answering the easier questions. In this book, we're going to do the same thing. So we will start with competitive markets.

When a market is competitive, its behavior is well described by a model known as the **supply and demand model**. And because many markets *are* competitive, the supply and demand model is a very useful one indeed.

There are five key elements in this model:

- The *demand curve*
- The *supply curve*
- The set of factors that cause the demand curve to shift, and the set of factors that cause the supply curve to shift
- The *equilibrium price*
- The way the equilibrium price changes when the supply or demand curves shift

To understand the supply and demand model, we will examine each of these elements.

A **competitive market** is a market in which there are many buyers and sellers of the same good or service.

The **supply and demand model** is a model of how a competitive market works.

The Demand Curve

How many people wanted to buy scalped tickets to see the New York Rangers and the Ottawa Senators play that April night? You might at first think the answer was: every hockey fan in Ontario who didn't already have a ticket. But although every hockey fan wanted to see Wayne Gretzky play one last time, most fans weren't willing to pay four or five times the normal ticket price. In general, the number of people who want to buy a hockey ticket, or any other good, depends on the price. The higher the price, the fewer people who want to buy the good; the lower the price, the more people who want to buy the good.

So the answer to the question "How many people will want to buy a ticket to Gretzky's last game?" depends on the price of a ticket. If you don't yet know what the price will be, you can start by making a table of how many tickets people would want

The announcement of Gretzky's retirement generated a *new* demand schedule, one in which the quantity demanded is greater at any given price than in the original demand schedule. The two curves in Figure 3-2 show the same information graphically. As you can see, the new demand schedule after the announcement corresponds to a new demand curve, D_2, that is to the right of the demand curve before the announcement, D_1. This **shift of the demand curve** shows the change in the quantity demanded at any given price, represented by the change in position of the original demand curve D_1 to its new location at D_2.

It's crucial to make the distinction between such shifts of the demand curve and **movements along the demand curve**, changes in the quantity demanded of a good that result from a change in that good's price. Figure 3-3 illustrates the difference.

The movement from point A to point B is a movement along the demand curve: the quantity demanded rises due to a fall in price as you move down D_1. Here, a fall in price from $350 to $215 generates a rise in the quantity demanded from 2,500 to 5,000 tickets. But the quantity demanded can also rise when the price is unchanged if there is an increase in demand—a rightward shift of the demand curve. This is illustrated in Figure 3-3 by the shift of the demand curve from D_1 to D_2. Holding price constant at $350, the quantity demanded rises from 2,500 tickets at point A on D_1 to 5,000 tickets at point C on D_2.

When economists say "the demand for X increased" or "the demand for Y decreased," they mean that the demand curve for X or Y shifted—*not* that the quantity demanded rose or fell because of a change in the price.

A **shift of the demand curve** is a change in the quantity demanded at any given price, represented by the change of the original demand curve to a new position, denoted by a new demand curve.

A **movement along the demand curve** is a change in the quantity demanded of a good that is the result of a change in that good's price.

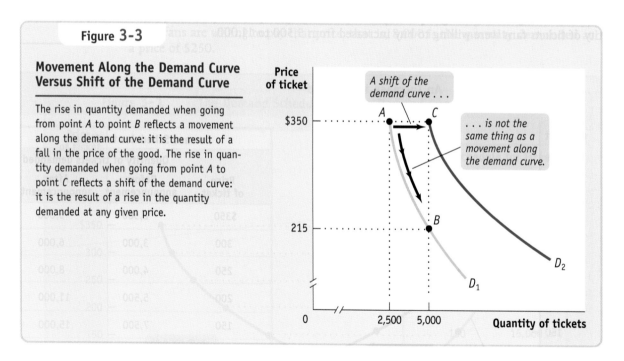

Figure 3-3

Movement Along the Demand Curve Versus Shift of the Demand Curve

The rise in quantity demanded when going from point A to point B reflects a movement along the demand curve: it is the result of a fall in the price of the good. The rise in quantity demanded when going from point A to point C reflects a shift of the demand curve: it is the result of a rise in the quantity demanded at any given price.

Understanding Shifts of the Demand Curve

Figure 3-4 illustrates the two basic ways in which demand curves can shift. When economists talk about an "increase in demand," they mean a *rightward* shift of the demand curve: at any given price, consumers demand a larger quantity of the good than before. This is shown in Figure 3-4 by the rightward shift of the original demand curve D_1 to D_2. And when economists talk about a "decrease in demand," they mean a *leftward* shift of the demand curve: at any given price, consumers demand a smaller quantity of the good than before. This is shown in Figure 3-4 by the leftward shift of the original demand curve D_1 to D_3.

One comm
by lowering t
service, hopir

An alterna
impose high
courage peop
bined with vi

However, 1
approach: red
in 2003, Lon
ing the city c

Complianc
plates. People
they have dri
imposed for
www.cclondo

Not surpri
ing to an Aug
and cars were

>> CHECK Y

1. Explain whet
   (ii) a *movem*
   a. A store o
   b. When XYZ
      ume of we
   c. People bu
      higher th;
   d. The sharp
      reduce the

The Supp

Ticket scalpers
ticket-holders
scalper depend
likely that you

So just as th
they have to p;
depends on th
market in scalp
less of the pri

The Supply

The table in Fi
varies with the
Gretzky's last
A supply sch
3-1: in this c;
willing to sell
to part with th
ing up the gar
quantity of tic
rises to 7,000,

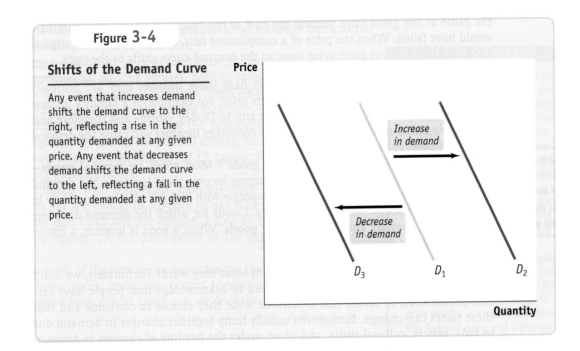

Figure 3-4

Shifts of the Demand Curve

Any event that increases demand shifts the demand curve to the right, reflecting a rise in the quantity demanded at any given price. Any event that decreases demand shifts the demand curve to the left, reflecting a fall in the quantity demanded at any given price.

But what causes a demand curve to shift? In our example, the event that shifts the demand curve for tickets is the announcement of Gretzky's imminent retirement. But if you think about it, you can come up with other things that would be likely to shift the demand curve for those tickets. For example, suppose there is a music concert the same evening as the hockey game, and the band announces that it will sell tickets at half-price. This is likely to cause a decrease in demand for hockey tickets: hockey fans who also like music will prefer to purchase half-price concert tickets rather than hockey game tickets.

Economists believe that there are four principal factors that shift the demand curve for a good:

- Changes in the prices of related goods
- Changes in income
- Changes in tastes
- Changes in expectations

Although this is not an exhaustive list, it contains the four most important factors that can shift demand curves. When we said before that the quantity of a good demanded falls as its price rises *other things equal,* we were referring to the factors that shift demand as remaining unchanged.

Changes in the Prices of Related Goods If you want to have a good night out but aren't too particular about what you do, a music concert is an alternative to the hockey game—it is what economists call a *substitute* for the hockey game. A pair of goods are **substitutes** if a fall in the price of one good (music concerts) makes consumers less willing to buy the other good (hockey games). Substitutes are usually goods that in some way serve a similar function: concerts and hockey games, muffins and doughnuts, trains and buses. A fall in the price of the alternative good induces some consumers to purchase it *instead of* the original good, shifting the demand for the original good to the left.

But sometimes a fall in the price of one good makes consumers *more* willing to buy another good. Such pairs of goods are known as **complements**. Complements are usually goods that in some sense are consumed together: sports tickets and parking at the stadium garage, hamburgers and buns, cars and gasoline. If the garage next to the hockey arena offered free parking, more people would be willing to buy tickets to see

Two goods are **substitutes** if a fall in the price of one of the goods makes consumers less willing to buy the other good.

Two goods are **complements** if a fall in the price of one good makes people more willing to buy the other good.

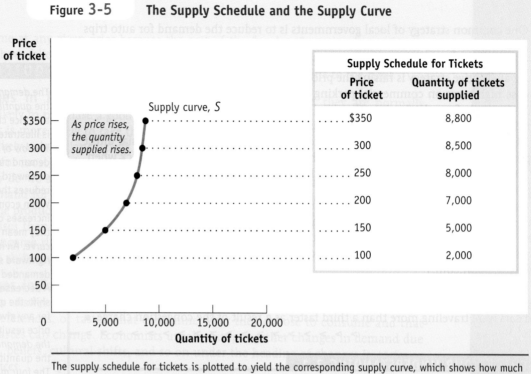

Figure 3-5   The Supply Schedule and the Supply Curve

Supply curve, *S*

As price rises, the quantity supplied rises.

Supply Schedule for Tickets	
Price of ticket	Quantity of tickets supplied
$350	8,800
300	8,500
250	8,000
200	7,000
150	5,000
100	2,000

The supply schedule for tickets is plotted to yield the corresponding supply curve, which shows how much of a good people are willing to sell at any given price. The supply curve and the supply schedule reflect the fact that supply curves are usually upward sloping: the quantity supplied rises when the price rises.

A **supply curve** shows graphically how much of a good or service people are willing to sell at any given price.

In the same way that a demand schedule can be represented graphically by a demand curve, a supply schedule can be represented by a **supply curve,** as shown in Figure 3-5. Each point on the curve represents an entry from the table.

Suppose that the price scalpers offer rises from $200 to $250; we can see from Figure 3-5 that the quantity of tickets sold to them rises from 7,000 to 8,000. This is the normal situation for a supply curve, reflecting the general proposition that a higher price leads to a higher quantity supplied. So just as demand curves normally slope downward, supply curves normally slope upward: the higher the price being offered, the more hockey tickets people will be willing to part with—the more of any good they will be willing to sell.

Shifts of the Supply Curve

When Gretzky's retirement was announced, the immediate effect was that people who already had tickets for the April 15 game became less willing to sell those tickets to scalpers at any given price. So the quantity of tickets supplied at any given price fell: the number of tickets people were willing to sell at $350 fell, the number they were willing to sell at $300 fell, and so on. Figure 3-6 shows us how to illustrate this event in terms of the supply schedule and the supply curve for tickets.

The table in Figure 3-6 shows two supply schedules; the schedule after the announcement is the same one as in Figure 3-5. The first supply schedule shows the supply of scalped tickets *before* Gretzky announced his retirement. And just as a change in demand schedules leads to a shift of the demand curve, a change in supply schedules leads to a **shift of the supply curve**—a change in the quantity supplied at any given price. This is shown in Figure 3-6 by the shift of the supply curve before the announcement, S_1, to its new position after the announcement, S_2. Notice that S_2 lies to the left of S_1, a reflection of the fact that quantity supplied decreased at any given price in the aftermath of Gretzky's announcement.

A **shift of the supply curve** is a change in the quantity supplied of a good at any given price. It is represented by the change of the original supply curve to a new position, denoted by a new supply curve.

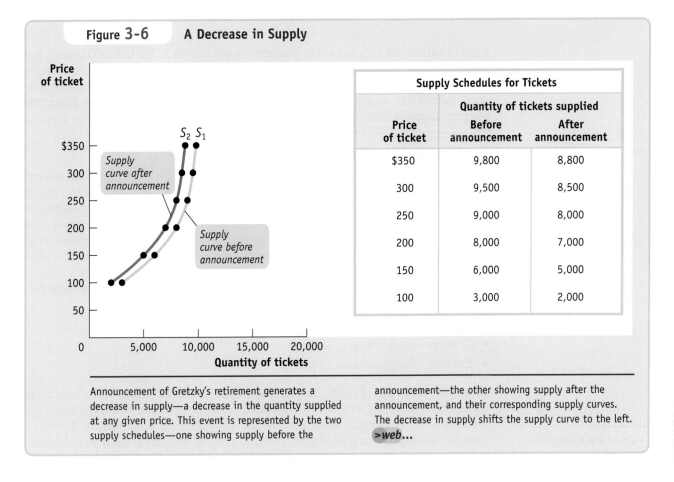

Figure 3-6   **A Decrease in Supply**

Supply Schedules for Tickets		
	Quantity of tickets supplied	
Price of ticket	Before announcement	After announcement
$350	9,800	8,800
300	9,500	8,500
250	9,000	8,000
200	8,000	7,000
150	6,000	5,000
100	3,000	2,000

Announcement of Gretzky's retirement generates a decrease in supply—a decrease in the quantity supplied at any given price. This event is represented by the two supply schedules—one showing supply before the announcement—the other showing supply after the announcement, and their corresponding supply curves. The decrease in supply shifts the supply curve to the left. >web...

As in the analysis of demand, it's crucial to draw a distinction between such shifts of the supply curve and **movements along the supply curve**—changes in the quantity supplied that result from a change in price. We can see this difference in Figure 3-7. The movement from point A to point B is a movement along the supply curve: the quantity supplied falls along S_1 due to a fall in price. Here, a fall in price from

A **movement along the supply curve** is a change in the quantity supplied of a good that is the result of a change in that good's price.

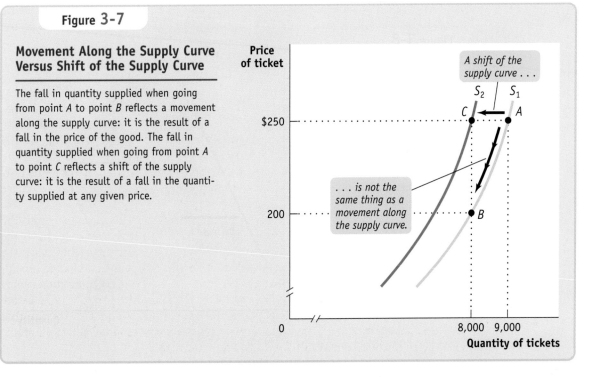

Figure 3-7

Movement Along the Supply Curve Versus Shift of the Supply Curve

The fall in quantity supplied when going from point A to point B reflects a movement along the supply curve: it is the result of a fall in the price of the good. The fall in quantity supplied when going from point A to point C reflects a shift of the supply curve: it is the result of a fall in the quantity supplied at any given price.

$250 to $200 leads to a fall in the quantity supplied from 9,000 to 8,000 tickets. But the quantity supplied can also fall when the price is unchanged if there is a decrease in supply—a leftward shift of the supply curve. This is shown in Figure 3-7 by the leftward shift of the supply curve from S_1 to S_2. Holding price constant at $250, the quantity supplied falls from 9,000 tickets at point A on S_1 to 8,000 at point C on S_2.

Understanding Shifts of the Supply Curve

Figure 3-8 illustrates the two basic ways in which supply curves can shift. When economists talk about an "increase in supply," they mean a *rightward* shift of the supply curve: at any given price, people will supply a larger quantity of the good than before. This is shown in Figure 3-8 by the shift to the right of the original supply curve S_1 to S_2. And when economists talk about a "decrease in supply," they mean a *leftward* shift of the supply curve: at any given price, people supply a smaller quantity of the good than before. This is represented in Figure 3-8 by the leftward shift of S_1 to S_3.

Economists believe that shifts of supply curves are mainly the result of three factors (though, as in the case of demand, there are other possible causes):

- Changes in input prices
- Changes in technology
- Changes in expectations

Changes in Input Prices To produce output, you need inputs—for example, to make vanilla ice cream, you need vanilla beans, cream, sugar, and so on. (Actually, you only need vanilla beans to make *good* vanilla ice cream; see Economics in Action on page 66.) An **input** is any good that is used to produce another good. Inputs, like output, have prices. And an increase in the price of an input makes the production of the final good more costly for those who produce and sell the good. So sellers are less willing to supply the good at any given price, and the supply curve shifts to the left. For example, newspaper publishers buy large quantities of newsprint (the paper on which newspapers are printed). When newsprint prices rose sharply in 1994–1995, the supply of newspapers fell: several newspapers went out of business and a number of new publishing ventures were canceled. Similarly, a fall in the price of an input makes the production of the final good less costly for sellers. They are more willing to supply the good at any given price, and the supply curve shifts to the right.

An **input** is a good that is used to produce another good.

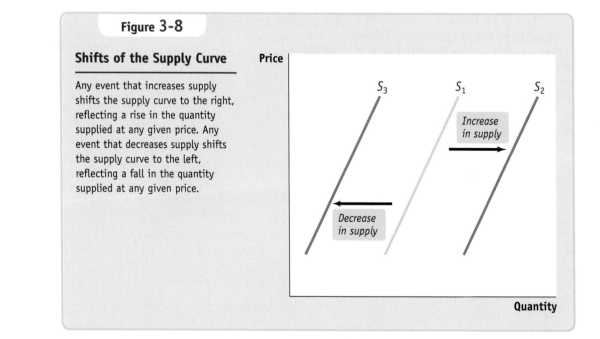

Figure 3-8

Shifts of the Supply Curve

Any event that increases supply shifts the supply curve to the right, reflecting a rise in the quantity supplied at any given price. Any event that decreases supply shifts the supply curve to the left, reflecting a fall in the quantity supplied at any given price.

Price

S_3 S_1 S_2

Increase in supply

Decrease in supply

Quantity

Changes in Technology When economists talk about "technology," they don't necessarily mean high technology—they mean all the ways in which people can turn inputs into useful goods. The whole complex of activities that turns corn from an Iowa farm into cornflakes on your breakfast table is technology in this sense. And when a better technology becomes available, reducing the cost of production—that is, letting a producer spend less on inputs yet produce the same output—supply increases, and the supply curve shifts to the right. For example, an improved strain of corn that is more resistant to disease makes farmers willing to supply more corn at any given price.

Changes in Expectations Imagine that you had a ticket for the April 15 game but couldn't go. You'd want to sell the ticket to a scalper. But if you heard a credible rumor about Gretzky's imminent retirement, you would know that the ticket would soon sky-rocket in value. So you'd hold off on selling the ticket until his decision to retire was made public. This illustrates how expectations can alter supply: an expectation that the price of a good will be higher in the future causes supply to decrease today, but an expectation that the price of a good will be lower in the future causes supply to increase today.

economics in action

Down (and Up) on the Farm

Many countries have designed farm policies based on the belief—or maybe the hope—that producers *won't* respond much to changes in the price of their product. But they have found out, to their dismay, that the price does indeed matter.

Advanced countries (including the United States) have historically tried to legislate farm prices *up*. (Chapter 4 describes how such price floors work in practice.) The point was to raise farmers' incomes, not to increase production—but production nonetheless did go up. Until the nations of the European Union began guaranteeing farmers high prices in the 1960s, they had limited agricultural production and imported much of their food. Once price supports were in place, production expanded rapidly, and European farmers began growing more grains and producing more dairy products than consumers wanted to buy.

In poorer countries, especially in Africa, governments have often sought to keep farm prices *down*. The typical strategy was to require farmers to sell their produce to a "marketing board," which then resold it to urban consumers or overseas buyers. A famous example is Ghana, once the world's main supplier of cocoa, the principal ingredient in chocolate. From 1965 until the 1980s, farmers were required to sell their cocoa beans to the government at prices that lagged steadily behind those chocolate manufacturers were paying elsewhere. The Ghanaian government hoped that cocoa production would be little affected by this policy and that it could profit by buying low and selling high. In fact, production fell sharply. By 1980, Ghana's share of the world market was down to 12 percent, while other cocoa-exporting countries that did not follow the same policy—including its African neighbors—were steadily increasing their sales.

Today Europe is trying to reform its agricultural policy, and most developing countries have abandoned their efforts to hold farm prices down. Governments seem finally to have learned that supply curves really do slope upward after all. ■

> > > > > > > > > > > > > > > > > > >

>>CHECK YOUR UNDERSTANDING 3-2

1. Explain whether each of the following events represents (i) a *shift of* the supply curve or (ii) a *movement along* the supply curve.
   a. More homeowners put their houses up for sale during a real estate boom that causes house prices to rise.
   b. Many strawberry farmers open temporary roadside stands during harvest season, even though prices are usually low at that time.
   continued

>>QUICK REVIEW

➤ The *supply schedule* shows how the *quantity supplied* depends on the price. The relationship between the two is illustrated by the *supply curve.*

➤ Supply curves are normally upward sloping: at a higher price, people are willing to supply more of the good.

➤ A change in price results in a *movement along the supply curve* and a change in the quantity supplied.

➤ As with demand, when economists talk of increases or decreases in supply, they mean *shifts of the supply curve*, not changes in the quantity supplied. An increase in supply is a rightward shift: the quantity supplied rises for any given price. A decrease in supply is a leftward shift: the quantity supplied falls for any given price.

➤ The three main factors that can shift the supply curve are changes in (1) input prices, (2) technology, and (3) expectations.

continued

c. Immediately after the school year begins, fast-food chains must raise wages to attract workers.
d. Many construction workers temporarily move to areas that have suffered hurricane damage, lured by higher wages offered.
e. Since new technologies have made it possible to build larger cruise ships (which are cheaper to run per passenger), Caribbean cruise lines have offered more berths, at lower prices, than before.

Solutions appear at back of book.

Supply, Demand, and Equilibrium

We have now covered the first three key elements in the supply and demand model: the supply curve, the demand curve, and the set of factors that shift each curve. The next step is to put these elements together to show how they can be used to predict the actual price at which a good will be bought and sold.

What determines the price at which a good is bought and sold? In Chapter 1 we learned the general principle that *markets move toward equilibrium*, a situation in which no individual would be better off taking a different action. In the case of a competitive market, we can be more specific: a competitive market is in equilibrium when the price has moved to a level at which the quantity demanded of a good equals the quantity supplied of that good. At that price, no individual seller could make herself better off by offering to sell either more or less of the good and no individual buyer could make himself better off by offering to buy more or less of the good.

The price that matches the quantity supplied and the quantity demanded is the **equilibrium price;** the quantity bought and sold at that price is the **equilibrium quantity.**

The equilibrium price is also known as the **market-clearing price:** it is the price that "clears the market" by ensuring that every buyer finds a seller, and vice versa.

You may notice from this point on that we will no longer focus on middlemen such as scalpers but focus directly on the market price and quantity. Why? Because the function of a middleman is to bring buyers and sellers together to trade. But what makes buyers and sellers willing to trade is in reality not the middleman, but the price they agree upon—the equilibrium price. By going deeper and examining how price functions within a market, we can safely assume that the middlemen are doing their job and leave them in the background.

So, how do we find the equilibrium price and quantity?

Finding the Equilibrium Price and Quantity

The easiest way to determine the equilibrium price and quantity in a market is by putting the supply curve and the demand curve on the same diagram. Since the supply curve shows the quantity supplied at any given price and the demand curve shows the quantity demanded at any given price, the price at which the two curves cross is the equilibrium price: the price at which quantity supplied equals quantity demanded.

Figure 3-9 combines the demand curve from Figure 3-1 and the supply curve from Figure 3-5. They *intersect* at point E, which is the equilibrium of this market; that is, $250 is the equilibrium price and 8,000 tickets is the equilibrium quantity.

Let's confirm that point E fits our definition of equilibrium. At a price of $250 per ticket, 8,000 ticket-holders are willing to resell their tickets and 8,000 people who do not have tickets are willing to buy. So at the price of $250 the quantity of tickets supplied equals the quantity demanded. Notice that at any other price the market would not clear: every willing buyer would not be able to find a willing seller, or vice versa. In other words, if the price were more than $250, the quantity supplied would exceed the quantity demanded; if the price were less than $250, the quantity demanded would exceed the quantity supplied.

A competitive market is in equilibrium when price has moved to a level at which the quantity demanded of a good equals the quantity supplied of that good. The price at which this takes place is the **equilibrium price**, also referred to as the **market-clearing price**. The quantity of the good bought and sold at that price is the **equilibrium quantity**.

PITFALLS

BOUGHT *AND* SOLD?

We have been talking about the price at which a good is bought *and* sold, as if the two were the same. But shouldn't we make a distinction between the price received by sellers and that paid by buyers? In principle, yes; but it is helpful at this point to sacrifice a bit of realism in the interests of simplicity—by assuming away the difference between the prices received by sellers and those paid by buyers. In reality, people who sell hockey tickets to scalpers, although they sometimes receive high prices, generally receive less than those who eventually buy these tickets pay. No mystery there: that difference is how a scalper or any other "middleman"—someone who brings buyers and sellers together—makes a living. In many markets, however, the difference between the buying and selling price is quite small. It is therefore not a bad approximation to think of the price paid by buyers as being the *same* as the price received by sellers. And that is what we will assume in the remainder of this chapter.

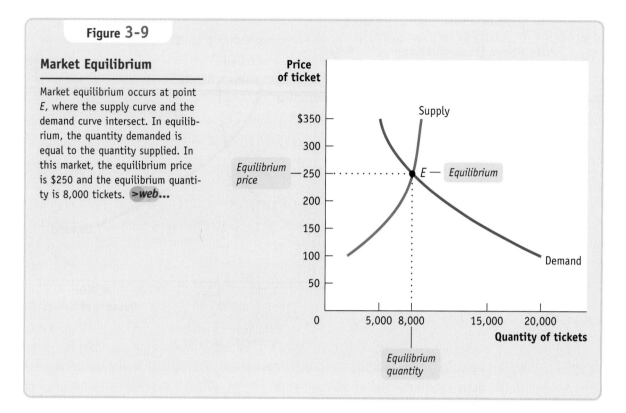

Figure 3-9

Market Equilibrium

Market equilibrium occurs at point *E*, where the supply curve and the demand curve intersect. In equilibrium, the quantity demanded is equal to the quantity supplied. In this market, the equilibrium price is $250 and the equilibrium quantity is 8,000 tickets. **>web...**

The model of supply and demand, then, predicts that given the demand and supply curves shown in Figure 3-9, 8,000 tickets would change hands at a price of $250 each.

But how can we be sure that the market will arrive at the equilibrium price? We begin by answering three simpler questions:

1. Why do all sales and purchases in a market take place at the same price?
2. Why does the market price fall if it is above the equilibrium price?
3. Why does the market price rise if it is below the equilibrium price?

Why Do All Sales and Purchases in a Market Take Place at the Same Price?

There are some markets where the same good can sell for many different prices, depending on who is selling or who is buying. For example, have you ever bought a souvenir in a "tourist trap" and then seen the same item on sale somewhere else (perhaps even in the next store) for a lower price? Because tourists don't know which shops offer the best deals and don't have time for comparison shopping, sellers in tourist areas can charge different prices for the same good.

But in any market where the buyers and sellers have both been around for some time, sales and purchases tend to converge at a generally uniform price, so that we can safely talk about *the* market price. It's easy to see why. Suppose a seller offered a potential buyer a price noticeably above what the buyer knew other people to be paying. The buyer would clearly be better off shopping elsewhere—unless the seller was prepared to offer a better deal. Conversely, a seller would not be willing to sell for significantly less than the amount he knew most buyers were paying; he would be better off waiting to get a more reasonable customer. So in any well-established, ongoing market, all sellers receive and all buyers pay approximately the same price. This is what we call the *market price*.

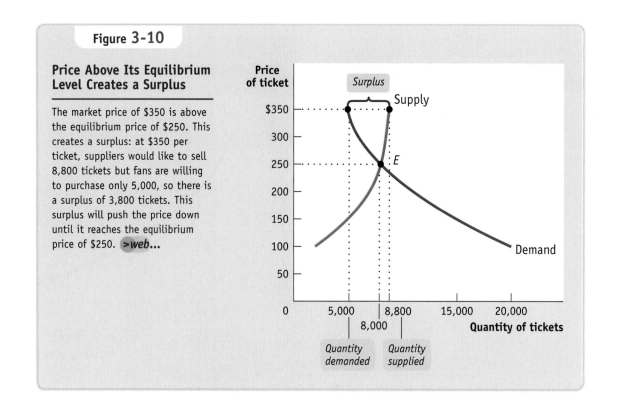

Figure 3-10

Price Above Its Equilibrium Level Creates a Surplus

The market price of $350 is above the equilibrium price of $250. This creates a surplus: at $350 per ticket, suppliers would like to sell 8,800 tickets but fans are willing to purchase only 5,000, so there is a surplus of 3,800 tickets. This surplus will push the price down until it reaches the equilibrium price of $250. **>web...**

Why Does the Market Price Fall If It Is Above the Equilibrium Price?

Suppose the supply and demand curves are as shown in Figure 3-9 but the market price is above the equilibrium level of $250—say, $350. This situation is illustrated in Figure 3-10. Why can't the price stay there?

As the figure shows, at a price of $350 there would be more tickets available than hockey fans wanted to buy: 8,800 versus 5,000. The difference of 3,800 is the **surplus**—also known as the *excess supply*—of tickets at $350.

This surplus means that some would-be sellers are being frustrated: they cannot find anyone to buy what they want to sell. So the surplus offers an incentive for those 3,800 would-be sellers to offer a lower price in order to poach business from other sellers. It also offers an incentive for would-be buyers to seek a bargain by offering a lower price. Sellers who reject the lower price will fail to find buyers, and the result of this price cutting will be to push the prevailing price down until it reaches the equilibrium price. So, the price of a good will fall whenever there is a surplus—that is, whenever the price is above its equilibrium level.

There is a **surplus** of a good when the quantity supplied exceeds the quantity demanded. Surpluses occur when the price is above its equilibrium level.

There is a **shortage** of a good when the quantity demanded exceeds the quantity supplied. Shortages occur when the price is below its equilibrium level.

Why Does the Market Price Rise If It Is Below the Equilibrium Price?

Now suppose the price is below its equilibrium level—say, at $150 per ticket, as shown in Figure 3-11. In this case, the quantity demanded (15,000 tickets) exceeds the quantity supplied (5,000 tickets), implying that there are 10,000 would-be buyers who cannot find tickets: there is a **shortage**, also known as an *excess demand*, of 10,000 tickets.

When there is a shortage, there are frustrated would-be buyers—people who want to purchase tickets but cannot find willing sellers at the current price. In this situation, either buyers will offer more than the prevailing price or sellers will realize that they can charge higher prices. Either way, the result is to drive up the prevailing price. This bidding up of prices happens whenever there are shortages—and there will be shortages whenever the price is below its equilibrium level. So the price will always rise if it is below the equilibrium level.

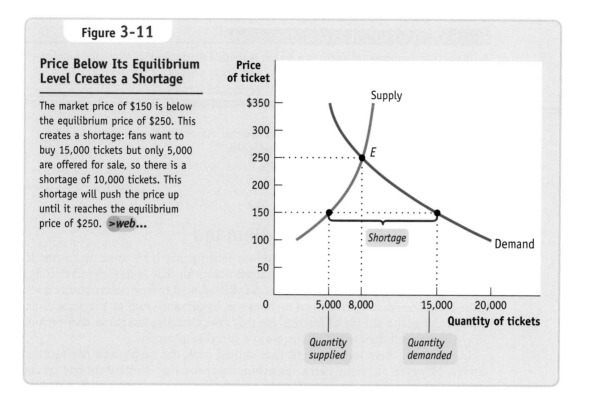

Figure 3-11

Price Below Its Equilibrium Level Creates a Shortage

The market price of $150 is below the equilibrium price of $250. This creates a shortage: fans want to buy 15,000 tickets but only 5,000 are offered for sale, so there is a shortage of 10,000 tickets. This shortage will push the price up until it reaches the equilibrium price of $250. **>web...**

Using Equilibrium to Describe Markets

We have now seen that a market tends to have a single price; that the market price falls if it is above the equilibrium level but rises if it is below that level. So the market price always *moves toward* the equilibrium price, the price at which there is neither surplus nor shortage.

economics in action

A Fish Story

In market equilibrium, something remarkable supposedly happens: everyone who wants to sell a good finds a willing buyer, and everyone who wants to buy that good finds a willing seller. It's a beautiful theory—but is it realistic?

In New York City the answer can be seen every day, just before dawn, at the famous Fulton Fish Market, which has operated since 1835 (though it has moved from its original Fulton Street location). There, every morning, fishermen bring their catch and haggle over prices with restaurant owners, shopkeepers, and a variety of middlemen and brokers.

The stakes are high. Restaurant owners who can't provide their customers with the fresh fish they expect stand to lose a lot of business, so it's important that would-be buyers find willing sellers. It's even more important for fishermen to make a sale: unsold fish loses much, if not all, of its value. But the market does reach equilibrium: just about every would-be buyer finds a willing seller, and vice versa. The reason is that every day the price of each type of fish quickly converges to a level that matches the quantity supplied and the quantity demanded.

So the tendency of markets to reach equilibrium isn't just theoretical speculation. You can see (and smell) it happening, early every morning. ■

> > > > > > > > > > > > > > > > > > > >

>>QUICK REVIEW

➤ Price in a competitive market moves to the *equilibrium price*, or *market-clearing price*, where the quantity supplied is equal to the quantity demanded. This quantity is the *equilibrium quantity*.

➤ All sales and purchases in a market take place at the same price. If the price is above its equilibrium level, there is a *surplus* that drives the price down. If the price is below its equilibrium level, there is a *shortage* that drives the price up.

1. In the following three situations, the market is initially in equilibrium. After each instance described below, does a surplus or shortage exist at the original equilibrium price? What will happen to the equilibrium price as a result?
   a. 1997 was a very good year for California wine-grape growers, who produced a bumper-size crop.
   b. After a hurricane, Florida hoteliers often find that many people cancel their upcoming vacations, leaving them with empty hotel rooms.
   c. After a heavy snowfall, many people want to buy secondhand snowblowers at the local tool shop.

Solutions appear at back of book.

Changes in Supply and Demand

Wayne Gretzky's announcement that he was retiring may have come as a surprise, but the subsequent rise in the price of scalped tickets for that April game was no surprise at all. Suddenly the number of people who wanted to buy tickets at any given price increased—that is, there was an increase in demand. And at the same time, because those who already had tickets wanted to see Gretzky's last game, they became less willing to sell them—that is, there was a decrease in supply.

In this case, there was an event that shifted both the supply and the demand curves. However, in many cases something happens that shifts only one of the curves. For example, a freeze in Florida reduces the supply of oranges but doesn't change the demand. A medical report that eggs are bad for your health reduces the demand for eggs but does not affect the supply. That is, events often shift either the supply curve or the demand curve, but not both; it is therefore useful to ask what happens in each case.

We have seen that when a curve shifts, the equilibrium price and quantity change. We will now concentrate on exactly how the shift of a curve alters the equilibrium price and quantity.

What Happens When the Demand Curve Shifts

Coffee and tea are substitutes: if the price of tea rises, the demand for coffee will increase, and if the price of tea falls, the demand for coffee will decrease. But how does the price of tea affect the *market* for coffee?

Figure 3-12 shows the effect of a rise in the price of tea on the market for coffee. The rise in the price of tea increases the demand for coffee. Point E_1 shows the equilibrium corresponding to the original demand curve, with P_1 the equilibrium price and Q_1 the equilibrium quantity bought and sold.

An increase in demand is indicated by a rightward *shift* of the demand curve from D_1 to D_2. At the original market price P_1, this market is no longer in equilibrium: a shortage occurs because the quantity demanded exceeds the quantity supplied. So the price of coffee rises and generates an increase in the quantity supplied, an upward *movement along the supply curve*. A new equilibrium is established at point E_2, with a higher equilibrium price P_2 and higher equilibrium quantity Q_2. This sequence of events reflects a general principle: *When demand for a good increases, the equilibrium price and the equilibrium quantity of the good both rise.*

And what would happen in the reverse case, a fall in the price of tea? A fall in the price of tea decreases the demand for coffee, shifting the demand curve to the *left*. At the original price, a surplus occurs as quantity supplied exceeds quantity demanded. The price falls and leads to a decrease in the quantity supplied, with a lower equilibrium price and a lower equilibrium quantity. This illustrates another general principle: *When demand for a good decreases, the equilibrium price of the good and the equilibrium quantity both fall.*

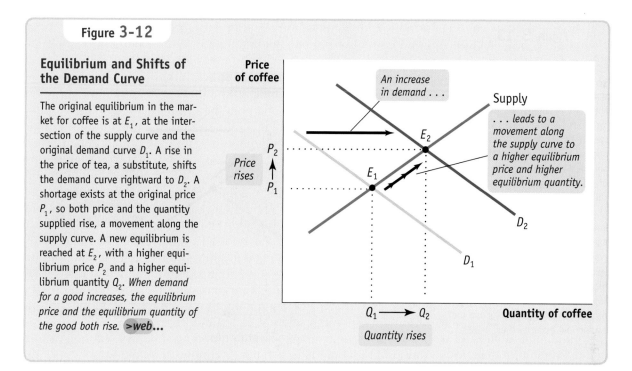

Figure 3-12

Equilibrium and Shifts of the Demand Curve

The original equilibrium in the market for coffee is at E_1, at the intersection of the supply curve and the original demand curve D_1. A rise in the price of tea, a substitute, shifts the demand curve rightward to D_2. A shortage exists at the original price P_1, so both price and the quantity supplied rise, a movement along the supply curve. A new equilibrium is reached at E_2, with a higher equilibrium price P_2 and a higher equilibrium quantity Q_2. *When demand for a good increases, the equilibrium price and the equilibrium quantity of the good both rise.* **>web...**

To summarize how a market responds to a change in demand: *An increase in demand leads to a rise in both the equilibrium price and the equilibrium quantity. A decrease in demand leads to a fall in both the equilibrium price and the equilibrium quantity.*

What Happens When the Supply Curve Shifts

In the real world, it is a bit easier to predict changes in supply than changes in demand. Physical factors that affect supply, like the availability of inputs, are easier to get a handle on than the fickle tastes that affect demand. Still, with supply as with demand, what we really know are the *effects* of shifts of the supply curve.

A spectacular example of a change in technology increasing supply occurred in the manufacture of semiconductors—the silicon chips that are the core of computers, video games, and many other devices. In the early 1970s, engineers learned how to use a process known as photolithography to put microscopic electronic components onto a silicon chip; subsequent progress in the technique has allowed ever more components to be put on each chip. Figure 3-13 (page 64) shows the effect of such an innovation on the market for silicon chips. The demand curve does not change. The original equilibrium is at E_1, the point of intersection of the original supply curve S_1 and the demand curve, with equilibrium price P_1 and equilibrium quantity Q_1. As a result of the technological change, supply increases and S_1 shifts rightward to S_2. At the original price P_1, a surplus of chips now exists and the market is no longer in equilibrium. The surplus causes a fall in price and a rise in quantity demanded, a downward movement along the demand curve. The new equilibrium is at E_2, with an equilibrium price P_2 and an equilibrium quantity Q_2. In the new equilibrium E_2, the price is lower and the equilibrium quantity higher than before. This may be stated as a general principle: *An increase in supply leads to a fall in the equilibrium price and a rise in the equilibrium quantity.*

What happens to the market when supply decreases? A decrease in supply leads to a *leftward* shift of the supply curve. At the original price, a shortage now exists; as a result, the equilibrium price rises and the quantity demanded falls. This describes the sequence of events in the newspaper market in 1994–1995, which we

Figure 3-13

Equilibrium and Shifts of the Supply Curve

The original equilibrium in the market for silicon chips is at E_1, at the intersection of the demand curve and the original supply curve S_1. After a technological change increases the supply of silicon chips, the supply curve shifts rightward to S_2. A surplus exists at the original price P_1, so price falls and the quantity demanded rises, a movement along the demand curve. A new equilibrium is reached at E_2, with a lower equilibrium price P_2 and a higher equilibrium quantity Q_2. *When supply of a good increases, the equilibrium price of the good falls and the equilibrium quantity rises.* **>web...**

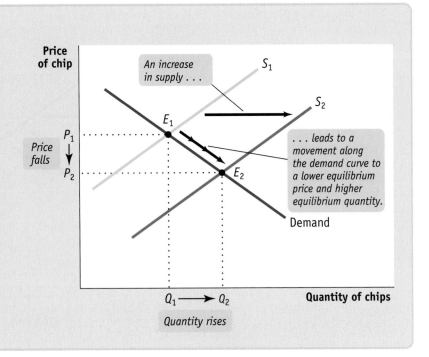

discussed earlier: a decrease in the supply of newsprint led to a rise in the price and the closure of many newspapers. We can formulate a general principle: *A decrease in supply leads to a rise in the equilibrium price and a fall in the equilibrium quantity.*

To summarize how a market responds to a change in supply: *An increase in supply leads to a fall in the equilibrium price and a rise in the equilibrium quantity. A decrease in supply leads to a rise in the equilibrium price and a fall in the equilibrium quantity.*

Simultaneous Shifts in Supply and Demand

Finally, it sometimes happens that events shift *both* the demand and supply curves. In fact, this chapter began with an example of such a simultaneous shift. Wayne Gretzky's announcement that he was retiring increased the demand for scalped tickets because more people wanted to see him play one last time; but it also decreased the supply because those who already had tickets became less willing to part with them.

Figure 3-14 illustrates what happened. In both panels we show an increase in demand—that is, a rightward shift of the demand curve, from D_1 to D_2. Notice that the rightward shift in panel (a) is relatively larger than the one in panel (b). Both panels also show a decrease in supply—that is, a leftward shift of the supply curve, from S_1 to S_2. Notice that the leftward shift in panel (b) is relatively larger than the one in panel (a).

In both cases, the equilibrium price rises, from P_1 to P_2, as the equilibrium moves from E_1 to E_2. But what happens to the equilibrium quantity, the quantity of scalped tickets bought and sold? In panel (a) the increase in demand is large relative to the decrease in supply, and the equilibrium quantity rises as a result. In panel (b) the decrease in supply is large relative to the increase in demand, and the equilibrium quantity falls as a result. That is, when demand increases and

PITFALLS

WHICH CURVE IS IT, ANYWAY?

When the price of some good changes, in general we can say that this reflects a change in either supply or demand. But it is easy to get confused about which one. A helpful clue is the direction of change in the quantity. If the quantity sold changes in the *same* direction as the price—for example, if both the price and the quantity rise—this suggests that the demand curve has shifted. If the price and the quantity move in *opposite* directions, the likely cause is a shift in the supply curve.

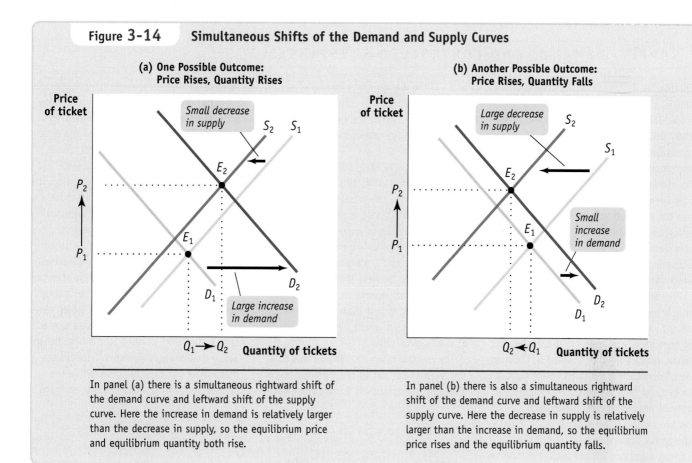

Figure 3-14 Simultaneous Shifts of the Demand and Supply Curves

(a) One Possible Outcome:
Price Rises, Quantity Rises

(b) Another Possible Outcome:
Price Rises, Quantity Falls

In panel (a) there is a simultaneous rightward shift of the demand curve and leftward shift of the supply curve. Here the increase in demand is relatively larger than the decrease in supply, so the equilibrium price and equilibrium quantity both rise.

In panel (b) there is also a simultaneous rightward shift of the demand curve and leftward shift of the supply curve. Here the decrease in supply is relatively larger than the increase in demand, so the equilibrium price rises and the equilibrium quantity falls.

supply decreases, the actual quantity bought and sold can go either way, depending on *how much* the demand and supply curves have shifted.

In general, when supply and demand shift in opposite directions, we can't predict what the ultimate effect will be on the quantity bought and sold. What we can say is that a curve that shifts a disproportionately greater distance than the other curve will have a disproportionately greater effect on the quantity bought and sold. That said, we can make the following prediction about the outcome when the supply and demand curves shift in opposite directions:

- When demand increases and supply decreases, the price rises but the change in the quantity is ambiguous.

- When demand decreases and supply increases, the price falls but the change in the quantity is ambiguous.

But suppose that the demand and supply curves shift in the same direction. Can we safely make any predictions about the changes in price and quantity? In this situation, the change in quantity bought and sold can be predicted but the change in price is ambiguous. The two possible outcomes when the supply and demand curves shift in the same direction (which you should check for yourself) are as follows:

- When both demand and supply increase, the quantity increases but the change in price is ambiguous.

- When both demand and supply decrease, the quantity decreases but the change in price is ambiguous.

SUPPLY, DEMAND, AND CONTROLLED SUBSTANCES

The big "issue" movie of the year 2000 was *Traffic*, a panoramic treatment of the drug trade. The movie was loosely based on the 1989 British TV miniseries *Traffik*. Despite the lapse of 11 years, the basic outlines of the situation—in which the drug trade flourishes despite laws that are supposed to prevent it—had not changed. Not only has the so-called war on drugs by law enforcement officials not succeeded in eliminating the trade in illegal drugs; according to most assessments, it has not even done much to reduce consumption.

The failure of the war on drugs has a historical precedent: during Prohibition, from 1920 to 1933, the sale and consumption of alcohol was illegal in the United States. But liquor, produced and distributed by "bootleggers," nonetheless remained widely available. In fact, by 1929 per capita consumption of alcohol was higher than it had been a decade earlier. As with illegal drugs today, the production and distribution of the banned substance became a large enterprise that flourished despite its illegality.

Why is it so hard to choke off markets in alcohol and drugs? Think of the war on drugs as a policy that shifts the supply curve but has not done much to shift the demand curve.

Although it is illegal to use drugs such as cocaine, just as it was once illegal to drink alcohol, in practice the war on drugs focuses mainly on the suppliers. As a result, the cost of supplying drugs includes the risk of being caught and sent to jail, perhaps even of being executed. This undoubtedly reduces the quantity of drugs supplied *at any given price*, in effect shifting the supply curve for drugs to the left. In Figure 3-15, this is shown as a shift in the supply curve from S_1

to S_2. If the war on drugs had no effect on the price of drugs, this leftward shift would reflect a reduction in the quantity of drugs supplied equal in magnitude to the leftward shift of supply.

But as we have seen, when the supply curve for a good shifts to the left, the effect is to raise the market price of that good. In Figure 3-15 the effect of the war on drugs would be to move the equilibrium from E_1 to E_2, and to raise the price of drugs from P_1 to P_2, a movement along the demand curve. Because the market price rises, the actual decline in the quantity of drugs supplied is less than the decline in the quantity that would have been supplied at the original price.

The crucial reason Prohibition was so ineffective was that as the market price of alcohol rose, consumers trimmed back only

slightly on their consumption—yet the higher prices were enough to induce many potential suppliers to take the risk of jail time. So while Prohibition raised the price of alcohol, it did not do much to reduce consumption. Unfortunately, the same seems to be true of current drug policy. The policy raises the price of drugs to those who use them, but this does not do much to discourage consumption. Meanwhile, the higher prices are enough to induce suppliers to provide drugs despite the penalties.

What is the answer? Some argue that the policy should be refocused on the demand side—more antidrug education, more counseling, and so on. If these policies worked, they would shift demand to the left. Others argue that drugs, like alcohol, should be made legal but heavily taxed. While the debate goes on, so does the war on drugs.

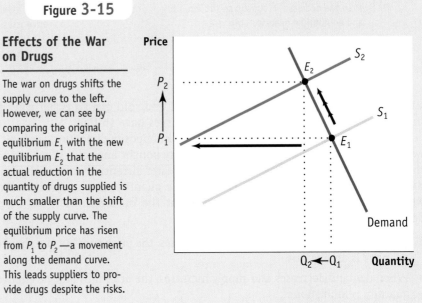

Figure 3-15

Effects of the War on Drugs

The war on drugs shifts the supply curve to the left. However, we can see by comparing the original equilibrium E_1 with the new equilibrium E_2 that the actual reduction in the quantity of drugs supplied is much smaller than the shift of the supply curve. The equilibrium price has risen from P_1 to P_2—a movement along the demand curve. This leads suppliers to provide drugs despite the risks.

economics in action

Plain Vanilla Gets Fancy

Vanilla doesn't get any respect. It's such a common flavoring that "plain vanilla" has become a generic term for ordinary, unembellished products. But between 2000 and 2003, plain vanilla got quite fancy—at least if you looked at the price. At the supermarket, the price of a small bottle of vanilla extract rose from about $5 to about $15. The wholesale price of vanilla beans rose 400 percent.

The cause of the price spike was bad weather—not here, but in the Indian Ocean. Most of the world's vanilla comes from Madagascar, an island nation off Africa's southeast coast. A huge cyclone struck there in 2000, and a combination of colder-than-normal weather and excessive rain impeded recovery.

The higher price of vanilla led to a fall in the quantity demanded: worldwide consumption of vanilla fell about 35 percent from 2000 to 2003. Consumers didn't stop eating vanilla-flavored products; instead, they switched (often without realizing it) to ice cream and other products flavored with synthetic vanillin, which is a by-product of wood pulp and petroleum production.

Notice that there was never a shortage of vanilla: you could always find it in the store if you were willing to pay the price. That is, the vanilla market remained in equilibrium. ■

> >

>>CHECK YOUR UNDERSTANDING 3-4

1. In each of the following examples, determine (i) the market in question; (ii) whether a shift in demand or supply occurred, the direction of the shift, and what induced the shift; and (iii) the effect of the shift on the equilibrium price and the equilibrium quantity.
   a. As the price of gasoline fell in the United States during the 1990s, more people bought large cars.
   b. As technological innovation has lowered the cost of recycling used paper, fresh paper made from recycled stock is used more frequently.
   c. As a local cable company offers cheaper pay-per-view films, local movie theaters have more unfilled seats.

2. Periodically, a computer chip maker like Intel introduces a new chip that is faster than the previous one. In response, demand for computers using the earlier chip decreases as customers put off purchases in anticipation of machines containing the new chip. Simultaneously, computer makers increase their production of computers containing the earlier chip in order to clear out their stocks of those chips.

   Draw two diagrams of the market for computers containing the earlier chip: (a) one in which the equilibrium quantity falls in response to these events and (b) one in which the equilibrium quantity rises. What happens to the equilibrium price in each diagram?

Solutions appear at back of book.

Competitive Markets—And Others

Early in this chapter, we defined a competitive market and explained that the supply and demand framework is a model of competitive markets. But we took a rain check on the question of why it matters whether or not a market is competitive. Now that we've seen how the supply and demand model works, we can offer some explanation.

To understand why competitive markets are different from other markets, compare the problems facing two individuals: a wheat farmer who must decide whether to grow more wheat, and the president of a giant aluminum company—say, Alcoa—who must decide whether to produce more aluminum.

For the wheat farmer, the question is simply whether the extra wheat can be sold at a price high enough to justify the extra production cost. The farmer need not worry about whether producing more wheat will affect the price of the wheat he or she was already planning to grow. That's because the wheat market is competitive. There are thousands of wheat farmers, and no one farmer's decision will have much impact on the market.

For the Alcoa executive, things are not that simple because the aluminum market is *not* competitive. There are only a few big players, including Alcoa, and each of them is well aware that its actions *do* have a noticeable impact on the market price. This adds a whole new level of complexity to the decisions producers have to make. Alcoa can't decide whether or not to produce more aluminum just by asking whether the additional product will sell for more than it costs to make. The company also has to ask whether producing more aluminum will drive down the market price and reduce its profit.

When a market is competitive, individuals can base decisions on less complicated analyses than those used in a noncompetitive market. This in turn means that it's easier for economists to build a model of a competitive market than of a noncompetitive market.

Don't take this to mean that economic analysis has nothing to say about noncompetitive markets. On the contrary, economists can offer some very important insights into how other kinds of markets work. But those insights require other models. In the next chapter, we will focus on what we can learn about competitive markets from the very useful model we have just developed: supply and demand.

• A LOOK AHEAD •

We've now developed a model that explains how markets arrive at prices and why markets "work" in the sense that buyers can almost always find sellers, and vice versa. But this model could use a little more clarification.

But, nothing demonstrates a principle quite as well as what happens when people try to defy it. And governments do, fairly often, try to defy the principles of supply and demand. In the next chapter we consider what happens when they do—the revenge of the market.

SUMMARY

1. The **supply and demand model** illustrates how a **competitive market**, one with many buyers and sellers, works.

2. The **demand schedule** shows the **quantity demanded** at each price and is represented graphically by a **demand curve**. The **law of demand** says that demand curves slope downward.

3. A **movement along the demand curve** occurs when the price changes and causes a change in the quantity demanded. When economists talk of increasing or decreasing demand, they mean **shifts of the demand curve**—a change in the quantity demanded at any given price. An increase in demand causes a rightward shift of the demand curve. A decrease in demand causes a leftward shift.

4. There are four main factors that shift the demand curve:
   - A change in the prices of related goods, such as **substitutes** or **complements**
   - A change in income: when income rises, the demand for **normal goods** increases and the demand for **inferior goods** decreases.
   - A change in tastes
   - A change in expectations

5. The **supply schedule** shows the **quantity supplied** at each price and is represented graphically by a **supply curve**. Supply curves usually slope upward.

6. A **movement along the supply curve** occurs when the price changes and causes a change in the quantity supplied. When economists talk of increasing or decreasing supply, they mean **shifts of the supply curve**—a change in the quantity supplied at any given price. An increase in supply causes a rightward shift of the supply curve. A decrease in supply causes a leftward shift.

7. There are three main factors that shift the supply curve:
   - A change in **input** prices
   - A change in technology
   - A change in expectations

8. The supply and demand model is based on the principle that the price in a market moves to its **equilibrium price, or market-clearing price,** the price at which the quantity demanded is equal to the quantity supplied. This quantity is the **equilibrium quantity**. When the price is above its market-clearing level, there is a **surplus** that pushes the price down. When the price is below its market-clearing level, there is a **shortage** that pushes the price up.

9. An increase in demand increases both the equilibrium price and the equilibrium quantity; a decrease in demand has the opposite effect. An increase in supply reduces the equilibrium price and increases the equilibrium quantity; a decrease in supply has the opposite effect.

10. Shifts of the demand curve and the supply curve can happen simultaneously. When they shift in opposite directions, the change in price is predictable but the change in quantity is not. When they shift in the same direction, the change in quantity is predictable but the change in price is not. In general, the curve that shifts the greater distance has a greater effect on the changes in price and quantity.

KEY TERMS

Competitive market, p. 57
Supply and demand model, p. 57
Demand schedule, p. 58
Demand curve, p. 58
Quantity demanded, p. 58
Law of demand, p. 59
Shift of the demand curve, p. 60
Movement along the demand curve, p. 60

Substitutes, p. 61
Complements, p. 61
Normal good, p. 62
Inferior good, p. 62
Quantity supplied, p. 63
Supply schedule, p. 63
Supply curve, p. 64
Shift of the supply curve, p. 64

Movement along the supply curve, p. 65
Input, p. 66
Equilibrium price, p. 68
Equilibrium quantity, p. 68
Market-clearing price, p. 68
Surplus, p. 70
Shortage, p. 70

PROBLEMS

1. A survey indicated that chocolate ice cream is America's favorite ice-cream flavor. For each of the following, indicate the possible effects on demand and/or supply and equilibrium price and quantity of chocolate ice cream.

   a. A severe drought in the Midwest causes dairy farmers to reduce the number of milk-producing cattle in their herds by a third. These dairy farmers supply cream that is used to manufacture chocolate ice cream.

   b. A new report by the American Medical Association reveals that chocolate does, in fact, have significant health benefits.

   c. The discovery of cheaper synthetic vanilla flavoring lowers the price of vanilla ice cream.

   d. New technology for mixing and freezing ice cream lowers manufacturers' costs of producing chocolate ice cream.

2. In a supply and demand diagram, draw the shift in demand for hamburgers in your hometown due to the following events. In each case show the effect on equilibrium price and quantity.

   a. The price of tacos increases.

   b. All hamburger sellers raise the price of their french fries.

   c. Income falls in town. Assume that hamburgers are a normal good for most people.

   d. Income falls in town. Assume that hamburgers are an inferior good for most people.

   e. Hot dog stands cut the price of hot dogs.

3. The market for many goods changes in predictable ways according to the time of year, in response to events such as holidays, vacation times, seasonal changes in production, and so on. Using supply and demand, explain the change in price in each of the following cases. Note that supply and demand may shift simultaneously.

   a. Lobster prices usually fall during the summer peak harvest season, despite the fact that people like to eat lobster during the summer months more than during any other time of year.

   b. The price of a Christmas tree is lower after Christmas than before, despite the fact that tree growers harvest and supply fewer trees for sale after Christmas than before.

   c. The price of a round-trip ticket to Paris on Air France falls by more than $200 after the end of school vacation in September. This happens despite the fact that generally worsening weather increases the cost of operating flights to Paris, and Air France therefore reduces the number of flights to Paris at any given price.

4. Show in a diagram the effect on the demand curve, the supply curve, the equilibrium price, and the equilibrium quantity of each of the following events.

   a. The market for newspapers in your town.

   Case 1:   The salaries of journalists go up.
   Case 2:   There is a big news event in your town, which is reported in the newspapers.

   b. The market for St. Louis Rams cotton T-shirts.

   Case 1:   The Rams win the national championship.
   Case 2:   The price of cotton increases.

   c. The market for bagels.

   Case 1:   People realize how fattening they are.
   Case 2:   People have less time to make themselves a cooked breakfast.

   d. The market for the Krugman and Wells economics textbook.

   Case 1:   Your professor makes it required reading for all of his or her students.
   Case 2:   Printing costs for textbooks are lowered by the use of synthetic paper.

5. Suppose that the supply schedule of Maine lobsters is as follows:

Price of lobster (per pound)	Quantity of lobster supplied (pounds)
$25	800
20	700
15	600
10	500
5	400

Suppose that Maine lobsters can be sold only in the United States. The U.S. demand schedule for Maine lobsters is as follows:

Price of lobster (per pound)	Quantity of lobster demanded (pounds)
$25	200
20	400
15	600
10	800
5	1,000

a. Draw the demand curve and the supply curve for Maine lobsters. What is the equilibrium price and quantity of lobsters?

Price of lobster (per pound)	Quantity of lobster demanded (pounds)
$25	100
20	300
15	500
10	700
5	900

Now suppose that Maine lobsters can be sold in France. The French demand schedule for Maine lobsters is as follows:

b. What is the demand schedule for Maine lobsters now that French consumers can also buy them? Draw a supply and demand diagram that illustrates the new equilibrium price and quantity of lobsters. What will happen to the price at which fishermen can sell lobster? What will happen to the price paid by U.S. consumers? What will happen to the quantity consumed by U.S. consumers?

6. Find the flaws in reasoning in the following statements, paying particular attention to the distinction between shifts of and movements along the supply and demand curves. Draw a diagram to illustrate what actually happens in each situation.

a. "A technological innovation that lowers the cost of producing a good might seem at first to result in a reduction

in the price of the good to consumers. But a fall in price will increase demand for the good, and higher demand will send the price up again. It is not certain, therefore, that an innovation will really reduce price in the end."

b. "A study shows that eating a clove of garlic a day can help prevent heart disease, causing many consumers to demand more garlic. This increase in demand results in a rise in the price of garlic. Consumers, seeing that the price of garlic has gone up, reduce their demand for garlic. This causes the demand for garlic to decrease and the price of garlic to fall. Therefore, the ultimate effect of the study on the price of garlic is uncertain."

7. Some points on a demand curve for a normal good are given here:

Price	Quantity demanded
$23	70
21	90
19	110
17	130

Do you think that the increase in quantity demanded (from 90 to 110 in the table) when price decreases (from 21 to 19) is due to a rise in consumers' income? Explain clearly (and briefly) why or why not.

8. Aaron Hank is a star hitter for the Bay City baseball team. He is close to breaking the major league record for home runs hit during one season, and it is widely anticipated that in the next game he will break that record. As a result, tickets for the team's next game have been a hot commodity. But today it is announced that, due to a knee injury, he will not in fact play in the team's next game. Assume that season ticket-holders are able to resell their tickets if they wish. Use supply and demand diagrams to explain the following.

a. Show the case in which this announcement results in a lower equilibrium price and a lower equilibrium quantity than before the announcement.

b. Show the case in which this announcement results in a lower equilibrium price and a higher equilibrium quantity than before the announcement.

c. What accounts for whether case a or case b occurs?

d. Suppose that a scalper had secretly learned before the announcement that Aaron Hank would not play in the next game. What actions do you think he would take?

9. In *Rolling Stone* magazine, several fans and rock stars, including Pearl Jam, were bemoaning the high price of concert tickets. One superstar argued, "It just isn't worth $75 to see me play. No one should have to pay that much to go to a concert." Assume this star sold out arenas around the country at an average ticket price of $75.

a. How would you evaluate the arguments that ticket prices are too high?

b. Suppose that due to this star's protests, ticket prices were lowered to $50. In what sense is this price too low? Draw a diagram using supply and demand curves to support your argument.

c. Suppose Pearl Jam really wanted to bring down ticket prices. Since the band controls the supply of its services, what do you recommend they do? Explain using a supply and demand diagram.

d. Suppose the band's next CD was a total dud. Do you think they would still have to worry about ticket prices being too high? Why or why not? Draw a supply and demand diagram to support your argument.

e. Suppose the group announced their next tour was going to be their last. What effect would this likely have on the demand for and price of tickets? Illustrate with a supply and demand diagram.

10. The accompanying table gives the annual U.S. demand and supply schedules for pickup trucks.

Price of truck	Quantity of trucks demanded (millions)	Quantity of trucks supplied (millions)
$20,000	20	14
25,000	18	15
30,000	16	16
35,000	14	17
40,000	12	18

a. Plot the demand and supply curves using these schedules. Indicate the equilibrium price and quantity on your diagram.

b. Suppose the tires used on pickup trucks are found to be defective. What would you expect to happen in the market for pickup trucks? Show this on your diagram.

c. Suppose that the U.S. Department of Transportation imposes restrictions on manufacturers that cause them to reduce supply by one-third at any given price. Calculate and plot the new supply schedule and indicate the new equilibrium price and quantity on your diagram.

11. After several years of decline, the market for handmade acoustic guitars is making a comeback. These guitars are usually made in small workshops employing relatively few highly skilled luthiers. Assess the impact on the equilibrium price and quantity of handmade acoustic guitars as a result of each of the following events. In your answers indicate which curve(s) shift(s) and in which direction.

a. Environmentalists succeed in having the use of Brazilian rosewood banned in the United States, forcing luthiers to seek out alternative, more costly woods.

b. A foreign producer reengineers the guitar-making process and floods the market with identical guitars.

c. Music featuring handmade acoustic guitars makes a comeback as audiences tire of heavy metal and grunge music.

d. The country goes into a deep recession and the income of the average American falls sharply.

12. *Demand twisters*: Sketch and explain the demand relationship in each of the following statements.

a. I would never buy a Britney Spears CD! You couldn't even give me one for nothing.

b. I generally buy a bit more coffee as the price falls. But once the price falls to $2 per pound, I'll buy out the entire stock of the supermarket.

c. I spend more on orange juice even as the price rises. (Does this mean that I must be violating the law of demand?)

d. The price of meals in my dormitory cafeteria has risen. But since I quit my part-time job, I now eat more meals there than at restaurants. (This one requires that you draw both the demand and the supply curves for dormitory cafeteria meals.) Assume that the demand curve slopes downward, and the supply curve slopes upward.

13. Will Shakespeare is a struggling playwright in sixteenth-century London. As the price he receives for writing a play increases, he is willing to write more plays. For the following situations, use a diagram to illustrate how each event affects the equilibrium price and quantity in the market for Shakespeare's plays.

a. The playwright Christopher Marlowe, Shakespeare's chief rival, is killed in a bar brawl.

b. The bubonic plague, a deadly infectious disease, breaks out in London.

c. To celebrate the defeat of the Spanish Armada, Queen Elizabeth declares several weeks of festivities, which involves commissioning new plays.

14. The small town of Middling experiences a sudden doubling of the birth rate. After three years, the birth rate returns to normal. Use a diagram to illustrate the effect of these events on the following.

a. The market for an hour of babysitting services in Middling today

b. The market for an hour of babysitting services 14 years into the future, after the birth rate has returned to normal, by which time children born today are old enough to work as babysitters.

c. The market for an hour of babysitting services 30 years into the future, when children born today are likely to be having children of their own.

15. Use a diagram to illustrate how each of the following events affects the equilibrium price and quantity of pizza.

a. The price of mozzarella cheese rises.

b. The health hazards of hamburgers are widely publicized.

c. The price of tomato sauce falls.

d. The incomes of consumers rise and pizza is an inferior good.

e. Consumers expect the price of pizza to fall next week.

16. Although he was a prolific artist, Pablo Picasso painted only 1,000 canvases during his "Blue Period." Picasso is now dead, and all of his Blue Period works are currently on display in museums and private galleries throughout Europe and the United States.

a. Draw a supply curve for Picasso Blue Period works. Why is this supply curve different from ones you have seen?

b. Given the supply curve from part a, the price of a Picasso Blue Period work will be entirely dependent on what factor(s)? Draw a diagram showing how the equilibrium price of such a work is determined.

c. Suppose that rich art collectors decide that it is essential to acquire Picasso Blue Period art for their collections. Show the impact of this on the market for these paintings.

17. Draw the appropriate curve in each of the following cases. Is it like or unlike the curves you have seen so far? Explain.

a. The demand for cardiac bypass surgery, given that the government pays the full cost for any patient

b. The demand for elective cosmetic plastic surgery, given that the patient pays the full cost

c. The supply of Rembrandt paintings

d. The supply of reproductions of Rembrandt paintings

> *web*... To continue your study and review of concepts in this chapter, please visit the Krugman/Wells website for quizzes, animated graph tutorials, web links to helpful resources, and more.
>
> ## www.worthpublishers.com/krugmanwells

>> The Market Strikes Back

BIG CITY, NOT-SO-BRIGHT IDEAS

NEW YORK CITY IS A PLACE WHERE YOU can find almost anything—that is, almost anything, except a taxicab when you need one or a decent apartment at a rent you can afford. You might think that New York's notorious shortages of cabs and apartments are the inevitable price of big-city living. However, they are largely the product of government policies—specifically, of government policies that have, one way or another, tried to prevail over the market forces of supply and demand.

In the previous chapter, we learned the principle that a market moves to equilibrium—that the market price rises or falls to the level at which the quantity of a good that people are willing to supply is equal to the quantity that other people want to buy. But sometimes governments try to defy that principle. When they do, the market strikes back in predictable ways. And our ability to predict what will happen when governments try to defy supply and demand shows the power and usefulness of supply and demand analysis itself.

The shortages of apartments and taxicabs in New York are particular examples that illuminate what happens when the logic of the market is defied. New York's housing shortage is the result of *rent control,* a law that prevents landlords from raising rents except when specifically given permission. Rent control was introduced during World War II to protect the interests of tenants, and it still remains in force. Many other American cities have had rent control at one time or another, but with the notable exceptions of New York and San Francisco, these controls have largely been done away with. Similarly, New York's limited supply of taxis is the result of a licensing system introduced in the 1930s. New York taxi licenses are known as "medallions," and only taxis with medallions are allowed to pick up passengers. And although this

New York City: An empty taxi is hard to find.

system was originally intended to protect the interests of both drivers and customers, it has generated a shortage of taxis in the city. The number of medallions remained fixed from 1937 until 1995, and only a handful of additional licenses have been issued since then.

What you will learn in this chapter:

➤ The meaning of **price controls** and **quantity controls,** two kinds of government intervention in markets

➤ How price and quantity controls create problems and make a market **inefficient**

➤ Why economists are often deeply skeptical of attempts to intervene in markets

➤ Who benefits and who loses from market interventions, and why they are used despite their well-known problems

➤ What an **excise tax** is and why its effect is similar to a quantity control

➤ Why the **deadweight loss** of a tax means that its true cost is more than the amount of tax revenue collected

83

In this chapter, we begin by examining what happens when governments try to control prices in a competitive market, keeping the price in a market either below its equilibrium level—a *price ceiling* such as rent control—or above it—a *price floor*. We then turn to schemes such as taxi medallions that attempt to dictate the quantity of a good bought or sold. Finally, we consider the effects of taxes on sales or purchases.

Why Governments Control Prices

You learned in Chapter 3 that a market moves to equilibrium—that is, the market price moves to the level at which the quantity supplied equals the quantity demanded. But this equilibrium price does not necessarily please either buyers or sellers.

After all, buyers would always like to pay less if they could, and sometimes they can make a strong moral or political case that they should pay lower prices. For example, what if the equilibrium between supply and demand for apartments in a major city leads to rental rates that an average working person can't afford? In that case, a government might well be under pressure to impose limits on the rents landlords can charge.

Sellers, however, would always like to get more money for what they sell, and sometimes they can make a strong moral or political case that they should receive higher prices. For example, consider the labor market: the price for an hour of a worker's time is the wage rate. What if the equilibrium between supply and demand for less-skilled workers leads to wage rates that are below the poverty level? In that case, a government might well find itself pressured to require employers to pay a rate no lower than some specified minimum wage.

In other words, there is often a strong political demand for governments to intervene in markets. When a government intervenes to regulate prices, we say that it imposes **price controls**. These controls typically take the form either of an upper limit, a **price ceiling**, or a lower limit, a **price floor**.

Unfortunately, it's not that easy to tell a market what to do. As we will now see, when a government tries to legislate prices—whether it legislates them *down* by imposing a price ceiling or *up* by imposing a price floor—there are certain predictable and unpleasant side effects.

We should note an important caveat here: our analysis in this chapter considers only what happens when price controls are imposed on *competitive markets*, which, as you should recall from Chapter 3, are markets with many buyers and sellers in which no buyer or seller can have any influence on the price. When markets are *not* competitive—as in a monopoly, where there is only one seller—price controls don't necessarily cause the same problems. In practice, however, price controls often *are* imposed on competitive markets—like the New York apartment market. And so the analysis in this chapter applies to many important real-world situations.

Price controls are legal restrictions on how high or low a market price may go. They can take two forms: a **price ceiling,** a maximum price sellers are allowed to charge for a good, or a **price floor,** a minimum price buyers are required to pay for a good.

Price Ceilings

Aside from rent control, there are not many price ceilings in the United States today. But at times they have been widespread. Price ceilings are typically imposed during crises—wars, harvest failures, natural disasters—because these events often lead to sudden price increases that hurt many people but produce big gains for a lucky few. The U.S. government imposed ceilings on many prices during World War II: the war sharply increased demand for raw materials, such as aluminum and steel, and price controls prevented those with access to these raw materials from earning huge profits. Price controls on oil were imposed in 1973, when an embargo by Arab oil-exporting countries seemed likely to generate huge profits for U.S. oil companies. (See

Economics in Action on page 79.) Price controls were imposed on California's whole-sale electricity market in 2001, when a shortage was creating big profits for a few power-generating companies but leading to higher bills for consumers.

Rent control in New York is, believe it or not, a legacy of World War II: it was imposed because the war produced an economic boom, which increased demand for apartments at a time when the labor and raw materials that might have been used to build them were being used to win the war instead. Although most price controls were removed soon after the war ended, New York's rent limits were retained and gradually extended to buildings not previously covered, leading to some very strange situations.

You can rent a one-bedroom apartment in Manhattan on fairly short notice—if you are able and willing to pay about $1,700 a month and live in a less-than-desirable area. Yet some people pay only a small fraction of this for comparable apartments and others pay hardly more for bigger apartments in better locations.

Aside from producing great deals for some renters, however, what are the broader consequences of New York's rent control system? To answer this question, we turn to the model we developed in Chapter 3 on supply and demand.

Modeling a Price Ceiling

To see what can go wrong when a government imposes a price ceiling on a competitive market, consider Figure 4-1, which shows a simplified model of the market for apartments in New York. For the sake of simplicity, we imagine that all apartments are exactly the same and would therefore rent for the same price in an uncontrolled market. The table in the figure shows the demand and supply schedules; the implied demand and supply curves are shown on the left of the diagram. We show the quantity of apartments on the horizontal axis and the monthly rent per apartment on the vertical axis. You can see that in an unregulated market the equilibrium would be at point E: 2 million apartments would be rented for $1,000 each per month.

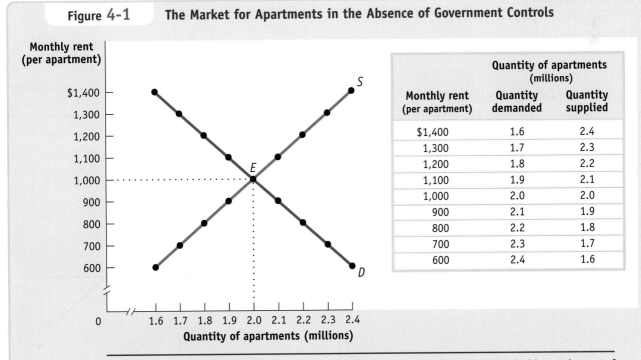

Figure 4-1   The Market for Apartments in the Absence of Government Controls

Monthly rent (per apartment)	Quantity of apartments (millions)	
	Quantity demanded	Quantity supplied
$1,400	1.6	2.4
1,300	1.7	2.3
1,200	1.8	2.2
1,100	1.9	2.1
1,000	2.0	2.0
900	2.1	1.9
800	2.2	1.8
700	2.3	1.7
600	2.4	1.6

Without government intervention, the market for apartments reaches equilibrium at point E with a market rent of $1,000 per month and 2 million apartments rented. **>web...**

Now suppose that the government imposes a price ceiling, limiting rents to a price below the equilibrium price—say no more than $800.

Figure 4-2 shows the effect of the price ceiling, represented by the line at $800. At the enforced rental rate of $800, landlords will have less incentive to offer apartments, so they won't be willing to supply as many as they would at the equilibrium rate of $1,000. So they will choose point *A* on the supply curve, offering only 1.8 million apartments for rent, 200,000 fewer than in the free-market situation. At the same time, more people will want to rent apartments at a price of $800 than at the equilibrium price of $1,000; as shown at point *B* on the demand curve, at a monthly rent of $800 the quantity of apartments demanded rises to 2.2 million, 200,000 more than in the free-market situation and 400,000 more than are actually available at the price of $800. So there is now a persistent shortage of rental housing: at that price, 400,000 more people want to rent than are able to find apartments.

Do price ceilings always cause shortages? No. If a price ceiling is set above the equilibrium price, it won't have any effect. Suppose that the equilibrium rental rate on apartments is $1,000 per month and the city government sets a ceiling of $1,200. Who cares? In this case, the price ceiling won't be binding—it won't actually constrain market behavior—and it will have no effect.

Why a Price Ceiling Causes Inefficiency

The housing shortage shown in Figure 4-2 is not merely annoying: like any shortage induced by price controls, it can be seriously harmful because it leads to *inefficiency*. We introduced the concept of *efficiency* back in Chapter 1, where we learned that an economy is efficient if there is no way to make some people better off without making others worse off and learned the basic principle that a market economy, left to itself, is usually efficient.

A market or an economy becomes **inefficient** when there are missed opportunities—ways in which production or consumption could be rearranged that would make some people better off at no cost to anyone else.

A market or an economy is **inefficient** if there are missed opportunities: some people could be made better off without making other people worse off.

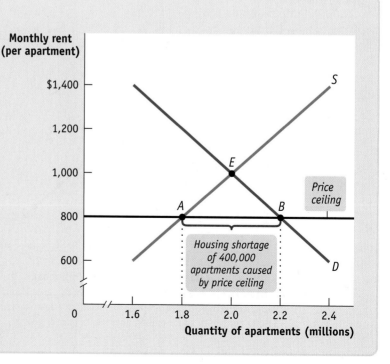

Figure 4-2

The Effects of a Price Ceiling

The dark horizontal line represents the government-imposed price ceiling on rents of $800 per month. This price ceiling reduces the quantity of apartments supplied to 1.8 million, point *A*, and increases the quantity demanded to 2.2 million, point *B*. This creates a persistent shortage of 400,000 units: 400,000 people who want apartments at the legal rent of $800 but cannot get them.

Rent control, like all price ceilings, creates inefficiency in at least three distinct ways: in the allocation of apartments to renters, in the time wasted searching for apartments, and in the inefficiently low quality or condition in which landlords maintain apartments. In addition to inefficiency, price ceilings give rise to illegal behavior as people try to circumvent them.

Inefficient Allocation to Consumers

In the case shown in Figure 4-2, 2.2 million people would like to rent an apartment at $800 per month, but only 1.8 million apartments are available. Of those 2.2 million who are seeking an apartment, some want an apartment badly and are willing to pay a high price to get one. Others have a less urgent need and are only willing to pay a low price, perhaps because they have alternative housing. An efficient allocation of apartments would reflect these differences: people who really want an apartment will get one and people who aren't all that anxious to find an apartment won't. In an inefficient distribution of apartments, the opposite will happen: some people who are not especially anxious to find an apartment will get one but others who are very anxious to find an apartment won't. And because under rent control people usually get apartments through luck or personal connections, rent control generally results in an **inefficient allocation to consumers** of the few apartments available.

To see the inefficiency involved, consider the plight of the Lees, a family with young children who have no alternative housing and would be willing to pay up to $1,500 for an apartment—but are unable to find one. Also consider George, a retiree who lives most of the year in Florida but still has a lease on the New York apartment he moved into 40 years ago. George pays $800 per month for this apartment, but if the rent were even slightly more—say, $850—he would give it up and stay with his children when he is in New York.

This allocation of apartments—George has one and the Lees do not—is a missed opportunity: there is a way to make the Lees and George both better off at no additional cost. The Lees would be happy to pay George, say, $1,200 a month to sublet his apartment, which he would happily accept since the apartment is worth no more than $850 a month to him. George would prefer the money he gets from the Lees to keeping his apartment; the Lees would prefer to have the apartment rather than the money. So both would be made better off by this transaction—and nobody else would be hurt.

Generally, if people who really want apartments could sublet them from people who are less eager to stay in them, both those who gain apartments and those who trade their leases for more money would be better off. However, subletting is illegal under rent control because it would occur at prices above the price ceiling. But just because subletting is illegal doesn't mean it never happens; in fact, it does occur in New York, although not on a scale that would undo the effects of rent control. This illegal subletting is a kind of *black market activity*, which we will discuss shortly.

Wasted Resources

A second reason a price ceiling causes inefficiency is that it leads to **wasted resources**. The Economics in Action on page 79 describes the gasoline shortages of 1979, when millions of Americans spent hours each week waiting in lines at gas stations. The *opportunity cost* of the time spent in gas lines—the wages not earned, the leisure time not enjoyed—constituted wasted resources from the point of view of consumers and of the economy as a whole. Because of rent control, the Lees will spend all their spare time for several months searching for an apartment, time they would rather have spent working or in family activities. That is, there is an opportunity cost to the Lees' prolonged search for an apartment—the leisure or income they had to forgo. If the market for apartments worked freely, the Lees would quickly find an apartment at $1,000 and have time to earn more or to enjoy themselves—an outcome that would make them better off at no expense to anyone else. Again, rent control creates missed opportunities.

Inefficiently Low Quality

A third way a price ceiling causes inefficiency is by causing goods to be of **inefficiently low quality**.

Price ceilings often lead to inefficiency in the form of **inefficient allocation to consumers**: people who want the good badly and are willing to pay a high price don't get it, and those who care relatively little about the good and are only willing to pay a low price do get it.

Price ceilings typically lead to inefficiency in the form of **wasted resources**: people spend money and expend effort in order to deal with the shortages caused by the price ceiling.

Price ceilings often lead to inefficiency in that the goods being offered are of **inefficiently low quality**: sellers offer low-quality goods at a low price even though buyers would prefer a higher quality at a higher price.

Again, consider rent control. Landlords have no incentive to provide better conditions because they cannot raise rents to cover their repair costs but are still able to find tenants easily. In many cases tenants would be willing to pay much more for improved conditions than it would cost for the landlord to provide them—for example, the upgrade of an antiquated electrical system that cannot safely run air conditioners or computers. But any additional payment for such improvements would be legally considered a rent increase, which is prohibited. Indeed, rent-controlled apartments are notoriously badly maintained, rarely painted, subject to frequent electrical and plumbing problems, sometimes even hazardous to inhabit. As one former manager of Manhattan buildings described his job: "At unregulated apartments we'd do most things that the tenants requested. But on the rent-regulated units, we did absolutely only what the law required. . . . We had a perverse incentive to make those tenants unhappy. With regulated apartments, the ultimate objective is to get people out of the building."

This whole situation is a missed opportunity—some tenants would be happy to pay for better conditions, and landlords would be happy to provide them for payment. But such an exchange would occur only if the market were allowed to operate freely.

Black Markets And that leads us to a last aspect of price ceilings: the incentive they provide for *illegal activities*, specifically the emergence of **black markets**. We have already described one kind of black market activity—illegal subletting by tenants. But it does not stop there. Clearly, there is a temptation for a landlord to say to a potential tenant, "Look, you can have the place if you slip me an extra few hundred in cash each month"—and for the tenant to agree, if he or she is one of those people who would be willing to pay much more than the maximum legal rent.

What's wrong with black markets? In general, it's a bad thing if people break *any* law, because it encourages disrespect for the law in general. Worse yet, in this case illegal activity worsens the position of those who try to be honest. If the Lees are scrupulous about not breaking the rent control law but others—who may need an apartment less than the Lees do—are willing to bribe landlords, the Lees may *never* find an apartment.

A **black market** is a market in which goods or services are bought and sold illegally—either because it is illegal to sell them at all or because the prices charged are legally prohibited by a price ceiling.

So Why Are There Price Ceilings?

We have seen three common results of price ceilings:

- A persistent shortage of the good
- Inefficiency arising from this persistent shortage in the form of inefficient allocation of the good to consumers, resources wasted in searching for the good, and the inefficiently low quality of the good offered for sale
- The emergence of illegal, black market activity

Given these unpleasant consequences, why do governments still sometimes impose price ceilings—and why does rent control, in particular, persist in New York?

One answer is that although price ceilings may have adverse effects, they do benefit some people. In practice, New York's rent control rules—which are more complex than our simple model—hurt most residents but give a small minority of renters much cheaper housing than they would get in an unregulated market. And those who benefit from the controls are typically better organized and more vocal than those who are harmed by them.

Also, when price ceilings have been in effect for a long time, buyers may not have a realistic idea of what would happen without them. In our previous example, the rental rate in an uncontrolled market (Figure 4-1) would be only 25 percent higher than in the controlled market (Figure 4-2)—$1,000 instead of $800. But how would renters know that? Indeed, they might have heard about black market transactions at much higher prices—the Lees or some other family paying George $1,200 or more—and would not realize that these black market prices are much higher than the price that would prevail in a fully free market.

A last answer is that government officials often do not understand supply and demand analysis! It is a great mistake to suppose that economic policies in the real world are always sensible or well informed.

economics in action

Oil Shortages in the 1970s

In 1979 a revolution overthrew the government of Iran, one of the world's major petroleum-exporting countries. The political chaos in Iran disrupted oil production there, and the sudden fall in world supply caused the price of crude oil to shoot up by 300 percent.

In most of the world this price increase made gasoline more expensive at the pump but did not lead to shortages. In the United States, however, gasoline was subject to a price ceiling, imposed six years earlier during an oil crisis sparked by the Arab–Israeli war of 1973. The main purpose of those price controls was to prevent U.S. oil producers from reaping large profits as a result of temporary disruptions of supply.

As we learned in Chapter 3, a fall in supply generally raises prices. But here, because the price of gasoline at the pump couldn't rise, the reduction in supply showed up as shortages. As it turned out, these shortages became much worse because of panic: drivers who weren't sure when they would next be able to get gas rushed to fill up even if they still had plenty in their tanks. This produced a temporary surge in demand and long lines at gas stations.

For a few months the gasoline shortage dominated the national scene. Hours were wasted sitting in gasoline lines; families canceled vacations for fear of being stranded. Eventually, higher production began to work its way through the refineries, increasing supply. And the end of the summer driving season reduced demand. Both together led to a fall in price.

In 1981 price controls on gasoline, now discredited as a policy, were abolished. But the uncontrolled gasoline market faced a major test in the spring of 2000. Oil-producing nations restricted their output in order to drive up prices and achieved unexpected success, more than doubling world prices over a period of a few months. Prices at the pump rose sharply—many people altered their driving plans and some felt distinctly poorer as a result of the higher prices. But there were no shortages and life continued in the United States without nearly as much disruption as price controls had generated in the 1970s.

Interestingly, however, the oil price shock of 2000 *did* cause serious disruptions in some European countries—because truck drivers and farmers, protesting the high price of fuel, blocked deliveries. This protest was an extreme illustration of the reasons why governments sometimes try to control prices despite the known problems with price controls! ∎

> >

1. Homeowners near Middletown University's stadium used to rent parking spaces in their driveways to fans at a going rate of $11. A new town ordinance now sets a maximum parking fee of $7. Use the accompanying supply and demand diagram to explain how each of the following corresponds to a price-ceiling concept.

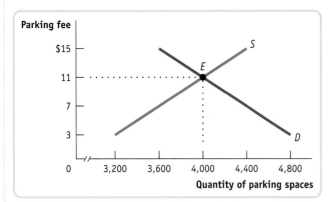

   a. Some homeowners now think it's not worth the hassle to rent out spaces.
   b. Some fans who used to carpool to the game now drive alone.
   c. Some fans can't find parking and leave without seeing the game.
   Explain how each of the following arises from the price ceiling.
   d. Some fans now arrive several hours early to find parking.
   e. Friends of homeowners near the stadium regularly attend games, even if they aren't big fans. But some serious fans have given up because of the parking situation.
   f. Some homeowners rent spaces for more than $7 but pretend that the buyers are non-paying friends or family.

2. True or false? Explain your answer. Compared to a free market, price ceilings at a price below the equilibrium price do the following:
   a. Increase quantity supplied
   b. Make some people who want to consume the good worse off
   c. Make all producers worse off

Solutions appear at back of book.

Price Floors

Sometimes governments intervene to push market prices up instead of down. *Price floors* have been widely legislated for agricultural products, such as wheat and milk, as a way to support the incomes of farmers. Historically, there were also price floors on such services as trucking and air travel, although these were phased out by the United States in the 1970s. If you have ever worked in a fast-food restaurant, you are likely to have encountered a price floor: the United States and many other countries maintain a lower limit on the hourly wage rate of a worker's labor—that is, a floor on the price of labor, called the **minimum wage**.

Just like price ceilings, price floors are intended to help some people but generate predictable and undesirable side effects. Figure 4-3 shows hypothetical supply and demand curves for butter. Left to itself, the market would move to equilibrium at point *E*, with 10 million pounds of butter bought and sold at a price of $1 per pound.

But now suppose that the government, in order to help dairy farmers, imposes a price floor on butter of $1.20 per pound. Its effects are shown in Figure 4-4, where the line at $1.20 represents the price floor. At a price of $1.20 per pound, producers would want to supply 12 million pounds (point *B* on the supply curve) but consumers would want to buy only 9 million pounds (point *A* on the demand curve). There would therefore be a persistent surplus of 3 million pounds of butter.

Does a price floor always lead to an unwanted surplus? No. Just as in the case of a price ceiling, the floor may not be binding—that is, it may be irrelevant. If the equilibrium price of butter is $1 per pound but the floor is set at only $0.80, the floor has no effect.

But suppose that a price floor is binding: what happens to the unwanted surplus? The answer depends on government policy. In the case of agricultural price floors, governments buy up unwanted surplus. Therefore the U.S. government has at times found itself warehousing thousands of tons of butter, cheese, and other farm products. (The European Commission, which administers price floors for a number of European countries, once found itself the owner of a so-called butter mountain, equal in weight to the entire population of Austria.) The government then has to find a way to dispose of these unwanted goods.

Some countries pay exporters to sell products at a loss overseas; this is standard procedure for the European Union. (See For Inquiring Minds on page 82.) At one point the United States tried giving away surplus cheese to the poor. In some cases, governments have actually destroyed the surplus production. To avoid the problem of

The **minimum wage** is a legal floor on the wage rate, which is the market price of labor.

Figure 4-3   The Market for Butter in the Absence of Government Controls

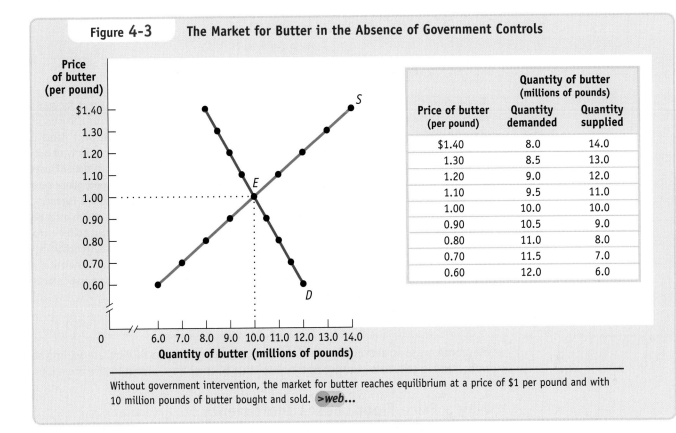

Price of butter (per pound)	Quantity of butter (millions of pounds)	
	Quantity demanded	Quantity supplied
$1.40	8.0	14.0
1.30	8.5	13.0
1.20	9.0	12.0
1.10	9.5	11.0
1.00	10.0	10.0
0.90	10.5	9.0
0.80	11.0	8.0
0.70	11.5	7.0
0.60	12.0	6.0

Without government intervention, the market for butter reaches equilibrium at a price of $1 per pound and with 10 million pounds of butter bought and sold. **>web...**

dealing with the unwanted supplies, the U.S. government typically pays farmers not to produce the products at all.

When the government is not prepared to purchase the unwanted surplus, a price floor means that would-be sellers cannot find buyers. This is what happens when there is a price floor on the wage rate paid for an hour of labor, the *minimum wage*: when the

Figure 4-4

The Effects of a Price Floor

The dark horizontal line represents the government-imposed price floor of $1.20 per pound of butter. The quantity of butter demanded falls to 9 million pounds while the quantity supplied rises to 12 million pounds, generating a persistent surplus of 3 million pounds of butter. **>web...**

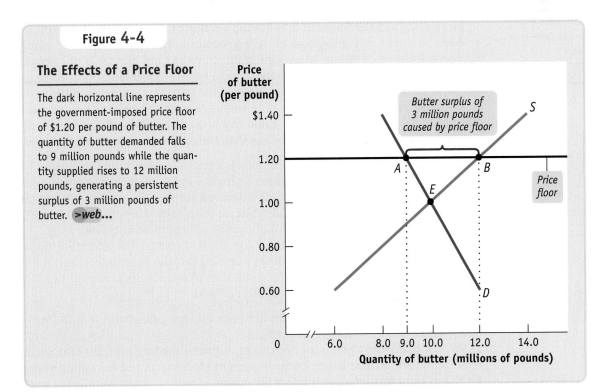

minimum wage is above the equilibrium wage rate, some people who are willing to work—that is, sell labor—cannot find buyers—that is, employers willing to give them jobs.

Why a Price Floor Causes Inefficiency

The persistent surplus that results from a price floor creates missed opportunities—inefficiencies—that resemble those created by the shortage that results from a price ceiling. These include inefficient allocation of sales among sellers, wasted resources, inefficiently high quality, and the temptation to break the law by selling below the legal price.

Inefficient Allocation of Sales Among Sellers Like a price ceiling, a price floor can lead to *inefficient allocation*—but in this case **inefficient allocation of sales among sellers** rather than inefficient allocation to consumers.

An episode from the Belgian movie *Rosetta*, a realistic fictional story, illustrates the problem of inefficient allocation of selling opportunities quite well. Like many European countries, Belgium has a high minimum wage, and jobs for young people are scarce. At one point Rosetta, a young woman who is very anxious to work, loses her job at a fast-food stand because the owner of the stand replaces her with his son—a very reluctant worker. Rosetta would be willing to work for less money, and with the money he would save, the owner could give his son an allowance and let him do something else. But to hire Rosetta for less than the minimum wage would be illegal.

Wasted Resources Also like a price ceiling, a price floor generates inefficiency by *wasting resources*. The most graphic examples involve agricultural products with price floors when the government buys up the unwanted surplus. The surplus production is sometimes destroyed, which is a pure waste; in other cases the stored produce goes, as officials euphemistically put it, "out of condition" and must be thrown away.

Price floors also lead to wasted time and effort. Consider the minimum wage. Would-be workers who spend many hours searching for jobs, or waiting in line in the hope of getting jobs, play the same role in the case of price floors as hapless families searching for apartments in the case of price ceilings.

Inefficiently High Quality Again like price ceilings, price floors lead to ineffi-ciency in the quality of goods produced.

We saw that when there is a price ceiling, suppliers produce products that are of inefficiently low quality: buyers prefer higher-quality products and are willing to pay for them, but sellers refuse to improve the quality of their products because the price

---

Price floors lead to **inefficient alloca-tion of sales among sellers:** those who would be willing to sell the good at the lowest price are not always those who actually manage to sell it.

ceiling prevents their being compensated for doing so. This same logic applies to price floors, but in reverse: suppliers offer goods of **inefficiently high quality**.

How can this be? Isn't high quality a good thing? Yes, but only if it is worth the cost. Suppose that suppliers spend a lot to make goods of very high quality but that this quality is not worth all that much to consumers, who would rather receive the money spent on that quality in the form of a lower price. This represents a missed opportunity: suppliers and buyers could make a mutually beneficial deal in which buyers got goods of somewhat lower quality for a much lower price.

A good example of the inefficiency of excessive quality comes from the days when transatlantic airfares were set artificially high by international treaty. Forbidden to compete for customers by offering lower ticket prices, airlines instead offered expensive services, like lavish in-flight meals that went largely uneaten. At one point the regulators tried to restrict this practice by defining maximum service standards—for example, that snack service should consist of no more than a sandwich. One airline then introduced what it called a "Scandinavian Sandwich," a towering affair that forced the convening of another conference to define *sandwich*. All of this was wasteful, especially considering that what passengers really wanted was less food and lower airfares.

Since the deregulation of U.S. airlines in the 1970s, American passengers have experienced a large decrease in ticket prices accompanied by a decrease in the quality of in-flight service—smaller seats, lower-quality food, and so on. Everyone complains about the service—but thanks to lower fares, the number of people flying on U.S. carriers has grown several hundred percent since airline deregulation.

Illegal Activity Finally, like price ceilings, price floors can provide an incentive for *illegal activity*. For example, in countries where the minimum wage is far above the equilibrium wage rate, workers desperate for jobs sometimes agree to work off the books for employers who conceal their employment from the government—or bribe the government inspectors. This practice, known in Europe as "black labor," is especially common in Southern European countries such as Italy and Spain (see Economics in Action below).

> Price floors often lead to inefficiency in that goods of **inefficiently high quality** are offered: sellers offer high-quality goods at a high price, even though buyers would prefer a lower quality at a lower price.

So Why Are There Price Floors?

To sum up, a price floor creates various negative side effects:

- A persistent surplus of the good
- Inefficiency arising from the persistent surplus in the form of inefficient allocation of sales among sellers, wasted resources, and an inefficiently high level of quality offered by suppliers
- The temptation to engage in illegal activity, particularly bribery and corruption of government officials

So why do governments impose price floors when they have so many negative side effects? The reasons are similar to those for imposing price ceilings. Government officials often disregard warnings about the consequences of price floors either because they believe that the relevant market is poorly described by the supply and demand model or, more often, because they do not understand the model. Above all, just as price ceilings are often imposed because they benefit some influential buyers of a good, price floors are often imposed because they benefit some influential *sellers*.

economics in action

"Black Labor" in Southern Europe

The best-known example of a price floor is the minimum wage. Most economists believe, however, that the minimum wage has relatively little effect on the job market in the United States, mainly because the floor is set so low. (This effectively makes

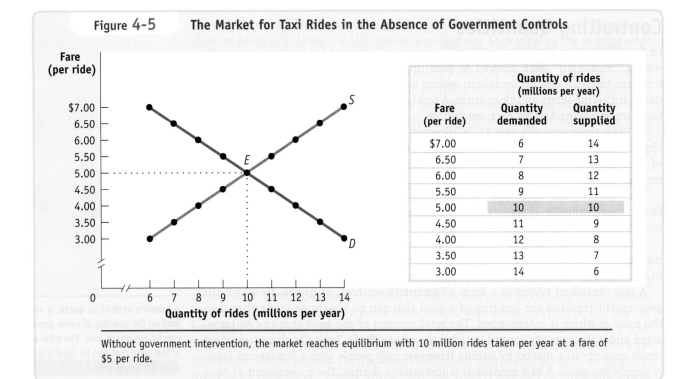

Figure 4-5   **The Market for Taxi Rides in the Absence of Government Controls**

Fare (per ride)	Quantity of rides (millions per year)	
	Quantity demanded	Quantity supplied
$7.00	6	14
6.50	7	13
6.00	8	12
5.50	9	11
5.00	10	10
4.50	11	9
4.00	12	8
3.50	13	7
3.00	14	6

Without government intervention, the market reaches equilibrium with 10 million rides taken per year at a fare of $5 per ride.

---

quantity. You can see from the demand schedule in Figure 4-5 that the demand price of 6 million rides is $7, the demand price of 7 million rides is $6.50, and so on.

Similarly, the supply curve represents the answer to questions of the form: "How many taxi rides would taxi drivers supply at a price of $5 each?" But we can also reverse this question to ask: "At what price will suppliers be willing to supply 10 million rides per year?" The price at which suppliers will supply a given quantity—in this case, 10 million rides at $5 per ride—is the **supply price** of that quantity. We can see from the supply schedule in Figure 4-5 that the supply price of 6 million rides is $3, the supply price of 7 million rides is $3.50, and so on.

The **supply price** of a given quantity is the price at which producers will supply that quantity.

Now we are ready to analyze a quota. We have assumed that the city government limits the quantity of taxi rides to 8 million per year. Medallions, each of which carries the right to provide a certain number of taxi rides per year, are made available to selected people in such a way that a total of 8 million rides will be provided. Medallion holders may then either drive their own taxis or rent their medallions to others for a fee.

Figure 4-6 shows the resulting market for taxi rides, with the line at 8 million rides per year representing the quota limit. Because the quantity of rides is limited to 8 million, consumers must be at point *A* on the demand curve, corresponding to the shaded entry in the demand schedule: the demand price of 8 million rides is $6. Meanwhile, taxi drivers must be at point *B* on the supply curve, corresponding to the shaded entry in the supply schedule: the supply price of 8 million rides is $4.

But how can the price received by taxi drivers be $4 when the price paid by taxi riders is $6? The answer is that in addition to the market in taxi rides, there will also be a market in medallions. Medallion-holders may not always want to drive their taxis: they may be ill or on vacation. So those who do not want to drive their own taxis will sell the right to use the medallion to someone else. So we need to consider two sets of transactions here, and hence two prices: (1) the transactions in taxi rides and the price at which these will occur, and (2) the transactions in medallions and the price at which these will occur. It turns out that since we are looking at two markets, the $4 and $6 prices will both be right.

To see how this all works, consider two imaginary New York taxi drivers, Sunil and Harriet. Sunil has a medallion but can't use it because he's recovering from a severely sprained wrist. So he's looking to rent his medallion out to someone else. Harriet

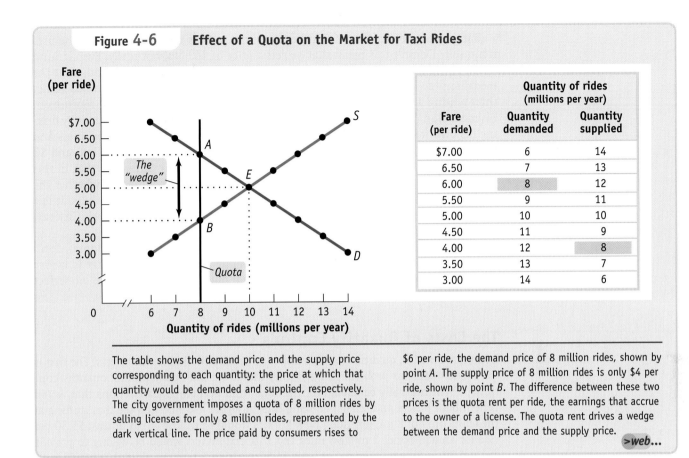

Figure 4-6   Effect of a Quota on the Market for Taxi Rides

Fare (per ride)	Quantity of rides (millions per year)	
	Quantity demanded	Quantity supplied
$7.00	6	14
6.50	7	13
6.00	8	12
5.50	9	11
5.00	10	10
4.50	11	9
4.00	12	8
3.50	13	7
3.00	14	6

The table shows the demand price and the supply price corresponding to each quantity: the price at which that quantity would be demanded and supplied, respectively. The city government imposes a quota of 8 million rides by selling licenses for only 8 million rides, represented by the dark vertical line. The price paid by consumers rises to $6 per ride, the demand price of 8 million rides, shown by point A. The supply price of 8 million rides is only $4 per ride, shown by point B. The difference between these two prices is the quota rent per ride, the earnings that accrue to the owner of a license. The quota rent drives a wedge between the demand price and the supply price.

>*web*...

doesn't have a medallion but would like to rent one. Furthermore, at any point in time there are many other people like Harriet who would like to rent a medallion as well as many others like Sunil who have a medallion to rent. Suppose Sunil agrees to rent his medallion to Harriet. To make things simple, assume that any driver can give only one ride per day and that Sunil is renting his medallion to Harriet for one day. What rental price will they agree on?

To answer this question, we need to look at the transactions from the viewpoints of both drivers. Once she has the medallion, Harriet knows she can make $6 per day—the demand price of a ride under the quota. And she is willing to rent the medallion only if she makes at least $4 per day—the supply price of a ride under the quota. So Sunil cannot demand a rent of more than $2—the difference between $6 and $4. And if Harriet offered Sunil less than $2—say, $1.50—there would be other eager drivers willing to offer him more, up to $2. Hence, in order to get the medallion, Harriet must offer Sunil at least $2. Therefore, since the rent can be no more than $2 and no less than $2, it must be exactly $2.

It is no coincidence that $2 is exactly the difference between $6, the demand price of 8 million rides, and $4, the supply price of 8 million rides. In every case in which the supply of a good is legally restricted, there is a **wedge** between the demand price of the quantity transacted and the supply price of the quantity transacted. This wedge, illustrated by the double-headed arrow in Figure 4-6, has a special name: the **quota rent**. It is the earnings that accrue to the license-holder from ownership of a valuable commodity, the license. In the case of Sunil and Harriet, the quota rent of $2 goes to Sunil because he owns the license, and the remaining $4 from the total fare of $6 goes to Harriet.

So Figure 4-6 also illustrates the quota rent in the market for New York taxi rides. The quota limits the quantity of rides to 8 million per year, a quantity at which the demand price of $6 exceeds the supply price of $4. The wedge between these two prices, $2, is the quota rent that results from the restrictions placed on the quantity of taxi rides in this market.

A quantity control, or quota, drives a **wedge** between the demand price and the supply price of a good; that is, the price paid by buyers ends up being higher than that received by sellers. The difference between the demand and supply price at the quota limit is the **quota rent**, the earnings that accrue to the license-holder from ownership of the right to sell the good. It is equal to the market price of the license when the licenses are traded.

But wait a second. What if Sunil doesn't rent out his medallion? What if he uses it himself? Doesn't this mean that he gets a price of $6? No, not really. Even if Sunil doesn't rent out his medallion, he could have rented it out, which means that the medallion has an *opportunity cost* of $2: if Sunil decides to drive his own taxi rather than renting it to Harriet, the $2 represents his opportunity cost of not renting out his medallion. That is, the $2 quota rent is now the rental income he forgoes by driving his own taxi. In effect, Sunil is in two businesses—the taxi-driving business and the medallion-renting business. He makes $4 per ride from driving his taxi and $2 per ride from renting out his medallion. It doesn't make any difference that in this particular case he has rented his medallion to himself! So regardless of whether the medallion owner uses the medallion himself or herself, or rents it to others, it is a valuable asset. And this is represented in the going price for a New York City taxi medallion: in 2004, it was around $250,000.

Notice, by the way, that quotas—like price ceilings and price floors—don't always have a real effect. If the quota were set at 12 million rides—that is, above the equilibrium quantity in an unregulated market—it would have no effect because it would not be binding.

The Costs of Quantity Controls

Like price controls, quantity controls can have some undesirable side effects. The first is the by-now-familiar problem of *inefficiency* due to missed opportunities: quantity controls prevent mutually beneficial transactions from occurring, transactions that would benefit both buyers and sellers. Looking back at Figure 4-6, you can see that starting at the quota limit of 8 million rides, New Yorkers would be willing to pay at least $5.50 per ride for an additional 1 million rides and that taxi drivers would be willing to provide those rides as long as they got at least $4.50 per ride. These are rides that would have taken place if there were no quota limit. The same is true for the next 1 million rides: New Yorkers would be willing to pay at least $5 per ride when the quantity of rides is increased from 9 to 10 million, and taxi drivers would be willing to provide those rides as long as they got at least $5 per ride. Again, these rides would have occurred without the quota limit. Only when the market has reached the free-market equilibrium quantity of 10 million rides are there no "missed-opportunity rides"—the quota limit of 8 million rides has caused 2 million "missed-opportunity rides." Generally, *as long as the demand price of a given quantity exceeds the supply price, there is a missed opportunity.* A buyer would be willing to buy the good at a price that the seller would be willing to accept, but such a transaction does not occur because it is forbidden by the quota.

And because there are transactions that people would like to make but are not allowed to, quantity controls generate an incentive to evade them or even to break the law. New York's taxi industry again provides clear examples. Taxi regulation applies only to those drivers who are hailed by passengers on the street. A car service that makes prearranged pickups does not need a medallion. As a result, such hired cars provide much of the service that might otherwise be provided by taxis, as in other cities. In addition, there are substantial numbers of unlicensed cabs that simply defy the law by picking up passengers without a medallion. Because these cabs are illegal, their drivers are completely unregulated, and they generate a disproportionately large share of traffic accidents in New York.

In fact, in 2004 the hardships caused by the limited number of New York taxis led city leaders to authorize an increase in the number of licensed taxis, from the original number of 12,187 to a little over 13,000 by 2007—a move that certainly cheered New York riders. But those who already owned medallions were less happy with the increase; they understood that the nearly 900 new taxis would reduce or eliminate the shortage of taxis. As a result, taxi drivers might find their revenues decline as they would no longer always be assured of finding willing customers. And, in turn, the value of a medallion would fall. So to placate the medallion owners, city officials also agreed in 2004 to raise fares by 25 percent, a move that slightly diminished the new-found cheer of New York riders.

In sum, quantity controls typically create the following undesirable side effects:

- Inefficiencies, or missed opportunities, in the form of mutually beneficial transactions that don't occur
- Incentives for illegal activities

economics in action

The Clams of New Jersey

Forget the refineries along the Jersey Turnpike; one industry that New Jersey *really* dominates is clam fishing. The Garden State supplies 80 percent of the world's surf clams, whose tongues are used in fried-clam dinners, and 40 percent of the quahogs, which are used to make clam chowder.

In the 1980s, however, excessive fishing threatened to wipe out New Jersey's clam beds. To save the resource, the U.S. government introduced a clam quota, which sets an overall limit on the number of bushels of clams that may be caught and allocates licenses to owners of fishing boats based on their historical catches.

Notice, by the way, that this is an example of a quota that is probably justified by broader economic and environmental considerations—unlike the New York taxicab quota, which has long since lost any economic rationale. Still, whatever its rationale, the New Jersey clam quota works the same way as any other quota.

Once the quota system was established, many boat owners stopped fishing for clams. They realized that rather than operate a boat part time, it was more profitable to sell or rent their licenses to someone else, who could then assemble enough licenses to operate a boat full time. Today, there are about 50 boats fishing for clams; the license required to operate one is worth more than the boat itself. ■

> > > > > > > > > > > > > > > > > > > >

>> **CHECK YOUR UNDERSTANDING 4-3**

1. Suppose that the supply and demand for taxi rides is given by Figure 4-5 but the quota is set at 6 million rides instead of 8 million. Find the following and indicate them on Figure 4-5.
   a. The price of a ride
   b. The quota rent
   c. Suppose the quota limit on taxi rides is increased to 9 million. What happens to the quota rent?

2. Assume that the quota limit is 8 million rides. Suppose demand decreases due to a decline in tourism. What is the smallest parallel leftward shift in demand that would result in the quota no longer having an effect on the market? Illustrate your answer using Figure 4-5.

Solutions appear at back of book.

A Surprise Parallel: Taxes

To provide the services we want, from national defense to public parks, governments must collect taxes. But taxes impose costs on the economy. Among the most important roles of economics is tax analysis: figuring out the economic costs of taxation, determining who bears those costs, and suggesting ways to change the tax system that will reduce the costs it imposes. It turns out that the same analysis we have just used to understand quotas can be used, with hardly any modification, to make a preliminary analysis of taxes, too.

Why Is a Tax Like a Quota?

Suppose that the supply and demand curves for New York taxis were exactly as shown in Figure 4-5. This means that in the absence of government action, the equilibrium price of a taxi ride will be $5 and 10 million rides will be bought and sold.

Figure 4-7

Effect of an Excise Tax Levied on Sales of Taxi Rides

S_1 is the supply curve before the tax. After the city requires drivers to pay a tax of $2 for every ride they give, the supply curve shifts upward by $2, to the new supply curve S_2. This means that the price drivers receive net of tax is $4, represented by point B on the old supply curve S_1. And the price paid by riders is $6, represented by point A on the new supply curve S_2. The tax drives a wedge between the demand price, $6, and the original supply price, $4.

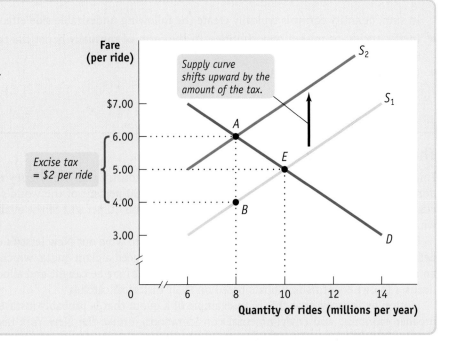

An **excise tax** is a tax on sales of a good or service.

Now suppose that instead of imposing a quota on the quantity of rides, the city imposes an **excise tax**—a tax on sales. Specifically, it charges taxi drivers $2 for each ride they provide. What is the effect of the tax?

From the point of view of a taxi driver, the tax means that he or she doesn't get to keep all of the fare: if a passenger pays $5, $2 is collected as a tax, so the driver gets only $3. For any given quantity of rides supplied, the *post-tax supply price* is higher than the pre-tax supply price. For example, drivers will now require a price of $6 to supply as many rides as they would have been willing to supply at a price of $4 in the absence of the $2 tax.

So the tax on sales shifts the supply curve upward, by the amount of the tax. This is shown in Figure 4-7, where S_1 is the supply curve before the tax is imposed and S_2 is the supply curve after the tax is imposed. The market equilibrium moves from E, where the price is $5 per ride and 10 million rides are bought and sold, to A, where the price is $6 per ride and 8 million rides are bought and sold. A is, of course, on both the demand curve D and the new supply curve S_2.

But how do we know that 8 million rides will be supplied at a price of $6? Because the price *net of the tax* is $4 and the pre-tax supply price of 8 million rides is $4, as shown by point B in Figure 4-7.

Does all this look familiar? It should. The equilibrium with a $2 tax on rides, which reduces the quantity bought and sold to 8 million rides, looks just like the equilibrium with a quota of 8 million rides, which leads to a quota rent of $2 per ride. Just like a quota, the tax *drives a wedge* between the demand price and the original, pre-tax supply price.

The only difference is that instead of paying a $2 rent to the owner of a license, drivers pay a $2 tax to the city. In fact, there is a way to make an excise tax and a quota completely equivalent. Imagine that instead of issuing a limited number of licenses, the city simply sold licenses at $2 each. This $2 license fee would, for all practical purposes, be a $2 excise tax.

Finally, imagine that instead of selling licenses at a fixed price, the city were to issue 8 million licenses and auction them off—that is, sell them for whatever price the, um, traffic will bear. What would be the price of a license? Surely it would be $2—the quota rent. And so in this case the quota rent would act just like an excise tax.

Who Pays an Excise Tax?

We have just imagined a tax that must be paid by the *sellers* of a good. But what would happen if the tax were instead paid by the *buyers*—say, if you had to pay a special $2 tax to ride in a taxicab?

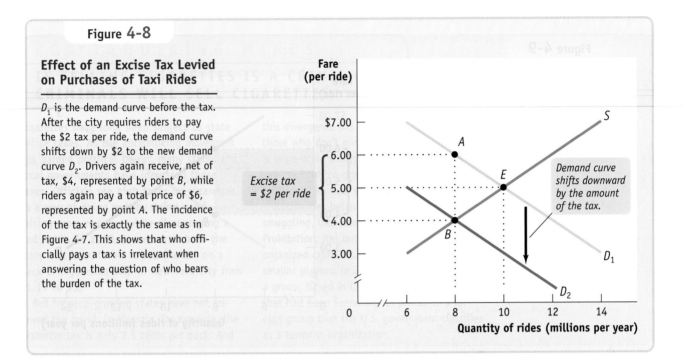

Figure 4-8

Effect of an Excise Tax Levied on Purchases of Taxi Rides

D_1 is the demand curve before the tax. After the city requires riders to pay the $2 tax per ride, the demand curve shifts down by $2 to the new demand curve D_2. Drivers again receive, net of tax, $4, represented by point B, while riders again pay a total price of $6, represented by point A. The incidence of the tax is exactly the same as in Figure 4-7. This shows that who officially pays a tax is irrelevant when answering the question of who bears the burden of the tax.

The answer is shown in Figure 4-8. If a taxi rider must pay a $2 tax on each ride, then the price riders pay must be $2 less in order for the quantity of taxi rides demanded post-tax to be the same quantity as that demanded pre-tax. So the demand curve shifts *downward*, from D_1 to D_2, by the amount of the tax. This shifts the equilibrium from E to B, where the market price is $4 per ride and 8 million rides are bought and sold. In this case, $4 is the supply price of 8 million rides and $6 is the demand price—but in effect riders do pay $6, when you include the tax. So it is just as if riders were on their original demand curve at point A.

If you compare Figures 4-7 and 4-8, you will immediately notice that they show the same price effect. In each case, buyers pay an effective price of $6, sellers receive an effective price of $4, and 8 million rides are bought and sold. *It doesn't seem to make any difference who officially pays the tax.*

This insight is a general one in analyzing taxes: the **incidence** of a tax—who really bears the burden of the tax—is often not a question you can answer by asking who actually writes the check to the government. In this particular case, a $2 tax on taxi rides is reflected in a $1 increase in the price paid by buyers and a $1 decrease in the price received by sellers; so the incidence of the tax is actually evenly split between buyers and sellers. This incidence is the same regardless of whether the check to the city government is made out by buyers or by sellers.

The incidence of an excise tax isn't always split evenly between buyers and sellers as in this example. Depending on the shapes of supply and demand curves, the incidence of an excise tax may be divided differently.

The **incidence** of a tax is a measure of who really pays it.

The Revenue from an Excise Tax

Although both buyers and sellers lose from an excise tax, the government does collect revenue—which is the whole point of the tax. How much revenue does the government collect? The revenue is equal to the area of the shaded rectangle in Figure 4-9 on page 92.

To see why this is the revenue collected by a $2 tax on taxi rides, notice that the *height* of the rectangle is $2. This is the amount of the tax per ride; it is also, as we have seen, the size of the wedge that the tax drives between the supply price and the demand price. Meanwhile, the *width* of the rectangle is 8 million rides, which is the equilibrium quantity of rides given that $2 tax.

Panel (c) shows a case of elastic demand when the toll is raised from $0.90 to $1.10. The 20% price increase causes the quantity demanded to fall from 1,200 to 800—a 40% decline, so the price elasticity of demand is 40%/20% = 2.

Why does it matter whether demand is unit-elastic, inelastic, or elastic? Because this classification predicts how changes in the price of a good will affect the *total revenue* earned by producers from the sale of that good. In many real-life situations, such as the one faced by Tellez, it is crucial to know how price changes affect total revenue. **Total revenue** is defined as the total value of sales of a good: the price multiplied by the quantity sold.

> The **total revenue** is the total value of sales of a good. It is equal to the price of a good multiplied by the quantity sold.

(5-6) Total revenue = Price × quantity sold

Total revenue has a useful graphical representation that can help us understand why knowing the price elasticity of demand is crucial when we ask whether a price rise will increase or reduce total revenue. Panel (a) of Figure 5-4 shows the same demand curve as panel (a) of Figure 5-3. We see that 1,100 drivers will use the bridge if the toll is $0.90. The total revenue at a price of $0.90 is therefore $0.90 × 1,100 = $990. This value is equal to the area of the green rectangle, which is drawn with the bottom left corner at the coordinates (0, 0) and the top right corner at the coordinates (1,100, 0.90). In general, the total revenue at any given price is equal to the area of a rectangle whose height is the price and whose width is the quantity demanded at that price.

To get an idea of why total revenue is important, consider the following scenario. Suppose that the toll on the bridge is currently $0.90 but that the highway department must raise extra money for road repairs. One way to do this is to raise the toll on the bridge. But this plan might backfire, since a higher toll will reduce the number of drivers who use the bridge. And if traffic on the bridge dropped a lot, a higher toll would actually reduce total revenue instead of increasing it. So it's important for the highway department to know how drivers will respond to a toll increase.

We can see graphically how the toll increase affects total bridge revenue by examining panel (b) of Figure 5-4. At a toll of $0.90, total revenue is given by the sum of the areas A and B. After the toll is raised to $1.10, total revenue is given by the sum of areas B and

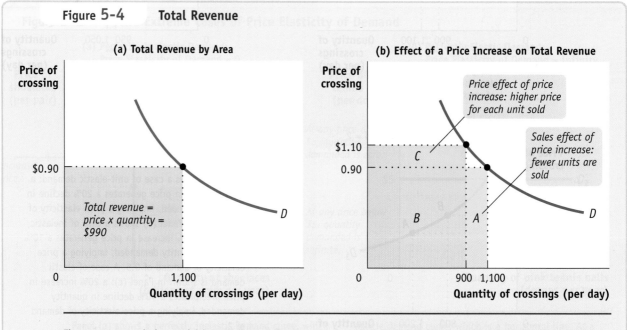

Figure 5-4 **Total Revenue**

(a) Total Revenue by Area

Price of crossing

$0.90

Total revenue = price x quantity = $990

0   1,100
Quantity of crossings (per day)

D

(b) Effect of a Price Increase on Total Revenue

Price of crossing

Price effect of price increase: higher price for each unit sold

Sales effect of price increase: fewer units are sold

$1.10

C

0.90

B   A

0   900 1,100
Quantity of crossings (per day)

D

The green rectangle in panel (a) represents total revenue generated from 1,100 drivers who each pay a toll of $0.90. Panel (b) shows how total revenue is affected when the price increases from $0.90 to $1.10. Due to the sales effect, total revenue falls by area A. Due to the price effect, total revenue increases by the area C. The overall effect can go either way, depending upon the price elasticity of demand.

C. So when the toll is raised, revenue represented by area A is lost but revenue represented by area C is gained. These two areas have important interpretations. Area C represents the revenue gain that comes from the additional $0.20 paid by drivers who continue to use the bridge. That is, the 900 who continue to use the bridge contribute an additional $0.20 × 900 = $180 per day to total revenue, represented by area C. On the other hand, 200 drivers who would have used the bridge at a price of $0.90 no longer do so, generating a loss to total revenue of $0.90 × 200 = $180 per day, represented by area A.

Except in the rare case of a good with perfectly elastic or perfectly inelastic demand, when a seller raises the price of a good, two countervailing effects are present:

- *A price effect*. After a price increase, each unit sold sells at a higher price, which tends to raise revenue.

- *A sales effect*. After a price increase, fewer units are sold, which tends to lower revenue.

But then, you may ask, what is the ultimate effect on total revenue: does it go up or down? The answer is that, in general, the effect on total revenue can go either way—a price rise may increase total revenue or may lower it. If the price effect, which tends to raise total revenue, is the stronger of the two effects, then total revenue goes up. If the sales effect, which tends to reduce total revenue, is the stronger, then total revenue goes down. And if the strengths of the two effects are exactly equal—as in our toll bridge example, where a $180 gain offsets a $180 loss—total revenue is unchanged by the price increase.

The price elasticity of demand tells us what happens to total revenue when price changes: its size determines which effect—the price effect or the sales effect—is stronger. Specifically:

- If demand for a good is *elastic* (the price elasticity of demand is greater than 1), an increase in price reduces total revenue. In this case, the sales effect is stronger than the price effect.

- If demand for a good is *inelastic* (the price elasticity of demand is less than 1), a higher price increases total revenue. In this case, the price effect is stronger than the sales effect.

- If demand for a good is *unit-elastic* (the price elasticity of demand is 1), an increase in price does not change total revenue. In this case, the sales effect and the price effect exactly offset each other.

Table 5-2 shows how the effect of a price increase on total revenue depends on the price elasticity of demand, using the same data as in Figure 5-3. An increase in the price from $0.90 to $1.10 leaves total revenue unchanged at $990 when demand is unit-elastic. When demand is inelastic, the price effect dominates the sales effect; the same price increase leads to an increase in total revenue from $945 to $1,045. And when demand is elastic, the sales effect dominates the price effect; the price increase leads to a decline in total revenue from $1,080 to $880.

TABLE 5-2

Price Elasticity of Demand and Total Revenue

	Price of crossing = $0.90	Price of crossing = $1.10
Unit-elastic demand (price elasticity of demand = 1)		
Quantity demanded	1,100	900
Total revenue	$990	$990
Inelastic demand (price elasticity of demand = 0.5)		
Quantity demanded	1,050	950
Total revenue	$945	$1,045
Elastic demand (price elasticity of demand = 2)		
Quantity demanded	1,200	800
Total revenue	$1,080	$880

The price elasticity of demand also predicts the effect of a *fall* in price on total revenue. When the price falls, the same two countervailing effects are present, but they work in the opposite directions as in the case of a price rise. There is the price effect of a lower price per unit sold, which tends to lower revenue. This is countered by the sales effect of more units sold, which tends to raise revenue. Which effect dominates depends on the price elasticity. Here is a quick summary:

- When demand is *elastic*, the sales effect dominates the price effect; so a fall in price increases total revenue.
- When demand is *inelastic*, the price effect dominates the sales effect; so a fall in price reduces total revenue.
- When demand is *unit-elastic*, the two effects exactly balance; so a fall in price has no effect on total revenue.

Price Elasticity Along the Demand Curve

Suppose that an economist says that "the price elasticity of demand for coffee is 0.25." What he or she means is that *at the current price* the elasticity is 0.25. In the previous discussion of the toll bridge, what we were really describing was the elasticity *at the price* of $0.90. Why this qualification? Because for the vast majority of demand curves, the price elasticity of demand at one point along the curve is different from the price elasticity at other points along the same curve.

To see this, consider the table in Figure 5-5, which shows a hypothetical demand schedule. It also shows in the last column the total revenue generated at any given price in the demand schedule. The upper panel of the graph in Figure 5-5 shows the correspond- ing demand curve. The lower panel illustrates the same data on total revenue: the height of a bar at each quantity demanded—which corresponds to a particular price—measures the total revenue generated at that price.

In Figure 5-5, you can see that when the price is low, a higher price increases total revenue: starting at a price of $1, raising the price to $2 increases total revenue from $9 to $16. This means that when the price is low, demand is inelastic. Moreover, you can see that demand is inelastic on the entire section of the demand curve from a price of $0 to a price of $5.

When the price is high, however, raising it further reduces total revenue: starting at a price of $8, raising the price to $9 reduces total revenue, from $16 to $9. This means that when the price is high, demand is elastic. Furthermore, you can see that demand is elastic over the section of the demand curve from a price of $5 to $10.

For the vast majority of goods, the price elasticity of demand changes along the demand curve. So whenever you measure the elasticity, you are really measuring it at a particular point or section of the demand curve.

What Factors Determine the Price Elasticity of Demand?

1998 was not the first time Americans had been subject to an attempt by oil-exporting countries to increase revenue by raising oil prices. In the 1970s, gasoline prices in the United States jumped significantly after oil exporters reduced output and raised oil prices. Americans initially reacted by changing their consumption of gasoline very little. Over time, however, they gradually adapted to the higher prices. After a few years, drivers had cut their consumption of gasoline in various ways: increased carpooling, greater use of public transportation, and, most importantly, replacement of large, gas-guzzling cars with smaller, more fuel-efficient models.

The experience of the 1970s illustrates the three main factors that determine elasticity: whether close substitutes are available, whether the good is a necessity or a luxury, and how much time has elapsed since the price change. We'll briefly examine each of these three factors.

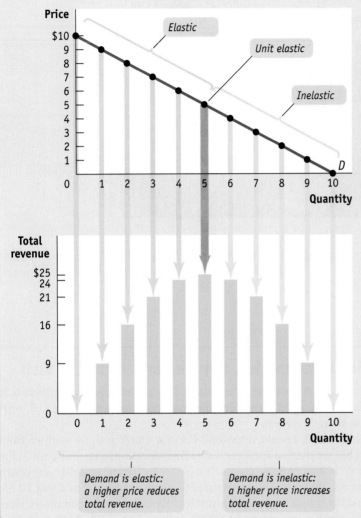

Figure 5-5   **The Price Elasticity of Demand Changes Along the Demand**

Price	Quantity demanded	Total revenue
$ 0	10	$ 0
1	9	9
2	8	16
3	7	21
4	6	24
5	5	25
6	4	24
7	3	21
8	2	16
9	1	9
10	0	0

The upper panel shows a demand curve. The lower panel shows how total revenue changes along that demand curve: at each price and quantity combination, the height of the bar represents the total revenue generated. You can see that at a low price, raising the price increases total revenue. Therefore demand is inelastic at low prices. At a high price, however, a rise in price reduces total revenue. Therefore demand is elastic at high prices.

Demand is elastic: a higher price reduces total revenue.

Demand is inelastic: a higher price increases total revenue.

Whether Close Substitutes Are Available The price elasticity of demand tends to be high if there are other goods that consumers regard as similar and would be willing to consume instead. The price elasticity of demand tends to be low if there are no close substitutes.

Whether the Good Is a Necessity or a Luxury The price elasticity of demand tends to be low if a good is something you must have, like a life-saving medicine. The price elasticity of demand tends to be high if the good is a luxury—something you can live without.

Time In general, the price elasticity of demand tends to increase as consumers have more time to adjust to a price change. This means that the long-run price elasticity of demand is often higher than the short-run elasticity.

So when gasoline prices first increased dramatically in the United States at the end of the 1970s, consumption fell very little because there were no close substitutes for gasoline and because driving their cars was necessary for people to carry out the ordinary tasks of life. Over time, however, Americans changed their habits in ways that enabled them to gradually reduce their gasoline consumption. The result was a steady

Mike Thompson, Detroit Free Press. Reprinted by permission.

decline in gasoline consumption over the next decade, even though the price of gasoline did not continue to rise, confirming that the long-run price elasticity of demand for gasoline was indeed much larger than the short-run elasticity.

economics in action

America's a Nice Place to Live, but We Can't Afford to Visit

In 1992, 18.6 million Canadians visited the United States, but only 11.8 million U.S. residents visited Canada. By 2002, however, roles had been reversed: more U.S. residents visited Canada than vice versa.

Why did the tourist traffic reverse direction? Canada didn't get any warmer from 1992 to 2002—but it did get cheaper for Americans. The reason was a large change in the exchange rate between the two nations' currencies: in 1992 a Canadian dollar was worth more than $0.80, but by 2002 it had fallen in value by nearly 20 percent to about $0.65. This meant that Canadian goods and services, particularly hotel rooms and meals, were about 20 percent cheaper for Americans in 2002 compared to 1992. So Canada had become a cheap vacation destination for Americans by 2002. Things were not so rosy, however, when viewed from the other side of the border: American vacations had become 20 percent more expensive for Canadians. Canadians responded by vacationing in their own country or in other parts of the world besides the United States.

Foreign travel is an example of a good that has a high price elasticity of demand: as we saw in Table 5-1, it has been estimated at about 4.1. One reason is that foreign travel is a luxury good for most people—you may regret not going to Paris this year, but you can live without it. A second reason is that a good substitute for foreign travel typically exists—domestic travel. A Canadian who finds it too expensive to vacation in San Francisco this year is likely to find that Vancouver is a pretty good alternative. ■

< < < < < < < < < < < < < < < < < <

>>CHECK YOUR UNDERSTANDING 5-2

1. For each case, choose the condition that characterizes demand: elastic demand, inelastic demand, or unit-elastic demand.
   a. Total revenue decreases when price increases.
   b. The additional revenue generated by an increase in quantity sold is exactly offset by revenue lost from the fall in price received per unit.
   c. Total revenue falls when output increases.
   d. Producers in an industry find they can increase their total revenues by working together to reduce industry output.

continued

2. For the following goods, what is the elasticity of demand? Explain. What is the shape of the demand curve?
  a. Demand by a snake-bite victim for an antidote
  b. Demand by students for green erasers

Solutions appear at back of book.

Other Demand Elasticities

The quantity of a good demanded depends not only on the price of that good but on other variables. In particular, demand curves shift because of changes in the prices of related goods and changes in consumers' incomes. It is often important to have a measure of these other effects, and the best measures are—you guessed it—elasticities. Specifically, we can best measure how the demand for a good is affected by prices of other goods using a measure called the *cross-price elasticity of demand*, and we can best measure how demand is affected by changes in income using the *income elasticity of demand*.

The Cross-Price Elasticity of Demand

In Chapter 3 you learned that the demand for a good is often affected by the prices of other, related goods—goods that are substitutes or complements. There you saw that a change in the price of a related good shifts the demand curve of the original good, reflecting a change in the quantity demanded at any given price. The strength of such a "cross" effect on demand can be measured by the **cross-price elasticity of demand**, defined as the ratio of the percent change in the quantity demanded of one good to the percent change in the price of the other.

> The **cross-price elasticity of demand** between two goods measures the effect of the change in one good's price on the quantity demanded of the other good. It is equal to the percent change in the quantity demanded of one good divided by the percent change in the other good's price.

(5-7) Cross-price elasticity of demand between goods A and B

$$= \frac{\% \text{ change in quantity of A demanded}}{\% \text{ change in price of B}}$$

When two goods are substitutes, like hot dogs and hamburgers, the cross-price elasticity of demand is positive: a rise in the price of hot dogs increases the demand for hamburgers—that is, it causes a rightward shift of the demand curve for hamburgers. If the goods are close substitutes, the cross-price elasticity will be positive and large; if they are not close substitutes, the cross-price elasticity will be positive and small. So when the cross-price elasticity of demand is positive, it is a measure of how closely substitutable for each other two goods are.

When two goods are complements, like hot dogs and hot dog buns, the cross-price elasticity is negative: a rise in the price of hot dogs decreases the demand for hot dog buns—that is, it causes a leftward shift of the demand curve for hot dog buns. As with substitutes, the size of the cross-price elasticity of demand between two complements tells us how strongly complementary they are: if the cross-price elasticity is only slightly below zero, they are weak complements; if it is very negative, they are strong complements.

Note that in the case of the cross-price elasticity of demand, the sign (plus or minus) is very important: it tells us whether the two goods are complements or substitutes. So we cannot drop the minus sign as we did for the price elasticity of demand.

Our discussion of the cross-price elasticity of demand is a useful place to return to a point we made earlier: elasticity is a *unit-free* measure—that is, it doesn't depend on the units in which goods are measured.

To see the potential problem, suppose someone told you that "if the price of hot dog buns rises by $0.30, Americans will buy 10 million fewer hot dogs this year." If you've ever bought hot dog buns, you'll immediately wonder: is that a $0.30 increase in the price *per bun*, or is it a $0.30 increase in the price *per package* (buns are usually sold by the dozen)? It makes a big difference what units we are talking about! However, if someone says that the cross-price elasticity of demand between buns and hot dogs is −0.3, it doesn't matter whether buns are sold individually or by the package. So elasticity is defined as a ratio of percent changes, as a way of making sure that confusion over units doesn't arise.

The Income Elasticity of Demand

The **income elasticity of demand** is a measure of how much the demand for a good is affected by changes in consumers' incomes. It allows us to determine whether a good is a normal or inferior good as well as measure how intensely the demand for the good responds to changes in income.

The **income elasticity of demand** is the percent change in the quantity of a good demanded when a consumer's income changes divided by the percent change in the consumer's income.

$$\textbf{(5-8)} \quad \text{Income elasticity of demand} = \frac{\% \text{ change in quantity demanded}}{\% \text{ change in income}}$$

Just as the cross-price elasticity of demand between two goods can be either positive or negative, depending on whether the goods are substitutes or complements, the income elasticity of demand for a good can also be either positive or negative. Recall from Chapter 3 that goods can be either *normal goods*, for which demand increases when income rises, or *inferior goods*, for which demand decreases when income rises. These definitions relate directly to the sign of the income elasticity of demand:

- When the income elasticity of demand is positive, the good is a normal good—that is, the quantity demanded at any given price increases as income increases.

- When the income elasticity of demand is negative, the good is an inferior good—that is, the quantity demanded at any given price decreases as income increases.

Economists often use estimates of the income elasticity of demand to predict which industries will grow most rapidly as the incomes of consumers grow over time. In doing this, they often find it useful to make a further distinction among normal goods, identifying which are *income-elastic* and which are *income-inelastic*.

The demand for a good is **income-elastic** if the income elasticity of demand for that good is greater than 1.

The demand for a good is **income-inelastic** if the income elasticity of demand for that good is positive but less than 1.

The demand for a good is **income-elastic** if the income elasticity of demand for that good is greater than 1. When income rises, the demand for income-elastic goods rises *faster* than income. Luxury goods such as second homes and international travel tend to be income-elastic. The demand for a good is **income-inelastic** if the income elasticity of demand for that good is positive but less than 1. When income rises, the demand for income-inelastic goods rises, but more slowly than income. Necessities such as food and clothing tend to be income-inelastic.

FOR INQUIRING MINDS

WHERE HAVE ALL THE FARMERS GONE?

What percentage of Americans live on farms? Sad to say, the U.S. government no longer publishes that number. In 1991 the official percentage was 1.9, but in that year the government decided it was no longer a meaningful indicator of the size of the agricultural sector because a large proportion of those who live on farms actually make their living doing something else. But in the days of the Founding Fathers, the great majority of Americans lived on farms. As recently as the 1940s, one American in six—or approximately 17%—still did.

Why do so few people now live and work on farms in the United States? There are two main reasons, both involving elasticities.

First, the income elasticity of demand for food is much less than 1—it is income-inelastic. As consumers grow richer, other things equal, spending on food rises less than income. As a result, as the U.S. economy has grown, the share of income it spends on food—and therefore the share of total income earned by farmers—has fallen.

Second, agriculture has been a technologically progressive sector for approximately 150 years in the United States, with steadily increasing yields over time. You might think that technological progress would be good for farmers. But competition among farmers means that technological progress leads to lower food prices. Meanwhile, the demand for food is price-inelastic, so falling prices of agricultural goods, other things equal, reduce the total revenue of farmers. That's right: progress in farming is good for consumers but bad for farmers.

The combination of these effects explains the relative decline of farming. Even if farming weren't such a technologically progressive sector, the low income elasticity of demand for food would ensure that the income of farmers grows more slowly than the economy as a whole. The combination of rapid technological progress in farming with price-inelastic demand for farm products reinforces this effect, further reducing the growth of farm income. In short, the U.S. farm sector has been a victim of success—the U.S. economy's success as a whole (which reduces the importance of spending on food) and its own success in increasing yields.

economics in action

Spending It

The U.S. Bureau of Labor Statistics carries out extensive surveys of how families spend their incomes. This is not just a matter of intellectual curiosity. Quite a few government programs involve some adjustment for changes in the cost of living; to estimate those changes, the government must know how people spend their money. But an additional payoff to these surveys is evidence on the income elasticity of demand for various goods.

What stands out from these studies? The classic result is that the income elasticity of demand for "food eaten at home" is considerably less than 1: as a family's income rises, the share of its income spent on food consumed at home falls. Correspondingly, the lower a family's income, the higher the share of income spent on food consumed at home. In poor countries, many families spend more than half their income on food consumed at home. While the income elasticity of "food eaten at home" is estimated at less than 0.5 in the United States, "food eaten away from home" (restaurant meals) is estimated to be much higher—close to 1. Families with higher incomes eat out more often and at fancier places. In 1950,

Judging from the activity at this busy McDonald's, incomes are rising in Jakarta, Indonesia.

about 19 percent of U.S. income was spent on food consumed at home, a number which has dropped to 8 percent today. But over the same time period, the share of U.S. income spent on food away from home has stayed constant at 5 percent. In fact, a sure sign of rising income levels in developing countries is the arrival of fast-food restaurants that cater to newly affluent customers. For example, McDonald's can now be found in Jakarta, Shanghai, and Bombay.

There is one clear example of an inferior good found in the surveys: rental housing. Families with higher income actually spend less on rent than families with lower income, because they are much more likely to own their own homes. And the category identified as "other housing"—which basically means second homes—is highly income-elastic. Only higher-income families can afford a vacation home at all, so "other housing" has an income elasticity of demand greater than 1.

> > > > > > > > > > > > > > > > > > >

>> CHECK YOUR UNDERSTANDING 5-3

1. After Chelsea's income increased from $12,000 to $18,000 a year, her purchases of CDs increased from 10 to 40 CDs a year. Calculate Chelsea's income elasticity of demand for CDs using the midpoint method.

2. Expensive restaurant meals are income-elastic goods for most people, including Sanjay. Suppose his income falls by 10% this year. What can you predict about the change in Sanjay's consumption of expensive restaurant meals?

3. As the price of margarine rises by 20%, a manufacturer of baked goods increases its quantity of butter demanded by 5%. Calculate the cross-price elasticity of demand between butter and margarine. Are butter and margarine substitutes or complements for this manufacturer?

Solutions appear at back of book.

The Price Elasticity of Supply

The Tellez plan to drive up the price of oil would have been much less effective if a higher price had induced large increases in output by countries that were not party to the agreement. For example, if American oil producers had responded to the higher price by significantly increasing their production, they could have pushed the price of oil back down. But they didn't—in fact, producers of oil who were not members of OPEC did not respond much to the higher price. This was another critical element in the success of the Tellez plan: a low responsiveness in output to a higher price of oil from other oil producers. To measure the response of producers to price changes, we need a measure parallel to the price elasticity of demand—the *price elasticity of supply*.

Measuring the Price Elasticity of Supply

The **price elasticity of supply** is a measure of the responsiveness of the quantity of a good supplied to the price of that good. It is the ratio of the percent change in the quantity supplied to the percent change in the price as we move along the supply curve.

The **price elasticity of supply** is defined the same way as the price elasticity of demand:

$$(5\text{-}9) \quad \text{Price elasticity of supply} = \frac{\%\ \text{change in quantity supplied}}{\%\ \text{change in price}}$$

The only difference is that this time we consider movements along the supply curve rather than movements along the demand curve.

Suppose that the price of tomatoes rises by 10%. If the quantity of tomatoes supplied also increases by 10% in response, the price elasticity of supply of tomatoes is 1 (10%/10%), and supply is unit-elastic. If the quantity supplied increases by 5 percent, the price elasticity of supply is 0.5 and supply is inelastic; if the quantity increases by 20%, the price elasticity of supply is 2 and supply is elastic.

As in the case of demand, the extreme values of the price elasticity of supply have a simple graphical representation.

Panel (a) of Figure 5-6 shows the supply of cell phone frequencies, the portion of the radio spectrum which is suitable for sending and receiving cell phone signals. Governments own the right to sell the use of this part of the radio spectrum to cell phone operators inside their borders. In Chapter 7, we will discuss how governments recently sold off their cell phone frequencies to the highest bidder in an auction. But

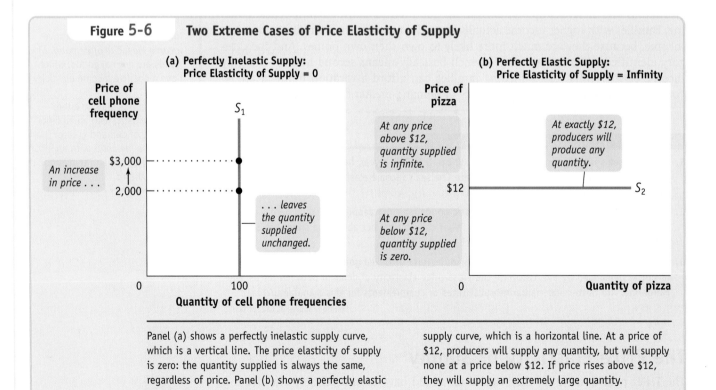

Figure 5-6 **Two Extreme Cases of Price Elasticity of Supply**

Panel (a) shows a perfectly inelastic supply curve, which is a vertical line. The price elasticity of supply is zero: the quantity supplied is always the same, regardless of price. Panel (b) shows a perfectly elastic supply curve, which is a horizontal line. At a price of $12, producers will supply any quantity, but will supply none at a price below $12. If price rises above $12, they will supply an extremely large quantity.

governments can't increase or decrease the number of cell phone frequencies that they have to offer—for technical reasons, the quantity of frequencies suitable for cell phone operation is a fixed quantity. So the supply curve for cell phone frequencies is a vertical line, which we have assumed is set at the quantity of 100 frequencies. As you move up and down that curve, the change in the quantity supplied by the government is zero, whatever the change in price. So panel (a) illustrates a case in which the price elasticity of supply is zero. This is a case of **perfectly inelastic supply.**

Panel (b) shows the supply curve for pizza. We suppose that it costs $12 to produce a pizza, including all opportunity costs such as the implicit cost of capital invested in pizza parlors. At any price below $12, it would be unprofitable to produce pizza and all the pizza parlors in America would go out of business. Alternatively, there are many producers who could operate pizza parlors if they were profitable. The ingredients—dough, tomatoes, cheese—are plentiful. And if necessary, more tomatoes could be grown, more milk could be produced to make mozzarella, and so on. So any price above $12 would elicit an unlimited quantity of pizzas supplied. The implied supply curve is therefore a horizontal line at $12. Since even a tiny increase in the price would lead to a huge increase in the quantity supplied, the price elasticity of supply would be more or less infinite. This is a case of **perfectly elastic supply**.

As our cell phone frequencies and pizza examples suggest, real-world instances of both perfectly inelastic and perfectly elastic supply are easy to find—much easier than their counterparts in demand.

What Factors Determine the Price Elasticity of Supply?

Our examples tell us the main determinant of the price elasticity of supply: the availability of inputs. In addition, as with the price elasticity of demand, time may also play a role in the price elasticity of supply. Here we briefly summarize the two factors.

The Availability of Inputs The price elasticity of supply tends to be large when inputs are easily available. It tends to be small when inputs are difficult to obtain.

Time The price elasticity of supply tends to become larger as producers have more time to respond to a price change. This means that the long-run price elasticity of supply is often higher than the short-run elasticity.

The price elasticity of pizza supply is very high because the inputs needed to expand the industry are readily available. The price elasticity of cell phone frequencies is zero because an essential input—the radio spectrum—cannot be increased at all.

Many industries are like pizza and have large price elasticities of supply: they can be readily expanded because they don't require any special or unique resources. On the other hand, the price elasticity of supply is usually substantially less than perfectly elastic for goods that involve limited natural resources: minerals like gold or copper, agricultural products like coffee that flourish only on certain types of land, renewable resources like ocean fish that can only be exploited up to a point without destroying the resource.

But given enough time, producers are often able to significantly change the amount they produce in response to a price change, even when production involves a limited natural resource. For example, consider again the effects of a surge in oil prices, but this time focus on the supply response. If oil prices were to rise to $40 per barrel and stay there for a number of years, there would almost certainly be a substantial increase in oil production. Oil companies would search for and exploit oil in inaccessible places, such as deep-sea waters; costly equipment would be put in place to squeeze still more oil out of already-exploited reservoirs; and so on. But Rome wasn't built in a day, and all these oil-production efforts can't take place in a month or even a year.

There is **perfectly inelastic supply** when the price elasticity of supply is zero, so that changes in the price of the good have no effect on the quantity supplied. A perfectly inelastic supply curve is a vertical line.

There is **perfectly elastic supply** when even a tiny increase or reduction in the price will lead to very large changes in the quantity supplied, so that the price elasticity of supply is infinite. A perfectly elastic supply curve is a horizontal line.

For this reason, economists often make a distinction between the short-run elasticity of supply, usually referring to a few weeks or months, and the long-run elasticity of supply, usually referring to several years. In most industries, the long-run elasticity of supply is larger than the short-run elasticity.

economics in action

European Farm Surpluses

One of the policies we analyzed in Chapter 4 was the imposition of a *price floor*, a lower limit on the price of a good. We saw that price floors are often used by governments to support the incomes of farmers but create large unwanted surpluses of farm produce. The most dramatic example of this is found in the European Union, where price floors have created a "butter mountain," a "wine lake," and so on.

Were European politicians unaware that their price floors would create huge surpluses? They probably knew that surpluses would arise, but underestimated the price elasticity of agricultural supply. In fact, when the agricultural price supports were put in place, many analysts thought they were unlikely to lead to big increases in production. After all, European countries are densely populated and there was little new land available for cultivation.

What the analysts failed to realize, however, was how much farm production could expand by adding other resources, especially fertilizer and pesticides. So although farm acreage didn't increase much, farm production did! ∎

< < < < < < < < < < < < < < < < < < <

>> CHECK YOUR UNDERSTANDING 5-4

1. Using the midpoint method, calculate the elasticity of supply for web-design services when the price per hour rises from $100 to $150 and the number of hours transacted increases from 300,000 hours to 500,000. Is supply elastic, inelastic, or unit-elastic?

2. True or false? If the demand for milk were to rise, then, in the long run, milk-drinkers would be better off if supply were elastic rather than inelastic.

3. True or false? Long-run price elasticities of supply are generally larger than short-run price elasticities of supply. Therefore the short-run supply curves are generally flatter than the long-run supply curves.

4. True or false? When supply is perfectly elastic, changes in demand have no effect on price.

Solutions appear at back of book.

An Elasticity Menagerie

We've just run through quite a few different elasticities. Keeping them all straight can be a problem. So in Table 5-3 we provide a summary of all the elasticities we have discussed and their implications.

Using Elasticity: The Incidence of an Excise Tax

In Chapter 4 we introduced the concept of the *incidence* of a tax—the measure of who really bears the burden of the tax. We saw in the case of an excise tax—a tax on sales or purchases of a product—that the incidence does not depend on who literally pays the money to the government. It doesn't matter, in other words, whether the tax is assessed on the sellers or the buyers. But we also noted that to determine who really pays the tax, we need the concept of elasticity.

We are now ready to see how the price elasticity of demand and the price elasticity of supply determine the incidence of an excise tax.

TABLE **5-3**

An Elasticity Menagerie

Name	Possible values	Significance
Price elasticity of demand = $\dfrac{\text{\% change in quantity demanded}}{\text{\% change in price}}$		(use absolute value)
Perfectly inelastic demand	0	Price has no effect on quantity demanded (vertical demand curve).
Inelastic demand	Between 0 and 1	A rise in the price increases total revenue.
Unit-elastic demand	Exactly 1	Changes in the price have no effect on total revenue.
Elastic demand	Greater than 1, less than ∞	A rise in the price reduces total revenue.
Perfectly elastic demand	∞	A rise in price causes quantity demanded to fall to 0. A fall in price leads to an infinite quantity demanded (horizontal demand curve).
Cross-price elasticity of demand = $\dfrac{\text{\% change in quantity demanded}}{\text{\% change in price } of\ another\ good}$		
Complements	Negative	Quantity demanded of one good falls when the price of another rises.
Substitutes	Positive	Quantity demanded of one good rises when the price of another rises.
Income elasticity of demand = $\dfrac{\text{\% change in quantity demanded}}{\text{\% change in income}}$		
Inferior good	Negative	Quantity demanded falls when income rises.
Normal good, income-inelastic	Positive, less than 1	Quantity demanded rises when income rises, but not as rapidly as income.
Normal good, income-elastic	Greater than 1	Quantity demanded rises when income rises, and more rapidly than income.
Price elasticity of supply = $\dfrac{\text{\% change in quantity supplied}}{\text{\% change in price}}$		
Perfectly inelastic supply	0	Price has no effect on quantity supplied— vertical supply curve.
	Greater than 0, less than ∞	Ordinary upward-sloping supply curve.
Perfectly elastic supply	∞	Any fall in price causes quantity supplied to fall to 0. Any rise in price elicits unlimited supply (horizontal supply curve).

When an Excise Tax Is Paid Mainly by Consumers

Figure 5-7 on page 128 shows an excise tax that falls mainly on consumers: an excise tax on gasoline, which we set at $1 per gallon. (There really is a federal excise tax on gasoline, though it is actually only about $0.50 per gallon in the United States.) According to Figure 5-7, in the absence of the tax, gasoline would sell for $1 per gallon.

Two key assumptions are reflected in the supply and demand curves. First, the price elasticity of demand for gasoline is very low, so the demand curve is steep. Second, the price elasticity of supply is very high, so the supply curve is flat.

We know from Chapter 4 that an excise tax drives a wedge, equal to the size of the tax, between the price paid by consumers and the price received by producers. This

Figure 5-7

An Excise Tax Paid Mainly by Consumers

The steep demand curve here reflects a low price elasticity of demand for gasoline. The flat supply curve reflects a high price elasticity of supply. The pre-tax price of a gallon of gas is $1.00, and a tax of $1.00 per gallon is imposed. The cost to consumers rises by $0.95 to $1.95, reflecting the fact that most of the burden of the tax falls on consumers. Only a small portion of the tax is borne by producers: the price they receive falls by only $0.05 to $0.95.

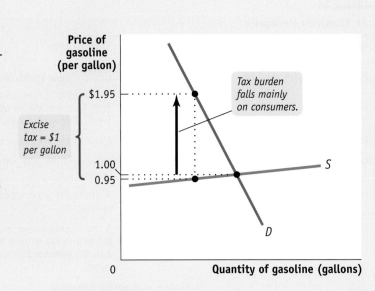

wedge drives the price paid by consumers up, and the price received by producers down. But as we can see from the figure, in this case those two effects are very unequal in size. The price received by producers falls only slightly, from $1.00 to $0.95, while the price paid by consumers rises by a lot, from $1.00 to $1.95.

This example illustrates a general principle: When the price elasticity of demand is low and the price elasticity of supply is high, the burden of an excise tax falls mainly on consumers. This is probably a good description of the main excise taxes actually collected in the United States today, such as taxes on cigarettes and alcoholic beverages.

When an Excise Tax Is Paid Mainly by Producers

Figure 5-8 shows an excise tax paid mainly by producers. In this case, we consider a $5.00 per day tax on downtown parking in a small city. In the market equilibrium, parking would cost $6.00 per day in the absence of the tax.

The price elasticity of supply is assumed to be very low because the lots used for parking have very few alternative uses. So the supply curve is steep. The price elasticity of demand, however, is high: consumers can easily switch to other parking spaces a few minutes' walk from downtown. So the demand curve is relatively flat.

The tax drives a wedge between the price paid by consumers and the price received by producers. This time, however, the price to consumers rises only slightly, from $6.00 to $6.50, but the price received by producers falls a lot, from $6.00 to $1.50. So a consumer bears only $0.50 of the $5 tax, with a producer bearing the remaining $4.50.

Again, this example illustrates a general principle: When the price elasticity of demand is high and the price elasticity of supply is low, the burden of an excise tax falls mainly on producers. A real-world example is the tax on purchases of existing houses. Over the past few years, house prices in many towns in desirable locations have gone up as well-off outsiders move in, a process called gentrification. Some of these towns have imposed taxes on house sales in an effort to extract money from the new arrivals. But this ignores the fact that the elasticity of demand for houses in a particular town is often high, because buyers can choose to move to other towns. Furthermore, the elasticity of supply is probably low, because most sellers must sell their houses due to things like job transfers to other locations. So taxes on home purchases are actually paid mainly by the sellers—not, as town officials imagine, by wealthy buyers.

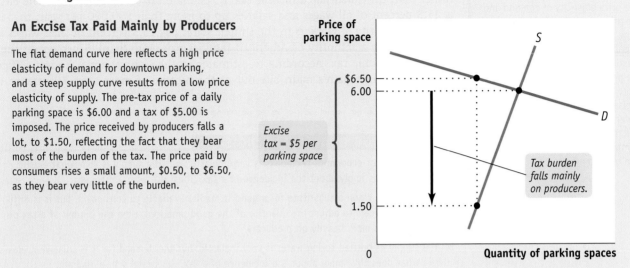

Figure 5-8

An Excise Tax Paid Mainly by Producers

The flat demand curve here reflects a high price elasticity of demand for downtown parking, and a steep supply curve results from a low price elasticity of supply. The pre-tax price of a daily parking space is $6.00 and a tax of $5.00 is imposed. The price received by producers falls a lot, to $1.50, reflecting the fact that they bear most of the burden of the tax. The price paid by consumers rises a small amount, $0.50, to $6.50, as they bear very little of the burden.

Putting It All Together

We've just seen that when the price elasticity of supply is high and the price elasticity of demand is low, an excise tax falls mainly on consumers; when the price elasticity of supply is low and the price elasticity of demand is high, an excise tax falls mainly on producers. This leads us to the general rule: When the price elasticity of demand is higher than the price elasticity of supply, an excise tax falls mainly on the producers. When the price elasticity of supply is higher than the price elasticity of demand, an excise tax falls mainly on consumers. So elasticity—not who literally pays the tax—determines the incidence of an excise tax.

economics in action

So Who Does Pay the FICA?

As we explained in Chapter 4, one of the main taxes levied by the federal government is the FICA, or payroll tax. Half of this tax is paid by workers, half by their employers. But we have learned that this tells us nothing about who *really* pays the tax, that is, about the incidence of the FICA.

So who does pay the FICA? Almost all economists who have studied the issue agree that the answer is that the FICA is a tax on workers, not on their employers.

The reason for this conclusion lies in a comparison of the price elasticities of the supply of labor by households and the demand for labor by firms. The evidence suggests that the price elasticity of demand for labor is quite high, at least 3. That is, an increase in average wages of 1 percent would lead to at least a 3 percent decline in the number of hours of work demanded. The price elasticity of supply of labor, however, is generally believed to be very low. The reason is that although a rise in the wage rate increases the incentive to work, it also makes people richer and more able to afford leisure. So the number of hours people are willing to work increases very little—if at all—when the wage per hour goes up.

Our analysis already tells us that when the price elasticity of demand is much higher than the price elasticity of supply, the burden of an excise tax falls mainly on the suppliers. So the FICA falls mainly on the suppliers of labor, that is, workers—even though on paper half the tax is paid by employers.

This conclusion tells us something important about our tax system: that the FICA, rather than the much-hated income tax, is the main tax on most families. The FICA is 15.3 percent of all wages and salaries up to more than $80,000 per year; that is, the great majority of workers in the United States pay 15.3 percent of their wages in FICA. But only a minority of American families pay more than 15 percent of their income in income tax. According to estimates by the Congressional Budget Office, the FICA is Uncle Sam's main bite out of the income of more than 70 percent of families.

‹ ‹ ‹ ‹ ‹ ‹ ‹ ‹ ‹ ‹ ‹ ‹ ‹ ‹ ‹ ‹ ‹ ‹ ‹

▶▶CHECK YOUR UNDERSTANDING 5-5

1. The demand for economics textbooks is very inelastic, but the supply is somewhat elastic. What does this imply about the incidence of a tax? Illustrate with a diagram.

2. True or false? When a substitute for a good is readily available to consumers, but it is difficult for producers to adjust the quantity of the good produced, then the burden of a tax on the good falls more heavily on producers.

3. The supply of bottled spring water is very inelastic, but the demand for it is somewhat elastic. What does this imply about the incidence of a tax? Illustrate with a diagram.

4. True or false? Other things equal, consumers would prefer to face a less elastic supply curve when a tax is imposed.

Solutions appear at back of book.

● A LOOK AHEAD ●

The concept of elasticity deepens our understanding of supply and demand, among other things helping us predict not only in which direction prices will move but also by how much. For example, we now know that supply and demand elasticities determine how the burden of a tax will be divided between producers and consumers. And, to come back to an example from very early on in this chapter, the concept of elasticity was just what Luis Tellez needed to be able to engineer a reduction in output by oil-exporting countries that led to an increase in oil prices and an increase in their oil revenues.

But we don't yet have a way to translate the changes in prices that result from a tax, or from any other change in the situation, into a measure of gains or losses to individuals. In the next chapter, we show how to make that translation—how to use the supply and demand curves to calculate gains and losses to producers and consumers.

SUMMARY

1. Many economic questions depend on the size of consumer or producer response to changes in prices or other variables. *Elasticity* is a general measure of responsiveness that can be used to answer such questions.

2. The **price elasticity of demand**—the percent change in the quantity demanded divided by the percent change in the price (dropping the minus sign)—is a measure of the responsiveness of the quantity demanded to changes in prices. In practical calculations, it is usually best to use the **midpoint method**, which calculates percent changes in prices and quantities based on the average of starting and final values.

3. The responsiveness of the quantity demanded to price can range from **perfectly inelastic demand**, where the quantity demanded is unaffected by the price, to **perfectly elastic demand**, where there is a unique price at which consumers will buy as much or as little as they are offered. When demand is perfectly inelastic, the demand curve is a vertical line; when it is perfectly elastic, the demand curve is a horizontal line.

4. The price elasticity of demand is classified according to whether it is more or less than 1. If it is greater than 1, demand is **elastic**; if it is less than 1, demand is **inelastic**; if it is exactly 1, demand is **unit-elastic**. This classification

determines how **total revenue**, the total value of sales, changes when the price changes. If demand is elastic, total revenue falls when the price increases and rises when the price decreases. If demand is inelastic, total revenue rises when the price increases and falls when the price decreases.

5. The price elasticity of demand depends on whether there are close substitutes for the good in question, whether the good is necessary, and the length of time that has elapsed since the price change.

6. The **cross-price elasticity of demand** measures the effect of a change in one good's price on the quantity of another good demanded. The cross-price elasticity of demand can be positive, in which case the goods are substitutes, or negative, in which case they are complements.

7. The **income elasticity of demand** is the percent change in the quantity of a good demanded when a consumer's income changes divided by the percent change in income. The income elasticity of demand indicates how intensely the demand for a good responds to changes in income. It can be negative; in that case the good is an inferior good. Goods with positive income elasticities of demand are normal goods. If the income elasticity is greater than 1, a good is **income-elastic**; if it is positive and less than 1, the good is **income-inelastic**.

8. The **price elasticity of supply** is the percent change in the quantity of a good supplied when the price changes divided by the percent change in the price. If the quantity supplied does not change at all, we have an instance of **perfectly inelastic supply**; the supply curve is a vertical line. If the quantity supplied is zero below some price but unlimited above that price, we have an instance of **perfectly elastic supply**; the supply curve is a horizontal line.

9. The price elasticity of supply depends on the availability of resources to expand production and on time. It is higher when inputs are easily available and the longer the time elapsed since the price change.

10. The incidence of an excise tax depends on the price elasticities of supply and demand. If the price elasticity of demand is higher than the price elasticity of supply, the tax falls mainly on producers; if the price elasticity of supply is higher than the price elasticity of demand, the tax falls mainly on consumers.

KEY TERMS

Price elasticity of demand, p. 111
Midpoint method, p. 112
Perfectly inelastic demand, p. 114
Perfectly elastic demand, p. 114
Elastic demand, p. 114

Inelastic demand, p. 114
Unit-elastic demand, p. 114
Total revenue, p. 116
Cross-price elasticity of demand, p. 121
Income elasticity of demand, p. 122

Income-elastic demand, p. 122
Income-inelastic demand, p. 122
Price elasticity of supply, p. 124
Perfectly inelastic supply, p. 125
Perfectly elastic supply, p. 125

PROBLEMS

1. TheNile.com, the online bookseller, wants to increase its total revenue. Currently, every book it sells is priced at $10.50. One suggested strategy is to offer a discount that lowers the price of a book to $9.50, a 10% reduction in price using the midpoint method. TheNile.com knows that its customers can be divided into two distinct groups according to their likely responses to the discount. The accompanying table shows how the two groups respond to the discount.

	Group A (sales per week)	Group B (sales per week)
Volume of sales before the 10% discount	1.55 million	1.50 million
Volume of sales after the 10% discount	1.65 million	1.70 million

a. Using the midpoint method, calculate the price elasticities of demand for Group A and Group B.

b. Explain how the discount will affect total revenue from each group.

c. Suppose TheNile.com knows which group each customer belongs to when he or she logs on and can choose whether or not to offer the 10% discount. If TheNile.com wants to increase its total revenue, should discounts be offered to Group A or to Group B, to neither group, or to both groups?

2. Do you think the price elasticity of demand for Ford sport-utility vehicles (SUVs) will increase, decrease, or remain the same when each of the following events occurs? Explain your answer.

a. Other car manufacturers, such as General Motors, decide to make and sell SUVs.

b. SUVs produced in foreign countries are banned from the American market.

c. Due to ad campaigns, Americans believe that SUVs are much safer than ordinary passenger cars.

d. The time period over which you measure the elasticity lengthens. During that longer time, new models such as four-wheel-drive cargo vans appear.

3. U.S. winter wheat production increased dramatically in 1999 after a bumper harvest. The supply curve shifted rightward; as a result, the price decreased and the quantity demanded increased (a movement along the demand curve). The accompanying table describes what happened to prices and the quantity demanded of wheat.

	1998	1999
Quantity demanded (bushels)	1.74 billion	1.9 billion
Average price (per bushel)	$3.70	$2.72

a. Using the midpoint method, calculate the price elasticity of demand for winter wheat.

b. What is the total revenue for U.S. wheat farmers in 1998 and 1999?

c. Did the bumper harvest increase or decrease the incomes of American wheat farmers? How could you have predicted this from your answer to part a?

4. The accompanying table gives part of the supply schedule for personal computers in the United States.

Price of computer	Quantity of computers supplied (thousands)
$1,100	12,000
900	8,000

a. Calculate the price elasticity of supply when the price increases from $900 to $1,100 using the midpoint method.

b. Suppose firms produce 1,000 more computers at any given price due to improved technology. As price increases from $900 to $1,100, is the price elasticity of demand now greater than, less than, or the same as it was in part a?

c. Suppose a longer time period under consideration means that the quantity supplied at any given price is 20% higher than the figures given in the table. As price increases from $900 to $1,100, is the price elasticity of demand now greater than, less than, or the same as it was in part a?

5. The accompanying table lists the cross-price elasticities of demand for several goods, where the percentage price change is measured for the first good of the pair, and the percentage quantity change is measured for the second good.

Good	Cross-price elasticities of demand
Air-conditioning units and kilowatts of electricity	−0.34
Coke and Pepsi	+0.63
High-fuel-consuming sport-utility vehicles (SUVs) and gasoline	−0.28
McDonald's burgers and Burger King burgers	+0.82
Butter and margarine	+1.54

a. Explain the sign of each of the cross-price elasticities. What does it imply about the relationship between the two goods in question?

b. Compare the absolute values of the cross-price elasticities and explain their magnitudes. For example, why is the cross-price elasticity of McDonald's and Burger King less than the cross-elasticity of butter and margarine?

c. Use the information in the table to calculate how a 5% increase in the price of Pepsi affects the quantity of Coke demanded.

d. Use the information in the table to calculate how a 10% decrease in the price of gasoline affects the quantity of SUVs demanded.

6. What can you conclude about the price elasticity of demand in each of the following statements?

a. "The pizza delivery business in this town is very competitive. I'd lose half my customers if I raised the price by as little as 10%."

b. "I owned both of the two Jerry Garcia autographed lithographs in existence. I sold one on Ebay for a high price. But when I sold the second one, the price dropped a lot."

c. "My economics professor has chosen to use the Krugman/Wells textbook for this class. I have no choice but to buy this book."

d. "I always spend exactly $10 per week on coffee."

7. Take a linear demand curve like that shown in Figure 5-5, where the range of prices for which demand is elastic and inelastic is labeled. In each of the following scenarios, the supply curve shifts. Show along which portion of the demand curve (that is, the elastic or the inelastic portion) the supply curve must have shifted in order to generate the event described. In each case, show on the diagram the sales effect and the price effect.

a. Recent attempts by the Colombian army to stop the flow of illegal drugs into the United States have actually benefited drug dealers.

b. New construction increased the number of seats in the football stadium and resulted in greater total revenue from box-office ticket sales.

c. A fall in input prices has led to higher output of Porsches. But total revenue for the Porsche Company has declined as a result.

8. The accompanying table shows the price and yearly quantity sold of souvenir T-shirts in the town of Crystal Lake according to the average income of the tourists visiting.

Price of T-shirt	Quantity of T-shirts demanded when average tourist income is $20,000	Quantity of T-shirts demanded when average tourist income is $30,000
$4	3,000	5,000
5	2,400	4,200
6	1,600	3,000
7	800	1,800

a. Using the midpoint method, calculate the price elasticity of demand when the price of a T-shirt rises from $5 to $6 when the average tourist income is $20,000. Also calculate it when the average tourist income is $30,000.

b. Using the midpoint method, calculate the income elasticity of demand when the average tourist income increases from $20,000 to $30,000 when the price of a T-shirt is $4. Also calculate it when the price is $7.

9. A recent study determined the following elasticities for Volkswagen Beetles:

Price elasticity of demand = 2
Income elasticity of demand = 1.5

Based on this information, are the following statements true or false? Explain your reasoning.

a. A 10% increase in the price of a Beetle will reduce the quantity demanded by 20%.

b. An increase in consumer income will increase the price and quantity sold of Beetles. Since price elasticity of demand is greater than 1, total revenue will go down.

10. In each of the following cases, do you think the price elasticity of supply is (i) perfectly elastic; (ii) perfectly inelastic; (iii) elastic, but not perfectly elastic; or (iv) inelastic, but not perfectly inelastic? Explain using a diagram.

a. An increase in demand this summer for luxury cruises leads to a huge jump in the sales price of a cabin on the Queen Mary.

b. The price of a kilowatt of electricity is the same during periods of high electricity demand as during periods of low electricity demand.

c. Fewer people want to fly during February than during any other month. The airlines cancel about 10% of their flights as ticket prices fall about 20% during this month.

d. Owners of vacation homes in Maine rent them out during the summer. Due to the soft economy this year, a 30% decline in the rental rate leads more than half of homeowners to occupy their vacation homes themselves during the summer.

11. Use an elasticity concept to explain each of the following observations.

a. During economic boom times, the number of new personal care businesses, such as gyms and tanning salons, is

proportionately greater than the number of other new businesses, such as grocery stores.

b. Cement is the primary building material in Mexico. After new technology makes cement cheaper to produce, the supply curve for the Mexican cement industry becomes flatter.

c. Some goods that were once considered luxuries, like a telephone, are now considered virtual necessities. As a result, the demand curve for telephone services has become steeper over time.

d. Consumers in a less developed country like Guatemala spend proportionately more of their income on equipment for producing things at home, like sewing machines, than consumers in a more developed country like Canada.

12. Taiwan is a major world supplier of semiconductor chips. A recent earthquake severely damaged the production facilities of Taiwanese chip-producing companies, sharply reducing the amount of chips they could produce.

a. Assume that the total revenue of a typical non-Taiwanese chip manufacturer rises due to these events. In terms of an elasticity, what must be true for this to happen? Illustrate the change in total revenue with a diagram, indicating the price effect and the sales effect of the Taiwan earthquake on this company's total revenue.

b. Now assume that the total revenue of a typical non-Taiwanese chip manufacturer falls due to these events. In terms of an elasticity, what must be true for this to happen? Illustrate the change in total revenue with a diagram, indicating the price effect and the sales effect of the Taiwan earthquake on this company's total revenue.

13. There is a debate about whether sterile hypodermic needles should be passed out free of charge in cities with high drug use. Proponents argue that doing so will reduce the incidence of diseases, such as HIV/AIDS, that are often spread by needle sharing among drug users. Opponents believe that doing so will encourage more drug use by reducing the risks of this behavior. As an economist asked to assess the policy, you must know the following: (i) how responsive the spread of diseases like HIV/AIDS is to the price of sterile needles; and (ii) how responsive drug use is to the price of sterile needles. Assuming that you know these two things, use the concepts of price elasticity of demand for sterile needles and the cross-price elasticity between drugs and sterile needles to answer the following questions.

a. In what circumstances do you believe this is a beneficial policy?

b. In what circumstances do you believe this is a bad policy?

14. Suppose the government imposes an excise tax of $1 for every gallon of gas sold. Before the tax, the price of a gallon of gas is $2. Consider the following four after-tax scenarios. In each case, (i) use an elasticity concept to explain what must be true for this scenario to arise; (ii) determine who bears relatively more of the burden of the tax, producers or consumers; and (iii) illustrate your answer with a diagram.

a. The price of gasoline paid by consumers rises to $3 per gallon. Assume that the demand curve is downward sloping.

b. The price paid by consumers remains at $2 per gallon after the tax is imposed. Assume that the supply curve is upward sloping.

c. The price of gasoline paid by consumers rises to $2.75.

d. The price of gasoline paid by consumers rises to $2.25.

15. Describe how the following events will affect the incidence of taxation—that is, after the event, will the tax fall more heavily on consumers or producers in comparison to before the event? Use the concept of elasticity to explain your answer.

a. Sales of gasoline are taxed. Ethanol, a substitute for gasoline, becomes widely available.

b. Sales of electricity to California residents are taxed. Regulations are introduced that make it much more difficult for California utility companies to divert supplies of electricity from the California market to markets in neighboring states like Nevada.

c. Sales of electricity to California residents are taxed. Regulations are introduced that make it much easier for California utility companies to divert supplies of electricity from the California market to markets in neighboring states like Nevada.

d. The sale of municipally provided water is taxed. Legislation is introduced that forbids the use of private sources of water such as wells and the diversion of rivers.

16. In devising taxes, there is often a debate about (i) who bears the burden of the tax and (ii) whether the tax achieves some desirable social goal, such as discouraging undesirable behavior by making it more expensive. In the case of cigarettes, smokers tend to be highly addicted and have lower income than the average nonsmoker. Taxes on cigarettes have historically had the effect of raising the price to consumers almost one for one with the size of the tax.

a. Why might such a tax be undesirable when considering issues of tax equity—that is, whether or not more of the tax burden falls more heavily on lower-income people? How do the elasticities of supply and demand for cigarettes affect the equity of cigarette taxation?

b. How do the elasticities of supply and demand for cigarettes affect the effectiveness of the tax in discouraging smoking?

c. In light of your answers to parts a and b and the historical response of price to the tax, what trade-offs must policy makers make when considering a cigarette tax?

17. Worldwide, the average coffee grower has increased the amount of acreage under cultivation over the past few years. The result has been that the average coffee plantation produces significantly more coffee than it did 10 to 20 years ago. Unfortunately for the growers, however, this has also been a period in which their average revenues have plunged. In terms of an elasticity, what must be true for these events to have occurred? Illustrate these events with a diagram, indicating the sales effect and the price effect that gave rise to these events.

>web... To continue your study and review of concepts in this chapter, please visit the Krugman/Wells website for quizzes, animated graph tutorials, web links to helpful resources, and more.

www.worthpublishers.com/krugmanwells

>>Consumer and Producer Surplus

chapter 6

MAKING GAINS BY THE BOOK

There is a lively market in second-hand college textbooks. At the end of each term, some students who took a course decide that the money they can get by selling their used books is worth more to them than keeping the books. And some students who are taking the course next term prefer to buy a somewhat battered but inexpensive used textbook rather than pay the full price for a new one.

Textbook publishers and authors are not happy about these transactions, because they cut into sales of new books. But both the students who sell used books and those who buy them clearly benefit from the existence of the market. That is why many college bookstores facilitate their trade, buying used textbooks and selling them alongside the new books.

But can we put a number on what used textbook buyers and sellers gain from these transactions? Can we answer the question, "*How much* do the buyers and sellers of textbooks gain from the existence of the used-book market?"

Yes, we can. In this chapter we will see how to measure benefits, such as those to buyers of used textbooks, from being able to purchase a good—known as *consumer surplus*. And we will see that there is a corresponding measure, *producer surplus*, of the benefits sellers receive from being able to sell a good.

The concepts of consumer surplus and producer surplus are extremely useful for analyzing a wide variety of economic issues.

How much am I willing to pay for that used textbook?

They let us calculate how much benefit producers and consumers receive from the existence of a market. They also allow us to calculate how the welfare of consumers and producers is affected by changes in market

What you will learn in this chapter:

➤ The meaning of **consumer surplus** and its relationship to the demand curve

➤ The meaning of **producer surplus** and its relationship to the supply curve

➤ The meaning and importance of **total surplus** and how it can be used both to measure the gains from trade and to evaluate the efficiency of a market

➤ How to use changes in total surplus to measure the deadweight loss of taxes

prices. Such calculations play a crucial role in evaluating many economic policies.

What information do we need to calculate consumer and producer surplus? The answer, surprisingly, is that all we need are the demand and supply curves for a good. That is, the supply and demand model isn't just a model of how a market works—it's also a model of how much consumers and producers gain from participating in that market. So our first step will be to learn how consumer and producer surplus can be derived from the demand and supply curves. We will then see how these concepts can be applied to actual economic issues.

Consumer Surplus and the Demand Curve

The market in used textbooks is not a big business in terms of dollars and cents. But it is a convenient starting point for developing the concepts of consumer and producer surplus.

So let's look at the market for used textbooks, starting with the buyers. The key point, as we'll see in a minute, is that the demand curve is derived from their preferences—and that those same preferences also determine how much they gain from the opportunity to buy used books.

Willingness to Pay and the Demand Curve

A consumer's **willingness to pay** for a good is the maximum price at which he or she would buy that good.

A used book is not as good as a new book—it will be battered and coffee-stained, may include someone else's highlighting, and may not be completely up to date. How much this bothers you depends on your own preferences. Some potential buyers would prefer to buy the used book if it is only slightly cheaper, while others would buy the used book only if it is considerably cheaper than a new book. Let's define a potential buyer's **willingness to pay** as the maximum price at which he or she would buy a good, in this case a used textbook. An individual won't buy the book if it costs more than this amount but is eager to do so if it costs less. If the price is just equal to an individual's willingness to pay, he or she is indifferent between buying and not buying.

The table in Figure 6-1 shows five potential buyers of a used book that costs $100 new, listed in order of their willingness to pay. At one extreme is Aleisha, who will buy a second-hand book even if the price is as high as $59. Brad is less willing to have a used book and will buy one only if the price is $45 or less. Claudia is willing to pay only $35, Darren only $25. And Edwina, who really doesn't like the idea of a used book, will buy one only if it costs no more than $10.

How many of these five students will actually buy a used book? It depends on the price. If the price of a used book is $55, only Aleisha buys one; if the price is $40, Aleisha and Brad both buy used books, and so on. So the information in the table on willingness to pay also defines the *demand schedule* for used textbooks.

As we saw in Chapter 3, we can use this demand schedule to derive the market demand curve shown in Figure 6-1. Because we are considering only a small number of consumers, this curve doesn't look like the smooth demand curves of earlier chapters, where markets contained hundreds or thousands of consumers. This demand curve is step-shaped, with alternating horizontal and vertical segments. Each horizontal segment—each step—corresponds to one potential buyer's willingness to pay. However, we'll see shortly that for the analysis of consumer surplus it doesn't matter whether the demand curve is stepped, as in this figure, or whether there are many consumers, making the curve smooth.

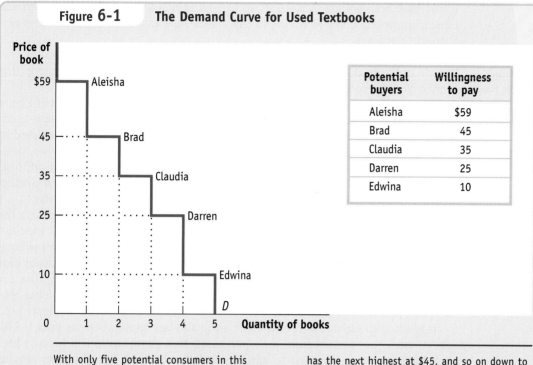

Figure 6-1   **The Demand Curve for Used Textbooks**

Potential buyers	Willingness to pay
Aleisha	$59
Brad	45
Claudia	35
Darren	25
Edwina	10

With only five potential consumers in this market, the demand curve is step-shaped. Each step represents one consumer, and its height indicates that consumer's willingness to pay, the maximum price at which each student will buy a used textbook, as indicated in the table. Aleisha has the highest willingness to pay at $59, Brad has the next highest at $45, and so on down to Edwina with the lowest at $10. At a price of $59 the quantity demanded is one (Aleisha); at a price of $45 the quantity demanded is two (Aleisha and Brad), and so on until you reach a price of $10 at which all five students are willing to purchase a book.

Willingness to Pay and Consumer Surplus

Suppose that the campus bookstore makes used textbooks available at a price of $30. In that case Aleisha, Brad, and Claudia will buy books. Do they gain from their purchases, and if so, how much?

The answer, shown in Table 6-1, is that each student who purchases a book does achieve a net gain but that the amount of the gain differs among students.

Aleisha would have been willing to pay $59, so her net gain is $59 − $30 = $29. Brad would have been willing to pay $45, so his net gain is $45 − $30 = $15. Claudia

TABLE 6-1

Consumer Surplus When the Price of a Used Textbook Is $30

Potential buyer	Willingness to pay	Price paid	Individual consumer surplus = willingness to pay − price paid
Aleisha	$59	$30	$29
Brad	45	30	15
Claudia	35	30	5
Darren	25	—	—
Edwina	10	—	—

Total consumer surplus: $49

would have been willing to pay $35, so her net gain is $35 − $30 = $5. Darren and Edwina, however, won't be willing to buy a used book at a price of $30, so they neither gain nor lose.

The net gain that a buyer achieves from the purchase of a good is called that buyer's **individual consumer surplus**. What we learn from this example is that every buyer of a good achieves some individual consumer surplus.

The sum of the individual consumer surpluses achieved by all the buyers of a good is known as the **total consumer surplus** achieved in the market. In Table 6-1, the total consumer surplus is the sum of the individual consumer surpluses achieved by Aleisha, Brad, and Claudia: $29 + $15 + $5 = $49.

Economists often use the term **consumer surplus** to refer to both individual and total consumer surplus. We will follow this practice; it will always be clear in context whether we are referring to the consumer surplus achieved by an individual or by all buyers.

Total consumer surplus can be represented graphically. Figure 6-2 reproduces the demand curve from Figure 6-1. Each step in that demand curve is one book wide and represents one consumer. For example, the height of Aleisha's step is $59, her willingness to pay. This step forms the top of a rectangle, with $30—the price she actually pays for a book—forming the bottom. The area of Aleisha's rectangle, ($59 − $30) × 1 = $29, is her consumer surplus from purchasing a book at $30. So the individual consumer surplus Aleisha gains is the *area of the dark blue rectangle* shown in Figure 6-2.

In addition to Aleisha, Brad and Claudia will also buy books when the price is $30. Like Aleisha, they benefit from their purchases, though not as much, because they each have a lower willingness to pay. Figure 6-2 also shows the consumer surplus gained by Brad and Claudia; again, this can be measured by the areas of the appropriate rectangles. Darren and Edwina, because they do not buy books at a price of $30, receive no consumer surplus.

The total consumer surplus achieved in this market is just the sum of the individual consumer surpluses received by Aleisha, Brad, and Claudia. So total consumer surplus is equal to the combined area of the three rectangles—the entire shaded area in Figure 6-2. Another way to say this is that total consumer surplus is equal to the area that is under the demand curve but above the price.

[sidebar]

... the net
... n the purchase of a good. It is equ... the difference between the buyer's willingness to pay and the price paid.

Total consumer surplus is the sum of the individual consumer surpluses of all the buyers of a good.

The term **consumer surplus** is often used to refer to both individual and to total consumer surplus.

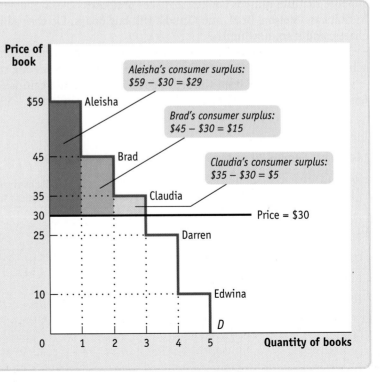

Figure 6-2

Consumer Surplus in the Used-Textbook Market

At a market price of $30, Aleisha, Brad, and Claudia each buy a book but Darren and Edwina do not. Aleisha, Brad, and Claudia get individual consumer surpluses equal to the difference between their willingness to pay and the market price, illustrated by the areas of the shaded rectangles. Both Darren and Edwina have a willingness to pay less than $30, so they are unwilling to buy a book in this market; they receive zero consumer surplus. The total consumer surplus is given by the entire shaded area—the sum of the individual consumer surpluses of Aleisha, Brad, and Claudia—equal to $29 + $15 + $5 = $49.

Aleisha's consumer surplus: $59 − $30 = $29

Brad's consumer surplus: $45 − $30 = $15

Claudia's consumer surplus: $35 − $30 = $5

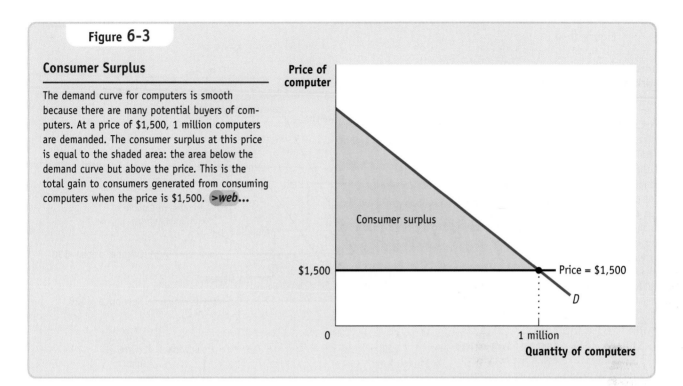

Figure 6-3

Consumer Surplus

The demand curve for computers is smooth because there are many potential buyers of computers. At a price of $1,500, 1 million computers are demanded. The consumer surplus at this price is equal to the shaded area: the area below the demand curve but above the price. This is the total gain to consumers generated from consuming computers when the price is $1,500. **>web...**

(Graph labels: Price of computer; Consumer surplus; $1,500; Price = $1,500; D; 0; 1 million; Quantity of computers)

This illustrates the following general principle: *The total consumer surplus generated by purchases of a good at a given price is equal to the area below the demand curve but above that price.* The same principle applies regardless of the number of consumers.

When we consider large markets, this graphical representation becomes extremely helpful. Consider, for example, the sales of personal computers to millions of potential buyers. Each potential buyer has a maximum price that he or she is willing to pay. With so many potential buyers, the demand curve will be smooth, like the one shown in Figure 6-3.

Suppose that at a price of $1,500, a total of 1 million computers are purchased. How much do consumers gain from being able to buy those 1 million computers? We could answer that question by calculating the consumer surplus of each individual buyer and then adding these numbers up to arrive at a total. But it is much easier just to look at Figure 6-3 and use the fact that the total consumer surplus is equal to the shaded area. As in our original example, consumer surplus is equal to the area below the demand curve but above the price.

How Changing Prices Affect Consumer Surplus

It is often important to know how much consumer surplus *changes* when the price changes. For example, we may want to know how much consumers are hurt if a frost in Florida drives up orange prices or how much consumers gain if the introduction of fish farming makes salmon less expensive. The same approach we have used to derive consumer surplus can be used to answer questions about how changes in prices affect consumers.

Let's return to the example of the market for used textbooks. Suppose that the bookstore decided to sell used textbooks for $20 instead of $30. How much would this increase consumer surplus?

The answer is illustrated in Figure 6-4 on page 140. As shown in the figure, there are two parts to the increase in consumer surplus. The first part, shaded dark blue, is the gain of those who would have bought books even at the higher price. Each of the students who would have bought books at $30—Aleisha, Brad, and Claudia—pays $10 less, and therefore each gains $10 in consumer surplus from the fall in price to

Figure 6-4

Consumer Surplus and a Fall in the Market Price of Used Textbooks

There are two parts to the increase in consumer surplus generated by a fall in market price from $30 to $20. The first is given by the dark blue rectangle: each person who would have bought at the original price of $30—Aleisha, Brad, and Claudia—receives an increase in consumer surplus equal to the total fall in price, $10. So the area of the dark blue rectangle corresponds to an amount equal to 3 × $10 = $30. The second part is given by the light blue rectangle: the increase in consumer surplus for those who would *not* have bought at the original price of $30 but who buy at the new price of $20—namely, Darren. Darren's willingness to pay is $25, so he now receives a consumer surplus of $5. The total increase in consumer surplus is 3 × $10 + $5 = $35, represented by the sum of the shaded areas. Likewise, a rise in market price from $20 to $30 would decrease consumer surplus by an amount equal to the sum of the shaded areas.

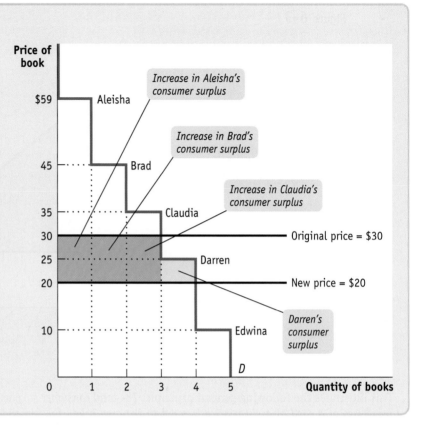

$20. So the dark blue area represents the $30 increase in consumer surplus to those three buyers. The second part, shaded light blue, is the gain of those who would not have bought a book at $30 but are willing to pay more than $20. In this case that means Darren, who would not have bought a book at $30 but does buy one at $20. He gains $5—the difference between the new price of $20 and his willingness to pay, $25. So the light blue area represents a further $5 gain in consumer surplus. The total increase in consumer surplus is the sum of the shaded areas, $35. Likewise, a rise in market price from $20 to $30 would decrease consumer surplus by an amount equal to the sum of the shaded areas.

Figure 6-4 illustrates that when the price of a good falls, the area under the demand curve but above the price—which we have seen is equal to the total consumer surplus—increases. Figure 6-5 shows the same result for the case of a smooth demand curve, the demand for personal computers. Here we assume that the price of computers falls from $5,000 to $1,500, leading to an increase in the quantity demanded from 200,000 to 1 million units. As in the used-textbook example, we divide the gain in consumer surplus into two parts. The dark blue rectangle in Figure 6-5 corresponds to the dark blue area in Figure 6-4: it is the gain to the 200,000 people who would have bought computers even at the higher price of $5,000. As a result of the price fall, each receives additional surplus of $3,500. The light blue triangle in Figure 6-5 corresponds to the light blue area in Figure 6-4: it is the gain to people who would not have bought the good at the higher price but are willing to do so at a price of $1,500. For example, the light blue triangle includes the gain to someone who would have been willing to pay $2,000 for a computer and therefore gains $500 in consumer surplus when he or she is able to buy a computer for only $1,500. As before, the total gain in consumer surplus is the sum of the shaded areas, the increase in the area under the demand curve but above the market price.

What would happen if the price of a good were to rise instead of fall? We would do the same analysis in reverse. Suppose, for example, that for some reason the price

Figure 6-5

A Fall in the Market Price Increases Consumer Surplus

A fall in the market price of a computer from $5,000 to $1,500 leads to an increase in the quantity demanded and an increase in consumer surplus. The change in the total consumer surplus is given by the sum of the shaded areas: the total area below the demand curve but between the old and new prices. Here, the dark blue area represents the increase in consumer surplus for the 200,000 consumers who would have bought a computer at the original price of $5,000; they each receive an increase in consumer surplus of $3,500. The light blue area represents the increase in consumer surplus for those willing to buy at a price equal to or greater than $1,500 but less than $5,000. Similarly, a rise in the market price of a computer from $1,500 to $5,000 generates a decrease in consumer surplus equal to the sum of the two shaded areas. **>web...**

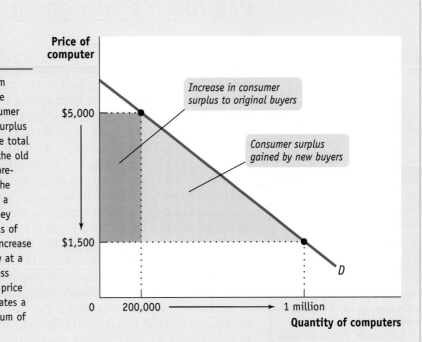

of computers rises from $1,500 to $5,000. This would lead to a fall in consumer surplus, equal to the shaded area in Figure 6-5. This loss consists of two parts. The dark blue rectangle represents the losses to consumers who would still buy a computer, even at a price of $5,000. The light blue triangle represents the loss to consumers who decide not to buy a computer at the higher price.

FOR INQUIRING MINDS

I WANT A NEW DRUG . . .

The pharmaceutical industry is constantly introducing new prescription drugs. Some of these drugs do the same thing as other, existing drugs, but a bit better—for example, pretty good allergy medicines have been around for years, but newer versions that are somewhat more effective or have fewer side effects keep emerging. Other drugs do something that was previously considered impossible—a famous example from the late 1990s was Propecia, the pill that slows and in some cases reverses hair loss.

Such innovations raise a difficult question for the people who are supposed to measure economic growth: how do you calculate the contribution of a new product to the economy?

You might at first say that it's just a matter of dollars and cents. But that could be wrong, in either direction. A new painkiller that is just slightly better than aspirin might have huge sales, because it would take over the painkiller market—but it wouldn't really add much to

consumer welfare. On the other hand, the benefits of a drug that cures the previously incurable might be much larger than the money actually spent on it—after all, people *would have been willing* to pay much more.

Consider, for example, the benefits of antibiotics. When penicillin was introduced in 1941, it transformed the treatment of infectious disease; illnesses that had previously crippled or killed millions of people were suddenly easy to treat. Presumably most people would be willing to pay a lot not to go back to the days before penicillin. Yet the average American spends only a few dollars per year on antibiotics.

The right way to measure the gains from a new drug—or any new product—is therefore to try to figure out what people would have been willing to pay for the good, and subtract what they actually pay. In other words, the gains from a new drug should be measured by calculating consumer surplus!

economics in action

When Money Isn't Enough

The key insight we get from the concept of consumer surplus is that purchases yield a net benefit to the consumer, because the consumer pays a price that is less than the amount he or she would have been willing to pay for the good. Another way to say this is that the right to buy a good at the going price is a valuable thing in itself.

Most of the time we don't think about the value associated with the right to buy a good. In a market economy, we take it for granted that we can buy whatever we want, as long as we are willing to pay the price. But that hasn't always been true. For example, during World War II many goods were rationed in order to make resources available for the war effort. To buy sugar, meat, coffee, gasoline, and many other goods, you not only had to pay cash; you also had to present stamps or coupons from special books that were issued to each family by the government. These pieces of paper, which represented nothing but the right to buy goods at the market price, quickly became valuable commodities in themselves. As a result, black markets in meat stamps and gasoline coupons sprang into existence. Moreover, criminals began stealing coupons and even counterfeiting stamps.

The funny thing was that even if you had bought a gasoline coupon on the black market, you still had to pay the regular price of gasoline to fill your tank. So what you were buying on the black market was not the good but *the right to buy the good*—that is, people who bought ration coupons on the black market were paying for the right to get some consumer surplus. ∎

< < < < < < < < < < < < < < < < < <

>>CHECK YOUR UNDERSTANDING 6-1

1. Consider the market for cheese-stuffed jalapeno peppers. There are two consumers, Casey and Josie, and their willingness to pay for each pepper is given in the accompanying table. Use the table (i) to construct the demand schedule for peppers for prices of $0.00, $0.10, and so on, up to $0.90; and (ii) to calculate the total consumer surplus when the price per pepper is $0.40.

Solutions appear at back of book.

Quantity of peppers	Casey's willingness to pay	Josie's willingness to pay
1st pepper	$0.90	$0.80
2nd pepper	0.70	0.60
3rd pepper	0.50	0.40
4th pepper	0.30	0.30

Producer Surplus and the Supply Curve

Just as buyers of a good would have been willing to pay more for their purchase than the price they actually pay, sellers of a good would have been willing to sell it for less than the price they actually receive. We can therefore carry out an analysis of producer surplus and the supply curve that is almost exactly parallel to that of consumer surplus and the demand curve.

Cost and Producer Surplus

Consider a group of students who are potential sellers of used textbooks. Because they have different preferences, the various potential sellers differ in the price at which they are willing to sell their books. The table in Figure 6-6 shows the prices at which several different students would be willing to sell. Andrew is willing to sell the book as long as he can get anything more than $5; Betty won't sell unless she can get at least $15; Carlos, unless he can get $25; Donna, unless she can get $35; Engelbert, unless he can get $45.

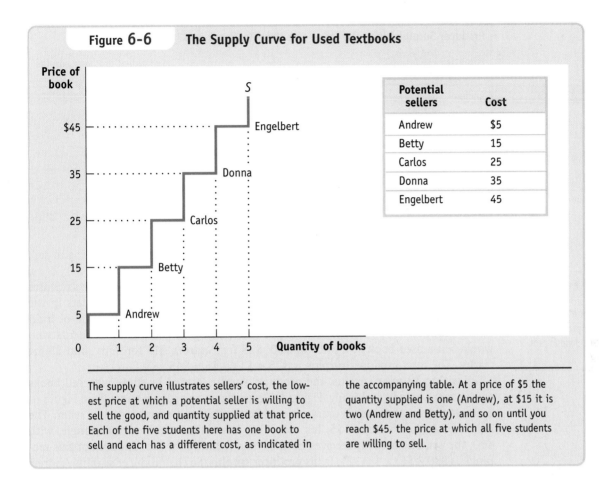

Figure 6-6   The Supply Curve for Used Textbooks

Potential sellers	Cost
Andrew	$5
Betty	15
Carlos	25
Donna	35
Engelbert	45

The supply curve illustrates sellers' cost, the lowest price at which a potential seller is willing to sell the good, and quantity supplied at that price. Each of the five students here has one book to sell and each has a different cost, as indicated in the accompanying table. At a price of $5 the quantity supplied is one (Andrew), at $15 it is two (Andrew and Betty), and so on until you reach $45, the price at which all five students are willing to sell.

The lowest price at which a potential seller is willing to sell has a special name in economics: it is called the seller's **cost**. So Andrew's cost is $5, Betty's is $15, and so on.

Using the term *cost*, which people normally associate with the monetary cost of producing a good, may sound a little strange when applied to sellers of used textbooks. The students don't have to manufacture the books, so it doesn't cost the student who sells a book anything to make that book available for sale, does it?

Yes, it does. A student who sells a book won't have it later, as part of a personal collection. So there is an *opportunity cost* to selling a textbook, even if the owner has completed the course for which it was required. And remember that one of the basic principles of economics is that the true measure of the cost of doing anything is always its opportunity cost—the real cost of something is what you give up to get it.

So it is good economics to talk of the minimum price at which someone will sell a good as the "cost" of selling that good, even if he or she doesn't spend any money to make the good available for sale. Of course, in most real-world markets the sellers are also those who produce the good—and therefore *do* expend money to make the good available for sale. In this case the cost of making the good available for sale *includes* monetary costs—but it may also include other opportunity costs.

Getting back to the example, suppose that Andrew sells his book for $30. Clearly he has gained from the transaction: he would have been willing to sell for only $5, so he has gained $25. This gain, the difference between the price he actually gets and his cost—the minimum price at which he would have been willing to sell—is known as his **individual producer surplus.**

Just as we derived the demand curve from the willingness to pay of different consumers, we can derive the supply curve from the cost of different producers. The step-shaped curve in Figure 6-6 shows the supply curve implied by the costs shown in the

A potential seller's **cost** is the lowest price at which he or she is willing to sell a good.

Individual producer surplus is the net gain to a seller from selling a good. It is equal to the difference between the price received and the seller's cost.

TABLE 6-2

Producer Surplus When the Price of a Used Textbook Is $30

Potential seller	Cost	Price received	Individual producer surplus = price received − cost
Andrew	$5	$30	$25
Betty	15	30	15
Carlos	25	30	5
Donna	35	—	—
Engelbert	45	—	—
Total producer surplus: $45			

Total producer surplus in a market is the sum of the individual producer surpluses of all the sellers of a good. Economists use the term **producer surplus** to refer both to individual and to total producer surplus.

accompanying table. At a price less than $5, none of the students are willing to sell; at a price between $5 and $15, only Andrew is willing to sell, and so on.

As in the case of consumer surplus, we can add the individual producer surpluses of sellers to calculate the **total producer surplus**, the total gains to sellers in the market. Economists use the term **producer surplus** to refer to either total or individual producer surplus. Table 6-2 shows the net gain to each of the students who would sell a used book at a price of $30: $25 for Andrew, $15 for Betty, and $5 for Carlos. The total producer surplus is $25 + $15 + $5 = $45.

As with consumer surplus, the producer surplus gained by those who sell books can be represented graphically. Figure 6-7 reproduces the supply curve from Figure 6-6. Each step in that supply curve is one book wide and represents one seller. The height of Andrew's step is $5, his cost. This forms the bottom of a rectangle, with $30, the price he actually receives for his book, forming the top. The area of this rectangle, ($30 − $5) × 1 = $25, is his producer surplus. So the producer surplus Andrew gains from selling his book is the *area of the dark red rectangle* shown in the figure.

Let's assume that the campus bookstore is willing to buy all the used copies of this book that students are willing to sell at a price of $30. Then, in addition to Andrew, Betty and Carlos will also sell their books. They will also benefit from their sales, though not as much as Andrew, because they have higher costs. Andrew, as we have

Figure 6-7

Producer Surplus in the Used-Textbook Market

At a market price of $30, Andrew, Betty, and Carlos each sell a book but Donna and Engelbert do not. Andrew, Betty, and Carlos get individual producer surpluses equal to the difference between the market price and their cost, illustrated here by the shaded rectangles. Donna and Engelbert each have a cost that is greater than the market price of $30, so they are unwilling to sell a book and therefore receive zero producer surplus. The total producer surplus is given by the entire shaded area, the sum of the individual producer surpluses of Andrew, Betty, and Carlos, equal to $25 + $15 + $5 = $45.

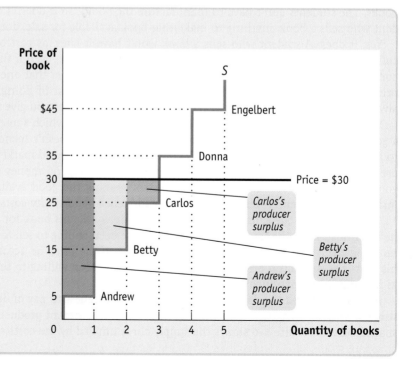

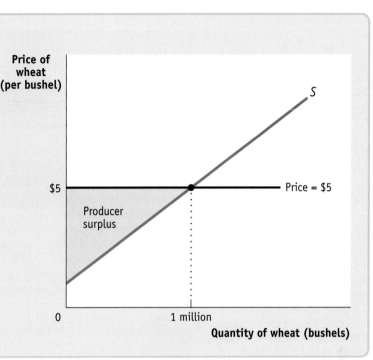

Figure 6-8

Producer Surplus

Here is the supply curve for wheat. At a price of $5 per bushel, farmers supply 1 million bushels. The producer surplus at this price is equal to the shaded area: the area above the supply curve but below the price. This is the total gain to producers—farmers in this case—from supplying their product when the price is $5. **>web...**

seen, gains $25. Betty gains a smaller amount: since her cost is $15, she gains only $15. Carlos gains even less, only $5.

Again, as with consumer surplus, we have a general rule for determining the total producer surplus from sales of a good: *The total producer surplus from sales of a good at a given price is the area above the supply curve but below that price.*

This rule applies both to examples like the one shown in Figure 6-7, where there are a small number of producers and a step-shaped supply curve, and to more realistic examples where there are many producers and the supply curve is more or less smooth.

Consider, for example, the supply of wheat. Figure 6-8 shows how the producer surplus depends on the price per bushel. Suppose that, as shown in the figure, the price is $5 per bushel and farmers supply 1 million bushels. What is the benefit to the farmers from selling their wheat at a price of $5? Their producer surplus is equal to the shaded area in the figure—the area above the supply curve but below the price of $5 per bushel.

Changes in Producer Surplus

If the price of a good rises, producers of the good will experience an increase in producer surplus, though not all producers gain the same amount. Some producers would have produced the good even at the original price; they will gain the entire price increase on every unit they produce. Other producers will enter the market because of the higher price; they will gain only the difference between the new market price and their cost.

Figure 6-9 (page 146) is the supply counterpart of Figure 6-5. It shows the effect on producer surplus of a rise in the price of wheat from $5 to $7 per bushel. The increase in producer surplus is the entire shaded area, which consists of two parts. First, there is a red rectangle corresponding to the gains of those farmers who would have supplied wheat even at the original $5 price. Second, there is an additional pink triangle that corresponds to the gains of those farmers who would not have supplied wheat at the original price but are drawn into the market by the higher price.

If the price were to fall from $7 to $5 per bushel, the story would run in reverse. The whole shaded area would now be the decline in producer surplus, the fall in the area above the supply curve but below the price. The loss would consist of two parts, the loss to farmers who would still grow wheat at a price of $5 (the red rectangle) and the loss to farmers who decide not to grow wheat because of the lower price (the pink triangle).

Figure 6-9

A Rise in the Market Price Increases Producer Surplus

A rise in the market price of wheat from $5 to $7 leads to an increase in the quantity supplied and an increase in producer surplus. The change in the total producer surplus is given by the sum of the shaded areas: the total area above the supply curve but between the old and new prices. The red area represents the gain to the farmers who would have supplied 1 million bushels at the original price of $5; they each receive an increase in producer surplus of $2 for each of those bushels. The triangular pink area represents the increase in producer surplus achieved by the farmers who supply the additional 500,000 bushels because of the higher price. Similarly, a fall in the market price of wheat generates a decrease in producer surplus equal to the shaded areas. **>web...**

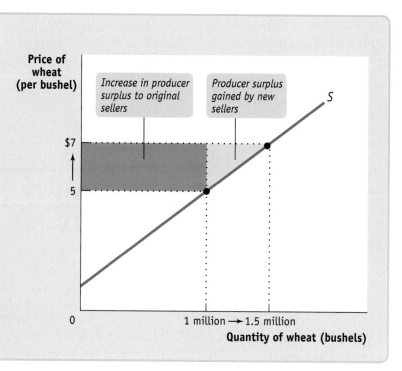

economics in action

Gaining from Disaster

In 1992 Hurricane Andrew swept through Florida, destroying thousands of homes and businesses. The state quickly began rebuilding, with the help of thousands of construction workers who moved temporarily to Florida to help out.

These construction workers were not motivated mainly by sympathy for Florida residents. They were lured by the high wages available there—and took home billions of dollars.

But how much did the temporary workers actually gain? Certainly we should not count all the money they earned in Florida as a net benefit. For one thing, most of these workers would have earned something—though not as much—if they had stayed home. In addition to this opportunity cost, the temporary move to Florida had other costs: the expense of motel rooms and of transportation, the wear and tear of being away from families and friends.

Clearly the workers viewed the benefits as being larger than the costs—otherwise they wouldn't have gone down to Florida in the first place. But the producer surplus earned by those temporary workers was much less than the money they earned. ■

< < < < < < < < < < < < < < < < < < < <

>> CHECK YOUR UNDERSTANDING 6-2

1. Consider the market for cheese-stuffed jalapeno peppers. There are two producers, Cara and Jamie, and their costs of producing each pepper are given in the accompanying table. Use the table (i) to construct the supply schedule for pepper for prices of $0.00, $0.10, and so on, up to $0.90; and (ii) to calculate the total producer surplus when the price per pepper is $0.70.

Solutions appear at back of book.

Quantity of peppers	Cara's cost	Jamie's cost
1st pepper	$0.10	$0.30
2nd pepper	0.10	0.50
3rd pepper	0.40	0.70
4th pepper	0.60	0.90

Consumer Surplus, Producer Surplus, and the Gains from Trade

One of the nine core principles of economics we introduced in Chapter 1 is that markets are a remarkably effective way to organize economic activity: they generally make society as well off as possible given the available resources. The concepts of consumer surplus and producer surplus can help us deepen our understanding of why this is so.

The Gains from Trade

Let's go back to the market in used textbooks but now consider a much bigger market—say, one at a large state university—where there are many potential buyers and sellers. Let's line up incoming students—who are potential buyers of the book—in order of their willingness to pay, so that the entering student with the highest willingness to pay is potential buyer number 1, the student with the next highest willingness to pay is number 2, and so on. Then we can use their willingness to pay to derive a demand curve like the one in Figure 6-10. Similarly, we can line up outgoing students, who are potential sellers of the book, in order of their cost, starting with the student with the lowest cost, then the student with the next lowest cost, and so on, to derive a supply curve like the one shown in the same figure.

As we have drawn the curves, the market reaches equilibrium at a price of $30 per book, and 1,000 books are bought and sold at that price. The two shaded triangles show the consumer surplus (blue) and the producer surplus (red) generated by this market. The sum of consumer and producer surplus is known as the **total surplus** generated in a market.

The striking thing about this picture is that both consumers and producers gain—that is, both consumers and producers are better off because there is a market in this good. But this should come as no surprise—it illustrates another core principle of economics: there are *gains from trade*. These gains from trade are the reason everyone is better off participating in a market economy than they would be if each individual tried to be self-sufficient.

But are we as well off as we could be? This brings us to the question of the efficiency of markets.

The **total surplus** generated in a market is the total net gain to consumers and producers from trading in the market. It is the sum of the producer and the consumer surplus.

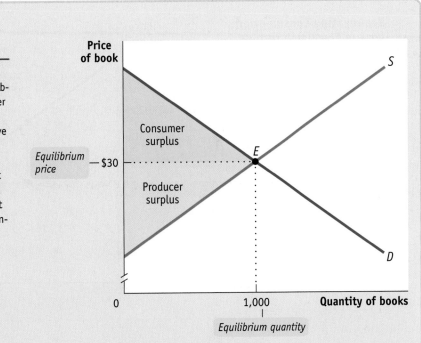

Figure 6-10

Total Surplus

In the market for used textbooks, the equilibrium price is $30 and the equilibrium quantity is 1,000 books. Consumer surplus is given by the blue area, the area below the demand curve but above the market price. Producer surplus is given by the red area, the area above the supply curve but below the market price. The sum of the blue and the red areas is total surplus, the total benefit to society from the production and consumption of the good. **>web...**

The Efficiency of Markets: A Preliminary View

Markets produce gains from trade, but in Chapter 1 we made a bigger claim: that markets are usually *efficient*. That is, we claimed that once the market has produced its gains from trade, there is usually no way to make anyone better off without making someone else worse off (with some well-defined exceptions).

We're not yet ready to carry out a full discussion of the efficiency of markets—that will have to wait until we've looked in more detail at the behavior of producers and consumers. However, we can get an intuitive sense of the efficiency of markets by noticing a key feature of the market equilibrium shown in Figure 6-10: the maximum possible total surplus is achieved at market equilibrium. That is, the market equilibrium allocates the consumption of the good among potential consumers and sales of the good among potential sellers in a way that achieves the highest possible gain to society.

How do we know this? By comparing the total surplus generated by the consumption and production choices in the market equilibrium to the surplus generated by a different set of production and consumption choices. We can show that any change from the market equilibrium reduces total surplus.

Let's consider three ways in which you might try to increase the total surplus:

1. *Reallocate consumption among consumers*—take the good away from buyers who would have purchased the good in the market equilibrium, and instead give it to potential consumers who would not have bought it in equilibrium.

2. *Reallocate sales among sellers*—take sales away from sellers who would have sold the good in the market equilibrium, and instead compel potential sellers who would not have sold the good in equilibrium to sell it.

3. *Change the quantity traded*—compel consumers and producers to transact either more or less than the equilibrium quantity.

It turns out that each of these actions will not only fail to increase the total surplus; in fact, each will reduce the total surplus.

Figure 6-11 shows why reallocating consumption of the good among consumers will reduce the total surplus. Points A and B show the positions on the demand curve of two potential buyers of a used book, Ana and Bob. As we can see from the figure,

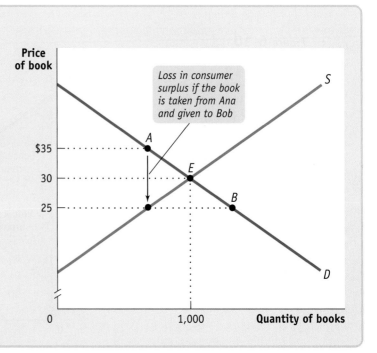

Figure 6-11

Reallocating Consumption Lowers Consumer Surplus

Ana (point *A*) has a willingness to pay of $35. Bob (point *B*) has a willingness to pay of only $25. At the market equilibrium price of $30, Ana purchases a book but Bob does not. If we rearrange consumption by taking a book from Ana and giving it to Bob, consumer surplus declines by $10 and, as a result, total surplus declines by $10. The market equilibrium generates the highest possible consumer surplus by ensuring that those who consume the good are those who value it the most. *>web...*

Ana is willing to pay $35 for a book, but Bob is willing to pay only $25. Since the equilibrium price is $30, Ana buys a book and Bob does not.

Now suppose that we try to reallocate consumption. This would mean taking a book away from somebody who *would* have bought one at the equilibrium price of $30, like Ana, and giving that book to someone who would *not* have bought at that price, like Bob. But since the book is worth $35 to Ana, but only $25 to Bob, this would *reduce total consumer surplus* by $35 − $25 = $10.

This result doesn't depend on which two students we pick. Every student who buys a book in equilibrium has a willingness to pay that is *more* than $30, and every student who doesn't buy a book has a willingness to pay that is *less* than $30. So reallocating the good among consumers always means taking a book away from a student who values it more and giving it to a student who values it less, which necessarily reduces consumer surplus.

A similar argument, illustrated by Figure 6-12, holds for producer surplus. Here points *X* and *Y* show the positions on the supply curve of Xavier, who has a cost of $25, and Yvonne, who has a cost of $35. At the equilibrium price of $30, Xavier would sell his book but Yvonne would not. If we reallocated sales, forcing Xavier to keep his book and forcing Yvonne to give up hers, total producer surplus would be reduced by $35 − $25 = $10. Again, it doesn't matter which two students we choose. Any student who sells a book in equilibrium has a lower cost than any student who does not, so reallocating sales among sellers necessarily increases total cost and reduces producer surplus. In this way the market equilibrium generates the highest possible producer surplus: it ensures that those who sell their books are those who most value the right to sell them.

Finally, changing the quantity bought and sold reduces the sum of producer and consumer surplus. Figure 6-13 (page 150) shows all four students: potential buyers Ana and Bob, potential sellers Xavier and Yvonne. To reduce sales, we would have to prevent someone like Xavier, who would have sold the book in equilibrium, from making the sale; and the book would then not be made available to someone like Ana who would have bought it in equilibrium. As we've seen, however, Ana would be willing to pay $35, but Xavier's cost is only $25. So preventing this sale would reduce total surplus by $35 − $25 = $10. Once again, this result doesn't depend on which two students we pick: any student who would have sold the book in equilibrium has

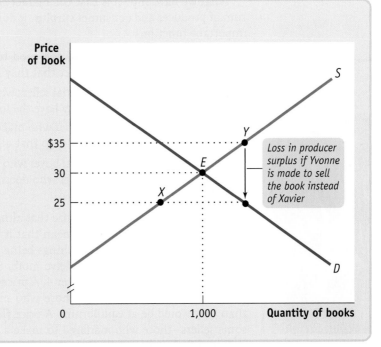

Figure 6-12

Reallocating Sales Lowers Producer Surplus

Yvonne (point *Y*) has a cost of $35, $10 more than Xavier (point *X*) who has a cost of $25. At the market equilibrium price of $30, Xavier sells a book, but Yvonne does not. If we rearrange sales by preventing Xavier from selling his book and compelling Yvonne to sell hers, producer surplus declines by $10 and, as a result, total surplus declines by $10. The market equilibrium generates the highest possible producer surplus by assuring that those who sell the good are those who value the right to sell it the most. **>web...**

Figure 6-13

Changing the Quantity Lowers Total Surplus

If Xavier (point *X*) were prevented from selling his book to someone like Ana (point *A*), total surplus would fall by $10, the difference between Ana's willingness to pay ($35) and Xavier's cost ($25). This means that total surplus falls whenever fewer than 1,000 books—the equilibrium quantity—are transacted. Likewise, if Yvonne (point *Y*) were compelled to sell her book to someone like Bob (point *B*), total surplus would also fall by $10, the difference between Yvonne's cost ($35) and Bob's willingness to pay ($25). This means that total surplus falls whenever more than 1,000 books are transacted. These two examples show that at market equilibrium, all beneficial transactions—and only beneficial transactions—occur.

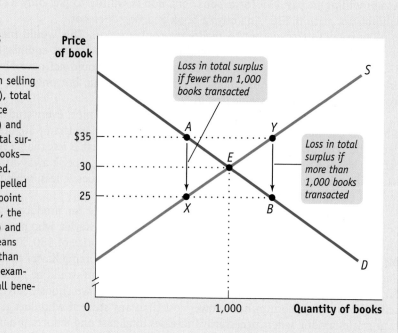

a cost of *less* than $30, and any student who would have purchased the book at equilibrium would be willing to pay *more* than $30, so preventing any sale that would have taken place in equilibrium reduces total surplus.

Finally, to increase sales would mean forcing someone like Yvonne, who would not have sold her book in equilibrium, to sell it, and giving it to someone like Bob, who would not have bought a book in equilibrium. Because Yvonne's cost is $35 but Bob is only willing to pay $25, this reduces total surplus by $10. And once again it doesn't matter which two students we pick—anyone who wouldn't have bought the book is willing to pay less than $30, and anyone who wouldn't have sold has a cost of more than $30.

What we have shown is that the market equilibrium maximizes total surplus—the sum of producer and consumer surplus. It does this because the market performs four important functions:

1. It allocates consumption of the good to the potential buyers who value it the most, as indicated by the fact that they have the highest willingness to pay.

2. It allocates sales to the potential sellers who most value the right to sell the good, as indicated by the fact that they have the lowest cost.

3. It ensures that every consumer who makes a purchase values the good more than every seller who makes a sale, so that all transactions are mutually beneficial.

4. It ensures that every potential buyer who doesn't make a purchase values the good less than every potential seller who doesn't make a sale, so that no mutually beneficial transactions are missed.

A caveat: it's important to realize that although the market equilibrium maximizes the total surplus, this does not mean that it is the best outcome for every individual consumer and producer. Other things being equal, each buyer would like to pay less and each seller would like to receive more. So some people would benefit from the price controls discussed in Chapter 4. A price ceiling that held down the market price would leave some consumers—those who managed to make a purchase—better off than they would be at equilibrium. A price floor that kept the price up would benefit some sellers—those who managed to make a sale.

But in the market equilibrium there is no way to make some people better off without making others worse off—and that's the definition of efficiency.

Maximizing total surplus at your local hardware store.

Photodisc Red/Getty Images

A Few Words of Caution

Markets are an amazingly effective way to organize economic activity; we've just demonstrated that, under certain conditions, a market is actually efficient—there is literally no way to make anyone better off without making someone else worse off.

But how secure is this result? Are markets really that good?

The answer is "not always." As we discussed briefly in Chapter 1 in our ninth and final principle of economics (*when markets don't achieve efficiency, government intervention can improve society's welfare*), markets can fail to be efficient for a number of reasons. When a market is not efficient, we have what is known as a case of **market failure**. We will examine various causes of *market failure* in depth in later chapters; for now, let's review the three main reasons why markets sometimes fall short of efficiency in reality.

First, markets can fail when, in an attempt to capture more resources, one party prevents mutually beneficial trades from occurring. This situation arises, for instance, when a market contains only a single seller of a good, known as a *monopolist*. In this case, the assumption we have relied on in supply and demand analysis—that no individual buyer and seller can have a noticeable effect on the market price—is no longer valid; the monopolist can determine the market price. As we'll see in Chapter 14, this gives rise to inefficiency as a monopolist manipulates the market price in order to increase profits, thereby preventing mutually beneficial trades from occurring.

Second, actions of individuals sometimes have *side effects* on the welfare of other individuals that markets don't take into account. The best-known example of such an *externality* is pollution. We'll see in Chapter 19 that pollution and other externalities also give rise to inefficiency.

Third, markets for some goods can fail because these goods, by their very nature, are unsuited for efficient management by markets. In Chapter 18 we will analyze goods that fall into this category because of problems of *private information*—information about a good that some people possess but others don't. In Chapter 20, we will encounter other types of goods that fall into this category—*public goods*, *common resources*, and *artificially scarce goods*. These are goods for which markets fail because of problems in limiting people's access to and consumption of the good. And in Chapter 22 we will learn about *information goods*: goods like a downloaded tune, that are costly to create but, once created, cost nothing to consume.

But even with these caveats, it's remarkable how well markets work at maximizing the gains from trade.

> **Market failure** occurs when a market fails to be efficient.

economics in action

eBay and Efficiency

Garage sales are an old American tradition: they are a way for families to sell items they don't want to other families that have some use for them, to the benefit of both parties. But many potentially beneficial trades were missed. For all Mr. Smith knew, there was someone 1,000 miles away who would really have loved that 1930s gramophone he had in the basement; for all Ms. Jones knew, there was someone 1,000 miles away who had that 1930s gramophone she had always wanted. But there was no way for Mr. Smith and Ms. Jones to find each other.

Enter eBay, the online auction service. eBay was founded in 1995 by Pierre Omidyar, a programmer whose fiancée was a collector of Pez candy dispensers and wanted a way to find potential sellers. The company, which says that its mission is "to help practically anyone trade practically anything on earth," provides a way for would-be buyers and would-be sellers of unique or used items to find each other, even if they don't live in the same neighborhood or even the same city.

"I got it from eBay"

EW

es the gains
et.
efficient. We can
demonstr... / considering what happens to total surplus if we start from the equilibrium and rearrange consumption, rearrange sales, or change the quantity traded. Any outcome other than the market equilibrium reduces total surplus, which means that the market equilibrium is efficient.

➤ Under certain conditions, *market failure* occurs and the market produces an inefficient outcome. The three principal sources are attempts to capture more resources that produce inefficiencies, side effects from certain transactions, and problems in the nature of the goods themselves.

The potential gains from trade were evidently large: in 2002, 86 million people were registered by eBay, and in the same year almost $15 billion in goods were bought and sold using the service. The Omidyars now possess a large collection of Pez dispensers. They are also billionaires.

< < < < < < < < < < < < < < < < < <

>>CHECK YOUR UNDERSTANDING 6-3

1. Using the tables in Check Your Understanding 6-1 and 6-2, find the equilibrium price and quantity in the market for cheese-stuffed jalapeno peppers. What is total surplus in the equilibrium in this market, and who receives it?

2. Show how each of the following three actions reduces total surplus:
   a. Having Josie consume one less pepper, and Casey one more pepper, than in the market equilibrium
   b. Having Cara produce one less pepper, and Jamie one more pepper, than in the market equilibrium
   c. Having Josie consume one less pepper, and Cara produce one less pepper, than in the market equilibrium

Solutions appear at back of book.

Applying Consumer and Producer Surplus: The Efficiency Costs of a Tax

The concepts of consumer and producer surplus are extremely useful in many economic applications. Among the most important of these is assessing the efficiency cost of taxation.

In Chapter 4 we introduced the concept of an *excise tax*, a tax on the purchase or sale of a good. We saw that such a tax drives a *wedge* between the price paid by consumers and that received by producers: the price paid by consumers rises, and the price received by producers falls, with the difference equal to the tax per unit. The *incidence* of the tax—how much of the burden falls on consumers, how much on producers—does not depend on who actually writes the check to the government. Instead, as we saw in Chapter 5, the burden of the tax depends on the price elasticities of supply and demand: the higher the price elasticity of demand, the greater the burden on producers; the higher the price elasticity of supply, the greater the burden on consumers.

We also learned that there is an additional cost of a tax, over and above the money actually paid to the government. A tax causes a *deadweight loss* to society, because less of the good is produced and consumed than in the absence of the tax. As a result, some mutually beneficial trades between producers and consumers do not take place.

Now we can complete the picture, because the concepts of consumer and producer surplus are what we need to pin down precisely the deadweight loss that an excise tax imposes.

Figure 6-14 shows the effects of an excise tax on consumer and producer surplus. In the absence of the tax, the equilibrium is at E, and the equilibrium price and quantity are P_E and Q_E, respectively. An excise tax drives a wedge equal to the amount of the tax between the price received by producers and the price paid by consumers, reducing the quantity bought and sold. In this case, where the tax is T dollars per unit, the quantity bought and sold falls to Q_T. The price paid by consumers rises to P_C, the demand price of the reduced quantity, and the price received by producers falls to P_P, the supply price of that quantity. The difference between these prices, $P_C - P_P$, is equal to the excise tax, T.

What we can now do, using the concepts of producer and consumer surplus, is show exactly how much surplus producers and consumers lose as a result of the tax.

We saw earlier, in Figure 6-5, that a fall in the price of a good generates a gain in consumer surplus that is equal to the sum of the areas of a rectangle and a triangle. A price increase causes a loss to consumers that looks exactly the same. In the case of an excise tax, the rise in the price paid by consumers causes a loss equal to the sum

Figure 6-14

A Tax Reduces Consumer and Producer Surplus

Before the tax, the equilibrium price and quantity are P_E and Q_E, respectively. After an excise tax of T per unit is imposed, the price to consumers rises to P_C and consumer surplus falls by the sum of the dark blue rectangle, labeled A, and the light blue triangle, labeled B. The tax also causes the price to producers to fall to P_P; producer surplus falls by the sum of the red rectangle, labeled C, and the pink triangle, labeled F. The government receives revenue from the tax, $Q_T \times T$, which is given by the sum of the areas A and C. Areas B and F represent the losses to consumer and producer surplus that are not collected by the government as revenue; they are the deadweight loss to society of the tax. **>web...**

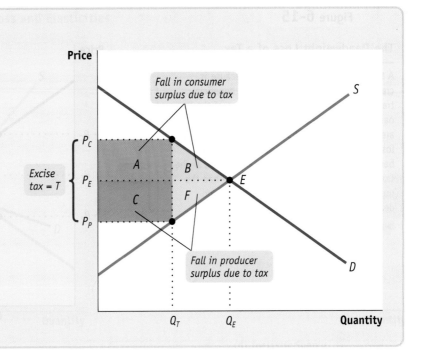

of the area of the dark blue rectangle labeled A and the area of the light blue triangle labeled B in Figure 6-14.

Meanwhile, the fall in the price received by producers causes a fall in producer surplus. This, too, is the sum of the areas of a rectangle and a triangle. The loss in producer surplus is the sum of the areas of the red rectangle labeled C and the pink triangle labeled F in Figure 6-14.

Of course, although consumers and producers are hurt by the tax, the government gains revenue. The revenue the government collects is equal to the tax per unit sold, T, multiplied by the quantity sold, Q_T. This revenue is equal to the area of a rectangle Q_T wide and T high. And we already have that rectangle in the figure: it is the sum of rectangles A and C. So the government gains part of what consumers and producers lose from an excise tax.

But there is a part of the loss to producers and consumers from the tax that is not offset by a gain to the government—specifically, the two triangles B and F. The deadweight loss caused by the tax is equal to the combined area of these triangles. It represents the total surplus that would have been generated by transactions that do not take place because of the tax.

Figure 6-15 (page 154) is a version of the same picture, leaving out the shaded rectangles—which represent money shifted from consumers and producers to the government—and showing only the deadweight loss, this time as a triangle shaded yellow. The base of that triangle is the tax wedge, T; the height of the triangle is the reduction the tax causes in the quantity sold, $Q_E - Q_T$. Notice that if the excise tax *didn't* reduce the quantity bought and sold in this market—if Q_T weren't less than Q_E—the deadweight loss represented by the yellow triangle would disappear. This observation ties in with the explanation given in Chapter 4 of why an excise tax generates a deadweight loss to society: the tax causes inefficiency because it discourages mutually beneficial transactions between buyers and sellers.

The idea that deadweight losses can be measured by the area of a triangle recurs in many economic applications. Deadweight-loss triangles are produced not only by excise taxes but also by other types of taxation. They are also produced by other kinds of distortions of markets, such as monopoly. And triangles are often used to evaluate other public policies besides taxation—for example, decisions about whether to build new highways.

economics in action

Missing the Boats

Because of deadweight losses, the costs of a tax to consumers and producers can sometimes be much larger than the actual value of taxes paid. In fact, if demand or supply, or both, is sufficiently elastic, a tax can inflict considerable losses even though it raises hardly any revenue.

A case in point was the infamous "yacht tax" of 1990, a special sales tax imposed by the U.S. government on yachts whose price exceeded $100,000. The purpose was to raise taxes on the wealthy, the only people who could afford such boats. But the tax generated much less revenue than expected, only $7 million. The reason for the low yield was that sales of $100,000-plus yachts in the United States fell sharply, by 71 percent. The number of jobs in the yacht industry, in both manufacturing and sales, also fell, by about 25 percent.

What happened? Basically, potential yacht buyers changed their behavior to avoid the tax. Some decided not to buy yachts at all; others bought their boats in places where the sales tax did not apply, such as the Bahamas; and still others scaled back, buying boats costing less than $100,000 and thereby avoiding the tax. In other words, the demand for yachts was very elastic. And the size of the job losses in the industry indicates that supply was relatively elastic as well.

Despite the fact that few potential yacht buyers ended up paying the tax, you would not want to say that it imposed no costs on consumers and producers. For consumers, avoiding the tax had its own costs, such as the expense and inconvenience of buying a boat overseas or the loss in satisfaction from buying a $99,000 boat when you really wanted something fancier. Moreover, the sales force and boat builders suffered a loss in producer surplus. Policy makers eventually concluded that pain had been inflicted for little gain in tax revenue, and the tax was repealed in 1993.

< < < < < < < < < < < < < < < < < < <

>>CHECK YOUR UNDERSTANDING 6-4

1. Suppose that an excise tax of $0.40 is imposed on cheese-stuffed jalapeno peppers, raising the price paid by consumers to $0.70 and lowering the price received by producers to $0.30. Compared to the market equilibrium without the tax from Check Your Understanding 6-3, calculate the following:
   a. The loss in consumer surplus and who loses consumer surplus
   b. The loss in producer surplus and who loses producer surplus
   c. The government revenue from this tax
   d. The deadweight loss of the tax

2. In each of the following cases, focus on the elasticity of demand and use a diagram to illustrate the likely size—small or large—of the deadweight loss resulting from a tax. Explain your reasoning.
   a. Gasoline
   b. Milk chocolate bars

Solutions appear at back of book.

• A LOOK AHEAD •

We have now almost completed our tour of the supply and demand model. But there is one more topic we need to address: how do producers and consumers make decisions? Up to now we have looked at simple situations where it is immediately clear what an individual should do. For example, a consumer should buy if the price is less than his or her willingness to pay. But not all situations are that simple. In the next chapter, we take a deeper look at how producers and consumers make decisions.

SUMMARY

1. The **willingness to pay** of each individual consumer determines the demand curve. When price is less than the willingness to pay, the potential consumer purchases the good. The difference between them is the net gain to the consumer, the **individual consumer surplus.**

2. The **total consumer surplus** in a market, the sum of all individual consumer surpluses in a market, is equal to the area below the demand curve but above the market price. A rise in the price of a good reduces consumer surplus; a fall in the price increases consumer surplus. The term **consumer surplus** is often used to refer both to individual and to total consumer surplus.

3. The **cost** of each potential producer, the lowest price at which he or she is willing to supply a unit of that good, determines the supply curve. If the price of a good is above a producer's cost, a sale generates a net gain to the producer, known as the **individual producer surplus.**

4. The **total producer surplus,** the sum of the individual producer surpluses, is equal to the area above the supply curve but below the market price. A rise in the price of a good increases producer surplus; a fall in the price reduces producer surplus. The term **producer surplus** is often used to refer both to the individual and to the total producer surplus.

5. **Total surplus,** the total gain to society from the production and consumption of a good, is the sum of consumer and producer surplus.

6. Usually, markets are efficient and achieve the maximum total surplus. Any possible rearrangement of consumption or sales, or change in the quantity bought and sold, reduces total surplus.

7. Under certain conditions, **market failure** occurs and markets fail to be efficient. This situation arises from three principal sources: attempts to capture more resources that create inefficiencies, side effects of some transactions, and problems in the nature of the good.

8. Economic policies can be evaluated by their effect on total surplus. For example, an excise tax generates revenue for the government but lowers total surplus. The loss in total surplus exceeds the tax revenue, resulting in a deadweight loss to society. The value of this deadweight loss is shown by the triangle that represents the value of the transactions discouraged by the tax. The greater the elasticity of demand or supply, or both, the larger the deadweight loss of a tax.

KEY TERMS

Willingness to pay, p. 136
Individual consumer surplus, p. 138
Total consumer surplus, p. 138
Consumer surplus, p. 138

Cost, p. 143
Individual producer surplus, p. 143
Total producer surplus, p. 144

Producer surplus, p. 144
Total surplus, p. 147
Market failure, p. 151

PROBLEMS

1. Determine the amount of consumer surplus generated in each of the following situations.

   a. Paul goes to the clothing store to buy a new T-shirt, for which he is willing to pay up to $10. He picks out one he likes with a price tag of exactly $10. At the cash register, he is told that his T-shirt is on sale for half the posted price.

   b. Robin goes to the CD store hoping to find a used copy of the *Eagles Greatest Hits* for up to $10. The store has one copy selling for $10.

   c. After soccer practice, Phil is willing to pay $2 for a bottle of mineral water. The 7-Eleven sells mineral water for $2.25 per bottle.

2. Determine the amount of producer surplus generated in each of the following situations.

   a. Bob lists his old Lionel electric trains on eBay. He sets a minimum acceptable price, known as his *reserve price*, of $75. After five days of bidding, the final high bid is exactly $75.

   b. Jenny advertises her car for sale in the used-car section of the student newspaper for $2,000, but she is willing to sell the car for any price higher than $1,500. The best offer she gets is $1,200.

   c. Sanjay likes his job so much that he would be willing to do it for free. However, his annual salary is $80,000.

3. Hollywood writers have a new agreement with movie producers that they will receive 10 percent of the revenue from every video rental of a movie they worked on. They have no such agreement for movies shown on pay-per-view television.

   a. When the new writers' agreement comes into effect, what will happen in the market for video rentals—that is, will supply or demand shift, and how? As a result, how will consumer surplus in the market for video rentals change? Illustrate with a diagram. Do you think the writers' agreement will be popular with consumers who rent videos?

   b. Consumers consider video rentals and pay-per-view movies substitutable to some extent. When the new writers' agreement comes into effect, what will happen in the market for pay-per-view movies—that is, will supply or demand shift, and how? As a result, how will producer surplus in the market for pay-per-view movies change? Illustrate with a diagram. Do you think the writers' agreement will be popular with cable television companies that show pay-per-view movies?

4. There are six potential consumers of computer games, each willing to buy only one game. Consumer 1 is willing to pay $40 for a computer game, consumer 2 is willing to pay $35, consumer 3 is willing to pay $30, consumer 4 is willing pay $25, consumer 5 is willing to pay $20, and consumer 6 is willing to pay $15.

   a. Suppose the market price is $29. What is the total consumer surplus?

   b. Now the market price decreases to $19. What is the total consumer surplus now?

   c. When the price fell from $29 to $19, how much did each consumer's individual consumer surplus change?

5. In an effort to provide more affordable rental housing for low-income families, the city council of Collegetown decides to impose a rent ceiling well below the current market equilibrium rent.

   a. Illustrate the effect of this policy in a diagram. Indicate consumer and producer surplus before and after the introduction of the rent ceiling.

   b. Will this policy be popular with renters? With landlords?

   c. An economist explains to the city council that this policy is creating a deadweight loss. Illustrate the deadweight loss in your diagram.

6. On Thursday nights, a local restaurant has a pasta special. Ari likes the restaurant's pasta, and his willingness to pay for each serving is shown in the accompanying table.

Quantity of pasta (servings)	Willingness to pay for pasta (per serving)
1	$10
2	8
3	6
4	4
5	2
6	0

   a. If the price of a serving of pasta is $4, how many servings will Ari buy? How much consumer surplus does he receive?

   b. The following week, Ari is back at the restaurant again, but now the price of a serving of pasta is $6. By how much does his consumer surplus decrease compared to the previous week?

   c. One week later, he goes to the restaurant again. He discovers that the restaurant is offering an "all you can eat"

special for $25. How much pasta will Ari eat, and how much consumer surplus does he receive now?

   d. Suppose you own the restaurant and Ari is a "typical" customer. What is the highest price you can charge for the "all you can eat" special and still attract customers?

7. The accompanying diagram shows the market for cigarettes. The current equilibrium price per pack is $4, and every day 40 million packs of cigarettes are sold. In order to recover some of the health care costs associated with smoking, the government imposes a tax of $2 per pack. This will raise the equilibrium price to $5 per pack and reduce the equilibrium quantity to 30 million packs.

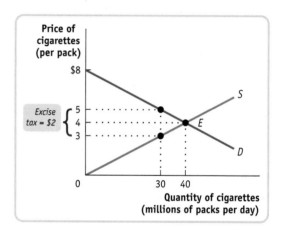

The economist working for the tobacco lobby claims that this tax will reduce consumer surplus for smokers by $40 million per day, since 40 million packs now cost $1 more per pack. The economist working for the lobby for sufferers of second-hand smoke argues that this is an enormous overestimate and that the reduction in consumer surplus will be only $30 million per day, since after the imposition of the tax only 30 million packs of cigarettes will be bought and each of these packs will now cost $1 more. They are both wrong. Why?

8. Consider the original market for pizza in Collegetown, illustrated in the accompanying table. Collegetown officials decide to impose an excise tax on pizza of $4 per pizza.

Price of pizza	Quantity of pizza demanded	Quantity of pizza supplied
$10	0	6
9	1	5
8	2	4
7	3	3
6	4	2
5	5	1
4	6	0
3	7	0
2	8	0
1	9	0

a. What is the quantity of pizza bought and sold after the imposition of the tax? What is the price paid by consumers? What is the price received by producers?

b. Calculate the consumer surplus and the producer surplus after the imposition of the tax. By how much has the imposition of the tax reduced consumer surplus? By how much has it reduced producer surplus?

c. How much tax revenue does Collegetown earn from this tax?

d. Calculate the deadweight loss from this tax.

9. Consider once more the original market for pizza in Collegetown, illustrated in the table in Problem 8. Now Collegetown officials impose a price floor on pizza of $8.

a. What is the quantity of pizza bought and sold after the imposition of the price floor?

b. Calculate the consumer surplus and the producer surplus after the imposition of the price floor.

10. You are the manager of Fun World, a small amusement park. The accompanying diagram shows the demand curve of a typical customer at Fun World.

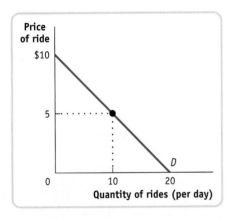

a. Suppose that the price of each ride is $5. At that price, how much consumer surplus does an individual consumer get? (Recall that the area of a triangle is ½ × the base of the triangle × the height of the triangle.)

b. Suppose that Fun World considers charging an admission fee, even though it maintains the price of each ride at $5. What is the maximum admission fee it could charge? (Assume that all potential customers have enough money to pay the fee.)

c. Suppose that Fun World lowered the price of each ride to zero. How much consumer surplus does an individual consumer get? What is the maximum admission fee Fun World could therefore charge?

11. The accompanying diagram illustrates a taxi driver's individual supply curve (assume that each taxi ride is the same distance).

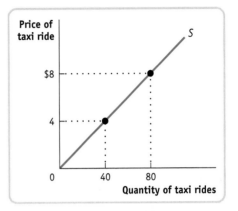

a. Suppose the city sets the price of taxi rides at $4 per ride. What is this taxi driver's producer surplus? (Recall that the area of a triangle is ½ × the base of the triangle × the height of the triangle.)

b. Suppose now that the city keeps the price of a taxi ride set at $4, but it decides to charge taxi drivers a "licensing fee." What is the maximum licensing fee the city could extract from this taxi driver?

c. Suppose that the city allowed the price of taxi rides to increase to $8 per ride. How much producer surplus does an individual taxi driver now get? What is the maximum licensing fee the city could charge this taxi driver?

12. The state needs to raise money, and the governor has a choice of imposing an excise tax of the same amount on one of two previously untaxed goods: the state can tax either sales of restaurant meals or sales of gasoline. Both the demand for and the supply of restaurant meals is more elastic than the demand for and the supply of gasoline. If the governor wants to minimize the deadweight loss caused by the tax, which good should be taxed? For each good, draw a diagram that illustrates the deadweight loss from taxation.

>**web**... To continue your study and review of concepts in this chapter, please visit the Krugman/Wells website for quizzes, animated graph tutorials, web links to helpful resources, and more.

www.worthpublishers.com/krugmanwells

>> Making Decisions

A TALE OF TWO INVASIONS

O N JUNE 6, 1944, ALLIED SOLDIERS stormed the beaches of Norman-dy, beginning the liberation of France from German rule. Long before the assault, however, Allied generals had to make a crucial decision: *where* would the soldiers land?

They had to make what we call an "either-or" decision. *Either* the invasion force could cross the English Channel at its narrowest point, Calais—which was what the Germans expected—*or* it could try to surprise the Germans by landing farther west, in Normandy. Since men and landing craft were in limit-ed supply, the Allies could not do both. In fact they chose to rely on surprise. The German defenses in Normandy were too weak to stop the landings, and the Allies went on to liberate France and win the war.

Thirty years earlier, at the beginning of World War I, German generals had to make a different kind of decision. They, too, planned to invade France, in this case via land, and had decided to mount that invasion through Belgium. The decision they had to make was not an "either-or" but a "how much" decision: *how much* of their army should be allocated to the invasion force, and

how much should be used to defend Germany's border with France? The original plan, devised by General Alfred von Schlieffen, allocated most of the German army to the invasion force; on his deathbed, Schlieffen is supposed to have pleaded, "Keep the right wing [the invasion force] strong!" But his successor, General Helmuth von Moltke, weakened the plan: he reallocated some of the divisions that were supposed to race through Belgium to the defense. The weakened invasion force wasn't strong

Decision: Attack here? Or there?

MGM/The Kobal Collection

enough: the defending French army stopped it 30 miles from Paris. Most military histori-ans believe that by allocating too few men to the attack, von Moltke cost Germany the war.

So Allied generals made the right deci-sion in 1944; German generals made the wrong decision in 1914. The important point for this chapter is that in both cases the generals had to apply the same logic that applies to economic decisions, like production decisions by businesses and consumption decisions by households.

In this chapter we will survey the principles involved in making economic decisions. These principles will help us understand how any individual—whether a consumer or a producer—makes an economic decision. We begin by taking a deeper look at the significance of opportunity cost for economic decisions and the role it plays in "either–or" decisions. Next we turn to the problem of making "how much" decisions and the usefulness of *marginal analysis*. We then examine what kind of costs should be ignored in making a decision—costs which economists call *sunk costs*. We end by considering the concept of *present value* and its importance for making decisions when costs and benefits arrive at different times.

Opportunity Cost and Decisions

In Chapter 1 we introduced some core principles underlying economic decisions. We've just seen two of those principles at work in our tale of two invasions. The first is that *resources are scarce*—the invading Allies had a limited number of landing craft, and the invading Germans had a limited number of divisions. Because resources are scarce, the true cost of anything is its *opportunity cost*—that is, the real cost of something is what you must give up to get it. When it comes to making decisions, it is crucial to think in terms of opportunity cost, because the opportunity cost of an action is often considerably more than the simple monetary cost.

Explicit Versus Implicit Costs

Suppose that, after graduating from college, you have two options: to go to school for an additional year to get an advanced degree or to take a job immediately. You would like to take the extra year in school but are concerned about the cost.

But what exactly is the cost of that additional year of school? Here is where it is important to remember the concept of opportunity cost: the cost of that year spent getting an advanced degree is what you forgo by not taking a job for that year.

This cost, like any cost, can be broken into two parts: the *explicit costs* of the year's schooling and the *implicit costs*.

An **explicit cost** is a cost that requires an outlay of money. For example, the explicit cost of the additional year of schooling includes tuition. An **implicit cost,** on the other hand, does not involve an outlay of money; instead, it is measured by the value, in dollar terms, of all the benefits that are forgone. For example, the implicit cost of the year spent in school includes the income you would have earned if you had taken that job instead.

A common mistake, both in economic analysis and in real business situations, is to ignore implicit costs and focus exclusively on explicit costs. But often the implicit cost of an activity is quite substantial—indeed, sometimes it is much larger than the explicit cost.

Table 7-1 on page 162 gives a breakdown of hypothetical explicit and implicit costs associated with spending an additional year in school instead of taking a job. Explicit costs consist of tuition, books, supplies, and a home computer for doing assignments—all of which require you to spend money. Implicit costs are the salary you would have earned if you had taken a job instead. As you can see, the forgone salary is $35,000 and explicit costs are $9,500, making implicit costs more than three times as much as explicit costs. So ignoring the implicit costs of an action can lead to a seriously misguided decision.

An **explicit cost** is a cost that involves actually laying out money. An **implicit cost** does not require an outlay of money; it is measured by the value, in dollar terms, of the benefits that are forgone.

"I've done the numbers, and I will marry you."

This means that Kathy would be better off financially if she closed the business and devoted her time and capital to something else.

In real life, discrepancies between accounting profits and economic profits are extremely common. As the following Economics in Action explains, this is a message that has found a receptive audience among real-world businesses.

economics in action

Farming in the Shadow of Suburbia

Beyond the sprawling suburbs, most of New England is covered by dense forest. But this is not the forest primeval: if you hike through the woods, you encounter many stone walls, relics of the region's agricultural past when stone walls enclosed fields and pastures. In 1880, more than half of New England's land was farmed; by 2002, the amount was down to 10 percent.

The remaining farms of New England are mainly located close to large metropolitan areas. There farmers get high prices for their produce from city dwellers who are willing to pay a premium for locally grown, extremely fresh fruit and vegetables.

But now even these farms are under economic pressure caused by a rise in the implicit costs of farming close to a metropolitan area. As metropolitan areas have expanded during the last two decades, farmers increasingly ask themselves whether they could do better by selling their land to property developers.

In 2002, the average value of an acre of farmland in the United States as a whole was $1,210; in Rhode Island, the most densely populated of the New England states, the average was $7,300. The Federal Reserve Bank of Boston has noted that "high land prices put intense pressure on the region's farms to generate incomes that are substantial enough to justify keeping the land in agriculture." The important point is that the pressure is intense even if the farmer owns the land because the land is a form of capital used to run the business. So maintaining the land as a farm instead of selling it to a developer constitutes a large implicit cost of capital. A fact provided by the U.S. Department of Agriculture (USDA) helps us put a dollar figure on the portion of the implicit cost of capital due to development pressure for some Rhode Island farms. In 2003, a USDA program to prevent development of Rhode Island farmland by paying owners for the "development rights" to their land paid an average of $9,850 per acre for those rights alone.

About two-thirds of New England's farms remaining in business earn very little money. They are maintained as "rural residences" by people with other sources of income—not so much because they are commercially viable, but more out of a personal commitment and the satisfaction these people derive from farm life. Although many businesses have important implicit costs, they can also have important benefits to their owners that go beyond the revenue earned. ■

< < < < < < < < < < < < < < < < < < <

> **QUICK REVIEW**

➤ All costs are opportunity costs. They can be divided into *explicit costs* and *implicit costs*.

➤ Companies report their *accounting profit*, which is not necessarily equal to their *economic profit*.

➤ Due to the *implicit cost of capital*, the opportunity cost of a company's *capital*, and the opportunity cost of the owner's time, economic profit is often substantially less than accounting profit.

> **CHECK YOUR UNDERSTANDING 7-1**

1. Karma and Don run a furniture-refinishing business from their home. Which of the following represent explicit costs of the business and which represent implicit costs?
   a. Supplies such as paint stripper, varnish, polish, sandpaper, and so on
   b. Basement space that has been converted into a workroom
   c. Wages paid to a part-time helper
   d. A van that they inherited and use only for transporting furniture
   e. The job at a larger furniture restorer that Karma gave up in order to run the business

Solutions appear at back of book.

Making "How Much" Decisions: The Role of Marginal Analysis

As the story of the two wars at the beginning of this chapter demonstrated, there are two types of decisions: "either–or" decisions and "how much" decisions. To help you get a better sense of that distinction, Table 7-3 offers some examples of each kind of decision.

Although many decisions in economics are "either–or," many others are "how much." Not many people will stop driving if the price of gasoline goes up, but many people will drive less. How much less? A rise in wheat prices won't necessarily persuade a lot of people to take up farming for the first time, but it will persuade farmers who were already growing wheat to plant more. How much more?

TABLE **7-3**

"How Much" Versus "Either–Or" Decisions

"How much" decisions	"Either–or" decisions
How many days before you do your laundry?	Tide or Cheer?
How many miles do you go before an oil change in your car?	Buy a car or not?
How many jalapenos on your nachos?	An order of nachos or a sandwich?
How many workers should you hire in your company?	Run your own business or work for someone else?
How much should a patient take of a drug that generates side effects?	Prescribe drug A or drug B for your patients?
How many troops do you allocate to your invasion force?	Invade at Calais or at Normandy?

To understand "how much" decisions, we use an approach known as *marginal analysis*. Marginal analysis involves comparing the benefit of doing a little bit more of some activity with the cost of doing a little bit more of that activity. The benefit of doing a little bit more of something is what economists call its *marginal benefit*, and the cost of doing a little bit more of something is what they call its *marginal cost*.

Why is this called "marginal" analysis? A margin is an edge; what you do in marginal analysis is push out the edge a bit and see whether that is a good move.

We will begin our study of marginal analysis by focusing on marginal cost, and we'll do that by considering a hypothetical company called Felix's Lawn-Mowing Service, operated by Felix himself with his tractor-mower.

Marginal Cost

Felix is a very hard-working individual; if he works continuously, he can mow 7 lawns in a day. It takes him an hour to mow each lawn. The opportunity cost of an hour of Felix's time is $10.00 because he could make that much at his next best job.

His one and only mower, however, presents a problem when Felix works this hard. Running his mower for longer and longer periods on a given day takes an increasing toll on the engine and ultimately necessitates more—and more costly—maintenance and repairs.

The second column of Table 7-4 on page 166 shows how the total daily cost of Felix's business depends on the quantity of lawns he mows in a day. For simplicity, we assume that Felix's only costs are the opportunity cost of his time and the cost of upkeep for his mower.

At only 1 lawn per day, Felix's daily cost is $10.50: $10 for an hour of his time plus $0.50 for some oil. At 2 lawns per day, his daily cost is $21.75: $20 for 2 hours of his time and $1.75 for mower repair and maintenance. At 3 lawns per day, the daily cost has risen to $35.00: $30 for 3 hours of his time and $5.00 for mower repair and maintenance.

TABLE **7-4**

Felix's Marginal Cost of Mowing Lawns

Quantity of lawns mowed	Felix's total cost	Felix's marginal cost of lawn mowed
0	$0	
		$10.50
1	10.50	
		11.25
2	21.75	
		13.25
3	35.00	
		15.50
4	50.50	
		18.00
5	68.50	
		20.75
6	89.25	
		23.75
7	$113.00	

The third column of Table 7-4 contains the cost incurred by Felix for each *additional* lawn he mows, calculated from information in the second column. The 1st lawn he mows costs him $10.50; this number appears in the third column between the lines representing 0 lawn and 1 lawn because $10.50 is Felix's cost of going from 0 to 1 lawn mowed. The next lawn, going from 1 to 2, costs him an additional $11.25. So $11.25 appears in the third column between the lines representing the 1st and 2nd lawn, and so on.

The **marginal cost** of an activity is the additional cost incurred by doing one more unit of that activity.

The increase in Felix's cost when he mows one more lawn is his **marginal cost** of lawn-mowing. In general, the marginal cost of any activity is the additional cost incurred by doing one more unit of that activity.

The marginal costs shown in Table 7-4 have a clear pattern: Felix's marginal cost is greater the more lawns he has already mowed. That is, each time he mows a lawn, the additional cost of doing yet another lawn goes up. Felix's lawn-mowing business has what economists call **increasing marginal cost:** each additional lawn costs more to mow than the previous one. Or, to put it slightly differently; with increasing marginal cost, the marginal cost of an activity rises as the quantity already done rises.

There is **increasing marginal cost** from an activity when each additional unit of the activity costs more than the previous unit.

Figure 7-1 is a graphical representation of the third column in Table 7-4. The horizontal axis measures the quantity of lawns mowed, and the vertical axis measures the

---

Figure 7-1

The Marginal Cost Curve

The height of each bar is equal to the marginal cost of mowing the corresponding lawn. For example, the 1st lawn mowed has a marginal cost of $10.50, equal to the height of the bar extending from 0 to 1 lawn. The bars ascend in height, reflecting increasing marginal cost: each additional lawn is more costly to mow than the previous one. As a result, the marginal cost curve (drawn by plotting points in the top center of each bar) is upward sloping.

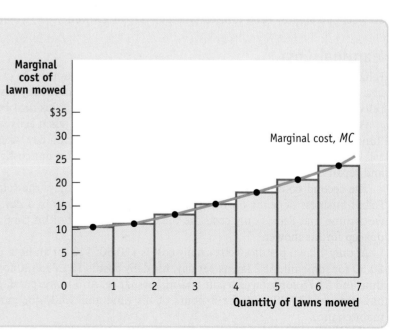

marginal cost of a mowed lawn. The height of each shaded bar indicates the marginal cost incurred by mowing a given lawn. For example, the bar stretching from 4 to 5 lawns is at a height of $18.00, equal to the cost of mowing the 5th lawn. Notice that the bars form a series of ascending steps, a reflection of the increasing marginal cost of lawn-mowing. The **marginal cost curve,** the red curve in Figure 7-1, shows the relationship between marginal cost and the quantity of the activity already done. We draw it by plotting a point in the center at the top of each bar and connecting the points.

The marginal cost curve is upward sloping, due to increasing marginal cost. Not all activities have increasing marginal cost; for example, it is possible for marginal cost to be the same regardless of the number of lawns already mowed. Economists call this case *constant* marginal cost. It is also possible for some activities to have a marginal cost that initially falls as we do more of the activity and then eventually rises. These sorts of activities involve gains from specialization: as more output is produced, more workers are hired, allowing each one to specialize in the task that he or she performs best. The gains from specialization yield a lower marginal cost of production.

Now that we have established the concept of marginal cost, we move to the parallel concept of marginal benefit.

Marginal Benefit

Felix's business is in a town where some of the residents are very busy but others are not so busy. For people who are very busy, the opportunity cost of an hour of their time spent mowing the lawn is very high. So they are willing to pay Felix a fairly high sum to do it for them. People with lots of free time, however, have a lower opportunity cost of an hour of their time spent mowing the lawn. So they are willing to pay Felix only a relatively small sum. And between these two extremes lie other residents who are moderately busy and so are willing to pay a moderate price to have their lawns mowed.

We'll assume that on any given day, Felix has one potential customer who will pay him $35 to mow her lawn, another who will pay $30, a third who will pay $26, a fourth who will pay $23, and so on. Table 7-5 lists what he can receive from each of his seven potential customers per day, in descending order according to price. So if Felix goes from 0 to 1 lawn mowed, he can earn $35; if he goes from 1 to 2 lawns mowed, he can earn an additional $30; and so on. The third column of Table 7-5 shows the **marginal benefit** to Felix of each additional lawn mowed. In general, marginal benefit is the additional benefit derived from undertaking one more unit of an activity. Because it arises from doing one more lawn, each marginal benefit value appears between the lines associated with successive quantities of lawns.

It's clear from Table 7-5 that the more lawns Felix has already mowed, the smaller his marginal benefit from mowing one more. So Felix's lawn-mowing business has what

The **marginal cost curve** shows how the cost of undertaking one more unit of an activity depends on the quantity of that activity that has already been done.

PITFALLS

INCREASING TOTAL COST VERSUS INCREASING MARGINAL COST

The concept of *increasing marginal cost* plays an important role in economic analysis, but students sometimes get confused about what it means. That's because it is easy to wrongly conclude that whenever total cost is increasing, marginal cost must also be increasing. But the following example shows that this conclusion is misguided.

Suppose that we change the numbers of our example: the marginal cost of mowing the 6th lawn is now $20.00, and the marginal cost of mowing the 7th lawn is now $15.00. In both instances total cost increases as Felix does an additional lawn: it increases by $20.00 for the 6th lawn and by $15.00 for the 7th lawn. But in this example marginal cost is *decreasing*: the marginal cost of the 7th lawn is less than the marginal cost of the 6th lawn. So we have a case of increasing total cost and decreasing marginal cost. What this shows us is that, in fact, totals and marginals can sometimes move in opposite directions.

The **marginal benefit** from an activity is the additional benefit derived from undertaking one more unit of that activity.

TABLE 7-5

Felix's Marginal Benefit of Mowing Lawns

Quantity of lawns mowed	Felix's total benefit	Felix's marginal benefit of lawn mowed
0	$0	
		$35.00
1	35.00	
		30.00
2	65.00	
		26.00
3	91.00	
		23.00
4	114.00	
		21.00
5	135.00	
		19.00
6	154.00	
		18.00
7	$172.00	

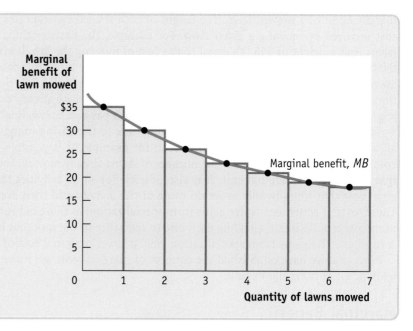

Figure 7-2

The Marginal Benefit Curve

The height of each bar is equal to the marginal benefit of mowing the corresponding lawn. For example, the 1st lawn mowed has a marginal benefit of $35, equal to the height of the bar extending from 0 to 1 lawn. The bars descend in height, reflecting decreasing marginal cost: each additional lawn produces a smaller benefit than the previous one. As a result, the marginal benefit curve (drawn by plotting points in the top center of each bar) is downward sloping. *>web...*

There is **decreasing marginal benefit** from an activity when each additional unit of the activity produces less benefit than the previous unit.

The **marginal benefit curve** shows how the benefit from undertaking one more unit of an activity depends on the quantity of that activity that has already been done.

economists call **decreasing marginal benefit:** each additional lawn mowed produces less benefit than the previous lawn. Or, to put it slightly differently, with decreasing marginal benefit, each additional unit produces less benefit than the unit before.

Just as marginal cost could be represented with a marginal cost curve, marginal benefit can be represented with a **marginal benefit curve,** shown in blue in Figure 7-2. The height of each bar shows the marginal benefit of each additional lawn mowed; the curve through the middle of each bar's top shows how the benefit of each additional unit of the activity depends on the number of units that have already been undertaken.

Felix's marginal benefit curve is downward sloping because he faces decreasing marginal benefit from lawn-mowing. Not all activities have decreasing marginal benefit; in fact, there are many activities for which marginal benefit is constant—that is, it is the same regardless of the number of units already undertaken. In later chapters where we study firms, we will see that the shape of a firm's marginal benefit curve from producing output has important implications for how it behaves within its industry. We'll also see in Chapters 10 and 11 why economists assume that declining marginal benefit is the norm when considering choices made by consumers. Like increasing marginal cost, decreasing marginal benefit is so common that for now we can take it as the norm.

Now we are ready to see how the concepts of marginal benefit and marginal cost can be brought together to answer the question of "how much" of an activity an individual should undertake.

Marginal Analysis

Table 7-6 shows the marginal cost and marginal benefit numbers from Tables 7-4 and 7-5. It also adds an additional column: the net gain to Felix from one more lawn mowed, equal to the difference between the marginal benefit and the marginal cost.

We can use Table 7-6 to determine how many lawns Felix should mow. To see this, imagine for a moment that Felix planned to mow only 3 lawns today. We can immediately see that this is too small a quantity. If Felix mows an additional lawn, increasing the quantity from 3 to 4, he realizes a marginal benefit of $23 and incurs a marginal cost of only $15.50—so his net gain would be $23.00 − $15.50 = $7.50. But even 4 lawns is still too few: if Felix increases the quantity from 4 to 5, his marginal benefit is $21.00 and his marginal cost is only $18.00, for a net gain of $21.00 − $18.00 = $3.00 (as indicated by the highlighting in the table).

TABLE **7-6**

Felix's Net Gain from Mowing Lawns

Quantity of lawns mowed	Felix's marginal benefit of lawn mowed	Felix's marginal cost of lawn mowed	Felix's net gain of lawn mowed
0			
	$35.00	$10.50	$24.50
1			
	30.00	11.25	18.75
2			
	26.00	13.25	12.75
3			
	23.00	15.50	7.50
4			
	21.00	18.00	3.00
5			
	19.00	20.75	−1.75
6			
	18.00	23.75	−5.75
7			

But if Felix goes ahead and mows 7 lawns, that is too many. We can see this by looking at the net gain from mowing that 7th lawn: Felix's marginal benefit is $18.00, but his marginal cost is $23.75. So mowing that 7th lawn would produce a net gain of $18.00 − $23.75 = −$5.75; that is, a net *loss* for his business. Even 6 lawns is too many: by increasing the quantity of lawns mowed from 5 to 6, Felix incurs a marginal cost of $20.75 compared with a marginal benefit of only $19.00. He is best off at mowing 5 lawns, the largest quantity of lawns for which marginal benefit is at least as great as marginal cost.

The upshot is that Felix should mow 5 lawns—no more and no less. If he mows fewer than 5 lawns, his marginal benefit from one more is greater than his marginal cost; he would be passing up a net gain by not mowing more lawns. If he mows more than 5 lawns, his marginal benefit from the last lawn mowed is less than his marginal cost, resulting in a loss for that lawn. So 5 lawns is the quantity that generates Felix's maximum possible total net gain; it is what economists call the **optimal quantity** of lawns mowed.

Figure 7-3 on page 170 shows graphically how the optimal quantity can be determined. Felix's marginal benefit and marginal cost curves are both shown. If Felix mows fewer than 5 lawns, the marginal benefit curve is *above* the marginal cost curve, so he can make himself better off by mowing more lawns; if he mows more than 5 lawns, the marginal benefit curve is *below* the marginal cost curve, so he would be better off mowing fewer lawns.

The table in Figure 7-3 confirms our result. The second column repeats information from Table 7-6, showing marginal benefit minus marginal cost—or the net gain—for each lawn. The third column shows total net gain according to the quantity of lawns mowed. The total net gain after doing a given lawn is simply the sum of numbers in the second column up to and including that lawn. For example, the net gain is $24.50 for the first lawn and $18.75 for the second. So the total net gain after doing the first lawn is $24.50, and the total net gain after doing the second lawn is $24.50 + $18.75 = $43.25. Our conclusion that 5 is the optimal quantity is confirmed by the fact that the greatest total net gain, $66.50, occurs when the 5th lawn is mowed.

The example of Felix's lawn-mowing business shows how you go about finding the optimal quantity: increase the quantity as long as the marginal benefit from one more unit is greater than the marginal cost, but stop before the marginal benefit becomes less than the marginal cost.

In many cases, however, it is possible to state this rule more simply. When a "how much" decision involves relatively large quantities, the rule simplifies to this: the optimal quantity is the quantity at which marginal benefit is equal to marginal cost.

The **optimal quantity** of an activity is the level that generates the maximum possible total net gain.

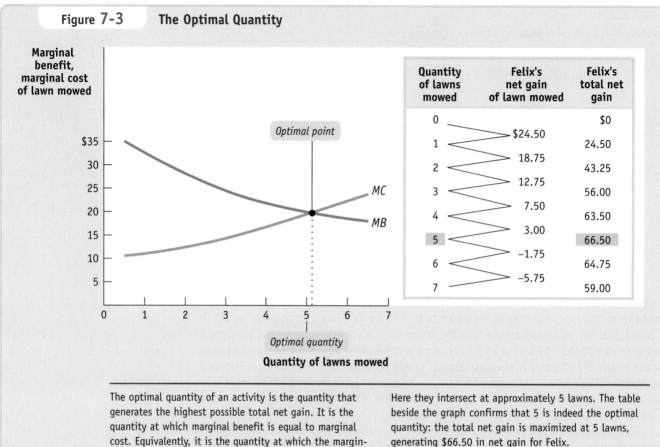

Figure 7-3 **The Optimal Quantity**

The optimal quantity of an activity is the quantity that generates the highest possible total net gain. It is the quantity at which marginal benefit is equal to marginal cost. Equivalently, it is the quantity at which the marginal benefit curve and the marginal cost curve intersect.

Here they intersect at approximately 5 lawns. The table beside the graph confirms that 5 is indeed the optimal quantity: the total net gain is maximized at 5 lawns, generating $66.50 in net gain for Felix.

The **principle of marginal analysis** says that the optimal quantity of an activity is the quantity at which marginal benefit is equal to marginal cost.

PITFALLS

MUDDLED AT THE MARGIN

The idea of setting marginal benefit *equal* to marginal cost sometimes confuses people. Aren't we trying to maximize the *difference* between benefits and costs? And don't we wipe out our gains by setting benefits and costs equal to each other? But what we are doing is setting *marginal*, not *total*, benefit and cost equal to each other.

Once again, the point is to maximize the total net gain from an activity. If the marginal benefit from the activity is greater than the marginal cost, doing a bit more will increase that gain. If the marginal benefit is less than the marginal cost, doing a bit less will increase the total net gain. So only when the *marginal* benefit and cost are equal is the difference between *total* benefit and cost at a maximum.

To see why this is so, consider the example of a farmer who finds that her optimal quantity of wheat produced is 5,000 bushels. Typically, she will find that in going from 4,999 to 5,000 bushels, her marginal benefit is only very slightly greater than her marginal cost—that is, the difference between marginal benefit and marginal cost is close to zero. Similarly, in going from 5,000 to 5,001 bushels, her marginal cost is only very slightly greater than her marginal benefit—again, the difference between marginal cost and marginal benefit is very close to zero. So a simple rule for her in choosing the optimal quantity of wheat is to produce the quantity at which the difference between marginal benefit and marginal cost is approximately zero—that is, the quantity at which marginal benefit equals marginal cost.

Economists call this rule the **principle of marginal analysis.** It says that the optimal quantity of an activity is the level at which marginal benefit equals marginal cost. Graphically, the optimal quantity is the level of an activity at which the marginal benefit curve *intersects* the marginal cost curve. In fact, this graphical method works quite well even when the numbers involved aren't that large. For example, in Figure 7-3 the marginal benefit and marginal cost curves cross each other at about 5 lawns mowed—that is, marginal benefit equals marginal cost at about 5 lawns mowed, which we have already seen is Felix's optimal quantity.

A Principle with Many Uses

The principle of marginal analysis can be applied to just about any "how much" decision—including those decisions where the benefits and costs are not necessarily expressed in dollars and cents. Here are a few examples:

- The number of traffic deaths can be reduced by spending more on highways, requiring better protection in cars, and so on. But these measures are expensive. So we can talk about the marginal cost to society of eliminating one more traffic fatality. And we can then ask whether the marginal benefit of that life saved is large enough to warrant doing this. (If you think no price is too high to save a life, see the following Economics in Action.)

- Many useful drugs have side effects that depend on the dosage. So we can talk about the marginal cost, in terms of these side effects, of increasing the dosage of a drug. The drug also has a marginal benefit in helping fight the disease. So the optimal quantity of the drug is the quantity that makes the best of this trade-off.

- Studying for an exam has costs because you could have done something else with the time, such as studying for another exam or sleeping. So we can talk about the marginal cost of devoting another hour to studying for your chemistry final. The optimal quantity of studying is the level at which the marginal benefit in terms of a higher grade is just equal to the marginal cost.

economics in action

The Cost of a Life

What's the marginal benefit to society of saving a human life? You might be tempted to answer that human life is infinitely precious. But in the real world, resources are scarce, so we must decide how much to spend on saving lives since we cannot spend infinite amounts. After all, we could surely reduce highway deaths by dropping the speed limit on interstates to 40 miles per hour, but the cost of such a lower speed limit—in time and money—is more than anyone is willing to pay.

Generally, people are reluctant to talk in a straightforward way about comparing the marginal cost of a life saved with the marginal benefit—it sounds too callous. Sometimes, however, the question becomes unavoidable.

For example, the cost of saving a life became an object of intense discussion in the United Kingdom in 1999, after a horrifying train crash near London's Paddington Station killed 31 people. There were accusations that the British government was spending too little on rail safety. However, the government estimated that improving rail safety would cost an additional $4.5 million per life saved. But if that amount was worth spending—that is, if the estimated marginal benefit to saving a life exceeded $4.5 million—then the implication was that the British government was spending way too little on *traffic safety*. The estimated marginal cost per life saved through highway improvements was only $1.5 million, making it a much better deal than saving lives through greater rail safety.

> > > > > > > > > > > > > > > > > > > >

>>CHECK YOUR UNDERSTANDING 7-2

1. For each of the "how much" decisions listed in Table 7-3, describe the nature of the marginal cost and of the marginal benefit.

2. Suppose that Felix's marginal cost, instead of increasing, is the same for every lawn he mows.
   a. Assume Felix's marginal cost is $18.50. Using Table 7-6, find the optimal quantity of mowed lawns. What is his total net gain?
   b. Is there any marginal cost for which Felix's optimal quantity of lawns mowed is 0? Can you specify a marginal cost for which the optimal quantity is 3?

Solutions appear at back of book.

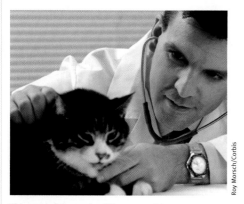

This vet left law school to pursue his dream career. The cost for a year of law school was lost—a sunk cost. But he and his patients are now happy.

Sunk Costs

When making decisions, knowing what to ignore is important. Although we have devoted much attention in this chapter to costs that are important to take into account when making a decision, some costs should be ignored when doing so. In this section we will focus on the kinds of costs that people should ignore—what economists call *sunk costs*—and why they should be ignored.

To gain some intuition, consider the following scenario. You own a car that is a few years old, and you have just replaced the brake pads at a cost of $250. But then you find out that the entire brake system is defective and must be replaced—including the newly installed brake pads. This will cost you an additional $1,500. Alternatively, you could sell the car and buy another of comparable quality, but with no brake defects, by spending an additional $1,600. What should you do: fix your old car, or sell it and buy another?

Some might say that you should take the latter option. After all, this line of reasoning goes, if you repair your car, you will end up having spent $1,750: $1,500 for the brake system and $250 for the brake pads you replaced. If you were instead to sell your old car and buy another, you would spend only $1,600.

But this reasoning, although it sounds plausible, is wrong. It is wrong because it ignores the fact that you have *already* spent $250 on brake pads, and that $250 is *nonrecoverable*. That is, having been spent already, the $250 cannot be recouped. Therefore, it should be ignored and should have no effect on your decision whether to repair your car and keep it or not. From an economist's viewpoint, the real cost at this time of repairing and keeping your car is $1,500, not $1,750. Therefore, the correct decision is to repair your car and keep it rather than spend $1,600 on a new car.

In this example, the $250 that has already been spent and cannot be recovered is what economists call a **sunk cost.** Sunk costs should be ignored in making decisions about future actions because they have no influence on their costs and benefits. It's like the old saying, "There's no use crying over spilled milk": once something is gone and can't be recovered, it is irrelevant in making decisions about what to do in the future.

It is often psychologically hard to ignore sunk costs. And if, in fact, the costs haven't yet been incurred, then they should be taken into consideration. That is, if you had known at the beginning that it would cost $1,750 to repair your car, then the right choice *at that time* would have been to buy a new car for $1,600. But once the $250 has already been paid for brake pads, it is no longer something that should be included in your decision making about your next actions. It may be hard to accept that "bygones are bygones," but it is the right thing to do.

> A **sunk cost** is a cost that has already been incurred and is nonrecoverable. A sunk cost should be ignored in decisions about future actions.

economics in action

The Next Generation

Recently, several European countries held "spectrum auctions," auctions in which telephone companies bid for portions of a country's airwave space. The telephone companies planned to use this airwave space to offer new mobile phone services to consumers. Companies believed they could earn large profits by providing these new services, so-called third-generation, or 3G, mobile phone services, which include features such as videocalling and mobile Internet access. Eager to capture what they expected to be large future profits, telephone companies paid billions of dollars for portions of the European airwave space.

But some technology experts were worried. They believed that the companies had exaggerated expectations of future profits and, as a result, had paid too much for the airwave space. These experts feared that once the companies realized that the airwave space was worth much less than what they had paid, the companies would be unwilling to put up the additional money needed for physical infrastructure, such as the towers used to transmit the signals that are necessary to the 3G services.

It turned out that the technology experts were right about the exaggerated expectations: within a few months of the spectrum auctions, telephone companies realized that they had paid far more for the portions of airwave space than they were really worth.

But was the experts' second conjecture correct: would the overpayment for the airwaves really prevent the future investment needed to provide 3G services? The answer at this point is no. Several companies, including Vodaphone, the British company that owns a substantial part of the American company Verizon, have pushed ahead in building the required infrastructure. As of 2004, 3G was available in selected cities in the United Kingdom, Ireland, Austria, Finland, Norway, and Sweden.

Technology experts were wrong about the effect of overpayment because they didn't understand the concept of sunk costs. That is, they didn't understand that once made, those payments for airwave space couldn't be recovered; therefore, they wouldn't affect the telephone companies' willingness to spend additional money to complete the project. After the companies came to the painful—and quite embarrassing—realization of their overpayment, it didn't change the fact that it was still profitable to build the infrastructure needed to provide the new services. In the end, they appear to have made the right economic calculation—and in the process admitted to themselves that "there's no use crying over a lost billion or two."

> > > > > > > > > > > > > > > > > > > >

>>CHECK YOUR UNDERSTANDING 7-3

1. You have decided to go into the ice-cream business and have bought a used ice-cream truck for $8,000. Now you are reconsidering. What is your sunk cost in the following scenarios?
   a. The truck cannot be resold.
   b. It can be resold, but only at a 50 percent discount.

2. You have gone through two years of medical school but are suddenly wondering whether you wouldn't be happier as a musician. Which of the following statements are potentially valid arguments and which are not?
   a. "I can't give up now, after all the time and money I've put in."
   b. "If I had thought about it from the beginning, I never would have gone to med school, so I should give it up now."
   c. "I wasted two years, but never mind—let's start from here."
   d. "My parents would kill me if I stopped now." (*Hint:* we're discussing *your* decision-making ability, not your parents'.)

Solutions appear at back of book.

The Concept of Present Value

In many cases, individuals must make decisions whose consequences extend some ways into the future. For example, when you decide to attend college, you are committing yourself to years of study, which you expect will pay off for the rest of your life. So the decision to attend college is the decision to embark on a long-term project.

As we have already seen, the basic rule in deciding whether or not to undertake a project is that you should compare the benefits of that project with its costs, implicit as well as explicit. But sometimes there can be a problem in making these comparisons: the benefits and costs of a project may not arrive at the same time.

Sometimes the costs of a project come at an earlier date than the benefits. For example, going to college involves large immediate costs: tuition, income forgone because you are in school, and so on. The benefits, such as a higher salary in your future career, come later, often much later.

In other cases, the benefits of a project come at an earlier date than the costs. If you take out a loan to pay for a vacation cruise, the satisfaction of the vacation will come immediately, but the burden of making payments will come later.

But why is time an issue?

Borrowing, Lending, and Interest

In general, having a dollar today is worth more than having a dollar a year from now. To see why, let's consider two examples.

First, suppose that you get a new job that comes with a $1,000 bonus, which will be paid at the end of the first year. But you would like to spend the extra money now—say, on new clothes for work. Can you do that?

The answer is yes—you can borrow money today and use the bonus to repay the debt a year from now. But if that is your plan, you cannot borrow the full $1,000 today. You must borrow less than that, because a year from now you will have to repay the amount borrowed *plus interest*.

Now consider a different scenario. Suppose that you are paid a bonus of $1,000 today, and you decide that you don't want to spend the money right now. What do you do with it? You put it in the bank; in effect, you are lending the $1,000 to the bank, which in turn lends it out to its customers who wish to borrow. At the end of a year, you will get more than $1,000 back—you will have the $1,000 plus the interest earned.

What all of this means is that $1,000 today is worth more than $1,000 a year from now. The reason is that if you want to have the money today, you must borrow it and pay interest. That is, you must pay a price for using the money today. And, correspondingly, if you forgo using the money today and lend it to someone else, you earn interest on the money. That is, you earn something by letting someone else use your money. When someone borrows money for a year, the **interest rate** is the price, calculated as a percentage of the amount borrowed, charged by the lender.

Because of the interest paid on borrowing, you can't evaluate a project just by adding up all the costs and benefits when those costs and benefits arrive at different times. You must take time into account when evaluating the project because a $1 benefit that comes today is worth more than a $1 benefit that comes a year from now; and a $1 cost that comes today is more burdensome to you than a $1 cost that comes next year. Fortunately, there is a simple way to adjust for these complications.

What we will now see is that the interest rate can be used to convert future benefits and costs into what economists call their *present values*. By using present values in evaluating a project, you can evaluate a project *as if* all its costs and benefits were occurring today rather than at different times. This allows people to "factor out" the complications created by time. We'll start by defining exactly what the concept of present value is.

When someone borrows money for a year, the **interest rate** is the price, calculated as a percentage of the amount borrowed, charged by the lender.

Defining Present Value

The key to the concept of present value is to understand that you can use the interest rate to compare the value of a dollar realized today with the value of a dollar realized later. Why the interest rate? Because the interest rate correctly measures the cost of delaying a dollar of benefit and, correspondingly, the benefit of delaying a dollar of cost. Let's illustrate this with some examples.

Suppose, first, that you are evaluating whether or not to take a job in which your employer promises to pay you a bonus at the end of the first year. What is the value to you today of $1 of bonus money to be paid to you one year into the future? A slightly different way of asking the same question: what would you be willing to accept today in place of receiving $1 one year in the future?

The way to answer this question is to observe that you need *less* than $1 today in order to be assured of having $1 one year from now. Why? Because any money that you have today can be lent out at interest, turning it into a greater sum at the end of the year.

The symbol r is used to represent the rate of interest, expressed as a fraction—that is, if the interest rate is 10%, then $r = 0.10$. If you lend out X, at the end of a year you will receive your X back, plus the interest on your X, which is $X \times r$. Thus, at the end of the year you will receive $\$X + \$X \times r$, which is $\$X \times (1+r)$. What we want to know is how much you would have to lend out today to have $1 a year from now. If the amount you lend out is $\$X$, it must be true that

(7-1) $\$X \times (1+r) = \$1$

Rearranging, we can solve for $\$X$, the amount you need today in order to generate $1 one year from now.

(7-2) $\$X = \$1/(1+r)$

This means that you would be willing to accept $\$X$ today for every $1 to be paid one year from now. The reason is that by lending out $\$X$ today, you can be assured of having $1 one year from now. If we plug into the equation the value of the yearly interest rate—say it is 10%, which means that $r = 0.10$—then we can solve for $\$X$: $\$X$ is equal to $1/1.10, which is approximately $0.91. So you would be willing to accept $0.91 today in exchange for every $1 to be paid to you one year from now. Economists have a special name for $\$X$—it's called the **present value** of $1.

To see that this technique works for future costs as well as future benefits, consider the following example. Suppose you enter into an agreement that obliges you to pay $1 one year from now—say, to pay off your student loan when you graduate in a year. How much money would you need today to ensure that you have $1 in a year? The answer is $\$X$, the present value of $1, which in our example is $0.91. The reason $0.91 is the right answer is that if you lend it out for one year at an interest rate of 10%, you will receive $1 in return at the end.

> The **present value** of $1 realized one year from now is equal to $1/(1 + r)$: the amount of money you must lend out today in order to have $1 in one year. It is the value to you today of $1 realized one year from now.

What these two examples show us is that the present value concept provides a way to calculate the value today of $1 that is realized in the future—regardless of whether that $1 is realized as a benefit (the bonus) or a cost (the student loan payback). This means that to evaluate a project today that has benefits and/or costs to be realized in the future, we just use the relevant interest rate to convert those future dollars into their present values. In that way we have "factored out" the complication that time creates for decision making.

In the next section we will work out an example of using the present value concept to evaluate a project. But before we do that, it is worthwhile to note that the present value method can be used for projects in which the $1 is realized more than a year later—say, two, three, or even more years.

Suppose you are considering a project that will pay you $1 *two* years from today. What is the value to you today of $1 received two years into the future? We can find the answer to that question by expanding our formula for present value.

Let's call $\$V$ the amount of money you need to lend today at an interest rate of r in order to have $1 in two years. So if you lend $\$V$ today, you will receive $\$V \times (1+r)$ in one year. And if you *re-lend* that sum for yet another year, you will receive $\$V \times (1+r) \times (1+r) = \$V \times (1+r)^2$ at the end of the second year. At the end of two years, $\$V$ will be worth $\$V \times (1+r)^2$; if $r = 0.10$, then this becomes $\$V \times (1.10)^2 = \$V \times (1.21)$.

Now we are ready to answer the question of what $1 realized two years in the future is worth today. In order for the amount lent today, $\$V$, to be worth $1 two years from now, it must satisfy this formula:

(7-3) $\$V \times (1+r)^2 = \$1$

Or equivalently, given $r = 0.10$,

(7-4) $\$V = \$1/(1+r)^2 = \$1/1.21 = \$0.83$

So when the interest rate is 10%, $1 realized two years from today is worth $0.83 today because by lending out $0.83 today you can be assured of having $1 in two years. And that means that the present value of $1 realized two years into the future is $0.83.

From this example we can see how the present value concept can be expanded to a number of years even greater than two. If we ask what value of $1 realized N number of years into the future is, the answer is given by a generalization of the present value formula: it is equal to $1/(1 + r)^N$.

Using Present Value

Suppose you have to choose one of three projects to undertake. Project A has an immediate payoff to you of $100, while project B requires that you put up $10 of your own money today in order to receive $115 a year from now. Project C gives you an immediate payoff of $119 but requires that you pay $20 a year from now. We'll assume that the annual interest rate is 10%—that is, $r = 0.10$.

The problem in evaluating these three projects is that they have costs and benefits that are realized at different times. That is, of course, where the concept of present value becomes extremely helpful: by using present value to convert any dollars realized in the future into today's value, you factor out the issue of time. This allows you to calculate the **net present value** of a project—the present value of current and future benefits minus the present value of current and future costs. And the best project is the one with the highest net present value.

Table 7-7 shows how this is done for each of the three projects. The second and third columns show how many dollars are realized and when they are realized; costs are indicated by a minus sign. The fourth column shows the equations used to convert the flows of dollars into their present value, and the fifth column shows the actual amounts of the total net present value for each of the three projects.

For instance, to calculate the net present value of project B, we need to calculate the present value of $115 received in one year. The present value of $1 received in one year would be $1/(1 + r)$. So the present value of $115 is 115 times $1/(1 + r)$; that is, $115/(1 + r)$. The net present value of project B is the present value of today's and future benefits minus the present value of today's and future costs: $-$10 + $115/(1 + r)$.

From the fifth column, we can immediately see which is the preferred project—it is project C. That's because it has the highest net present value, $100.82, which is higher than the net present value of project A ($100) and much higher than the net present value of project B ($94.55).

This example shows how important the concept of present value is. If we had failed to use the present value calculations and instead had simply added up the dollars generated by each of the three projects, we could have easily been misled into believing that project B was the best project and project C was the worst one.

The **net present value** of a project is the present value of current and future benefits minus the present value of current and future costs.

TABLE 7-7

The Net Present Value of Three Projects

Project	Dollars realized today	Dollars realized one year from today	Present value formula	Net present value given $r = 0.10$
A	$100	—	$100	$100.00
B	−10	$115	$-10 + 115/(1 + r)$	94.55
C	119	−20	$119 - 20/(1 + r)$	100.82

economics in action

How Big Is That Jackpot, Anyway?

For a clear example of present value at work, consider the case of lottery jackpots.

Recently, the Pennsylvania State Lottery's "Super 6" offered the lucky winner $4 million. Well, sort of. That $4 million was available only if you chose to take your winnings in the form of an "annuity," consisting of $200,000 per year for the next 20 years. If you wanted cash up front, the jackpot was only $2 million.

Why was Pennsylvania so stingy about quick payoffs? It was all a matter of present value.

In fact, the lottery budgeted only $2 million for the jackpot. If the winner had been willing to take the annuity, the lottery would have invested that money, buying U.S. government bonds (in effect lending the money to the federal government). The money would have been invested in such a way that the investments would pay $200,000 each year, just enough to pay the annuity. This worked, of course, because at the interest rates prevailing at the time, the present value of a $4 million annuity spread over 20 years was just about $2 million. Or to put it another way, the opportunity cost to the lottery of that annuity was $2 million.

So why didn't they just call it a $2 million jackpot? Hey, $4 million sounds more impressive! But it was really the same thing.

> >

>> QUICK REVIEW

➤ When costs or benefits arrive at different times, you must take the complication created by time into account. This is done by transforming any dollars realized in the future into their *present value*.

➤ $1 in benefit realized a year from now is worth $1/(1 + r)$ today, where r is the *interest rate*. Similarly, $1 in cost realized a year from now is valued today at a cost of $1/(1 + r)$ today.

➤ When comparing several projects in which costs and benefits arrive at different times, you should choose the project that generates the highest *net present value*.

>>CHECK YOUR UNDERSTANDING 7-4

1. Consider the three alternative projects shown in Table 7-7. This time, however, suppose that the interest rate is only 2%.
   a. Calculate the net present values of the three projects. Which one is now preferred?
   b. Explain why the preferred choice is different with a 2% interest rate than with a 10% rate.

Solutions appear at back of book.

• A LOOK AHEAD •

This chapter laid out the basic concepts that we need to understand economic decisions. These concepts, as we will soon see, provide the necessary tools for understanding not only the behavior behind the supply and demand curves but also the implications of markets for consumer and producer welfare.

But to get there we need a bit more context—we need to know something more about the kinds of decisions that producers and consumers must make. We start with producers: in the next two chapters we will see how marginal analysis determines how much a profit-maximizing producer chooses to produce.

SUMMARY

1. All economic decisions involve the allocation of scarce resources. Some decisions are "either–or" decisions, in which the question is whether or not to do something. Other decisions are "how much" decisions, in which the question is how many resources to put into some use.

2. The cost of using a resource for a particular activity is the opportunity cost of that resource. Some opportunity costs are **explicit costs**; they involve a direct payment of cash. Other opportunity costs, however, are **implicit** costs; they involve no outlay of money but represent the inflows of cash that are forgone. Both explicit and implicit costs should be taken into account in decisions. Companies use **capital** and their owners' time. So companies should base decisions on **economic profit,** which takes into account implicit costs such as the opportunity cost of the owners' time and **the implicit cost of capital.** The **accounting profit,** which companies calculate for the purposes of taxes and public reporting, is often considerably larger than the economic

table gives the data that are available about the effects of a smallpox vaccination program.

Percent of population vaccinated	Deaths due to smallpox	Deaths due to vaccination side effects
0	200	0
10	180	4
20	160	10
30	140	18
40	120	33
50	100	50
60	80	74

a. Calculate the marginal benefit (in terms of lives saved) and the marginal cost (in terms of lives lost) of each 10% increment of smallpox vaccination. Calculate the net gain of a 10% increment in population vaccinated.

b. Using marginal analysis, decide what percentage of the population should optimally be vaccinated.

10. Patty delivers pizza using her own car, and she is paid according to how many pizzas she delivers. The accompanying table shows Patty's total benefit and total cost when she works a specific number of hours.

Quantity of hours worked	Total benefit	Total cost
0	$0	$0
1	30	10
2	55	21
3	75	34
4	90	50
5	100	70

a. Use marginal analysis to decide how many hours Patty should work. In other words, what is the optimal number of hours Patty should work?

b. Calculate the total net gain to Patty from working 0 hours, 1 hour, 2 hours, and so on. Now suppose Patty chooses to work for 1 hour. Compare her total net gain from working for 1 hour with her total net gain from working the optimal number of hours. How much would she lose by working for only 1 hour?

11. De Beers is the sole producer of diamonds. When it wants to sell more diamonds, it must lower its price in order to induce consumers to buy more. Furthermore, each additional diamond that is produced costs more than the previous one due to the difficulty of mining for diamonds. De Beers's total benefit schedule is given in the accompanying table, along with its total cost schedule.

Quantity of diamonds	Total benefit	Total cost
0	$0	$0
1	1,000	50
2	1,900	100
3	2,700	200
4	3,400	400
5	4,000	800
6	4,500	1,500
7	4,900	2,500
8	5,200	3,800

a. Draw the marginal cost curve and the marginal benefit curve and, from your diagram, graphically derive the optimal quantity of diamonds to produce.

b. Calculate the total net gain to De Beers from producing each quantity of diamonds. Which quantity gives De Beers the highest total net gain?

12. You have won the state lottery. There are two ways in which you can receive your prize. You can either have $1 million in cash now, or you can have $1.2 million that is paid out as follows: $300,000 now, $300,000 in one year's time, $300,000 in two years' time, and $300,000 in thee years' time. The interest rate is 20%. How would you prefer to receive your prize?

13. The drug company Pfizer is considering whether to invest in the development of a new cancer drug. Development will require an initial investment of $10 million now; beginning one year from now, the drug will generate annual profits of $4 million for three years.

a. If the interest rate is 12%, should Pfizer invest in the development of the new drug? Why or why not?

b. If the interest rate is 8%, should Pfizer invest in the development of the new drug? Why or why not?

>web... To continue your study and review of concepts in this chapter, please visit the Krugman/Wells website for quizzes, animated graph tutorials, web links to helpful resources, and more.

www.worthpublishers.com/krugmanwells

>>Behind the Supply Curve: Inputs and Costs

THE FARMER'S MARGIN

Oh beautiful, for spacious skies, for amber waves of grain." So begins the song "America the Beautiful." And those amber waves of grain are for real: though farmers are now only a small minority of America's population, our agricultural industry is immensely productive and feeds much of the world.

If you look at agricultural statistics, however, something may seem a bit surprising: when it comes to yield per acre, U.S. farmers are often nowhere near the top. For example, farmers in western European countries grow about three times as much wheat per acre as their U.S. counterparts. Are the Europeans better at growing wheat than we are?

No: European farmers are very skillful, but no more so than Americans. They produce more wheat per acre because they employ more inputs—more fertilizer and, especially, more labor—per acre. Of course, this means that European farmers have higher costs than their American counterparts. But because of government policies, European farmers receive a much higher price for their wheat than American farmers. This gives them an incentive to use more inputs and to expend more effort at the margin to increase the crop yield per acre.

Notice our use of the phrase "at the margin." Like most decisions that involve a comparison of benefits and costs, decisions about production and inputs involve a comparison of marginal quantities—the marginal cost versus the marginal benefit of producing a bit more from each acre.

In Chapter 7 we used the example of Felix's Lawn-Mowing Service to illustrate the *principle of marginal analysis,* showing

What you will learn in this chapter:

➤ The importance of the firm's **production function,** the relationship between quantity of inputs and quantity of output

➤ Why production is often subject to **diminishing returns to inputs**

➤ What the various forms of a firm's costs are and how they generate the firm's **marginal** and **average cost curves**

➤ Why a firm's costs may differ in the **short run** versus the **long run**

➤ How the firm's technology of production can generate **economies of scale**

American farming practices (at left) or European farming practices (at right)? How intensively an acre of land is worked—a decision at the margin—depends on the price of wheat a farmer faces.

how Felix could use marginal analysis to determine the optimal number of lawns to mow daily—that is, the number that generates the maximum total net gain or profit. In this chapter and in Chapter 9, we will show how marginal analysis can be used to understand the output decisions that lie behind the supply curve. The first step in this analysis is to show how the relationship between a firm's inputs and its output—its *production function*—determines its *cost curves,* the relationship between cost and quantity of output produced. That is what we do in this chapter. In Chapter 9, we will see how to go from the firm's cost curves to the supply curve.

The Production Function

A *firm* is an organization that produces goods or services for sale. To do this, it must transform inputs into output. The quantity of output a firm produces depends on the quantity of inputs; this relationship is known as the firm's **production function**. As we'll see, a firm's production function underlies its *cost curves.* But as a first step, let's look at the characteristics of a hypothetical production function.

Inputs and Output

To understand the concept of a production function, let's consider a farm that we assume, for the sake of simplicity, produces only one output, wheat, and uses only two inputs, land and labor. This particular farm is owned by a couple named George and Martha. They hire workers to do the actual physical labor on the farm. Moreover, we will assume that all potential workers are of the same quality—they are all equally knowledgeable and capable of performing farmwork.

George and Martha's farm sits on 10 acres of land; no more acres are available to them, and they are currently unable to either increase or decrease the size of their farm by selling, buying, or leasing acreage. Land here is what economists call a **fixed input**—an input whose quantity is fixed and cannot be varied. On the other hand, George and Martha are free to decide how many workers to hire. The labor provided by these workers is called a **variable input**—an input whose quantity the firm can vary. (In Chapter 7, when we considered the example of Felix's Lawn-Mowing Service, Felix's fixed input was his lawn mower and his variable input was his own labor.)

In reality, whether or not the quantity of an input is really fixed depends on the time horizon. In the **long run**—that is, given that a long enough period of time has elapsed—firms can adjust the quantity of any input. So there are no fixed inputs in the long run, only in the **short run**. Later in this chapter we'll look more carefully at the distinction between the short run and the long run. But for now, we will restrict our attention to the short run and assume that at least one input is fixed.

George and Martha know that the quantity of wheat they produce depends on the number of workers they hire. Given modern farming techniques, one worker can cultivate the 10-acre farm, albeit not very intensively. When an additional worker is added, the land is divided equally among all the workers: each worker has 5 acres to cultivate when 2 workers are employed, each cultivates 3⅓ acres when 3 are employed, and so on. So as additional workers are employed, the 10 acres of land are cultivated more intensively and more bushels of wheat are produced. The relationship between the quantity of labor and the quantity of output, for a given amount of the fixed input, constitutes the farm's production function. The production function for George and Martha's farm is given in the first two columns of the table in Figure 8-1; the diagram there shows the same information graphically. The curve in Figure 8-1 shows how the quantity of output depends on the quantity of the variable input, for a given amount of the fixed input; it is called the farm's **total product curve**. The physical quantity of output, bushels of wheat, is measured on the vertical axis, while the quantity of the

A **production function** is the relationship between the quantity of inputs a firm uses and the quantity of output it produces.

A **fixed input** is an input whose quantity is fixed and cannot be varied.

A **variable input** is an input whose quantity the firm can vary.

The **long run** is the time period in which all inputs can be varied.

The **short run** is the time period in which at least one input is fixed.

The **total product curve** shows how the quantity of output depends on the quantity of the variable input, for a given amount of the fixed input.

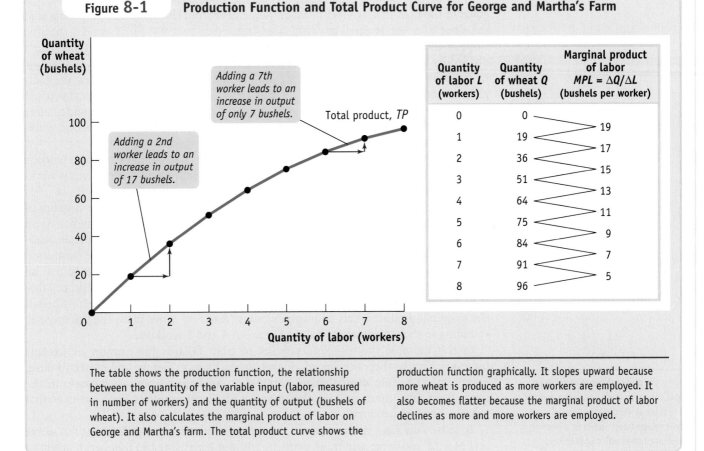

Figure **8-1**   **Production Function and Total Product Curve for George and Martha's Farm**

Quantity of labor L (workers)	Quantity of wheat Q (bushels)	Marginal product of labor $MPL = \Delta Q/\Delta L$ (bushels per worker)
0	0	
		19
1	19	
		17
2	36	
		15
3	51	
		13
4	64	
		11
5	75	
		9
6	84	
		7
7	91	
		5
8	96	

The table shows the production function, the relationship between the quantity of the variable input (labor, measured in number of workers) and the quantity of output (bushels of wheat). It also calculates the marginal product of labor on George and Martha's farm. The total product curve shows the production function graphically. It slopes upward because more wheat is produced as more workers are employed. It also becomes flatter because the marginal product of labor declines as more and more workers are employed.

variable input, labor, that is, the number of workers employed, is measured on the horizontal axis. The total product curve here is upward sloping, reflecting the fact that more bushels of wheat are produced as more workers are employed.

Although the total product curve in Figure 8-1 slopes upward along its entire length, the slope isn't constant: as you move up the curve to the right, it flattens out. To understand this changing slope, look at the third column of the table in Figure 8-1, which shows the *change in the quantity of output* that is generated by adding one more worker. That is, it shows the **marginal product** of labor: the additional quantity of output from using one more unit of labor (that is, one more worker).

In this case, we have data at intervals of 1 worker—that is, we have information on the quantity of output when there are 3 workers, 4 workers, and so on. Sometimes data aren't available in increments of 1 unit—for example, you might have information only on the quantity of output when there are 40 workers and when there are 50 workers. In this case, you can use the following equation to figure out the marginal product of labor:

The **marginal product** of an input is the additional quantity of output that is produced by using one more unit of that input.

$$\textbf{(8-1)} \quad \begin{array}{c} \text{Marginal} \\ \text{product} \\ \text{of labor} \end{array} = \frac{\text{Change in quantity of output}}{\text{Change in quantity of labor}} = \begin{array}{c} \text{Change in quantity of} \\ \text{output generated by one} \\ \text{additional unit of labor} \end{array}$$

or

$$MPL = \Delta Q/\Delta L$$

In this equation, Δ, the Greek capital delta, represents the change in a variable.

Now we can explain the significance of the slope of the total product curve: it is equal to the marginal product of labor. Remember from the Chapter 2 Appendix that the slope of a line is equal to "rise" over "run" (see page 44). This implies that the slope of the total product curve is the change in the quantity of output (the "rise") divided by the change in the quantity of labor (the "run"). And this, as we can see from Equation 8-1, is simply the marginal product of labor. So the fact that the marginal product of the first worker is 19 also means that the slope of the total product curve in going from 0 to 1 worker is 19. Similarly, the slope of the total product curve in going from 1 to 2 workers is the same as the marginal product of the second worker, 17, and so on.

In this example, the marginal product of labor steadily declines as more workers are hired—that is, each successive worker adds less to output than the previous worker. So as employment increases, the total product curve gets flatter.

Figure 8-2 shows how the marginal product of labor depends on the number of workers employed on the farm. The marginal product of labor, *MPL*, is measured on the vertical axis in units of physical output—bushels of wheat—produced per additional worker, and the number of workers employed is measured on the horizontal axis. You can see from the table in Figure 8-1 that if 5 workers are employed instead of 4, output rises from 64 to 75 bushels; so in this case the marginal product of labor is 11 bushels—the same number found in Figure 8-2. To indicate that 11 bushels is the marginal product when employment rises from 4 to 5, we place the point corresponding to that information halfway between 4 and 5 workers.

In this example the marginal product of labor falls as the number of workers increases. That is, there are *diminishing returns to labor* on George and Martha's farm. In general, there are **diminishing returns to an input** when an increase in the quantity of that input, holding the quantity of all other inputs fixed, reduces that input's marginal product.

To grasp why diminishing returns can occur, think about what happens as George and Martha add more and more workers, without increasing the number of acres. As the number of workers increases, the land is farmed more intensively and the number of bushels increases. But each additional worker is working with a smaller share of the 10 acres—the fixed input—than the previous worker. As a result, the additional

There are **diminishing returns to an input** when an increase in the quantity of that input, holding the levels of all other inputs fixed, leads to a decline in the marginal product of that input.

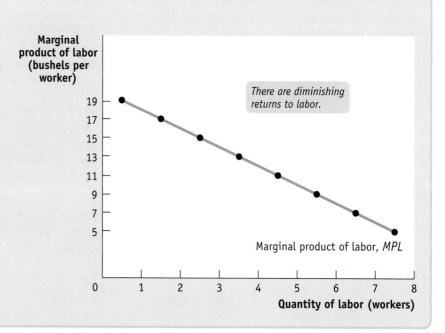

Figure 8-2

Marginal Product of Labor Curve for George and Martha's Farm

The marginal product of labor curve plots each worker's marginal product, the increase in the quantity of output generated by each additional worker. The change in the quantity of output is measured on the vertical axis and the number of workers employed on the horizontal axis. The first worker employed generates an increase in output of 19 bushels, the second worker generates an increase of 17 bushels, and so on. The curve slopes downward due to diminishing returns. **>web...**

There are diminishing returns to labor.

Marginal product of labor, *MPL*

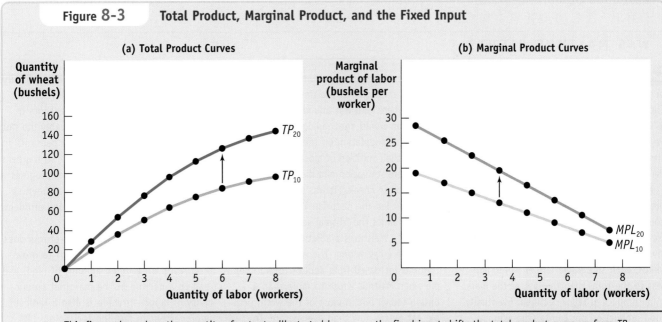

Figure 8-3   **Total Product, Marginal Product, and the Fixed Input**

This figure shows how the quantity of output—illustrated by the total product curve—and marginal product depend on the level of the fixed input. Panel (a) shows two total product curves for George and Martha's farm, TP_{10} when their farm is 10 acres and TP_{20} when it is 20 acres. Panel (b) shows the corresponding marginal product of labor curves. With more land, each worker can produce more wheat. So an increase in the fixed input shifts the total product curve up from TP_{10} to TP_{20}. This also implies that the marginal product of each worker is higher when the farm is 20 acres than when it is 10 acres. As a result, an increase in acreage also shifts the marginal product of labor curve up from MPL_{10} to MPL_{20}. Note that both marginal product of labor curves still slope downward due to diminishing returns.

worker cannot produce as much output as the previous worker. So it's not surprising that the marginal product of the additional worker falls.

The crucial thing to emphasize about diminishing returns is that, like many propositions in economics, it is an "other things equal" proposition: each successive unit of an input will raise production by less than the last *if the quantity of all other inputs is held fixed.*

What would happen if the levels of other inputs were allowed to change? You can see the answer in Figure 8-3. Panel (a) shows two total product curves, TP_{10} and TP_{20}. TP_{10} is the farm's total product curve when its total area is 10 acres (the same curve as in Figure 8-1). TP_{20} is the total product curve when the farm has increased to 20 acres. Except when no workers are employed, TP_{20} lies everywhere above TP_{10} because with more acres available, any given number of workers produces more output. Panel (b) shows the corresponding marginal product of labor curves. MPL_{10} is the marginal product of labor curve given 10 acres to cultivate (the same curve as in Figure 8-2) and MPL_{20} is the marginal product of labor curve given 20 acres. Both curves slope downward because, in each case, the amount of land is fixed, albeit at different levels. But MPL_{20} lies everywhere above MPL_{10}, reflecting the fact that the marginal product of the same worker is higher when he or she has more of the fixed input to work with.

Figure 8-3 demonstrates a general result: the position of the total product curve depends on the quantities of other inputs. If you change the quantity of the other inputs, both the total product curve and the marginal product curve of the remaining input will shift. The importance of the "other things equal" assumption in discussing diminishing returns is illustrated in the following For Inquiring Minds.

PITFALLS

WHAT'S A UNIT?

The marginal product of labor (or any other input) is defined as the increase in the quantity of output when you increase the quantity of that input by one unit. But what do we mean by a "unit" of labor? Is it an additional hour of labor, an additional week, or a person-year?

The answer is that it doesn't matter, *as long as you are consistent.* One common source of error in economics is getting units confused—say, comparing the output added by an additional *hour* of labor with the cost of employing a worker for a *week.* Whatever units you use, always be careful that you use the same units throughout your analysis of any problem.

WAS MALTHUS RIGHT?

The idea of diminishing returns first became influential with the writings of Thomas Malthus, an English pastor whose 1798 book *An Essay on the Principle of Population* was deeply influential in its own time and continues to provoke heated argument to this day.

Malthus argued that as its population grew (while its land area remained fixed), a country would find it increasingly difficult to grow enough food. Though more intensive cultivation of the land could increase yields, each successive farmer would add less to the total than the last as the marginal product of labor declined. Eventually, food production per capita (the average output of an existing worker) would decline as the population exceeded some level.

He drew a powerful conclusion from this argument—namely, that misery was the normal condition of humankind. Imagine a country in which land was abundant and population low, so that everyone had plenty

to eat. Then families would, he argued, be large (as they were at the time in the United States, where land was abundant), and the population would grow rapidly—until the pressure of population on the land had reduced the condition of most people to a level where starvation and disease held the population in check. (It was arguments like these that led the historian Thomas Carlyle to dub economics the "dismal science").

Happily, Malthus's prediction has turned out to be quite wrong. The world's population has increased from about 1 billion people when Malthus wrote to more than 6 billion today, but in most of the world people eat better now than ever before. In England, in particular, a fivefold increase in population was accompanied by a dramatic rise in the standard of living.

So was Malthus completely wrong? And does the wrongness of his prediction refute the whole idea of diminishing returns? No, on both counts.

First of all, the Malthusian story actually works pretty well as a description of 57 out of the last 59 centuries: peasants in eighteenth-century France probably did not live much better than Egyptian peasants in the age of the pyramids. It just so happens that scientific and technological progress since the eighteenth century has been so rapid that it has far outpaced any problems caused by diminishing returns.

The concept of diminishing returns does not mean that using more labor to grow food, even on a given amount of land, will lead to a decline in the marginal productivity of labor—*if* there is also a radical improvement in farming technology. It does mean that the marginal productivity declines when *all* other things—land, farming technology, and a host of other factors—remain the same. And so the happy fact that Malthus's predictions were wrong does not invalidate the concept of diminishing returns.

From the Production Function to Cost Curves

Once George and Martha know their production function, they know the relationship between inputs of labor and land and output of wheat. But if they want to maximize their profits, they need to translate this knowledge into information about the relationship between the quantity of output and cost. Let's see how they can do this.

To translate information about a firm's production function into information about its costs, we need to know how much the firm must pay for its inputs. We will assume that George and Martha face either an explicit or an implicit cost of $400 for the use of the land. As we learned in Chapter 7, it is irrelevant whether George and Martha must rent the land for $400 from someone else, or they own the land themselves and forgo earning $400 by renting it to someone else. Either way, they pay an opportunity cost of $400 by using the land to grow wheat. Moreover, since the land is a fixed input, the $400 George and Martha pay for it is a **fixed cost**, denoted by *FC*—a cost that does not depend on the quantity of output produced. In business, fixed cost is often referred to as "overhead cost."

We also assume that George and Martha must pay each worker $200. Using their production function, George and Martha know that the number of workers they must hire depends on the amount of wheat they intend to produce. So the cost of labor, which is equal to the number of workers multiplied by $200, is a **variable cost**, denoted by *VC*—a cost that depends on the quantity of output produced. Adding the fixed cost and the variable cost of a given quantity of output gives the **total cost**, or *TC*, of that quantity of output. We can express the relationship among fixed cost, variable cost, and total cost as an equation:

A **fixed cost** is a cost that does not depend on the quantity of output produced. It is the cost of the fixed input.

A **variable cost** is a cost that depends on the quantity of output produced. It is the cost of the variable input.

The **total cost** of producing a given quantity of output is the sum of the fixed cost and the variable cost of producing that quantity of output.

(8-2) Total cost = Fixed cost + Variable cost

or

$$TC = FC + VC$$

The table in Figure 8-4 shows how total cost is calculated for George and Martha's farm. The second column shows the number of workers employed. The third column shows the corresponding level of output, taken from the table in Figure 8-1. The fourth column shows the variable cost, equal to the number of workers multiplied by $200. The fifth column shows the fixed cost, which is $400 regardless of how many workers are employed. The sixth column shows the total cost of output, which is the variable cost plus the fixed cost.

The first column labels each row of the table with a letter, from A to I. These labels will be helpful in understanding our next step: drawing the **total cost curve**, a curve that shows how total cost depends on the quantity of output.

George and Martha's total cost curve is shown in the diagram in Figure 8-4, where the horizontal axis measures the quantity of output in bushels of wheat and the vertical

The **total cost curve** shows how total cost depends on the quantity of output.

Figure 8-4

Total Cost Curve for George and Martha's Farm

The table shows the variable cost, fixed cost, and total cost for various output quantities on George and Martha's 10-acre farm. The total cost curve shows how total cost (measured on the vertical axis) depends on the quantity of output (measured on the horizontal axis). The labeled points on the curve correspond to the rows of the table. The total cost curve slopes upward because the number of workers employed, and hence total cost, increases as the quantity of output increases. The curve gets steeper as output increases due to the diminishing returns to additional workers.

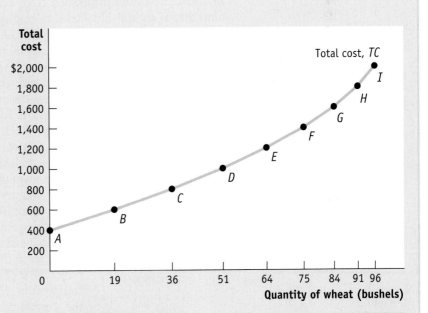

Point on graph	Quantity of labor L (workers)	Quantity of wheat Q (bushels)	Variable cost VC	Fixed cost FC	Total cost TC = FC + VC
A	0	0	$0	$400	$400
B	1	19	200	400	600
C	2	36	400	400	800
D	3	51	600	400	1,000
E	4	64	800	400	1,200
F	5	75	1,000	400	1,400
G	6	84	1,200	400	1,600
H	7	91	1,400	400	1,800
I	8	96	1,600	400	2,000

axis measures total cost in dollars. Each point on the curve corresponds to one row of the table in Figure 8-4. For example, point *A* shows the situation when 0 workers are employed: output is zero, and total cost is equal to fixed cost, $400. Similarly, point *B* shows the situation when 1 worker is employed: output is 19 bushels, and total cost is $600, equal to the sum of $400 in fixed cost and $200 in variable cost.

Like the total product curve, the total cost curve is upward sloping: due to the variable cost, the more output produced, the higher the farm's total cost. But unlike the total product curve, which gets flatter as employment rises, the total cost curve gets *steeper*. That is, the slope of the total cost curve is greater as the amount of output produced increases. And as we will soon see, the steepening of the total cost curve is also due to diminishing returns to the variable input. Before we can understand this, we must first look at the relationships among several useful measures of cost.

economics in action

The Mythical Man-Month

The concept of diminishing returns to inputs was first formulated by economists during the late eighteenth century. These economists, notably including Thomas Malthus, drew their inspiration from agricultural examples; they noticed, in particular, that as an individual tried to employ more workers in agriculture, he or she was forced to cultivate poorer quality land. Although still valid, such examples can seem somewhat musty and old-fashioned in our modern information economy.

However, the idea of diminishing returns to inputs applies with equal force to the most modern of economic activities—such as, say, the design of software. In 1975 Frederick P. Brooks Jr., a project manager at IBM during the days when it dominated the computer business, published a book titled *The Mythical Man-Month* that soon became a classic—so much so that a special anniversary edition was published 20 years later.

The chapter that gave its title to the book is basically about diminishing returns in the writing of software. Brooks observed that multiplying the number of programmers assigned to a project did not produce a proportionate reduction in the time it took to get the program written. A project that could be done by 1 programmer in 12 months could *not* be done by 12 programmers in 1 month—hence the "mythical man-month," the false notion that the number of lines of programming code produced was proportional to the number of code writers employed. In fact, above a certain number, adding another programmer on a project actually *increased* the time to completion.

The argument of *The Mythical Man-Month* is summarized in Figure 8-5. The upper part of the figure shows how the quantity of the project's output, as measured by the number of lines of code produced per month, varies with the number of programmers. Each additional programmer accomplishes less than the previous one, and beyond a certain point an additional programmer is actually counterproductive. The lower part of the figure shows the marginal product of each successive programmer, which falls as more programmers are employed and eventually becomes negative. In other words, programming is subject to diminishing returns so severe that at some point more programmers

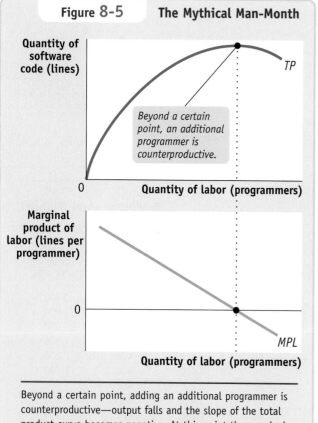

Figure 8-5   The Mythical Man-Month

Quantity of software code (lines)

Beyond a certain point, an additional programmer is counterproductive.

TP

0   Quantity of labor (programmers)

Marginal product of labor (lines per programmer)

0

MPL

Quantity of labor (programmers)

Beyond a certain point, adding an additional programmer is counterproductive—output falls and the slope of the total product curve becomes negative. At this point the marginal product of labor curve crosses the horizontal axis—and the marginal product of labor becomes negative.

actually have negative marginal product. The source of the diminishing returns lies in the nature of the production function for a programming project: each programmer must coordinate his or her work with that of all the other programmers on the project, leading to each person spending more and more time communicating with others as the number of programmers increases. In other words, other things equal, there are diminishing returns to labor. It is likely, however, that if fixed inputs devoted to programming projects are increased—say, installing a faster e-mail system—the problem of diminishing returns for additional programmers can be mitigated.

A reviewer of the reissued edition of *The Mythical Man-Month* summarized the reasons for these diminishing returns: "There is an inescapable overhead to yoking up programmers in parallel. The members of the team must 'waste time' attending meetings, drafting project plans, exchanging e-mail, negotiating interfaces, enduring performance reviews, and so on . . . At Microsoft, there will be at least one team member that just designs T-shirts for the rest of the team to wear." (from www.ercb.com, Dr. Dobb's Electronic Review of Computer Books.) ∎

> > > > > > > > > > > > > > > > > >

▶▶CHECK YOUR UNDERSTANDING 8-1

1. Bernie's ice-making company produces ice cubes using a 10-ton machine and electricity. The quantity of output, measured in terms of pounds of ice, is given in this table:

Quantity of electricity (kilowatts)	Quantity of ice (pounds)
0	0
1	1,000
2	1,800
3	2,400
4	2,800

a. What is the fixed input? What is the variable input?
b. Construct a table showing the marginal product of the variable input. Does it show diminishing returns?
c. Suppose a 50 percent increase in the size of the fixed input increases output by 100 percent for any given amount of the variable input. What is the fixed input now? Construct a table showing the total product and marginal product in this case.

Solutions appear at back of book.

Two Key Concepts: Marginal Cost and Average Cost

We've just seen how to derive a firm's total cost curve from its production function. Our next step is to take a deeper look at total cost by deriving two extremely useful measures: *marginal cost* and *average cost*. As we'll see, these two measures of the cost of production have a somewhat surprising relationship to each other. Moreover, they will prove to be vitally important in Chapter 9, where we will use them to analyze the firm's output decision and the market supply curve.

Marginal Cost

We defined marginal cost in Chapter 7: it is the change in total cost generated by producing one more unit of output. We've already seen that marginal product is easiest to calculate if data on output are available in increments of one unit of input. Similarly, marginal cost is easiest to calculate if data on total cost are available in increments of one unit of output. When the data come in less convenient increments, it's

b. On one diagram, draw the AFC, AVC, and ATC curves.

c. What principle explains why the AFC declines as output increases? What principle explains why the AVC increases as output increases? Explain your answers.

d. How many cups of frozen yogurt are produced when average total cost is minimized?

4. The accompanying table shows a car manufacturer's total cost of producing cars.

Quantity of cars	TC
0	$ 500,000
1	540,000
2	560,000
3	570,000
4	590,000
5	620,000
6	660,000
7	720,000
8	800,000
9	920,000
10	1,100,000

a. What is this manufacturer's fixed cost?

b. For each level of output, calculate the variable cost (VC). For each level of output except zero output, calculate the average variable cost (AVC), average total cost (ATC), and average fixed cost (AFC). What is the minimum-cost output?

c. For each level of output, calculate this manufacturer's marginal cost (MC).

d. On one diagram, draw the manufacturer's AVC, ATC, and MC curves.

5. Magnificent Blooms is a florist specializing in floral arrangements for weddings, graduations, and other events. Magnificent Blooms has a fixed cost associated with space and equipment of $100 per day. Each worker is paid $50 per day. The production function for Magnificent Blooms is shown in the accompanying table.

Quantity of labor (workers)	Quantity of floral arrangements
0	0
1	5
2	9
3	12
4	14
5	15

a. What is the marginal product, MPL, of the first, second, third, fourth, and fifth workers? What principle explains why the marginal product per worker declines as the number of workers employed increases?

b. What is the marginal cost (MC) of producing each of the first 5 floral arrangements? The sixth through ninth floral arrangements? The remaining levels of output? What principle explains why the marginal cost per floral arrangement increases as the number of arrangements increases?

6. You have the information shown in the accompanying table about a firm's costs. Complete the missing data.

Quantity	TC	MC	ATC	AVT
0	$20			
1	?	$20	?	?
2	?	10	?	?
3	?	16	?	?
4	?	20	?	?
5	?	24	?	?

7. Evaluate each of the following statements: If a statement is true, explain why; if it is false, identify the mistake and try to correct it.

a. A decreasing marginal product tells us that marginal cost must be rising.

b. An increase in fixed cost increases the minimum-cost output.

c. An increase in fixed cost increases marginal cost.

d. When marginal cost is above average total cost, average total cost must be falling.

8. Mark and Jeff operate a small company that produces souvenir footballs. Their fixed cost is $2,000 per month. They can hire workers for $1,000 per worker per month. Their monthly production function for footballs is as given in the accompanying table.

Quantity of labor (workers)	Quantity of footballs
0	0
1	300
2	800
3	1,200
4	1,400
5	1,500

a. For each level of employment, calculate average variable cost (AVC), average fixed cost (AFC), average total cost (ATC), and marginal cost (MC).

b. On one diagram, draw in the AVC, ATC, and MC curves.

c. At what level of output is Mark and Jeff's average total cost minimized?

9. You produce widgets. Currently you produce 4 widgets at a total cost of $40.

a. What is your average total cost?

b. Suppose you could produce one more (the fifth) widget at a marginal cost of $5. If you do produce that fifth widget, what will your average total cost be? Has your average total cost increased or decreased? Why?

c. Suppose instead that you could produce one more (the fifth) widget at a marginal cost of $20. If you do produce that fifth widget, what will your average total cost be? Has your average total cost increased or decreased? Why?

10. In your economics class, each homework problem set is graded on the basis of a maximum score of 100. You have completed 9 out of 10 of the problem sets for the term, and your current average grade is 88. What range of grades for your 10th problem set will raise your overall average? What range will lower your overall average? Explain.

11. Don owns a small concrete-mixing company. His fixed cost is the cost of the concrete-batching machinery and his mixer trucks. His variable cost is the cost of the sand, gravel, and other inputs for producing concrete; the gas and maintenance for the machinery and trucks; and his workers. He is trying to decide how many mixer trucks to purchase. He has estimated the costs shown in the accompanying table based on estimates of the number of orders his company will receive per week.

Quantity of trucks	FC	VC 20 orders	VC 40 orders	VC 60 orders
2	$6,000	$2,000	$5,000	$12,000
3	7,000	1,800	3,800	10,800
4	8,000	1,200	3,600	8,400

a. For each level of fixed cost, calculate Don's total cost for producing 20, 40, and 60 orders per week.

b. If Don is producing 20 orders per week, how many trucks should he purchase and what will his average total cost be? Answer the same questions for 40 and 60 orders per week.

12. Consider Don's concrete-mixing business described in Problem 11. Suppose Don purchased three trucks, expecting to produce 40 orders per week.

a. Suppose that, in the short run, business declines to 20 orders per week. What is Don's average total cost per order in the short run? What will his average total cost per order in the short run be if his business booms to 60 orders per week?

b. What is Don's long-run average total cost for 20 orders per week? Explain why his short-run average total cost of producing 20 orders per week when the number of trucks is fixed at 3 is greater than his long-run average total cost of producing 20 orders per week.

c. Sketch Don's long-run average total cost curve. Sketch his short-run average total cost curve if he owns three trucks.

13. True or False? Explain your reasoning.

a. The short-run average total cost can never be less than the long-run average total cost.

b. The short-run average variable cost can never be less than the long-run average total cost.

c. In the long run, choosing a higher level of fixed cost shifts the long-run average total cost curve upward.

14. Wolfsburg Wagon (WW) is a small automaker. The accompanying table shows WW's long-run average total cost.

Quantity of cars	LRATC of car
1	$30,000
2	20,000
3	15,000
4	12,000
5	12,000
6	12,000
7	14,000
8	18,000

a. For which levels of output does WW experience economies of scale?

b. For which levels of output does WW experience diseconomies of scale?

c. For which levels of output does WW experience constant returns to scale?

>web... To continue your study and review of concepts in this chapter, please visit the Krugman/Wells website for quizzes, animated graph tutorials, web links to helpful resources, and more.

www.worthpublishers.com/krugmanwells

Perfect Competition and the
>> Supply Curve

DOING WHAT COMES NATURALLY

What you will learn in this chapter:

➤ The meaning of **perfect competition** and the characteristics of a **perfectly competitive industry**

➤ How a **price-taking producer** determines its profit-maximizing quantity of output

➤ How to assess whether or not a producer is profitable and why an unprofitable producer may continue to operate in the short run

➤ Why industries behave differently in the short run and the long run

➤ What determines the **industry supply curve** in both the short run and the long run

Food consumers in the United States are concerned about health issues. Demand for "natural" foods and beverages, such as bottled water and organically grown fruits and vegetables, increased rapidly over the past decade. The small group of farmers who had pioneered organic farming techniques prospered thanks to higher prices.

But everyone knew that the high prices of organic produce were unlikely to persist even if the new, higher demand for naturally grown food continued: the supply of organic food, while not that price-elastic in the short run, was surely much more price-elastic in the long run. Over time, farms already producing organically would increase their capacity, and conventional farmers would enter the organic food business. So the increase in the quantity supplied in response to the increase in price would be much larger in the long run than in the short run.

Where does the supply curve come from? Why is there a difference between the short-run and the long-run supply curve? In this chapter we will use our understanding of costs, developed in Chapter 8, as the basis for an analysis of the supply curve. As we'll see, this will require that we understand the behavior both of individual firms and of an entire industry, composed of these many individual firms.

Our analysis in this chapter assumes that the industry in question is characterized by

perfect competition. We begin by explaining the concept of perfect competition, providing a brief introduction to the conditions that give rise to a perfectly competitive industry. We then show how a producer under perfect competition decides how much to produce. Finally, we use the cost curves of the individual producers to derive the *industry supply curve* under perfect competition. By analyzing the way a competitive industry evolves over time, we will come to understand the distinction between the short-run and long-run effects of changes in demand on a competitive industry—such as, for example, the effect of America's new taste for organic food on the organic farming industry. We will conclude with a deeper discussion of the conditions necessary for perfect competition.

Peter Dean/Agriculture/Grant Heilman Photography

Whether it's organic strawberries or satellites, how a good is produced determines its cost of production.

Perfect Competition

Suppose that Yves and Zoe are neighboring farmers, both of whom grow organic tomatoes. Both sell their output to the same grocery store chains that carry organic foods; so, in a real sense, Yves and Zoe compete with each other.

Does this mean that Yves should try to stop Zoe from growing tomatoes or that Yves and Zoe should form an agreement to grow less? Almost certainly not: there are hundreds or thousands of organic tomato farmers, and Yves and Zoe are competing with all those other growers as well as with each other. Because so many farmers sell organic tomatoes, if any one of them produced more or less, there would be no measure able effect on market prices.

When people talk about business competition, the image they often have in mind is a situation in which two or three rival firms are intensely struggling for advantage. But economists know that when a business focuses on a few main competitors, it's actually a sign that competition is fairly limited. As the example of organic tomatoes suggests, when there is enough competition it doesn't even make sense to identify your opponents: there are so many competitors that you cannot single out any one of them as a rival.

We can put it another way: Yves and Zoe are **price-taking producers.** A producer is a price-taker when its actions cannot affect the market price of the good it sells. As a result, a price-taking producer considers the market price as given. When there is enough competition—when competition is what economists call "perfect"—then every producer is a price-taker. And there is a similar definition for consumers: a **price-taking consumer** is a consumer who cannot influence the market price of the good by his or her actions. That is, the market price is unaffected by how much or how little of the good the consumer buys.

A **price-taking producer** is a producer whose actions have no effect on the market price of the good it sells.

A **price-taking consumer** is a consumer whose actions have no effect on the market price of the good he or she buys.

Defining Perfect Competition

In a **perfectly competitive market**, all market participants, both consumers and producers, are price-takers. That is, neither consumption decisions by individual consumers nor production decisions by individual producers affect the market price of the good.

The supply and demand model, which we introduced in Chapter 3 and have used repeatedly since then, is a model of a perfectly competitive market. It depends fundamentally on the assumption that no individual buyer or seller of a good, such as scalped tickets to a hockey game or organic tomatoes, believes that he or she can affect the price at which he or she can sell or buy the good.

As a general rule, consumers are indeed price-takers. Instances in which consumers are able to affect the prices they pay are rare. It is, however, quite common for producers to have a significant ability to affect the prices they receive, a phenomenon we'll address in Chapter 14. So the model of perfect competition is appropriate for some but not all markets. An industry in which producers are price-takers is called a **perfectly competitive industry.** Clearly, some industries aren't perfectly competitive; in later chapters we'll see how to analyze industries that don't fit the perfectly competitive model.

A **perfectly competitive market** is a market in which all market participants are price-takers.

A **perfectly competitive industry** is an industry in which producers are price-takers.

Under what circumstances will all producers be price-takers? In the next section we will see that there are two necessary conditions for a perfectly competitive industry and that a third condition is often present as well.

Two Necessary Conditions for Perfect Competition

The markets for major grains, like wheat and corn, are perfectly competitive: individual wheat and corn farmers, as well as individual buyers of wheat and corn, take market prices as given. In contrast, the markets for some of the food items made from these grains—in particular, breakfast cereals—are by no means perfectly competitive. There is intense competition among cereal brands, but not *perfect*

207

competition. To understand the difference between the market for wheat and the market for shredded wheat cereal is to understand the two necessary conditions for perfect competition.

A producer's **market share** is the fraction of the total industry output represented by that producer's output.

First, for an industry to be perfectly competitive, it must contain many producers, none of whom have a large **market share**. A producer's market share is the fraction of the total industry output represented by that producer's output. The distribution of market share constitutes a major difference between the grain industry and the breakfast cereal industry. There are thousands of wheat farmers, none of whom account for more than a small fraction of 1 percent of total wheat sales. The breakfast cereal industry, however, is dominated by four producers: Kellogg's, General Mills, Post, and Quaker Foods. Kellogg's alone accounts for about one-third of all cereal sales. Kellogg's executives know that if they try to sell more corn flakes, they are likely to drive down the market price of corn flakes. That is, they know that their actions influence market prices, simply because they are so large a part of the market that changes in their production will significantly affect the overall quantity supplied. It makes sense to assume that producers are price-takers only when an industry does *not* contain any large players like Kellogg's.

A good is a **standardized product**, also known as a **commodity**, when consumers regard the products of different producers as the same good.

Second, an industry can be perfectly competitive only if consumers regard the products of all producers as equivalent. This clearly isn't true in the breakfast cereal market: consumers don't consider Cap'n Crunch to be a good substitute for Wheaties. As a result, the maker of Wheaties has some ability to increase its price without fear that it will lose all its customers to the maker of Cap'n Crunch. Contrast this with the case of a **standardized product,** sometimes known as a **commodity.** Consumers regard the output of one wheat producer as a perfect substitute for that of another producer. Consequently, one farmer cannot increase the price for his wheat without losing all his sales to other wheat farmers. So the second necessary condition for a competitive industry is that the industry output is a standardized product.

FOR INQUIRING MINDS

WHAT'S A STANDARDIZED PRODUCT?

A perfectly competitive industry must produce a standardized product. But is it enough for the products of different firms actually to be the same? No: people must also *think* that they are the same. And producers often go to great lengths to convince consumers that they have a distinctive, or *differentiated*, product, even when they don't.

Consider, for example, champagne—not the superexpensive premium champagnes but the more ordinary stuff. Most people cannot tell the difference between champagne actually produced in the Champagne region of France, where the product originated, and similar products from Spain or California. But the French government has sought and obtained legal protection for the firms of Champagne, ensuring that around the world only bubbly wine from that region

In the end, only kimchi eaters can tell you if there is truly a difference between Korean-produced kimchi and the Japanese-produced variety.

AP/Wide World Photos

can be called champagne. If it's from someplace else, all the seller can do is say that it was produced by the *méthode Champenoise*. This creates a differentiation in the minds of consumers and lets the champagne producers of Champagne charge higher prices.

In a less Eurocentric example, Korean producers of *kimchi*, the spicy fermented cabbage that is the national side dish, are doing their best to convince consumers that the same product packaged by Japanese firms is just not the real thing. The purpose is, of course, to ensure higher prices for Korean *kimchi*.

So is an industry perfectly competitive if it sells products that are indistinguishable except in name but that consumers, for whatever reason, don't think are standardized? No. When it comes to defining the nature of competition, the consumer is always right.

Free Entry and Exit

All perfectly competitive industries have many producers with small market shares, producing a standardized product. Most perfectly competitive industries are also characterized by one more feature: it is easy for new firms to enter the industry or for firms that are currently in the industry to leave. That is, no obstacles in the form of government regulations or limited access to key resources prevent new producers from entering the market. And no additional costs are associated with shutting down a company and leaving the industry. Economists refer to the arrival of new firms into an industry as *entry*; they refer to the departure of firms from an industry as *exit*. When there are no obstacles to entry into or exit from an industry, we say that the industry has **free entry and exit.**

Free entry and exit is not strictly necessary for perfect competition. In Chapter 4 we described the case of New Jersey clam fishing, where regulations have the effect of limiting the number of fishing boats. Despite this, there are enough boats operating that the fishermen are price-takers. But free entry and exit is a key factor in most competitive industries. It ensures that the number of producers in an industry can adjust to changing market conditions. And, in particular, it ensures that producers in an industry cannot artificially keep other firms out.

To sum up, then, perfect competition depends on two necessary conditions. First, the industry must contain many producers, each having a small market share. Second, the industry must produce a standardized product. In addition, perfectly competitive industries are normally characterized by free entry and exit.

How does an industry that meets these three criteria behave? As a first step toward answering that question, let's look at how an individual producer in a perfectly competitive industry maximizes profit.

> There is **free entry and exit** into and from an industry when new producers can easily enter into or leave that industry.

economics in action

The Pain of Competition

Sometimes it is possible to see an industry become perfectly competitive. In fact, it happens on a regular basis in the case of pharmaceuticals: the conditions for perfect competition are often met as soon as the patent on a popular drug expires.

When a company develops a new drug, it is usually able to receive a patent—a legal monopoly that gives it the exclusive right to sell that drug for 20 years from the date of filing. When the patent expires, the field is open for other companies to sell their own versions of the drug—marketed as "generics" and sold under the medical name of the drug rather than the brand name used by the original producer. Generics are standardized products, much like aspirin, and are often sold by many producers.

A good example came in 1984, when Upjohn's patent on ibuprofen—a painkiller that the company still markets under the brand name Motrin—expired. Most people who use ibuprofen, like most people who use aspirin, now purchase a generic version made by one of many producers.

The shift to perfect competition, not coincidentally, is accompanied by a sharp fall in market price. When its patent expired, Upjohn immediately cut the price of Motrin by 35 percent, but as more companies started selling the generic drug, the price of ibuprofen eventually fell by another two-thirds.

Ten years later the patent on the painkiller naproxen—sold under the brand name Naprosyn—expired. The generic version of naproxen was soon selling at only one-tenth of the original price of Naprosyn. ■

> >

> ➤➤ **QUICK REVIEW**
> ➤ Neither the actions of a *price-taking producer* nor those of a *price-taking consumer* can influence the market price of a good.
> ➤ In a *perfectly competitive market* all producers and consumers are price-takers. Consumers are almost always price-takers, but this is often not true of producers. An industry in which producers are price-takers is a *perfectly competitive industry*.
> ➤ A perfectly competitive industry contains many producers, each of which produces a *standardized product* (also known as a *commodity*) but none of which has a large *market share*.
> ➤ Most perfectly competitive industries are also characterized by *free entry and exit*.

1. In each of the following situations, do you think the industry described will be perfectly competitive or not? Explain your answer.
   a. There are two producers of aluminum in the world, a good sold in many places.
   b. Only a handful of companies produce natural gas from the North Sea. The price of natural gas is determined by global supply and demand, of which North Sea production represents a small share.
   c. Dozens of designers sell high-fashion clothes. Each designer has a distinctive style and a loyal clientele.
   d. There are many baseball teams in the United States, one or two in each major city, and each selling tickets to its events.

Solutions appear at back of book.

Production and Profits

Consider Jennifer and Jason, who run an organic tomato farm. Suppose that the market price of organic tomatoes is $18 per bushel and that Jennifer and Jason are price-takers—they can sell as much as they like at that price. Then we can use the data in Table 9-1 to find their profit-maximizing level of output by direct calculation.

TABLE **9-1**

Profit for Jennifer and Jason's Farm When Market Price Is $18

Quantity of tomatoes Q (bushels)	Total revenue of output TR	Total cost of output TC	Profit $TR - TC$
0	$0	$14	$-14
1	18	30	-12
2	36	36	0
3	54	44	10
4	72	56	16
5	90	72	18
6	108	92	16
7	126	116	10

The first column shows the quantity of output in bushels, and the second column shows Jennifer and Jason's total revenue from their output: the market value of their output. Total revenue, TR, is equal to the market price multiplied by the quantity of output:

(9-1) $TR = P \times Q$

In this example, total revenue is equal to $18 per bushel times the quantity of output in bushels.

The third column of Table 9-1 shows Jennifer and Jason's total cost. The fourth column of Table 9-1 shows their profit, equal to total revenue minus total cost:

(9-2) Profit $= TR - TC$

As indicated by the numbers in the table, profit is maximized at an output of 5 bushels, where profit is equal to $18. But we can gain more insight into the profit-maximizing choice of output by viewing it as a problem of marginal analysis, a task we'll do next.

Using Marginal Analysis to Choose the Profit-Maximizing Quantity of Output

Recall from Chapter 7 the *principle of marginal analysis:* the optimal amount of an activity is the level at which marginal benefit is equal to marginal cost. To apply this principle, consider the effect on a producer's profit of increasing output by 1 unit. The marginal benefit of that unit is the additional revenue generated by selling it; this measure has a name—it is called the **marginal revenue** of that output. The general formula for marginal revenue is:

Marginal revenue is the change in total revenue generated by an additional unit of output.

$$\text{(9-3)} \quad \text{Marginal revenue} = \frac{\text{Change in total revenue}}{\text{Change in output}} = \begin{array}{c}\text{Change in total revenue}\\ \text{generated by one}\\ \text{additional unit of output}\end{array}$$

or

$$MR = \Delta TR/\Delta Q$$

So Jennifer and Jason would maximize their profit by producing bushels up to the point at which the marginal revenue is equal to marginal cost. We can summarize this as the producer's **optimal output rule:** profit is maximized by producing the quantity at which the marginal revenue of the last unit produced is equal to its marginal cost. That is, $MR = MC$ at the optimal quantity of output.

The **optimal output rule** says that profit is maximized by producing the quantity of output at which the marginal cost of the last unit produced is equal to its marginal revenue.

We can learn how to apply the optimal output rule with the help of Table 9-2, which provides various short-run cost measures for Jennifer and Jason's farm. The second column contains the farm's variable cost, and the third column shows its total cost of output based on the assumption that the farm incurs a fixed cost of $14. The fourth column shows their marginal cost. Notice that, in this example, the marginal cost falls as output increases from a low level before rising, so that the marginal cost curve has the "swoosh" shape described in Chapter 8. (Shortly it will become clear that this shape has important implications for short-run production decisions.)

TABLE 9-2

Short-Run Costs for Jennifer and Jason's farm

Quantity of tomatoes Q (bushels)	Variable cost of output VC	Total cost of output TC	Marginal cost of bushel $MC = \Delta TC/\Delta Q$	Marginal revenue of bushel	Net gain of bushel = $MR - MC$
0	$0	$14			
			$16	$18	$2
1	16	30			
			6	18	12
2	22	36			
			8	18	10
3	30	44			
			12	18	6
4	42	56			
			16	18	2
5	58	72			
			20	18	-2
6	78	92			
			24	18	-6
7	102	116			

The fifth column contains the farm's marginal revenue, which has an important feature: Jennifer and Jason's marginal revenue is constant for every output level at $18. The sixth and final column of Table 9-2 shows the calculation of the net gain per bushel of tomatoes, which is equal to marginal revenue minus marginal cost—or, equivalently, market price minus marginal cost. As you can see, it is positive for the 1st through 5th bushels; producing each of these bushels raises Jennifer and Jason's profit. For the 6th and 7th bushels, however, net gain is negative: producing

WHAT IF MARGINAL REVENUE AND MARGINAL COST AREN'T EXACTLY EQUAL?

The optimal output rule says that to maximize profit, you should produce the quantity at which marginal revenue is equal to marginal cost. But what do you do if there is no output level at which marginal revenue equals marginal cost? In that case, you produce the largest quantity for which marginal revenue exceeds marginal cost. This is the case in Table 9-2 at an output of 5 bushels. The simpler version of the optimal output rule applies when production involves large numbers, such as hundreds or thousands of units. In such cases marginal cost comes in small increments, and there is always a level of output at which marginal cost almost exactly equals marginal revenue.

The **price-taking firm's optimal output rule** says that a price-taking firm's profit is maximized by producing the quantity of output at which the marginal cost of the last unit produced is equal to the market price.

The **marginal revenue curve** shows how marginal revenue varies as output varies.

them would decrease, not increase, profit. (You can verify this by examining Table 9-1.) So 5 bushels are Jennifer and Jason's profit-maximizing output; it is the level of output at which marginal cost is approximately equal to the market price, $18.

This example, in fact, illustrates another general rule derived from marginal analysis—the **price-taking firm's optimal output rule,** which says that a price-taking firm's profit is maximized by producing the quantity of output at which the marginal cost of the last unit produced is equal to the market price. That is, $P = MC$ at the *price-taking firm's* optimal quantity of output. In fact, the price-taking firm's optimal output rule is just an application of the optimal output rule to the particular case of a price-taking firm. Why? Because in the case of a price-taking firm, *marginal revenue is equal to price.* A price-taking firm cannot influence the market price by its actions. It always takes the market price as given because it cannot lower the market price by selling more or raise the market price by selling less. So, for a price-taking firm, the additional revenue generated by producing one more unit is always the market price. We will need to keep this fact in mind in future chapters, where we will learn that marginal revenue is not equal to the market price if the industry is not perfectly competitive and, as a result, firms are not price-takers.

For the remainder of this chapter, we will assume that the firms in question are, like Jennifer and Jason's farm, perfectly competitive. Figure 9-1 shows that Jennifer and Jason's profit-maximizing quantity of output is, indeed, the number of bushels at which the marginal cost of production is equal to price. The figure shows the marginal cost curve, *MC,* drawn from the data in the last column of Table 9-1. As in Chapter 8, we plot the marginal cost of increasing output from 1 to 2 bushels halfway between 1 and 2, and so on. The horizontal line at $18 is Jennifer and Jason's **marginal revenue curve, MR.** Note that whenever a firm is a price-taker, its marginal revenue curve is a horizontal line at the market price: it can sell as much as it likes at the market price. Regardless of whether it sells more or less, the market price is unaffected. In effect, the individual firm faces a horizontal, perfectly elastic demand curve for its output—an individual demand curve for its output that is equivalent to

Figure 9-1

The Price-Taking Firm's Profit-Maximizing Quantity of Output

At the profit-maximizing quantity of output, marginal cost is equal to the market price. It is located at the point where the marginal cost curve crosses the marginal revenue curve, which is a horizontal line at the market price. Here, the profit-maximizing point is at an output of 5 bushels of tomatoes, the output quantity at point *E.*

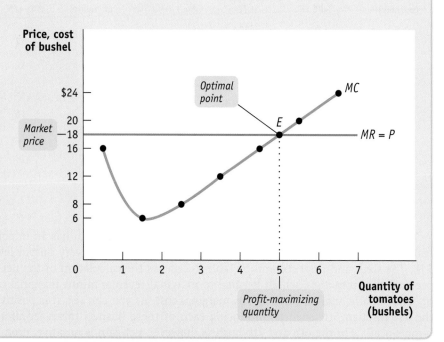

its marginal revenue curve. The marginal cost curve crosses the marginal revenue curve at point E. Sure enough, the quantity of output at E is 5 bushels.

Does this mean that the firm's production decision can be entirely summed up as "produce up to the point where the marginal cost of production is equal to the price"? No, not quite. Before applying the principle of marginal analysis to determine how much to produce, a potential producer must as a first step answer an "either–or" question: should it produce at all? If the answer to that question is yes, it then proceeds to the second step—a "how much" decision: maximizing profit by choosing the quantity of output at which marginal cost is equal to price.

To understand why the first step in the production decision involves an "either–or" question, we need to ask how we determine whether it is profitable or unprofitable to produce at all.

When Is Production Profitable?

Recall from Chapter 7 that a firm's decision whether or not to stay in a given business depends on its *economic profit*—a measure based on the opportunity cost of resources used in the business. To put it a slightly different way: in the calculation of profit, a firm's total cost incorporates implicit costs—the benefits forgone in the next best use of the firm's resources—as well as explicit costs in the form of actual cash outlays.

We will assume that all costs, implicit as well as explicit, are included in the cost numbers given in Table 9-1; as a result, the profit numbers in Table 9-2 are economic profit. So what determines whether Jennifer and Jason's farm earns a profit or generates a loss? The answer is that, given the farm's cost curves, whether or not it is profitable depends on the market price of tomatoes—specifically, *whether the market price is more or less than the farm's minimum average total cost.*

Table 9-3 calculates short-run average variable cost and short-run average total cost for Jennifer and Jason's farm. These are short-run values, because we take fixed cost as given. (We'll turn to the effects of changing fixed cost shortly.) The short-run average total cost curve, *ATC*, is shown in Figure 9-2 on page 214, along with the marginal cost curve, *MC*, from Figure 9-1. As you can see, average total cost is minimized at point C, corresponding to an output of 4 bushels—the *minimum-cost output*—and an average total cost of $14 per bushel.

To see how these curves can be used to decide whether production is profitable or unprofitable, recall that profit is equal to total revenue minus total cost, *TR – TC*. This means:

- If *TR > TC*, the firm is profitable.
- If *TR = TC*, the firm breaks even.
- If *TR < TC*, the firm incurs a loss.

TABLE 9-3

Average Costs for Jennifer and Jason's Farm

Quantity of tomatoes Q (bushels)	Average variable cost of bushel AVC	Average total cost of bushel ATC	Average variable cost of tomatoes AVC = VC/Q	Average total cost of tomatoes ATC = TC/Q
1	$16.00	$30.00	$16.00	$30.00
2	22.00	36.00	11.00	18.00
3	30.00	44.00	10.00	14.67
4	42.00	56.00	10.50	14.00
5	58.00	72.00	11.60	14.40
6	78.00	92.00	13.00	15.33
7	102.00	116.00	14.57	16.57

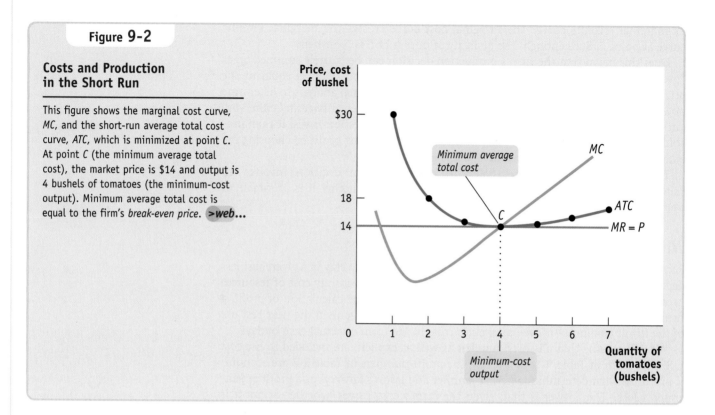

Figure 9-2

Costs and Production in the Short Run

This figure shows the marginal cost curve, MC, and the short-run average total cost curve, ATC, which is minimized at point C. At point C (the minimum average total cost), the market price is $14 and output is 4 bushels of tomatoes (the minimum-cost output). Minimum average total cost is equal to the firm's *break-even price*. **>web**...

We can also express this idea in terms of revenue and cost per unit of output. If we divide profit by the number of units of output, Q, we obtain the following expression for profit per unit of output:

(9-4) $\text{Profit}/Q = TR/Q - TC/Q$

TR/Q is average revenue—that is, the market price. TC/Q is average total cost. So a firm is profitable if the market price for its product exceeds the average total cost of the quantity the firm produces; a firm loses money if the market price is less than average total cost of the quantity the firm produces. This means:

- If $P > ATC$, the firm is profitable.
- If $P = ATC$, the firm breaks even.
- If $P < ATC$, the firm incurs a loss.

Figure 9-3 illustrates this result, showing how the market price determines whether a firm is profitable. It also shows how profits are depicted graphically. Each panel shows the marginal cost curve, MC, and the short-run average total cost curve, ATC. Average total cost is minimized at point C. Panel (a) shows the case we have already analyzed, in which the market price of tomatoes is $18 per bushel. Panel (b) shows the case in which the market price of tomatoes is lower, $10 per bushel.

In panel (a), we see that at a price of $18 per bushel the profit-maximizing quantity of output is 5 bushels, indicated by point E where the marginal cost curve, MC, intersects the marginal revenue curve—which for a price-taking firm is a horizontal line at the market price. At that quantity of output, average total cost is $14.40 per bushel, indicated by point Z. Since the price per bushel exceeds average total cost per bushel, Jennifer and Jason's farm is profitable.

Jennifer and Jason's total profits when the market price is $18 are represented by the area of the shaded rectangle in panel (a). To see why, notice that total profit can be expressed in terms of profit per unit:

(9-5)   Profit = $TR - TC = (TR/Q - TC/Q) \times Q$

or, equivalently,

Profit = $(P - ATC) \times Q$

since P is equal to TR/Q and ATC is equal to TC/Q. The height of the shaded rectangle in panel (a) corresponds to the vertical distance between points E and Z. It is equal to $P - ATC = \$18.00 - \$14.40 = \$3.60$ per bushel. The shaded rectangle has a width equal to the output: $Q = 5$ bushels. So the area of that rectangle is equal to

---

Figure 9-3

Profitability and the Market Price

In panel (a) the market price is $18. The farm is profitable because price exceeds minimum average total cost, the break-even price, $14. The farm's optimal output choice is indicated by point E, corresponding to an output of 5 bushels. The average total cost of producing 5 bushels is indicated by point Z on the ATC curve, corresponding to an amount of $14.40. The vertical distance between E and Z corresponds to the farm's per-unit profit, $18.00 - $14.40 = $3.60. Total profit is given by the area of the shaded rectangle, $5 \times \$3.60 = \$18.00$.

In panel (b) the market price is $10; the farm is unprofitable because the price falls below the minimum average total cost, $14. The farm's optimal output choice when producing is indicated by point A, corresponding to an output of three bushels. The farm's per-unit loss, $14.67 - $10.00 = $4.67, is represented by the vertical distance between A and Y. The farm's total loss is represented by the shaded rectangle, $3 \times \$4.67 = \$14.00$ (adjusted for rounding error). **>web...**

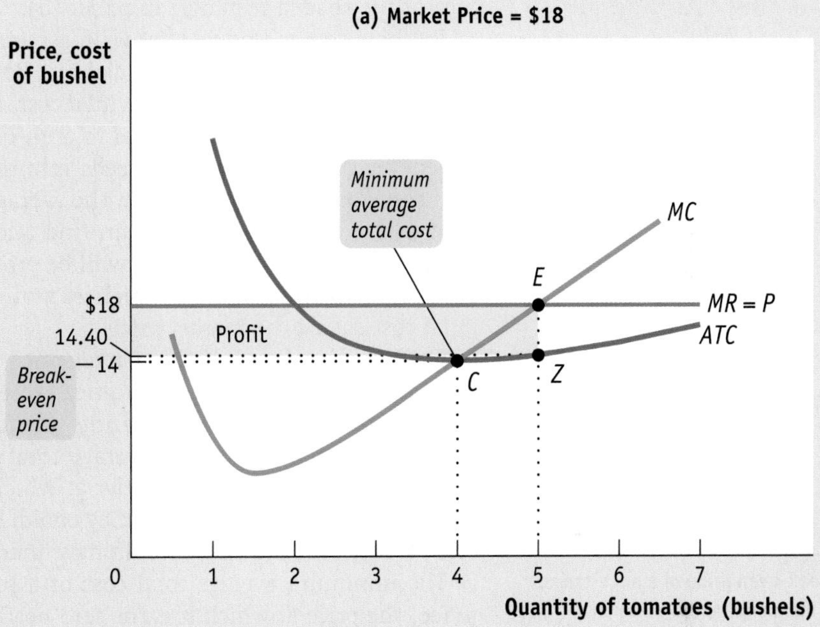

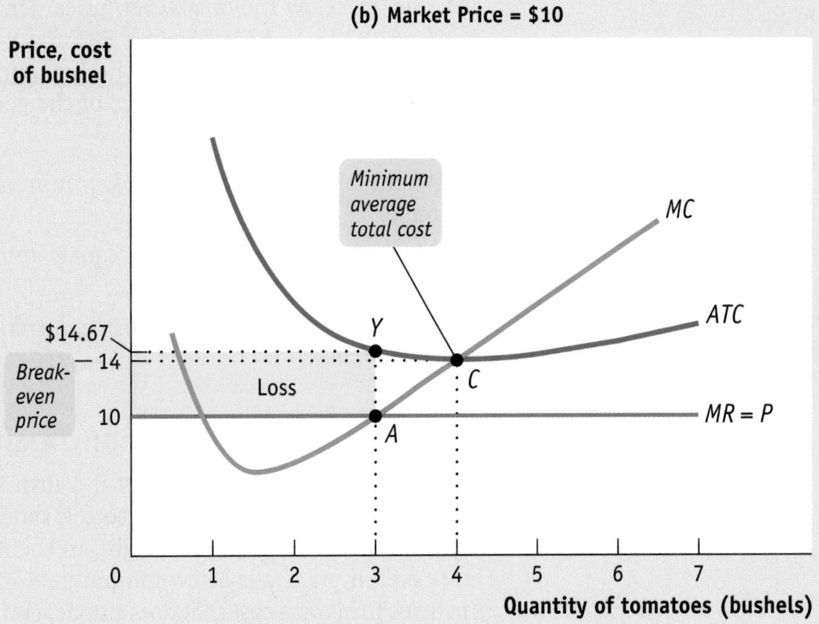

(a) Market Price = $18

(b) Market Price = $10

Jennifer and Jason's profit: 5 bushels × $3.60 profit per bushel = $18—the same number we calculated in Table 9-2.

What about the situation illustrated in panel (b)? Here the market price of tomatoes is $10 per bushel. Setting price equal to marginal cost leads to a profit-maximizing output of 3 bushels, indicated by point A. At this output, Jennifer and Jason have an average total cost of $14.67 per bushel, indicated by point Y. At their profit-maximizing output quantity—3 bushels—average total cost exceeds the market price. This means that Jennifer and Jason's farm generates losses, not profits.

How much do they lose by producing when the market price is $10? On each bushel they lose $ATC - P = \$14.67 - \$10.00 = \$4.67$, an amount corresponding to the vertical distance between points A and Y. And, they would produce 3 bushels, which corresponds to the width of the shaded rectangle. So, the total value of the losses is $4.67 × 3 = $14.00 (adjusted for rounding error), an amount that corresponds to the area of the shaded rectangle in panel (b).

But how does a producer know, in general, whether or not its business will be profitable? It turns out that the crucial test lies in a comparison of the market price to the producer's *minimum average total cost*. On Jennifer and Jason's farm, minimum average total cost, which is equal to $14, occurs at an output quantity of 4 bushels. Whenever the market price exceeds minimum average total cost, the producer can find some output level for which the average total cost is less than the market price. That means that the producer can find a level of output at which the firm makes a profit. Jennifer and Jason's farm will be profitable whenever the market price exceeds $14. And they will achieve the highest profit by producing the quantity at which marginal cost equals the market price.

On the other hand, if the market price is less than minimum average total cost, there is no output level at which price exceeds average total cost. As a result, the firm will be unprofitable at any quantity of output. As we saw, at a price of $10—an amount less than minimum average total cost—Jennifer and Jason did indeed lose money. By producing the quantity at which marginal cost equals the market price, Jennifer and Jason did the best they could, but the best that they could do was a loss of $14. Any other quantity would have increased the size of their loss.

The minimum average total cost of a price-taking firm is called its **break-even price,** the price at which it earns zero profits. A firm will earn positive profits when the market price is above the break-even price, and it will suffer losses when the market price is below the break-even price. Jennifer and Jason's break-even price of $14 is the price at point C in Figures 9-2 and 9-3.

So the rule for determining whether a producer of a good is profitable depends on a comparison of the market price of the good to the producer's break-even price—its minimum average total cost:

- Whenever market price exceeds minimum average total cost, the producer is profitable.

- Whenever the market price equals minimum average total cost, the producer breaks even.

- Whenever market price is less than minimum average total cost, the producer is unprofitable.

The **break-even price** of a price-taking firm is the market price at which it earns zero profits.

The Short-Run Production Decision

You might be tempted to say that if a firm is unprofitable because the market price is below its minimum average total cost, it shouldn't produce any output. In the short run, however, this conclusion isn't right. In the short run, sometimes the firm should produce even if price falls below minimum average total cost. The reason is that total cost includes *fixed cost*—cost that does not depend on the amount of output produced. In the short run, fixed cost must still be paid, regardless of whether or not a firm produces. For

These profits will induce new producers to enter the industry, shifting the short-run industry supply curve to the right. For example, the short-run industry supply curve when the number of producers has increased to 167 is S_2. Corresponding to this supply curve is a new short-run market equilibrium labeled D_{MKT}, with a market price of $16 and a quantity of 750 bushels. At $16, each firm produces 4.5 bushels, so that industry output is $167 \times 4.5 = 750$ bushels (rounded). From panel (a) you can see the effect of the entry of 67 new producers on an existing firm: the fall in price causes it to reduce its output, and its profit falls to the area represented by the shaded rectangle labeled B.

Although diminished, the profit of existing firms at D_{MKT} means that entry will continue and the number of firms will continue to rise. If the number of producers rises to 250, the short-run industry supply curve shifts out again to S_3, and the market equilibrium is at C_{MKT}, with a quantity supplied and demanded of 1,000 bushels and a market price of $14 per bushel.

Like E_{MKT} and D_{MKT}, C_{MKT} is a short-run equilibrium. But it is also something more. Because the price of $14 is each firm's break-even price, an existing producer makes zero economic profits—neither a profit nor a loss—when producing its profit-maximizing output of 4 bushels. At this price there is no incentive either for potential producers to enter or for existing producers to exit the industry. So C_{MKT} corresponds to a **long-run market equilibrium**—a situation in which quantity supplied equals the quantity demanded given that sufficient time has elapsed for producers to either enter or exit the industry. In a long-run market equilibrium, all existing and potential producers have fully adjusted to their optimal long-run choices; as a result, no producer has an incentive to either enter or exit the industry.

To explore further the significance of the difference between short-run and long-run equilibrium, consider the effect of an increase in demand on an industry with free entry that is initially in long-run equilibrium. Panel (b) in Figure 9-7 on page 224 shows the market adjustment; panels (a) and (c) show how an existing individual firm behaves during the process.

In panel (b)of Figure 9-7, D_1 is the initial demand curve and S_1 is the initial short-run industry supply curve. Their intersection at point X_{MKT} is both a short-run and a long-run market equilibrium, because the equilibrium price of $14 leads to zero economic profits—and therefore neither entry nor exit. It corresponds to point X in panel (a), where an individual existing firm is operating at the minimum of its average total cost curve.

Now suppose that the demand curve shifts out for some reason to D_2. As shown in panel (b), in the short run, industry output moves along the short-run industry supply curve S_1 to the new short-run market equilibrium at Y_{MKT}, the intersection of S_1 and D_2. The market price rises to $18 per bushel and industry output increases from Q_X to Q_Y. This corresponds to the movement from X to Y in panel (a), as an existing firm increases its output in response to the rise in the market price.

But we know that Y_{MKT} is not a long-run equilibrium, because $18 is higher than minimum average total cost, so existing producers are making economic profits. This will lead additional firms to enter the industry. Over time entry will cause the short-run industry supply curve to shift to the right. In the long run, the short-run industry supply curve will have shifted out to S_2, and the equilibrium will be at Z_{MKT}—with the price falling back to $14 per bushel and industry output increasing yet again, from Q_Y to Q_Z. Like X_{MKT} before the increase in demand, Z_{MKT} is both a short-run and a long-run market equilibrium.

The effect of entry on an existing firm is illustrated in panel (c), in the movement from Y to Z along the firm's individual supply curve. The firm reduces its output in response to the fall in price, ultimately arriving back at its original output quantity, corresponding to the minimum of its average total cost curve. In fact, every firm that is now in the industry—the initial set of firms and the new entrants—will operate at the minimum of its average total cost curves, at point Z. This means that the entire increase in industry output, from Q_X to Q_Z, comes from production by new entrants.

A market is in **long-run market equilibrium** when the quantity supplied equals the quantity demanded, given that sufficient time has elapsed for entry into and exit from the industry to occur.

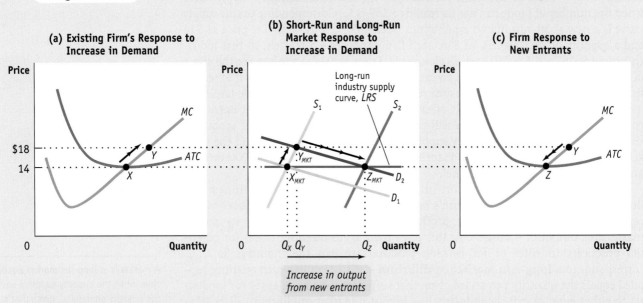

Figure 9-7   The Effect of an Increase in Demand in the Short Run and the Long Run

Panel (b) shows how an industry adjusts in the short and long run to an increase in demand; panels (a) and (c) show the corresponding adjustments by an existing firm. Initially the market is a point X_{MKT} in panel (b), a short-run and long-run equilibrium at a price of $14 and industry output of Q_X. An existing firm makes zero profit, operating at point X in panel (a) at minimum average total cost. Demand increases as D_1 shifts rightward to D_2, and raises the market price to $18. Existing firms increase their output and industry output moves along the short-run industry supply curve S_1 to a short-run equilibrium at Y_{MKT}. Correspondingly, the existing firm in panel (a) moves from point X to point Y. But at a price of $18 existing firms are profitable. As shown in panel (b), in the long run new entrants arrive and the short-run industry suppply curve shifts rightward, from S_1 to S_2. There is a new equilibrium at point Z_{MKT}, at a lower price of $14 and higher industry output of Q_Z. An existing firm responds by moving from Y to Z in panel (c), returning to its initial output level and zero profit. Production by new entrants accounts for the total increase in industsy output, $Q_Z - Q_X$. Like X_{MKT}, Z_{MKT} is also a short-run and long-run equilibrium: with existing firms earning zero economic profits, there is no incentive for any firms to enter or exit the industry. The horizontal line passing through X_{MKT} and Z_{MKT}, LRS, is the *long-run industry supply curve*: at the break-even price of $14, producers will produce any amount that consumers demand in the long run.

The **long-run industry supply curve** shows how the quantity supplied responds to the price once producers have had time to enter or exit the industry.

The line LRS that passes through X_{MKT} and Z_{MKT} in panel (b) is the **long-run industry supply curve.** It shows how the quantity supplied by an industry responds to the price given that producers have had time to enter or exit the industry.

In this particular case, the long-run industry supply curve is horizontal at $14. In other words, in this industry supply is *perfectly elastic* in the long run—given time to enter or exit, producers will supply any quantity consumers demand at a price of $14. Perfectly elastic long-run supply is actually a good assumption for many industries. However, in other industries even the long-run industry supply curve is upward sloping. The usual reason even the long-run industry supply curve is upward sloping is that producers must use some input that is in limited supply and as the industry expands, the price of that input is driven up. For example, beach-resort hotels must compete for a limited quantity of prime beachfront property.

Whether the long-run industry supply curve is horizontal or upward sloping, however, the long-run price elasticity of supply is *higher* than the short-run price elasticity whenever there is free entry and exit. As shown in Figure 9-8, the long-run industry supply curve is always flatter than the short-run industry supply curve. The reason is entry and exit: a high price attracts entry by new producers, resulting in a

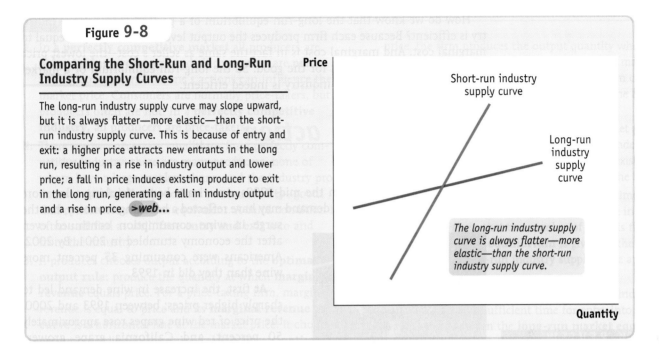

Figure 9-8

Comparing the Short-Run and Long-Run Industry Supply Curves

The long-run industry supply curve may slope upward, but it is always flatter—more elastic—than the short-run industry supply curve. This is because of entry and exit: a higher price attracts new entrants in the long run, resulting in a rise in industry output and lower price; a fall in price induces existing producer to exit in the long run, generating a fall in industry output and a rise in price. **>web...**

Price

Short-run industry supply curve

Long-run industry supply curve

The long-run industry supply curve is always flatter—more elastic—than the short-run industry supply curve.

Quantity

rise in industry output and a fall in price; a low price induces existing firms to exit, leading to a fall in industry output and an increase in price.

The distinction between the short-run industry supply curve and the long-run industry supply curve is very important in practice. We often see a sequence of events like that shown in Figure 9-7: an increase in demand initially leads to a large price increase, but prices return to their initial level once new firms have entered the industry. Or we see the sequence in reverse: a fall in demand reduces prices in the short run, but they return to their initial level as producers exit the industry.

The Cost of Production and Efficiency in Long-run Equilibrium

Our analysis leads us to three conclusions about the cost of production and efficiency in the long-run equilibrium of a perfectly competitive industry. These results will be important in our discussion in Chapter 14 of how monopoly gives rise to inefficiency.

First, in a perfectly competitive industry in equilibrium, the value of marginal cost is the same for all firms. That's because all firms produce the quantity of output at which marginal cost equals the market price, and as price-takers they all face the same market price.

Second, in a perfectly competitive industry with free entry and exit, each firm will have zero economic profits in long-run equilibrium. Each firm produces the quantity of output that minimizes its average total cost—corresponding to point Z in panel (c) of Figure 9-7. So the total cost of production of the industry's output is minimized in a perfectly competitive industry.

The third and final conclusion is that the long-run market equilibrium of a perfectly competitive industry is efficient: no mutually beneficial transactions go unexploited. To understand this we need to recall a fundamental requirement for efficiency from Chapter 6: all consumers who have a willingness to pay greater than or equal to sellers' costs actually get the good. And we also learned that a market is efficient (except under certain, well-defined conditions)—the market price matches all consumers with a willingness to pay greater than or equal to the market price to all sellers who have a cost of producing the good less than or equal to the market price.

10

>>The Rational Consumer

A CLAM TOO FAR

To entice customers, restaurants sometimes offer "all-you-can-eat" specials: all-you-can-eat salad bars, all-you-can-eat breakfast buffets, and all-you-can-eat fried-clam dinners.

But how can a restaurant owner who offers such a special be sure she won't be eaten out of business? If she charges $12.99 for an all-you-can-eat clam dinner, what prevents her average customer from wolfing down $30 worth of clams?

The answer is that even though every once in a while you see someone really take advantage of the offer—heaping a plate high with 30 or 40 fried clams—it's a rare occurrence. And even those of us who like fried clams shudder a bit at the sight. Five or even 10 fried clams can be a treat, but 30 clams is ridiculous. Anyone who pays for an all-you-can-eat meal wants to make the most of it, but a sensible person knows when one more clam would be one clam too many.

Notice what we just did in that last sentence. We said that customers in a restaurant want to "make the most" of their meal; that sounds as if they are trying to maximize something. And we also said that they will stop when consuming one more clam would be a mistake; that sounds as if they are making a marginal decision.

When we analyze the behavior of *producers*, it makes sense to assume that they maximize profits. But what do consumers maximize? Isn't it all a matter of taste?

The answer is yes, it is a matter of taste—and economists can't say much about where tastes come from. But economists *can* say a lot about how a rational individual goes about satisfying his or her tastes. And that is in fact the way that economists think about consumer choice. They work with a model of a *rational consumer*—a consumer who knows what he or she wants and makes the most of the available opportunities.

In this chapter we will show how to analyze the decisions of a rational consumer and how this analysis can be used to derive the market demand curve.

When is more of a good thing too much?

What you will learn in this chapter:

➤ How consumers choose to spend their income on goods and services

➤ Why consumers make choices by maximizing **utility,** a measure of satisfaction from consumption

➤ Why the **principal of diminishing marginal utility** applies to the consumption of most goods and services

➤ How to use marginal analysis to find the **optimal consumption bundle**

➤ How choices by individual consumers give rise to the market demand curve

➤ What **income** and **substitution effects** are

We will begin by showing how the concept of *utility*—a measure of consumer satisfaction—allows us to begin thinking about rational consumer choice. We will then look at how *budget constraints* determine what a consumer can buy and how marginal analysis can be used to determine the consumption choice that maximizes utility. Finally, we will see how to use marginal analysis to derive the demand curve.

Utility: Getting Satisfaction

When analyzing consumer behavior, we're talking about people trying to get what they want—that is, about subjective feelings. Yet there is no simple way to measure subjective feelings. How much satisfaction do I get from my third fried clam? Is it less or more than yours? Does it even make sense to ask the question?

Luckily, it turns out that we don't need to make comparisons between your feelings and mine. All that is required to analyze consumer behavior is to suppose that each individual is trying to maximize some personal measure of the satisfaction gained from consumption of goods and services. That measure is known as the consumer's **utility,** a concept we use to understand behavior but don't expect to measure in practice. Nonetheless, we'll see that the assumption that consumers maximize utility helps us think clearly about consumer choice.

The **utility** of a consumer is a measure of the satisfaction the consumer derives from consumption of goods and services

Utility and Consumption

An individual's utility depends on everything that individual consumes, from apples to Ziploc bags. The set of all the goods and services an individual consumes is known as the individual's **consumption bundle.** The relationship between an individual's consumption bundle and the total amount of utility it generates is known as the **utility function.** The utility function is a personal matter; two people with different tastes will have different utility functions. Someone who actually likes to consume 40 fried clams at a sitting must have a utility function that looks different from that of someone who would rather stop at 5 clams.

An individual's **consumption bundle** is the collection of all the goods and services consumed by that individual.

An individual's total **utility function** gives the total utility generated by his or her consumption bundle.

This terminology is closely parallel to the terminology we used to describe producer decisions in Chapters 8 and 9. A producer uses inputs to produce output according to a production function; a consumer uses consumption to "produce" utility according to a utility function.

Obviously, people do not have a little computer in their heads that calculates the utility generated by their consumption choices. Nonetheless, people must make choices, and they usually base them on at least a rough attempt to decide which choice will give them greater satisfaction. I can have either soup or salad with my dinner. Which will I enjoy more? I can go to Disney World this year or save the money toward buying a new car. Which will make me happier?

The concept of a utility function is just a way of representing the fact that people must make such choices and that they make those choices in a more or less rational way.

How do we measure utility? For the sake of simplicity, it is useful to suppose that we can measure utility in hypothetical units called—what else?—**utils.**

A **util** is a unit of utility.

Figure 10-1, on page 232, illustrates a utility function. It shows the total utility that Cassie, who likes fried clams, gets from an all-you-can-eat clam dinner. We suppose that her consumption bundle consists of a side of cole slaw, which comes with the meal, plus a number of clams to be determined. The table that accompanies the figure shows how Cassie's total utility depends on the number of clams; the curve in panel (a) of the figure shows that same information graphically.

Cassie's utility function is upward sloping over most of the range shown, but it gets flatter as the number of clams consumed increases. And in this example it eventually

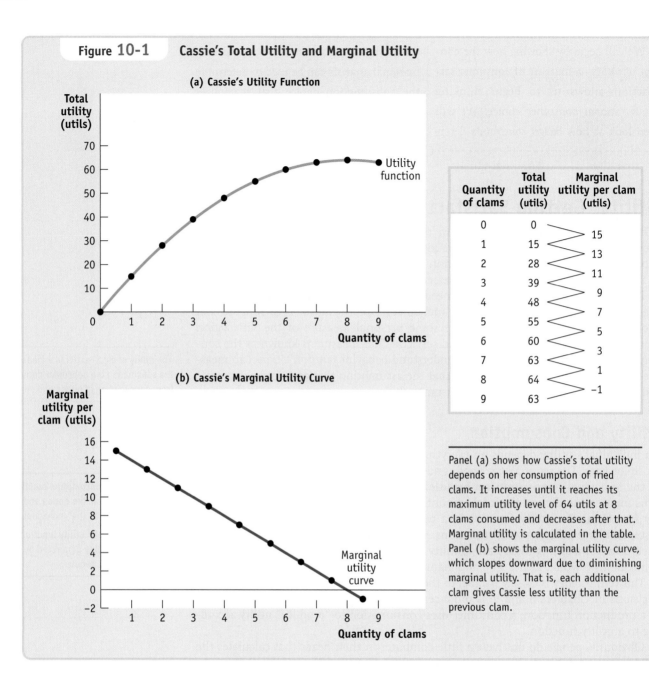

Figure 10-1   Cassie's Total Utility and Marginal Utility

(a) Cassie's Utility Function

Quantity of clams	Total utility (utils)	Marginal utility per clam (utils)
0	0	
		15
1	15	
		13
2	28	
		11
3	39	
		9
4	48	
		7
5	55	
		5
6	60	
		3
7	63	
		1
8	64	
		−1
9	63	

(b) Cassie's Marginal Utility Curve

Panel (a) shows how Cassie's total utility depends on her consumption of fried clams. It increases until it reaches its maximum utility level of 64 utils at 8 clams consumed and decreases after that. Marginal utility is calculated in the table. Panel (b) shows the marginal utility curve, which slopes downward due to diminishing marginal utility. That is, each additional clam gives Cassie less utility than the previous clam.

turns downward. According to the information in the table in Figure 10-1, nine clams is a clam too far: adding that additional clam actually makes Cassie worse off. If she's rational, of course, Cassie will realize that and not consume the ninth clam.

So when Cassie chooses how many clams to consume, she will make this decision by considering the *change* in her total utility from consuming one more clam. This illustrates the general point: to maximize *total* utility, consumers must focus on *marginal* utility.

The **marginal utility** of a good or service is the change in total utility generated by consuming one additional unit of that good or service. The **marginal utility curve** shows how marginal utility depends on the quantity of a good or service consumed.

The Principle of Diminishing Marginal Utility

In addition to showing how Cassie's total utility depends on the number of clams she consumes, the table in Figure 10-1 also shows the **marginal utility** generated by consuming each additional clam—that is, the *change* in total utility from consuming one additional clam. Panel (b) shows the implied **marginal utility curve.** Following our practice in Chapters 7, 8, and 9 with the marginal cost curve, the marginal utility curve is constructed by plotting points at the midpoint of the unit in intervals.

FOR INQUIRING MINDS

IS MARGINAL UTILITY REALLY DIMINISHING?

Are all goods really subject to diminishing marginal utility? Of course not; there are a number of goods for which, at least over some range, marginal utility is surely *increasing*.

For example, there are goods that require some experience to enjoy. The first time you do it, downhill skiing involves a lot more fear than enjoyment—or so they say: the authors have never tried it! It only becomes a pleasurable activity if you do it enough to become reasonably competent. And even some less strenuous forms of consumption

take practice; people who are not accustomed to drinking coffee say it has a bitter taste and can't understand its appeal. (The authors, on the other hand, regard coffee as one of the basic food groups.)

Another example would be goods that only deliver if you buy enough; the great Victorian economist Alfred Marshall, who more or less invented the supply and demand model, gave the example of wallpaper: buying only enough to do half a room is worse than useless. If you need two rolls of wallpaper to finish a room, the marginal

utility of the second roll is larger than the marginal utility of the first roll.

So why does it make sense to assume diminishing marginal utility? For one thing, most goods don't suffer from these qualifications: nobody needs to learn to like ice cream. Also, although most people don't ski and some people don't drink coffee, those who do ski or drink coffee do enough of it that the marginal utility of one more ski run or one more cup is less than that of the last. So *in the relevant range,* marginal utility is still diminishing.

The marginal utility curve is downward sloping: each successive clam adds less to total utility than the previous clam. This is reflected in the table: marginal utility falls from a high of 15 utils for the first clam consumed to −1 for the ninth clam consumed. The fact that the ninth clam has negative marginal utility means that consuming it actually reduces total utility. (Restaurants that offer all-you-can-eat meals depend on the proposition that you can have too much of a good thing.) Not all marginal utility curves eventually become negative. But it is a generally accepted proposition that marginal utility curves do slope downward—that consumption of most goods and services is subject to *diminishing marginal utility*.

The basic idea behind the **principle of diminishing marginal utility** is that the additional satisfaction a consumer gets from one more unit of a good or service declines as the amount of that good or service consumed rises. Or, to put it slightly differently, the more of a good or service you consume, the closer you are to being satiated—reaching a point at which an additional unit of the good adds nothing to your satisfaction. For someone who almost never gets to eat a banana, the occasional banana is a marvelous treat (as it was in Eastern Europe before the fall of communism, when bananas were very hard to find). For someone who eats them all the time, a banana is just, well, a banana.

The principle of diminishing marginal utility plays the same role in the analysis of consumer behavior that the principle of diminishing returns to an input plays in the analysis of producer behavior. Like the principle of diminishing returns to an input, the principle of diminishing marginal utility isn't always true. But it is true in the great majority of cases, enough to serve as a foundation for our analysis of consumer behavior.

The **principle of diminishing marginal utility** says that each successive unit of a good or service consumed adds less to total utility than the previous unit.

economics in action

Oysters versus Chicken

Is a particular food a special treat, something you consume on special occasions? Or is it an ordinary, take-it-or-leave-it dish? The answer depends a lot on how much of that food people normally consume, which determines how much utility they get *at the margin* from having a bit more.

Consider chicken. Modern Americans eat a lot of chicken, so much that they regard it as nothing special. Yet this was not always the case. Traditionally chicken was a luxury dish because chickens were expensive to raise. Restaurant menus from two centuries ago show chicken dishes as the most expensive items listed. Even as recently as 1928, Herbert Hoover ran for president on the slogan "A chicken in every pot," a promise of great prosperity.

What changed the status of chicken was the emergence of new, technologically advanced methods for raising and processing the birds. (You don't want to know.) These methods made chicken abundant, cheap, and also—thanks to the principle of diminishing marginal utility—nothing to get excited about.

The reverse evolution took place for oysters. Not everyone likes oysters, or for that matter has ever tried them—they are definitely not ordinary food. But they are regarded as a delicacy by some; at restaurants that serve them, an oyster appetizer often costs more than the main course.

Yet oysters were once very cheap and abundant—and were regarded as poverty food. In *The Pickwick Papers* by Charles Dickens, published in the 1830s, the author remarks that "poverty and oysters always seem to go together."

What changed? Pollution, which destroyed many oyster beds, greatly reduced the supply, but human population growth greatly increased the demand. As a result, thanks to the principle of diminishing marginal utility, oysters went from being a common food, regarded as nothing special, to being a highly prized luxury good. ■

>> CHECK YOUR UNDERSTANDING 10-1

1. Explain why a rational consumer who has diminishing marginal utility for a good would never consume an additional unit when it generates negative marginal utility, even when that unit is free.

2. Marta drinks three cups of coffee a day, for which she has diminishing marginal utility. Which of her three cups generates the greatest increase in total utility? Which generates the least?

3. In each of the following cases, does the consumer have diminishing, constant, or increasing marginal utility? Explain your answers.
   a. The more Mabel exercises, the more she enjoys each additional visit to the gym.
   b. Although Mei's classical CD collection is huge, her enjoyment from buying another CD has not changed as her collection has grown.
   c. When Dexter was a struggling student, his enjoyment from a good restaurant meal was greater than now, when he has them more frequently.

Solutions appear at back of book.

Budgets and Optimal Consumption

The principle of diminishing marginal utility explains why most people eventually reach a limit, even at an all-you-can-eat buffet where the cost of another clam is measured only in future indigestion. Under ordinary circumstances, however, it costs some additional resources to consume more of a good, and consumers must take that cost into account when making choices.

What do we mean by cost? As always, the fundamental measure of cost is *opportunity cost*. Because the amount of money a consumer can spend is limited, a decision to consume more of one good is also a decision to consume less of some other good.

Budget Constraints and Budget Lines

Consider Sammy, whose appetite is exclusively for clams and potatoes (there's no accounting for tastes). He has a weekly income of $20 and since, given his appetite, more of either good is better than less, he spends all of it on clams and potatoes. We will assume that clams cost $4 per pound and potatoes, $2 per pound. What are his possible choices?

Whatever Sammy chooses, we know that the cost of his consumption bundle cannot exceed the amount of money he has to spend. That is,

(10-1) Expenditure on clams + expenditure on potatoes ≤ total income

Consumers always have limited income, which constrains how much they can consume. So the requirement illustrated by Equation 10-1—that a consumer must choose a consumption bundle that costs no more than his or her total income—is known as the consumer's **budget constraint.** It's a simple way of saying that consumers can't spend more than the total amount of income available to them. In other words, consumption bundles are affordable when they obey the budget constraint. We call the set of all of Sammy's affordable consumption bundles his **consumption possibilities.** As we will see, which consumption bundles are in this set depends on the consumer's income and the prices of goods and services.

Figure 10-2 shows Sammy's consumption possibilities. The quantity of clams in his consumption bundle is measured on the horizontal axis and the quantity of potatoes on the vertical axis. The downward-sloping line connecting points A through F shows which consumption bundles are affordable and which are not. Every bundle on or inside this line (the shaded area) is affordable; every bundle outside this line is unaffordable. As an example of one of the points, let's look at point C, representing 2 pounds of clams and 6 pounds of potatoes, and check whether it satisfies Sammy's budget constraint. The cost of bundle C is 6 pounds of potatoes × $2 per pound + 2 pounds of clams × $4 per pound = $12 + $8 = $20. So bundle C does indeed satisfy Sammy's budget constraint: it costs no more than his weekly income of $20. In fact,

> A **budget constraint** requires that the cost of a consumer's consumption bundle be no more than the consumer's total income.
>
> A consumer's **consumption possibilities** is the set of all consumption bundles that can be consumed given the consumer's income and prevailing prices.

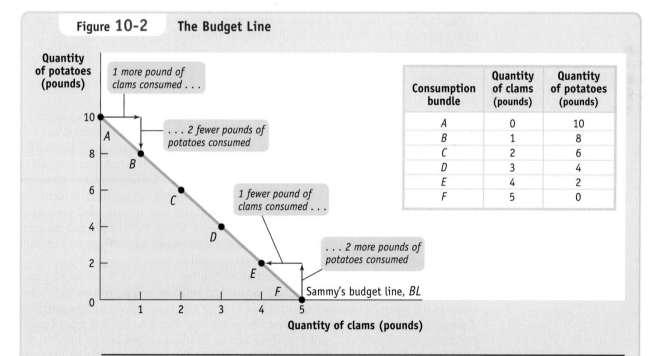

Figure 10-2   The Budget Line

Consumption bundle	Quantity of clams (pounds)	Quantity of potatoes (pounds)
A	0	10
B	1	8
C	2	6
D	3	4
E	4	2
F	5	0

The *budget line* represents all the possible combinations of quantities of potatoes and clams that Sammy can purchase if he spends all of his income. Also, it is the boundary between the set of affordable consumption bundles (the *consumption possibilities*) and unaffordable ones. Given that clams cost $4 per pound and potatoes cost $2 per pound, if Sammy spends all of his income on clams (bundle F), he can purchase 5 pounds of clams; if he spends all of his income on potatoes (bundle A), he can purchase 10 pounds of potatoes. The slope of the budget line here is −2: 2 pounds of potatoes must be forgone for 1 more pound of clams, reflecting the opportunity cost of clams in terms of potatoes. So the location and slope of the budget line depend on the consumer's income and the prices of the goods.

A consumer's **budget line** shows the consumption bundles available to a consumer who spends all of his or her income.

bundle *C* costs exactly as much as Sammy's income. By doing the arithmetic, you can check that all the other points lying on the downward-sloping line are also bundles at which Sammy spends all of his income.

The downward-sloping line has a special name, the **budget line.** It shows all the consumption bundles available to Sammy when he spends all of his income. Let's use Figure 10-2 to gain an intuitive understanding of Sammy's budget line. For brevity's sake, we will denote the quantity of clams (in pounds) by Q_C and the quantity of potatoes (in pounds) by Q_P. We will also define P_C to be the price of one pound of clams, P_P to be the price of one pound of potatoes, and N to be Sammy's income. So if we restate Sammy's budget constraint of Equation 10-1 in terms of this new notation, it becomes

(10-2) $(Q_C \times P_C) + (Q_P \times P_P) \leq N$

Whenever Sammy consumes a bundle on his *budget line*, he spends all of his income, so that his expenditure on clams and potatoes is exactly equal to his income. The equation for Sammy's budget line is therefore

(10-3) $(Q_C \times P_C) + (Q_P \times P_P) = N$

Now consider what happens when Sammy spends all $20 of his income on clams (that is, $Q_P = 0$). In that case the greatest amount of clams he can consume is

$Q_C = N/P_C = \$20/\$4$ per pound of potatoes $= 5$ pounds of clams

So the horizontal intercept of the budget line—Sammy's clam consumption when he consumes zero potatoes—is at point *F*, where he consumes 5 pounds of clams.

Now consider the other extreme consumption choice given that Sammy spends all of his income: Sammy consumes all potatoes and no clams (that is, $Q_C = 0$). Then the greatest amount of potatoes he can consume would be

$Q_P = N/P_P = \$20/\$2$ per pound of potatoes $= 10$ pounds of potatoes

So the vertical intercept of the budget line—Sammy's potato consumption when he consumes zero clams—is at point *A*, where he consumes 10 pounds of potatoes.

The remaining four bundles indicated on the budget line—points *B*, *C*, *D*, and *E*—can be understood by considering the trade-offs Sammy faces when spending all of his income. Starting at bundle *A*, consider what happens if Sammy wants to consume 1 pound of clams while still consuming as many pounds of potatoes as possible. Consuming 1 pound of clams, which costs $4, requires that he give up 2 pounds of potatoes, which cost $2 per pound. In order to move 1 unit to the right (an increase of 1 pound of clams), Sammy must also move 2 units down (a decrease of 2 pounds of potatoes). This places him at bundle *B* on his budget line.

Similarly, if we start at bundle *F* and allow Sammy to give up 1 pound of clams (moving 1 unit to the left), how many pounds of potatoes will he receive in return? Giving up 1 pound of clams frees up $4 of Sammy's income, which goes to purchase 2 pounds of potatoes at $2 per pound. So by moving 1 unit to the left from bundle *F*, Sammy also moves up 2 units, putting him at bundle *E* on his budget line.

This exercise shows that when Sammy spends all of his income, he trades off more clams for fewer potatoes, or vice versa, by "sliding" along his budget line. In particular, if we assume that Sammy can consume fractions of pounds of clams and potatoes as well as whole pounds, his budget line is indeed the line connecting the points *A* through *F* in Figure 10-2.

Do we need to consider the other bundles in Sammy's consumption possibilities, the ones that lie *within* the shaded region in Figure 10-2 bounded by the budget line? The answer is, for all practical situations, no: as long as Sammy doesn't get satiated— that is, his marginal utility from consuming either good is always positive—and he doesn't get any utility from saving income rather than spending it, then he will always choose to consume a bundle that lies on his budget line.

Because changing a consumption bundle involves sliding up or down the budget line, the *slope* of the budget line tells us the opportunity cost of each good in terms of the other. Recall from Chapter 2 that we used the slope of the production possibility frontier to illustrate the opportunity cost to the economy of an additional unit of one good in terms of how much of the other good must be forgone, a cost that arose from the economy's limited productive resources. In this case, the slope of the budget line illustrates the opportunity cost to an individual of consuming one more unit of one good in terms of how much of the other good in his or her consumption bundle must be forgone. The scarce "resource" here is money—the consumer has a limited budget.

The slope of Sammy's budget line—the rise over run—is −2; 2 pounds of potatoes must be forgone to obtain another pound of clams. Economists call the number of pounds of potatoes that must be forgone in order to obtain one more pound of clams the *relative price* of one pound of clams in terms of potatoes. The relative price of the good on the horizontal axis in terms of the good on the vertical axis is equal to minus the slope of the budget line.

One important point about the budget line may be obvious but nonetheless needs emphasizing: the position of a consumer's budget line—how far *out* it is from the origin—depends on that consumer's income. Suppose that Sammy's income were to rise to $32 per week. Then he could afford to buy 8 pounds of clams, or 16 pounds of potatoes, or any consumption bundle in between; as shown in Figure 10-3, his budget line would move *outward*. However, if his income were to shrink to $12 per week, his budget line would shift *inward*: he would be able to consume at most 3 pounds of clams or 6 pounds of potatoes. In all these cases, the slope of the budget line would not change because the relative price of clams in terms of potatoes does not change: for 1 more pound of clams, Sammy still has to give up 2 pounds of potatoes.

Clearly, a larger income would increase Sammy's consumption possibilities; and utility analysis can tell us how he would take advantage of those possibilities to increase his total utility by consuming more of one or both goods. Conversely, a smaller income would reduce Sammy's consumption possibilities. He would be forced to consume less, and his utility would be lower. But for now let's continue to assume that Sammy's income is fixed at $20 per week.

Given that $20 per week budget, what point on his budget line will Sammy choose?

Figure 10-3

Changes in Income Shift the Budget Line

If Sammy's income increases from $20 to $32 per week, he is clearly better off: his consumption possibilities have increased, and his budget line shifts, from BL_1, outward to its new position at BL_2. If Sammy's income decreases from $20 to $12, he is clearly worse off: his consumption possibilities have decreased and his budget line shifts inward toward the origin, from BL_1 to BL_3. **>web...**

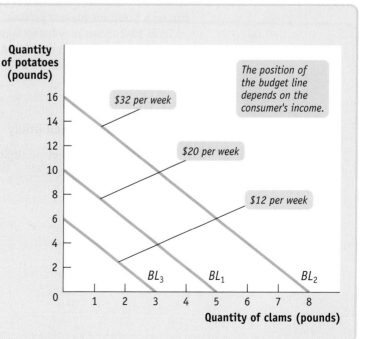

Optimal Consumption Choice

Because Sammy has a budget constraint, which means that he will consume a consumption bundle on the budget line, a choice to consume a given quantity of clams also determines his potato consumption, and vice versa. We want to find the consumption bundle—the point on the budget line—that maximizes Sammy's total utility. This bundle is Sammy's **optimal consumption bundle,** the consumption bundle that maximizes total utility given the budget constraint.

The **optimal consumption bundle** is the consumption bundle that maximizes a consumer's total utility given his or her bud-get constraint.

TABLE 10-1

Sammy's Utility from Clam and Potato Consumption

Utility from clam consumption		Utility from potato consumption	
Quantity of clams (pounds)	Utility from clams (utils)	Quantity of potatoes (pounds)	Utility from potatoes (utils)
0	0	0	0
1	15	1	11.5
2	25	2	21.4
3	31	3	29.8
4	34	4	36.8
5	36	5	42.5
		6	47.0
		7	50.5
		8	53.2
		9	55.2
		10	56.7

Table 10-1 shows how much utility Sammy gets from different levels of consumption of clams and potatoes, respectively. According to the table, Sammy has a healthy appetite; the more of either good he consumes, the higher his utility.

But because he has a limited budget, he must make a trade-off: the more pounds of clams he consumes, the fewer pounds of potatoes, and vice versa. That is, he must choose a point on his budget line.

Table 10-2 shows how his total utility varies as he slides down his budget line. Each of six possible consumption bundles, A through F from Figure 10-2, is given in the first column. The second column shows the level of clam consumption corresponding to each

TABLE 10-2

Sammy's Budget and Total Utility

Consumption Bundle	Quantity of clams (pounds)	Utility from clams (utils)	Quantity of potatoes (pounds)	Utility from potatoes (utils)	Total utility (utils)
A	0	0	10	56.7	56.7
B	1	15	8	53.2	68.2
C	2	25	6	47.0	72.0
D	3	31	4	36.8	67.8
E	4	34	2	21.4	55.4
F	5	36	0	0	36.0

choice. The third column shows the utility Sammy gets from consuming those clams. The fourth column shows the quantity of potatoes Sammy can afford *given* the level of clam consumption; this quantity goes down as his clam consumption goes up, because he is sliding down the budget line. The fifth column shows the utility he gets from consuming those potatoes. And the final column shows his *total utility*. In this example, Sammy's total utility is the sum of the utility he gets from clams and the utility he gets from potatoes.

Figure 10-4 illustrates the result graphically. Panel (a) shows Sammy's budget line, to remind us that when he decides to consume more clams he is also deciding to consume fewer potatoes. Panel (b) then shows how his total utility depends on that choice. The horizontal axis in panel (b) has two sets of labels: it shows both the quantity of clams, increasing from left to right, and the quantity of potatoes, increasing from right to left. The reason we can use the same axis to represent consumption of both goods is, of course, the budget line: the more pounds of clams Sammy consumes, the fewer pounds of potatoes he can afford, and vice versa.

Figure 10-4

Optimal Consumption Bundle

Panel (a) shows Sammy's budget line and his six possible consumption bundles. Panel (b) shows how his total utility is affected by his consumption bundle, which must lie on his budget line. The quantity of clams is measured from left to right on the horizontal axis, and the quantity of potatoes is measured from right to left. His total utility is maximized at bundle *C*, where he consumes 2 pounds of clams and 6 pounds of potatoes. This is Sammy's *optimal consumption bundle.* **>web**...

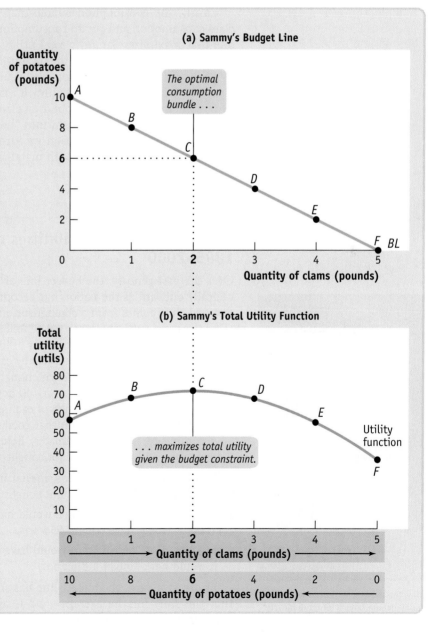

(a) Sammy's Budget Line

The optimal consumption bundle . . .

(b) Sammy's Total Utility Function

. . . *maximizes total utility given the budget constraint.*

Utility function

Clearly, the consumption bundle that makes the best of the trade-off between clam consumption and potato consumption, the optimal consumption bundle, is the one that maximizes Sammy's total utility. That is, Sammy's optimal consumption bundle puts him at the top of the total utility curve.

As always, we can find the top of the curve by direct observation. We can see from Figure 10-4 that Sammy's total utility is maximized at point C—that his optimal consumption bundle contains 2 pounds of clams and 6 pounds of potatoes. But we know that we usually gain more insight into "how-much" problems when we use marginal analysis. So in the next section we turn to representing and solving the optimal consumption choice problem with marginal analysis.

economics in action

The Consumption Possibilities of American Workers, 1895–2000

Over the past century, the budget line of the average American worker has shifted radically outward as the nation has become vastly richer. A good illustration of this outward shift comes from a comparison made by the economist J. Bradford DeLong (find the article at http://econ161.berkeley.edu/TCEH/Slouch_wealth2.html).

He compared the cost of a number of items in the 1895 Montgomery Ward catalog to the cost of similar items today by calculating the number of hours an average worker would need to work to earn enough money to buy them. If we assume that a worker puts in 2,000 hours per year—40 hours per week, with two weeks of vacation—we can calculate how many units of each good a worker could purchase by spending an entire year's income only on that good.

According to DeLong's estimates, here are the amounts of various goods that workers then and now could have bought:

- In 1895, an average worker's annual income would have bought 7.7 one-speed bicycles; in 2000, it would have bought 278 bicycles.

- In 1895, the worker's income would have bought 45 full sets of dinner plates; in 2000, it would have bought 556 sets.

- In 1895, a worker's income would have bought 0.83 of a Steinway piano; in 2000, it would have bought 1.8 pianos.

By any standard, the budget line has shifted out enormously. DeLong estimates that the shift for the average good is approximately sevenfold. That is, today's workers can on average purchase seven times as much of a randomly chosen good

Today, the average American worker's annual income buys a lot more bicycle than it did in 1895.

as their predecessors could have in 1895. Of course, in a way this understates the rise in purchasing power: there are many goods, like computers, that were not available in 1895 at any price. ∎

> > > > > > > > > > > > > > > > > > > >

1. In the following two examples, draw the budget line. Make sure that you calculate the following: (i) the vertical intercept of the budget line; (ii) the horizontal intercept of the budget line; (iii) the slope of the budget line; (iv) the opportunity cost of the good on the horizontal axis in terms of the good on the vertical axis.
   a. A consumption bundle consisting of movie tickets and buckets of popcorn. Each ticket costs $5.00, each bucket of popcorn costs $2.50, and the consumer's income is $10.00. Movie tickets are on the vertical axis and buckets of popcorn are on the horizontal axis.
   b. A consumption bundle consisting of underwear and socks. Each pair of underwear costs $4.00, each pair of socks costs $1.50, and the consumer's income is $12.00. Pairs of socks are on the vertical axis and pairs of underwear are on the horizontal axis.

Solutions appear at back of book.

Spending the Marginal Dollar

Marginal analysis is often the best way to think about "how much" decisions. In this case, Sammy is making a decision about the quantity of clams to consume, taking into account the fact that the more clams he consumes, the fewer potatoes he can afford. As we've seen, we can find his optimal consumption choice by finding the total utility he receives from each consumption bundle on his budget line and then choosing the bundle at which total utility is maximized. But is there a way to use marginal analysis instead?

The answer is yes: we can think about the problem of choosing an optimal consumption bundle in terms of the decision a consumer must make about how much to spend on each good. The marginal decision then becomes one of how to *spend the marginal dollar*—how to allocate an additional dollar between clams and potatoes. As we'll see in a moment, looking at Sammy's decision in terms of how he allocates his income gives us an important insight into the relationship between prices and consumer decisions.

Our first step is to ask how much additional utility Sammy gets from spending an additional dollar on either good—the **marginal utility per dollar** spent on either clams or potatoes.

Marginal Utility per Dollar

We've already introduced the concept of marginal utility, the additional utility a consumer gets from consuming one more unit of a good or service; now let's see how this concept can be used to derive the related measure of marginal utility per dollar.

Table 10-3, on page 242, shows how to calculate the marginal utility per dollar spent on clams and potatoes, respectively.

In panel (a) of the table, the first column shows different possible levels of clam consumption. The second column shows the utility Sammy derives from each level of clam consumption; the third column then shows the marginal utility, the increase in utility Sammy gets from consuming an additional pound of clams. Panel (b) does the same thing for potatoes. The next step is to derive marginal utility *per dollar* for each good. To do this, we must divide the marginal utility of the good by its price in dollars.

To see why we must divide by the price, compare the third and fourth columns of panel (a). Consider what happens if Sammy increases his clam consumption from 2 pounds to 3 pounds. As we can see, this increase in clam consumption raises his total utility by 6 utils. But he must spend $4 for that additional pound, so the increase in his utility per additional dollar spent on clams is 6 utils/$4 = 1.5 utils per dollar.

The **marginal utility per dollar** spent on a good or service is the additional utility from spending one more dollar on that good or service.

THE RIGHT MARGINAL COMPARISON

Marginal analysis helps us understand "how-much" decisions by showing that they involve setting the marginal *benefit* of some activity equal to its marginal *cost*. But to get this right, it's important to be careful what "marginals" you compare. In the case of consumption, it's tempting but wrong to say that the marginal utility of consumption of any two goods must be the same.

The right answer is that the marginal utility *per dollar* must be the same. This takes prices into account. If a milkshake costs four times as much as an order of french fries, the optimal consumption choice isn't where you gain the same amount of utility from an extra milkshake as from an extra order of french fries; it's where the milkshake adds four times as much to utility. With the money that buys one milkshake you could have bought four orders of french fries, so the one milkshake has to add four times as much to your utility as one order of french fries. In other words, the marginal utility per dollar has to be the same for milkshakes and french fries.

TABLE 10-3

Marginal Utility per Dollar

(a) Clams (price of clams = $4 per pound)				(b) Potatoes (price of potatoes = $2 per pound)			
Quantity of clams (pounds)	Utility from clams (utils)	Marginal utility per pound of clams (utils)	Marginal utility per dollar (utils)	Quantity of potatoes (pounds)	Utility from potatoes (utils)	Marginal utility per pound of potatoes (utils)	Marginal utility per dollar (utils)
0	0			0	0		
		15	3.75			11.5	5.75
1	15			1	11.5		
		10	2.50			9.9	4.95
2	25			2	21.4		
		6	1.50			8.4	4.20
3	31			3	29.8		
		3	0.75			7.0	3.50
4	34			4	36.8		
		2	0.50			5.7	2.85
5	36			5	42.5		
						4.5	2.25
				6	47.0		
						3.5	1.75
				7	50.5		
						2.7	1.35
				8	53.2		
						2.0	1.00
				9	55.2		
						1.5	0.75
				10	56.7		

Similarly, if he increases his clam consumption from 3 pounds to 4 pounds, his marginal utility is 3 utils per clam but his marginal utility per dollar is 3 utils/$4 = 0.75 utils per dollar. Notice that because of diminishing marginal utility per pound of clams, Sammy's marginal utility per pound of clams falls as the quantity of clams he consumes rises. As a result, his marginal utility per dollar spent on clams also falls as the quantity of clams he consumes rises.

So the last column of panel (a) shows how Sammy's marginal utility per dollar spent on clams depends on the quantity of clams he consumes. Similarly, the last column of panel (b) shows how his marginal utility per dollar spent on potatoes depends on the quantity of potatoes he consumes. Again, marginal utility per dollar spent on each good declines as the quantity of that good consumed rises, because of diminishing marginal utility.

We will use the symbols MU_C and MU_P to represent the marginal utility per pound of clams and potatoes, respectively. Then the marginal utility per dollar spent on clams is MU_C/P_C and the marginal utility per dollar spent on potatoes is MU_P/P_P. In general, the additional utility generated from an additional dollar spent on a good is equal to:

(10-4)   Marginal utility per dollar spent on a good
= Marginal utility of one unit of the good / Price of one unit of the good
= MU_{good}/P_{good}

Now let's see how this concept helps us derive a consumer's optimal consumption using marginal analysis.

Optimal Consumption

The curve in panel (a) of Figure 10-5 shows Sammy's marginal utility per dollar spent on clams, MU_C/P_C, as derived in Table 10-3. The curve in panel (b) shows his marginal utility per dollar spent on potatoes, MU_P/P_P. We already know from Figure

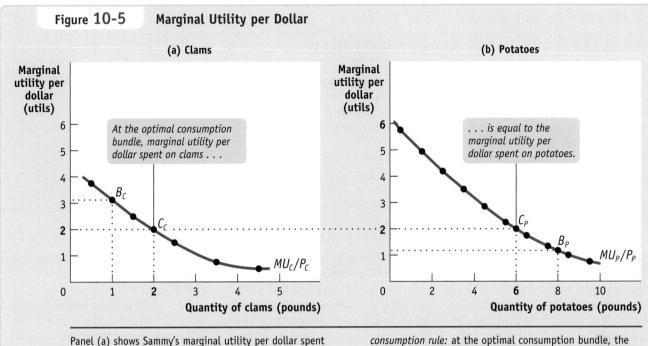

Figure 10-5 — Marginal Utility per Dollar

(a) Clams

At the optimal consumption bundle, marginal utility per dollar spent on clams . . .

MU_C/P_C

Quantity of clams (pounds)

Marginal utility per dollar (utils)

(b) Potatoes

. . . is equal to the marginal utility per dollar spent on potatoes.

MU_P/P_P

Quantity of potatoes (pounds)

Marginal utility per dollar (utils)

Panel (a) shows Sammy's marginal utility per dollar spent on clams; panel (b) shows his marginal utility per dollar spent on potatoes. Points C_C in panel (a) and C_P in panel (b) correspond to bundle C in Figure 10-4, Sammy's optimal consumption bundle of 2 pounds of clams and 6 pounds of potatoes. At these points his marginal utility per dollar spent on each good is 2. This illustrates the *optimal consumption rule:* at the optimal consumption bundle, the marginal utility per dollar spent on each good and service is the same. At any other consumption bundle along Sammy's budget line, such as bundle B in Figure 10-4, which is represented here by points B_C and B_P, consumption is not optimal: he can increase his utility at no additional cost by reallocating his spending.

10-4 that Sammy's optimal consumption bundle, C, consists of 2 pounds of clams and 6 pounds of potatoes. From Figure 10-5 we can read off the marginal utility per dollar spent on clams and potatoes, respectively, at that optimal consumption bundle, which corresponds to points C_C and C_P. And we see something interesting: when Sammy consumes 2 pounds of clams and 6 pounds of potatoes, his marginal utility per dollar spent is the same, 2, for both goods. That is, at the optimal consumption bundle $MU_C/P_C = MU_P/P_P = 2$.

This isn't an accident. Consider another one of Sammy's possible consumption bundles, say B in Figure 10-4, at which he consumes 1 pound of clams and 8 pounds of potatoes. The marginal utility per dollar spent on each good is shown by points B_C and B_P in Figure 10-5. At that consumption bundle, Sammy's marginal utility per dollar spent on clams would be approximately 3, but his marginal utility per dollar spent on potatoes would be only approximately 1. This shows that he has made a mistake: he is consuming too many potatoes and not enough clams.

How do we know this? If Sammy's marginal utility per dollar spent on clams is higher than his marginal utility per dollar spent on potatoes, he has a simple way to make himself better off while staying within his budget: spend $1 less on potatoes and $1 more on clams. By spending an additional dollar on clams, he adds about 3 utils to his total utility; meanwhile, by spending $1 less on potatoes, he subtracts only about 1 util from his total utility. Because his marginal utility per dollar spent is higher for clams than for potatoes, reallocating his spending toward clams and away from potatoes would increase his total utility. On the other hand, if his marginal utility per dollar spent on potatoes is higher, he can increase his utility by spending less on clams and more on potatoes. So if Sammy has in fact chosen his optimal consumption bundle, his marginal utility per dollar spent on clams and potatoes must be equal.

BUT ARE CONSUMERS REALLY RATIONAL?

Many companies offer retirement plans that allow their employees to put aside part of their salaries tax-free. These plans, called 401(k)s, can save a worker thousands of dollars in taxes each year. But the plans sometimes have disadvantages: some companies invest their employees' savings mainly in their own stock, which can be disastrous if the company gets in trouble, leaving the employee with no savings *and* no job. (That's what happened to the employees of Enron.)

Clearly, then, people should carefully decide how much of their money to put in an employer-administered retirement plan. They should compare the marginal utility of a dollar spent on current consumption with the marginal utility of a dollar saved for retirement. They should weigh the tax advantages of saving through the employer plan against the risks of letting the employer decide where their savings are invested.

But recent economic research suggests that most people aren't careful at all. For example, some companies have an "opt-in" system for 401(k)s—that is, in some companies employees must ask to be enrolled. Other companies have an "opt-out" system—employees are automatically enrolled unless they request otherwise. This shouldn't make a difference—if the plan is managed well, people should opt in; if it's managed poorly (that is, investing mainly in company's own stock), they should opt out. Yet when companies switch to automatic enrollment, the number of employees in their 401(k) plans

rises dramatically. As the National Bureau of Economic Research put it, workers seem to follow the path of least resistance, instead of comparing their options and maximizing their utility.

Studies of saving behavior are one example of a growing field known as "behavioral economics." Behavioral economists question the whole concept of the rational consumer. Their research focuses on situations in which people don't seem to be rational—that is, when they behave in ways that can't easily be explained by utility maximization.

One key insight in behavioral economics comes from the work of Herbert Simon, who won the Nobel prize in economics in 1978. Simon argued that sometimes individuals find that it isn't actually rational to go to great lengths to maximize utility, since searching for the perfect answer is itself a costly activity. Instead, he argued, they engage in *bounded rationality*: individuals save time and effort by making decisions that are "good enough," rather than perfect. In the case of savings plans, this might involve following the path of least resistance: not bothering to participate in a well-managed

opt-in plan, and not bothering to opt out of a poorly managed automatic plan.

Today's behavioral economists use insights from psychology to understand behavior seemingly at odds with rationality. The 2002 Nobel prize went to Daniel Kahneman, a psychologist who, with his late co-author Amos Tversky, laid out a theory of how people make choices in the face of uncertainty. This work and other insights into nonrational behavior are having an important influence on analysis of financial markets, labor markets, and other economic concerns.

But it's hard to find a behavioral economist who thinks that the insights of this field should replace the analysis of utility maximization. The theory of the rational consumer remains the main way in which economists analyze consumer behavior.

Great new car, but are you saving enough for retirement?

The **optimal consumption rule** says that when a consumer maximizes utility, the marginal utility per dollar spent must be the same for all goods and services in the consumption bundle.

This is a general principle, known as the **optimal consumption rule**: when a consumer maximizes utility in the face of a budget constraint, the marginal utility per dollar spent on each good or service in the consumption bundle is the same. That is, for any two goods C and P the optimal consumption rule says that at the optimal consumption bundle

$$(10\text{-}5)\ MU_C/P_C = MU_P/P_P$$

It's easiest to understand this rule using examples in which the consumption bundle contains only two goods, but it applies no matter how many goods or services a consumer buys: in the optimal consumption bundle, the marginal utilities per dollar spent for each and every good or service in that bundle are equal.

economics in action

Self-Service Gasoline

At the end of the 1970s the price of gasoline in the United States shot up because of a combination of world oil shortages and deregulation. At the same time, many gas stations began offering drivers a discount if they pumped their own gas.

Many people argued that the rise of self-service gas was a response to higher gas prices and that if gas prices ever went down again, people would once again be willing to pay the price of full service.

But economists in general were skeptical of this conclusion. Consumers, they argued, were making a calculation: the extra utility gained from spending on other goods was worth the extra effort. And gas stations offered a price break on self-service gas because it saved them labor; so the price break would remain even if gas prices went down. So economists argued that people would continue to use self-service pumps even if gas prices fell back to traditional levels.

In the event, gas prices did fall; by the late 1990s they were actually lower, adjusted for inflation, than they had been for generations. But most drivers continued to use self-service gas. ∎

> > > > > > > > > > > > > > > > > > > >

>> CHECK YOUR UNDERSTANDING 10-3

1. In Figure 10-5 you can see that marginal utility per dollar spent on clams and marginal utility per dollar spent on potatoes are approximately equal at a consumption bundle consisting of 3 pounds of clams and 8 pounds of potatoes. Explain why this is not Sammy's optimal consumption bundle. Illustrate your answer using the budget line in Figure 10-4.

2. Explain what is faulty about the following statement, using data from Table 10-3: "In order to maximize utility, Sammy should consume the bundle that gives him the maximum marginal utility per dollar for each good."

Solutions appear at back of book.

From Utility to the Demand Curve

We have now analyzed the optimal consumption choice of a consumer whose income we take as given and who faces one particular set of prices—in our Sammy example, $20 of income per week, $4 per pound of clams, and $2 per pound of potatoes.

But the main reason we want to understand consumer behavior is to go behind the market demand curve—to understand how the market demand curve is explained by the utility-maximizing behavior of individual consumers.

Individual Demand and Market Demand

Let's begin by reviewing the relationship between prices and quantity demanded, both at the individual level and at the level of the market as a whole.

The **individual demand curve** for a good shows the relationship between the quantity of a good demanded by an individual consumer and the market price of that good. For example, suppose that Bert is a consumer of fried clams and that panel (a) of Figure 10-6 (page 246) shows how many pounds of clams he will buy at any given market price per pound. Then D_{Bert} is Bert's individual demand curve.

The *market demand curve* shows how the quantity of a good demanded by all consumers depends on the market price of that good. The market demand curve is the *horizontal sum* of the individual demand curves of all consumers. To see what we mean by the term *horizontal sum*, assume for a moment that there are only two consumers of fried clams, Bert and Ernie. Ernie's individual demand curve is shown in panel (b). Panel (c) shows the market demand curve. At any given price, the quantity demanded

The **individual demand curve** for a good shows the relationship between quantity demanded and price for an individual consumer.

9. Damien Matthews is a busy actor. He allocates his free time to watching movies and working out at the gym. The accompanying table shows his utility from the number of times per week he watches a movie or goes to the gym.

Quantity of gym visits per week	Utility from gym visits (utils)	Quantity of movies per week	Utility from movies (utils)
1	100	1	60
2	180	2	110
3	240	3	150
4	280	4	180
5	310	5	190
6	330	6	195

Damien has 14 hours per week to spend on watching movies and going to the gym. Each movie takes 2 hours and each gym visit takes 2 hours. (*Hint:* Damien's free time is analogous to income he can spend. The hours needed for each activity are analogous to the price of that activity.)

a. Which bundles of gym visits and movies can Damien consume per week if he spends all his time either going to the gym or watching movies? Draw Damien's budget line in a diagram with gym visits on the horizontal axis and movies on the vertical axis.

b. Calculate the marginal utility of each gym visit and the marginal utility of each movie. Then calculate the marginal utility per hour spent at the gym and the marginal utility per hour spent watching movies.

c. Draw a diagram like Figure 10-5 in which the marginal utility per hour spent at the gym is shown in one panel and the marginal utility per hour spent watching movies is shown in the other panel. Using this diagram and the optimal spending rule, decide how Damien should allocate his time.

10. Anna Jenniferson is an actress, and on the set of a new movie she meets Damien from Problem 9. She tells him that she likes watching movies much more than going to the gym. In fact, she says that if she had to give up seeing 1 movie, she would need to go to the gym twice to make up for the loss in utility from not seeing the movie. A movie takes 2 hours, and a gym visit also lasts 2 hours. Damien tells Anna that she is not watching enough movies. Is he right?

11. Sven is a poor student who covers most of his dietary needs by eating cheap breakfast cereal, since it contains most of the important vitamins. As the price of cereal increases, he decides to buy even less of other foods and even more breakfast cereal to maintain his intake of important nutrients. This makes breakfast cereal a Giffen good for Sven. Describe in words the substitution effect and the income effect from this increase in the price of cereal. In which direction does each effect move, and why? What does this imply for the slope of Sven's demand curve for cereal?

12. In each of the following situations, describe the substitution effect and (if it is significant) the income effect. In which direction does each of these effects move? Why?

a. Ed spends a large portion of his income on his children's education. Because tuition fees rise, one of his children has to withdraw from college.

b. Homer spends much of his monthly income on home mortgage payments. The interest on his adjustable-rate mortgage falls, lowering his mortgage payments, and Homer decides to move to a larger house.

c. Pam thinks that Spam is an inferior good. Yet as the price of Spam rises, she decides to buy less of it.

>*web*... To continue your study and review of concepts in this chapter, please visit the Krugman/Wells website for quizzes, animated graph tutorials, web links to helpful resources, and more.

www.worthpublishers.com/krugmanwells

>>Consumer Preferences and Consumer Choice

A TALE OF TWO CITIES

Do you want to earn a high salary? Maybe you should consider moving to San Jose, California, the metropolitan area that contains much of Silicon Valley, America's leading cluster of high-tech industries. The average family in San Jose has an income far higher than that of the average American family. According to bestplaces.net, a website that compares living conditions in different cities, average household income in San Jose is more than twice as high as that in Cincinnati.

But before you rush to San Jose, there's something else you should know: housing is very expensive there—about four times as expensive per square foot of living space as in Cincinnati. Understandably, the average apartment or house in San Jose is small by American standards.

So is life better or worse in San Jose than in Cincinnati? It depends a lot on what you want. For young people without children, the high wage they can earn in San Jose probably outweighs the high price of housing. They are willing to accept more cramped living quarters in return for the ability to consume greater quantities of other goods such as restaurant meals or clothing. People with large families, however, might prefer midwestern locations like Cincinnati, where the average wage is lower than in San Jose but a dollar buys many more square feet of living space. That is, they would choose to eat fewer restaurant meals but live in more spacious housing.

For individuals whose preferences lie somewhere between those of childless yuppies and those of proud parents, the choice between San Jose and Cincinnati may not be easy. In fact, some people would be *indifferent* between living in the two locations. That's not to say that they would live the same way in San Jose and in Cincinnati; in San Jose they would live in small apartments and eat out a lot, but in Cincinnati they would be homebodies.

What you will learn in this chapter:

➤ Why economists use **indifference curves** to illustrate a person's preferences

➤ The importance of the **marginal rate of substitution,** the rate at which a consumer is just willing to substitute one good for another

➤ An alternative way of finding a consumer's optimal consumption bundle using indifference curves and the budget line

➤ How the shape of indifference curves helps determine whether goods are substitutes or complements

➤ An in-depth understanding of income and substitution effects

Ariel Skelley/Masterfile

Carol Halebein for the *New York Times*

Spacious house in the suburbs or cozy apartment in the city—how would you choose?

253

Figure 11-3 An Indifference Curve Map

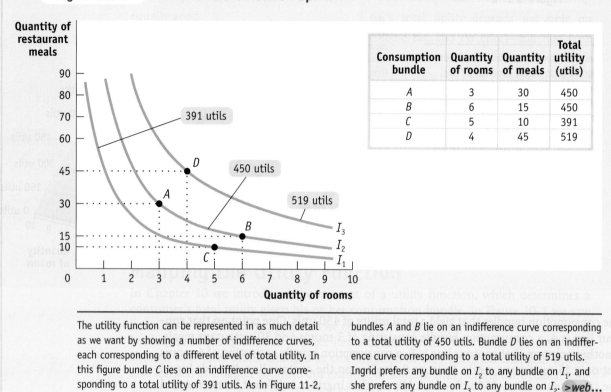

Consumption bundle	Quantity of rooms	Quantity of meals	Total utility (utils)
A	3	30	450
B	6	15	450
C	5	10	391
D	4	45	519

The utility function can be represented in as much detail as we want by showing a number of indifference curves, each corresponding to a different level of total utility. In this figure bundle C lies on an indifference curve corresponding to a total utility of 391 utils. As in Figure 11-2, bundles A and B lie on an indifference curve corresponding to a total utility of 450 utils. Bundle D lies on an indifference curve corresponding to a total utility of 519 utils. Ingrid prefers any bundle on I_2 to any bundle on I_1, and she prefers any bundle on I_3 to any bundle on I_2. **>web...**

The entire utility function of an individual can be represented by an **indifference curve map**, a collection of indifference curves in which each curve corresponds to a different total utility level.

A collection of indifference curves that represents a consumer's entire utility function, with each indifference curve corresponding to a different level of total utility, is known as an **indifference curve map.** Figure 11-3 shows three indifference curves, I_1, I_2, and I_3, from Ingrid's indifference curve map, as well as several consumption bundles, A, B, C, and D. The accompanying table lists each bundle, its composition of rooms and restaurant meals, and the total utility it yields. Because bundles A and B generate the same number of utils, 450, they lie on the same indifference curve, I_2. Although Ingrid is indifferent between A and B, she is certainly not indifferent between A and C: as you can see from the table, C generates only 391 utils, a lower total utility than A or B. So Ingrid prefers consumption bundles A and B to bundle C. This is represented by the fact that C is on indifference curve I_1, and I_1 lies below I_2. Bundle D, though, generates 519 utils, a higher total utility than A and B. It is on I_3, an indifference curve that lies above I_2. Clearly, Ingrid prefers D to either A or B. And, even more strongly, she prefers D to C.

FOR INQUIRING MINDS

ARE UTILS USEFUL?

In the table that accompanies Figure 11-3 we give the number of utils achieved at each of the indifference curves shown in the figure. But is this information actually needed?

The answer is no. As you will see shortly, the indifference curve map tells us all we need to know in order to find a consumer's optimal consumption bundle. That is, it's

important that Ingrid has higher total utility along indifference curve I_2 than she does along I_1, but it doesn't matter *how much* higher her total utility is. In other words, we don't have to measure utils in order to understand how consumers make choices.

Economists say that consumer theory requires an "ordinal" measure of utility—one that ranks consumption bundles in terms of

desirability—so that we can say that bundle X is better than bundle Y. The theory does not, however, require "cardinal" utility, which actually assigns a specific number to the total utility yielded by each bundle.

So why introduce the concept of utils at all? The answer is that it is much easier to understand the basis of rational choice by using the concept of measurable utility.

Properties of Indifference Curves

No two individuals have the same indifference curve map because no two individuals have the same preferences. But economists believe that every indifference curve map has two general properties, illustrated in panel (a) of Figure 11-4:

- *Indifference curves never cross.* Suppose that we tried to draw an indifference curve map like the one depicted in the left diagram in panel (a), in which two indifference curves cross at A. What is the total utility at A? Is it 100 utils or 200 utils? Indifference curves cannot cross because each consumption bundle must correspond to a unique total utility level—not, as shown at A, two different total utility levels.

Figure 11-4   Properties of Indifference Curves

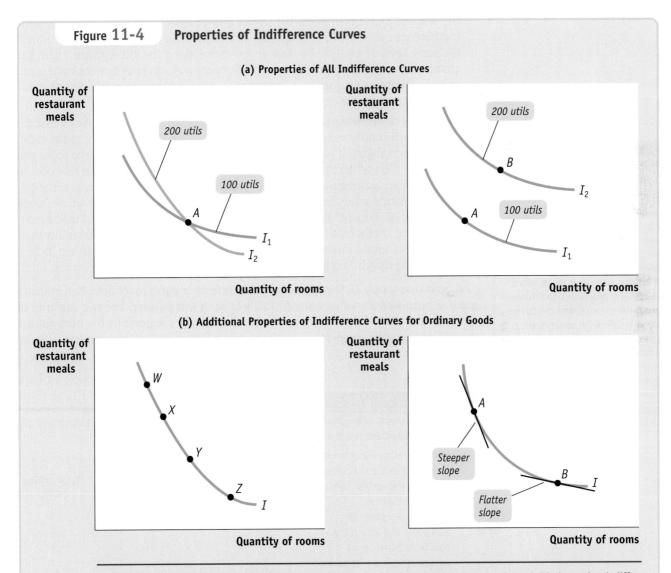

Panel (a) represents two general properties that all indifference curve maps share. The left diagram shows why indifference curves cannot cross: if they did, a consumption bundle such as A would yield both 100 and 200 utils, a contradiction. The right diagram of panel (a) shows that indifference curves that are farther out yield higher total utility: bundle B, which contains more of both goods than bundle A, yields higher total utility. Panel (b) depicts two additional properties of indifference curves for ordinary goods. The left diagram of panel (b) shows that indifference curves slope downward: as you move down the curve from bundle W to bundle Z, consumption of rooms increases. To keep total utility constant, this must be offset by a reduction in quantity of restaurant meals. The right diagram of panel (b) shows a convex-shaped indifference curve. The slope of the indifference curve gets flatter as you move down the curve to the right, a feature arising from diminishing marginal utility.

■ *The farther out an indifference curve lies—the farther it is from the origin—the higher the level of total utility it indicates.* The reason, illustrated in the right diagram in panel (a), is that we assume that more is better—over the set of consumption bundles we are considering, the consumer is not satiated. Bundle *B*, on the outer indifference curve, contains more of both goods than bundle *A* on the inner indifference curve. So *B* generates a higher total utility level (200 utils) and therefore lies on a higher indifference curve than *A*.

Furthermore, economists believe that, for most goods, consumers' indifference curve maps also have two additional properties. They are illustrated in panel (b) of Figure 11-4:

■ *Indifference curves are downward sloping.* Here, too, the reason is that more is better. The left diagram in panel (b) shows four consumption bundles on the same indifference curve: *W*, *X*, *Y*, and *Z*. By definition these consumption bundles yield the same level of total utility. But as you move along the curve to the right, the quantity of rooms consumed increases. The only way a person can consume more rooms without gaining utility is by giving up some restaurant meals. So the indifference curve must be downward sloping.

■ *Indifference curves have a convex shape.* The right diagram in panel (b) shows that the slope of each indifference curve changes as you move down the curve to the right: the curve gets flatter. If you move up an indifference curve to the left, the curve gets steeper. So the indifference curve is steeper at *A* than it is at *B*. When this occurs, we say that an indifference curve has a *convex* shape—it is bowed-in towards the origin. This feature arises from diminishing marginal utility, a principle we discussed in Chapter 10. Recall that when a consumer has diminishing marginal utility, consumption of another unit of a good generates a smaller increase in total utility than the previous unit consumed. In the next section, we will examine in detail how diminishing marginal utility gives rise to convex-shaped indifference curves.

Goods that satisfy all four properties of indifference curve maps are called *ordinary goods*, a term we will define more formally later in this chapter. The vast majority of goods in any consumer's utility function fall into this category. In the next section we will define ordinary goods and see the key role that diminishing marginal utility plays for them. ■

< < < < < < < < < < < < < < < < < < <

>> **CHECK YOUR UNDERSTANDING 11-1**

1. The accompanying table shows Samantha's preferences for consumption bundles composed of chocolate kisses and licorice drops.

   a. With chocolate kisses on the horizontal axis and licorice drops on the vertical axis, draw hypothetical indifference curves for Samantha and locate the bundles on the curves. Assume that both items are ordinary goods.

Consumption bundle	Quantity of chocolate kisses	Quantity of licorice drops	Total utility (utils)
A	1	3	6
B	2	3	10
C	3	1	6
D	2	1	4

   b. Suppose you don't know the number of utils provided by each bundle. Assuming that more is better, predict Samantha's ranking of each of the four bundles to the extent possible.

2. On the left diagram in panel (a) of Figure 11-4, draw a point *B* anywhere on the 200 utils indifference curve and a point *C* anywhere on the 100 utils indifference curve (but *not* at the same location as point *A*). By comparing the utils generated by bundles *A* and *B* and those generated by bundles *A* and *C*, explain why indifference curves cannot cross.

Solutions appear at back of book.

Indifference Curves and Consumer Choice

At the beginning of the last section we used indifference curves to represent the preferences of Ingrid, whose consumption bundles consist of rooms and restaurant meals. Our next step is to show how to use Ingrid's indifference curve map to find her utility-maximizing consumption bundle given her budget constraint.

It's important to understand how our analysis here relates to what we did in Chapter 10. We are not offering a new theory of consumer behavior in this chapter—just as in Chapter 10, consumers are assumed to maximize total utility. In particular, we know that consumers will follow the *optimal consumption rule* from Chapter 10: the optimal consumption bundle lies on the budget line, and the marginal utility per dollar is the same for every good in the bundle.

But as we'll see shortly, we can derive this optimal consumer behavior in a somewhat different way—a way that yields deeper insights into consumer choice.

The Marginal Rate of Substitution

The first component of our approach is a new concept, the *marginal rate of substitution*. The essence of this concept is illustrated in Figure 11-5.

Recall from the last section that for most goods, consumers' indifference curves are downward sloping and convex. Figure 11-5 shows such an indifference curve. The points labeled *V*, *W*, *X*, *Y*, and *Z* all lie on this indifference curve—that is, they represent consumption bundles that yield Ingrid the same level of total utility. The table accompanying the figure shows the components of each of the bundles. As we move along the indifference curve from *V* to *Z*, Ingrid's consumption of housing steadily increases from 2 rooms to 6 rooms, but her total utility is kept constant. As we move

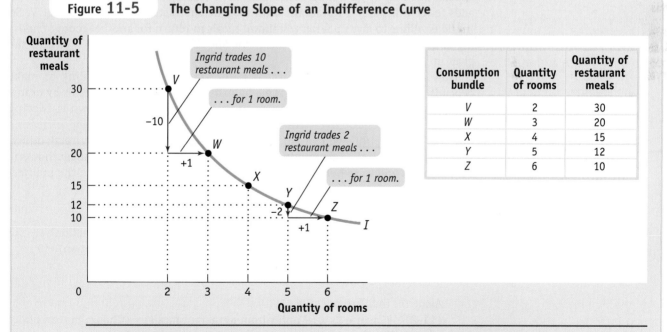

Figure 11-5 The Changing Slope of an Indifference Curve

Consumption bundle	Quantity of rooms	Quantity of restaurant meals
V	2	30
W	3	20
X	4	15
Y	5	12
Z	6	10

This indifference curve is downward sloping and convex, implying that restaurant meals and rooms are ordinary goods for Ingrid. As Ingrid moves down her indifference curve from *V* to *Z*, she trades off reduced consumption of restaurant meals for increased consumption of housing. However, the terms of that trade-off change. As she moves from *V* to *W*, she is willing to give up 10 restaurant meals in return for 1 more room. As her consumption of rooms rises and her consumption of restaurant meals falls, she is willing to give up fewer restaurant meals in return for each additional room. The flattening of the slope as you move from left to right arises from diminishing marginal utility. **>web...**

down the indifference curve, then, Ingrid is trading more of one good for less of the other, with the *terms* of that trade-off—the ratio of additional rooms consumed to restaurant meals sacrificed—chosen to keep her total utility constant.

Notice that the quantity of restaurant meals that Ingrid is willing to give up in return for an additional room changes along the indifference curve. As we move from V to W, housing consumption rises from 2 to 3 rooms and restaurant meal consumption falls from 30 to 20—a trade-off of 10 restaurant meals for 1 additional room. But as we move from Y to Z, housing consumption rises from 5 to 6 rooms and restaurant meal consumption falls from 12 to 10, a trade-off of only 2 restaurant meals for an additional room.

To put it in terms of slopes, the slope of the indifference curve between V and W is −10: the change in restaurant meal consumption, −10, divided by the change in housing consumption, 1. Similarly, the slope of the indifference curve between Y and Z is −2. So the indifference curve gets flatter as we move down it to the right—that is, it has a convex shape, one of the four properties of an indifference curve for ordinary goods.

Why does the trade-off change in this way? Let's think about it intuitively, then work through it more carefully. When Ingrid moves down her indifference curve, whether from V to W or from Y to Z, she gains utility from her additional consumption of housing but loses an equal amount of utility from her reduced consumption of restaurant meals. But at each step, the initial position from which Ingrid begins is different. At V, Ingrid consumes only a small quantity of rooms, so because of diminishing marginal utility her marginal utility per room at that point is high. At V, then, an additional room adds a lot to Ingrid's total utility. But at V she already consumes a large quantity of restaurant meals, so her marginal utility of restaurant meals is low at that point. This means that it takes a large reduction in her quantity of restaurant meals consumed to offset the increased utility she gets from the extra room of housing.

At Y, in contrast, Ingrid consumes a much larger quantity of rooms and a much smaller quantity of restaurant meals than at V. This means that an additional room adds fewer utils, and a restaurant meal forgone subtracts more utils, than at V. So Ingrid is willing to give up fewer restaurant meals in return for another room of housing at Y (where she gives up two meals for one room) than she is at V (where she gives up 10 meals for one room).

Now let's express the same idea—that the trade-off Ingrid is willing to make depends on where she is starting from—by using a little math. We do this by examining how the slope of the indifference curve changes as we move down it. Moving down the indifference curve—reducing restaurant meal consumption and increasing housing consumption—will produce two opposing effects on Ingrid's total utility: lower restaurant meal consumption will reduce her total utility, but higher housing consumption will raise her total utility. And since we are moving down the indifference curve, these two effects must exactly cancel out:

> *Along the indifference curve:*
> **(11-1)** (Change in total utility because of lower restaurant consumption) + (Change in total utility because of higher housing consumption) = 0

or, rearranging terms,

> *Along the indifference curve:*
> **(11-2)** −(Change in total utility from restaurant meals) = (Change in total utility from housing)

Let's now focus on what happens as we move only a short distance down the indifference curve, trading off a small increase in housing consumption for a small decrease in restaurant meal consumption. Following our notation from Chapter 10, let's use MU_R and MU_M to represent the marginal utility of rooms and restaurant meals, respectively, and ΔQ_R and ΔQ_M to represent the changes in room and meal consumption, respectively. In general, the change in total utility caused by a small change in consumption of a good is equal to the change in consumption multiplied by the *marginal utility* of that good. This means that we can calculate the change in Ingrid's total utility generated by a change in her consumption bundle using the following equations:

(11-3) Change in total utility arising from a change in consumption of restaurant meals = $MU_M \times \Delta Q_M$

and

(11-4) Change in total utility arising from a change in consumption of rooms $= MU_R \times \Delta Q_R$

So we can write Equation 11-2 in symbols as

(11-5) *Along the indifference curve:* $-MU_M \times \Delta Q_M = MU_R \times \Delta Q_R$

Note that the left-hand side of Equation 11-5 has a minus sign; it represents the loss in total utility from decreased restaurant meal consumption. This must equal the gain in total utility from increased room consumption, represented by the right-hand side of the equation.

What we want, of course, is to know how this translates into the slope of the indifference curve. To find the slope, we divide both sides of Equation 11-5 by ΔQ_R, and again by MU_M, in order to get the ΔQ_M, ΔQ_R terms on one side and the MU_R, MU_M terms on the other. This results in:

(11-6) *Along the indifference curve:* $\dfrac{-\Delta Q_M}{\Delta Q_R} = \dfrac{MU_R}{MU_M}$

The left-hand side of Equation 11-6 is *minus* the slope of the indifference curve; it is the rate at which Ingrid is willing to trade a higher quantity of rooms (the good on the horizontal axis) in place of restaurant meals (the good on the vertical axis). The right-hand side of Equation 11-6 is the ratio of the marginal utility of rooms to the marginal utility of restaurant meals—that is, the ratio of what she gains from one more room to what she gains from one more meal.

Putting all this together, we see that Equation 11-6 shows that, along the indifference curve, the quantity of restaurant meals Ingrid is willing to give up in return for a room, $\Delta Q_M/\Delta Q_R$, is exactly equal to the ratio of the marginal utility of a room to that of a meal, MU_R, MU_M. Only when this condition is met will her total utility level remain constant as she consumes more rooms and fewer restaurant meals.

Economists have a special name for the ratio of the marginal utilities found in the right-hand side of Equation 11-6: it is called the **marginal rate of substitution,** or **MRS,** of rooms (the good on the horizontal axis) in place of restaurant meals (the good on the vertical axis). That's because as we slide down Ingrid's indifference curve, we are substituting more rooms for fewer restaurant meals in her consumption bundle. As we'll see shortly, the marginal rate of substitution plays an important role in finding the optimal consumption bundle.

> The **marginal rate of substitution**, or **MRS**, of good *R* in place of good *M* is equal to MU_R/MU_M, the ratio of the marginal utility of *R* to the marginal utility of *M*.

Recall that indifference curves get flatter as you move down them to the right. The reason, as we've just discussed, is diminishing marginal utility: as Ingrid consumes more housing and fewer restaurant meals, her marginal utility from housing falls and her marginal utility from restaurant meals rises. So her marginal rate of substitution, which is equal to minus the slope of her indifference curve, falls as she moves down the indifference curve.

The flattening of indifference curves as you slide down them to the right—which reflects the same logic as the principle of diminishing marginal utility—is known as the principle of **diminishing marginal rate of substitution.** It says that an individual who consumes only a little bit of good *A* and a lot of good *B* will be willing to trade off a lot of *B* in return for one more unit of *A*; an individual who already consumes a lot of *A* and not much *B* will be less willing to make that trade-off.

> The principle of **diminishing marginal rate of substitution** states that the more of good *R* a person consumes in proportion to good *M*, the less *M* he or she is willing to substitute for another unit of *R*.

We can illustrate this point by referring back to Figure 11-5 on page 259. At point V, a bundle with a high proportion of restaurant meals to rooms, Ingrid is willing to forgo 10 restaurant meals in return for 1 room. But at point Y, a bundle with a low proportion of restaurant meals to rooms, she is willing to forgo only 2 restaurant meals in return for 1 room.

From this example we can see that, in Ingrid's utility function, rooms and restaurant meals possess the two additional properties that characterize ordinary goods. Ingrid requires additional rooms to compensate her for the loss of a meal, and vice versa; so her indifference curves for these two goods are downward sloping. And her indifference curves are convex: the slope of her indifference curve—*minus* the marginal rate of substitution—becomes flatter as we move down it. In fact, an indifference curve is convex only when it has diminishing marginal rate of substitution—these two conditions are equivalent.

With this information we can define **ordinary goods,** which account for the great majority of goods in any consumer's utility function. A pair of goods are ordinary goods in a consumer's utility function if they possess two properties: the consumer requires more of one good to compensate for less of the other, and the consumer experiences a diminishing marginal rate of substitution when substituting one good for the other.

Next we will see how to determine Ingrid's optimal consumption bundle using indifference curves.

Two goods, *R* and *M*, are **ordinary goods** in a consumer's utility function when (1) the consumer requires additional units of *R* to compensate for less *M*, and vice versa; and (2) the consumer experiences a diminishing marginal rate of substitution in substituting one good for another.

The Tangency Condition

Now let's put some of Ingrid's indifference curves on the same diagram as her budget line, to get an alternative way of representing her optimal consumption choice. Figure 11-6 shows Ingrid's budget line, *BL*, when her income is $2,400 per month, housing costs $150 per room each month, and restaurant meals cost $30 each. What is her optimal consumption bundle?

To answer this question, we show several of Ingrid's indifference curves: I_1, I_2, and I_3. Ingrid would like to achieve the total utility level represented by I_3, the highest of the three curves, but she cannot afford to because she is constrained by her income: no consumption bundle on her budget line yields that much total utility. But she shouldn't

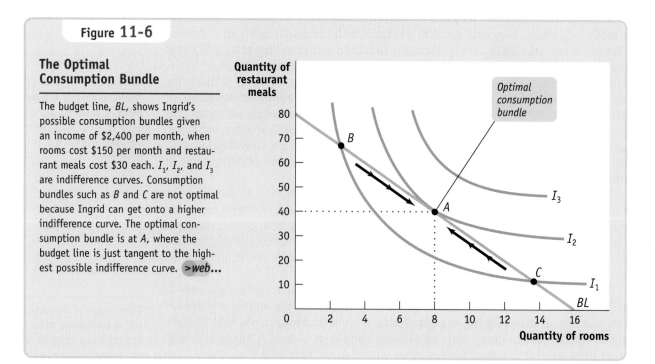

Figure 11-6

The Optimal Consumption Bundle

The budget line, *BL*, shows Ingrid's possible consumption bundles given an income of $2,400 per month, when rooms cost $150 per month and restaurant meals cost $30 each. I_1, I_2, and I_3 are indifference curves. Consumption bundles such as *B* and *C* are not optimal because Ingrid can get onto a higher indifference curve. The optimal consumption bundle is at *A*, where the budget line is just tangent to the highest possible indifference curve. **>web...**

settle for the level of total utility generated by *B*, which lies on I_1: there are other bundles on her budget line, such as *A*, that clearly yield higher total utility than *B*.

In fact, *A*—a consumption bundle consisting of 8 rooms and 40 restaurant meals per month—is Ingrid's optimal consumption choice. The reason is that *A* lies on the highest indifference curve Ingrid can reach given her income.

At the optimal consumption bundle *A*, Ingrid's budget line just touches the relevant indifference curve—the budget line is *tangent* to the indifference curve. This **tangency condition** between the indifference curve and the budget line applies to the optimal consumption bundle when the indifference curves have the typical convex shape: *At the optimal consumption bundle, the budget line just touches the indifference curve.*

To see why, let's look more closely at how we know that a consumption bundle that *doesn't* satisfy the tangency condition can't be optimal. Re-examining Figure 11-6, we can see that the consumption bundles *B* and *C* are both affordable because they lie on the budget line. However, neither is optimal. Both of them lie on the indifference curve I_1, which cuts through the budget line at both points. But because I_1 cuts through the budget line, Ingrid can do better: she can move down the budget line from *B* or up the budget line from *C*, as indicated by the arrows. In each case this allows her to get onto a higher indifference curve, I_2, which increases her total utility.

Ingrid cannot, however, do any better than I_2: any other indifference curve either cuts through her budget line or doesn't touch it at all. And the bundle that allows her to achieve I_2 is, of course, her optimal consumption bundle, *A*.

Prices and the Marginal Rate of Substitution

Let's note one final point about the optimal consumption bundle shown in Figure 11-6. At point *A*, the slope of the indifference curve is just equal to the slope of the budget line.

From rearranging Equation 11-6 we know that the slope of the indifference curve at any point is equal to minus the marginal rate of substitution:

(11-7) Slope of indifference curve $= -MU_R/MU_M$

But what is the slope of the budget line? As in Chapter 10, let's use the symbol *N* to represent Ingrid's income. As we saw in Chapter 10, the horizontal intercept of her budget line—the number of rooms she can afford if she spends all her income on rooms—is N/P_R. The vertical intercept of her budget line—the number of restaurant meals she can afford if she spends all her income on restaurant meals—is N/P_M. So the slope of her budget line when *R* is measured on the horizontal axis and *M* is measured on the vertical axis is:

(11-8) Slope of budget line $= -\dfrac{N/P_M}{N/P_R} = -P_R/P_M$

The quantity P_R/P_M is known as the **relative price** of rooms in terms of restaurant meals (to distinguish it from an ordinary price in terms of dollars). Because giving up one room allows you to buy P_R/P_M quantity of restaurant meals, we can interpret the relative price P_R/P_M as the rate at which a room trades for restaurant meals in the market.

Putting Equations 11-7 and 11-8 together, we arrive at the **relative price rule,** which says:

(11-9) *At the optimal consumption bundle:* $\dfrac{MU_R}{MU_M} = \dfrac{P_R}{P_M}$

That is, at the optimal consumption bundle, the marginal rate of substitution between any two goods is equal to the ratio of their prices. Or to put it in a more intuitive way, at Ingrid's optimal consumption bundle, the rate at which she would trade a room in exchange for having more restaurant meals along her indifference curve, MU_R/MU_M, is *equal* to the rate at which rooms are traded for restaurant meals in the market, P_R/P_M.

The **tangency condition** between the indifference curve and the budget line holds when the indifference curve and the budget line just touch. This condition determines the optimal consumption bundle when the indifference curves have the typical convex shape.

The **relative price** of good *R* in terms of good *M* is equal to P_R/P_M.

The **relative price rule** says that at the optimal consumption bundle, the marginal rate of substitution between two goods is equal to their relative price.

Figure 11-7

Understanding the Relative Price Rule

The *relative price* of rooms in terms of restaurant meals is equal to minus the slope of the budget line. The *marginal rate of substitution* of rooms in place of restaurant meals is equal to minus the slope of the indifference curve. The *relative price rule* says that at the optimal consumption bundle, the marginal rate of substitution must equal the relative price. This point can be demonstrated by considering what happens when the marginal rate of substitution is not equal to the relative price. At consumption bundle *B*, the marginal rate of substitution is larger than the relative price; Ingrid can increase her total utility by moving down her budget line, *BL*. At *C*, the marginal rate of substitution is smaller than the relative price, and Ingrid can increase her total utility by moving up the budget line. Only at *A*, where the relative price rule holds, is her total utility maximized, given her budget constraint.

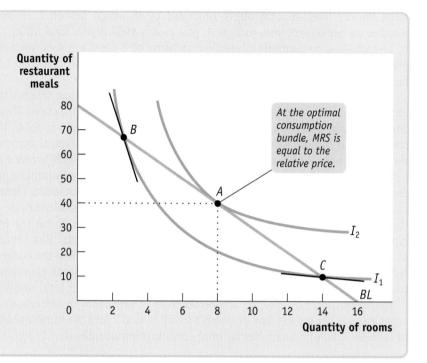

At the optimal consumption bundle, MRS is equal to the relative price.

What would happen if this equality did not hold? We can see by examining Figure 11-7. There, at point *B*, the slope of the indifference curve, $-MU_R/MU_M$, is greater than the slope of the budget line, $-P_R/P_M$. This means that, at *B*, Ingrid values an additional room in place of meals *more* than it costs her to buy an additional room and forgo some meals. As a result, Ingrid would be better off moving down her budget line toward *A*, consuming more rooms and fewer restaurant meals—and that *A* could not have been her optimal bundle! Likewise, at *C*, the slope of Ingrid's indifference curve is less than the slope of the budget line. The implication is that, at *C*, Ingrid values additional meals in place of a room *more* than it costs her to buy additional meals and forgo a room. Again, Ingrid would be made better off by moving along her budget line—consuming more restaurant meals and fewer rooms—until she reaches *A*, her optimal consumption bundle.

But suppose that we do the following transformation to Equation 11-9: divide both sides by P_R and multiply both by MU_M. Then the relative price rule becomes:

(11-10) *At the optimal consumption bundle:* $\dfrac{MU_R}{P_R} = \dfrac{MU_M}{P_M}$

which is the *optimal consumption rule*, from Chapter 10, Equation 10-5. So using either the optimal consumption rule (from Chapter 10) or the relative price rule (from this chapter), we find the same optimal consumption bundle.

Preferences and Choices

Now that we have seen how to represent optimal consumption choice in an indifference curve diagram, we can turn briefly to the relationship between consumer preferences and consumer choices.

When we say that two consumers have different preferences, we mean that they have different utility functions. This in turn means that they will have indifference curve maps with different shapes. And those different maps will translate into different consumption choices, even among consumers with the same income who face the same prices.

To see this, suppose that Ingrid's friend Lars also consumes only housing and restaurant meals. However, Lars has a stronger preference for restaurant meals and a

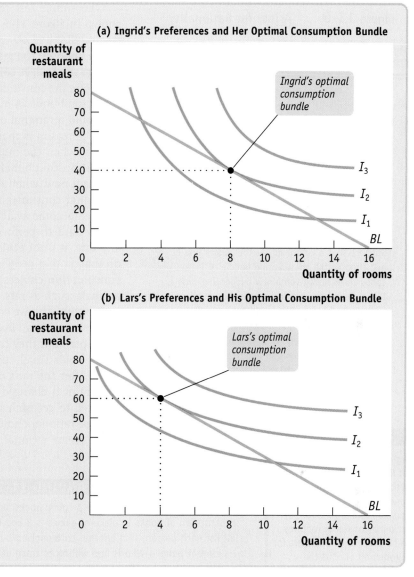

Figure 11-8

Differences in Preferences

Ingrid and Lars have different preferences, reflected in the different shapes of their indifference curve maps. So they will choose different consumption bundles even when they have the same possible choices. Both of them have an income of $2,400 per month and face prices of $30 per meal and $150 per room. Panel (a) shows Ingrid's consumption choice: 8 rooms and 40 restaurant meals. Panel (b) shows Lars's choice: even though he has the same budget line, he consumes fewer rooms and more restaurant meals.

(a) Ingrid's Preferences and Her Optimal Consumption Bundle

(b) Lars's Preferences and His Optimal Consumption Bundle

weaker preference for housing. This difference in preferences is shown in Figure 11-8, which shows *two* sets of indifference curves: panel (a) shows Ingrid's preferences and panel (b) shows Lars's preferences. Note the difference in their shapes.

Suppose, as before, that rooms cost $150 per month and restaurant meals cost $30. Let's also assume that both Ingrid and Lars have incomes of $2,400 per month, giving them identical budget lines. Nonetheless, because they have different preferences, they will make different consumption choices, as shown in Figure 11-8. Ingrid will choose 8 rooms and 40 restaurant meals; Lars will choose 4 rooms and 60 restaurant meals.

economics in action

Rats and Rational Choice

Let's admit it: the theory of consumer choice does not bear much resemblance to the way most of us think about our consumption decisions. The purpose of the theory is, however, to help economists think systematically about how a rational consumer would behave. The practical question is whether consumers actually behave rationally.

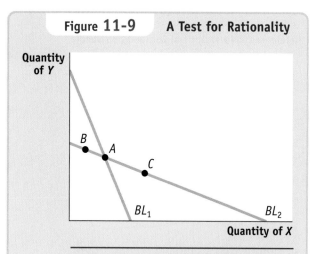

Figure 11-9   **A Test for Rationality**

Suppose that a consumer has the budget line BL_1 and chooses the consumption bundle A. If that consumer is now given a new budget line such as BL_2, it would be irrational to choose a bundle such as B; the consumer could have afforded that bundle before but chose A instead. A rational consumer would always at least stay at A or choose a new consumption bundle that was not affordable before, such as C. It's difficult to test people in this way—but it works for rats!

One simple test for rationality would look like the one shown in Figure 11-9. First, give a consumer the budget line labeled BL_1, and observe what consumption bundle the consumer chooses; the result is indicated in the figure as A. Then change the budget constraint, so that the new budget line is BL_2. Here the consumer is still able to afford the original consumption bundle A but also has some new choices available.

Would a rational consumer then choose a bundle like B? No. The reason is that B lies *inside* the original budget line—that is, when the budget line was BL_1, the consumer could have afforded it but chose A instead. It would be irrational to choose it now, when A is still available. So the new choice for a rational consumer must be either A or some bundle that has just become available, such as C.

It's hard to perform experiments like this on people—at any rate, it's not ethical (though more indirect experiments do suggest that people behave more or less rationally in their consumption choices). However, there is clear evidence that animals, such as rats, are able to make rational choices!

Economists have conducted experiments in which rats are presented with a "budget constraint"—a limited number of times per hour they can push either of two levers. One of the levers yields small cups of water; the other yields pellets of food. After the rat's choices have been observed, the budget constraint is changed by varying the number of lever pushes required to get each good. Sure enough, the rats satisfy the rule for rational choice.

If rats are rational, can people be far behind? ∎

< < < < < < < < < < < < < < < < < <

>> **QUICK REVIEW**

➤ The *marginal rate of substitution* (MRS) of R in place of M, MU_R/MU_M, is equal to minus the slope of the indifference curve.

➤ With *diminishing marginal rate of substitution*, a consumer requires more and more R to compensate for each forgone unit of M as the amount of R consumed grows relative to the amount of M consumed.

➤ Most goods are *ordinary goods*—goods with diminishing marginal rate of substitution.

➤ P_R/P_M, the *relative price* of good R in terms of good M, is equal to minus the slope of the budget line when R is measured on the horizontal axis and M is measured on the vertical axis. A utility-maximizing consumer chooses the bundle that satisfies the *tangency condition*: the indifference curve and the budget line just touch. So at the optimal consumption bundle, $MU_R/MU_M = P_R/P_M$, a condition called the *relative price rule*.

➤ Any two consumers will have different indifference curve maps because they have different preferences. Faced with the same budget and prices, they will make different consumption choices.

>> **CHECK YOUR UNDERSTANDING 11-2**

1. Lucinda and Kyle each consume 3 comic books and 6 video games. Lucinda's marginal rate of substitution of books in place of games is 2 and Kyle's is 5.
   a. For each person, find another consumption bundle that yields the same total utility as the current bundle. Who is less willing to trade games for books? In a diagram with books on the horizontal axis and games on the vertical axis, how would this be reflected in differences in the shapes of their indifference curves?
   b. Find the relative price of books in terms of games at which Lucinda's current bundle is optimal. Is Kyle's bundle optimal given this relative price? If not, how should Kyle rearrange his consumption?

Solutions appear at back of book.

Using Indifference Curves: Substitutes and Complements

Now that we've seen how to analyze consumer choice using indifference curves, we can get some payoffs from our new technique. First up is a new insight into the distinction between *substitutes* and *complements*.

Way back in Chapter 3 we pointed out that the price of one good often affects the demand for another but that the direction of this effect can go either way: a rise in the price of tea increases the demand for coffee, but a rise in the price of cream reduces the demand for coffee. Tea and coffee are substitutes; cream and coffee are complements.

But what determines whether two goods are substitutes or complements? It depends on the shape of a consumer's indifference curves. This relationship can be illustrated with two extreme cases: the cases of *perfect substitutes* and *perfect complements*.

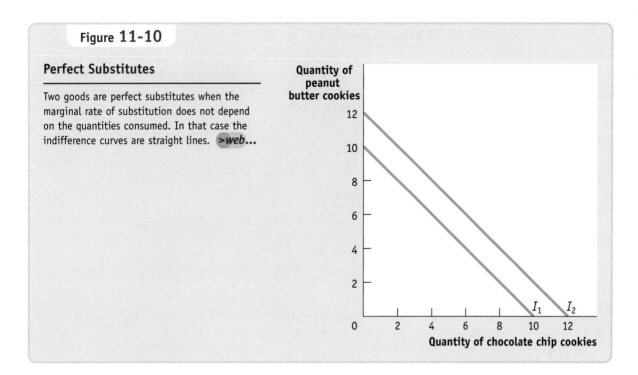

Figure 11-10

Perfect Substitutes

Two goods are perfect substitutes when the marginal rate of substitution does not depend on the quantities consumed. In that case the indifference curves are straight lines. **>web...**

Perfect Substitutes

Consider Cokie, who likes cookies. She isn't particular: it doesn't matter to her whether she has 3 peanut butter cookies and 7 chocolate chip cookies, or vice versa. What would her indifference curves between peanut butter and chocolate chip cookies look like?

The answer is that they would be straight lines like I_1 and I_2 in Figure 11-10. For example, I_1 shows that any combination of peanut butter cookies and chocolate chip cookies that adds up to 10 cookies yields Cokie the same utility.

A consumer whose indifference curves are straight lines is always willing to substitute the same amount of one good for one unit of the other, regardless of how much of either good he or she consumes. Cokie, for example, is always willing to accept one fewer peanut butter cookie in exchange for one more chocolate chip cookie, making her marginal rate of substitution *constant*.

When indifference curves are straight lines, we say that goods are **perfect substitutes.** When two goods are perfect substitutes, there is only one relative price at which consumers will be willing to purchase both goods; a slightly higher or lower relative price will cause consumers to buy only one of the two goods.

Figure 11-11 illustrates this point. The indifference curves are the same as those in Figure 11-10, but now we include Cokie's budget line, *BL*. In each panel we assume that Cokie has $12 to spend. In panel (a) we assume that chocolate chip cookies cost $1.20 and peanut butter cookies cost $1.00. Cokie's optimal consumption bundle is then at point *A*: she buys 12 peanut butter cookies and no chocolate chip cookies. In panel (b) the situation is reversed: chocolate chip cookies cost $1.00 and peanut butter cookies cost $1.20. In this case her optimal consumption is at point *B*, where she consumes only chocolate chip cookies.

Why does such a small change in the price cause Cokie to switch all her consumption from one good to the other? Because her marginal rate of substitution doesn't depend on the composition of her consumption bundle. If the relative price of chocolate chip cookies is more than the marginal rate of substitution, she buys only peanut butter cookies; if it is less, she buys only chocolate chip. And if the relative price of chocolate chip cookies is equal to the marginal rate of substitution, Cokie can maximize her utility by buying any bundle on her budget line. That is, she will be

Two goods are **perfect substitutes** if the marginal rate of substitution of one good in place of the other good is constant, regardless of how much of each an individual consumes.

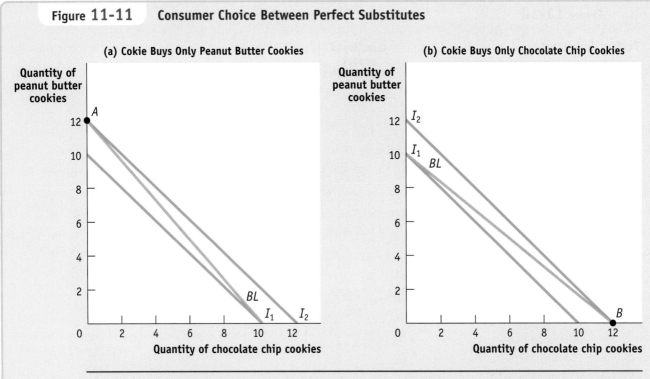

Figure 11-11   **Consumer Choice Between Perfect Substitutes**

(a) Cokie Buys Only Peanut Butter Cookies

Quantity of peanut butter cookies

(b) Cokie Buys Only Chocolate Chip Cookies

Quantity of peanut butter cookies

When two goods are perfect substitutes, small price changes can lead to large changes in the consumption bundle. In panel (a), the relative price of chocolate chip cookies is slightly higher than the marginal rate of substitution of chocolate chip in place of peanut butter cookies; this is enough to induce Cokie to choose consumption bundle A, which consists entirely of peanut butter cookies. In panel (b), the relative price of chocolate chip cookies is slightly lower than the marginal rate of substitution; this induces Cokie to choose bundle B, consisting entirely of chocolate chip cookies.

equally happy with any combination of chocolate chip cookies and peanut butter cookies that she can afford. As a result, we cannot predict which particular bundle she will choose among all the bundles that lie on her budget line.

Perfect Complements

The case of perfect substitutes represents one extreme form of consumer preferences; the case of perfect complements represents the other. Goods are **perfect complements** when a consumer wants to consume two goods in the same ratio, regardless of their relative price.

Suppose that Aaron likes cookies and milk—but only together. An extra cookie without an extra glass of milk yields no utility; neither does an extra glass of milk without another cookie. In this case, his indifference curves will form right angles, as shown in Figure 11-12.

To see why, consider the three bundles labeled A, B, and C. At B, on I_4, Aaron consumes 4 cookies and 4 glasses of milk. At A, directly above B, he consumes 4 cookies and 5 glasses of milk; but the extra glass of milk adds nothing to his utility. So A is on the same indifference curve as B, I_4. Similarly, at C he consumes 5 cookies and 4 glasses of milk, but this yields the same total utility as 4 cookies and 4 glasses of milk. So C is also on the same indifference curve, I_4.

Also shown in Figure 11-12 is a budget line that would allow Aaron to choose bundle B. The important point is that the slope of the budget line has no effect on his

Two goods are **perfect complements** when a consumer wants to consume the goods in the same ratio regardless of their relative price.

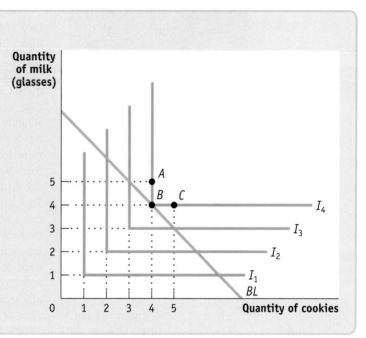

Figure 11-12

Perfect Complements

When two goods are perfect complements, a consumer wants to consume the goods in the same ratio regardless of their relative price. Indifference curves take the form of right angles. In this case, Aaron will choose to consume 4 glasses of milk and 4 cookies (bundle *B*) regardless of the slope of the budget line passing through *B*. The reason is that neither an additional glass of milk without an additional cookie (bundle *A*) nor an additional cookie without an additional glass of milk (bundle *C*) adds to his total utility. *>web*...

relative consumption of cookies and milk. This means that he will always consume the two goods in the same proportions regardless of prices—which makes the goods perfect complements.

You may be wondering what happened to the marginal rate of substitution in Figure 11-12. That is, exactly what is Aaron's marginal rate of substitution between cookies and milk, given that he is unwilling to make any substitutions between them? The answer is that in the case of perfect complements, the marginal rate of substitution is *undefined* because an individual's preferences don't allow *any* substitution between goods.

Less Extreme Cases

There are real-world examples of pairs of goods that are very close to being perfect substitutes. For example, the list of ingredients on a package of Bisquick pancake mix says that it contains "soybean and/or cottonseed oil": the producer uses whichever is cheaper, since consumers can't tell the difference. There are other pairs of goods that are very close to being perfect complements—for example, cars and tires.

In most cases, however, the possibilities for substitution lie somewhere between these extremes. In some cases, as illustrated by the following Economics in Action, it isn't easy to be sure whether goods are substitutes or complements.

economics in action

Who Needs Fleshmeets?

In the information technology community, "fleshmeet" is slang for a face-to-face (sorry, F2F) meeting, as opposed to an electronic interaction. Clearly the term is meant to be a bit derogatory; actually getting together with someone in the same room is so, well, twentieth-century—a crude, old-fashioned way of doing business.

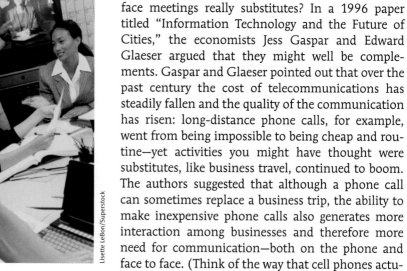

Lisette LeBon/Superstock

Video conferencing might cut your commute time, but there's really no substitute for being there.

But are electronic communication and face-to-face meetings really substitutes? In a 1996 paper titled "Information Technology and the Future of Cities," the economists Jess Gaspar and Edward Glaeser argued that they might well be complements. Gaspar and Glaeser pointed out that over the past century the cost of telecommunications has steadily fallen and the quality of the communication has risen: long-distance phone calls, for example, went from being impossible to being cheap and routine—yet activities you might have thought were substitutes, like business travel, continued to boom. The authors suggested that although a phone call can sometimes replace a business trip, the ability to make inexpensive phone calls also generates more interaction among businesses and therefore more need for communication—both on the phone and face to face. (Think of the way that cell phones actually encourage people to get together with their friends.) In the past the net effect has actually been to increase the demand for face-to-face meetings, and the authors suggested that newer technologies will continue to be complements rather than substitutes for direct personal interaction.

Some futurists believe that we are heading for a world in which people live wherever they please and interact via the Internet; in such a world not only business travel but also big cities, which exist mainly to facilitate face-to-face interaction, would lose much of their purpose. Gaspar and Glaeser argued, however, that this remains unlikely for the foreseeable future.

< < < < < < < < < < < < < < < < < <

>> CHECK YOUR UNDERSTANDING 11-3

In each of the following cases, determine whether the two goods are perfect substitutes, perfect complements, or ordinary goods. Explain your answer, paying particular attention to the marginal rate of substitution of one good in place of the other good.

1. Sanjay cares only about the number of jelly beans he receives and not about whether they are banana-flavored or pineapple-flavored.

2. Hillary's marginal utility of cherry pie goes up as she has more scoops of vanilla ice cream to go with each slice. But she is willing to consume some cherry pie without any vanilla ice cream.

3. Despite repeated reductions in price, customers won't buy software programs made by Omnisoft Corporation unless the company also sells the computer operating system that enables a computer to read these software programs.

4. Darnell works part time at the campus bookstore. The manager has asked him to work additional hours this week. Darnell is willing to do additional work, but he finds that the more hours he has already worked, the less willing he is to work yet another hour. (*Hint:* Think of the goods in question as being income and leisure time.)

Solutions appear at back of book.

Prices, Income, and Demand

Let's now return to Ingrid's consumption choices. In the situation we've considered, her income was $2,400 per month, housing cost $150 per room, and restaurant meals cost $30 each. Her optimal consumption bundle, as seen in Figure 11-7 on page 264, contained 8 rooms and 40 restaurant meals.

Let's now ask how her consumption choice would change if either the rent per room or her income changed. As we'll see, we can put these pieces together to deepen our understanding of consumer demand.

Figure 11-13

Effects of a Price Increase on the Budget Line

An increase in the price of rooms, holding the price of restaurant meals constant, increases the relative price of rooms in terms of restaurant meals. As a result, Ingrid's original budget line, BL_1, rotates inward to BL_2. Her maximum possible purchase of restaurant meals is unchanged, but her maximum possible purchase of rooms is reduced.
>web...

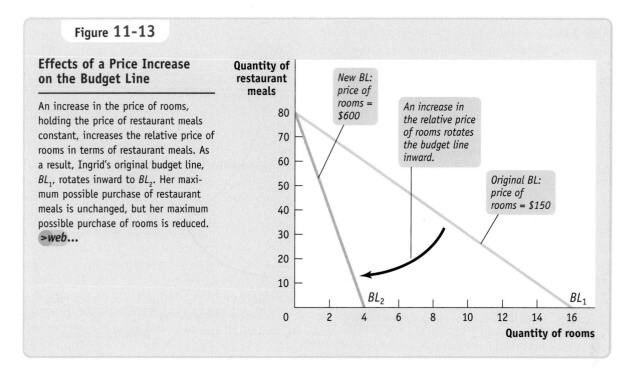

The Effects of a Price Increase

Suppose that for some reason there is a sharp increase in housing prices. Ingrid must now pay $600 per room instead of $150. Meanwhile, the price of restaurant meals and her income remain unchanged. How does this change affect her consumption choices?

When the price of rooms rises, the relative price of rooms in terms of restaurant meals rises; as a result, Ingrid's budget line changes (for the worse—but we'll get to that). She responds to that change by choosing a new consumption bundle.

Figure 11-13 shows Ingrid's original (BL_1) and new (BL_2) budget lines—again, under the assumption that her income remains constant at $2,400 per week. With housing costing $150 per room and a restaurant meal costing $30, her budget line, BL_1, intersected the horizontal axis at 16 rooms and the vertical axis at 80 restaurant meals. After the price of a room rises to $600 per room, the budget line, BL_2, still hits the vertical axis at 80 restaurant meals, but it hits the horizontal axis at only 4 rooms. Her budget line has rotated inward, reflecting the new, higher relative price of a room in terms of restaurant meals.

Figure 11-14, on page 272, shows how Ingrid responds to her new circumstances. Her original optimal consumption bundle consists of 8 rooms and 40 meals. After her budget line rotates in response to the change in relative price, she finds her new optimal consumption bundle by choosing the point on BL_2 that brings her to as high an indifference curve as possible. At the new optimal consumption bundle, she consumes fewer rooms and more restaurant meals than before: 1 room and 60 restaurant meals.

PITFALLS

"OTHER THINGS EQUAL," REVISITED

One of the biggest sources of confusion and error in economics—both in the classroom and in the real world—is failure to keep in mind the principle that all economic relationships are defined "other things equal." You may recall from Chapter 3 that a demand curve shows the effect of a good's price on its quantity demanded, *other things equal*—that is, all other things that influence demand being unchanged. Among those "other things" are the prices of other goods and the incomes of consumers.

To see how important it is to be clear about what is being held constant, let's compare two experiments. First, what happens to Ingrid's budget line if we increase the price of rooms, holding the price of restaurant meals and Ingrid's income constant? Second, what happens to her budget line if we increase the price of housing and *at the same time also increase the price of restaurant meals and Ingrid's income*?

We've just seen the effects of raising the price of rooms from $150 per month to $600. But now imagine that the price of restaurant meals also quadruples from $30 to $120 and that Ingrid's income quadruples from $2,400 to $9,600 per month. How does her budget line change?

The answer (check it yourself) is that quadrupling all three numbers—the price of rooms, the price of restaurant meals, and Ingrid's income—has *no* effect on her budget line. Because the relative price is unchanged, it won't affect her consumption choice. So the law of demand, which says that increasing the price of a good reduces the quantity demanded, is only an "other things equal" proposition; a higher price results in a lower quantity demanded, holding other prices and income constant.

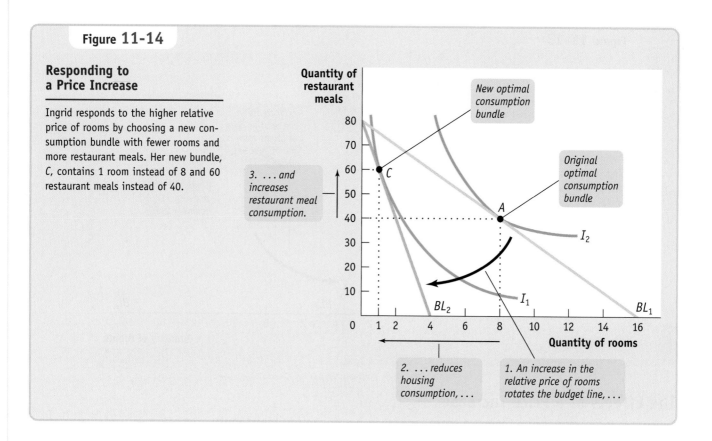

Figure 11-14

Responding to a Price Increase

Ingrid responds to the higher relative price of rooms by choosing a new consumption bundle with fewer rooms and more restaurant meals. Her new bundle, C, contains 1 room instead of 8 and 60 restaurant meals instead of 40.

Why does Ingrid's consumption of rooms fall? Part—but only part—of the reason is that the rise in the price of rooms reduces her purchasing power, making her poorer. That is, the higher relative price of rooms rotates her budget line inward towards the origin, reducing her consumption possibilities and putting her on a lower indifference curve. In a sense, when she faces a higher price of housing, it as if her income declined.

To understand this effect, and to see why it isn't the whole story, let's consider a different change in Ingrid's circumstances: a change in her income.

Income and Consumption

In Chapter 10 we learned about the individual demand curve, which shows how a consumer's consumption choice will change as the price of one good changes, holding income and the prices of other goods constant. That is, movement along the individual demand curve shows the substitution effect—how quantity consumed changes in response to changes in the *relative price* of the two goods. But we can also ask how the consumption choice will change if *income* changes, holding relative price constant.

In the previous section we considered an example in which a rise in the price of housing put Ingrid on a lower indifference curve. As we noted, it was as if her income had fallen. In this section we will consider how Ingrid responds to a direct change in income—that is, a change in her income level holding relative price constant. Figure 11-15 compares Ingrid's budget line and

Figure 11-15

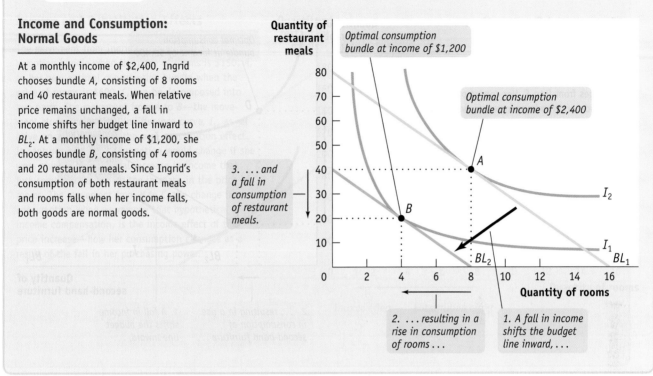

Income and Consumption: Normal Goods

At a monthly income of $2,400, Ingrid chooses bundle *A*, consisting of 8 rooms and 40 restaurant meals. When relative price remains unchanged, a fall in income shifts her budget line inward to BL_2. At a monthly income of $1,200, she chooses bundle *B*, consisting of 4 rooms and 20 restaurant meals. Since Ingrid's consumption of both restaurant meals and rooms falls when her income falls, both goods are normal goods.

Optimal consumption bundle at income of $1,200

Optimal consumption bundle at income of $2,400

3. ... and a fall in consumption of restaurant meals.

2. ... resulting in a rise in consumption of rooms ...

1. A fall in income shifts the budget line inward, ...

optimal consumption choice with an income of $2,400 per month ($BL_1$) with her budget line and optimal consumption choice with an income of $1,200 per month ($BL_2$), while keeping prices at $150 per room and $30 per restaurant meal. *A* is Ingrid's optimal consumption bundle at an income of $2,400 and *B* is her optimal consumption bundle at an income of $1,200. In each case, her optimal consumption bundle is given by the point at which the budget line is tangent to the indifference curve. As you can see, at the lower income her budget line shifts *inward* compared to her budget line at the higher income but maintains the same slope because relative price has not changed. This means that she must reduce her consumption of either housing or restaurant meals, or both. As a result she is at a lower level of total utility, represented by a lower indifference curve.

As it turns out, Ingrid chooses to consume less of both goods when her income falls: as her income goes from $2,400 to $1,200, her consumption of housing falls from 8 to 4 rooms and her consumption of restaurant meals falls from 40 to 20. This is because in her utility function both goods are *normal goods*, as defined in Chapter 5: goods for which demand increases when income rises and for which demand decreases when income falls.

Although most goods are normal goods, we also pointed out in Chapter 5 that some goods are *inferior goods*, goods for which demand moves in the opposite direction to the change in income: demand decreases when income rises, and demand increases when income falls. An example might be second-hand furniture. Whether a good is an inferior good depends on the consumer's indifference curve map. Figure 11-16 on page 274 illustrates such a case, where second-hand furniture is measured on the horizontal axis and restaurant meals are measured on the vertical axis. Note that when Ingrid's income falls from $2,400 ($BL_1$) to $1,200 ($BL_2$), and her optimal consumption bundle goes from *D* to *E*, her consumption of second-hand furniture increases—implying that second-hand furniture is an inferior good. Simultaneously, her consumption of restaurant meals decreases—implying that restaurant meals are a normal good.

Draw Sabine's budget line for Coke and Pepsi on the same diagram.

   d. What is Sabine's optimal consumption bundle? Show this on your diagram.

   e. If the price of Coke and Pepsi is the same, what combination of Coke and Pepsi will Sabine buy?

8. For Norma, both nachos and salsa are normal goods. Although she likes consuming them together, they are not perfect complements (her indifference curves are convex-shaped, not right angle–shaped). The price of nachos rises, while the price of salsa remains unchanged.

   a. Can you determine definitively whether she consumes more or fewer nachos? Explain with a diagram, placing nachos on the horizontal axis and salsa on the vertical axis.

   b. Can you determine definitively whether she consumes more or less salsa? Explain with a diagram, placing nachos on the horizontal axis and salsa on the vertical axis.

9. Tyrone is a utility maximizer. His income is $100, which he can spend on cafeteria meals and on notepads. Each meal costs $5, and each notepad costs $2. At these prices Tyrone chooses to buy 16 cafeteria meals and 10 notepads.

   a. Draw a diagram that shows Tyrone's choice using an indifference curve and his budget line, placing notepads on the vertical axis and cafeteria meals on the horizontal axis. Label the indifference curve I_1 and the budget line BL_1.

   b. The price of notepads falls to $1; the price of cafeteria meals remains the same. On the same diagram, draw Tyrone's budget line with the new prices and label it BL_S.

   c. Lastly, Tyrone's income falls to $90. On the same diagram, draw his budget line with this income and the new prices and label it BL_2. Is he worse off, better off, or equally as well off with these new prices and lower income than compared to the original prices and higher income? (Hint: Determine whether Tyrone can afford to buy his original consumption bundle of 16 meals and 10 notepads with the lower income and new prices.) Illustrate your answer using an indifference curve and label it I_2.

   d. Give an intuitive explanation of your answer to (c).

10. Gus spends his income on gas for his car and food. The government raises the tax on gas, thereby raising the price of gas. But the government also lowers the income tax, thereby increasing Gus's income. And this rise in income is just enough to place Gus on the same indifference curve as the one he was on before the price of gas rose. Will Gus buy more, less, or the same amount of gas as before these changes?

11. Pam spends her money on bread and Spam, and her indifference curves obey the four properties of indifference curves for ordinary goods. Suppose that, for Pam, Spam is an inferior, but not a Giffen, good; bread is a normal good. Bread costs $2 per loaf, and Spam costs $2 per can. Pam has $20 to spend.

   a. Draw a diagram of Pam's budget line, placing Spam on the horizontal axis and bread on the vertical axis. Suppose

her optimal consumption bundle is 4 cans of Spam and 6 loaves of bread. Illustrate that bundle also, and draw the indifference curve on which it lies.

   b. The price of Spam falls to $1; the price of bread remains the same. Pam now buys 7 loaves of bread and 6 cans of Spam. Illustrate her new budget line and new optimal consumption bundle in your diagram. Also draw the indifference curve on which this bundle lies.

   c. In your diagram, show the income and substitution effects from this fall in the price of Spam. Remember that Spam is an inferior good for Pam.

12. Katya commutes to work. She can either use public transport or her own car. Her indifference curves obey the four properties of indifference curves for ordinary goods.

   a. Draw Katya's budget line with car travel on the vertical axis and public transport on the horizontal axis. Suppose that Katya consumes some of both goods. Draw an indifference curve that helps you illustrate that optimal consumption bundle.

   b. Now the price of public transport falls. Draw Katya's new budget line.

   c. For Katya, public transport is an inferior, but not a Giffen, good. Draw an indifference curve that illustrates her optimal consumption bundle after the price of public transport has fallen. Is Katya consuming more or less public transport?

   d. Show the income and substitution effects from this fall in the price of public transport.

13. For Crandall, cheese cubes and crackers are perfect complements: he wants to consume exactly 1 cheese cube with each cracker. He has $2.40 to spend on cheese and crackers. One cheese cube costs 20 cents, and 1 cracker costs 10 cents. Draw a diagram, with crackers on the horizontal axis and cheese cubes on the vertical axis, to answer the following questions.

   a. Which bundle will Crandall consume?

   b. The price of crackers rises to 20 cents. How many cheese cubes and how many crackers will Crandall consume?

   c. In your diagram, show the income and substitution effects from this price rise.

14. Carmen consumes nothing but cafeteria meals and CDs. Her indifference curves exhibit the four general properties of indifference curves. Cafeteria meals cost $5 each, and CDs cost $10. Carmen has $50 to spend.

   a. Draw Carmen's budget line and an indifference curve that illustrates her optimal consumption bundle. Place cafeteria meals on the horizontal axis and CDs on the vertical axis. You do not have enough information to know the specific tangency point, so choose one arbitrarily.

   b. Now Carmen's income rises to $100. Draw her new budget line on the same diagram, as well as an indifference curve that illustrates her optimal consumption bundle. Assume that cafeteria meals are an inferior good.

   c. Can you draw an indifference curve showing that cafeteria meals and CDs are both inferior goods?

Factor Markets and the
>> Distribution of Income

THE VALUE OF A DEGREE

Does higher education pay? Yes, it does: in the modern economy, employers are willing to pay a premium for workers with more education. And the size of that premium has increased a lot over the last few decades. Back in 1973 workers with advanced degrees, such as law degrees or MBAs, earned only 76 percent more than those who had only graduated from high school. By 2003 the premium for an advanced degree had risen to 120 percent.

Who decided that the wages of workers with advanced degrees would rise so much compared with those of high school grads? The answer, of course, is that nobody decided it. Wage rates are prices, the prices of different kinds of labor; and they are decided, like other prices, by supply and demand.

Still, there is a difference between the wage rate of high school grads and the price of used textbooks: the wage rate isn't the price of a *good*, it's the price of a *factor of production*. And although markets for factors of production are in many ways similar to those

for goods, there are also some important differences.

In this chapter, we examine *factor markets*, the markets in which factors of production such as labor are traded. Factor markets, like goods markets, play a crucial role in the economy: they allocate productive resources to producers and help ensure that those resources are used efficiently.

This chapter begins by describing the major factors of production. Then we consider the demand for factors of production, which leads us to a crucial insight: the *marginal productivity theory of income distribution*.

If you've ever had doubts about attending college, consider this: factory workers with only high school degrees will make much less than college grads. The present discounted value of the difference in lifetime earnings is as much as $300,000.

We then consider some challenges to the marginal productivity theory. The final section of the chapter looks at the supply of the most important factor, labor.

What you will learn in this chapter:

➤ How factors of production—resources like land, labor, and both **physical capital** and **human capital**—are traded in factor markets, determining the **factor distribution of income**

➤ How the demand for factors leads to the **marginal productivity theory of income distribution**

➤ An understanding of the sources of wage disparities and the role of discrimination

➤ The way in which a worker's decision about **time allocation** gives rise to labor supply

The Marginal Productivity Theory of Income Distribution

We've now seen that each perfectly competitive producer in a perfectly competitive factor market maximizes profit by hiring labor up to the point at which its value of the marginal product is equal to its price—that is, to the point where $VMPL = W$.

The same logic works for other factors of production. Suppose, for example, that a farmer is considering whether to rent an additional acre of land for the next year. He or she will compare the cost of renting that acre with the value of the additional output generated by employing an additional acre—the value of the marginal product of an acre of land. To maximize profit, the farmer must employ land up to the point where the value of the marginal product of an acre is equal to the rent per acre.

What if the farmer already owns the land? We already saw the answer back in Chapter 7, which dealt with economic decisions: even if you own land, there is an implicit cost—the opportunity cost—of using it for a given activity, because it could be used for something else. So a profit-maximizing producer will employ additional acres of land up to the point where the cost of the last acre employed, explicit or implicit, is equal to the value of the marginal product of that acre.

The same is true for capital. In general, economists say that both land and capital are employed up to the point where the **rental rate**—the cost, explicit or implicit, of using a unit of land or capital for a set period of time—is equal to that unit's value of the marginal product over that time period.

The **rental rate** of either land or capital is the cost, explicit or implicit, of using a unit of that asset for a given period of time.

So we have learned that when the markets for goods and services and the factor markets are perfectly competitive, factors of production will be employed up to the point at which their value of the marginal product is equal to their price. What does this say about the factor distribution of income?

Suppose that the labor market is in equilibrium: at the going wage rate, the number of workers that producers want to employ is equal to the number of workers willing to work. Then all employers will pay the *same* wage rate, and *each* employer, whatever he or she is producing, will employ labor up to the point where the value of the marginal product of one more worker is equal to that wage rate.

This situation is illustrated in Figure 12-5, which shows the value of the marginal product curves of two producers—Farmer Jones, who produces wheat, and Farmer

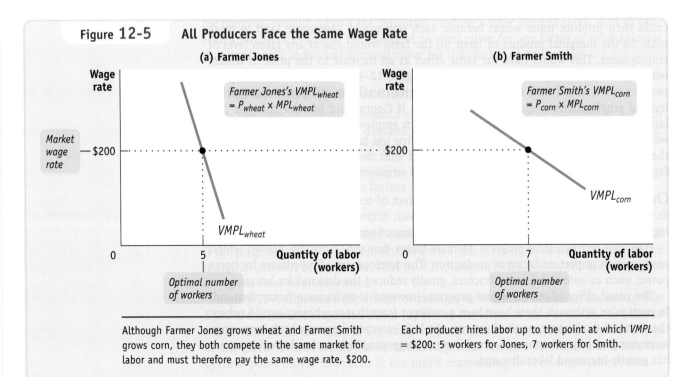

Figure 12-5   All Producers Face the Same Wage Rate

(a) Farmer Jones

Wage rate

Farmer Jones's $VMPL_{wheat}$ = $P_{wheat} \times MPL_{wheat}$

Market wage rate — $200

$VMPL_{wheat}$

0   5   Quantity of labor (workers)

Optimal number of workers

(b) Farmer Smith

Wage rate

Farmer Smith's $VMPL_{corn}$ = $P_{corn} \times MPL_{corn}$

$200

$VMPL_{corn}$

0   7   Quantity of labor (workers)

Optimal number of workers

Although Farmer Jones grows wheat and Farmer Smith grows corn, they both compete in the same market for labor and must therefore pay the same wage rate, $200.

Each producer hires labor up to the point at which $VMPL$ = $200: 5 workers for Jones, 7 workers for Smith.

Smith, who produces corn. Despite the fact that they produce different products, they compete for the same workers, and so must pay the same wage rate, $200. So when both farmers maximize profit, both hire labor up to the point where its value of the marginal product is equal to the wage rate. In the figure, this corresponds to employment of 5 workers by Jones and 7 by Smith.

Figure 12-6 illustrates the general situation in the labor market as a whole. The *market labor demand curve*, like the market demand curve for a good (shown in Figure 10-6), is the horizontal sum of all the individual labor demand curves—which is the same as each producer's value of the marginal product curve. For now, let's simply assume an upward-sloping supply curve for labor; we'll discuss labor supply later in this chapter. Then the equilibrium wage rate is the wage rate at which the quantity of labor supplied is equal to the quantity of labor demanded. In Figure 12-6, this equilibrium wage rate is W^* and the corresponding equilibrium employment level is L^*.

And as we showed in the examples of the farms of George and Martha and of Farmer Jones and Farmer Smith (where the equilibrium wage rate corresponds to $200), each firm will hire labor up to the point at which the value of the marginal product of labor is equal to the equilibrium wage rate. This means that, in equilibrium, the marginal product of labor will be the same for all employers. So the equilibrium (or market) wage rate is equal to the **equilibrium value of the marginal product** of labor—the additional value produced by the last unit of labor employed in the labor market as a whole. It doesn't matter where that additional unit is employed, since VMPL is the same for all producers.

What we have just learned, then, is that the market wage rate is equal to the equilibrium value of the marginal product of labor. And the same is true of each factor of production: in a perfectly competitive market economy, the market price of each factor is equal to its equilibrium value of the marginal product.

The theory that each factor is paid the value of the output generated by the last unit employed in the factor market as a whole is known as the **marginal productivity theory of income distribution**.

> The **equilibrium value of the marginal product** of a factor is the additional value produced by the last unit of that factor employed in the factor market as a whole.

> According to the **marginal productivity theory of income distribution**, every factor of production is paid its equilibrium value of the marginal product.

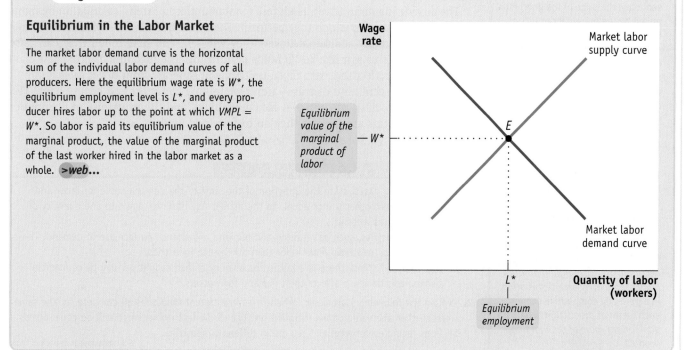

Figure 12-6

Equilibrium in the Labor Market

The market labor demand curve is the horizontal sum of the individual labor demand curves of all producers. Here the equilibrium wage rate is W^*, the equilibrium employment level is L^*, and every producer hires labor up to the point at which VMPL = W^*. So labor is paid its equilibrium value of the marginal product, the value of the marginal product of the last worker hired in the labor market as a whole. **>web...**

To understand why the marginal productivity theory of income distribution is an important theory, take a look back at Figure 12-1, which showed the factor distribution of income in the United States, and ask yourself this question: who or what decided that labor would get 71 percent of total U.S. income? Why not 90 percent or 50 percent?

The answer, according to the marginal productivity theory of income distribution, is that the division of income among the economy's factors of production isn't arbitrary: it is determined by each factor's marginal productivity at the economy's equilibrium. The wage rate earned by *all* workers in the economy is equal to the increase in the value of output generated by the last worker employed in the economy-wide labor market.

Here we have assumed that all workers are of the same ability. But in reality workers may differ considerably in ability. Rather than thinking of one labor market for all workers in the economy, we can instead think of different markets for different types of workers, where workers are of equivalent ability within each market. For example, the market for computer programmers is different from the market for pastry chefs. And in the market for computer programmers, all participants are assumed to have equal ability; likewise for the market for pastry chefs. In this scenario, the marginal productivity theory of income distribution still holds. That is, when the labor market for computer programmers is in equilibrium, the wage rate earned by all computer programmers is equal to the market's equilibrium value of the marginal product—the value of the marginal product of the last computer programmer hired in that market.

economics in action

Star Power

If you want to be rich, don't become a classical musician or an opera singer. Most musical artists earn quite little considering the many years of training required.

There are, however, a handful of performers who command very large fees, in the vicinity of $30,000 for a single performance. Can the fees paid to stars be explained by the marginal productivity theory of income distribution?

The answer is a definite yes. High fees for stars reflect a careful calculation by managers of the theaters in which they perform. These managers know—with considerable precision—how many additional tickets they will sell, and how much they can raise ticket prices, when a star like Yo-Yo Ma is performing. The high fees paid to these classical superstars reflect the extra revenues they will generate from ticket sales.

All this may seem kind of crass—aren't we talking about art and beauty here? Yes, but music—even classical music—is also a business, and the principles of economics apply to opera stars as much as they do to fast-food workers. ∎

< < < < < < < < < < < < < < < < < <

▶▶ CHECK YOUR UNDERSTANDING 12-2

1. In the following cases, state the direction of the shift of the demand curve for labor and what will happen, other things equal, to the market equilibrium wage rate and quantity of labor employed as a result.
   a. Service industries, such as retailing and banking, experience an increase in demand. These industries use relatively more labor than nonservice industries.
   b. Due to over-fishing, there is a fall in the amount of fish caught per day by commercial fishers; this decrease affects their demand for workers.

2. Explain the following statement: "When firms in different industries all compete for the same workers, then the value of the marginal product of the last worker hired will be equal across all firms regardless of whether they are in different industries."

Solutions appear at back of book.

Is the Marginal Productivity Theory of Income Distribution Really True?

Although the marginal productivity theory of income distribution is a well-established part of economic theory, closely linked to the analysis of markets in general, it is a source of some controversy. There are two main objections to it.

First, in the real world we see large disparities in income between factors of production that, in the eyes of some observers, should receive the same payment. Perhaps the most conspicuous examples in the United States are the large differences in the average wages between women and men and among various racial and ethnic groups. Do these wage differences really reflect differences in marginal productivity, or is something else going on?

Second, many people wrongly believe that the marginal productivity theory of income distribution gives a *moral* justification for the distribution of income, implying that the existing distribution is fair and appropriate. (We'll explain in Chapter 13 why this is a misconception.) This misconception sometimes leads people who believe that the current distribution of income is unfair to reject marginal productivity theory.

To address these controversies, we'll start by looking at income disparities across gender and ethnic groups. Then we'll ask what factors might account for these disparities and whether these explanations are consistent with the marginal productivity theory of income distribution.

Wage Disparities in Practice

Wage rates in the United States cover a very wide range. In 2003, hundreds of thousands of workers received the legal federal minimum of $5.15 per hour. At the other extreme, the chief executives of several companies were paid more than $100 million, which is $20,000 per hour even if they worked 100-hour weeks. Even leaving out these extremes, there is a huge range of wage rates. Are people really that different in their marginal productivities?

A particular source of concern is the existence of systematic wage differences across gender and ethnicity. Figure 12-7 compares annual median earnings in 2002 of workers classified by gender and ethnicity. As a group, white males had the highest

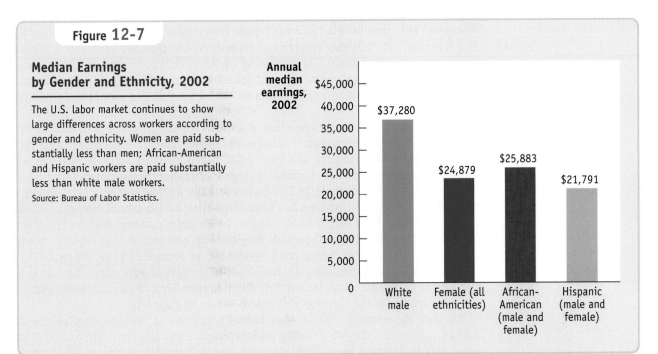

Figure 12-7

Median Earnings by Gender and Ethnicity, 2002

The U.S. labor market continues to show large differences across workers according to gender and ethnicity. Women are paid substantially less than men; African-American and Hispanic workers are paid substantially less than white male workers.

Source: Bureau of Labor Statistics.

earnings. Other data show that women (averaging across all ethnicities) earned only about 67 percent as much; African-American workers (male and female combined) only 69 percent as much; Hispanic workers only 58 percent as much.

We are a nation founded on the belief that all men are created equal—and if the Constitution were rewritten today, we would say that *all people* are created equal. So why do they receive such unequal pay? Let's start with the marginal productivity explanations, then look at other influences.

Marginal Productivity and Wage Inequality

A large part of the observed inequality in wages can be explained by considerations that are consistent with the marginal productivity theory of income distribution. In particular, there are three well-understood sources of wage differences across occupations and individuals.

Compensating differentials are wage differences across jobs that reflect the fact that some jobs are less pleasant than others.

First is the existence of **compensating differentials:** across different types of jobs, wages are often higher or lower depending on how attractive or unattractive the job is. Workers with unpleasant or dangerous jobs demand a higher wage in comparison to workers with jobs that require the same skill and effort but lack the unpleasant or dangerous qualities. For example, truckers who haul hazardous loads are paid more than truckers who haul normal loads. But for any *given* job, the marginal productivity theory of income distribution generally holds true. For example, hazardous-load truckers are paid a wage equal to the equilibrium value of the marginal product of the last person employed in the market for hazardous-load truckers.

A second reason for wage inequality that is clearly consistent with marginal productivity theory is differences in talent. People differ in their abilities: a high-ability person, by producing a better product that commands a higher price compared to a lower-ability person, generates a higher value of the marginal product. And these differences in the value of the marginal product translate into differences in earning potential. We all know that this is true in sports: practice is important, but 99.99 percent (at least) of the population just doesn't have what it takes to hit golf balls like Tiger Woods or skate like Michelle Kwan. The same is true, though less obvious, in other fields of endeavor.

A third, very important reason for wage differences is differences in the quantity of *human capital*. Recall that human capital—education and training—is at least as important in the modern economy as physical capital in the form of buildings and machines. Different people "embody" quite different quantities of human capital, and a person with a higher quantity of human capital typically generates a higher value of the marginal product by producing a product that commands a higher price. So differences in human capital account for substantial differences in wages. People with high levels of human capital, such as skilled surgeons or engineers, generally receive high wages.

The most direct way to see the effect of human capital on wages is to look at the relationship between educational levels and earnings. Figure 12-8 shows earnings differentials by gender, ethnicity, and three educational levels in 2002. As you can see from it, regardless of gender or ethnicity, higher education is associated with higher median earnings. For example, in 2002 white females without a high school diploma had median earnings 31 percent less than those with a high school diploma and 58 percent less than those with a college degree—and similar patterns exist for the other five groups. Additional data show that surgeons—an occupation that requires steady hands and many years of formal training—earned an average of $161,348 in 2001.

Because even now men typically have had more years of education than women and whites more years than nonwhites, differences in level of education are part of the explanation for the earnings differences shown in Figure 12-7.

It's also important to realize that formal education is not the only source of human capital; on-the-job training and experience are also very important. This point was highlighted by a 1999 National Science Foundation report on earnings

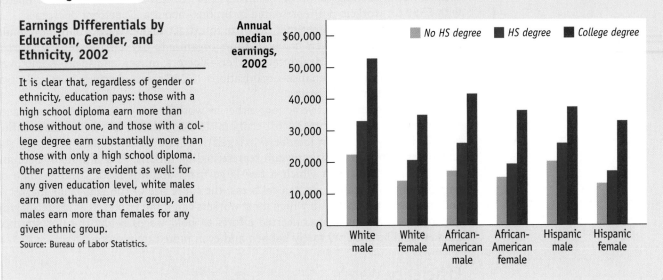

Figure 12-8

Earnings Differentials by Education, Gender, and Ethnicity, 2002

It is clear that, regardless of gender or ethnicity, education pays: those with a high school diploma earn more than those without one, and those with a college degree earn substantially more than those with only a high school diploma. Other patterns are evident as well: for any given education level, white males earn more than every other group, and males earn more than females for any given ethnic group.

Source: Bureau of Labor Statistics.

differences between male and female engineers. The study was motivated by concerns over the male–female earnings gap: on average, men with engineering degrees earn about 25 percent more than women with equivalent degrees. The study found that women in engineering are, on average, younger than men and have considerably less experience than their male counterparts. This difference in age and experience, according to the study, explained most of the earnings differential. Differences in job tenure and experience can partly explain one notable aspect of Figure 12-8: that, across all ethnicities, women's median earnings are less than men's median earnings for any given education level.

But it's also important to emphasize that earnings differences that arise from differences in human capital are not necessarily "fair." A society in which nonwhite children typically receive a poor education because they live in underfunded school districts, then go on to earn low wages because they are poorly educated, may have labor markets that are well described by marginal productivity theory (and would be consistent with the earnings differentials across ethnic groups shown in Figure 12-7). Yet many people would still consider the resulting distribution of income unfair.

Still, many observers think that actual wage differentials cannot be entirely explained by compensating differentials, differences in talent, and human capital. They believe that market power, *efficiency wages,* and discrimination also play an important role. We will examine these forces next.

Market Power

The marginal productivity theory of income distribution is based on the assumption that factor markets are perfectly competitive. In such markets we can expect workers to be paid their equilibrium value of the marginal product, regardless of who they are. But how valid is this assumption?

We haven't yet studied markets that are *not* perfectly competitive (we'll get there in Chapter 14), but let's touch briefly on the ways in which labor markets may deviate from the competitive assumption.

One undoubted source of differences in wages between otherwise similar workers is the role of **unions**—organizations that try to raise wages and improve working conditions for their members. Labor unions, when they are successful, replace one-on-one wage deals between workers and employers with "collective bargaining," in which the employer must negotiate wages with union representatives. Without question, this

Unions are organizations of workers that try to raise wages and improve working conditions for their members.

leads to higher wages for those workers who are represented by unions. In 2003 the median weekly earnings of union members in the United States were $760, compared with $599 for workers not represented by unions—about a 22 percent difference.

Just as workers can sometimes organize to extract higher wages than they would otherwise receive, employers can sometimes organize to pay *lower* wages than would result from competition. Health care workers—doctors, nurses, and so on—sometimes argue that health maintenance organizations (HMOs) are engaged in a collective effort to hold down their wages.

How much does collective action, either by workers or by employers, affect wages in the modern United States? Most economists think that it is a fairly minor influence. To begin with, union membership is relatively limited: less than 9 percent of the employees of private businesses are represented by unions. And although there are fields like health care in which a few large firms account for a sizeable share of employment in certain geographical areas, the sheer size of the U.S. labor market is enormous and the ease with which most workers can move in search of higher-paying jobs probably means that concerted efforts to hold wages below the unrestrained market equilibrium level rarely happen and even more rarely succeed.

Efficiency Wages

A second source of wage inequality is the phenomenon of *efficiency wages*—a type of incentive scheme to motivate workers to work hard and reduce worker turnover used by employers. Suppose that a worker performs a job that is extremely important but in which the employer can observe only at infrequent intervals how well the job is being performed—say, serving as a caregiver for the employer's child. Then it often makes sense for the employer to pay more than the worker could earn in an alternative job—that is, more than the equilibrium wage. Why? Because earning a premium makes losing this job and having to take the alternative job quite costly for the worker. So a worker who happens to be observed performing poorly and is therefore fired is now worse off for having to accept a lower-paying job. The threat of losing a job that pays a premium motivates the worker to perform well and avoid being fired. Likewise, paying a premium also reduces worker turnover—the frequency with which an employee leaves a job voluntarily. Despite the fact that it may take no more effort and skill to be a child's caregiver than to be an office worker, efficiency wages show why it often makes economic sense for a parent to pay a caregiver more than the equilibrium wage of an office worker.

According to the **efficiency-wage model,** some employers pay an above-equilibrium wage as an incentive for better performance.

The **efficiency-wage model** explains why we may observe wages offered above their equilibrium level. Like the price floors that we studied in Chapter 4—and, in particular, much like the minimum wage—this phenomenon leads to a surplus of labor supplied in the markets for labor that are characterized by the efficiency wage model. This surplus of labor translates into unemployment—some workers are actively searching for a high-paying efficiency-wage job but are unable to get one, and other more fortunate but no more deserving workers are able to acquire one. As a result, two workers with exactly the same profile—the same skills and same job history—may earn unequal wages: the worker who is lucky enough to get an efficiency-wage job earns more than the worker who gets a standard job (or who remains unemployed while searching for a higher-paying job). Efficiency wages are a type of market failure that arises from the fact that some employees don't always perform as well as they should and are able to hide that fact. As a result, employers use nonequilibrium wages in order to motivate their employees, leading to an inefficient outcome.

Discrimination

It is a real and ugly fact that throughout history there has been discrimination against workers who are considered to be the wrong race, ethnicity, or gender. How does this fit into our economic models?

The main insight economic analysis offers is that discrimination is *not* a natural consequence of market competition. On the contrary, market forces tend to work against discrimination. To see why, consider the incentives that would exist if social convention dictated that women be paid, say, 30 percent less than men with equivalent qualifications and experience. A company whose management was itself unbiased would then be able to reduce its costs by hiring women rather than men—and such companies would have an advantage over other companies that hired men despite their higher cost. The result would be to create an excess demand for female workers, which would tend to drive up their wages.

But if market competition works against discrimination, how is it that so much discrimination has taken place? The answer is twofold. First, when labor markets don't work well, employers may have the ability to discriminate without hurting their profits. For example, market interferences (such as unions or minimum-wage laws) or market failures (such as efficiency wages) can lead to wages that are above their equilibrium levels. In these cases, there are more job applicants than there are jobs—leaving employers free to discriminate among applicants. In research published in 2003, two economists, Marianne Bertrand and Sendhil Mullainathan, documented discrimination in hiring by sending fictitious résumés to prospective employers on a random basis. Applicants with "white-sounding" names such as Emily Walsh were 50 percent more likely to be contacted than applicants with "African-American-sounding" names such as Lakisha Washington. Also, applicants with white-sounding names and good credentials were much more likely to be contacted than those without such credentials. By contrast, potential employers seemed to ignore the credentials of applicants with African-American-sounding names.

Second, discrimination has sometimes been institutionalized in government policy. This institutionalization of discrimination has made it easier to maintain it against market pressure, and historically it is the form that discrimination has typically taken. For example, at one time in the United States, African-Americans were barred from attending "whites-only" public schools and universities in many parts of the country and forced to attend inferior schools. So although market competition tends to work against *current* discrimination, it is not a remedy for past discrimination, which typically has had an impact on the education and experience of its victims and thereby reduces their income. Economics in Action below illustrates the way in which government policy enforced discrimination in the world's most famous racist regime, that of South Africa.

So Does Marginal Productivity Theory Work?

The main conclusion you should draw from this discussion is that marginal productivity theory is not a perfect description of how factor incomes are determined but that it works pretty well. The deviations are important. But, by and large, in a modern economy with well-functioning labor markets, factors of production are paid the equilibrium value of the marginal product—the value of the marginal product of the last unit employed in the market as a whole.

It's important to emphasize, once again, that this does not mean that the factor distribution of income is morally justified. We'll turn to issues of fairness and equity in Chapter 13.

economics in action

The Economics of Apartheid

The Republic of South Africa is the richest nation in Africa, but it also has a harsh political history. Until the peaceful transition to majority rule in 1994, the country was controlled by its white minority, Afrikaners, the descendants of European (mainly Dutch) immigrants. This minority imposed an economic system known as apartheid, which overwhelmingly favored white interests over those of native Africans and other groups considered "nonwhite," such as Asians.

South Africa is a democracy now, but the human legacy of apartheid persists.

The origins of apartheid go back to the early years of the twentieth century, when large numbers of white farmers began moving into South Africa's growing cities. There they discovered, to their horror, that they did not automatically earn higher wages than other races. But they had the right to vote—and nonwhites did not. And so the South African government instituted "job-reservation" laws designed to ensure that only whites got jobs that paid well. The government also set about creating jobs for whites in government-owned industries. As Allister Sparks notes in *The Mind of South Africa* (1990), in its efforts to provide high-paying jobs for whites, the country "eventually acquired the largest amount of nationalized industry of any country out-side the Communist bloc."

In other words, racial discrimination was possible because it was backed by the power of the government, which prevented markets from following their natural course.

A postscript: in 1994, in one of the political miracles of modern times, the white regime ceded power and South Africa became a full-fledged democracy. Apartheid was abolished. Unfortunately, large racial differences in earnings remain. The main reason is that apartheid created huge disparities in human capital, which will persist for many years to come. ■

< < < < < < < < < < < < < < < < < <

>>CHECK YOUR UNDERSTANDING 12-3

1. Assess each of the following statements. Do you think they are true, false, or ambiguous? Explain.
   a. The marginal productivity theory of income distribution is inconsistent with the presence of income disparities associated with gender, race, or ethnicity.
   b. Companies that engage in workplace discrimination but whose competitors do not are likely to have lower profits as a result of their actions.
   c. Workers who are paid less because they have less experience are not the victims of discrimination.

The Supply of Labor

Up to this point we have focused on the demand for factors, which determines the quantities demanded of labor, capital or land by producers as a function of their factor prices. What about the supply of factors?

In this section we focus exclusively on the supply of labor. We do this for two reasons. First, in the modern U.S. economy, labor is the most important factor of production, accounting for most of factor income. Second, as we'll see, labor supply is the area in which factor markets look most different from markets for goods and services.

Work Versus Leisure

In the labor market, the roles of firms and households are the reverse of what they are in markets for goods and services. On the one hand, a good such as wheat is supplied by firms and demanded by households; on the other hand, labor is demanded by firms and supplied by households. How do people decide how much labor to supply?

As a practical matter, most people have limited control over their work hours: either you take a job that involves working a set number of hours per week, or you don't get the job at all. To understand the logic of labor supply, however, it helps to put realism to one side for a bit and imagine an individual who can choose to work as many or as few hours as he or she likes.

Why wouldn't such an individual work as many hours as possible? Because workers are human beings, too, and have other uses for their time. An hour spent on the job is an hour not spent on other, presumably more pleasant, activities. So the decision about how much labor to supply involves making a decision about **time allocation**—how many hours to spend on different activities.

Decisions about labor supply result from decisions about **time allocation:** how many hours to spend on different activities.

By working, people earn income that they can use to buy goods. The more hours an individual works, the more goods he or she can afford to buy. But this increased purchasing power comes at the expense of a reduction in **leisure,** the time spent not working. (Leisure doesn't necessarily mean time goofing off. It could mean time spent with one's family, pursuing hobbies, exercising, and so on). And though purchased goods yield utility, so does leisure. Indeed, we can think of leisure itself as a normal good, which most people would like to consume more of as their incomes increase.

How does a rational individual decide how much leisure to consume? By making a marginal comparison, of course. In analyzing consumer choice, we asked how a utility-maximizing consumer uses a marginal *dollar*. In analyzing labor supply, we ask how an individual uses a marginal *hour*.

Consider Clive, an individual who likes both leisure and the goods money can buy. And suppose that his wage rate is $10 per hour. In deciding how many hours he wants to work, he must compare the marginal utility of an additional hour of leisure with the additional utility he gets from $10 worth of goods. If $10 worth of goods adds more to his total utility than an additional hour of leisure, he can increase his total utility by giving up an hour of leisure in order to work an additional hour. If an extra hour of leisure adds more to his total utility than $10 in income, he can increase his total utility by working one fewer hour in order to gain an hour of leisure.

At Clive's optimal labor supply choice, then, his marginal utility of one hour of leisure is equal to the marginal utility he gets from the goods that his hourly wage can purchase. This is very similar to the *optimal consumption rule* we encountered in Chapter 10, except that it is a rule about time rather than money.

Our next step is to ask how Clive's decision about time allocation is affected when his wage rate changes.

Wages and Labor Supply

Suppose that Clive's wage rate doubles, from $10 to $20 per hour. How will he change his time allocation?

You could argue that Clive will work longer hours, because his incentive to work has increased: by giving up an hour of leisure, he can now gain twice as much money as before. But you could equally well argue that he will work less, because he doesn't need to work as many hours to generate the income to pay for the goods he wants.

As these opposing arguments suggest, the quantity of labor Clive supplies can either rise or fall when his wage rate rises. To understand why, let's recall the distinction between *substitution effects* and *income effects* that we learned in Chapters 10 and 11. We saw there that a price change affects consumer choice in two ways: by changing the opportunity cost of a good in terms of other goods (the substitution effect) and by making the consumer richer or poorer (the income effect).

Now think about how a rise in Clive's wage rate affects his demand for leisure. On the one hand, the opportunity cost of leisure—the amount of money he gives up by taking an hour off instead of working—rises. That substitution effect gives him an incentive, other things equal, to consume less leisure and work longer hours. But on the other hand, a higher wage rate makes Clive richer—and this income effect leads him, other things equal, to want to consume *more* leisure and supply less labor, because leisure is a normal good.

So in the case of labor supply, the substitution effect and the income effect work in opposite directions. If the substitution effect is so powerful that it dominates the income effect, an increase in Clive's wage rate leads him to supply more hours of labor. If the income effect is so powerful that it dominates the substitution effect, an increase in the wage rate leads him to supply *fewer* hours of labor.

We see, then, that the **individual labor supply curve**—the relationship between the wage rate and the number of hours of labor supplied by an individual worker—is not necessarily upward sloping. If the income effect dominates, a higher wage rate will reduce the quantity of labor supplied.

Leisure is time available for purposes other than earning money to buy marketed goods.

The **individual labor supply curve** shows how the quantity of labor supplied by an individual depends on that individual's wage rate.

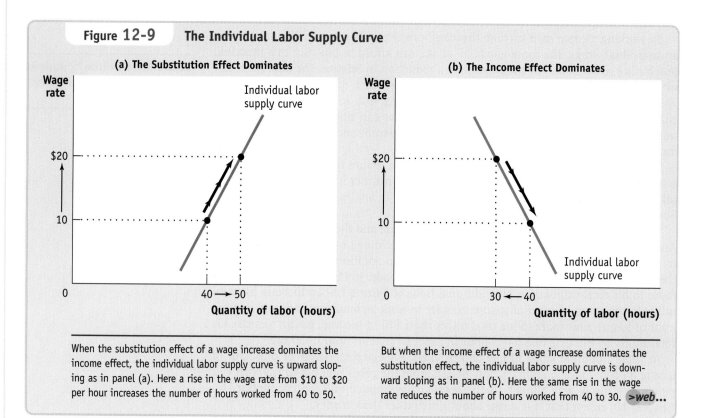

Figure 12-9 — The Individual Labor Supply Curve

(a) The Substitution Effect Dominates

Wage rate

Individual labor supply curve

$20

10

0 40 → 50

Quantity of labor (hours)

(b) The Income Effect Dominates

Wage rate

$20

10

Individual labor supply curve

0 30 ← 40

Quantity of labor (hours)

When the substitution effect of a wage increase dominates the income effect, the individual labor supply curve is upward sloping as in panel (a). Here a rise in the wage rate from $10 to $20 per hour increases the number of hours worked from 40 to 50.

But when the income effect of a wage increase dominates the substitution effect, the individual labor supply curve is downward sloping as in panel (b). Here the same rise in the wage rate reduces the number of hours worked from 40 to 30. **>web...**

Figure 12-9 illustrates the two possibilities for labor supply. If the substitution effect dominates the income effect, the individual labor supply curve slopes upward; panel (a) shows an increase in the wage rate from $10 to $20 per hour leading to a rise in the number of hours worked from 40 to 50. However, if the income effect dominates, the quantity of labor supplied goes down when the wage rate increases. Panel (b) shows the same rise in the wage rate leading to a *fall* in the number of hours worked from 40 to 30. (Economists refer to an individual labor supply curve that contains both upward-sloping and downward-sloping segments as a "backward-bending labor supply curve"— a concept that we analyze in detail in this chapter's appendix.)

Is a negative response of the quantity of labor supplied to the wage rate a real possibility? Yes: many labor economists believe that income effects on the supply of labor may be somewhat stronger than substitution effects. The most compelling piece of evidence for this belief comes from Americans' increasing consumption of leisure over the past century. At the end of the nineteenth century, wages adjusted for inflation

FOR INQUIRING MINDS

WHY YOU CAN'T FIND A CAB WHEN IT'S RAINING

Everyone says that you can't find a taxi in New York when you really need one—say, when it's raining. That could be because everyone else is trying to get a taxi at the same time. But according to a study published in the *Quarterly Journal of Economics*, it's more than that: cab drivers actually go home early when it's raining.

The reason is that the hourly wage rate of a taxi driver depends on the weather:

when it's raining, drivers get more fares and therefore earn more per hour. And it seems that the income effect of this higher wage rate outweighs the substitution effect.

This behavior leads the authors of the study to question drivers' rationality. They point out that if taxi drivers thought in terms of the long run, they would realize that rainy days and nice days tend to average out and that their high earnings on a

rainy day don't really affect their long-run income very much. Indeed, experienced drivers (who have probably figured this out) are less likely than inexperienced drivers to go home early on a rainy day. But leaving such issues to one side, the study does seem to show clear evidence of a labor supply curve that slopes downward instead of upward, thanks to income effects. (See source note on page xxii.)

were only about one-eighth what they are today; the typical work week was 70 hours, and very few workers retired at 65. Today the typical work week is less than 40 hours, and most people retire at 65 or earlier. So it seems that Americans have chosen to take advantage of higher wages in part by consuming more leisure.

Shifts of the Labor Supply Curve

Now that we have examined how income and substitution effects shape the individual labor supply curve, we can turn to the market labor supply curve. In any labor market, the market supply curve is the horizontal sum of the individual labor supply curves of all workers in that market. A change in any factor *other than the wage* that alters workers' willingness to supply labor causes a shift of the labor supply curve. A variety of factors can lead to such shifts, including changes in preferences and social norms, changes in population, changes in opportunities, and changes in wealth.

Changes in Preferences and Social Norms Changes in preferences and social norms can lead workers to increase or decrease their willingness to work at any given wage. A striking example of this phenomenon is the large increase in the number of employed women—particularly married employed women—that has occurred in the United States since the 1960s. Until that time, women who could afford to largely avoided working outside the home. Changes in preferences and norms in post–World War II America (helped along by the invention of labor-saving home appliances such as washing machines, increasing urbanization of the population, and higher female education levels) have induced large numbers of American women to join the workforce—a phenomenon often repeated in other countries that experience similar social and technological forces.

Changes in Population Changes in the population size generally lead to shifts of the labor supply curve. A larger population tends to shift the labor supply rightward as more workers are available at any given wage; a smaller population tends to shift the labor supply curve leftward. Currently the size of the U.S. labor force grows by approximately 1 percent per year, a result of immigration from other countries and, in comparison to other developed countries, a relatively high U.S. birth rate. As a result, many labor markets in the United States are experiencing rightward shifts of their labor supply curves.

Changes in Opportunities At one time, teaching was the only occupation considered suitable for well-educated women. However, as opportunities in other professions opened up to women starting in the 1960s, many women left teaching and potential female teachers chose other careers. This generated a leftward shift of the supply curve for teachers, reflecting a fall in the willingness to work at any given wage and forcing school districts to pay more to maintain an adequate teaching staff. These events illustrate a general result: when superior alternatives arise for workers in another labor market, the supply curve in the original labor market shifts leftward as workers move to the new opportunities. Similarly, when opportunities diminish in one labor market—say, layoffs in the manufacturing industry occur because of increased foreign competition—the supply in alternative labor markets increases as workers move to these other markets.

Changes in Wealth A person whose wealth increases will buy more normal goods, including leisure. So when a class of workers experiences a general rise in their wealth levels—say, due to a stock market boom—the income effect from the wealth increase will shift the labor supply curve associated with those workers leftward as workers consume more leisure and work less. Note that *the income effect caused by a change in wealth shifts the labor supply curve,* but *the income effect from a wage increase*—as we discussed in the case of the individual labor supply curve—*is a movement along the labor supply curve.* The following Economics in Action illustrates how such a change in the wealth levels of many families during the late 1990s led to a shift of the market labor supply curve associated with their employable children.

economics in action

The Decline of the Summer Job

In the summer of 2000, according to the *New York Times*, the New Jersey resort town of Ocean City found itself facing a serious shortage of lifeguards. Traditionally lifeguard positions, together with many other seasonal jobs, have been filled mainly by high school and college students. But in recent years a growing number of young Americans have chosen not to take summer jobs. In 1979, 71 percent of Americans between the ages of 16 and 19 were in the summer workforce. Twenty years later that number had fallen to 63 percent; and by 2003, it was 54 percent. Data show that it was young men in particular who became much less willing to take summer jobs during the 1990s.

One explanation for the decline in summer labor supply is that more students feel that they should devote their summers to additional study. But an important factor in the decline, according to the article, was that an economic and stock market boom in the late 1990s had made many more American families affluent—affluent enough that their children no longer felt pressure to make a financial contribution by working all summer.

In short, the income effect led to a reduced labor supply. ∎

< < < < < < < < < < < < < < < < < <

>> CHECK YOUR UNDERSTANDING 12-4

1. Formerly, Clive was free to work as many or as few hours per week as he wanted. But a new law limits the maximum number of hours he can work per week to 35. Explain under what circumstances, if at all, he is made:
   a. Worse off
   b. Equally as well off
   c. Better off

2. Explain in terms of the income and substitution effects how a fall in Clive's wage can induce him to work more hours than before.

Solutions appear at back of book.

• A LOOK AHEAD •

We have now put together all the pieces for understanding how a perfectly competitive market economy works. We've seen how supply and demand determine market prices, how profit maximization gives rise to the supply curve for each good, and how utility maximization gives rise to the demand curve. We've also just seen how factor markets determine the prices of factors of production and therefore the factor incomes of individuals.

But the ultimate purpose of an economy is to provide people with what they want. How well does a market economy do that job? In the next chapter we finally examine the *efficiency* of a market economy and the related but different question of *equity*.

SUMMARY

1. Just as there are markets for goods and services, there are markets for factors of production, including labor, land, and both **physical capital** and **human capital.** These markets determine the **factor distribution of income.**

2. Profit-maximizing price-taking producers will employ a factor up to the point at which its price is equal to its **value of the marginal product**—the marginal product of the factor multiplied by the price of the good. The **value of the marginal product curve** is therefore the individual price-taking producer's demand curve for a factor.

3. The market demand curve for labor is the sum of the individual demand curves of producers in that market. It shifts for three main reasons: changes in output price, changes in the supply of other factors, and technological changes.

4. When a competitive labor market is in equilibrium, the market wage is equal to the **equilibrium value of the marginal product** of labor, the additional value produced by the last worker hired in the labor market as a whole. The same principle applies to other factors of production: the **rental rate** of land or capital is equal to the equilibrium value of the marginal products. This insight leads to the **marginal productivity theory of income distribution,** according to which each factor is paid the value of the marginal product of the last unit of that factor employed in the factor market as a whole.

5. Large disparities in wages raise questions about the validity of the marginal productivity theory of income distribution. Many disparities can be explained by **compensating differentials** and by differences in talent, job experience, and human capital across workers. Market interference in the forms of **unions** and collective action by employers also creates wage disparities. The **efficiency-wage model,** which arises from a type of market failure, shows how wage disparities can arise from employers' attempts to increase worker performance. Free markets tend to diminish discrimination, but discrimination remains a real source of wage disparity. Discrimination is typically maintained either through problems in labor markets or (historically) through institutionalization in government policies.

6. Labor supply is the result of decisions about **time allocation,** where each worker faces a trade-off between **leisure** and work. An increase in the hourly wage rate tends to increase work hours by the substitution effect but to reduce work hours by the income effect. If the net result is that a worker increases the quantity of labor supplied in response to a higher wage, the **individual labor supply** curve slopes upward. If the net result is that a worker reduces their work hours, the individual labor supply curve—unlike supply curves for goods and services—slopes downward.

7. The market labor supply curve is the sum of the individual labor supply curves of all workers in that market. It shifts for four main reasons: changes in preferences and social norms, changes in population, changes in opportunities, and changes in wealth.

KEY TERMS

Physical capital, p. 282
Human capital, p. 282
Factor distribution of income, p. 282
Value of the marginal product, p. 286
Value of the marginal product curve, p. 286
Rental rate, p. 290

Equilibrium value of the marginal product, p. 291
Marginal productivity theory of income distribution, p. 291
Compensating differentials, p. 294
Unions, p. 295

Efficiency-wage model, p. 296
Time allocation, p. 298
Leisure, p. 299
Individual labor supply curve, p. 299

PROBLEMS

1. In 2001, national income in the United States was $8,122.0 billion. In the same year, 135 million workers were employed, at an average wage of $43,518 per worker per year.

   a. How much compensation of employees was paid in the United States in 2001?

   b. Analyze the factor distribution of income. What percentage of national income was received in terms of compensation of employees in 2001?

   c. Suppose that a huge wave of corporate downsizing leads many terminated employees to open their own businesses. What is the effect on the factor distribution of income?

   d. Suppose the supply of labor rises due to an increase in the retirement age. What happens to the percentage of national income received in terms of compensation of employees?

2. Marty's Frozen Yogurt has the production function per day shown in the accompanying table. The equilibrium wage rate for a worker is $80 per day. Each cup of frozen yogurt sells for $2.

Quantity of labor (workers)	Quantity of frozen yogurt (cups)
0	0
1	110
2	200
3	270
4	300
5	320
6	330

   a. Calculate the marginal product of labor for each worker and the value of the marginal product per worker.

   b. How many workers should Marty employ?

3. Patty's Pizza Parlor has the production function per hour shown in the accompanying table. The hourly wage rate for each worker is $10. Each pizza sells for $2.

Quantity of labor (workers)	Quantity of pizza
0	0
1	9
2	15
3	19
4	22
5	24

a. Calculate the marginal product of labor for each worker and the value of the marginal product per worker.

b. Draw the value of the marginal product curve. Use your diagram to determine how many workers Patty should employ.

c. Now the price of pizza increases to $4. Calculate the value of the marginal product per worker, and draw the new value of the marginal product curve into your diagram. Use your diagram to determine how many workers Patty should employ now.

4. The production function for Patty's Pizza Parlor is given in the table in Problem 3. The price of pizza is $2, but the hourly wage rate rises from $10 to $15. Use a diagram to determine how Patty's demand for workers responds as a result of this wage rate increase.

5. Patty's Pizza Parlor initially had the production function given in the table in Problem 3. A worker's hourly wage rate was $10, and pizza sold for $2. Now Patty buys a new high-tech pizza oven that allows her workers to become twice as productive as before. That is, the first worker now produces 18 pizzas per hour instead of 9, and so on.

a. Calculate the new marginal product of labor and the new value of the marginal product of labor.

b. Use a diagram to determine how Patty's hiring decision responds to this increase in the productivity of her workforce.

6. Jameel runs a driver education school. The more driving instructors he hires, the more driving lessons he can sell. But because he owns a limited number of training automobiles, each additional driving instructor adds less to Jameel's output of driving lessons. The accompanying table shows Jameel's production function per day. Each driving lesson can be sold at $35 per hour.

Quantity of labor (driving instructors)	Quantity of driving lessons (hours)
0	0
1	8
2	15
3	21
4	26
5	30
6	33

Determine Jameel's labor demand schedule (his demand schedule for driving instructors) for each of the following daily wage rates for driving instructors: $160, $180, $200, $220, $240, and $260.

7. Dale and Dana work at a self-service gas station and convenience store. Dale opens up everyday and Dana arrives later to help stock the store. They are both paid the current market wage of $9.50 per hour. But Dale feels he should be paid much more because the revenue generated from the gas pumps he turns on every morning is much higher than the revenue generated by the items that Dana stocks. Assess this argument.

8. In the Shire, farmers can rent land for $100 per acre per year. All the acres are identical. Merry Brandybuck rents 30 acres on which he grows carrots. Pippin Took rents 20 acres on which he grows corn. They sell their produce in a perfectly competitive market. Merry boasts that his value of the marginal product of land is twice as large as Pippin's. Pippin replies that, if this is true and if Merry wants to maximize his profit, Merry is renting too much land. Is Pippin right? Explain your answer.

9. For each of the following situations in which similar workers are paid different wages, give the most likely explanation for these wage differences.

a. Test pilots for new jet aircraft earn higher wages than airline pilots.

b. College graduates usually have higher earnings in their first year on the job than workers without college degrees have in their first year on the job.

c. Full professors command higher salaries than assistant professors for teaching the same class.

d. Unionized workers are generally better paid than non-unionized workers.

10. Research consistently finds that despite nondiscrimination policies, African-American workers on average receive lower wages than white workers do. What are the possible reasons for this? Are these reasons consistent with marginal productivity theory?

11. Greta is an enthusiastic amateur gardener and spends a lot of her free time working in her yard. She also has a demanding and well-paid job as a freelance advertising consultant. The advertising business is going through a difficult time and the hourly consulting fee Greta can charge falls. Greta decides to spend more time gardening and less time consulting. Explain her decision in terms of income and substitution effects.

12. Wendy works at a fast-food restaurant. When her wage rate was $5 per hour, she worked 30 hours per week. When her wage rate rose to $6 per hour, she decided to work 40 hours. But when her wage rate rose further to $7, she decided to work only 35 hours.

a. Draw Wendy's individual labor supply curve.

b. Is Wendy's behavior irrational, or can you find a rational explanation? Explain your answer.

13. You are the governor's economic policy adviser. The governor wants to put in place policies that encourage employed people to work more hours at their jobs and that encourage unemployed people to find and take jobs. Assess each of the following policies in terms of reaching that goal. Explain your

reasoning in terms of income and substitution effects, and indicate when the impact of the policy may be ambiguous.

a. The state income tax rate is lowered, which has the effect of increasing workers' after-tax wage rate.

b. The state income tax rate is increased, which has the effect of decreasing workers' after-tax wage rate.

c. The state property tax rate is increased, which reduces workers' after-tax income.

>**web**... To continue your study and review of concepts in this chapter, please visit the Krugman/Wells website for quizzes, animated graph tutorials, web links to helpful resources, and more.

www.worthpublishers.com/krugmanwells

Chapter 12 Appendix: Indifference >>Curve Analysis of Labor Supply

In the body of this chapter, we explained why the labor supply curve can slope downward instead of upward: the substitution effect of a higher wage rate, which provides an incentive to work longer hours, can be outweighed by the income effect of a higher wage rate, which may lead individuals to consume more leisure. In this appendix we show how this analysis can be carried out using the *indifference curves* introduced in Chapter 11.

The Time Allocation Budget Line

Let's return to the example of Clive, who likes leisure but also likes having money to spend. We now assume that Clive has a total of 80 hours per week that he could spend either working or enjoying as leisure time. (The remaining hours in his week, we assume, are taken up with necessary activities, mainly sleeping). Let's also assume, initially, that his hourly wage rate is $10.

> A **time allocation budget line** shows an individual's trade-offs between consumption of leisure and the income that allows consumption of marketed goods.

His consumption possibilities are defined by the **time allocation budget line** in Figure 12A-1, a budget line that shows Clive's trade-offs between consumption of leisure and income. Hours of leisure per week are measured on the horizontal axis, and the money he earns from working is measured on the vertical axis.

The horizontal intercept, point *X*, is at 80 hours: if Clive didn't work at all, he would have 80 hours of leisure per week but would not earn any money. The vertical intercept, point *Y*, is at $800: if Clive worked all the time, he would earn $800 per week.

Why can we use a budget line to describe Clive's time allocation choice? The budget lines found in Chapters 10 and 11 represented the trade-offs facing consumers deciding how to allocate their income among different goods. Here, instead of asking how

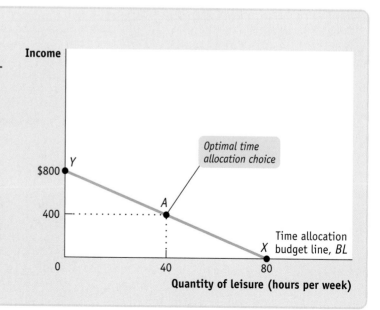

Figure 12A-1

The Time Allocation Budget Line

Clive's time allocation budget line shows his tradeoff between work, which pays a wage rate of $10 per hour, and leisure. At point *X* he allocates all his time, 80 hours, to leisure but has no income. At point *Y* he allocates all his time to work, earning $800, but consumes no leisure. His hourly wage rate of $10, the opportunity cost of an hour of leisure, is equal to minus the slope of the time allocation budget line. We have assumed that point *A*, at 40 hours of leisure and $400 in income, is Clive's optimal time allocation. It obeys the optimal time allocation rule: the additional utility Clive gets from one more hour of leisure must equal the additional utility he gets from the goods he can purchase with one hour's wages.

Clive allocates his income, we ask how he allocates his *time*. But the principles underlying the allocation of income and the allocation of time are the same: each involves allocating a fixed amount of a resource (80 hours of time in this case) with a constant trade-off (Clive must forgo $10 for each additional hour of leisure). So using a budget line is just as appropriate for time allocation as it is for income allocation.

As in the case of ordinary budget lines, opportunity cost plays a key role. The opportunity cost of an hour of leisure is what Clive must forgo by working one less hour—$10 in income. This opportunity cost is, of course, Clive's hourly wage rate and is equal to minus the slope of his time allocation budget line. You can verify this by noting that the slope is equal to minus the vertical intercept, point *Y*, divided by the horizontal intercept, point *X*—that is, −$800/(80 hours) = −$10 per hour.

To maximize his utility, Clive must choose the optimal point on the time allocation budget line in Figure 12A-1. In Chapter 10 we saw that a consumer who allocates spending to maximize utility finds the point on the budget line that satisfies the *optimal consumption rule:* the marginal utility per dollar spent on two goods must be equal. Although Clive's choice involves allocating time rather than money, the same principles apply.

Since Clive "spends" time rather than money, the counterpart of the optimal consumption rule is the **optimal time allocation rule:** the marginal utility Clive gets from the extra money earned from an additional hour spent working must equal the marginal utility of an additional hour of leisure.

> The **optimal time allocation rule** says that an individual should allocate time so that the marginal utility per hour spent working is equal to the marginal utility of an additional hour of leisure.

The Effect of a Higher Wage Rate

Depending on his tastes, Clive's utility-maximizing choice of hours of leisure and income could lie anywhere on the time allocation budget line in Figure 12A-1. Let's assume that his optimal choice is point *A*, at which he consumes 40 hours of leisure and earns $400. Now we are ready to link the analysis of time allocation to labor supply.

When Clive chooses a point like *A* on his time allocation budget line, he is also choosing the quantity of labor he supplies to the labor market. By choosing to consume 40 of his 80 available hours as leisure, he has also chosen to supply the other 40 hours as labor.

Now suppose that Clive's wage rate doubles, from $10 to $20 per hour. The effect of this increase in his wage rate is shown in Figure 12A-2 on page 308. His time allocation budget line rotates outward: the vertical intercept, which represents the amount he could earn if he devoted all 80 hours to work, shifts upward from point *Y* to point *Z*. As a result of the doubling of his wage, Clive would earn $1,600 instead of $800 if he devoted all 80 hours to working.

But how will Clive's time allocation actually change? As we saw in the chapter, this depends on the *income effect* and *substitution effect* that we learned about in Chapters 10 and 11.

The substitution effect of an increase in the wage rate works as follows. When the wage rate increases, the opportunity cost of an hour of leisure increases; this induces Clive to consume less leisure and work more hours—that is, to substitute hours of work for hours of leisure as the wage rate rises. If the substitution effect were the whole story, the individual labor supply curve would look like any ordinary supply curve and would always be upward sloping—a higher wage rate leads to greater labor supply.

What we learned in our analysis of demand was that for most consumer goods, the income effect isn't very important because most goods account for only a very small share of a consumer's spending. In addition, in the few cases of goods where the income effect is significant—for example, major purchases like housing—it usually reinforces the substitution effect: most goods are normal goods, so when a price increase makes a consumer poorer, he or she buys less of that good.

Figure 12A-2

An Increase in the Wage Rate

The two panels show Clive's initial optimal choice, point A, on BL_1 the time allocation budget line corresponding to a wage rate of $10. After his wage rate rises to $20, his budget line rotates out to the new budget line, BL_2: if he spends all his time working, the amount of money he earns rises from $800 to $1,600, reflected in the movement from Y to Z. This generates two opposing effects: the substitution effect pushes him to consume less leisure and to work more hours; the income effect pushes him to consume more leisure and to work fewer hours. Panel (a) shows the change in time allocation when the substitution effect is stronger: Clive's new optimal choice is point B, representing a decrease in hours of leisure to 30 hours and an increase in hours of labor to 50 hours. In this case the individual labor supply curve slopes upward. Panel (b) shows the change in time allocation when the income effect is stronger: point C is the new optimal choice, representing an increase in hours of leisure to 50 hours and a decrease in hours of labor to 30 hours. Now the individual labor supply curve slopes downward.

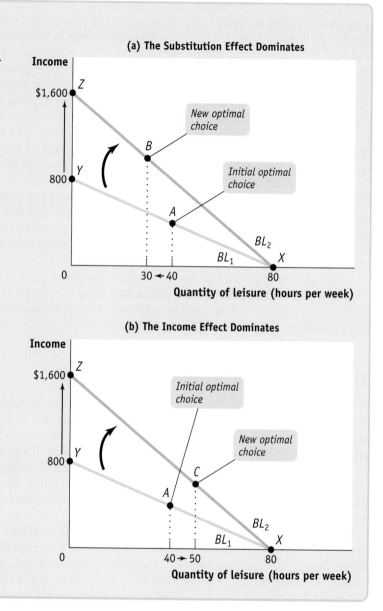

(a) The Substitution Effect Dominates

(b) The Income Effect Dominates

In the labor/leisure choice, however, the income effect takes on a new significance, for two reasons. First, most people get the great majority of their income from wages. This means that the income effect of a change in the wage rate is *not* small: an increase in the wage rate will generate a significant increase in income. Second, leisure is a normal good: when income rises, other things equal, people tend to consume more leisure and work fewer hours.

So the income effect of a higher wage rate tends to *reduce* the quantity of labor supplied, working in opposition to the substitution effect, which tends to *increase* the quantity of labor supplied. So the net effect of a higher wage rate on the quantity of labor Clive supplies could go either way—depending on his preferences, he might choose to supply more labor, or he might choose to supply less labor. The two panels of Figure 12-A2 illustrate these two outcomes. In each panel, point A represents Clive's initial consumption choice. Panel (a) shows the case in which Clive works more hours in response to a higher wage rate. An increase in the wage rate induces him to move from point A to point B, where he consumes less leisure than

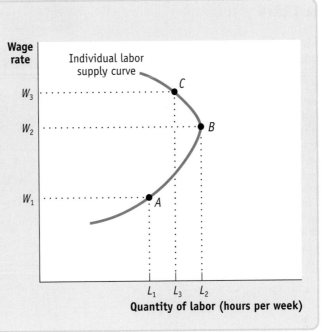

Figure 12A-3

A Backward-Bending Individual Labor Supply Curve

At lower wage rates, the substitution effect dominates the income effect for this individual. This is illustrated by the movement along the individual labor supply curve from point A to point B: a rise in the wage rate from W_1 to W_2 leads the quantity of labor supplied to increase from L_1 to L_2. But at higher wage rates, the income effect dominates the substitution effect, shown by the movement from point B to point C: here, a rise in the wage rate from W_2 to W_3 leads the quantity of labor supplied to decrease from L_2 to L_3.

at A and therefore works more hours. Here the substitution effect prevails over the income effect. Panel (b) shows the case in which Clive works fewer hours in response to a higher wage rate. Here, he moves from A to C, where he consumes more leisure and works *fewer* hours than at A. Here the income effect prevails over the substitution effect.

When the income effect of a higher wage rate is stronger than the substitution effect, the individual labor supply curve, which shows how much labor an individual will supply at any given wage rate, slopes the "wrong" way—downward: a higher wage rate leads to a smaller quantity of labor supplied.

Economists believe that the substitution effect usually dominates the income effect in the labor supply decision when an individual's wage rate is low. An individual labor supply curve is typically upward sloping for lower wage rates as people work more in response to rising wage rates. But they also believe that many individuals have stronger preferences for leisure and will choose to cut back the number of hours worked as their wage rate continues to rise. For these individuals, the income effect eventually dominates the substitution effect as the wage rate rises, leading their individual labor supply curves to change slope and to "bend backward" at high wage rates. An individual labor supply curve with this feature, called a **backward-bending individual labor supply curve,** is shown in Figure 12A-3. Although an *individual* labor supply curve may bend backward, *market* labor supply curves are almost always upward sloping over their entire range as higher wage rates draw more new workers into the labor market.

A **backward-bending individual labor supply curve** is an individual labor supply curve that is upward sloping at low to moderate wage rates and is downward sloping at higher wage rates.

Indifference Curve Analysis

In Chapter 11, we showed that consumer choice can be represented using the concept of *indifference curves,* which provide a "map" of consumer preferences. If you have covered Chapter 11, you may find it interesting to learn that indifference curves are also useful for addressing the issue of labor supply. In fact, this is one place where they are particularly helpful.

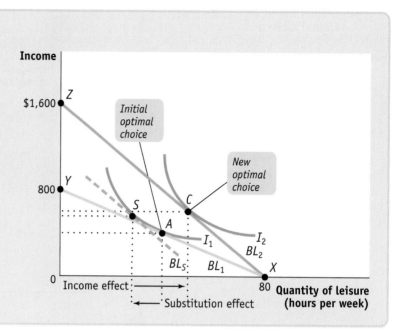

Figure 12A-4

Labor Supply Choice: The Indifference Curve Approach

Point A, on BL_1, is Clive's initial optimal choice. After a wage rate increase his income and utility level increase: his new time budget allocation line is BL_2 and his new optimal choice is point C. This change can be decomposed into the substitution effect—the fall in the hours of leisure from point A to point S, and the income effect—the increase in the number of hours of leisure from point S to point C. As shown here, the income effect dominates the substitution effect: the net result of an increase in the wage rate is an increase in the hours of leisure consumed and a decrease in the hours of labor supplied.

Using indifference curves, Figure 12A-4 shows how an increase in the wage rate can lead to a fall in the quantity of labor supplied. Point A is Clive's initial optimal choice, given an hourly wage rate of $10. It is the same as point A in Figure 12A-2; this time, however, we include an indifference curve to show that it is a point at which the budget line is tangent to the highest possible indifference curve.

Now consider the effect of a rise in the wage rate to $20. Imagine, for a moment, that at the same time Clive was offered a higher wage, he was told that he had to start repaying his student loan and that the good-news/bad-news combination left his utility unchanged. Then he would find himself at point S: on the same indifference curve as at A, but tangent to a steeper budget line, the dashed line BL_S in Figure 12A-4, which is parallel to BL_2. The move from A to S is the substitution effect of his wage increase: it leads him to consume less leisure and therefore supply more labor.

But now cancel the repayment on the student loan, and Clive is able to move to a higher indifference curve. His new optimum is at C, which corresponds to C in panel (b) of Figure 12A-2. The move from S to C is the income effect of his wage increase. And we see that this income effect can outweigh the substitution effect: at C he consumes more leisure, and therefore supplies less labor, than he did at A.

PROBLEMS

1. Leandro has 16 hours per day that he can allocate to work or leisure. His job pays a wage rate of $20. Leandro decides to consume 8 hours of leisure. His indifference curves have the usual shape: they are downward sloping, they do not cross, and they have the characteristic convex shape.

  a. Draw Leandro's time allocation budget line for a typical day. Then illustrate the indifference curve at his optimal choice.

  Now Leandro's wage rate falls to $10.

  b. Draw Leandro's new budget line.

  c. Suppose that Leandro now works only 4 hours as a result of his reduced wage rate. Illustrate the indifference curve at his new optimal choice.

  d. Leandro's decision to work less as the wage rate falls is the result of a substitution effect and an income effect. In your diagram, show the income effect and the substitution effect from this reduced wage rate. Which effect is stronger?

2. Florence is a highly paid fashion consultant who earns $100 per hour. She has 16 hours per day that she can allocate to work or leisure, and she decides to work for 12 hours.

a. Draw Florence's time allocation budget line for a typical day, and illustrate the indifference curve at her optimal choice.

One of Florence's clients is featured on the front page of *Vague*, an influential fashion magazine. As a result, Florence's consulting fee now rises to $500 per hour. Florence decides to work only 10 hours per day.

b. Draw Florence's new time allocation budget line, and illustrate the indifference curve at her optimal choice.

c. In your diagram, show the income effect and the substitution effect from this increase in the wage rate. Which effect is stronger?

3. Tamara has 80 hours per week that she can allocate to work or leisure. Her job pays a wage rate of $20 per hour, but Tamara is being taxed on her income in the following way. On the first $400 that Tamara makes, she pays no tax. That is, for the first 20 hours she works, her net wage—what she takes home after taxes—is $20 per hour. On all income above $400, Tamara pays a 75% tax. That is, for all hours above the first 20 hours, her net wage rate is only $5 per hour. Tamara

decides to work 30 hours. Her indifference curves have the usual shape.

a. Draw Tamara's time allocation budget line for a typical week. Also illustrate the indifference curve at her optimal choice.

The government changes the tax scheme. Now only the first $100 of income are tax-exempt. That is, for the first 5 hours she works, Tamara's net wage rate is $20 per hour. But the government reduces the tax rate on all other income to 50%. That is, for all hours above the first 5 hours, Tamara's net wage rate is now $10. After these changes, Tamara finds herself exactly equally as well off as before. That is, her new optimal choice is on the same indifference curve as her initial optimal choice.

b. Draw Tamara's new time allocation budget line on the same diagram. Also illustrate her optimal choice. Bear in mind that she is equally as well off (on the same indifference curve) as before the tax changes occurred.

c. Will Tamara work more or less than before the changes to the tax scheme? Why?

>> Efficiency and Equity

AFTER THE FALL

When the Berlin Wall came down in 1989, Western observers got their first good look at the centrally planned economy of East Germany. What they found was a stunningly inefficient system. Although investment had been lavished on politically favored industries such as energy production, producers of consumer goods and services were starved for capital. And the consumer goods that were produced were often not what consumers wanted to buy.

The revelation of East German inefficiency showed how badly such a planned economy worked compared with a market economy, like that of West Germany.

But even after the wall had come down, the government of the newly unified Federal Republic of Germany was not willing to let the free market run its course. Instead, both industry and individuals in East Germany received huge amounts of financial aid. The goal was to prevent the emergence of a politically unacceptable level of inequality between the former East Germans, many of whom lost their jobs in the aftermath of reunification, and West Germans.

Over time, many economists have come to believe that this aid actually delayed the reconstruction of the East German economy. They argue that the aid reduced incentives for workers to relocate to areas where more jobs were available or to learn new skills. But German officials insist that the price was well worth paying: sometimes a sense of fairness, they argue, is more important than efficiency.

Germany's experience reminds us that although we want our economy to be efficient, we also want it to be fair. In this chapter we will address both concerns. We begin by discussing the *efficiency* of a competitive market economy—the effectiveness of a competitive market economy at producing the goods and services that people want to consume. We then turn to the less well-defined

Goods produced in centrally planned economies (consider the East German–produced Trabant at left) are notorious for their poor quality compared to stylish, high-quality goods produced in market economies (consider the West German–produced Mercedes at right).

but equally important issue of *equity*—is the distribution of consumption among individuals "fair"? As we'll see, there is no generally accepted definition of *fairness*; nonetheless, societies often choose to sacrifice some efficiency in the pursuit of equity.

Supply, Demand, and the Virtues of the Market

Back in Chapter 6 we introduced the concepts of *consumer surplus* and *producer surplus*. Recall that consumer surplus is the difference between what buyers are willing to pay for a good and what they actually pay; it measures the gains to consumers from participating in the market. Similarly, producer surplus is the difference between the price that sellers of a good receive and their cost; it measures the gains to producers from participating in the market. The sum of consumer and producer surplus, *total surplus*, measures the gains from trade: the total benefits to buyers and sellers from participating in the market.

What we learned in that chapter was a remarkable fact: in equilibrium, a perfectly competitive market—a market in which both buyers and sellers are price-takers—is usually efficient. That is, in most cases such a market *maximizes total surplus*. Except in cases of market failure, there is no way to increase the gains from trade once a market has done its work.

But why is this true, and what are the conditions that make it possible?

To answer these questions, let's briefly look at this story again. It will set the stage for our discussion of efficiency in the economy as a whole.

Why a Market Maximizes Total Surplus

In Chapter 6 we showed that a market maximizes total surplus by considering the alternatives. That is, any attempt to rearrange consumption or production from the market equilibrium reduces total surplus.

How did we demonstrate this result? Figure 13-1 shows, once again, the example of a market in used textbooks. In this example the equilibrium is at *E*, where the price

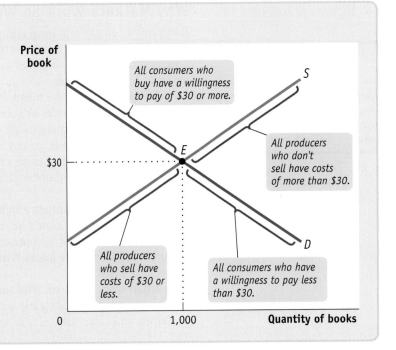

Figure 13-1

Why a Market Maximizes Total Surplus

How do we know that total surplus is maximized at the equilibrium price of $30 per book and the equilibrium quantity of 1,000? First, books go to the "right" consumers: every consumer who buys a book has a willingness to pay of $30 or more, and every potential consumer who does *not* buy a book has a willingness to pay less than $30. Second, books are supplied by the "right" producers: every seller who supplies a book has a cost of $30 or less, and every potential seller who does *not* supply a book has a cost of more than $30. Finally, the "right" quantity of 1,000 books are bought and sold: any additional books would cost more than $30 to produce but would be worth less than $30 to the consumers who receive them. If any fewer books were bought and sold, some consumers would be willing to pay more than it costs producers to supply these books.

All consumers who buy have a willingness to pay of $30 or more.

All producers who don't sell have costs of more than $30.

All producers who sell have costs of $30 or less.

All consumers who have a willingness to pay less than $30.

Price of book

$30

E

S

D

0   1,000   **Quantity of books**

is $30, and the quantity bought and sold is 1,000 books. We then laid out the three ways in which you might try to improve on this equilibrium and showed that none of them will succeed:

- *Reallocating consumption.* You might try to increase total surplus by giving books to different consumers. But in equilibrium every consumer who gets a book is to the left of *E* on the demand curve, and every consumer who does not get a book is to the right of *E*. That is, every consumer who gets a book has a higher willingness to pay than every consumer who does not get a book. So any reallocation of consumption away from the market equilibrium would reduce the total surplus.

- *Reallocating production.* You might try to increase total surplus by getting different people to sell books. (For simplicity, let's think of sellers as "producing" the books.) But every potential seller who sells a book is to the left of *E* on the supply curve, and every potential seller who does not sell a book is to the right of *E*. That is, every potential seller who sells a book has a lower cost than every potential seller who does not. So any reallocation of production away from the market equilibrium would reduce the total surplus.

- *Changing the level of production.* You might try to increase total surplus by either increasing or decreasing the number of books sold. But at point *E*, the willingness to pay of the last buyer is just equal to the cost of the last seller. So any change in production means either producing a book that is not worth as much to the buyer as it costs to provide or *not* producing a book that is worth more to a consumer than it costs.

So we saw in Chapter 6 that when an individual competetive market is in equilibrium, the consumers who are willing to pay the most for a good are the ones who get it; the producers with the lowest cost are the ones who produce it; and the quantity produced and consumed is right, in the sense that producing either more or less would reduce total surplus.

As we'll see in the next section, a similar case for efficiency applies to the economy as a whole. But before we lay out that case, let's look at the reasons why a market manages to get so much right.

Why Markets Work So Well: Property Rights

Economists can say and have said volumes about why markets are an effective way to organize an economy. But the effectiveness of markets comes down largely to the power of two features of a well-functioning market: *property rights* and the role of prices as *economic signals*.

By **property rights** we mean a system in which valuable items in the economy—whether they are resources or goods—have specific owners who can dispose of them as they choose. Property rights are what make the mutually beneficial transactions in the used-textbook market, or any market, possible.

To see why property rights are crucial, imagine that students do not have full property rights in their textbooks—that they are not allowed to resell books when the semester is over.

This restriction on property rights would prevent many mutually beneficial transactions. Some students would be stuck with textbooks they do not plan to reread and would be happier receiving some cash instead. Other students would be forced to pay full price for shiny new books when they would be happier getting slightly battered copies at a lower price.

In Chapter 20, we'll see that some of the major ways in which markets go wrong have to do with a lack of clearly defined property rights in valuable goods such as fish in the sea and clean air.

Property rights are the rights of owners of valuable items, whether resources or goods, to dispose of those items as they choose.

Why Markets Work So Well: Prices as Economic Signals

Because well-defined property rights give individuals the right to engage in mutually beneficial trades, the second necessary feature of well-functioning markets—economic signals—tell individuals *which* trades are mutually beneficial. An **economic signal** is any piece of information that helps people make better economic decisions. There are thousands of signals that businesses watch in the real world. For example, business forecasters say that sales of cardboard boxes are a good early indicator of changes in industrial production: if businesses are buying lots of cardboard boxes, you can be sure that they will soon increase their production.

An **economic signal** is any piece of information that helps people make better economic decisions.

But prices are far and away the most important signals in a market economy, because they convey essential information about other people's costs and their willingness to pay. If the equilibrium price of used books is $30, this in effect tells everyone both that there are consumers willing to pay $30 and up and that there are producers with a cost of $30 or less.

The signal given by the market price is what ensures that total surplus is maximized, by telling people whether to buy or sell books. If the price of a book is $30, any consumer who would not be willing to pay $30 knows that there are other consumers who are willing to pay more; any producer whose cost is more than $30 knows that there are other producers with lower costs. And consumers who *are* willing to pay $30 or more, like producers with costs of $30 or less, are in effect told that it is a good idea for them to consume and produce.

Why Markets Sometimes Don't Work Well: Market Failure

We'll want to keep these two crucial features of competitive markets—property rights and prices as economic signals—in mind in later chapters when we analyze in detail how markets sometimes fail. It's worth revisiting the caution found in Chapter 6 about cases of market failure—the situation in which a market fails to maximize total surplus. First, markets can fail when one party, in an attempt to capture more resources, prevents mutually beneficial trades from occurring. Second, markets can fail when actions have side effects on others that aren't properly taken into account by the market—side effects like pollution. Finally, markets can fail because some goods, by their very nature, are unsuited for efficient management by markets. We will see in the next section how all three of these cases can be interpreted as instances in which prices give incorrect signals—that is, they fail to help people make better economic decisions. And as we will discover shortly, the failure of a particular market in an economy has implications for how well the entire economy operates.

economics in action

Smoothing Out the Bumps

The area around the departure gate is crowded, so it's obvious the plane will be full. In fact, it turns out that it's more than full. The gate agent announces that the flight is overbooked and asks for volunteers to give up their seats in return for rebooking on a later flight plus additional incentives, such as $200 toward a future ticket. If not enough volunteers come forward immediately, the incentives are increased.

This scene is familiar to any frequent flier. But it didn't always work that way. In fact, it took a couple of economists to teach the airlines how to deal efficiently with overbooking.

On busy flights, airlines have always sold tickets for more seats than actually exist. There's a good reason for this: some people with reservations always fail to show up, and an empty seat is a seat wasted. But sometimes fewer people than expected are no-shows, and a flight ends up overbooked. What happens then?

Until 1978, airlines simply "bumped" some of their passengers—informed them that their reservations had been canceled. There were no uniform rules about who got bumped; some airlines, for example, bumped older passengers because they were less likely to complain. Needless to say, those who got bumped were not happy.

In 1968, however, the economist Julian Simon proposed a market approach, in which airlines would treat a flight reservation as if a seat were a property right given to the passenger, so that the airlines would have to buy that right back if the plane was overbooked. Airlines didn't think this idea was practical. But in 1978 another economist, Alfred Kahn, was appointed to head the Civil Aeronautics Board, which regulated airlines at that time. He required airlines to use an auction system to deal with overbooking, resulting in the familiar process of asking for volunteers.

What's the advantage of this voluntary, market solution? Under the old system, someone who urgently needed to get on the scheduled flight was as likely to get bumped as someone who could easily take a later connection. Since 1978, those who absolutely have to make the flight don't volunteer; those who aren't that anxious to board get something that's worth more to them. The airline pays a cost to get passengers to give up their reserved seats but more than makes up for it in higher overall customer satisfaction. In short, everyone gains. By using property rights to create a market, Simon and Kahn moved that piece of the economy toward efficiency. ∎

< < < < < < < < < < < < < < < < <

>>CHECK YOUR UNDERSTANDING 13-1

1. Imagine that eMarkets! is a company that implements a competitive market in MP3 players. Based on information it gathers, it tells producers what the equilibrium price will be so that they can decide how much to produce. And once production has occurred, it allocates output to consumers based on the price and their willingness to pay.
   a. What information would they need to know from consumers and producers in order to find the equilibrium price and quantity of MP3 players?
   b. Suppose that eMarkets! has determined that, once production occurs and trading happens, the equilibrium price will be $199 and the equilibrium quantity will be 10,000 units. But also suppose that due to a computer glitch, it informs some producers that the price will be $299, while it informs some producers that the price will be $99. How will producer surplus be affected? Can you determine the effect on the quantity produced—will it be equal to, less than, or more than the equilibrium quantity?
   c. Also suppose that due to the computer glitch, some consumers who have a willingness to pay less than $99 are allowed to purchase the good at their willingness to pay; some who have a willingness to pay of $199 are told that the price is $299. How will consumer surplus be affected?

Solutions appear at back of book.

Efficiency in the Economy as a Whole

We've seen how the equilibrium outcome of an individual competitive market usually maximizes the total surplus of participants in that market. Is there an equivalent result for the economy as a whole? That is, is there a corresponding concept of equilibrium for the whole economy? And if so, does this equilibrium outcome maximize the welfare of the economy's participants?

The economy as a whole consists not of one but of many, many markets, all interrelated in two ways:

- On the consumption side, the demand for each good is affected by the prices of other goods.
- On the production side, producers of different goods compete for the same factors of production.

To think about the economy as a whole, then, we have to think of many markets, for both goods and factors. A **competitive market economy** is an economy in which all of these markets are perfectly competitive, with equilibrium prices determined by

A **competitive market economy** is an economy in which all markets, for goods and for factors, are perfectly competitive.

supply and demand. In each market both the supply and demand curves are likely to be affected by events in other markets.

When all markets have reached equilibrium—when the quantity of each good and factor demanded is equal to the quantity of each good and factor supplied at the going market prices—we say that the economy is in **general equilibrium.** To put it another way, general equilibrium is the economy-wide counterpart of ordinary equilibrium in a single market.

Our next task is to show that, as with an individual competitive market in equilibrium, a competitive market economy in general equilibrium is usually *efficient*—that is, it is efficient except in certain well-defined cases. What do we mean by saying that the economy as a whole is efficient? Actually, we defined efficiency way back in Chapter 1. We will start by revisiting that definition to see why it is the right approach to analyzing the economy as a whole. Next, we will describe the three criteria that an economy as a whole must satisfy in order to be efficient. Finally, we will learn how failures of individual markets can lead to inefficiency in the economy as a whole—failures we can view as cases in which prices fail to perform as economic signals.

> An economy is in **general equilibrium** when the quantity supplied is equal to the quantity demanded in all markets.

Efficiency, Revisited

When economists discuss efficiency in an individual market, they usually use the concepts of consumer and producer surplus, which measure costs and benefits in monetary terms. This makes sense when you are talking about the market for just one good, because you can take the prices of other goods—and therefore the value of a dollar—as given. When we are analyzing the economy as a whole, however, measuring costs and benefits in dollar terms no longer makes sense, because all prices are "to be determined."

FOR INQUIRING MINDS
DEFINING ECONOMIC EFFICIENCY

The economist's definition of *efficiency*—that an economy is efficient if nobody can be made better off without making others worse off—may seem to be oddly indirect. Why can't we define efficiency in terms of a positive achievement rather than the absence of something?

Many other definitions of efficiency have been proposed, but none of them have survived careful scrutiny—all of them turn out either to be incomplete or to involve unacceptable implications. A good example is the fate of the principle known as utilitarianism, proposed by the nineteenth-century English philosopher Jeremy Bentham.

Bentham offered a simple principle: "the greatest good for the greatest number." In effect, he argued that society should try to maximize the total utility of its members. This sounded persuasive but eventually ran into two problems. First, how do we add up the utility of different people? We may loosely say that Ms. Martineau is happier than Mr. Ricardo, but is she twice as happy or three

Whose util counts more? Efficiency has been difficult to define because we can't compare utility across people.

times as happy? You may argue that it makes no sense even to ask that question—but in that case Bentham's principle becomes meaningless because we have no way to add up the total utility of all members of society.

Second, even if we imagine that it is somehow possible to add up the utility of different people, critics of Bentham point out that his doctrine has the disturbing

implication that we should cater to the tastes of "utility monsters"—people who derive especially high pleasure from excessive consumption. Bentham's criterion implies that if Martineau really likes owning luxury automobiles and going to fancy restaurants but Ricardo is a modest sort who can make do with a bicycle and macaroni-and-cheese dinners, we should take money from Ricardo and give it to Martineau—even if Ricardo is a hard worker and Martineau notably lazy. This doesn't seem right.

Because of these difficulties, Bentham's principle has pretty much vanished from economic thought. The same is true of other ideas, such as the Marxist slogan "from each according to his ability, to each according to his needs." The only definition of efficiency that has managed to survive practical and logical criticism is the negative one: an economy is inefficient if there is a way to make at least one person better off without making others worse off, and it is efficient if it is not inefficient.

Instead, economists focus on the basic definition of efficiency. Recall from Chapter 1: an economy is efficient if it does not pass up any opportunities to make some people better off without making other people worse off.

To achieve efficiency, an economy must meet three criteria, which closely parallel the three features ensuring that total surplus is maximized in an individual market. The economy must be *efficient in consumption, efficient in production,* and *efficient in output levels.* Let's look at these criteria and see how a competitive market economy satisfies them.

Efficiency in Consumption

An economy is **efficient in consumption** if there is no way to redistribute goods among consumers that makes some consumers better off without making others worse off.

To see what efficiency in consumption involves, it helps to imagine scenarios for inefficiency. Imagine, for example, an economy that produces both cornflakes and shredded wheat but that provides those who prefer shredded wheat with cornflakes, and vice versa. Then it would be possible to make at least one person better off without making anyone else worse off by redistributing the goods, giving people the breakfast cereal they prefer.

The first piece of good news is that as long as prices perform properly as economic signals, this kind of inefficiency won't occur in a competitive market economy. We've seen this already in the case of market equilibrium in one individual market: the consumers who actually receive a good at the market equilibrium are those with the greatest willingness to pay—thanks to the role prices play in helping people make the right economic decisions. Consumers who prefer an additional box of cornflakes will be willing to pay more for that box than consumers who would rather have an additional box of shredded wheat. So if the markets for cornflakes and shredded wheat are both in equilibrium, there won't be any way to make at least one consumer better off without making others worse off by redistributing the available quantities of breakfast cereals.

In other words, prices in goods markets ensure that you can't increase total surplus in a single market by taking a good away from one person and giving it to another. Similarly, prices also ensure that when all markets in an economy are in perfectly competitive general equilibrium, there is no way to redistribute goods that makes some consumers better off without making others worse off.

It's important, however, to realize the limitations of that statement: even though an economy is efficient, you can always make *some* consumers better off if you are willing to make others worse off. We'll come back to that point shortly.

Efficiency in Production

Economists say that an economy is **efficient in production** if it is not possible to produce more of some goods without producing less of others.

We can use the *production possibility frontier* model from Chapter 2 to understand this. This model uses a diagram like Figure 13-2 to illustrate the economy's trade-offs: the more wheat it produces, the less corn it can produce, and vice versa. If the economy produces the quantities at either point *A* or point *B* on the production possibility frontier, it is efficient in production: it is possible to produce more corn than the economy produces at *A*, but only by producing less wheat; it is possible to produce more wheat than the economy produces at *B*, but only by producing less corn. The economy is not efficient in production, however, if it produces at point *C:* it is possible to produce more wheat *and* more corn than the economy does at that point.

An economy will be efficient in production if it has an **efficient allocation of resources**—if there is no way to reallocate factors of production among producers to produce more of some goods without producing less of others. This is an important result: *An economy that is efficient in allocation of resources is efficient in production, and vice versa.*

Here is another way to think about Figure 13-2: at point *A* the economy can produce more corn only by taking resources away from wheat production. Similarly, at

---

An economy is **efficient in consumption** if there is no way to redistribute goods among consumers that makes some consumers better off without making others worse off.

An economy is **efficient in production** if there is no way to produce more of some goods without producing less of other goods.

An economy has an **efficient allocation of resources** if there is no way to reallocate factors of production among producers to produce more of some goods without producing less of others.

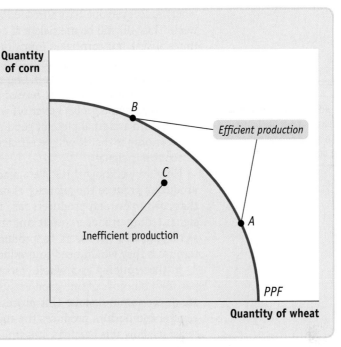

Figure 13-2

The Production Possibility Frontier and Efficiency in Production

An economy is efficient in production if it cannot produce more of one good without producing less of other goods. Equivalently, an economy is efficient in production if it is on its production possibility frontier. Here *A* and *B* are efficient production points—at each point the economy can produce more of one good only by producing less of the other. *C* is not an efficient production point because more corn *and* more wheat can be produced.

point *B* the economy can produce more wheat only by taking resources away from corn production.

Just as in the case of efficiency in consumption, it helps to imagine scenarios for inefficiency. In the United States, land in Iowa is ideally suited for growing corn, land in Minnesota is much better suited for growing wheat, and most land in Maine isn't suitable for growing either. It would clearly be inefficient if good land in the Midwest were left idle but farmers struggled with the stony soil of Maine; it would also be inefficient if Iowa farms grew wheat and Minnesota farms grew corn.

The second piece of good news is that, just as in the case of consumption, the role of prices as economic signals ensures that a competitive market economy in general equilibrium achieves efficiency in production. The logic is similar, but this time it applies to prices in factor markets rather than prices in goods markets. Corn farmers are willing to pay more for Iowa land than wheat farmers; wheat farmers are willing to pay more for Minnesota land than are corn farmers. And much of New England is no longer farmed but has returned to forest, because labor and capital can be more productively employed on richer lands elsewhere. In short, when factor markets are competitive, resources are allocated to the producers that can make the best use of them, and the economy is indeed efficient in production.

Notice, however, that this does not say *what* the economy produces. Both *A* and *B* in Figure 13-2 represent efficient production. We still need to ask whether the economy produces at the "right" place on the production possibility frontier—or, rather, *a* right place, because there may be many efficient outcomes. But let's hold off on that for a moment and finish our description of efficiency in the competitive market economy as a whole.

Efficiency in Output Levels

Suppose that a competitive market economy is efficient in production—it cannot produce more of some goods without producing less of others. Suppose also that it is efficient in consumption—there is no way to redistribute the goods produced that will make some consumers better off without making others worse off. There is still the question of whether the competitive market economy is producing the *right mix* of goods to start with. For example, suppose that point *A* in Figure 13-3 corresponds to producing enough wheat to let everyone have shredded wheat five times a week and cornflakes two times a week. This will still be inefficient if everyone prefers to have shredded wheat only three times a week but cornflakes four times a week—*and* if point *B* would allow them to do so. In that case, moving from *A* to *B*—that is, shifting resources into corn production—would make everyone better off. Our third criterion for efficiency, then, is that the economy be **efficient in output levels**: there must not be a different mix of output that would make some people better off without making others worse off.

An economy is **efficient in output levels** if there isn't a different mix of output that would make some people better off without making others worse off.

The third and final piece of good news about the equilibrium of a competitive market economy is that it will be efficient in output levels when prices perform properly as economic signals.

How do we know this? We already saw that in an individual competitive market producers produce the quantity of output that maximizes total surplus. The reason is that consumers and producers face the same price—the market price is an economic signal telling producers what one more unit of output is worth to consumers. This signal induces producers to produce that extra unit of output if the cost of the resources they would need to produce it is less than the market price.

In the economy as a whole, producers learn how much consumers are willing to pay for a bit more of one good versus a bit more of another when market prices operate as economic signals. This process ensures that a competitive market economy in general equilibrium produces the right mix of goods.

To see how this happens, imagine an economy in which the only resource that can be shifted between industries is labor, and all producers are hiring from the same labor market. (We'll also assume there are no complications like compensating differentials that make wages differ.) Imagine that right now consumers would prefer more corn and less wheat than the economy is currently producing. The economy can provide what consumers want by transferring labor from wheat production to corn production—by forgoing some wheat output in order to produce more corn. But will this adjustment take place?

Yes, it will, because consumers are willing to pay more for the additional corn that one more worker employed in corn production can produce than they are willing to pay for the wheat forgone by employing one fewer worker in wheat production. We can express this algebraically. The extra corn that a unit of labor can produce is MPL_{corn}, the marginal product of labor in corn. The wheat that unit of labor would have produced is MPL_{wheat}, the marginal product of labor in wheat. When we say that

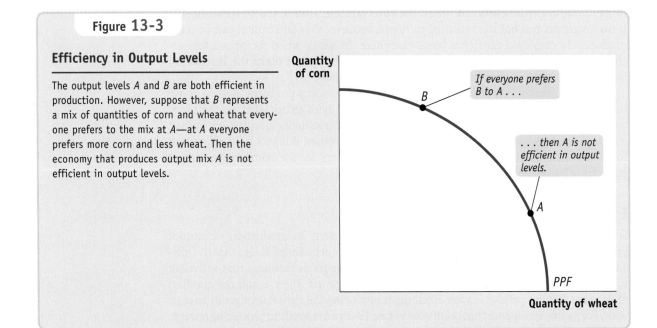

Figure 13-3

Efficiency in Output Levels

The output levels *A* and *B* are both efficient in production. However, suppose that *B* represents a mix of quantities of corn and wheat that everyone prefers to the mix at *A*—at *A* everyone prefers more corn and less wheat. Then the economy that produces output mix *A* is not efficient in output levels.

Quantity of corn

B

If everyone prefers *B* to *A* . . .

. . . then *A* is not efficient in output levels.

A

PPF

Quantity of wheat

consumers are willing to pay more for the extra corn than for the wheat, we are saying that at the current employment and output levels in the corn and wheat sectors

(13-1) $P_{corn} \times MPL_{corn} > P_{wheat} \times MPL_{wheat}$

where P_{corn} and P_{wheat} are the prices of corn and wheat respectively.

We've already seen the expressions in Equation 13-1 in Chapter 12. $P_{corn} \times MPL_{corn}$ is the *value of the marginal product* of labor in corn production, and $P_{wheat} \times MPL_{wheat}$ is the value of the marginal product of labor in wheat production. So we can restate Equation 13-1 as

(13-2) $VMPL_{corn} > VMPL_{wheat}$

This expression says that the value produced by an additional unit of labor employed in corn production is greater than that of an additional unit of labor employed in wheat production when consumers prefer more corn and less wheat than is being produced.

Can this be an equilibrium? No; we learned in Chapter 12 that producers maximize profits by hiring labor up until the point that $VMPL = W$, where W is the wage rate. That is, a producer hires labor until the value of the output produced by the last worker employed is equal to the current market wage rate. In this example, corn producers and wheat producers hire workers from the same labor market. So the direct implication of $VMPL_{corn} > VMPL_{wheat}$ is that, at current employment levels, corn producers are willing to pay a higher wage rate than wheat producers. Corn producers will hire workers away from wheat producers.

When will this process stop? When the wage rate that corn producers are willing to pay is equal to the wage rate that wheat producers are willing to pay; that is, when $VMPL_{corn} = VMPL_{wheat}$. The evolution of this process is illustrated in Figure 13-4.

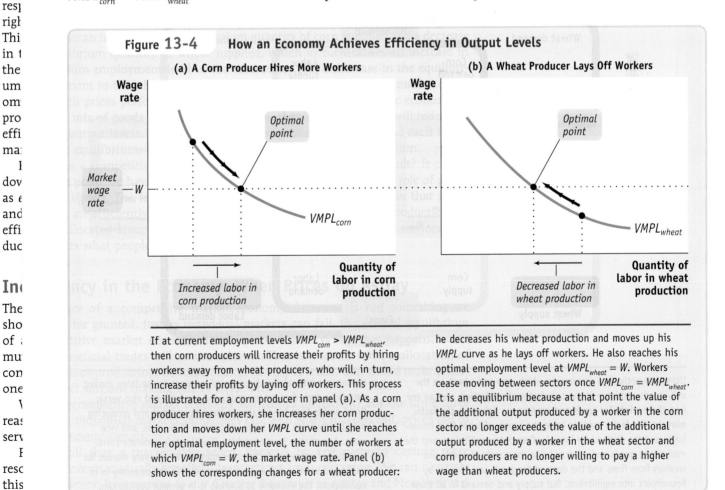

Figure 13-4   How an Economy Achieves Efficiency in Output Levels

(a) A Corn Producer Hires More Workers

(b) A Wheat Producer Lays Off Workers

If at current employment levels $VMPL_{corn} > VMPL_{wheat}$, then corn producers will increase their profits by hiring workers away from wheat producers, who will, in turn, increase their profits by laying off workers. This process is illustrated for a corn producer in panel (a). As a corn producer hires workers, she increases her corn production and moves down her $VMPL$ curve until she reaches her optimal employment level, the number of workers at which $VMPL_{corn} = W$, the market wage rate. Panel (b) shows the corresponding changes for a wheat producer: he decreases his wheat production and moves up his $VMPL$ curve as he lays off workers. He also reaches his optimal employment level at $VMPL_{wheat} = W$. Workers cease moving between sectors once $VMPL_{corn} = VMPL_{wheat}$. It is an equilibrium because at that point the value of the additional output produced by a worker in the corn sector no longer exceeds the value of the additional output produced by a worker in the wheat sector and corn producers are no longer willing to pay a higher wage than wheat producers.

Figure 14-5

A Monopolist's Demand, Total Revenue, and Marginal Revenue Curves

Panel (a) shows the monopolist's demand and marginal revenue curves for diamonds from Table 14-1. The marginal revenue curve lies below the demand curve. To see why, consider point *A* on the demand curve, where 9 diamonds are sold at $550 each, generating total revenue of $4,950. To sell a 10th diamond, the price on all 10 diamonds must be cut to $500, as shown by point *B*. As a result, total revenue increases by the green area (the quantity effect: $500) but decreases by the orange area (the price effect: –$450). So the marginal revenue from the 10th diamond is $50 (the difference between the green and orange areas) which is much lower than its price, $500.

Panel (b) shows the monopolist's total revenue curve for diamonds. As output goes from 0 to 10 diamonds, total revenue increases. It reaches its maximum at 10 diamonds—the level at which marginal revenue is equal to 0—and declines thereafter. The quantity effect dominates the price effect when total revenue is rising; the price effect dominates the quantity effect when total revenue is falling. **>web...**

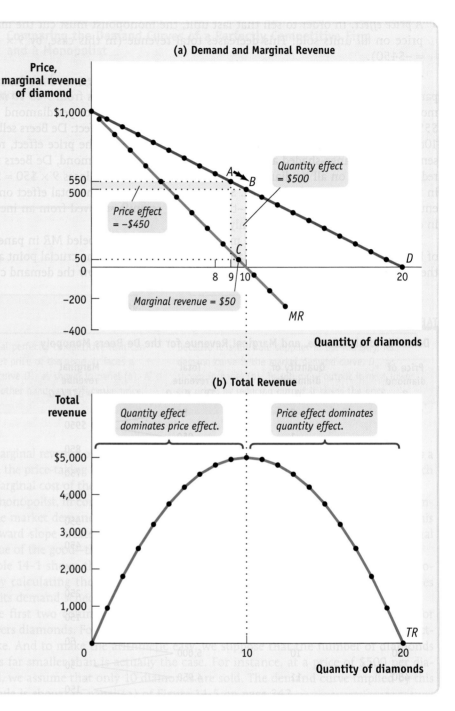

(a) Demand and Marginal Revenue

Price, marginal revenue of diamond

Quantity effect = $500

Price effect = –$450

Marginal revenue = $50

MR

Quantity of diamonds

(b) Total Revenue

Total revenue

Quantity effect dominates price effect.

Price effect dominates quantity effect.

TR

Quantity of diamonds

That's because of the price effect, which means that a monopolist's marginal revenue from selling an additional unit is always less than the price the monopolist receives for that unit. It is the price effect that creates the wedge between the monopolist's marginal revenue curve and the demand curve: in order to sell an additional diamond, De Beers must cut the market price on all units sold.

In fact, this wedge exists for any firm that possesses market power, such as oligopolists. Having market power means that the firm faces a downward-sloping demand curve. As a result, there will always be a price effect from an increase in its output. So for a firm with market power, the marginal revenue curve always lies below its demand curve.

Take a moment to compare the monopolist's marginal revenue curve with the marginal revenue curve for a perfectly competitive firm, one without market power. For such a firm there is no price effect from an increase in output: its marginal revenue curve is simply its horizontal demand curve. So for a perfectly competitive firm, market price and marginal revenue are always equal.

To emphasize how the quantity and price effects offset each other for a firm with market power, De Beers's total revenue curve is shown in panel (b) of Figure 14-5. Notice that it is hill-shaped: as output rises from 0 to 10 diamonds, total revenue increases. This reflects the fact that *at low levels of output, the quantity effect is stronger than the price effect:* as the monopolist sells more, it has to lower the price on only very few units, so the price effect is small. As output rises beyond 10 diamonds, total revenue actually falls. This reflects the fact that *at high levels of output, the price effect is stronger than the quantity effect:* as the monopolist sells more, it now has to lower the price on many units of output, making the price effect very large. Correspondingly, the marginal revenue curve lies below zero at output levels above 10 diamonds. For example, an increase in diamond production from 11 to 12 yields only $400 for the 12th diamond, simultaneously reducing the revenue from diamonds 1 through 11 by $550. As a result, the marginal revenue of the 12th diamond is −$150.

The Monopolist's Profit-Maximizing Output and Price

To complete the story of how a monopolist maximizes profit, we now bring in the monopolist's marginal cost. Let's assume that there is no fixed cost of production, and we'll also assume that the marginal cost of producing an additional diamond is constant at $200, no matter how many diamonds De Beers produces. Then marginal cost will always equal average total cost and the marginal cost curve (and the average total cost curve) is a horizontal line at $200, as shown in Figure 14-6.

Figure 14-6

The Monopolist's Profit-Maximizing Output and Price

This figure shows the demand, marginal revenue, and marginal cost curves. Marginal cost per diamond is $200, so the marginal cost curve is horizontal at $200. According to the optimal output rule, the profit-maximizing level of output for the monopolist is at $MR = MC$, shown by point A, where the marginal cost and marginal revenue curves cross at an output of 8 diamonds. The price De Beers can charge per diamond is found by going to the point on the demand curve directly above point A, which is point B here—a price of $600 per diamond. It makes a profit of $400 × 8 = $3,200. A perfectly competitive industry produces the output level at which $P = MC$, given by point C, where the demand curve and marginal cost curves cross. So a competitive industry produces 16 diamonds, sells at a price of $200, and makes zero profit.

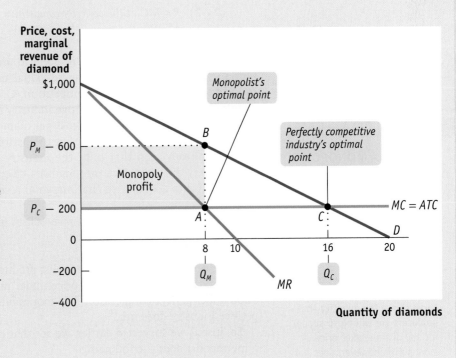

To maximize profit, the monopolist compares marginal cost with marginal revenue. If marginal revenue exceeds marginal cost, De Beers increases profit by producing more; if marginal revenue is less than marginal cost, De Beers increases profit by producing less. So the monopolist maximizes its profit by using the optimal output rule:

(14-1) *MR = MC at the monopolist's profit-maximizing quantity of output*

The monopolist's optimal point is shown in Figure 14-6. At *A*, the marginal cost curve, *MC*, crosses the marginal revenue curve, *MR*. The corresponding output level, 8 diamonds, is the monopolist's profit-maximizing quantity of output, Q_M. The price at which consumers demand 8 diamonds is $600, so the monopolist's price, P_M, is $600—corresponding to point *B*. The cost of producing each diamond is $200, so the monopolist earns a profit of $600 – $200 = $400 per diamond, and total profit is 8 × $400 = $3,200, as indicated by the shaded area.

Monopoly versus Perfect Competition

When Cecil Rhodes consolidated many independent diamond producers into De Beers, he converted a perfectly competitive industry into a monopoly. We can now use our analysis to see the effects of such a consolidation.

Let's look again at Figure 14-6 and ask how this same market would work if, instead of being a monopoly, the industry were perfectly competitive. We will continue to assume that there is no fixed cost, and that marginal cost is constant, so average total cost and marginal cost are equal.

If the diamond industry consists of many perfectly competitive firms, each of those producers takes the market price as given. That is, each producer acts as if its marginal revenue is equal to the market price. So each firm within the industry uses the price-taking firm's optimal output rule:

(14-2) *P = MC at the perfectly competitive firm's profit-maximizing quantity of output*

In Figure 14-6, this would correspond to producing at *C*, where the price per diamond, P_C, is $200, equal to the marginal cost of production. Profit-maximizing industry output under perfect competition, Q_C, is therefore 16 diamonds.

But does the perfectly competitive industry earn any profits at *C*? No: the price of $200 is equal to the production cost per diamond. So there are no economic profits for this industry when it produces at the perfectly competitive output level.

We've already seen that once the industry is consolidated into a monopoly, the result is very different. The monopolist's calculation of marginal revenue takes the price effect into account, so that marginal revenue is less than the price. That is,

(14-3) *P > MR = MC at the monopolist's profit-maximizing quantity of output*

As we've already seen, the monopolist produces less than the competitive industry—8 diamonds rather than 16. The price under monopoly is $600, compared with only $200 under perfect competition. The monopolist earns a positive profit, but the competitive industry does not.

So, just as we suggested earlier, we see that compared with a competitive industry, a monopolist does the following:

- Produces a smaller quantity: $Q_M < Q_C$
- Charges a higher price: $P_M > P_C$
- Earns a profit

FOR INQUIRING MINDS

MONOPOLY BEHAVIOR AND THE PRICE ELASTICITY OF DEMAND

A monopolist faces marginal revenue that is less than the market price. But how much lower? The answer depends on the *price elasticity of demand*.

Remember from Chapter 5 that the price elasticity of demand determines how *total revenue* from sales changes when the price falls. If the price elasticity is greater than 1, a fall in the price increases total revenue, because the rise in the quantity demanded outweighs the lower price of each unit sold. If the elasticity is less than 1, a lower price reduces total revenue.

When a monopolist increases output by one unit, it must reduce the market price in order to sell that unit. If the price elasticity of demand is less than 1, this will actually reduce revenue—that is, marginal revenue will be negative. The monopolist can only increase

revenue by producing more if the price elasticity of demand is greater than 1; the higher the elasticity, the closer the additional revenue is to the initial market price.

What this tells us is that the difference between monopoly behavior and perfect competition depends on the price elasticity of demand. A monopolist that faces highly elastic demand will behave almost like a firm in a perfectly competitive industry.

For example, Amtrak has a monopoly of intercity passenger service in the Northeast Corridor, but it has very little ability to raise prices: potential train travelers will switch to cars and planes. In contrast, a monopolist that faces less elastic demand—like most cable TV companies—will behave very differently from a perfect competitor: it will charge much higher prices and restrict output more.

Monopoly: The General Picture

Figure 14-6 involved specific numbers and assumed that the marginal cost curve was a horizontal line. Figure 14-7 shows a more general picture of monopoly in action: *D* is the market demand curve; *MR*, the marginal revenue curve; *MC*, the marginal cost curve; and *ATC*, the average total cost curve. Here we return to the usual assumption that the marginal cost curve is upward sloping and the average total cost curve is U-shaped.

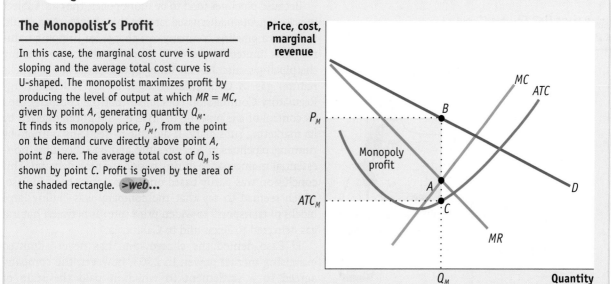

Figure 14-7

The Monopolist's Profit

In this case, the marginal cost curve is upward sloping and the average total cost curve is U-shaped. The monopolist maximizes profit by producing the level of output at which $MR = MC$, given by point A, generating quantity Q_M. It finds its monopoly price, P_M, from the point on the demand curve directly above point A, point B here. The average total cost of Q_M is shown by point C. Profit is given by the area of the shaded rectangle. **>web...**

Applying the optimal output rule, we see that the profit-maximizing level of output is the output at which marginal revenue equals marginal cost, indicated by point A. The profit-maximizing quantity of output is Q_M, and the price charged by the monopolist is P_M. At the profit-maximizing level of output, the monopolist's average total cost is ATC_M, shown by point C.

Recalling how we calculated profit in Equation 9-5 on page 215, profit is equal to the difference between total revenue and total cost. So we have

$$\textbf{(14-4)} \quad \text{Profit} = TR - TC$$
$$= (P_M \times Q_M) - (ATC_M \times Q_M)$$
$$= (P_M - ATC_M) \times Q_M$$

Profit is equal to the area of the shaded rectangle in Figure 14-7, with a height of $P_M - ATC_M$ and a width of Q_M.

In Chapter 9 we learned that a perfectly competitive industry can have profits *in the short run but not in the long run.* In the short run price can exceed average total cost, allowing a perfectly competitive firm to make a profit. But we also know that this cannot persist. In the long run, any profit in a perfectly competitive industry will be competed away as new firms enter the market. In contrast, a monopolist will make profits in both the short run and the long run.

economics in action

California Power Play?

The winter of 2000–2001 was a grim time for California, as power shortages gripped the state. One factor involved was the soaring price of natural gas, especially in the southern part of the state.

The strange thing was that natural gas prices in California were much higher than in Texas, the source of most of the state's natural gas. That is, the marginal cost of supplying natural gas to California—the cost of buying it in Texas, plus the small expense of shipping it across state lines—was much less than the price of California gas. So why wasn't more gas supplied?

The answer appears to have been that natural gas is transported via interstate pipelines and that the El Paso Corporation, which held a near-monopoly of pipelines supplying southern California, deliberately restricted the quantity of gas available in order to drive up market prices.

Because pipelines tend to be monopolies, they are subject to *price regulation,* discussed later in this chapter. As a result, the price a pipeline company can charge for shipping natural gas is limited. However, El Paso, in addition to running the pipelines, also has an unregulated subsidiary that sells natural gas in California. A judge at the Federal Energy Regulatory Commission concluded that the company used its control of the pipeline to drive up the prices received by its marketing subsidiary. It did this by reducing output—by running pipelines at low pressure and by scheduling nonessential maintenance during periods of peak demand. This conclusion was partly based on internal memos at El Paso, which seemed to say that the company was "idling large blocks of transport" to widen price spreads between natural gas delivered to Texas and to California.

El Paso denied the charges and has never admitted exercising market power. In 2003, however, the company agreed to a settlement in which it paid the state of

California $1.7 billion. Many analysts—including the staff at the Federal Energy Regulatory Commission—believe that El Paso's exercise of market power in the natural gas market was part of a broad pattern of market manipulation that played a key role in California's energy crisis during 2000–2001. ∎

> >

>>CHECK YOUR UNDERSTANDING 14-2

1. Use the accompanying total revenue schedule of Emerald, Inc., a monopoly producer of 10-carat emeralds, to calculate the answers to parts a–d. Then answer part e.
   a. The demand schedule
   b. The marginal revenue schedule
   c. The quantity effect component of marginal revenue per output level
   d. The price effect component of marginal revenue per output level
   e. What additional information is needed to determine Emerald, Inc.'s profit-maximizing output?

Quantity of emeralds demanded	Total revenue
1	$100
2	$186
3	$252
4	$280
5	$250

2. Use Figure 14-6 to show what happens to the following when the marginal cost of diamond production rises from $200 to $400.
   a. Marginal cost curve
   b. Profit-maximizing quantity
   c. Profit of the monopolist
   d. Perfectly competitive industry profits

Solutions appear at back of book.

>>QUICK REVIEW

➤ The crucial difference between a firm with market power, such as a monopolist, and a firm in a perfectly competitive industry is that perfectly competitive firms are price-takers that face horizontal demand curves, but a firm with market power faces a downward-sloping demand curve.

➤ Due to the price effect of an increase in output, the marginal revenue curve of a firm with market power always lies below its demand curve. So a profit-maximizing monopolist chooses the output level at which marginal cost is equal to marginal revenue—*not* to price.

➤ As a result, the monopolist produces less and sells its output at a higher price than a perfectly competitive industry would. It earns a profit in the short run and the long run.

Monopoly and Public Policy

It's good to be a monopolist, but it's not so good to be a monopolist's customer. A monopolist, by reducing output and raising prices, benefits at the expense of consumers. But buyers and sellers always have conflicting interests. Is the conflict of interest under monopoly any different than it is under perfect competition?

The answer is yes, because monopoly is a source of inefficiency: the losses to consumers from monopoly behavior are larger than the gains to the monopolist. Because monopoly leads to net losses for the economy, governments often try either to prevent the emergence of monopolies or to limit their effects. In this section we will see why monopoly leads to inefficiency and examine the policies governments adopt in an attempt to prevent this inefficiency.

Welfare Effects of Monopoly

By restricting output below the level at which marginal cost is equal to the market price, a monopolist increases its profit but hurts consumers. To assess whether this is a net benefit or loss to society, we must compare the monopolist's gain in profit to the consumer loss. And what we learn is that the consumer loss is larger than the monopolist's gain. Monopoly causes a net loss for the economy.

To see why, let's return to the case where the marginal cost curve is horizontal, as shown in the two panels of Figure 14-8 on page 348. Here the marginal cost curve is MC, the demand curve is D, and, in panel (b), the marginal revenue curve is MR.

Panel (a) shows what happens if this industry is perfectly competitive. Equilibrium output is Q_C; the price of the good, P_C, is equal to marginal cost, and marginal cost is also equal to average total cost because there is no fixed cost and marginal cost is constant. Each firm is earning exactly its cost per unit of output, so there is no producer surplus in this equilibrium. The consumer surplus generated by the market is equal to the area of the blue-shaded triangle CS_C shown in panel (a). Since there is no producer surplus when the industry is perfectly competitive, CS_C also represents the total surplus.

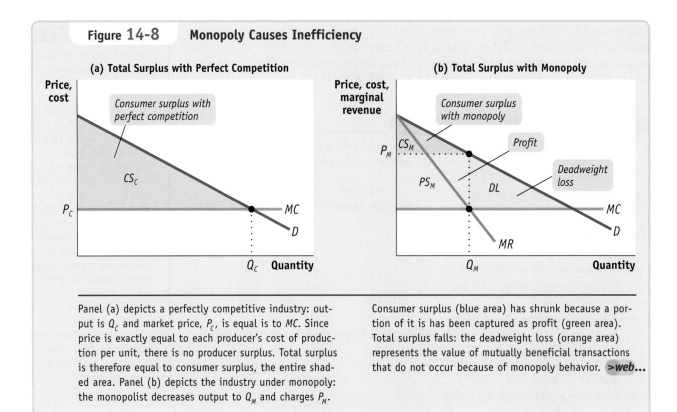

Figure 14-8   **Monopoly Causes Inefficiency**

(a) Total Surplus with Perfect Competition

(b) Total Surplus with Monopoly

Panel (a) depicts a perfectly competitive industry: output is Q_C and market price, P_C, is equal is to MC. Since price is exactly equal to each producer's cost of production per unit, there is no producer surplus. Total surplus is therefore equal to consumer surplus, the entire shaded area. Panel (b) depicts the industry under monopoly: the monopolist decreases output to Q_M and charges P_M.

Consumer surplus (blue area) has shrunk because a portion of it is has been captured as profit (green area). Total surplus falls: the deadweight loss (orange area) represents the value of mutually beneficial transactions that do not occur because of monopoly behavior. **>web...**

Panel (b) shows the results for the same market, but this time assuming that the industry is a monopoly. The monopolist produces the level of output, Q_M, at which marginal cost is equal to marginal revenue, and it charges the price P_M. The industry now earns profit—which is also the producer surplus—equal to the area of the green rectangle, PS_M. Note that this profit is surplus that has been captured from consumers as consumer surplus shrinks to the area of the blue triangle, CS_M.

By comparing panels (a) and (b), we see that in addition to the redistribution of surplus from consumers to the monopolist, another important change has occurred: the sum of profit and consumer surplus—total surplus—is *smaller* under monopoly than under perfect competition. That is, the sum of CS_M and PS_M is less than the area CS_C in panel (a). In Chapter 6, we analyzed the concept of *deadweight loss*, the net loss caused by government policies such as taxes. Here we show that monopoly creates a deadweight loss to society equal to the area of the orange triangle, DL. So monopoly produces a net loss for the economy.

This net loss exists because some mutually beneficial transactions do not occur. There are people for whom an additional unit of the good is worth more than the marginal cost of producing it, but who don't consume it because they are not willing to pay P_M.

Those who recall our discussion of the deadweight loss from taxes in Chapter 6 will notice that the deadweight loss from monopoly looks quite similar. Indeed, by driving a wedge between price and marginal cost, monopoly acts much like a tax on consumers and produces the same kind of inefficiency.

So monopoly hurts the welfare of society as a whole and is a source of market failure. Is there anything government policy can do about it?

Preventing Monopoly

Policy toward monopoly depends crucially on whether or not the industry in question is a natural monopoly, one in which economies of scale ensure that bigger producers have lower average total cost. If the industry is *not* a natural monopoly, the best policy is to prevent monopoly from arising or break it up if it already exists. Let's focus on that case first, then turn to the more difficult problem of dealing with natural monopoly.

The De Beers monopoly on diamonds didn't have to happen. Diamond production is not a natural monopoly: the industry's costs would be no higher if it consisted of a number of independent, competing producers (as is the case, for example, in gold production).

So if the South African government had been worried about how a monopoly would have affected consumers, it could have blocked Cecil Rhodes in his drive to dominate the industry or broken up his monopoly after the fact. Today, governments often try to prevent monopolies from forming and break up existing ones.

De Beers is a rather unique case: for complicated historical reasons, it was allowed to remain a monopoly. But over the last century, most similar monopolies have been broken up. The most celebrated example in the United States is Standard Oil, founded by John D. Rockefeller in 1870. By 1878 Standard Oil controlled almost all U.S. oil refining; but in 1911 a court order broke the company into a number of smaller units, including the companies that later became Exxon and Mobil (and more recently merged to become ExxonMobil).

The government policies used to prevent or eliminate monopolies are known as *antitrust policy*, which we will discuss in the next chapter.

Dealing with Natural Monopoly

Breaking up a monopoly that isn't natural is clearly a good idea: the gains to consumers outweigh the loss to the producer. But it's not so clear whether a natural monopoly, one in which large producers have lower average total costs than small producers, should be broken up, because this would raise average total cost. For example, a town government that tried to prevent a single company from dominating local gas supply—which, as we've discussed, is almost surely a natural monopoly—would raise the cost of providing gas to its residents.

Yet even in the case of a natural monopoly, a profit-maximizing monopolist acts in a way that causes inefficiency—it charges consumers a price that is higher than marginal cost, and therefore prevents some potentially beneficial transactions. Also, it can seem unfair that a firm that has managed to establish a monopoly position earns large profits at the expense of consumers.

What can public policy do about this? There are two common answers.

Public Ownership   In many countries, the preferred answer to the problem of natural monopoly has been **public ownership.** Instead of allowing a private monopolist to control an industry, the government establishes a public agency to provide the good and protect consumers' interests. For example, before 1984 in Britain, telephone service was provided by the state-owned British Telecom, and before 1987 airline travel was provided by the state-owned British Airways. (These companies still exist, but they have been privatized, competing with other firms in their respective industries.)

There are some examples of public ownership in the United States. Passenger rail service is provided by the public company Amtrak; regular mail delivery is provided by the U.S. Postal Service; some cities, including Los Angeles, have publicly owned electric power companies.

The advantage of public ownership, in principle, is that a publicly owned natural monopoly can set prices based on the criterion of efficiency rather than profit maximization. In a perfectly competitive industry, profit-maximizing behavior *is* efficient, because producers set prices equal to marginal cost; that is why there is no economic argument for public ownership of, say, wheat farms.

Experience suggests, however, that public ownership as a solution to the problem of natural monopoly often works badly in practice. One reason is that publicly owned firms are often less eager than private companies to keep costs down or offer high-quality products. Another is that publicly owned companies all too often end up serving political

In **public ownership** of a monopoly, the good supplied is by the government or by a firm owned by the government.

interests—providing contracts or jobs to people with the right connections. For example, Amtrak has notoriously provided train service at a loss to destinations that attract few passengers—but that are located in the districts of influential members of Congress.

Regulation In the United States, the more common answer has been to leave the industry in private hands but subject it to regulation. In particular, most local utilities like electricity, telephone service, natural gas, and so on are covered by **price regulation** that limits the prices they can charge.

We saw in Chapter 4 that imposing a *price ceiling* on a competitive industry is a recipe for shortages, black markets, and other nasty side effects. Doesn't imposing a limit on the price that, say, a local gas company can charge have the same effects?

Not necessarily: a price ceiling on a monopolist need not create a shortage—in the absence of a price ceiling, a monopolist would charge a price that is higher than its marginal cost of production. So even if forced to charge a lower price—as long as that price is above *MC* and the monolpolist at least breaks even on total output—the monopolist still has an incentive to produce the quantity demanded at that price.

Figure 14-9 shows an example of price regulation of a natural monopoly—a highly simplified version of a local gas company. The company faces a demand curve *D*, with an associated marginal revenue curve *MR*. For simplicity, we assume that the firm's total costs consist of two parts: a fixed cost and variable costs that are incurred at a constant proportion to output. So the marginal cost is constant in this case, and the marginal cost curve (which here is also the average variable cost curve) is a horizontal line at *MC*. The average total cost curve is the downward-sloping curve *ATC*; it is downward sloping because the higher the output, the lower the average fixed cost (the fixed cost per unit of output). Because average total cost is downward sloping over the range of output relevant for market demand, this is a natural monopoly.

> **Price regulation** limits the price that a monopolist is allowed to charge.

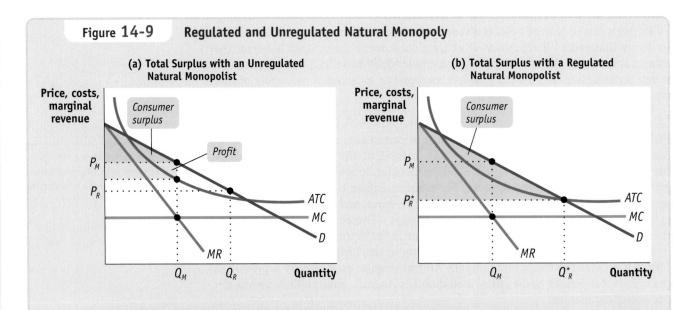

Figure 14-9   Regulated and Unregulated Natural Monopoly

(a) Total Surplus with an Unregulated Natural Monopolist

(b) Total Surplus with a Regulated Natural Monopolist

This figure shows the case of a natural monopolist. In panel (a), if the monopolist is allowed to charge P_M, it makes a profit, shown by the green area; consumer surplus is shown by the blue area. If it is regulated and must charge the lower price P_R, output increases from Q_M to Q_R, and consumer surplus increases.

Panel (b) shows what happens when the monopolist must charge a price equal to average total cost, the price P_R^*. Output expands to Q_R^*, and consumer surplus is now the entire blue area. The monopolist makes zero profit. This is the greatest consumer surplus possible when the monopolist is allowed to at least break even, making P_R^* the best regulated price.

Panel (a) illustrates a case of natural monopoly without regulation. The unregulated natural monopolist chooses the monopoly output Q_M and charges the price P_M. Since the monopolist receives a price greater than its average total cost, it earns a profit. This profit is exactly equal to the producer surplus in this market, represented by the green-shaded rectangle. Consumer surplus is given by the blue-shaded triangle.

Now suppose that regulators impose a price ceiling on local gas deliveries—one that falls below the monopoly price P_M but above ATC, say, at P_R in panel (a). At that price the quantity demanded is Q_R.

Does the company have an incentive to produce that quantity? Yes. If the price at which the monopolist can sell its product is fixed by regulators, the firm's output no longer affects the market price—so it ignores the MR curve and is willing to expand output to meet the quantity demanded as long as the price it receives for the next unit is greater than marginal cost and the monopolist at least breaks even on total output. So with price regulation, the monopolist produces more, at a lower price.

Of course, the monopolist will not be willing to produce at all if the imposed price means producing at a loss. That is, the price ceiling has to be set high enough to allow the firm to cover its average total cost. Panel (b) shows a situation in which regulators have pushed the price down as far as possible, at the level where the average total cost curve crosses the demand curve. At any lower price the firm loses money. The price here, P_R^*, is the best regulated price: the monopolist is just willing to operate and produces Q_R^*, the quantity demanded at that price. Consumers and society gain as a result.

The welfare effects of this regulation can be seen by comparing the shaded areas in the two panels of Figure 14-9. Consumer surplus is increased by the regulation, with the gains coming from two sources. First, profits are eliminated and added instead to consumer surplus. Second, the larger output and lower price leads to an overall welfare gain—an increase in total surplus.

This all looks terrific: consumers are better off, profits are eliminated, and overall welfare increases. Unfortunately, things are rarely that easy in practice. The main problem is that regulators don't have the information required to set the price exactly at the level at which the demand curve crosses the average total cost curve. Sometimes they set it too low, creating shortages; at other times they set it too high. Also, regulated monopolies, like publicly owned firms, tend to exaggerate their costs to regulators and to provide inferior quality to consumers.

Must Monopoly Be Controlled?   Sometimes the cure is worse than the disease. Some economists have argued that the best solution, even in the case of natural monopoly, may be to live with it. The case for doing nothing is that attempts to control monopoly will, one way or another, do more harm than good—for example, by the politicization of pricing, which leads to shortages or by the creation of opportunities for political corruption.

The following Economics in Action describes the case of cable television, a natural monopoly that has been alternately regulated and deregulated as politicians change their minds about the appropriate policy.

economics in action

Cable Dilemmas

Most price regulation in the United States goes back a long way: electricity, local phone service, water, and gas have been regulated in most places for generations. But cable television is a relatively new industry. Until the late 1970s only rural areas too remote to support local broadcast stations were served by cable. After 1972 new technology and looser rules made it profitable to offer cable service to major metropolitan areas; new networks like HBO and CNN emerged to take advantage of the possibilities.

But local cable TV is clearly a natural monopoly: there are large fixed costs to running cable through a town that don't depend on how many people actually subscribe, so that having more than one cable company would involve a lot of wasteful duplication. But if the local cable company is a monopoly, should its prices be regulated?

At first most local governments thought so, and cable TV was subject to price regulation. In 1984, however, Congress passed a law prohibiting most local governments from regulating cable prices. (The law was the result both of widespread skepticism about whether price regulation was actually a good idea and of intensive lobbying by the cable companies.)

After the law went into effect, however, cable television rates increased sharply. The resulting consumer backlash led to a new law, in 1992, which once again allowed local governments to set limits on cable prices.

Was the new regulation a success? As measured by the prices of "basic" cable service, it was: after rising rapidly during the period of deregulation, the cost of basic service leveled off.

However, price regulation in cable applies only to "basic" service. Cable operators can try to evade the restrictions by charging more for premium channels like HBO or by offering fewer channels in the "basic" package. So some skeptics have questioned whether the regulation has actually been effective.

The story of cable television shows that making policy for natural monopolies is harder than the simplified model suggests. It also shows that sometimes governments have a hard time making up their minds! ∎

— < < < < < < < < < < < < < < < < <

>> CHECK YOUR UNDERSTANDING 14-3

1. What policy should the government adopt in the following cases? Explain.
   a. Internet service in Anytown, OH, is provided by cable. Customers feel they are being overcharged, but the cable company claims it must charge prices that let it recover the costs of laying cable.
   b. The only two airlines that currently fly to Alaska need government approval to merge. Other airlines wish to fly to Alaska but need government-allocated landing slots to do so.

2. True or false? Explain your answer.
   a. Society's welfare is lower under monopoly because some consumer surplus is transformed into profit for the monopolist.
   b. A monopolist causes inefficiency because there are consumers who are willing to pay a price greater than or equal to marginal cost but less than the monopoly price.

3. Suppose a monopolist mistakenly believes that its marginal revenue is always equal to the market price. Assuming constant marginal cost and no fixed cost, draw a diagram comparing the level of profit, consumer surplus, total surplus, and deadweight loss for this misguided monopolist compared to a smart monopolist.

Solutions appear at back of book.

Price Discrimination

A **single-price monopolist** offers its product to all consumers at the same price.

Sellers engage in **price discrimination** when they charge different prices to different consumers for the same good.

Up to this point we have considered only the case of a **single-price monopolist**, one who charges all consumers the same price. As the term suggests, not all monopolists do this. In fact, many if not most monopolists find that they can increase their profits by charging different customers different prices for the same good: they engage in **price discrimination.**

The most striking example of price discrimination most of us encounter regularly involves airline tickets. Although there are several airlines, most routes in the United States are serviced by only one or two carriers, which, as a result, have market power and can set prices. So any regular airline passenger quickly becomes aware that the question "How much will it cost me to fly there?" rarely has a simple answer. If you are willing to buy a nonrefundable ticket a month in advance and stay over a Saturday night, the round trip may cost only $150—or less if you are a senior citizen or a student. But if you have to go on a business trip tomorrow, which happens to be Tuesday, and come back on Wednesday, the round trip might cost $550. Yet the business traveler and the visiting grandparent receive the same product—the same cramped seat, the same awful food.

You might object that airlines are not usually monopolists—that the airline industry is an oligopoly. In fact, price discrimination takes place under oligopoly and monopolistic competition as well as monopoly. But it doesn't happen under perfect competition. And once we've seen why monopolists sometimes price-discriminate, we'll be in a good position to understand why it happens in other cases, too.

The Logic of Price Discrimination

To get a preliminary view of why price discrimination might be more profitable than charging all consumers the same price, imagine that Air Sunshine offers the only nonstop flights between Bismarck, North Dakota, and Ft. Lauderdale, Florida. Assume that there are no capacity problems—the airline can fly as many planes as the number of passengers warrants. Also assume that there is no fixed cost. The marginal cost to the airline of providing a seat is $125, however many passengers it carries.

Further assume that the airline knows there are two kinds of potential passengers. First, there are business travelers, 2,000 of whom want to travel between the destinations each week. Second, there are students, 2,000 of whom also want to travel each week.

Will potential passengers take the flight? It depends on the price. The business travelers, it turns out, really want to fly; they will take the plane as long as the price is no more than $550. The students, however, have less money and more time; if the price goes above $150, they will take the bus.

So what should the airline do? If it has to charge everyone the same price, its options are limited. It could charge $550; that way it would get as much as possible out of the business travelers but lose the student market. Or it could charge only $150; that way it would get both types of travelers but would not make as much money on the business travelers as it might have.

We can quickly calculate the profits from each of these alternatives. If the airline charged $550, it would sell 2,000 tickets to the business travelers, getting total revenues of 550 × 2,000 = $1.1 million and incurring costs of 125 × 2,000 = $250,000; so its profit would be $850,000. If the airline charged only $150, it would sell 4,000 tickets, receiving revenue of 4,000 × 150 = $600,000 and incurring costs of 4,000 × 125 = $500,000; so its profit would be $100,000. If the airline must charge everyone the same price, charging the higher price is clearly more profitable.

What the airline would really like to do, however, is charge the business travelers the full $550 but offer $150 tickets to the students. That's a lot less than the price paid by business travelers, but it's still above marginal cost; so if the airline could sell those extra 2,000 tickets to students, it would make an additional $50,000 in profit.

In this example we assume that cutting the price below $550 will not lead to *any* additional business travel and that at a price above $150 *no* students will fly. The implied demand curve is shown in Figure 14-10 on page 354.

It would be more realistic to suppose that there is some "give" in the demand of each group. But this, it turns out, does not do away with the argument for price discrimination. The important point is that the two groups of consumers differ in their *sensitivity to price*—that a high price has a larger effect in discouraging purchases by students than by business travelers. As long as different groups of customers respond differently to the price, a monopolist will find that it can capture more consumer surplus and increase its profit by charging them different prices.

Figure 14-10

Two Types of Airline Customers

Air Sunshine has two types of customers, business travelers willing to pay $550 per ticket and students willing to pay $150 per ticket. There are 2,000 of each kind of customer. Air Sunshine has constant marginal cost of $125 per seat. If Air Sunshine could charge these two types of customers different prices, it would maximize its profit by charging business travelers $550 and students $150 per ticket. It would capture all of the consumer surplus as profit.

>web...

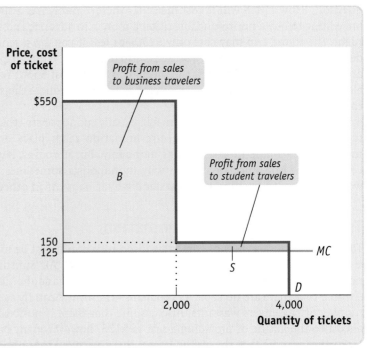

Price Discrimination and Elasticity

A more realistic description of the demand that airlines face would not specify particular prices at which different types of travelers would choose to fly. Instead, it would distinguish between the groups on the basis of their sensitivity to the price—their price elasticity of demand.

Suppose that a company sells its product to two easily identifiable groups of people—business travelers and students. It just so happens that business travelers are very insensitive to the price: there is a certain amount of the product they just have to have whatever the price, but they cannot be persuaded to buy much more than that no matter how cheap it is. Students, though, are more flexible: offer a good enough price and they will buy quite a lot, but raise the price too high and they will switch to something else. What should the company do?

The answer is the one already suggested by our simplified example: the company should charge business travelers, with their low price elasticity of demand, a higher price than it charges students, with their high price elasticity of demand.

The actual situation of the airlines is very much like this hypothetical example. Business travelers typically place a high priority on being at the right place at the right time and are not too sensitive to the price. But nonbusiness travelers faced with a high price might take the bus, drive to another airport to get a lower fare, or skip the trip altogether.

So why doesn't an airline simply announce different prices for business and nonbusiness customers? First, this would probably be illegal (U.S. law places severe limits on the ability of companies to practice open price discrimination). Second, even if it were legal, it would be a hard policy to enforce: business travelers might be willing to wear casual clothing and claim they were visiting family in Ft. Lauderdale in order to save $400.

So what the airlines do—quite successfully—is impose rules that indirectly have the effect of charging business and nonbusiness travelers different fares. Business travelers usually

On many airline routes, the fare you pay depends on the type of traveller you are.

travel during the week and want to be home on the weekend; so the round-trip fare is much higher if you don't stay over a Saturday night. The requirement of a weekend stay for a cheap ticket effectively separates business from nonbusiness travelers. Similarly, business travelers often visit several cities in succession rather than make a simple round trip; so round-trip fares are much lower than twice the one-way fare. Many business trips are scheduled on short notice; so fares are much lower if you book far in advance. Fares are also lower if you travel standby, taking your chances on whether you actually get a seat—business travelers have to make it to that meeting; people visiting their relatives don't. And by requiring customers to show their ID upon check-in, airlines make sure there are no resales of tickets between the two groups that would undermine their ability to price-discriminate—students can't buy cheap tickets and resell them to business travelers. Look at the rules that govern ticket-pricing, and you will see an ingenious implementation of profit-maximizing price discrimination.

Perfect Price Discrimination

Let's return to the example of business travelers and students traveling between Bismarck and Ft. Lauderdale, illustrated in Figure 14-10, and ask what would happen if the airline could distinguish between the two groups of customers in order to charge each a different price.

Clearly, then, the airline would charge each group its willingness to pay—that is, as we learned in Chapter 6, the maximum that each group is willing to pay. For business travelers, the willingness to pay is $550, and it is $150 for students. As we have assumed, the marginal cost is $125 and does not depend on output, so that the marginal cost curve is a horizontal line. We can easily read off the airline's profit: it is the sum of the areas of the rectangle B and the rectangle S.

In this case, the consumers do not get any consumer surplus! The entire surplus is captured by the monopolist in the form of profit. When a monopolist is able to capture the entire surplus in this way, we say that it achieves **perfect price discrimination.**

In general, the greater the number of different prices a monopolist is able to charge, the closer it can get to perfect price discrimination. Figure 14-11 on page 356 shows a monopolist facing a downward-sloping demand curve; we suppose that this monopolist is able to charge different prices to different groups of consumers, with the consumers who are willing to pay the most being charged the most. In panel (a) the monopolist charges two different prices; in panel (b) the monopolist charges three different prices. Two things are apparent:

- The greater the number of prices the monopolist charges, the lower the lowest price—that is, some consumers will pay prices that approach marginal cost.
- The greater the number of prices the monopolist charges, the more money it extracts from consumers.

With a very large number of different prices, the picture would look like panel (c), a case of perfect price discrimination. Here, consumers least willing to buy the good pay marginal cost, and the entire consumer surplus is extracted as profit.

Both our airline example and the example in Figure 14-11 can be used to make another point: a monopolist that can engage in perfect price discrimination doesn't cause any inefficiency! The reason is that the source of inefficiency is eliminated: there are no potential consumers who would be willing to purchase the good at a price equal to or above marginal cost but do not get the chance to do so. Instead, the monopolist manages to "scoop up" these consumers by offering them lower prices than it charges others.

Perfect price discrimination is probably never possible in practice. At a fundamental level, the inability to achieve perfect price discrimination is a problem of prices as economic signals, a phenomenon we noted in Chapter 13. When prices work as economic signals, they convey the information needed to ensure that all mutually beneficial transactions will indeed occur: the market price signals the seller's cost, and a

Perfect price discrimination takes place when a monopolist charges each consumer his or her willingness to pay—the maximum that consumer is willing to pay.

Figure 14-11   Price Discrimination

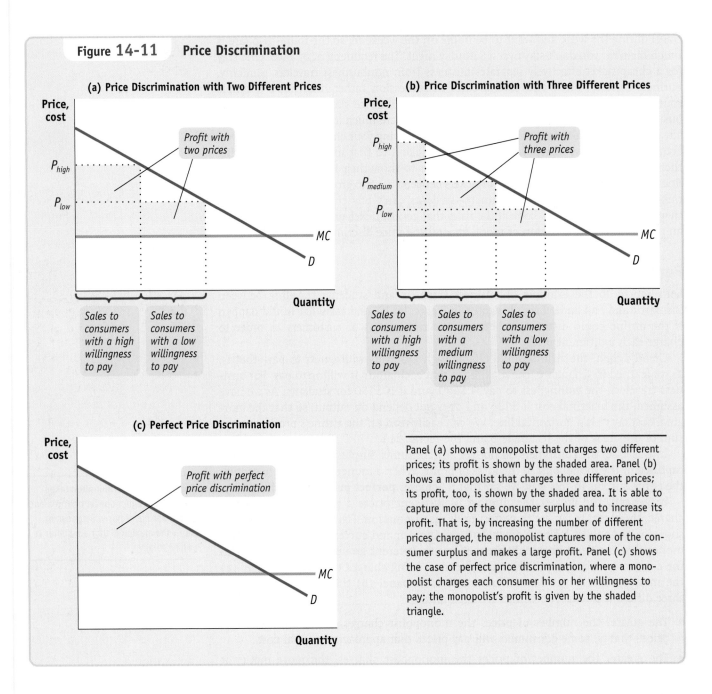

(a) Price Discrimination with Two Different Prices

Price, cost

P_{high}

P_{low}

Profit with two prices

MC

D

Quantity

Sales to consumers with a high willingness to pay

Sales to consumers with a low willingness to pay

(b) Price Discrimination with Three Different Prices

Price, cost

P_{high}

P_{medium}

P_{low}

Profit with three prices

MC

D

Quantity

Sales to consumers with a high willingness to pay

Sales to consumers with a medium willingness to pay

Sales to consumers with a low willingness to pay

(c) Perfect Price Discrimination

Price, cost

Profit with perfect price discrimination

MC

D

Quantity

Panel (a) shows a monopolist that charges two different prices; its profit is shown by the shaded area. Panel (b) shows a monopolist that charges three different prices; its profit, too, is shown by the shaded area. It is able to capture more of the consumer surplus and to increase its profit. That is, by increasing the number of different prices charged, the monopolist captures more of the consumer surplus and makes a large profit. Panel (c) shows the case of perfect price discrimination, where a monopolist charges each consumer his or her willingness to pay; the monopolist's profit is given by the shaded triangle.

consumer signals willingness to pay by purchasing the good whenever that willingness to pay is at least as high as the market price. The problem in reality, however, is that prices are often not perfect signals: a consumer's true willingness to pay can be disguised, as by a business traveler who claims to be a student when buying a ticket in order to obtain a lower fare. When such disguises work, a monopolist cannot achieve perfect price discrimination. However, monopolists do try to move in the direction of perfect price discrimination through a variety of pricing strategies. Common techniques for price discrimination include the following:

■ *Advance purchase restrictions.* Prices are lower for those who purchase well in advance (or in some cases for those who purchase at the last minute). This separates those who are likely to shop for better prices from those who won't.

■ *Volume discounts.* Often the price is lower if you buy a large quantity. For a consumer who plans to consume a lot of a good, the cost of the last unit—the marginal cost to the consumer—is considerably less than the average price. This separates those who plan to buy a lot and are therefore likely to be more sensitive to price from those who don't.

- *Two-part tariffs*. In a discount club like Sam's Club (which is not a monopolist but a monopolistic competitor), you pay an annual fee in addition to the cost of the items you purchase. So the cost of the first item you buy is in effect much higher than that of subsequent items, thereby making the two-part tariff behave like a volume discount.

Our discussion also helps explain why government policies on monopoly typically focus on preventing deadweight losses, not preventing price discrimination—unless it causes serious issues of equity. Compared to a single-price monopolist, price discrimination—even when it is not perfect—can increase the efficiency of the market. If sales to consumers formerly priced out of the market but now able to purchase the good at a lower price generate enough surplus to offset the loss in surplus to those now facing a higher price and no longer buying the good, then total surplus increases when price discrimination is introduced. An example of this might be a drug that is disproportionately prescribed to senior citizens, who are often on fixed incomes and so are very sensitive to price. A policy that allows a drug company to charge senior citizens a low price and everyone else a high price may indeed increase total surplus compared to a situation in which everyone is charged the same price. But price discrimination that creates serious concerns about equity is likely to be prohibited—for example, an ambulance service that charges patients based on the severity of their emergency.

economics in action

Sales, Factory Outlets, and Ghost Cities

Have you ever wondered why department stores occasionally hold sales, offering their merchandise for considerably less than the usual prices? Or why, driving along America's highways, you sometimes encounter clusters of "factory outlet" stores, often a couple of hours' drive from the nearest city? These familiar features of the economic landscape are actually rather peculiar if you think about them: why should sheets and towels be suddenly cheaper for a week each winter, or raincoats be offered for less in Freeport, Maine, than in Boston? In each case the answer is that the sellers—who are often oligopolists or monopolistic competitors—are engaged in a subtle form of price discrimination.

Why hold regular sales of sheets and towels? Stores are aware that some consumers buy these goods only when they discover that they need them; they are not likely to put a lot of effort into searching for the best price and so have a relatively low price elasticity of demand. So the store wants to charge high prices for customers who come in on an ordinary day. But shoppers who plan ahead, looking for the lowest price, will wait until there is a sale. So by scheduling such sales only now and then, the store is in effect able to discriminate between high-elasticity and low-elasticity customers.

An outlet store serves the same purpose: by offering merchandise for low prices, but only a considerable distance away from downtown, a seller is able to establish a separate market for those customers who are willing to make a significant effort to search out lower prices—and who therefore have a relatively high price elasticity of demand.

Finally, let's return to airline tickets to mention one of the truly odd features of their prices. Often a flight from one major destination to another—say, from Chicago to Los Angeles—is cheaper than a much shorter flight to a smaller city—say, from Chicago to Salt Lake City. Again, the reason is a difference in the price elasticity of demand: customers have a choice of many airlines between Chicago and Los Angeles, so the demand for any one flight is quite elastic; customers have very little choice in flights to a small city, so the demand is much less elastic.

But often there is a flight between two major destinations that makes a stop along the way—say, a flight from Chicago to Los Angeles with a stop in Salt Lake. In these cases, it is sometimes cheaper to fly to the more distant city than to the city that is a stop along the way. For example, it may be cheaper to purchase a ticket to Los Angeles and get off in Salt Lake City than to purchase a ticket to Salt Lake City! It sounds ridiculous but makes perfect sense given the logic of monopoly pricing.

So why don't passengers simply buy a ticket from Chicago to Los Angeles, but get off at Salt Lake? Well, some do—but the airlines, understandably, make it difficult for customers to find out about such "ghost cities." In addition, the airline will not allow you to check baggage only part of the way if you have a ticket for the final destination. (And airlines refuse to honor tickets for return flights when a passenger has not completed all the legs of the outbound flight.) All these restrictions are meant to enforce the separation of markets necessary to allow price discrimination. ∎

< < < < < < < < < < < < < < < < < <

>> CHECK YOUR UNDERSTANDING 14-4

1. True or false? Explain your answer.
   a. A single-price monopolist sells to some customers that a price-discriminating monopolist refuses to.
   b. A price-discriminating monopolist creates more inefficiency than a single-price monopolist because it captures more of the consumer surplus.
   c. Under price discrimination, a customer with highly elastic demand will pay a lower price than a customer with inelastic demand.

2. Which of the following are cases of price discrimination and which are not? In the cases of price discrimination, identify the consumers with high and those with low price elasticity of demand.
   a. Damaged merchandise is marked down.
   b. Restaurants have senior citizen discounts.
   c. Food manufacturers place discount coupons for their merchandise in newspapers.
   d. Airline tickets cost more during the summer peak flying season.

Solutions appear at back of book.

• A LOOK AHEAD •

We've now taken one large step away from the world of perfect competition. As we have seen, a monopolistic industry behaves quite differently from a perfectly competitive one.

But pure monopoly is actually quite rare in the modern economy. More typical are industries in which there is some competition, but not perfect competition—that is, where there is *imperfect competition*. In the next two chapters we examine two types of imperfect competition: oligopoly and monopolistic competition.

You might expect an oligopoly to act something like a cross between a monopoly and a perfectly competitive industry, but it turns out that oligopoly raises issues that arise neither in perfect competition nor in monopoly, issues of *strategic interaction* and *collusion* between firms. Likewise, monopolistic competition creates yet another set of issues, such as tastes, product differentiation, and advertising.

SUMMARY

1. There are four main types of market structure based on number of firms in the industry and product differentiation: perfect competition, monopoly, oligopoly, and monopolistic competition.

2. A **monopolist** is a producer who is the sole supplier of a good without close substitutes. An industry controlled by a monopolist is a **monopoly.**

3. The key difference between a monopoly and a perfectly competitive industry is that a perfectly competitive firm faces a horizontal demand curve but a monopolist faces a downward-sloping demand curve. This gives the monopolist **market power,** the ability to raise the market price by reducing output compared to a perfectly competitive industry.

4. To persist, a monopoly must be protected by a **barrier to entry.** This can take the form of control of natural resources or inputs, economies of scale that give rise to **natural monopoly,** technological advantage, or government rules that prevent entry by other firms.

5. The marginal revenue of a monopolist is composed of a quantity effect (the price received from the additional unit) and a price effect (the reduction in the price at which all units are sold). Because of the price effect, a monopolist's marginal revenue is always less than the market price, and the marginal revenue curve lies below the demand curve.

6. At the monopolist's profit-maximizing output level, marginal cost equals marginal revenue, which is less than market price. At the perfectly competitive firm's profit-maximizing output level, marginal cost equals the market price. So in comparison to perfectly competitive industries, monopolies produce less, charge higher prices, and earn higher profits in both the short run and the long run.

7. A monopoly creates deadweight losses by changing a price above marginal cost: the loss in consumer surplus exceeds the monopolist's profit. Thus monopolies are a source of market failure and should be prevented or broken up, except in the case of natural monopolies.

8. Natural monopolies can still cause deadweight losses. To limit these losses, governments sometimes impose **public ownership** and at other times impose **price regulation.** A price ceiling on a monopolist, as opposed to a perfectly competitive industry, need not cause shortages and can increase total surplus.

9. Not all monopolists are **single-price monopolists.** Monopolists, as well as oligopolists and monopolistic competitors, often engage in **price discrimination** to make higher profits, using various techniques to differentiate consumers based on their sensitivity to price and charging those with less elastic demand higher prices. A monopolist that achieves **perfect price discrimination** charges each consumer a price equal to his or her willingness to pay and captures the total surplus in the market. Although perfect price discrimination creates no inefficiency, it is practically impossible to implement.

KEY TERMS

Monopolist, p. 335
Monopoly, p. 335
Market power, p. 336
Barrier to entry, p. 337

Natural monopoly, p. 337
Public ownership, p. 349
Price regulation, p. 350
Single-price monopolist, p. 352

Price discrimination, p. 352
Perfect price discrimination, p. 355

PROBLEMS

1. Each of the following firms possesses market power. Explain its source.

   a. Merck, the producer of the patented cholesterol-lowering drug Zetia

   b. Verizon, a provider of local telephone service

   c. Chiquita, a supplier of bananas and owner of most banana plantations

2. Skyscraper City has a subway system, for which a one-way fare is $1.50. There is pressure on the mayor to reduce the fare by one-third, to $1.00. The mayor is dismayed, thinking that this will mean Skyscraper City is losing one-third of its revenue from sales of subway tickets. The mayor's economic adviser reminds her that she is focusing only on the price effect and ignoring the quantity effect. Explain why the mayor's estimate of a one-third loss of revenue is likely to be an overestimate. Illustrate with a diagram.

3. Consider an industry with the demand curve and marginal cost (MC) curve shown in the accompanying diagram. There is no fixed cost. If the industry is a single-price monopoly, the monopolist's marginal revenue curve would be MR. Answer the following questions by naming the appropriate points or areas.

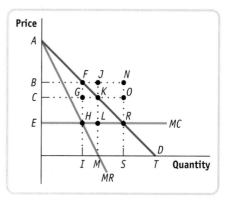

   a. If the industry is perfectly competitive, what will be the total quantity produced? At what price?

b. Which area reflects consumer surplus under perfect competition?

c. If the industry is a single-price monopoly, what quantity will the monopolist produce? Which price will it charge?

d. Which area reflects the single-price monopolist's profit?

e. Which area reflects consumer surplus under single-price monopoly?

f. Which area reflects the deadweight loss to society from single-price monopoly?

g. If the monopolist can price-discriminate perfectly, what quantity will the perfectly price-discriminating monopolist produce?

4. Bob, Bill, Ben, and Brad Baxter have just made a documentary movie about their basketball team. They are thinking about making the movie available for download on the Internet, and they can act as a single-price monopolist if they choose to. Each time the movie is downloaded, their Internet service provider charges them a fee of $4. The Baxter brothers are arguing about which price to charge customers per download. The accompanying table shows the demand schedule for their film.

Price of download	Quantity of downloads demanded
$10	0
8	1
6	3
4	6
2	10
0	15

a. Calculate the total revenue and the marginal revenue per download.

b. Bob is proud of the film and wants as many people as possible to download it. Which price would he choose? How many downloads would be sold?

c. Bill wants as much total revenue as possible. Which price would he choose? How many downloads would be sold?

d. Ben wants to maximize profit. Which price would he choose? How many downloads would be sold?

e. Brad wants to charge the efficient price. Which price would he choose? How many downloads would be sold?

5. Jimmy has a room that overlooks, from some distance, a major league baseball stadium. He decides to rent a telescope for $50.00 a week and charge his friends and classmates to use it to peep at the game for 30 seconds. He can act as a single-price monopolist for renting out "peeps." For each person who takes a 30-second peep, it costs Jimmy $0.20 to clean the eyepiece. The accompanying table shows the information Jimmy has gathered about the demand for the service.

Price of peep	Quantity of peeps demanded
$1.20	0
1.00	100
0.90	150
0.80	200
0.70	250
0.60	300
0.50	350
0.40	400
0.30	450
0.20	500
0.10	550

a. For each price in the table, calculate the total revenue from selling peeps and the marginal revenue per peep.

b. At what quantity will Jimmy's profit be maximized? What price will he charge? What will his total profit be?

c. Jimmy's landlady complains about all the visitors coming into the building and tells Jimmy to stop selling peeps. Jimmy discovers, however, that if he gives the landlady $0.20 for every peep he sells, she will stop complaining. What effect does the $0.20-per-peep bribe have on Jimmy's marginal cost per peep? What is the new profit-maximizing quantity of peeps? What effect does the $0.20-per-peep bribe have on Jimmy's total profit?

6. Suppose that De Beers is a single-price monopolist in the market for diamonds. De Beers has five potential customers: Raquel, Jackie, Joan, Mia, and Sophia. Each of these customers will buy at most one diamond—and only if the price is just equal to, or lower than, her willingness to pay. Raquel's willingness to pay is $400; Jackie's, $300; Joan's, $200; Mia's, $100; and Sophia's, $0. De Beers's marginal cost per diamond is $100. This leads to the demand schedule for diamonds shown in the accompanying table.

Price of diamond	Quantity of diamonds demanded
$500	0
400	1
300	2
200	3
100	4
0	5

a. Calculate De Beers's total revenue and its marginal revenue. From your calculation, draw the demand curve and the marginal revenue curve.

b. Explain why De Beers faces a downward-sloping demand curve.

c. Explain why the marginal revenue from an additional diamond sale is less than the price of the diamond.

d. Suppose De Beers currently charges $200 for its diamonds. If it lowered the price to $100, how large is the price effect? How large is the quantity effect?

e. Draw the marginal cost curve into your diagram and determine which quantity maximizes De Beers's profit and which price De Beers will charge.

7. Use the demand schedule for diamonds given in Problem 6. The marginal cost of producing diamonds is constant at $100.

a. If De Beers charges the monopoly price, how large is the individual consumer surplus that each buyer experiences? Calculate total consumer surplus by summing the individual consumer surpluses. How large is producer surplus?

Suppose that upstart Russian and Asian producers enter the market and the market becomes perfectly competitive.

b. What is the perfectly competitive price? What quantity will be sold in this perfectly competitive market?

c. At the competitive price and quantity, how large is the consumer surplus that each buyer experiences? How large is total consumer surplus? How large is producer surplus?

d. Compare your answer to part c to your answer to part a. How large is the deadweight loss associated with monopoly in this case?

8. Use the demand schedule for diamonds given in Problem 6. De Beers is a monopolist, but it can now price-discriminate perfectly among all five of its potential customers. De Beers's marginal cost is constant at $100.

a. If De Beers can price-discriminate perfectly, to which customers will it sell diamonds and at what prices?

b. How large is each individual consumer surplus? How large is total consumer surplus? Calculate producer surplus by summing the producer surplus generated by each sale.

9. Download Records decides to release an album by the group Mary and the Little Lamb. It produces the album with no fixed cost, but the total cost of downloading an album to a CD and paying Mary her royalty is $6 per album. Download Records can act as a single-price monopolist. Its marketing division finds that the demand schedule for the album is as shown in the accompanying table.

Price of album	Quantity of albums demanded
$22	0
20	1,000
18	2,000
16	3,000
14	4,000
12	5,000
10	6,000
8	7,000

a. Calculate the total revenue and the marginal revenue per album.

b. The marginal cost of producing each album is constant at $6. To maximize profit, what level of output should Download Records choose, and which price should it therefore charge?

c. Mary renegotiates her contract and now needs to be paid a royalty of $14 per album. So the marginal cost rises to be constant at $14. To maximize profit, what level of output should Download Records now choose, and which price should it charge for each album?

10. The accompanying diagram illustrates your local electricity company's natural monopoly. The diagram shows the demand curve for kilowatt-hours of electricity, the company's marginal revenue (*MR*) curve, the marginal cost (*MC*) curve, and its average total cost (*ATC*) curve. The government wants to regulate the monopolist by imposing a price ceiling.

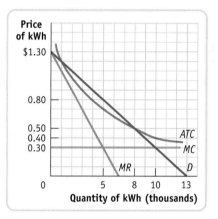

a. If the government does not regulate this monopolist, which price will it charge? Illustrate the inefficiency this creates by shading the deadweight loss from monopoly.

b. If the government imposes a price ceiling equal to the marginal cost, $0.30, will the monopolist make profits or lose money? Shade the area of profit (or losses) for the monopolist. If the government does impose this price ceiling, do you think the firm will continue to produce in the long run?

c. If the government imposes a price ceiling of $0.50, will the monopolist make a profit or lose money?

11. The movie theater in Collegetown serves two kinds of customers: students and professors. There are 900 students and 100 professors in Collegetown. Each student's willingness to pay for a movie ticket is $5. Each professor's willingness to pay for a movie ticket is $10. Each will buy at most one ticket. The movie theater's marginal cost per ticket is constant at $3, and there is no fixed cost.

a. Suppose the movie theater cannot price-discriminate and needs to charge both students and professors the same price per ticket. If the movie theater charges $5, who will buy tickets and what will the movie theater's profit be? How large is consumer surplus?

b. If the movie theater charges $10, who will buy movie tickets and what will the movie theater's profit be? How large is consumer surplus?

c. Now suppose that, if it chooses to, the movie theater can price-discriminate between students and professors by requiring students to show their student ID. If the movie theater charges students $5 and professors $10, how much profit will the movie theater make? How large is consumer surplus?

>web... To continue your study and review of concepts in this chapter, please visit the Krugman/Wells website for quizzes, animated graph tutorials, web links to helpful resources, and more.

www.worthpublishers.com/krugmanwells

>> Solutions to "Check Your Understanding" Questions

This section offers suggested answers to the "Check Your Understanding" questions found within chapters.

Chapter One

1-1

1. **a.** This illustrates the concept of opportunity cost. Given that a person can only eat so much, having an additional slice of chocolate cake requires that you forgo eating something else, such as a slice of the coconut cream pie.
   b. This illustrates the concept that resources are scarce. Even if there were more resources in the world, the total amount of those resources would be limited. As a result, scarcity would still arise. For there to be no scarcity, there would have to be unlimited amounts of everything (including unlimited time in a human life), which is clearly impossible.
   c. This illustrates the concept that people usually exploit opportunities to make themselves better off. Students will seek to make themselves better off by signing up for the tutorials of teaching assistants with good reputations and avoiding those teaching assistants with poor reputations.
   d. This illustrates the concept of marginal analysis. Your decision about allocating your time is a "how much" decision: how much time spent exercising versus how much time spent studying. You make your decision by comparing the benefit of an additional hour of exercising to its cost, the effect on your grades of one less hour spent studying.

2. **a.** Yes. The increased time, but not the total time, spent commuting is a cost you will incur if you accept the new job. That additional time spent commuting—or equivalently, the benefit you would get from spending that time doing something else—is an opportunity cost of the new job.
   b. Yes. One of the benefits of the new job is that you will be making $50,000. But if you take the new job, you will have to give up your current job; that is, you have to give up your current salary of $45,000. So $45,000 is one of the opportunity costs of taking the new job.
   c. No. A more spacious office is an additional benefit of your new job and does not involve forgoing something else. So, it is not an opportunity cost.

1-2

1. **a.** This illustrates the concept that markets usually lead to efficiency. Any seller who wants to sell a book for at least $X does indeed sell to someone who is willing to buy a book for $X. As a result, there is no way to change how used textbooks are distributed among buyers and sellers in a way that would make one person better off without making someone else worse off.
   b. This illustrates the concept that there are gains from trade. Students here trade tutoring services based on their different abilities in academic subjects.
   c. This illustrates the concept that when markets don't achieve efficiency, government intervention can improve society's welfare. In this case the market, left alone, will permit bars and nightclubs to impose costs on their neighbors in the form of loud music, costs that the bars and nightclubs have no incentive to take into account. This is an inefficient outcome because society as a whole can be made better off if bars and nightclubs are induced to reduce their noise.
   d. This illustrates the concept that resources should be used as efficiently as possible to achieve society's goals. By closing neighborhood clinics and shifting funds to the main hospital, better health care can be provided at a lower cost.
   e. This illustrates the concept that markets move toward equilibrium. Here, because books with the same amount of wear and tear sell for about the same price, no buyer or seller can be made better off by engaging in a different trade than he or she undertook. This means that the market for used textbooks has moved to an equilibrium.

2. **a.** This does not describe an equilibrium situation. Many students should want to change their behavior and switch to eating at the restaurants. Therefore, the situation described is not an equilibrium. An equilibrium will be established when students are equally as well off eating at the restaurants as eating at the dining hall—which would happen if, say, prices at the restaurants were higher than at the dining hall.
   b. This does describe an equilibrium situation. By changing your behavior and riding the bus, you would not be made better off. Therefore, you have no incentive to change your behavior.

Chapter Two

Check Your Understanding
2-1

1. **a.** False. An increase in the resources available to Tom for use in producing coconuts and fish changes his production possibility frontier by shifting it outward. This is because he can now produce more fish and coconuts than before. In the accompanying figure, the line labeled Tom's original *PPF* represents Tom's original production possibility frontier, and the line labeled Tom's new *PPF* represents the new production possibility frontier that results from an increase in resources.

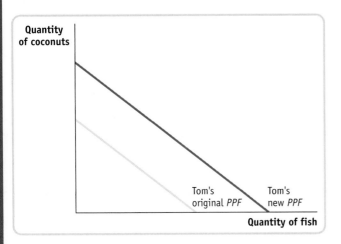

b. True. A technological change that allows Tom to catch more fish for any amount of coconuts gathered results in a change in his production possibility frontier. This is illustrated in the accompanying figure: the new production possibility frontier is represented by the line labeled Tom's new *PPF,* and the original production frontier is represented by the line labeled Tom's original *PPF.* Since the maximum amount of coconuts that Tom can gather is the same as before, the new production possibility frontier intersects the vertical axis at the same point as the old frontier. But since the maximum possible number of fish is now greater than before, the new frontier intersects the horizontal axis to the right of the old frontier.

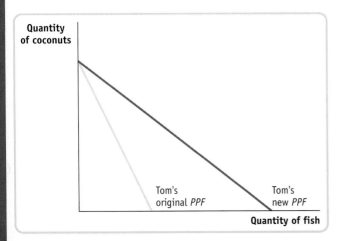

c. False. The production possibility frontier illustrates how much of one good an economy must give up to get more of another good only when resources are used efficiently. If an economy is producing inefficiently—that is, inside the frontier—then it does not have to give up a unit of one good in order to get another unit of the other good. Instead, by becoming more efficient, this economy can have more of both goods.

2. **a.** The United States has an absolute advantage in automobile production because it takes fewer Americans (6) to produce a car in one day than Italians (8). The United States also has an absolute advantage in washing machine production because it takes fewer Americans (2) to produce a washing machine in one day than Italians (3).

b. In Italy the opportunity cost of a washing machine in terms of an automobile is $3/8$: $3/8$ of a car can be produced with the same number of workers and in the same time it takes to produce 1 washing machine. In the United States the opportunity cost of a washing machine in terms of an automobile is $2/6 = 1/3$: $1/3$ of a car can be produced with the same number of workers and in the same time it takes to produce 1 washing machine. Since $1/3 < 3/8$, the United States has a comparative advantage in the production of washing machines: to produce a washing machine, only $1/3$ of a car must be given up in the United States but $3/8$ of a car must be given up in Italy. This means that Italy has a comparative advantage in automobiles. This can be checked as follows. The opportunity cost of an automobile in terms of a washing machine in Italy is $8/3$, equal to $2\frac{2}{3}$: $2\frac{2}{3}$ washing machines can be produced in the time it takes to produce 1 car in Italy. And the opportunity cost of an automobile in terms of a washing machine in the United States is $6/2$, equal to 3: 3 washing machines can be produced in the time it takes to produce 1 car in the United States.

c. The greatest gains are realized when each country specializes in producing the good for which it has a comparative advantage. Therefore the United States should specialize in washing machines and Italy should specialize in automobiles.

3. An increase in the amount of money spent by households results in an increase in the flow of goods to households. This, in turn, generates an increase in demand for factors of production by firms. Therefore there is an increase in the number of jobs in the economy.

Check Your Understanding
2-2

1. **a.** This is a normative statement because it stipulates what should be done. In addition, it may have no "right" answer. That is, should people be prevented from all dangerous personal behavior if they enjoy that behavior—like skydiving? Your answer may depend on your point of view.

b. This is a positive statement because it is a description of fact.

2. **a.** True. Economists often have different value judgments about the desirability of a particular social goal. But despite those differences in value judgments, they will tend to agree that society, once it has decided to pursue a given social goal, should adopt the most efficient policy to achieve that goal. Therefore economists are likely to agree on adopting policy choice B.

b. False. Disagreements between economists are more likely to arise because they base their conclusions on different models or because they have different value judgments about the desirability of the policy.

c. False. Deciding which goals a society should try to achieve is a matter of value judgments, not a question of economic analysis.

Chapter Three

Check Your Understanding
3-1

1. a. The quantity of umbrellas demanded is higher at any given price on a rainy day than on a dry day. This is a rightward *shift of* the demand curve, since at any given price the quantity demanded rises. This implies that any specific quantity can now be sold at a higher price. That price rise would be a *movement along* that new demand curve.

b. The quantity of weekend calls demanded rises in response to a price reduction. This is a *movement along* the demand curve for weekend calls.

c. The demand for roses increases the week of Valentine's Day. This is a rightward *shift of* the demand curve. Higher prices then imply a *movement along* that new demand curve.

d. The quantity of gasoline demanded falls in response to a rise in price. This is a *movement along* the demand curve.

Check Your Understanding
3-2

1. a. The quantity of houses supplied rises as a result of an increase in prices. This is a *movement along* the supply curve.

b. The quantity of strawberries supplied is higher at any given price. This is a rightward *shift of* the supply curve. Lower strawberry prices then lead to a *movement along* that new supply curve.

c. The quantity of labor supplied is lower at any given wage. This is a leftward *shift of* the supply curve compared to the supply curve during the school vacation. So, in order to attract workers, fast-food chains have to offer higher wages, a *movement along* that new supply curve.

d. The quantity of labor supplied rises in response to a rise in wages. This is a *movement along* the supply curve.

e. The quantity of berths supplied is higher at any given price. This is a rightward *shift of* the supply curve. A subsequent fall in price is a *movement along* that new supply curve.

Check Your Understanding
3-3

1. a. The supply curve shifts rightward. At the original equilibrium price of the year before, the quantity of grapes supplied exceeds the quantity demanded. This is a case of surplus. The price of grapes will fall.

b. The demand curve shifts leftward. At the original equilibrium price, the quantity of hotel rooms supplied exceeds the quantity demanded. This is a case of surplus. The rates for hotel rooms will fall.

c. The demand curve for secondhand snowblowers shifts rightward. At the original equilibrium price, the quantity of secondhand snowblowers demanded exceeds the quantity supplied. This is a case of shortage. The equilibrium price of secondhand snowblowers will rise.

Check Your Understanding
3-4

1. a. The market for large cars: This is a rightward shift in demand caused by a decrease in the price of a complement, gasoline. As a result of the shift, the equilibrium price of large cars will rise and the equilibrium quantity of large cars bought and sold will also rise.

b. The market for fresh paper made from recycled paper: this is a rightward shift in supply due to a technological innovation. As a result of this shift, the equilibrium price of fresh paper made from recycled paper will fall and the equilibrium quantity bought and sold will rise.

c. The market for movies at a local movie theatre: this is a leftward shift in demand caused by a fall in the price of a substitute, pay-per-view movies. As a result of this shift, the equilibrium price of movie tickets will fall and the equilibrium number of people who go to the movies will fall.

2. Upon the announcement of the new chip, the demand curve for computers using the earlier chip shifts leftward, as demand decreases, and the supply curve for these computers shifts rightward, as supply increases.

a. If demand decreases relatively more than supply increases, then the equilibrium quantity falls, as shown here:

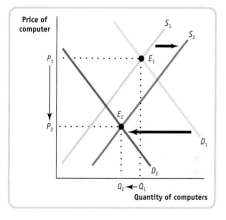

b. If supply increases relatively more than demand decreases, then the equilibrium quantity rises, as shown here:

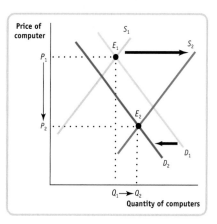

In both cases, the equilibrium price falls.

Chapter Four

Check Your Understanding
4-1

1. **a.** Fewer homeowners are willing to rent out their driveways because the price ceiling has caused a decrease in the payment they receive. This reflects the concept that the quantity supplied decreases as the price decreases. It is shown in the following diagram by the movement from point E to point A along the supply curve, a reduction in quantity of 400 parking spaces.

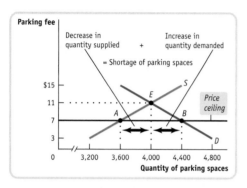

b. The quantity demanded increases by 400 spaces as the price decreases. At a lower price, more fans are willing to drive and rent a parking space. It is shown in the diagram by the movement from point E to point B along the demand curve.

c. Under a price ceiling, the quantity demanded exceeds the quantity supplied; as a result, shortages arise. In this case, there will be a shortage of 800 parking spaces. It is shown by the horizontal distance between points A and B.

d. Price ceilings result in wasted resources. The additional time fans spend to guarantee a parking space is wasted time.

e. Price ceilings lead to inefficient allocation of a good—here, the parking spaces—to consumers.

f. Price ceilings lead to black markets.

2. **a.** False. By lowering the price that producers receive, price ceilings lead to a decrease in the quantity supplied.

b. True. Price ceilings lead to a lower quantity supplied than in a free market. As a result, some people who would have been willing to pay the market price, and therefore would have gotten the good in a free market, are unable to obtain it when a price ceiling is imposed.

c. True. Those producers who still sell the product now receive less for it and are therefore worse off. Other producers will no longer find it worthwhile to sell the product at all and therefore will also be made worse off.

Check Your Understanding
4-2

1. **a.** Some gas station owners will benefit from getting a higher price. Point A indicates the sales (0.7 million gallons) made by these owners. But some will lose; there are those who made sales at the market price of $2 but do not make sales at the regulated price of $4. These missed sales are indicated on the graph by the fall in the quantity demanded along the demand curve, from point E to point A. Overall, the effect on station owners is ambiguous.

b. Those who buy gas at the higher price of $4 probably will receive better service; this is an example of *inefficiently high quality* caused by a price floor as gas station owners compete on quality rather than price. But opponents are correct to claim that consumers are generally worse off—those who buy at $4 would have been happy to buy at $2, and many who were willing to buy at a price between $2 and $4 are now unwilling to buy. This is indicated on the graph by the fall in the quantity demanded along the demand curve, from point E to point A.

c. Proponents are wrong because consumers and some gas station owners are hurt by the price floor, which creates "missed opportunities"—desirable transactions between consumers and station owners that never take place. Moreover, the inefficiency of wasted resources arises as consumers spend time and money driving to other states. The price floor tempts people to engage in black market activity. With the price floor of $4, only 0.7 million gallons are sold. But at prices between $2 and $4, there are drivers who cumulatively want to buy more than 0.7 million gallons and owners who are willing to sell to them, a situation likely to lead to illegal activity.

Check Your Understanding
4-3

1. **a.** The price of a ride is $7 since the quantity demanded at this price is 6 million: $7 is the *demand price* of 6 million rides. This is represented by point A in the following figure.

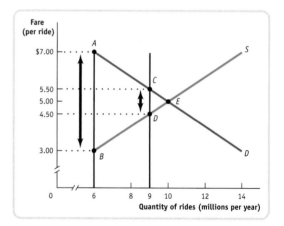

b. At 6 million rides, the supply price is $3, represented by point B in the figure. The wedge between the demand price of $7 and the supply price of $3 is the quota rent per ride, $4. This is represented in the figure above by the vertical distance between points A and B.

c. At 9 million rides, the demand price is $5.50, indicated by point C on the figure, and the supply price is $4.50, indicated by point D. The quota rent is the difference between the demand price and the supply price: $1.

2. The figure shows how a decrease in demand by 4 million rides, represented by a leftward shift of the demand curve from D_1 to D_2, eliminates the effect of a quota limit of 8 million rides. At point E_2, the new market equilibrium, the equilibrium quantity is equal to the quota limit; as a result, the quota has no effect on the market.

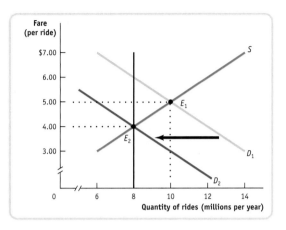

1. a. Under the quota, only 9 million pounds of butter are bought and sold. We can limit the amount of butter that dairies want to sell to 9 million pounds by setting the supply price to $0.90, as indicated by point D in the following figure, which is a replication of Figure 4-3. Similarly, we can limit the amount of butter consumers want to buy to 9 million pounds by setting the demand price to $1.20, as indicated by point C. The difference between these two prices, $0.30, is therefore equal to the tax that reduces sales to only 9 million pounds, indicated by the vertical distance between points C and D. Thus a tax of $0.30 per pound generates the same inefficiency as a quota of 9 million pounds.

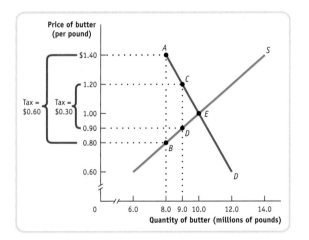

b. To answer this question, we must find a supply price and a demand price that generate the same quantity of butter but differ by $0.60. Examination of the supply and demand schedules shows that the supply price of $0.80 (indicated by point B) and the demand price of $1.40 (indicated by point A) satisfy these conditions: They give rise to the same quantity transacted, 8 million pounds, and they differ by $0.60. Therefore, a quota of 8 million pounds will generate the same level of inefficiency as a tax of $0.60. (Note that a supply price of $1.20 and a demand price of $0.60 also differ by $0.60 and give rise to the same quantity, 12 million pounds. Why is this choice not the right answer here? Because 12 million pounds is more than people want to buy in the free market, so it can't be a valid quota level.)

c. In part a, the unrestricted equilibrium price is $1 per pound. So consumers pay $0.20 ($1.20 − $1.00) of the $0.30 tax and producers pay $0.10 ($1.00 − $0.90).

Chapter Five

1. By the midpoint method, the percent change in the price of strawberries is

$$\frac{\$1.50 - \$1.00}{(\$1.50 + \$1.00)/2} \times 100 = \frac{\$0.50}{\$1.25} \times 100 = 40\%$$

Similarly, the percent change in the quantity of strawberries demanded is

$$\frac{200,000 - 100,000}{(100,000 + 200,000)/2} \times 100 = \frac{100,000}{150,000} \times 100 = 67\%$$

Therefore the price elasticity of demand using the midpoint method is $67\%/40\% = 1.7$.

2. By the midpoint method, the percent change in the quantity of movie tickets demanded in going from 4,000 tickets to 5,000 tickets is

$$\frac{5,000 - 4,000}{(4,000 + 5,000)/2} \times 100 = \frac{1,000}{4,500} \times 100 = 22\%$$

Since the price elasticity of demand is 1 at the current consumption level, it will take a 22% drop in the price of movie tickets to generate a 22% increase in quantity demanded.

3. Since price rises, we know that quantity demanded must fall. Given the current price of $0.50, a $0.05 increase in price represents a 10% change, using the method in Equation 5-2. This implies that

$$\frac{\% \text{ change in quantity demanded}}{10\%} = 1.2$$

so that the percent change in quantity demanded is 12%. A 12% decrease in quantity demanded represents $100,000 \times 0.12$, or 12,000 sandwiches.

Check Your Understanding Question 5-2

1. a. Elastic demand. Consumers are highly responsive to changes in price. For a rise in price, the sales effect (which tends to reduce total revenue) outweighs the price effect (which tends to increase total revenue). Overall, this leads to a fall in total revenue.

  b. Unit-elastic demand. Here the revenue lost to the fall in price is exactly equal to the revenue gained from higher sales. The sales effect exactly offsets the price effect.

  c. Inelastic demand. Consumers are relatively unresponsive to changes in price. For consumers to purchase a given percent increase in output, the price must fall by an even greater percent. The price effect of a fall in price (which tends to reduce total revenue) outweighs the sales effect (which tends to incease total revenue). As a result, total revenue decreases.

  d. Inelastic demand. Consumers are relatively unresponsive to price, so a given percent fall in output is accompanied by an even greater percent rise in price. The price effect of a rise in price (which tends to increase total revenue) outweighs the sales effect (which tends to reduce total revenue). As a result, total revenue increases.

2. a. Once bitten by a venomous snake, the victim's demand for an antidote is very likely to be perfectly inelastic because there is no substitute and it is necessary for survival. The demand curve will be vertical, at a quantity equal to the needed dose.

  b. Students' demand for green erasers is likely to be perfectly elastic because there are easily available substitutes: non-green erasers. The demand curve will be horizontal, at a price equal to the available price of nongreen erasers.

Check Your Understanding Question 5-3

1. By the midpoint method, the percent increase in Chelsea's income is

$$\frac{\$18{,}000 - \$12{,}000}{(\$12{,}000 + \$18{,}000)/2} \times 100 = \frac{\$6{,}000}{\$15{,}000} \times 100 = 40\%$$

Similarly, the percent increase in her consumption of CDs is

$$\frac{40 - 10}{(10 + 40)/2} \times 100 = \frac{30}{25} \times 100 = 120\%$$

Chelsea's income elasticity of demand for CDs is therefore 120%/40% = 3.

2. Sanjay's consumption of expensive restaurant meals will fall more than 10% because a given percent change in income (10% here) induces a larger percent change in consumption of an income-elastic good.

3. The cross-price elasticity of demand is 5%/20% = 0.25. Since the cross-price elasticity of demand is positive, the two goods are substitutes.

Check Your Understanding Question 5-4

1. By the midpoint method, the percent change in the number of hours of web-design services contracted is

$$\frac{500{,}000 - 300{,}000}{(300{,}000 + 500{,}000)/2} \times 100 = \frac{200{,}000}{400{,}000} \times 100 = 50\%$$

Similarly, the percent change in the price of web-design services is:

$$\frac{\$150 - \$100}{(\$100 + \$150)/2} \times 100 = \frac{\$50}{\$125} \times 100 = 40\%$$

The elasticity of supply is 50%/40% = 1.25; hence supply is elastic.

2. True. An increase in demand raises price. If the price elasticity of supply of milk is low, then relatively little additional supply will be forthcoming as the price rises. As a result, the price of milk will rise substantially to satisfy the increased demand for milk. If the price elasticity of supply is high, then a relatively large amount of additional supply will be produced as the price rises. As a result, the price of milk will rise only by a little to satisfy the higher demand for milk.

3. False. Long-run price elasticities of supply are generally larger than short-run elasticities of supply. This means that the short-run supply curves are generally steeper, not flatter, than the long-run supply curves.

4. True. When supply is perfectly elastic, the supply curve is a horizontal line at the supply price. A change in demand therefore has no effect on price; it affects only the quantity bought and sold.

Check Your Understanding Question 5-5

1. The fact that demand is very inelastic means that consumers will reduce their demand for textbooks very little in response to an increase in the price caused by the tax. The fact that supply is somewhat elastic means that suppliers will respond to the fall in the price received by reducing supply. As a result, the incidence of the tax will fall heavily on consumers of economics textbooks and very little on publishers as shown in the accompanying figure.

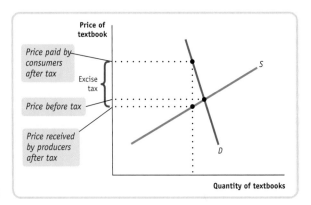

2. True. When a substitute is readily available, demand is elastic. This implies that producers cannot easily pass on the cost of the tax to consumers because consumers will respond to an increased price by switching to the substitute. Furthermore, when producers have difficulty adjusting the amount of the good produced, supply is inelastic. That is, producers cannot easily reduce output in response to a lower price net of the tax. So the tax burden will fall more heavily on producers than consumers.

3. The fact that supply is very inelastic means that producers will reduce their supply of bottled water very little in response to the fall in price received caused by the tax. Demand, on the other hand, will fall in response to an increase in price paid because demand is somewhat elastic. As a result, the incidence of the tax will fall heavily on producers of bottled spring water and very little on consumers as shown in the accompanying figure.

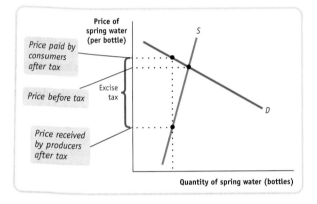

4. True. The lower the elasticity of supply, the more the burden of a tax will fall on producers rather than consumers, other things equal.

Chapter Six

1. A consumer buys each pepper if its price is less than (or just equal to) the consumer's willingness to pay for that pepper. The demand schedule is constructed by asking how many peppers will be demanded at any price. The accompanying table illustrates the demand schedule.

Price of pepper	Quantity of peppers demanded	Quantity of peppers demanded by Casey	Quantity of peppers demanded by Josie
$0.90	1	1	0
0.80	2	1	1
0.70	3	2	1
0.60	4	2	2
0.50	5	3	2
0.40	6	3	3
0.30	8	4	4
0.20	8	4	4
0.10	8	4	4
0.00	8	4	4

When the price is $0.40, Casey's consumer surplus from the first pepper is $0.50, from his second pepper $0.30, from his third pepper $0.10, and he does not buy any more peppers. Casey's individual consumer surplus is therefore $0.90. Josie's consumer surplus from her first pepper is $0.40, from her second pepper $0.20, from her third pepper $0.00 (she is just indifferent between buying it and not buying it, so let's assume she does buy it), and she does not buy any more peppers. Josie's individual consumer surplus is therefore $0.60. Total consumer surplus at a price of $0.40 is therefore $0.90 + $0.60 = $1.50.

1. A producer supplies each pepper if its price is greater than (or just equal to) the producer's cost of producing that pepper. The supply schedule is constructed by asking how many peppers will be supplied at any price. The accompanying table illustrates the supply schedule.

Price of pepper	Quantity of peppers demanded	Quantity of peppers supplied by Cara	Quantity of peppers supplied by Jamie
$0.90	8	4	4
0.80	7	4	3
0.70	7	4	3
0.60	6	4	2
0.50	5	3	2
0.40	4	3	1
0.30	3	2	1
0.20	2	2	0
0.10	2	2	0
0.00	0	0	0

When the price is $0.70, Cara's producer surplus from the first pepper is $0.60, from her second pepper $0.60, from her third pepper $0.30, from her fourth pepper $0.10, and she does not supply any more peppers. Cara's individual producer surplus is therefore $1.60. Jamie's producer surplus from his first pepper is $0.40, from his second pepper $0.20, from his third pepper $0.00 (he is just indifferent between supplying it and not supplying it, so let's assume he does supply it), and he does not supply any more peppers. Jamie's individual producer surplus therefore is $0.60. Total producer surplus at a price of $0.70 is therefore $1.60 + $0.60 = $2.20.

1. The quantity demanded equals the quantity supplied at a price of $0.50, the equilibrium price. At that price, a total quantity of five peppers will be bought and sold. Casey will buy three peppers and receive consumer surplus of $0.40 on his first, $0.20 on his second, and $0.00 on his third pepper. Josie will buy two peppers and receive consumer surplus of $0.30 on her first and $0.10 on her second pepper. Total consumer surplus is therefore $1.00. Cara will supply three peppers and receive producer surplus of $0.40 on her first, $0.40 on her second, and

c. A 50% increase in the size of the fixed input means that Bernie now has a 15-ton machine. So the fixed input is now the 15-ton machine. Since it generates a 100% increase in output for any given amount of electricity, the total product and marginal product are now as shown in the accompanying table.

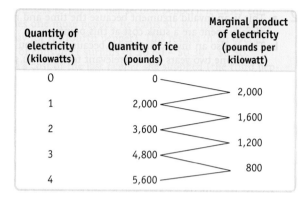

Quantity of electricity (kilowatts)	Quantity of ice (pounds)	Marginal product of electricity (pounds per kilowatt)
0	0	
		2,000
1	2,000	
		1,600
2	3,600	
		1,200
3	4,800	
		800
4	5,600	

Check Your Understanding

8-2

1. a. As shown in the accompanying table, the marginal cost for each pie is found by multiplying the marginal cost of the previous pie by 1.5. Variable cost for each output level is found by summing the marginal cost for all the pies produced to reach that output level. So, for example, the variable cost of three pies is $1.00 + $1.50 + $2.25 = $4.75. Average fixed cost for Q pies is calculated as $9/Q since fixed cost is $9. Average variable cost for Q pies is equal to variable cost for the Q pies divided by Q; for example, the average variable cost of five pies is $13.19/5, or approximately $2.64. Finally, average total cost can be calculated in two equivalent ways: as TC/Q or as $AVC + AFC$.

Quantity of pies	Marginal cost (of pie)	Variable cost	Average fixed cost (of pie)	Average variable cost (of pie)	Average total cost (of pie)
0		$0	—	—	—
	$1.00				
1		1.00	$9.00	$1.00	$10.00
	1.50				
2		2.50	4.50	1.25	5.75
	2.25				
3		4.75	3.00	1.58	4.58
	3.38				
4		8.13	2.25	2.03	4.28
	5.06				
5		13.19	1.80	2.64	4.44
	7.59				
6		20.78	1.50	3.46	4.96

b. The spreading effect dominates the diminishing returns effect when average total cost is falling: the fall in AFC dominates the rise in AVC for pies 1 to 4. The diminishing returns effect dominates when average total cost is rising: the rise in AVC dominates the fall in AFC for pies 5 and 6.

c. Alicia's minimum-cost output is 4 pies; this generates the lowest average total cost, $4.28. When output is less than 4, the marginal cost of a pie is less than the average total cost of the pies already produced. So making an additional pie lowers average total cost. For example, the marginal cost of pie 3 is $2.25, whereas the average total cost of pies 1 and 2 is $5.75. So making pie 3 lowers average total cost to $4.58, equal to (2 × $5.75 + $2.25)/3. When output is more than 4, the marginal cost of a pie is greater than the average total cost of the pies already produced. Consequently, making an additional pie raises average total cost. So, although the marginal cost of pie 6 is $7.59, the average total cost of pies 1 through 5 is $4.44. Making pie 6 raises average total cost to $4.96, equal to (5 × $4.44 + $7.59)/6.

Check Your Understanding

8-3

1. a. The accompanying table shows the average total cost of producing 12,000, 22,000, and 30,000 units for each of the three choices of fixed cost. For example, if the firm makes choice 1, the total cost of producing 12,000 units of output is $8,000 + 12,000 × $1.00 = $20,000. The average total cost of producing 12,000 units of output is therefore $20,000/12,000 = $1.67. The other average total costs are calculated similarly.

	12,000 units	22,000 units	30,000 units
Average total cost (per unit) from choice 1	$1.67	$1.36	$1.27
Average total cost (per unit) from choice 2	1.75	1.30	1.15
Average total cost (per unit) from choice 3	2.25	1.34	1.05

Therefore, if the firm wanted to produce 12,000 units, it would make choice 1 because this gives it the lowest average total cost. If it wanted to produce 22,000 units, it would make choice 2. If it wanted to produce 30,000 units, it would make choice 3.

b. Having historically produced 12,000 units, the firm would have adopted choice 1. When producing 12,000 units, the firm would have had an average total cost of $1.67. When output jumps to 22,000 units, the firm cannot alter its choice of fixed cost in the short run, so its average total cost in the short run will be $1.36. In the long run, however, it will adopt choice 2, giving it an average total cost of $1.30.

c. If the firm believes that the increase in demand is temporary, it should not alter its fixed cost from choice 1 because choice 2 generates higher average total cost as soon as output falls back to its original quantity of 12,000 units: $1.75 versus $1.67.

2. **a.** This firm is likely to experience constant returns to scale. To increase output, the firm must hire more workers, purchase more computers, and pay additional telephone charges. Because these inputs are easily available, their long-run costs are unlikely to change as output increases.

   b. This firm is likely to experience diseconomies of scale. As the firm takes on more projects, the costs of communication and coordination required to implement the expertise of the firm's owner are likely to increase.

   c. This firm is likely to experience economies of scale. Because diamond mining requires a large set-up cost for excavation equipment, long-run average cost will fall as output increases.

Chapter Nine

Check Your Understanding 9-1

1. **a.** With only two producers in the world, each producer will represent a sizable share of the market. So the industry will not be perfectly competitive.

   b. Because each producer of gas from the North Sea has only a small market share of total world supply of natural gas, and since natural gas is a standardized product, the natural gas industry will be perfectly competitive.

   c. Because each designer has a distinctive style, high-fashion clothes are not a standardized product. So the industry will not be perfectly competitive.

   d. The market described here is the market in each city for tickets to baseball games. Since there are only one or two teams in each major city, each team will represent a sizable share of the market. So the industry will not be perfectly competitive.

Check Your Understanding 9-2

1. **a.** The firm should shut down immediately when price is less than minimum average variable cost, the shut-down price. In the accompanying diagram, this is optimal for prices in the range 0 to P_1.

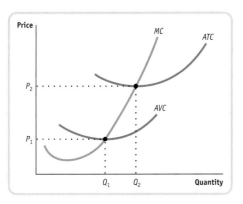

   b. When price is greater than minimum average variable cost (the shut-down price) but less than minimum average total cost (the break-even price), the firm should continue to operate in the short run even though it is making a loss. This is optimal for prices in the range P_1 to P_2 and quantities Q_1 to Q_2.

   c. When price exceeds minimum average total cost (the break-even price), the firm makes a profit. This happens for prices in excess of P_2 and results in quantities greater than Q_2.

2. This is an example of a temporary shut-down by a firm when the market price lies below the shut-down price, the minimum average variable cost. In this case, the market price is the price of a lobster meal and variable cost is the variable cost of serving such a meal, such as the cost of the lobster, employee wages, and so on. In this example, however, it is the average variable cost curve rather than the market price that shifts over time, due to seasonal changes in the cost of lobsters. Maine lobster shacks have relatively low average variable cost during the summer, when cheap Maine lobsters are available; during the rest of the year, their average variable cost is relatively high due to the high cost of imported lobsters. So the lobster shacks are open for business during the summer, when their minimum average variable cost lies below price; but they close during the rest of the year, when price lies below their minimum average variable cost.

Check Your Understanding 9-3

1. **a.** A fall in the fixed cost of production generates a fall in the average total cost of production and, in the short run, an increase in each firm's profit at the current output level. So in the long run new firms will enter the industry. The increase in supply drives down price and profits. Once profits are driven back to zero, entry will cease.

   b. An increase in wages generates an increase in the average total cost of production at every output level. In the short run, firms incur losses at the current output level, and so in the long run some firms will exit the industry. As firms exit, supply decreases, price rises, and losses are reduced. Exit will cease once losses return to zero.

   c. Price will rise as a result of the increased demand, leading to a short-run increase in profits at the current output level. In the long run, firms will enter the industry, generating an increase in supply, a fall in price, and a fall in profits. Once profits are driven back to zero, entry will cease.

   d. The shortage of a key input causes that input's price to increase, resulting in an increase in average total costs for producers. Firms incur losses in the short run, and some firms will exit the industry in the long run. The fall in supply generates an increase in price and decreased losses. Exit will cease when losses have returned to zero.

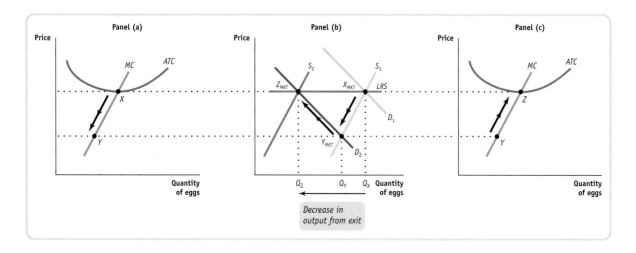

2. In the above diagram, point X_{MKT} in panel (b), the inter-section of S_1 and D_1, represents the long-run industry equilibrium before the change in consumer tastes. When tastes change, demand falls and the industry moves in the short run to point Y_{MKT} in panel (b), at the intersection of the new demand curve D_2 and S_1, the short-run supply curve representing the same number of egg producers as in the original equilibrium at point X_{MKT}. As the market price falls, an individual firm reacts by producing less—as shown in panel (a)—as long as the market price remains above the minimum average variable cost. If market price falls below average variable cost, the firm would shut down immediately. At point Y_{MKT} the price of eggs is below minimum average total cost, creating losses for producers. This leads some firms to exit, which shifts the short-run industry supply curve leftward to S_2. A new long-run equilibrium is established at point Z_{MKT}. As this occurs, the market price rises again, and, as shown in panel (c), each remaining producer reacts by increasing output (here, from point Y to point Z). All remaining producers again make zero profits. The decrease in the quantity of eggs supplied in the industry comes entirely from the exit of some producers from the industry. The long-run industry supply curve is the curve labeled LRS in panel (b).

Chapter Ten

10-1

1. Consuming a unit that generates negative marginal utility leaves the consumer with lower total utility than not con-suming that unit at all. A rational consumer, a consumer who maximizes utility, would not do that. For example, from Figure 10-1 you can see that Cassie receives 64 utils if she consumes 8 clams; but if she consumes the ninth clam, she loses a util, netting her a total utility of only 63 utils. So whenever consuming a unit generates negative marginal utility, the consumer is made better off by not consuming that unit.

2. Since Marta has diminishing marginal utility, her first cup of coffee of the day generates the greatest increase in total utility. Her third and last cup of the day generates the least.

3. a. Mabel has increasing marginal utility since each addi-tional unit consumed brings more additional enjoyment than the previous unit.

b. Mei has constant marginal utility because each additional unit generates the same additional satisfaction as the pre-vious unit.

c. Dexter has diminishing marginal utility since the addi-tional utility generated by a good restaurant meal is less when he consumes lots of them than when he consumed few of them.

10-2

1. a. At a price of $5.00 for a movie ticket and income of $10.00, the maximum quantity of tickets that can be pur-chased is $10/$5 = 2 as shown in the accompanying dia-gram. This is the vertical intercept. At a price of $2.50 for a bucket of popcorn, the horizontal intercept—the maximum quantity of popcorn that can be purchased given the budg-et—is $10.00/$2.50 = 4. The slope of the budget line is equal to the rise over run: $-2/4 = -1/2$ (there is a negative sign because the line is downward sloping). The opportuni-ty cost of a bucket of popcorn in terms of movie tickets is equal to minus the slope of the budget line, equal to $1/2$ in this case: 1 bucket of popcorn can be obtained if $1/2$ movie ticket is forgone.

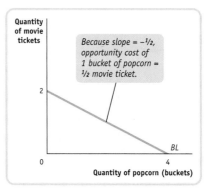

b. At a price of $1.50 for a pair of socks and income of $12.00, the vertical intercept—the maximum quantity of pairs of socks that can be purchased—is $12.00/$1.50 = 8, shown in the accompanying diagram. The horizontal intercept—the maximum quantity of pairs of underwear that can be purchased—is $12.00/$4.00 = 3. The slope of the budget line is $-8/3 = -2^2/3$. The opportunity cost of underwear in terms of socks is equal to minus the slope of the budget line, equal to $2^2/3$ in this case: 1 pair of underwear can be obtained if $2^2/3$ pairs of socks are forgone.

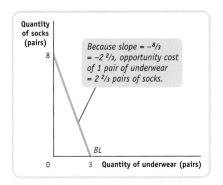

10-3

1. From Figure 10-5 you can see that the marginal utility per dollar at 3 pounds of clams and the marginal utility per dollar at 8 pounds of potatoes are approximately the same, at a value of about 1. But it is not Sammy's optimal consumption bundle because it is not affordable given his income of $20; 3 pounds of clams and 8 pounds of potatoes costs $4 × 3 + $2 × 8 = $28, $8 more than Sammy's income. This can be illustrated with Sammy's budget line from Figure 10-4: a bundle of 3 pounds of clams and 8 pounds of potatoes is represented by point X in the accompanying diagram, a point that lies outside Sammy's budget line.

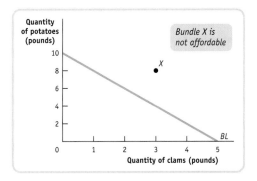

2. If Sammy chose the bundle that maximized his marginal utility per dollar for each good, he would choose to consume 1 pound of potatoes, where $MU_P/P_P = 5.75$, and 1 pound of clams, where $MU_C/P_C = 3.75$. But this bundle generates 26.5 utils for him. Instead, Sammy should choose the consumption bundle that satisfies his budget constraint and for which the marginal utility per dollar for both goods is equal.

10-4

1. Since spending on orange juice is a small share of Clare's spending, the income effect from a rise in the price of orange juice is insignificant. Only the substitution effect, represented by the substitution of lemonade for orange juice, is significant.

2. Since rent is a large share of Delia's expenditures, the increase in rent generates an income effect, making Delia feel poorer. Since housing is a normal good for Delia, the income and substitution effects move in the same direction, leading her to reduce her consumption of housing by moving to a smaller apartment.

3. Since a meal ticket is a significant share of the students' living costs, an increase in its price will generate an income effect. Students respond to the price increase by eating more often in the cafeteria. So the substitution effect (which would induce them to eat in the cafeteria less often) and the income effect (which would induce them to eat in the cafeteria more often than at restaurants because they are poorer) move in opposite directions. This happens because cafeteria meals are an inferior good. In fact, since the income effect outweighs the substitution effect (students eat in the cafeteria more as the price of meal tickets increases), cafeteria meals are a Giffen good.

Chapter Eleven

11-1

1. a. As you can see from the accompanying diagram, the four bundles are associated with three indifference curves: B on the 10-util indifference curve, A and C on the 6-util indifference curve, and D on the 4-util indifference curve.

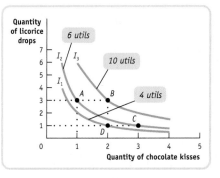

b. From comparing the quantities of chocolate kisses and licorice drops, you can predict that Samantha will prefer B to A because B gives her one more chocolate kiss and the same amount of licorice drops as A. Next, you can predict that she will prefer C to D because C gives her one more chocolate kiss and the same amount of licorice drops as D. You can also predict that she prefers B to D because B gives her two more licorice drops and the same amount of chocolate kisses as D. But without data about utils, you cannot predict how Samantha would rank *A* versus *C* or *D* because *C* and *D* have more chocolate kisses but fewer licorice drops than *A*. Neither can you rank *B* versus *C*, for the same reason.

2. Bundles *A* and *B* each generate 200 utils since they both lie on the 200 util indifference curve. Likewise, bundles *A* and *C* each generate 100 utils since they both lie on the 100 util indifference curve. But this implies that *A* generates 100 utils and also that *A* generates 200 utils. This is a contradiction and so cannot be true. It shows that indifference curves cannot cross.

Check Your Understanding 11-2

1. a. The marginal rate of substitution of books in place of games, MU_B/MU_G, is 2 for Lucinda and 5 for Kyle. This implies that Lucinda is willing to trade 1 more book for 2 fewer games and Kyle is willing to trade 1 more book for 5 fewer games. So starting from a bundle of 3 books and 6 games, Lucinda would be equally content with a bundle of 4 books and 4 games and Kyle would be equally content with a bundle of 4 books and 1 game. Lucinda finds it more difficult to trade games for books: she is willing to give up only 2 games for a book while Kyle is willing to give up 5 games for a book. If books are measured on the horizontal axis and games on the vertical axis, Kyle's indifference curve will be steeper than Lucinda's at the current consumption bundle.

   b. Lucinda's current consumption bundle is optimal if P_B/P_G, the relative price of books in terms of games, is 2. Kyle's current consumption bundle is not optimal at this relative price; his bundle would be optimal only if the relative price of books in terms of games is 5. Since, for Kyle, $MU_B/MU_G = 5$ but $P_B/P_G = 2$, Kyle should consume fewer games and more books, thereby lowering his MU_B/MU_G until it is equal to 2.

Check Your Understanding 11-3

1. Since Sanjay cares only about the number of jelly beans, not about whether they are banana- or pineapple-flavored, he is always willing to exchange one for the other at the same rate. This implies that his marginal rate of substitution of one flavor of jelly bean in place of another is constant. So they are perfect substitutes.

2. Cherry pie and vanilla ice cream are complements for Hillary since her marginal utility of cherry pie goes up as she has another scoop of vanilla ice cream. But they are ordinary goods, not perfect complements, because she gains some utility from having cherry pie without any vanilla ice cream.

3. Omnisoft's software programs and its operating system are perfect complements for its customers: they gain no utility from the software programs without the operating system. So their marginal rate of substitution of one good in place of the other is undefined, and their indifference curves have a right-angle shape.

4. Income and leisure are ordinary goods for Darnell: the more income he has made by working more hours, the less willing he is to earn yet more by giving up additional leisure time.

Check Your Understanding 11-4

1. a. Sammy's original budget line is illustrated in the accompanying diagram by BL_1. His original consumption is at point *A*. When the price of clams falls, his budget line rotates outward to BL_2, allowing him to achieve a higher level of utility. The pure substitution effect would involve the same change in the slope of his budget line, but without any increase in utility. So the pure substitution effect is illustrated by the movement from *A* to *B*. In fact, his utility does rise, so his consumption moves from *A* to *C*. The movement from *B* to *C* is the income effect.

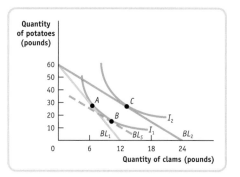

   b. Again, in the accompanying diagram Sammy's original budget line is BL_1, and his original consumption is at point *A*. The increase in the price of clams causes his budget line to rotate inward to BL_2. This reduces his total utility. The pure substitution effect is what would happen if the slope of the budget line changed but his total utility did not; it is shown as the movement from *A* to *B*. The full effect of the price change is the movement from *A* to *C*. The movement from *B* to *C* is the income effect.

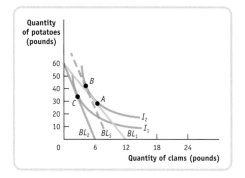

Chapter Twelve

Check Your Understanding 12-1

1. Many college professors will depart for other lines of work if the government imposes a wage that is lower than the market wage. Fewer professors will result in fewer courses taught and therefore fewer college degrees produced. It will adversely affect sectors of the economy that depend directly on colleges, such as the local shopkeepers who sell goods and services to students and facul-

ty, college textbook publishers, and so on. It will also adversely affect firms that use the "output" produced by colleges: new college graduates. Firms that need to hire new employees with college degrees will be hurt as a smaller supply results in a higher market wage for college graduates. Ultimately, the reduced supply of college-educated workers will result in a lower level of human capital in the entire economy relative to what it would have been without the policy. And this will hurt all sectors of the economy that depend on human capital. The sectors of the economy that might benefit are firms that compete with colleges in the hiring of would-be college professors. For example, accounting firms will find it easier to hire people who would otherwise have been professors of accounting, and publishers will find it easier to hire people who would otherwise have been professors of English (easier in the sense that the firms can recruit would-be professors with a lower wage than before). In addition, workers who already have college degrees will benefit; they will command higher wages as the supply of college-educated workers falls.

12-2

1. **a.** As the demand for services increases, the price of services will rise. And as the price of the output produced by the industries increases, this shifts the *VMPL* curve upward—that is, the demand for labor rises. This results in an increase in both the equilibrium wage rate and the quantity of labor employed.
   b. The fall in the catch per day means that the marginal product of labor in the industry declines. The *VMPL* curve shifts downward, generating a fall in the equilibrium wage rate and the equilibrium quantity of labor employed.

2. When firms from different industries compete for the same workers, then each worker in the various industries will be paid the same equilibrium wage, *W*. And since, by the marginal productivity theory of income distribution, $VMPL = P \times MPL = W$ for the last worker hired in equilibrium, the last worker hired in each of these different industries will have the same value of the marginal product of labor.

12-3

1. **a.** False. Income disparities associated with gender, race, or ethnicity can be explained by the marginal productivity theory of income distribution provided that differences in marginal productivity across people are correlated with gender, race, or ethnicity. One possible source for such correlation is past discrimination. Such discrimination can lower individuals' marginal productivity by, for example, preventing them from acquiring the human capital that would raise their productivity. Another possible source of the correlation is differences in work experience that are associated with gender, race, or ethnicity. For example, in jobs where work experience or length of tenure is important, women may earn lower wages because on average more women than men take child-care-related absences from work.

   b. True. Companies that discriminate when their competitors do not are likely to hire less able workers because they discriminate against more able workers who are considered of the wrong gender, race, or ethnicity. And with less able workers, such companies are likely to earn lower profits than their competitors who don't discriminate.
   c. Ambiguous. In general, workers who are paid less because they have less experience may or may not be the victims of discrimination. The answer depends on the reason for the lack of experience. If workers have less experience because they are young or have chosen to do something else rather than gain experience, then they are not victims of discrimination if they are paid less. But if workers lack experience because previous job discrimination prevented them from gaining experience, then they are indeed victims of discrimination when they are paid less.

12-4

1. **a.** Clive is made worse off if, before the new law, he had preferred to work more than 35 hours per week. As a result of the law, he can no longer choose his preferred time allocation; he now consumes fewer goods and more leisure than he would like.
   b. Clive's utility is unaffected by the law if, before the law, he had preferred to work 35 or fewer hours per week. The law has not changed his preferred time allocation.
   c. Clive can never be made better off by a law that restricts the number of hours he can work. He can only be made worse off (case a) or equally as well off (case b).

2. The substitution effect would induce Clive to work fewer hours and consume more leisure after his wage falls—the fall in wage means the price of an hour of leisure falls, leading Clive to consume more leisure. But a fall in his wage also generates a fall in Clive's income. The income effect of this is to induce Clive to consume less leisure and therefore work more hours, since he is now poorer and leisure is a normal good. If the income effect dominates the substitution effect, Clive will in the end work more hours than before.

Chapter Thirteen

13-1

1. **a.** eMarkets! will have to know the willingness to pay of every potential consumer—that is, the demand schedule. It will also have to know the seller's cost for each unit of output of every potential producer—that is, the supply schedule. (Equivalently, it must know the marginal cost curve of every potential producer.)
   b. Some producers who have a seller's cost greater than $99 will produce because they were mistakenly told that the price would be $299; some who have a seller's cost equal to or less than $199 will not produce because they were mistakenly told that the price would be $99. So producer surplus is lower because the market price cannot allocate production efficiently among producers. You cannot tell whether the output will be equal to, less than, or greater than the equilibrium output. Overproduction may occur

if a relatively high number of producers think the price will be $299, and underproduction may occur if a relatively high number of producers think the price will be $99.

c. Some consumers who have a willingness to pay less than $99 will get the good; some who have a willingness to pay of $99 or more, but less than $299, will not get the good. So consumer surplus is lower because the market price cannot allocate production efficiently among consumers.

Check Your Understanding 13-2

1. a. Before the change in preferences, the Bountifullian labor market is in equilibrium, defined by the condition $VMPL_C$ = wage rate = $VMPL_S$. After preferences change, a greater demand for breakfast cereal will induce an increase in the price of cereal, P_C. $VMPL_C = P_C \times MPL_C$ will therefore rise, with the result that $VMPL_C >$ wage rate. A lower demand for sausage will induce a decrease in the price of sausage, P_S. $VMPL_S = P_S \times MPL_S$ will fall, with the result that $VMPL_S <$ wage rate. Sausage producers will let some of their workers go; these workers will move to cereal producers, who are hiring additional workers. As labor moves from the sausage to the cereal industry, MPL_C and $VMPL_C$ fall, but MPL_S and $VMPL_S$ rise.

b. You will know that the economy has fully adjusted when the labor market has reattained equilibrium: when $VMPL_C$ = wage rate = $VMPL_S$ again. Because all consumers face the same price for cereal, P_C, and the same price for sausage, P_S, there will be *efficiency in consumption:* every consumer who consumes a good has a higher willingness to pay for it than someone who does not. Next, because cereal producers and sausage producers compete for workers in a perfectly competitive labor market, there will be no surplus of labor and all labor will be fully employed. So there will be *efficiency in production:* there is no way to produce more of one good without producing less of the other. Finally, there will be *efficiency in the output levels:* any other mix of cereal and sausage reduces welfare. Because $VMPL_C$ = wage rate = $VMPL_S$ in equilibrium, the allocation of labor to the two industries, and therefore the mix of outputs of the two goods, fully reflects consumers' valuations of the two goods.

Check Your Understanding 13-3

1. There is an objective way to determine whether an economy is efficient: determine whether there is another allocation of production and/or consumption that makes someone better off without making anyone else worse off. If not, it is efficient; if yes, it is inefficient. It is much harder to determine whether an economy is fair because there is no objective measure of determining this. What a person deems is fair typically depends upon his or her viewpoint.

2. a. The problem with this statement is that what one "should contribute" or "should receive" is subject to interpretation. Suppose one person has worked extremely hard to become wealthy but another is born wealthy and has never worked. Should each person be required to contribute the same to society? Some would say yes (those

who think amount of money is the only criterion) but others would say no (those who think that people should be rewarded for working hard relative to those who don't)—it depends upon the person's viewpoint. Similarly, suppose one person needs an operation to be able to see, another person needs an operation to be able to walk, and society doesn't have the resources to perform both operations. Whose need is more important? Again, the answer is unclear because society has no way of measuring whether one person's needs are more compelling than another's.

b. This statement is also subject to very different interpretations. First, how do we define "work hard"? Do people who spend years working on something they enjoy, such as writing a classical sonata, "work harder" than those who do less intense but very unappealing work? Also, this statement implies that people who cannot work hard for reasons outside their control—say, due to illness—should be rewarded less. Whether or not this is fair is again subject to a person's viewpoint.

Chapter Fourteen

Check Your Understanding 14-1

1. a. This does not support the conclusion. Texas Tea has a limited amount of oil, and the price has risen in order to equalize supply and demand.

b. This supports the conclusion because the market for home heating oil has become monopolized, and a monopolist will reduce the quantity supplied and raise price to generate profit.

c. This does not support the conclusion. Texas Tea has raised its price to consumers because the price of its input, home heating oil, has increased.

d. This supports the conclusion. The fact that other firms have begun to supply heating oil at a lower price implies that Texas Tea must have earned profits—profits that attracted the other firms to Frigid.

e. This supports the conclusion. It indicates that Texas Tea enjoys a barrier to entry because it controls access to the only Alaskan heating oil pipeline.

Check Your Understanding 14-2

1. a. The price at each output level is found by dividing the total revenue by the number of emeralds produced; for example, the price when 3 emeralds are produced is $252/3 = $84. The price at the various output levels is then used to construct the demand schedule.

b. The marginal revenue schedule is found by calculating the change in total revenue as output increases by one unit. For example, the marginal revenue generated by increasing output from 2 to 3 emeralds is ($252 − $186) = $66.

c. The quantity effect component of marginal revenue is the additional revenue generated by selling one more unit of the good at the market price. For example, as shown in the accompanying table, at 3 emeralds, the market price is $84; so, when going from 2 to 3 emeralds the quantity effect is equal to $84.

d. The price effect component of marginal revenue is the decline in revenue caused by the fall in price when one more unit is sold. For example, as shown in the table, when only 2 emeralds are sold, each emerald sells at a price of $186/2 = $93. However, when Emeralds, Inc. sells an additional emerald, the price must fall by $9 to $84. So the price effect component in going from 2 to 3 emeralds is (−$9) × 2 = −$18. That's because 2 emeralds can only be sold at a price of $84 when 3 emeralds in total are sold, although they could have been sold at a price of $93 when only 2 in total were sold.

Quantity of emerald demanded	Price of emerald	Marginal revenue	Quantity component	Price component
1	$100			
		$86	$93	−$7
2	93			
		66	84	−18
3	84			
		28	70	−42
4	70			
		−30	50	−80
5	50			

e. In order to determine Emerald, Inc.'s profit-maximizing output level, you must know its marginal cost at each output level. Its profit-maximizing output level is the one at which marginal revenue is equal to marginal cost.

2. As the accompanying diagram shows, the marginal cost curve shifts upward to $400. The profit-maximizing quantity falls, and so does profit, from $3,200 to $300 × 6 = $1,800. Competitive industry profits, though, are unchanged at zero.

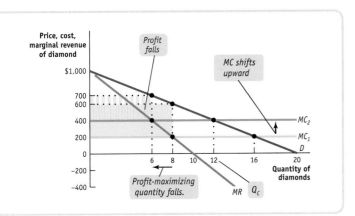

14-3

1. a. Cable Internet service is a natural monopoly. So the government should intervene only if it believes that price exceeds average total cost, where average total cost is based on the cost of laying the cable. In this case it should impose a price ceiling equal to average total cost. Otherwise, it should do nothing.

b. The government should approve the merger only if it fosters competition by transferring some of the company's landing slots to another, competing airline.

2. a. False. As can be see from Figure 14-8, panel (b), the inefficiency arises from the fact that some of the consumer surplus is transformed into deadweight loss (the orange area), not that it is transformed into profit (the green area).

b. True. If a monopolist sold to all customers who have a valuation greater than or equal to marginal cost, all mutually beneficial transactions would occur and there would be no deadweight loss.

3. As shown in the accompanying diagram, a monopolist produces Q_M, the output level at which $MR = MC$. A monopolist who mistakenly believes that $P = MR$ produces the output level at which $P = MC$ (when, in fact, $P > MR$, and at the true profit-maximizing level of output, $P > MR = MC$). This misguided monopolist will produce the output level Q_C, where the demand curve crosses the marginal cost curve—the same output level produced if the industry were perfectly competitive. It will charge the price P_C, which is equal to marginal cost, and make zero profit. The entire shaded area is equal to the consumer surplus, which is also equal to total surplus in this case (since the monopolist receives zero producer surplus). There is no deadweight loss since every consumer who is willing to pay as much as or more than marginal cost gets the good. A smart monopolist, however, will produce the output level Q_M, and charge the price P_M. Profit equals the green area, consumer surplus corresponds to the blue area, and total surplus is equal to the sum of the green and blue areas. The orange area is the deadweight loss generated by the monopolist.

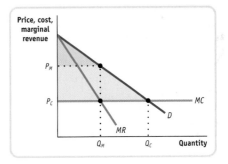

14-4

1. a. False. A price-discriminating monopolist will sell to some customers that a single-price monopolist will refuse to—namely, customers with a high price elasticity of demand who are willing to pay only a relatively low price for the good.

b. False. Although a price-discriminating monopolist does indeed capture more of the consumer surplus, inefficiency is lower: more mutually beneficial transactions occur because the monopolist makes more sales to customers with a low willingness to pay for the good.

c. True. Under price discrimination consumers are charged prices that depend on their price elasticity of demand. A consumer with a higher price elasticity of demand will pay a lower price than a consumer with inelastic demand.

2. **a.** This is not a case of price discrimination because all consumers, regardless of their price elasticities of demand, value the damaged merchandise less than undamaged merchandise. So the price must be lowered to sell the merchandise.

b. This is a case of price discrimination. Senior citizens have a higher price elasticity of demand for restaurant meals (their demand for restaurant meals is more responsive to price changes) than other patrons. Restaurants lower the price to high-elasticity consumers (senior citizens). Consumers with low price elasticity of demand will pay the full price.

c. This is a case of price discrimination. High-elasticity consumers will pay a lower price by collecting and using discount coupons. Low-elasticity consumers will not use coupons.

d. This is not a case of price discrimination; it is simply a case of supply and demand.

>> Index